Samuel Rawson Gardiner

Prince Charles and the Spanish Marriage: 1617-1623

A Chapter of English History - Vol. II

Samuel Rawson Gardiner

Prince Charles and the Spanish Marriage: 1617-1623
A Chapter of English History - Vol. II

ISBN/EAN: 9783743409828

Manufactured in Europe, USA, Canada, Australia, Japa

Cover: Foto ©ninafisch / pixelio.de

Manufactured and distributed by brebook publishing software (www.brebook.com)

Samuel Rawson Gardiner

Prince Charles and the Spanish Marriage: 1617-1623

PRINCE CHARLES

AND

THE SPANISH MARRIAGE:

1617–1623.

A CHAPTER OF ENGLISH HISTORY,

FOUNDED PRINCIPALLY UPON UNPUBLISHED DOCUMENTS IN THIS COUNTRY, AND IN THE ARCHIVES OF SIMANCAS, VENICE, AND BRUSSELS.

BY

SAMUEL RAWSON GARDINER,

AUTHOR OF THE "HISTORY OF ENGLAND FROM THE ACCESSION OF JAMES I. TO THE DISGRACE OF CHIEF JUSTICE COKE."

IN TWO VOLUMES.

VOL. II.

LONDON:
HURST AND BLACKETT, PUBLISHERS,
13, GREAT MARLBOROUGH STREET.
1869.

The Right of Translation is Reserved.

CHAPTER VII.—(*continued.*)

		PAGE
1621.	Abbot's accidental homicide	31
	Cranfield raised to the peerage	32
	Proclamation against monopolies	33
1593.	The early separatists	34
1604.	The congregation at Amsterdam	36
1606.	Emigration of the Gainsborough congregation	37
1603.	Clifton at Babworth	38
	Robinson at Norwich	40
1606.	The Scrooby congregation	41
1608.	Emigration to Holland	43
1617.	They determine to take refuge in America	45
1619.	Patent from the Virginia Company	47
1620.	The departure from Leyden	49
	The passage to Southampton	50
	The sailing of the May-flower	51
	Arrival at Cape Cod	52
	The instrument of government	53
	Exploration of Cape Cod	54
	The search for a home	55
	The landing at Plymouth	57
1621.	The return of the May-flower	59
	Prospects of toleration in England	60
	Robinson and Selden	61

CHAPTER VIII.

LORD DIGBY'S EMBASSY TO VIENNA.

1620.	Germany after the Battle of Prague	63
	Frederick's flight	66
1621.	The ban pronounced against him	67
	Mission of Sir E. Villiers	69
	Frederick at Segeberg	70
	The Danish loan	71
	Frederick's refusal to go to the Palatinate	72
	Pacific tendencies of Spain	74
	Morton at Heilbronn	75
	James and the Dutch Commissioners	76
	The expiration of the truce of Antwerp	77
	Digby at Brussels	79
	Death of Philip III.	80
	Dissolution of the Union	81
	Proposal for the transference of the Electorate	83
	Nethersole sent to England	84
	Mansfeld in Bohemia	85
	Soldiers of the Thirty Years' War	86
	Mansfeld in the Upper Palatinate	88
	Digby's instructions	89

CHAPTER VIII.—(*continued.*)

		PAGE
1621.	Preparations of Mansfeld and Jägerndorf	92
	Digby's arrival at Vienna	93
	Opening of negotiations	94
	Ferdinand determines to treat	95
	Policy of the new Spanish Government	97
	Death of the Archduke Albert	98
	Peace endangered by Frederick	99
	Frederick in the Dutch camp	100
	Pawel at Vienna	101
	The truce broken by Vere	103
	Digby's new plan	105
	Invasion of the Upper Palatinate	106
	Meeting between Digby and Mansfeld	107
	Conquest of the Upper Palatinate	108
	Spanish objections to the transference of the Electorate	109
	Sir E. Villiers at the Hague	110
	Digby at Heidelberg	111
	Mansfeld in the Lower Palatinate	112
	Mansell's attack upon Algiers	113
	The blockade of the Flemish ports	115
	Cranfield Lord Treasurer	117
	Lafuente's mission to Rome	119
	Meeting of the Houses	120
	Freedom of debate	121
	Debate on foreign affairs	122
	Resolution to grant a supply	129
	Pym's speech in the Committee on Religion	130
	The petition on religion	134
	Gondomar's interference	136
	The King's letter to the Speaker	137
	Explanatory petition	139
	The King's answer	140
	Debate upon it	142
	Liberty of speech	143
	Elizabethan precedents	144
	A protestation suggested by Wentworth	145
	Another letter from the King	146
	Coke supports Wentworth's proposal	147
	The protestation of the Commons	148
	The protestation torn out of the journals by James	152
	Gondomar's triumph	153
	Imprisonment of members	154
1622.	Dissolution of Parliament	155
	Digby's vexation	156
	Comparison between Digby and Gondomar	157

CHAPTER IX.

THE CONFERENCE AT BRUSSELS.

		PAGE
1622.	The blockade of the Flemish ports	160
	The scheme for an attack on the Dutch Republic revived	161
	Oxford in command in the narrow seas	162
	Marriage of Elizabeth Norris	163
	The bargain for York House	164
	Buckingham reconciled with the Howards	167
	The conference between Laud and Fisher	168
	Early history of De Dominis	170
	His visit to England	172
	He returns to Rome	174
	The civil war in France	177
	Doncaster's mission	178
	The French privateers	179
	The armies in the Palatinate	181
	A fresh benevolence	182
	Tom Tell-Truth	183
	Knight's sermon at Oxford	184
	Condemnation of Pareus's Commentaries	185
	Terms accepted by Frederick	186
	Mansfeld in Alsace	189
	Chichester's mission	190
	Schwarzenberg in England	191
	Ferdinand's intentions	192
	Mansfeld's intrigue with Raville	193
	Tilly's position in the Lower Palatinate	194
	Frederick joins Mansfeld	195
	Mansfeld takes the field	196
	Tilly's victory at Wimpfen	197
	Weston opens negotiations at Brussels	198
	The seizure of the Landgrave of Darmstadt	200
	Mansfeld driven back to Mannheim	201
	Chichester's arrival in the Palatinate	202
	His diplomatic failure	203
	Battle of Höchst	205
	Vere's position at Mannheim	206
	Fresh discussions at Brussels	208
	Frederick retires to Sedan	210
	The projected Assembly at Ratisbon	211
	Zuñiga's compromise adopted by the Spanish Council of State	214
	Hyacintho at Madrid	215
	Digby's return to Spain	216
	Plans of Zuñiga	217
	Digby's interview with the Infanta	219

CHAPTER IX.—(continued.)

		PAGE
1622.	Gondomar leaves England	220
	Decision taken at Madrid to enforce a suspension of arms	221
	Sequestration of the fortresses proposed at Brussels	222
	Mansfeld in Lorraine	223
	Indignation of the Emperor	225
	Weston's demand for a suspension of arms	226
	The Battle of Fleurus	227
	Rejection of Weston's demand	229
	Close of the Conference	230

CHAPTER X.

THE MISSION OF ENDYMION PORTER.

1622.	State of public opinion in England	232
	The directions to preachers	233
	Release of Catholic prisoners	235
	Liberation of Coke, Phelips, and Mallory	236
	Gage's instructions from the Cardinals	237
	His reception in England	239
	Buckingham's letter to Gondomar	240
	Hopelessness of James's position	243
	The fall of Heidelberg	246
	The siege of Mannheim	247
	Chichester at Frankfort	248
	Buckingham declares for war	250
	Character of the Prince of Wales	251
	He promises Gondomar to visit Madrid	254
	Proposes to send Porter to prepare the way	255
	Deliberations of the Privy Council	256
	James's letter to the Pope	257
	Cottington's return from Spain	258
	Orders carried by Porter	259
	Buckingham eager for war	260
	A Spanish fleet in the Channel	261
	Zuñiga's death	262
	Olivares succeeds to his position	263
	Bristol's confidence in Philip's intentions	264
	The Infanta Isabella instructed to intervene in James's favour	266
	Chichester's recall	267
	Porter's arrival at Madrid	269
	Fall of Mannheim	271
	Refusal of the Infanta Isabella to carry out her instructions	272
	Character of the Infanta Maria	273
	Her aversion to the marriage	274
	Philip directs Olivares to put an end to the treaty	276

CHAPTER X.—(continued.)

		PAGE
1622.	Scheme proposed by Olivares	277
	Its rejection by the Council of State	279
	Revisal of the marriage treaty	280
	Evasive answer about the Palatinate	281
1623.	The revised treaty accepted by James	283
1622.	James adopts the proposal for sequestrating Frankenthal	284
	Difficulties of the neutral Protestants in Germany.	285
	Mansfeld in East Friesland	286
1623.	Frederick's appeal to the Elector of Saxony	287
	His Electorate conferred upon Maximilian	289
	Frederick's objections to the sequestration of Frankenthal	291
	Settlement of the East India disputes	293
	Conway succeeds Naunton as Secretary	295

CHAPTER XI.

THE JOURNEY TO MADRID.

1623.	Project of Charles and Buckingham	297
	It is communicated to the King	298
	Buckingham's preparations	301
	The Prince's journey	302
	Dismay in England	303
	Outcry against Buckingham	304
	Arrival of the Prince at Madrid	305
	Expectations of Olivares	306
	Interview between Charles and Philip	309
	Attempts to convert the Prince	311
	Bristol asks Charles what his intentions are	312
	Charles's removal to the palace	313
	Fresh demands of Olivares	315
	Pastrana's mission to Rome	319
	Anxiety of Olivares about the Palatinate	320
	Continued resistance of the Infanta to the marriage	321
	Attempt to convert Buckingham	323
	The Prince's visit to the Infanta	324
	The dispensation granted	327
	The Prince takes part in a religious discussion	329
	The Prince's chaplains sent out	330
	Arrival of the dispensation at Madrid	331
	Quarrel between Buckingham and Olivares	332
	Charles's offers refused by the Council of State	333
	The Junta of Theologians	334
	Charles makes fresh offers	336
	Dismissal of his retinue	337
	The two favourites	339

CHAPTER XI.—(continued.)

		PAGE
1623.	Charles declares his intention of returning to England	340
	He gives way, and promises to remain	341
	Charles's correspondence with the Pope	342
	Decision of the Theologians that the Infanta must be detained for a year	343
	Fresh discussions	344
	Preparations in England for the reception of the Infanta	347
	James engages to confirm the articles	351
	Attempts of Charles to obtain better terms	352
	He again declares that he must go back to England	355
	But changes his mind and agrees to everything	356
	James hesitates to take the oath to the secret articles	357
	Advice of Williams	358
	The oath accepted by the Council	360
	The ceremony of swearing to the treaty	361
	Explanations given by the King	363
	Letter attributed to Abbot	365
	The sequestration of Frankenthal	367
	The treaty for the suspension of arms rejected by Frederick	368
	Christian of Brunswick's defeat at Stadtloo	371
	Frederick signs the treaty	372
	Dunkirk vessels blockaded in Scotland	373
	Seizure of a ship at Cowes by the Dutch	374
	Destruction of the Dunkirk vessel at Leith	375
	Excuses of the Prince of Orange	376
	Renewal of the scheme for the partition of the Netherlands	377
	Compromise with the Dutch	378
	The Dunkirk vessel convoyed from Aberdeen	379
	The fight at sea	380
	The Dunkirker convoyed to Mardike	381

CHAPTER XII.

THE BREACH WITH SPAIN.

1623.	Additional articles presented to Charles	382
	Olivares persuades the Infanta to accept the marriage	384
	Charles signs the marriage contract	385
	Continues to hope that he will bring the Infanta with him	386
	Buckingham's insolence	387
	His interview with the Infanta	389
	The fleet leaves England	390
	A pardon and dispensation promised to the recusants	391
	The agreement made at Salisbury	392

CHAPTER XII.—(*continued.*)

		PAGE
1623.	James orders his son to return	393
	Charles agrees to be married and remain till the spring	394
	Sir E. Verney's assault upon a priest	395
	Charles makes up his mind to go	396
	Discussions on the disposal of the Palatinate	398
	Resolution of Olivares adopted by the Council of State	399
	Bristol's opinion of the proposal	401
	Production of Philip's letter by Olivares	405
	Charles swears to the contract	407
	Takes leave of Philip	409
	Coolness of his feelings towards the Infanta	410
	His apprehension that she will go into a nunnery	411
	He sails from Santander	413
	Bristol's report of the Infanta	414
	Delays in issuing the pardon and dispensation	417
	Manœuvres of Williams	419
	The Prince's arrival	421
	His meeting with his father	422
	The Spanish plan for the pacification of Germany	423
	Liberation of the priests	424
	Bristol denies that the Infanta will become a nun	425
	James orders the postponement of the marriage	427
	Charles's letters to Bristol and Aston	428
	Frederick gives an evasive answer about his son's marriage with an archduchess	430
	Philip's declaration about the Palatinate	431
	Bristol complains of his orders to postpone the marriage	432
	James's anxiety	434
	The accident at Blackfriars	435
	Buckingham's report to the Committee of the Council	436
	James sends fresh orders to postpone the marriage	437
	Charles remonstrates with Bristol	439
	Bristol's resolution to proceed with the marriage	440
	Arrival of the Pope's approbation	443
	A better answer about the Palatinate promised	444
	The marriage postponed	445
	Philip summoned to restore the Palatinate	446
	Philip refuses to arm against the Emperor	447
	The Spanish terms laid before Frederick	448
	He refuses them	450
	The crisis comes at last	451
	Parliament summoned and Bristol recalled	452
	Bristol's character and policy	454
1624.	Offers made him by Olivares	457
	The marriage treaty at an end	458

PRINCE CHARLES

AND

THE SPANISH MARRIAGE.

CHAPTER VII.

THE JURISDICTION OF PARLIAMENT—THE VOYAGE OF THE MAYFLOWER.

UNCONSCIOUS of their high destiny, and utterly unembarrassed by any theories about their constitutional position, the Commons steadily pursued the course upon which they had entered, and continued to strike at practical abuses. The day after judgment had been delivered in the case of the late Lord Chancellor, they were summoned to the bar of the Upper House to hear Michell sentenced to degradation from the order of knighthood, to imprisonment during the King's pleasure, to a fine of 1000*l*., and to perpetual exclusion from public office.*

Not many days before, a fresh case of corruption had been laid before the Lords. It had been proved, to the satisfaction of the Commons, that Sir John Bennett, the Judge of the Prerogative Court, had abused the opportunities afforded by his jurisdiction, to extort large sums from those who had, in due course, applied to him for letters of administration.†

With these vigorous proceedings the King had no reason

CH. VII.
1621.
May 4.
Sentence upon Michell.

April 24.
Charge against Sir J. Bennett.

---

* *Lords' Journals,* iii. 89, 95, 108.
† *Proceedings and Debates,* i. 233, 241, 256, 279, 297. *Lords' Journals,* iii. 87.

CH. VII.
1621.
April 21.
The King's displeasure.

James, as soon as he heard what had passed, showed every sign of vexation. It was strange, he said to Cranfield, who was fast rising into the position of a medium between the Crown and the Commons, that the House could not remember what he had said till the sun had gone once about. Cranfield did what he could to pacify him. The House, he replied, had done nothing but what was for his Majesty's honour. James told him that he thanked them for that, but that he wished they would not be so careful for his honour as to destroy his service. He would not have the referees questioned, unless it could be shown that they had been influenced by corruption. Any man was capable of making a mistake.

April 24.
The Commons give way.

With consummate tact the Commons retreated, without loss of dignity, from the position which they had assumed. They examined Mandeville's certificate in favour of the patentees, and, affecting to be thoroughly satisfied with it, passed on to inquire into the conduct of the patentees themselves. Yet it was soon evident that there was no serious intention of prosecuting the matter further. The offenders were released on bail. They were examined by a committee, and a report was presented to the House. It was then ordered that the question should be taken into consideration at a future day, and the matter was allowed to drop.*

April 18.
Yelverton blames the King.

Another difficulty, which arose about the same time, was less easily settled. On the 18th of April, Yelverton was, by the King's permission, fetched from the Tower and examined in the House of Lords upon his knowledge of the circumstances attending the grant of the patent for inns, and the patent for the manufacture of gold and silver thread. Smarting under his imprisonment, he let fall some rash words about his own punishment. If ever, he said, he had deserved well of his Majesty, it was by his conduct in the affair of the patent for inns; and yet his behaviour on that occasion had been the cause of his present suffering.†

April 24.
The King demands

If James had been displeased with the Commons for their attack upon Mandeville, he was furious with the

---

* *Proceedings and Debates*, i. 308, ii. 52.
† *Lords' Journals*, iii. 77.

Lords for permitting such words to pass in silence. He fancied that he saw in their conduct evidence that they were ready to welcome an assault upon Buckingham. He went down at once to the House, gave his own account of Yelverton's proceedings, and called upon the Peers to punish him for the slander.*

Yelverton's spirit was now fully roused. Standing at bay, he refused to explain away his words. He had done his best, he said, to stop the proceedings in the Exchequer against the offenders who had kept open their inns in defiance of the patent. It was for this that he had been threatened with the ill-will of the all-powerful favourite, who stood "ever at his Majesty's hand, ready to hew him down." Mompesson had brought threatening messages, telling him that, if he did not take care, he would run himself upon the rocks, and that, unless he supported the patent, he should not hold his place for an hour. "My Lord," it had been said to him, "had obtained it by his favour, and would maintain it by his power." Yelverton then turned fiercely upon Buckingham. "Howbeit," he said, "I dare say if my Lord of Buckingham had but read the articles exhibited in this place against Hugh Spenser, and had known the danger of placing and displacing officers about a king, he would not have pursued me with such bitterness." † At this daring outburst, cries were heard on every side, bidding the speaker to hold his peace. But Buckingham, who was always more ready to bear down opposition than to silence it, bade him haughtily to proceed. "He that will seek to stop him," he said, "is more my enemy than his." After some interruption, Yelverton was permitted to go on, and concluded by asserting that he was ready to prove all that he had said.‡

As soon as the prisoner was removed, Buckingham rose again. Yelverton, he said, had objected to the proceedings in the Exchequer, and his objections had been accepted by the King; but he had originally assented to them, for the sake of his fee of ten shillings

---

* *Lords' Journals*, iii. 81. Salvetti's *News-Letter*, $\frac{\text{April 27}}{\text{May 7}}$.

† *Lords' Journals*, iii. 121.

‡ Elsing's *Notes*, April 30.

Ch. VII.
1621.
April 30.

upon each case. As for the charges against himself, he threw himself upon the House; but he must beg their lordships to remember that Mompesson, who was said to have carried the message, was absent, and could not be examined.

After some further conversation, Yelverton was recalled to be further questioned upon his conduct relating to the patent. As soon as the examination was at an end, Buckingham moved that he might be committed a close prisoner to the Tower for his reflection upon the King's honour, in declaring that he had allowed Royal authority to be usurped by a subject. Against this proposal Southampton protested. He was supported by Say, who pointed out that the words had been spoken, not against the King, but against Buckingham. The House finally decided upon sending Yelverton back to the Tower, without mentioning the cause of his committal.*

Question between the King and the Lords.

The next day a message was brought from the King. He had naturally been provoked by a comparison which implied a parallel between himself and Edward II., and by the suggestion that he had inflicted punishment upon Yelverton merely for his refusal to follow Buckingham's caprices. At Buckingham's request, he said, he should leave the insult which had been directed against his lordship in the hands of the House; but he should himself take care to vindicate his own honour. Such a message, no doubt, seemed simple enough to James. But there were some among the Lords who replied that the King had no right to take out of their hands the judgment of a fault which they were still engaged in investigating. In spite of the opposition of Buckingham and the Prince, these objections prevailed, and a remonstrance was drawn up to beg the King to leave the whole matter to the House. Before this remonstrance James gave way, and signified his intention of leaving Yelverton entirely to the Peers.†

May 8.
Debate on Yelverton's case.

It can hardly admit of a doubt that there were many amongst the Lords who took an ill-concealed pleasure at this attack upon the favourite. But Yelverton's un-

* Elsing's *Notes*, May 2.
† *Lords' Journals*, iii. 104, 114.

guarded speech had put him completely at the mercy of the Court, and it was impossible to vote for his acquittal without entering into a direct conflict with the Crown. Yet, even under these circumstances, a scene occurred which betrayed for a moment the passions which were smouldering beneath the surface. The notes of Yelverton's attack upon Buckingham were read, and a question was raised whether he should be heard in explanation of his words.* Arundel rose to dissuade the House from hearing the prisoner any further. We have his words, he said, and nothing more is necessary. In itself such a doctrine was not likely to meet with acceptance amongst the opponents of the Court, and it was specially unpalatable as coming from one who, as the representative of the Howards, might well seem to have strayed from his natural position in swelling the ranks of the supporters of the favourite. The feeling of the popular party was felicitously expressed by Spencer. He was surprised, he said, to hear such a doctrine from the Earl of Arundel, for he remembered that two of his ancestors, the Duke of Norfolk and the Earl of Surrey, had been unjustly condemned to death without a hearing. Stung by the retort which he had called down upon himself, Arundel sprung to his feet. "My Lords," he replied, with all the haughty insolence of his nature, "I do acknowledge that my ancestors have suffered, and it may be for doing the king and the country good service, and in such time as when, perhaps, the Lord's ancestors that spake last kept sheep."† An insult so uncalled for was received with a storm of reprobation on all sides. Suffolk attempted to interpose. He was even more nearly related than Arundel to those of whom Spencer had spoken, and he truly said that he thought that he had heard nothing but what was to their honour. The Prince then stepped forward, and demanded the adjournment of the House. For more than a week no further reference was made to the affair, and time was given for the angry passions which had been excited to calm down. Yet even then Arundel's indomitable pride was unconquered. To the House, he

Ch. VII.
1621.
May 8.

Quarrel between Arundel and Spencer.

---

* *Lords' Journals*, iii. 111, 115. Elsing's *Notes*, May 8.
† Words spoken in the House, May 8. *S. P. Dom.* cxxi. 15.

said, he was ready to apologize. To Lord Spencer he had nothing to say. He persisted in his refusal, and was sent as a prisoner to the Tower, from which he was only released at the special request of the King, and upon an engagement from the Prince of Wales that he would see a reconciliation effected between the two peers.* In the meanwhile Yelverton's case, which had been interrupted by Arundel's unseemly attack upon Spencer, had been brought again before the Lords. On the 12th of May, Buckingham moved that the House should proceed at once to censure him for his insult to the King. Again voices were raised, demanding that he should first be heard in his defence. Bishop Morton attempted to mediate. "The words," he said, "were scandalous, whatsoever their meaning was. But let us hear what meaning he places on them himself." Against the suggestion thus made, Arundel, who had not yet been sent to the Tower, rose defiantly. "Sir Henry Yelverton," he said, "is not judged unheard. He spake the words openly in this House. He had time to explain himself, and his speech we have in writing." But neither Arundel nor Buckingham was able to carry the House with him on such a question as this. The Lord Treasurer and the Archbishop of Canterbury joined in protesting against a doctrine that an accused person was not to be heard in his own defence. Dorset, Suffolk, and Southampton followed in their wake. At last, in order to satisfy the exigencies of the King, it was agreed that the words spoken touched the King's honour as the House did "yet conceive." No final judgment was to be passed on them till the prisoner had been heard.†

Accordingly, on the 14th, Yelverton was brought to the bar to answer for himself. Unable to offer any legal proof that Mompesson had not invented the messages

---

* Chamberlain to Carleton, May 19, June 9. *S. P. Dom.* cxxi. 44, 88. Salvetti's *News-Letter*, May $\frac{18}{28}$. It is worth while to compare this story as told at the time, with that which has been adopted by subsequent writers from Wilson's history. Wilson makes Spencer follow Arundel with an imaginary speech, "When my ancestors were keeping sheep, yours were plotting treason," omitting all reference to Spencer's real words. Both the letter and the spirit of the narrative are thus entirely sacrificed.

† Elsing's *Notes*, May 12.

which he had brought from Buckingham, he was reduced to explain away his words as best he might. There must have been many present who felt that the spirit of his accusation was true. But there was no evidence before them to show that it was literally true, and the Lords did not venture, perhaps did not wish, to cast upon the King the stigma which would be implied in a dismissal of the charge. Yelverton was accordingly declared to have attacked the honour of the King. With regard to the words spoken against Buckingham, the House was less unanimous. All were willing to declare them to be scandalous, but a minority, we know not how large, nor of whom it was composed, protested against declaring them to be false.* The prisoner was then sentenced to pay ten thousand marks to the King, and five thousand to Buckingham—to be imprisoned during pleasure, and to ask pardon for his offence.

By Buckingham this result was regarded in the light of a personal triumph. He was now, he was heard openly to boast, "Parliament proof." With that magnificent display of generosity which he knew well how to assume towards a beaten adversary, he at once remitted his share of the fine, and the Prince was requested by the House to express a hope that the King would be equally merciful.†

Not only had the favourite succeeded in bringing his own bark into smooth waters, but he had carried his brothers with him into a safe harbour. With the abandonment of the enquiry into the patent for ale-houses, the charge against Christopher Villiers fell to the ground, and Sir Edward, who had lately returned from his mission to Germany, was allowed to take his seat in the Commons without further molestation, though he prudently declined to avail himself of the permission till the storm had completely blown over.‡

Seldom has the unfitness of the Lords to act as a judicial body been more clearly brought out than in the

---

* Elsing's *Notes*, May 14, 15, 16.
† *Lords' Journals*, iii. 123, 124. Chamberlain to Carleton, May 19. *S. P. Dom.* cxxi. 44.
‡ *Lords' Journals*, iii. 76. *Proceedings and Debates*, ii. 3.

CH. VII.
1621.

treatment which Yelverton received at their hands. No real attempt was made to sound to the bottom that evil system of which Yelverton's hints had disclosed the abysses. No attempt was made to define the law which limited the free expression of opinion on the actions of persons in authority. It was enough that he had uttered or implied a condemnation of the King's proceedings; and even those who believed that what he said was true, shrunk from pronouncing a sentence in his favour.

Yet in truth, though much may be done by the substitution of trained and independent tribunals for a body composed, like the House of Lords, of men either dependent on the Court, or influenced by their own political feelings, the fault did not lie entirely with the composition of the tribunal by which Yelverton was tried. It is only when the great truth that liberty of speech is a good thing in itself has sunk deeply into the national conscience, that such scenes as those which attended Yelverton's condemnation become impossible, and unhappily the Peers did not stand alone in their ignorance of this cornerstone of freedom.

Proclamation against free speech.

During the early years of James's reign, indeed— except when actual treason was supposed to have been committed—little had been heard of penalties for words spoken or printed on political subjects. The times were quiet, and there was no general inclination to take part in the quarrel which divided the Crown from the House of Commons. But with the attack upon the Palatinate, all this was changed. The nation was resolutely bent upon following one line of policy. The King was no less resolutely bent upon following another. Hard words were spoken everywhere, if not of the King himself, of the King's ally, the King of Spain; and these words sometimes found their way into print, or into those sermons which, in those days, had a real political importance.

Dec. 24, 1620.

James was sorely irritated. Of the real benefits of freedom of utterance he knew as little as any of his contemporaries. He issued a proclamation forbidding men to speak on State affairs.* Scot, the author of the clever

---

* Proclamation, Dec. 24, 1620. *S. P. Dom.* clxxxvii. 87.

pamphlet, "Vox Populi,"* was forced to save himself by flight.† Dr. Everard, a London preacher, was summoned before the Council, and was committed to the Gatehouse, for inveighing in a sermon against the Spanish cruelties in the Indies.‡ But the case which most justly attracted public attention was that of Dr. Ward, of Ipswich, a man of considerable reputation as a preacher, who possessed the unusual accomplishment of ability to express his thoughts with his pencil as well as with his pen. He had lately put forth his skill as a caricaturist upon a picture which Gondomar had been able to represent as an insult to his master. On one side was to be seen the wreck of the Armada, driven in wild confusion before the storm. On the other side was the detection of the Gunpowder Plot. In the centre the Pope and the Cardinals appeared in consultation with the King of Spain and the Devil.§ Ward paid for his indiscretion by a short imprisonment, followed by an inhibition from preaching any more at Ipswich. By the people he was regarded as a martyr, and a story was freely circulated, telling how in reality he owed his punishment to the manly stand which he had taken against the election of a Papist as a knight of the shire for the county of Suffolk.‖

The invariable correlative of restraint upon speech is licentiousness of action. The repression to which James had subjected the spirit with which Englishmen were almost universally animated, only caused it to burst out in irregular channels. As Gondomar was one day passing down Fenchurch-street, in his litter, a saucy apprentice shouted after him, "There goes the Devil in a dung-cart." Stung by the taunt, one of his servants turned sharply upon the offender. "Sir," he said, "you shall see Bridewell ere long for your mirth." "What," was the reply, "shall we go to Bridewell for such a dog as thou?" Suiting his action to his words, the lad raised his fist, and knocked the Spaniard into the gutter. The ambassador

Ch. VII.
1621.
January:
Cases of Scot, Everard, and Ward.

March.

Insult to Gondomar.

* Vol. i. p. 394.
† Chamberlain to Carleton, Feb. 3. Locke to Carleton, Feb. 16. *S. P. Dom.* cxix. 64, 99.
‡ Mead to Stuteville, March 10. *Harl. MSS.* 389, fol. 37.
§ Description of Ward's Picture. *Harl. MSS.* 389, fol. 13.
‖ Mead to Stuteville, Feb. 24. *Harl. MSS.* 389, fol. 21. Petition of Ward, May 31. *S. P. Dom.* cxxx. 127.

appealed to the Lord Mayor for justice, and he, sorely against his will, sentenced the apprentice and his companions who had supported him, to be whipped through the streets. That an Englishman should be flogged for insulting a Spaniard was intolerable to the London populace. A crowd soon gathered round the cart, the youths were rescued, and the officials whose duty it was to carry out the sentence were themselves driven away with blows. Gondomar once more complained to the Lord Mayor, but the Lord Mayor, who in heart sympathized with the offenders, drily informed him that it was not to him that an account of the government of the city was to be rendered. James was next appealed to, and at once responded to the appeal. He came down in person to Guildhall. If such things were allowed, he said, he would place a garrison in the city, and seize its charter. The end of the affair was tragical enough. The original sentence was carried out, and one of the apprentices died under the lash.*

The feeling of indignation with which James's one-sided severity was received spread to higher regions. Chafing under the self-imposed silence which had for many weeks restrained their tongues from even mentioning the name of the Palatinate, the Commons were in a temper to catch eagerly at the first opportunity which offered itself, to give vent to the thoughts which were burning within. It was not long in coming. An aged Roman Catholic barrister, named Floyd, who had been imprisoned in the Fleet by the Council, had been guilty, as the House was informed, of the heinous offence of rejoicing at the news of the battle of Prague. "Goodman Palsgrave and Goodwife Palsgrave," he had been heard to say, "were now turned out of doors." At another time he had argued that Frederick had no more right than himself to the Bohemian Crown. Witnesses were called to prove the truth of the story. Floyd denied that he had ever said anything of the kind. The next day, however, additional witnesses corroborated the statements which had been previously made. Floyd persisted in his denial.

---

* Meddus to Mead, April 6. Mead to Stuteville, April 7. *Harl. MSS.* 389, fol. 50, 48. *Council Register*, April 2.

Then followed a scene, the like of which has seldom been exhibited in an English Parliament. Phelips proposed that Floyd should ride with his face to the horse's tail from Westminster to the Tower, bearing on his hat a paper with the inscription, "A popish wretch, that hath maliciously scandalized his Majesty's children," and that he should then be lodged in the horrible dungeon appropriately known as Little Ease, "with as much pain as he shall be able to endure without loss or danger of his life." Terrible as Phelips's suggestion was, it was not harsh enough for his hearers. All consideration for the rights of free speech, all thought of proportioning the punishment to the offence, was lost in the whirlpool of passion. A few words by Roe and Digges, not on behalf of Floyd, but on behalf of the Lords of the Council, who might resent any attempt to meddle with their prisoner, were followed by an immediate explosion. "If we have no precedent," said Sir George More, "let us make one. Let Floyd be whipped to the place from whence he came, and then let him be left to the Lords." "Let his beads be hung about his neck," cried Sir Francis Seymour, "and let him have as many lashes as he has beads." Sir Edward Giles hoped that he might be pilloried at Westminster, and whipped. Sir Francis Darcy was not content unless he might be twice pilloried, and twice whipped. Each member, as he shouted out his opinion, was more savage than the last. Let a hole be burnt in his tongue. Let his tongue be cut out. Let him be branded on the forehead. Let his nose and ears be lopped off. Let him be compelled to swallow his beads. Another member, with cruel irony, added that he had wished to recommend the heaviest possible punishment, but that, as "he perceived that the House was inclined to mercy, he would have him whipped more than twice as far as those who offended against the ambassador." At this stage John Finch, the future Lord Keeper of Charles I., attempted to interpose. The House, he said, had no evidence upon oath upon which to act. This reasonable suggestion was scouted by Walter, whose conduct on this day is the strongest evidence of the criminal follies into which even an honourable man may fall, in times when the principles upon

Ch. VII.
1621.
May 1.
Exasperation of the Commons.

<small>Ch. VII.
1621.
May 1.
Sentence upon Floyd.</small>

which freedom and morality rest, have not yet been engraved upon the public mind. "Let Floyd's lands and goods," he said, "be given to raise a force to recover the Palatinate. Let him be whipped for laughing at the loss of Prague, thereby to make him shed tears." Alone amongst the popular party, Sandys, the veteran champion of liberty, showed some glimmerings of sense. The real cause of Floyd's offence, he observed, was the difference in religion. If in his punishment his religion were touched, he would be looked upon as a martyr. Nor was it proper to whip a gentleman. This was not much to say. But it had its effect. All thought of branding and whipping was relinquished. Yet the poor old man, who had committed no real crime, was sentenced by the House to be pilloried three times, to ride from station to station on a bare-backed horse with his face to the tail, and a paper on his hat explaining the nature of his offence. Lastly, he was to pay a fine of 1000*l*.*

<small>May 2.
Objections of the King.</small>

When the members came down to take their places for the next morning's sitting, it was with the full expectation that they would be able to feast their eyes upon the sufferings of Floyd as they passed through Palace Yard. Nothing of the kind however was to be seen. They were told by the Chancellor of the Exchequer that the King had commanded him to thank them for their care of his honour, and then to ask them two questions. Could they show that they had authority to inflict punishment upon anyone, who, not being one of themselves, had neither offended against their House nor against any of its members? And if they could satisfy him on this point, would they inform him how they could condemn a man who denied his fault, without being able to take evidence on oath against him? A record was then handed in, from which it appeared that in the reign of Henry IV. the Commons had acknowledged that they had nothing to do with sentencing offenders.

<small>Hesitation of the Commons.</small>

Now that the excitement had passed off, there were few whose opinion was worth anything who did not know that the assertions implied in the King's questions were unanswerable. For it was certain that over Floyd

<small>* *Commons' Journals*, i. 601. *Proceedings and Debates*, i. 370.</small>

the Commons had no jurisdiction whatever. In fact, earlier in the session they had, in dealing with Mompesson, expressly renounced the right which they had now intemperately assumed. Noy, whose authority stood high on such questions, after denying the supposed right of the House, moved for a committee to search for precedents. Even this was more than Hakewill was willing to concede. It would, he said, be entirely useless. He had himself searched diligently for such precedents, and he was certain that none were to be found. Coke, who had been absent the day before, and who knew perfectly well what the law was, now interfered. He had no wish to bolster up an indefensible position, but he feared lest, in its recoil from a post which had been found to be untenable, the House might surrender claims which were fairly its own. The literal sense of the record presented to them would, he showed, debar them from scrutinising even the conduct of their own members. But they were not bound to acknowledge its force. It was no act of Parliament. "Let his tongue cleave to the roof of his mouth," he ended by saying, in his magisterial way, "who says that this House is no Court of Record. Though we have not the power of judicature in all things, yet we have it in some things."*

CH. VII.
1621.
May 2.

The only question which remained was, how to recede with dignity. It was finally decided that the King should be asked to put the sentence in force by his own authority, but that he should be told at the same time that the Commons did not consider themselves bound by the record which he had produced. Such a solution could not be satisfactory to anyone. In asking the King to confer by his mere prerogative validity upon an invalid sentence, the Commons were asking him to put forth powers which in another cause they would have been the first to dispute. After some further negotiation, James signified his intention of leaving the matter in the hands of the Lords.

May 3.
Negotiations with the King and the Lords.

Accordingly the Lords, as a preliminary to their investigation of the matter, proceeded to clear up the question of jurisdiction. At a conference held on the 5th of May,

* *Commons' Journals,* i. 603. *Proceedings and Debates,* ii. 5, 13.

Ch. VII.
1621.
May 5.

May 16.
The Commons give way.

May 26.
Floyd sentenced by the Lords.

Doctrine finally adopted on the jurisdiction of the Lords.

Coke had much to say on the right of the Commons to punish offences which affected their own House, but had nothing better to say about Floyd's case than that the words against the Electress "were spoken against the members of the House of Commons; for a daughter is part of her father, and the King is ever intended to be resident in that House." The result of the discussion was the acceptance by both sides of a declaration, which, under cover of leaving the law precisely as it stood before Floyd's name was mentioned, virtually gave the victory to the Lords.*

As far as the poor wretch who was the unwilling subject of the dispute was concerned, it would have been better if he had been left to the tender mercies of the Commons. The Lords, probably to show that they had no kindly feeling towards Papists, raised his fine from 1000*l.* to 5000*l.*, declared him an infamous person, whose testimony was never to be received in any court of justice, ordered him to be imprisoned for life, and to be whipped at the cart's tail from London Bridge to Westminster Hall.† It was no merit of the peers that the whipping was remitted by the King at the instance of the Prince of Wales.

Strangely enough this abominable sentence was, at least according to the doctrine which has been ultimately adopted, as unconstitutional as that which had been pronounced by the Commons. For the Lower House did not think it consistent with its dignity to prefer a definite charge against Floyd at the bar of the House of Lords, and, ever since that evil day on which, surrounded by a band of armed satellites, a misguided Sovereign attempted, against the express will of the Commons, to drag the leaders of the Long Parliament to a trial before the Peers, it has passed into a political axiom that, except in matters in which the privileges of their own members are concerned, the Lords can only exercise criminal jurisdiction upon the presentment of the House of Commons.‡

* *Commons' Journals,* i. 604, 608. *Lords' Journals,* iii. 119, 124. *Proceedings and Debates,* ii. 15, 19, 29.
† *Lords' Journals,* iii. 134.
‡ Hale, *Jurisdiction of the Lords,* 95. See, for Floyd's case, Hargrave's preface to this work, xvi.

Such a doctrine, indeed, may be supported by arguments far stronger than those which the lawyers of the seventeenth century derived from the analogy between the functions of the House of Commons and the functions of a grand jury; for, by requiring the co-operation of two independent bodies, it went far to lessen the chances of hasty and passionate injustice. But however the evil might be mitigated, it was none the less distinctly an evil, only to be tolerated because at the beginning of the seventeenth century the remedy would have been worse than the disease. For, however advisable it might be that political prosecutions should be conducted before judges and not before a political body, there were no judges in existence to whom the duty of conducting such trials could safely be entrusted. Revocable at the pleasure of the Crown, and since the overthrow of Coke, having the prospect of dismissal ever dangling before their eyes, the majority of the judges could not, as long as human nature is what it is, be impartial in such matters. If it was a bad thing that a court should be guided by its political sympathies like the House of Lords, it would have been far worse to trust questions of high political importance to a court warped by self-interest like the King's Bench or the Common Pleas. Nor were there wanting other reasons to justify, at least for the time, the renewed claim of Parliament to exercise jurisdiction over state offences. The time had come when the nation was beginning to watch with a jealous eye the conduct of the high officers of state. The time had not yet come when a vote of its representatives would be sufficient to remove them from office. It was only by the fear of a criminal charge that they could be in any way controlled, and no tribunal of less authority than Parliament could deal with them at all. It was by giving us at once a body of independent judges, and a House of Commons which was strong enough to control the Executive Government, that the Revolution of 1688 virtually put an end to parliamentary impeachments.*

CH. VII.
1621.
May 26.

* The case of Warren Hastings is an exception, which proves the rule, as a question of Indian, not of English government. The idea of impeachment has lately become again familiar to us from the events passing in

Ch. VII.
1621.
May 30.
Cases of Bishop Field;

The Lords had still two cases to dispose of. With the Bishop of Llandaff they dealt mercifully. It was proved that he had taken from Edward Egerton a recognizance for 6000*l.* upon a promise to do his best to procure for him the good will of the Chancellor. But the money had never been paid, and no service had been rendered in return. Such arguments would have availed Floyd but little. But a member of the House of Lords was not likely to appeal to the peers in vain. They contented themselves with handing over the offender to the Archbishop of Canterbury, who promised to admonish him publicly in convocation. He did not, however, take the admonition seriously to heart, for the first thing that he did after the Houses ceased to sit was to implore Buckingham to promote him to a better bishopric.*

May 31. and of Sir J. Bennett.

Sir John Bennett was still to be kept in suspense. Time would not allow a complete investigation of his case, and he was released on bail, with orders to prepare a reply to the depositions against him.†

May. Several patents condemned by the Commons.

Whilst the Lords had been mainly occupied with judicial business, the other House had not been idle. Patents for the sole engrossing of wills, for the levying of lighthouse tolls, for the importation of salmon and lobsters, for the making of gold leaf, and for the manufacture of glass were voted to be grievances. A monopoly bill had been passed by which the decision of the question, whether the protected manufacture was a new invention or not, would from henceforth be left to the ordinary tribunals. There had been long and anxious debates upon the alleged decline of trade, which seems to have been suffering temporarily from the effects of the war in Germany, and many rash and unwise restrictions were proposed in a vain hope that, with their aid, commerce might be restored to a flourishing condition. There had been an attempt also to set on foot an inquiry into the state of Ireland, which had been promptly checked by

America. There, too, the question would never have been raised, if the constitution had provided any ordinary means by which the representative body could control the executive.
* Field to Buckingham, June (?). *Harl. MSS.* 7000, fol. 57.
† *Lords' Journals,* iii. 143, 148.

the King, who held that this was a subject with which he was himself perfectly competent to deal.

On the 28th of May, however, in the very midst of their toils, the Commons were startled by a royal message directing them to bring their labours to an end within a week. The gentry, they were told, were wanted in their own neighbourhoods; the lawyers were wanted in Westminster Hall. Yet the House need not fear that their time had been wasted. There should be no prorogation to compel them to recommence their work at their next meeting. There would be a simple adjournment, and they would thus be able to resume their business at the stage at which they had left it.

The House was taken by surprise. There could be little doubt that more was intended than had been said. It may be that James was nettled at the contemptuous silence with which his demand for a fresh subsidy had been met, and with the pretensions of the Commons in their claim to jurisdiction over Floyd, or that he wished to hinder any renewed legislation upon recusancy. Rumour, too, was busy in bringing to his ear news of the proceedings of the opposition party in the Upper House. Their ill-will against Buckingham, it was told, had not relaxed, and suspicious meetings had been held at Southampton's house in Holborn, to which members of the House of Commons had been invited. It was even said that a scheme had been concocted for diverting future subsidies from the Exchequer, by sending them over directly to the fugitive King of Bohemia.*

In vain the Commons appealed to the Peers to aid them in obtaining a change in the King's intentions. All that James allowed the Lords to say was, that if the Lower House wished to get ready a few bills by the end of the week the King would give his assent to them, an act which, according to the notions of the day,

Ch. VII.
1621.

May 28.
The King directs an adjournment.

May 29.
Proposal of a prorogation.

---

* Compare the examinations in the Appendix to *Proceedings and Debates*, with a letter by Ashley to Buckingham, May 12. *Cabala*, 2. How any one, in the face of this letter, can maintain that Buckingham had taken part, except from timidity, in the overthrow of Bacon, I am unable to understand.

Ch. VII.
1621.
May 29.
Dissatisfaction of the Commons.

would bring the session to a close, thus involving a prorogation instead of an adjournment.*

Such an offer, in truth, was entirely illusory. There was not time to give a thorough discussion to the bills upon which the Commons had set their hearts. The statement made by the Lords was received with open discontent. Tongues were loosed which had for four months been placed under strict restraint. "The country," said Sandys, "is in a dangerous state. Our religion is rooted out of Bohemia and Germany. It will soon be rooted out of France." He then moved that nothing more should be done that day. Their hearts, he said, were full of grief and fear. Perhaps time might temper their passions. Cranfield then tried to speak, but the house refused to listen to him, and Sandys's motion was adopted.

May 30.

Reflection in this case did not bring a change of mood. The next morning Phelips painted in mournful colours the evil estate of religion abroad and at home, and urged that one more appeal should be made to the House of Lords. The Lords listened, but could give no hope whatever of inducing the King to prolong their sittings. They would do what they could. They would agree to the passing of an act declaring that, in this case at least, the royal assent to a few selected bills should not prevent the resumption of business, when they next met, at the stage at which it had been left. But the Commons would not hear of such a compromise. To an offer made by James to close the session after prolonging their sittings for a week or ten days, they were equally deaf. There was no time, they thought, left to do anything worthy of the name of a session. They would prefer the adjournment which had been originally proposed.†

June 4.
The last sitting.

Yet the last advances of James towards the Commons had not been wholly thrown away. Their temper had been ruffled, but only for a moment. They resolved to return thanks to the King for his offer of an additional week.‡ At their last sitting they listened with evident

---

* *Proceedings and Debates,* ii. 118. *Lords' Journals,* iii. 140.
† *Proceedings and Debates,* ii. 121—159. *Lords' Journals,* iii. 148, 153.
‡ *Proceedings and Debates,* ii. 161.

satisfaction to Cranfield's assurances that the burdens under which trade was suffering should have the immediate attention of the Government.

There were those, however, present who felt that this was not a fitting conclusion to the labours of the House. In the stormy discussions of the past week words had again been heard on that subject which the vast majority of the members had most deeply at heart, but they had not been always spoken wisely. For three months the House had disciplined itself into silence, by its earnest determination to act if possible in unison with the King. Carried away by the feelings of the moment, Sandys and Phelips had let fall expressions by which Gondomar might be led to imagine that England would no longer present an united front to the enemy. A few moments only now remained to wipe away such a mistake as that. Accordingly, whilst there was yet time, Sir John Perrot rose, in the midst of a discussion upon the mode of levying customs at the ports. It was Perrot who, at the commencement of the session, had moved that the Commons should partake of the Communion together as "a means of reconciliation," and as "a touchstone to try their faith."* In a similar spirit he now addressed them. The House, he said, had shown itself careful of the ports; but there was something still more necessary, namely, to provide for that port which would be the surest resting-place, and which would procure for them a perpetual rest when the merchandise, trade, and traffic of this life would have an end. True religion must be maintained. Abroad it was in sad case. At home it was in danger. At the beginning of the Parliament the King had declared that if the Palatinate could not be recovered by treaty, he would adventure his blood and life in its cause. Let them therefore, before they separated, make a public declaration that, if the treaty failed, they would upon their return be ready to adventure their lives and estates for the maintenance of the cause of God and of his Majesty's royal issue.

When Perrot sat down it was evident that he had touched the right chord in the hearts of his hearers.

Perrot's motion.

It is received with acclamation.

* *Commons' Journals*, i. 508.

Ch. VII.
1621.
June 4.

"This declaration," said Cecil, "comes from Heaven. It will do more for us than if we had ten thousand soldiers on the march." The motion was put and assented to amidst universal acclamation. "It was entertained," says one who took part in the scene,* "with much joy and a general consent of the whole House, and sounded forth with the voices of them all, withal lifting up their hats in their hands as high as they could hold them, as a visible testimony of their unanimous consent, in such sort that the like had scarce ever been seen in Parliament." †

The Commons' declaration.

A committee was at once appointed to prepare the declaration. In a few minutes its work was done. "The Commons assembled in Parliament," so ran the manifesto, " taking into consideration the present estate of the King's children abroad, and the general afflicted estate of the true professors of the same Christian religion professed by the Church of England and other foreign parts ; and being troubled with a true sense and fellow-feeling of their distresses as members of the same body, do, with one unanimous consent of themselves and of the whole body of the kingdom whom they do represent, declare unto the whole world their hearty grief and sorrow for the same ; and do not only join with them in their humble and devout prayers to Almighty God to protect his true Church, and to avert the dangers now threatened, but also with one heart and voice do solemnly protest that, if his Majesty's pious endeavours by treaty to procure their peace and safety shall not take that good effect he desireth, in the treaty whereof they humbly beseech his Majesty to make no long delay ;—that then, upon the signification of his pleasure in Parliament, they shall be ready to the uttermost of their powers, both with their lives and fortunes, to assist him ; so as, by the Divine help of Almighty God, who is never wanting unto those who, in His fear, shall undertake the defence of His own cause, he may be able to do that by his sword which by peaceable courses shall not be effected."

Adjourn-

Again, when the declaration had been read, the hats

* Edward Nicholas.
† *Proceedings and Debates*, ii. 170.

were waved high in the air. Again the shouts of acclamation rang out cheerily. Perrot had been just in time. The messengers from the Lords were at the door to notify the King's order to adjourn to the 14th of November. The Commons answered that, according to custom, they would adjourn themselves. Before the motion was put, Coke stood up, and with tears in his eyes, repeated the prayer for the Royal Family, adding, as he finished it, "and defend them from their cruel enemies."

For a time the work of the House of Commons was at an end. Complaints had been heard that the long months of labour had produced nothing with which the constituencies could be reasonably satisfied. With the exception of the act by which the subsidies had been granted, not a single bill had been passed. So far as legislation was concerned, monopolists were as safe as ever. The claims of the prerogative were as undefined as at the commencement of the session. Yet the Houses had not sat in vain. They had rescued from oblivion the right of impeachment, and had taught a crowd of hungry and unscrupulous adventurers that Court favour would not always suffice to screen them. They had made judicial corruption almost impossible for the future. Yet the highest of their achievements had not been of a nature to be quoted as a precedent, or to be noted down amongst the catalogue of constitutional changes. Far more truly than any member of that House dreamed, a crisis had come in which Protestantism was to be tried in the balance. There was a danger greater than any which was to be dreaded from the armies of Spinola or the policy of Maximilian, a danger lest moral superiority should pass over to the champions of the reactionary faith. And it was at such a crisis that the English House of Commons placed itself in the foremost ranks of those who were helping on the progress of the world. Cecil spoke truly when he said that their declaration would do more good than if ten thousand soldiers had been on the march. It showed that James and Frederick and John George were not the utmost that Protestantism could produce; that it had given birth to men who might be ignorant of much, but who were steeled with the armour of

Ch. VII.
1621.
June 4.

self-denial and self-restraint, and who were willing to sacrifice themselves for the common cause. It was of no political advantage to England that they were dreaming. They formed no schemes of national aggrandisement like Richelieu, they cherished no personal ambition like Gustavus. They thought of the poor inhabitants of the Palatinate, of the Bohemian churches empty or profaned, of the silenced voices of the ministers of the gospel, and though they never more than half-trusted James, they had the penetration to recognise the fact that it was only under James's leadership that they could help in averting the catastrophe. And so they disciplined themselves into silence, and restrained their zeal, lest by a moment's ill-considered speech, they should alienate the man who alone was in a position to give effect to their wishes. They had done more than gain a victory. They had ruled their own spirits. Once more moral greatness was on the side of Protestantism.

James accepts the declaration.

When James first heard that a declaration on the affairs of the Palatinate had been voted, he was much displeased; but as soon as he read it, his opinion changed. He ordered it to be translated into the chief languages of Europe, in order that foreign nations might learn to respect the loyalty of the English people.*

Bacon's imprisonment and release.

James was, no doubt, glad enough to regain his independence of action. No candid person will complain of his determination to moderate the harshness of Bacon's sentence. He was indeed far too indolent to set on foot on his own account, a thorough investigation of his late Chancellor's conduct. He probably thought, as every one else thought, that he was far more guilty than he really was. But the memory of old friendship and of years of devoted service indisposed him to harshness. For some days after the sentence was pronounced, Bacon was allowed to remain unmolested at York House, out of consideration for his health.† But before the Parliament broke up, he

* Chamberlain to Carleton, June 9. *S. P. Dom.* cxxi. 88.
† On the 12th of May, Southampton reminded the Lords that Bacon had not yet been sent to the Tower, and "hoped that the world may not think our sentence is in vain;" Buckingham replied that "the King hath respited his going to the Tower in this time of his great sickness." Elsing's *Notes,* May 12.

was conducted to the Tower.* It was never, however, intended that he should remain long a prisoner. A warrant for his release was sent to him with an intimation that he would do well not to use it till after the Houses had risen. So great, however, was his impatience, that he could not wait, and came away at once before the last sitting had taken place. Sir John Vaughan's house at Parson's Green was assigned him as a temporary residence. As, however, the place was within twelve miles of the Court, he could not be permitted to remain there long. A little breathing-time was granted him to settle his affairs; but on the 22nd of June, he was obliged, much against his will, to betake himself to Gorhambury.†

Any other man would have been crushed by the blow by which he had been surprised, and would have resigned himself, at least for a time, to lethargy. Bacon only saw in his exclusion from political life an additional reason for throwing himself heart and soul into other work. In less than five months after his liberation he had completed that noble history of the reign of Henry VII., which stands confessedly amongst the choicest first-fruits of the long harvest of English historical literature.

Two days before Bacon's removal to Gorhambury, the sentence of the House of Lords upon an offender of a very different kind was carried out. Sir Francis Michell was in due form degraded from knighthood. The spurs were hacked from his heels, the sword was broken over his head, and the heralds proclaimed to the applauding bystanders, that from henceforth he would be known as "Francis Michell, Knave." He was conducted back, amidst the hootings of the mob, to Finsbury Gaol, from which, about a fortnight later, he was contemptuously set at liberty.‡ Not long afterwards, Mompesson's fine was granted to trustees, for the use of his wife and child.§

---

* Chamberlain to Carleton, June 2. *S. P. Dom.* cxxi. 69.
† Chamberlain to Carleton, June 9. *S. P. Dom.* cxxi. 88. Bacon to Buckingham, May 31, June 4, 22, 30. *Works*, ed. Montagu, xii. 490, xiii. 32, xii. 408, xiii. 6. The letter to the Prince, xiii. 31, dated on the 1st of June, was really, as Mr. Spedding informs me, written on the 7th.
‡ Chamberlain to Carleton, June 23. *S. P. Dom.* cxxi. 120. Meddus to Mead, June 22. *Harl. MSS.* 389, fol. 96. Michell's petition, June 30. *S. P. Dom.* cxxi. 135.
§ Grant to St. John and Hungerford, July 7. *Sign Manuals*, xii. 71.

Ch. VII.
1621.
June 16.
Arrest of Southampton, Sandys, and Selden.

Against such lenity as this to men, for whose faults the Government was more than half responsible, there would have been little to be said, if it had not been sharply contrasted with harshness exercised in another direction. James had been deeply annoyed at the consultations which had been held between Southampton and certain members of the Lower House, with the object, it was said, of opening direct negotiations with Frederick and Elizabeth. On the 16th, Southampton, as he rose from the council-board, was ordered into confinement. On the same day, Sandys and Selden were arrested, the latter, though not a member of Parliament, having, it is said, given offence by an opinion delivered in support of the jurisdiction of the Commons over Floyd.

Anything more impolitic it is impossible to conceive. At once a belief in the unreality of the apparent concord between the Crown and the Lower House began to spread. A story was eagerly repeated that, when the searchers applied to Lady Sandys for Sir Edwin's keys, she had answered that she wished his Majesty had a key to her husband's heart, as he would then see that there was nothing there but loyalty. It was to no purpose that the world was carefully informed that the prisoners were not called in question for anything done in Parliament. Men shrugged their shoulders incredulously. The wildest rumours flew about. Coke, it was said, had been sent for. The Archbishop of Canterbury and the Bishop of Lichfield had been imprisoned. It was not long before another nobleman shared in reality Southampton's fate. A year before, the Earl of Oxford had surprised all who knew him by leaving those dissipations in which his youth had been passed, for the sake of hard service under Vere in the Palatinate. But he did not remain long upon the Continent. In company with the more demure Essex, he hurried back, as soon as the summer was over, to take his place in the House of Lords, and he now thought himself justified by the very moderate amount of hardship which he had undergone, in grumbling about the thankless reception which had been accorded to his services. One day he had inveighed over his wine against Popery and the Spanish match, and his words being reported to the

July 13.
Imprisonment of Oxford.

King, he was placed under arrest.* James was sufficiently vexed to issue a fresh proclamation "against excess of lavish and licentious speech of matters of state."†

Fortunately for James there was one amongst those to whom he willingly listened, who was able to warn him against the consequences of such blunders as these. Since he had warded off a breach with the Commons, Williams had found the King's ear open to him on all occasions. His first thought had been to claim his own reward. The see of London was vacant, and Williams lost no time in asking for it.‡ But, before his pretensions could be satisfied, a still more brilliant prospect opened itself before him. It was necessary to provide a successor to Bacon. Ley and Hobart had been pointed out by rumour as competitors for the office, but it was soon understood that the King's choice would rest upon Cranfield. Before, however, the selection had finally been made, it happened that Williams, who had learned many secrets as Ellesmere's chaplain, was consulted on a point of detail relating to the profits of the place, and that James was so struck with the ability of his reply, and with his thorough knowledge of the subject, that he at once declared that he would entrust the great seal to no one else.§

It is true that Williams was a clergyman only in name, and that he was not likely to be tainted with those faults by which so many ecclesiastical politicians have been ruined. Yet any sovereign who in our days should be guilty of such a choice, would justly be regarded as insane. For the last two centuries the equity administered in the Court of Chancery has been growing up into a body of scientific jurisprudence, which can only be grasped by those who have received a special legal training. It was far otherwise at the commencement of the seventeenth century. It was the business of Chancery to supply a correction to the highly artificial rules of the

---

* Examinations. App. to *Proceedings and Debates*. Meddus to Mead, June 22. Mead to Stuteville, June 23. *Harl. MSS.* 389, fol. 96, 98. Chamberlain to Carleton, June 23, July 14. *S. P. Dom.* cxxi. 121, cxxii. 23.
† Proclamation, July 26. *S. P. Dom.* clxxxvii. 95.
‡ Williams to Buckingham, April (?). *Cabala*, 374.
§ Hacket's *Life of Williams*, 52.

CH. VII.
1621.
July.

Common Law, and until the time came for the growth of a better and more coherent system, it was sufficient that the Chancellor should be possessed of a mind large enough to grasp the general principles of justice, and quick enough to apply those principles to the case before him. He would bear, in fact, very much the same relation to the other judges, which is in our day borne by a Secretary of State to the permanent officials of his department. Such a man, when he is first appointed, knows less of the details of business than his subordinates; but he brings to its transaction a mind less trammelled by routine, and therefore more open to the admission of new and enlarged conceptions.

and Bishop of Lincoln.

As might have been expected, many objections were raised against the King's choice. "I had thought," said Bacon, with a sneer, "that I should have known my successor." Yet it does not appear that any one complained of Williams's ignorance of law. Some said that he was too young; and that it was unfair to others "that so mean a man as a Dean should so suddenly leap over their heads." To remedy the last complaint as far as it was possible, James announced his intention to translate Bishop Montaigne to the see of London, and to give to Williams the Bishopric of Lincoln, which would be vacated by Montaigne. The great seal should not be placed in his hands till after the *congé d'élire* had been issued.*

On the 10th of July, he received the seal by the title of Lord Keeper. He had far too much tact not to be anxious that his promotion should be as unostentatious as possible. At his own request it was given out that he was appointed on probation, and that some of the common-law judges would take their seats with him on the bench as his assistants.†

His next step was to apply himself diligently to the study of law. Every day he shut himself up for hours with Serjeant Finch, in the hope of making himself fit for the duties of his office before Michaelmas term began.

How far was he fit for his post.

In addition to the Bishopric of Lincoln, he was allowed to retain *in commendam* the Deanery of Westminster and his other ecclesiastical appointments. It was to them

---

* Chamberlain to Carleton, June 23. *S. P. Dom.* cxxi. 121.
† Williams to Buckingham, July 27. *Cabala*, 260.

that he must look for the means to maintain the state of his office. The legitimate income of his post did not exceed 3000*l.* a-year, and he would not be allowed to eke out this revenue from those questionable sources which had supplied his predecessor. There must be no more taking of gratuities under any pretence whatever. "All my lawyers," said James," with pardonable exaggeration, "are so bred and nursed in corruption that they cannot leave it."* Williams was the very man to effect the necessary change. If his ideal of purity was lower than Bacon's, in practical shrewdness he was far his superior. He never was for a moment in doubt of that of which Bacon was certain to be ignorant, the precise light in which any action was likely to be regarded by ordinary men. He shunned everything approaching to corruption like the plague, but it was rather because corruption was stupid than because it was dishonourable.

Nor was it less as an adviser in domestic affairs that Williams was likely to prove useful to the King. At a time when united action between James and his people seemed once again to be possible, it was of no light moment that he should have some one at his ear who was not overburthened with plans and conceptions of his own, but who was quick to detect the changes of popular feeling, and who looked rather at what was practicable than at what was theoretically in agreement with a certain set of maxims. Williams was now the first to discern the impolicy of imprisoning such men as Sandys and Southampton. He lost no time in whispering his apprehensions into Buckingham's ear, and he did not whisper in vain. Nothing tickled the favourite's vanity so delicately as the display of a public forgiveness of his enemies. On the morning of the 16th of July, he hurried up from Theobalds, and visited all who for one reason or another were supposed to lie under his mortal displeasure. Within a few days the prison doors were flying open on every side. Southampton, Oxford, Sandys, Selden, Yelverton, and Floyd, regained their liberty. Nor was the

General liberation of prisoners.

* Chamberlain to Carleton, June 23. *S. P. Dom.* cxxi. 121.

1621. July.

been confined to those whose offences were still recent. Northumberland, after fifteen years' detention, was allowed once more to breathe the fresh air amongst the woods of Petworth. Naunton, too, was released from the confinement in which he had remained ever since the rash words which he had spoken in January; and even Captain North, whose voyage to the Amazon had given such offence to Gondomar, recovered his liberty at the same time.*

Arundel Earl Marshal.

On another point Williams's remonstrances were less successful. Arundel's services in the House of Lords could hardly be forgotten. Amongst the old nobility he alone had taken up Buckingham's cause with warmth. On the 15th of July the Earl Marshal's staff was placed in his hands. It was not long before two patents, one confirming him in this office, the other assigning him a pension of 2000l. a-year, were brought to Williams to be sealed. To the latter, remembering the penury of the Exchequer, the Lord Keeper gave an unwilling assent. To the former he entertained the strongest possible objection. By the wording of the patent powers over all cases in which rank and honour were concerned were conveyed, as it would seem, with studied vagueness; and of all men living, Arundel, with his passionate haughtiness, was the least fit to be trusted with authority of such a nature. Williams, however, uttered his remonstrances in vain, and Arundel was formally authorised to repeat before meaner audiences those outbursts of insolence which even in the presence of his peers he had not been able to restrain.†

Laud made Bishop of St. David's.

About this time accident brought Williams in contact with a man who was hereafter to prove his bitter enemy. Little had been heard of Laud since his injudicious proceedings at Gloucester. He had accompanied the King to Scotland, and is said to have given offence by the pertinacity with which he urged James to reduce the Church of Scotland to a complete conformity with her English

---

* Chamberlain to Carleton, July 21, Aug. 4. *S. P. Dom.* cxxii. 31, 60.
† Williams to Buckingham, Sept. 1. *Cabala*, 261. Grant of Office, Aug. 29. Grant of Pension, Aug. 30. Patent Rolls, 19 Jac. I. Parts 13 and 1. Locke to Carleton, Sept. 22, Sept. 99. *S. P. Dom.* cxxii. 140, 152.

sister. It is, however, not improbable that this story was invented at a later date. But whatever the truth may have been, if there was any estrangement between the Dean of Gloucester and the King, it quickly passed away. On the 3rd of June, the day before the adjournment of Parliament, James was heard speaking graciously to him. "I have given you," he said, "nothing but Gloucester. I know well that it is a shell without a kernel." At Court it was understood that he was to succeed Williams in the Deanery of Westminster. According to a story which afterwards found credence, Williams, bringing Buckingham to his aid, entreated earnestly that he might have the Bishopric of St. David's instead. It has with great probability been suspected* that Williams was actuated by the simple desire to keep the deanery for himself. At all events, he is said to have met with an unexpected obstacle in James, who objected to the harsh and impracticable nature of the man. At length the King yielded to the pressure put upon him. "Take him to you," he said, "but on my soul you will repent it." If the whole story is anything more than a pure invention, it may be that James, though he saw Laud's fitness for presiding over the public services of such a church as Westminster, and appreciated to the full his learning, his devotion to the throne, and his hatred of Puritanism, was yet well aware that he was singularly unfitted by nature for an office which, like that of a bishop, demanded no ordinary temper and discretion.†

Before the new Bishops were consecrated, an accident occurred which caused for some time a postponement of the ceremony. It happened that the Archbishop had gone down to Lord Zouch's estate at Bramshill, to consecrate a chapel. In the morning he was taken out to amuse himself by shooting with a bow at the deer. Unfortunately, the deer he was aiming at leapt up, and the arrow, missing its mark, struck a keeper who was passing

Ch. VII.
1621.
July.

July 24. Abbot's accidental homicide.

---

* By Dr. Bliss, in his notes to Laud's *Diary*.
† *Hacket*, 63. Some of the particulars of the story are in direct contradiction with Laud's *Diary*, (*Works*, iii. 136,) and Hacket, even when uncontradicted, is seldom to be fully trusted. But James's part in the conversation is characteristic, and the story, as I have given it above, may perhaps be hypothetically admitted.

along a sunken path out of the Archbishop's sight. In half an hour the man was dead.

Not a shadow of blame was to be imputed to Abbot. "No one but a fool or a knave," said James, as soon as he heard of the accident, "would think the worse of him. It might be any man's case."* The manner in which Williams received the news was no less characteristic of the man. About the moral nature of the action he did not trouble himself for a moment. But he thought much of what people would say about it. By the common law, he told Buckingham, the Archbishop had forfeited his estate to the Crown. By the canon law he had committed an irregularity, and was suspended from all ecclesiastical functions. It was difficult to say what was to be done. If the King were harsh, the Papists were certain to find fault. If the King were lenient, the Papists would find fault with that, too.† Williams, at all events, took care that no stain of irregularity should rest upon himself. He would not, he said, be consecrated by a man whose hands were dipped in blood; ‡ and his objection was shared by Laud, who bore no good will to the Archbishop.§

The scruples of the two Deans were respected, and Abbot was not allowed to take part in their consecration. The Archbishop's case was referred to a royal commission, and by its recommendation a special release from all irregularity was issued under the great seal.‖

Whilst Williams was thus engaged upon the whole in assuaging enmities, and in counselling moderation, Cranfield was rising no less rapidly into favour. It is not likely that he felt any great disappointment at the preference which had been shown to Williams. No one knew better than himself that the Court of Chancery was not the sphere in which he was best qualified to shine. It was as a financier that he had risen, and it was as a financier that he must retain his grasp upon power. James took care to let him feel that it was not from

---

* Lord Zouch to Sir Edward Zouch, July 24. Digges to Carleton, July 28. *S. P. Dom.* cxxii. 37, 47.
† Williams to Buckingham, July 27. *Cabala*, 260.
‡ Mead to Stuteville, Sept. 19. *Harl. MSS.* 389, fol. 118.
§ Chesterman to Conway, Aug. 28, *S. P. Dom.* cxxii. 94.
‖ *Hacket*, 68. *State Trials.*

ill-will that he had passed him by. On the day before the great seal was placed in the hands of Williams, the man who, not many years before, had been a mere city apprentice, was enrolled by the title of Baron Cranfield, on the peerage of England. It was not the first time that men of comparatively humble origin had won their way to that high place by sheer force of ability. But Cranfield was the first whose elevation can in any way be connected with success in obtaining the confidence of the House of Commons. In the earlier part of the session, he had placed himself at the head of the movement against the patents, and he had lost no opportunity of bringing the policy of the Crown into unison with that of the Lower House. In the last stormy debates before the adjournment he had done more than any one to allay the existing irritation by the readiness with which he assured the House that all their wishes with regard to trade would be carried out by the Government during the recess.

Ch. VII.
1621.
July.

Accordingly, on the 10th of July, the long deliberations of the Council were followed by a proclamation which swept away at a blow no less than eighteen monopolies and grants of a similar nature. A list of seventeen was added, against which any one who felt aggrieved was at liberty to appeal to a court of law. Other popular declarations followed. Informers were no longer to be tolerated. Excessive fees were not to be taken in the Courts. Certain restrictions placed upon trade by the merchant adventurers were to be abolished. On the other hand, the exportation of wool was to be prohibited, and that of the noted iron ordnance of England was to be fenced about with additional cautions.

July 10. Proclamation against monopolies.

It was the policy of Cranfield and of the House of Commons which had triumphed over the policy of Bacon. A system thoroughly logical and thoroughly wrong, was to be replaced by a system which was right by accident. But whatever its merits or its demerits might be, it was undoubtedly the system which the nation was willing to adopt. It was the will of the House of Commons which had prevailed. As far as the domestic government of the country was concerned, James had shown himself content

CH. VII.
1621.
July.

to walk in the track which had been marked out by his Parliament.

It would, indeed, have seemed strange to any of those who took part in these stirring events, and whose heads were full of questions about the Palatinate, or of questions about parliamentary privilege, if he had been told that there was not one of these points from which the Englishman of future times would not readily turn away in order to contemplate the fortunes of a little band of exiles who had lately made their way unknown and unheeded across the stormy waves of the Atlantic.

The early Separatists.

It was religious zeal which had driven these men from their native land. In many respects, their doctrines were those of the stricter English Puritans. But in one point they were peculiarly their own. Whilst the Puritan was anxious to reform as far as possible the existing Church, these men had made up their minds to break away from it altogether. Within its pale, they declared, was an unholy alliance between good and evil, which was utterly abhorrent to their minds. Their doctrine, indeed, was only a natural reaction against the systems of Whitgift and Bancroft. In every age there are found men who are discontented with the ordinary religious standard of the day, and who demand a society of their own, in which they may interchange their ideas and aspirations. To such the Mediæval Church offered the asylum of the cloister, or the active service of the mendicant orders. In the England of the nineteenth century, they would be at liberty to enter into any combination amongst themselves which the most unrestrained fancy could dictate. Religious societies and religious sects would welcome their co-operation. But, in the first century of the Reformed Church of England, nothing of the kind was possible. The parish church, and nothing but the parish church, was open to all. There the Puritan, who mourned over the dulness or the entire absence of the sermon, and to whom the Book of Common Prayer was not long enough or flexible enough to give expression to the emotions with which his heart was bursting, was seated side by side with men who thought that the shortest service was already too long, and who were only driven to take part in it at all by the ever present fear of a conviction for recusancy. If this had been all,—if, after having paid due obedience to the law, the Puritan had been left to himself,—if he had been permitted to meet for prayer in the afternoon as freely as other men were permitted to dance on the green, or to shoot at the butts, he might perhaps have been to some extent satisfied with the arrangements provided for him. In his private intercourse with neighbours like-minded with himself he would have found that of which he was in search, and he might have come in time to regard with reverence the large-heartedness of a Church which refused to content herself with claiming as her children the pious and the devoted, but which announced in the only way in which it was at that time possible to announce it, that the ignorant and the vicious, the publican and the harlot, were equally the object of her care with the wisest and best of her sons.

This, however, was not to be. Whitgift and Bancroft, Elizabeth and James, had set their faces against private associations; and the consequence was that men were found to declare that private associations were the only congregations to which they were justified in giving the name of churches. Feelings which might have formed a support to the general piety, were left to grow up in fierce opposition to the existing system. The Church, it was said, was, by the confession of the Articles themselves, "a congregation of faithful men." Such, at least, the Church of England was not. Her bishops and archdeacons, her chancellors and ecclesiastical commissioners, existed mainly for the purpose of forcing the faithful and the unfaithful into an unnatural union. The time had come when all true Christians must separate themselves from this antichristian Babylon, and must unite in churches from which the unbelieving and the profane would be rigorously excluded.*

---

* "If Mr. Johnson confess.... the Church of England a true Church, he must be able to prove it established by separation in a separated body in the constitution. He, with the rest, has formerly defined 'a true visible Church, a company of people called and separated from the world by the Word of God,' &c.; and proved the same by many Scriptures.

"And to conceive of a Church which is the body of Christ and household

Ch. VII.
1593.
Their unpopularity.

Towards the end of Elizabeth's reign, it was calculated that there were in England some 20,000 persons who had thus renounced communion with the Church, and who were popularly known by the name of Brownists. Such men would find but little sympathy even amongst Puritans. To ordinary Englishmen they were the object of contempt mingled with abhorrence. It was all very well, it might be said, for those who cared for such matters to raise questions about rites and ceremonies. But what was to be said to men who asserted that none but those who came up to their own arbitrary standard were sufficiently holy to take part with themselves in the assemblies of the Church.

Persecution.

Everywhere, therefore, the Separatist congregations were suppressed. Their members were committed to prison, in days when imprisonment was too often equivalent to the tortures of a lingering death; and they rotted away amongst the fevers which were rife in those infected abodes of misery. A few, by a cruel perversion of the law, were sent to the gallows. Some, who could not endure to remain at home and to wait for better times, made their way across the sea to a land where no bishops were to be found, and cowered for refuge under the shelter afforded by the tolerant magistrates of Amsterdam.

The congregation at Amsterdam.

The church thus planted did not prosper. It contained within itself many persons of piety and integrity; and one of its ministers, Henry Ainsworth, was distinguished no less by the suavity of his disposition than by the depth of his learning. But there were too many amongst his congregation whose temper was hasty and unwise. The very self-assertion and independence of character which had made them separatists, not unfrequently degenerated into an opinionativeness which augured ill for the peace of the community. It was peculiarly difficult to train to habits of mutual concession

---

of God not separated from the profane world which lieth in wickedness, is to confound heaven and earth, and to agree Christ with Belial, and, in truth, the most profane and dangerous error, which, this day, prevails amongst them that fear God." Robinson. Of Religious Communion. *Works*, iii. 129.

men who had already thrown off all restraints of custom and organization at home.

Amongst such men causes of dispute were certain to arise. Francis Johnson, who was associated in the ministry with Ainsworth, had since his arrival married the widow of a merchant. The lady, who had a little more money than the other members of the congregation, gave great offence by what in that strait-laced community was considered the magnificence of her dress. Whenever she made her appearance she was pointed at as a disgraceful example of female vanity. She had adopted the fashion of the day in wearing cork heels to her shoes and in stiffening her bodice with whalebone. A deputation accordingly waited upon Johnson to complain of the bad example set by his wife. The poor man did not know what to do. In a strait between his wife and his congregation, he tried to compromise the dispute. The lady pleaded that it was impossible for her to spoil her dress by making any alterations in its shape. But she promised that, as soon as it was worn out, her new clothes should be cut so as to give satisfaction to the complainants.* The congregation, however, was not to be bought off so cheaply as this, and this miserable dispute was only the commencement of a prolonged quarrel, of which glimpses are to be obtained from time to time in the fragmentary annals of the little community.

Two years later fresh seeds of contention were sown. In 1606 the Amsterdam Church was joined by a congregation which had emigrated from Gainsborough, under the guidance of their minister, John Smith.† He appears to have been a man of ability and eloquence, but of a singular angularity of character. He had scarcely set foot in Amsterdam before he had quarrelled with the original emigrants. He finally adopted Baptist opinions, so far at least as to assert the necessity of the re-baptism of adults. Not being able, however, to satisfy himself as to the proper quarter in which to apply for the administration of the rite, he finally solved the difficulty by

---

* Bradford's Dialogue in Young's Chronicles, 446.
† Hunter, Founders of Plymouth Colony, 32.

baptizing himself. He was not one in whose neighbourhood peace was likely to be found. The congregation which had followed him from England was infected by his spirit, and it speedily broke up, and came to nothing.*

Such stories as these, which lost nothing when recounted by the champions of the English Church, did not promise well for the future of the Separatists. In truth, there was a fund of intolerance inextricably involved in these men's opinions. The very principle upon which they had separated from the Church was calculated to foster a pharisaical spirit. And yet there were causes at work to draw them in an opposite direction. The theory that it was the duty of Christians to separate themselves from the profane and ungodly multitude led almost inevitably to the theory of the independence of each congregation so separated. The Roman Catholic, the Anglican, and the Presbyterian differed with respect to the principles upon which the Church ought to be organized; but they agreed in making that organization, whatever it might be, the central point of their system. To the Separatist, the one point of importance was, that a few faithful Christians had met together to strengthen one another with their mutual prayers and exhortations. He had, no doubt, a devout wish that others might be as pious as himself; but he was so far from entertaining a desire to compel them to join him against their will, that he would have regarded any one who proposed such a course with the utmost horror. He would, therefore, be the first to take a stand against the prevalent belief that it was the duty of a government to enforce conformity by penal legislation.

That, not without occasional relapses, the better principle became predominant, was mainly the work of a little group of men who had not yet made up their minds to forsake their native country, and of whom, as yet, the central figure was Richard Clifton, a man who is scarcely known to us, excepting by the influence which he exercised over others.† At the end of Elizabeth's

---

* Robinson. *Works*, iii. 108.
† Hunter. *Founders of Plymouth*, 40.

reign he was rector of Babworth, a village in the north-east corner of Nottinghamshire. He was devoted to his duties; and his earnestness attracted from the neighbouring villages all who were dissatisfied with the ministrations of their own parishes. Such a one was William Bradford,* at the time when James ascended the throne, a mere boy of thirteen, whose early piety and precocious thoughtfulness seemed to mark him for future eminence. The walk over the fields to Babworth from his Yorkshire home at Austerfield was nine or ten miles, and this distance he regularly paced backwards and forwards whenever Clifton's voice was to be heard in the pulpit. On his way he passed through the village of Scrooby, with its old manor-house, once a country seat of the Archbishops of York, but made over not long before by Archbishop Sandys, in a fit of nepotism, to his eldest son. It was now occupied by William Brewster, the postmaster of the place, which was a station on the great road to Scotland and the north.† Brewster was a man of congenial temperament with Bradford, and doubtless took a kindly interest in the boy. He was not without experience of the world. He had been attached to the service of the Puritan Secretary, Davison, and had accompanied him when he visited the Netherlands in 1585 to receive the keys of the cautionary towns. Upon Davison's disgrace, Brewster had returned to Scrooby, his native village, where he obtained the appointment which he held by means of the interest which he still retained at Court. He brought with him the strong Puritan opinions which he had imbibed in Davison's household; but there is every reason to believe that as long as Clifton was still preaching, he continued to regard himself as a member of the Church of England, and that, like many others in the neighbourhood, he made his way from time to time across the fields to Babworth.

 Evil days were in store for the non-conforming clergy. Elizabeth and Whitgift had chastised them with whips. James and Bancroft would chastise them with scorpions. The millenary petition was rejected. Its supporters were

* Hunter. *Founders of Plymouth*, 99.
† Ibid. 66.

CH. VII.
1603.

Bradford.

Brewster.

1604.
Clifton ejected.

driven with contumely from Hampton Court. The Canons of 1604 passed through convocation, and received the Royal assent. Conformity, thorough and unhesitating conformity, was to be the unbending rule of the English Church.

Like so many others, Clifton, it would seem, refused to comply with the requirements of the new reign. He was accordingly deprived of his rectory, and the voice was silenced which had sounded like the messenger of God to so many pious souls.* To those to whom the parish church of Babworth had been as the gate of heaven, there was a void which nothing could replace. The system under which the preacher whom they loved had been driven from his pulpit, grew more odious to them every day. They saw in it faults which they had never seen before. A conviction, ripening as the weeks passed by, settled deeper and deeper in their minds, that the Church which counted amongst her children the formalist and the worldling, and which drove the Papist under heavy penalties to take a hypocritical part in her most solemn rites, but which could find no room for Clifton amongst her ministers, was already condemned of God.

Robinson at Norwich.

The blow which had fallen upon Clifton at Babworth, fell at Norwich upon a man of equal piety, but far superior abilities. John Robinson had long striven to do his duty with such amount of compliance with the Prayer Book as the Puritan clergy were accustomed to render. When he was dismissed from his post, his heart clung to the Church, as the heart of Wesley clung to it a century and a half later. He entreated the magistrates of the city to grant him the mastership of the hospital, or at least to assign to him the lease of some premises in which he might continue to render spiritual aid to such of his old congregation as might be inclined to seek his assistance. Even this was denied him, and with a heavy heart

---

* There is no direct evidence of the date of Clifton's ejectment. But Cotton (*Magnalia Christi Americana*, ii. 1, § 2,) speaks of Bradford as reading the Scriptures at the age of twelve, and as subsequently attending Clifton's ministry. Bradford was twelve in 1602, and during the two following years James had not yet broken with the Puritans. Nor is it likely that Clifton could have escaped the clean sweep in the autumn of 1604, especially as we find him an ejected minister so soon afterwards.

he turned his steps towards Gainsborough, his native town.*

For two years after Clifton's expulsion, nothing is known of his proceedings, but it is certain that those who gathered round him grew more and more estranged from the Church. The line of demarcation between the ejected and the ejectors, was widening into an impassable gulf. It is by no means unlikely that they placed themselves in communication with Smith and his Gainsborough congregation. At all events, when Smith emigrated in 1606, they determined to form themselves into a separate congregation.† Brewster readily offered his house for their meetings, and Clifton was, as a matter of course, chosen to be the pastor of the little flock. Robinson, who it may safely be conjectured looked askance upon a man of Smith's quarrelsome temper, had taken no part in the emigration of his fellow-townsmen, but consented at once to act as Clifton's assistant at Scrooby. Brewster was to be the Elder, an office for which he was eminently fitted. His quiet unobtrusive goodness, as well as his position in the house in which the congregation met, enabled him, without the risk of giving offence, to speak words of kindly reproof, and to soften down those inevitable asperities which were working such mischief at Amsterdam. Bradford was, as yet, too young to take any prominent part in the community, but his more practical nature was likely to stand them in good stead when the time came for the exercise of the more energetic virtues.

The step which these men had taken was not without its dangers. Everyone who met at Brewster's house, knew that he was acting in defiance of the law. There was no

Ch. VII.
1606.

The congregation at Scrooby.

1607.
Determination to emigrate.

---

* Hunter. *Founders of Plymouth*, 92. Hall. Apology against the Brownists. *Works*, ix. 91. Ashton's Life of Robinson, prefixed to the collected edition of his Works.

† Morton (*Memorial*, 1.) places the date of the formation of the Scrooby Church in 1602. But this is most improbable in itself, and is contradicted by the far better evidence of Bradford, who says :—"After they had continued together about a year, ... they resolved to get over into Holland." (*History of New England*, 10.) Mr. Palfrey, indeed, (Ibid. i. 135, note 1,) observes, that Bradford perhaps reckoned from the time of Robinson's joining the Church. But the more natural interpretation is corroborated by another passage. In speaking of Brewster's death, in April, 1643, Bradford says, (*Hist.* 468), that he "had borne his part with this poor persecuted Church above thirty-six years," *i.e.* from the winter of 1606-7.

longer any peace for them in England. They were none of them rich men. For the most part, they were engaged in agriculture, the pursuit which, of all others, is the least suggestive of movement and change. Time out of mind, their forefathers had ploughed the same fields, and had been buried in the same green churchyards, under the shelter of the old familiar churches. Their English homes were very dear to them. To dwell in a foreign land was to be cut off from all intercourse with those they loved, to a degree which, in these days, we are hardly capable of comprehending. Yet all this, and more than this, they were resolved to face. They had made up their minds that it was their duty to go, and, in spite of the hardships which awaited them, there was no shrinking back.

But, if it was illegal to hold their assemblies in England, it was no less illegal to leave the country without the Royal licence.* It was therefore necessary to make their preparations in secret. At last it seemed that all difficulties were at an end. A vessel was hired to meet them at Boston. On the appointed day they moved down cautiously towards the coast, and timed their journey so as to arrive at the water's edge shortly after nightfall. They went on board at once, fancying they had nothing more to fear. But even then, they were doomed to disappointment. The captain proved a rogue. He had already pocketed their passage money, and he wanted to be relieved from the fulfilment of his bargain. He accordingly gave notice to the magistrates, and just as the poor emigrants were watching for the weighing of the anchor, the officers came on board, and hurried them on shore. The unhappy men were stripped of everything which they possessed, and were brought up for examination on the following morning. The magistrates, as frequently proved the case, were disposed to be lenient to anything that bore the name of Protestantism, but they were hampered by the necessity of waiting for instructions from the Privy Council. In due time these instructions were received, and it was only after long imprisonment, that the poor men were allowed to return to their homes.

* By 13 Ric. II. stat. 1, cap. 20, persons not being soldiers or merchants might not leave the realm without licence, excepting at Dover or Plymouth.

Brewster and six of his companions were detained still longer, and were only dismissed after having been bound over to answer for their conduct at the next assizes.

It is hard to stop resolute men. In the course of the following year, they all, in one way or another, succeeded in effecting their escape. When, in the autumn of 1608, they met together once more at Amsterdam, there were few who had not some tale to tell of sufferings endured. But even at Amsterdam there was no rest possible for them. The little Church there was still distracted by disputes, and it was not from a love of theological polemics that they had left their homes. Smith and Johnson might quarrel as much as they pleased; but as for themselves, they had come to Holland in search of peace, and, if peace was not to be found at Amsterdam, it must be sought elsewhere. Accordingly, before they had been many months upon the Continent, they removed in a body to Leyden, leaving the theologians to fight out their battles amongst themselves. Clifton, worn out by the trials of his life, and sinking into a premature old age, was unable or unwilling to accompany them, and his place was taken by Robinson.*

The years of residence at Leyden were, in every respect, beneficial to the exiles. Whatever intolerance might be lurking in their hearts was no longer influenced by the opposition of an intolerant Church. It was true that in Holland, as well as in England, they found themselves face to face with that world from which they had done their best to separate themselves. It was a world in which there was sin and error enough, a world in which evil men and evil habits were to be met at every turn; but it was not a world in which was to be found either a Bancroft or a James. In their own little circle, the emigrants might pray and preach as they pleased. There was no Court of High Commission to visit them with fines, no informer to dog their steps, no justice of the peace to send them to prison. Was it strange that, although their recollections were still full of bitterness towards the system under which they had suffered, their sentiments towards individual men grew more kindly, and that they were

* Bradford. *History of Plymouth Plantation*, 16.

more ready to make allowances than they had been before? On the other hand, their position drove them to grasp more firmly than ever their theory of the separation between the spiritual and the temporal, upon which the principles of toleration rest. Strangers in a foreign land, the wildest fancy could not lead them to expect a time when they might hope to win over the magistrates of the Republic to their own peculiar views. They knew that as long as they remained in Holland, they must either be tolerated or oppressed. Their only safeguard lay in throwing their whole weight into the scale of toleration, and in restricting to the uttermost the right of the civil magistrate to interfere in spiritual questions. What Knox and Calvin had failed to comprehend, was reserved for these poor Separatists to teach.

At such a time, the presence of a man like Robinson was invaluable to them. If the Leyden congregation was to be saved from the fate of the Church at Amsterdam, it could only be by the acceptance of some systematized belief, and the task of laying the foundations of such a system was one for which Robinson was eminently fitted. It was by him that the opinions of his companions were welded into a coherent whole. Separation from sinners, resistance to a dominant clergy, the right of individual congregations to manage their own affairs, and the other peculiarities which the current of events had brought to the surface, all assumed their proper place in a theory so complete that those who accepted it were able to imagine that it contained all wisdom, human and Divine. Nor was it solely to his intellectual powers that Robinson owed the influence which he had acquired. Even amongst men who could measure gentleness of disposition by Brewster's standard, he was noted for the kindness of his heart.

And yet the exiles were not at ease even at Leyden. Their sober industry kept them from want; but most of them had to struggle hard. Their fingers had been trained to handle the plough better than the loom, and it was with difficulty that they were able to compete with the skilled workmen by whom they were surrounded. From their lodgings amidst the close alleys of the town they looked

back with sadness to the pure air and the pleasant hedge- Ch. VII.
rows of their native England. Nor were other causes of 1617.
discontent wanting. They had come to Holland in order
to keep themselves separate from the world. Were they
sure that they had succeeded? Their longing for a land
in which tares never mingled with the wheat was still
unsatisfied. Their children, as they grew up, were not
always content with the hard life of their parents. Some
of them had enlisted in the armies of the Republic; with
what danger to their souls, who could tell? Some, still
worse, had strayed into folly and vice. Even in that
land of Calvinism, the Sabbath rest was not observed as
they would fain have seen it. And so, again and again,
the question was raised, whether the world did not afford
some spot where the young might be preserved from con-
tamination. Nor was it only for themselves and for their
children that they were anxious. They knew that there
were many still in England whose opinions coincided with
their own, and they had fondly hoped that their little
Church would prove the nucleus round which a large
number of emigrants would gather. But, as long as they
remained where they were, nothing of the kind was to
be hoped for. The spiritual advantages of becoming a
member of Robinson's congregation were of little weight
with the hundreds who shrunk from the drudgery of
daily life at Leyden.*

All these considerations urged the exiles to seek another Deter-
home. The ideal of the pure and sinless community mination
which they hoped to found was still floating before their grate to
eyes, and was drawing them on as it receded before them. America.
Let us not stop to inquire whether such an ideal was at-
tainable on earth. It is enough that in striving to realise
it, they did that which the world will not willingly
forget.

In what part of the globe was a home to be found for
the new Christian commonwealth? Very tempting were
the accounts borne across the Atlantic of the fertility of
Guiana; but, even though Raleigh's hopes had not yet

---

* Bradford. *History of Plymouth Plantation*, 22. Winslow's Brief Narrative, in *Young's Chronicle*, 381.

been wrecked on the banks of the Orinoco, prudence forbade the exposure of their scanty and unwarlike numbers to the hostility of the whole Spanish monarchy. Harsh, too, as their treatment had been in England, their hearts were still English, and not only were they unwilling to settle themselves out of the dominions of the English Crown, but all their hopes of attracting additional emigrants lay in their finding some spot where there was nothing to aggravate the ordinary difficulties in the way of a free communication with the mother country. With these hopes before them, their choice was limited to the Atlantic coast of North America.

Even with this limitation they had a wide range before them. From the Spanish possessions in Florida to the French colony in Nova Scotia, the little settlement at James Town was, with the exception of a Dutch factory on the Hudson, the only spot where Europeans were to be found. The Plymouth Company, to which the northern part of the coast had been assigned, had accomplished nothing. At the time when the sister company was sending out the last settlers to Virginia, an attempt had been made to establish a colony as far north as the mouth of the Kennebec. But the hardships of winter in such a latitude had been too much for the emigrants, and no Captain Smith was to be found in their ranks. As soon as the summer weather enabled them to move, they made the best of their way back to England with diminished numbers. Fresh efforts were made by Smith, who, since his recall from Virginia had transferred his allegiance to the Plymouth Company, but from various causes all his attempts at colonisation had proved abortive. All that he had been able to do was to bring home a survey of the coast, and to give to the land which he had hoped to fill with happy English homes the now familiar name of New England.

Between the rival companies the exiles of Leyden hesitated long. On the one hand, they were repelled by the known severity of the northern climate. On the other hand, they feared the neighbourhood of the James Town colonists, and they fancied, not without reason, that the arrival of a body of non-conformists would hardly be regarded with friendly eyes by the Virginian adventurers.

Ch. VII.
1617.

At last they resolved upon a middle course. They would come as far south as they dared without approaching too near to James Town. Near the mouth of the Hudson, somewhere on the coast of the present State of New Jersey, they might find a spot which would be free from both dangers. It was just within the limits of the Southern Company, the officials of which had practical experience in colonisation, and which, as long as it counted Sir Edwin Sandys among its leading members, was likely to abstain from investigating too narrowly the theology of the settlers who were taken under its patronage.

Two messengers were accordingly despatched to England to enter into negotiations with the Virginia Company of London. With the support of Sandys they had little difficulty in obtaining a favourable hearing for their project. But the King's assent was less easily won. Yet even with James they did not meet the obstacles that might have been expected. They hoped, they said, that he would allow them to enjoy liberty of conscience in America. In return they would extend his dominions, and would spread the Gospel amongst the heathen. James inquired how they meant to live. "By fishing," they said. "So God have my soul," replied the King, "'tis an honest trade; 'twas the Apostles' own calling." Their case was referred to the Archbishop of Canterbury and the Bishop of London, and they were finally told that, though they must not expect any public assurance of toleration, yet, as long as they behaved peaceably, their proceedings would be connived at. In accepting this offer, they probably thought that if they could only make good their footing in America, the King's arm would hardly be long enough to reach them.

1618.
Negotiations in England.

Further delay was caused by the dissensions with which the company was at this time agitated, and it was not till the summer of 1619 that they obtained a patent from it authorising them to establish a settlement near the mouth of the Hudson.* As soon as the patent arrived in

1619.
Patent from the Virginia Company.

* Bradford. *History of Plymouth Plantation*, 27—41. Winslow's Brief

Ch. VII.
1619.

Leyden, the first step of the congregation was to hold "a solemn meeting, and a day of humiliation to seek the Lord for his direction." In the midst of all their difficulties, Robinson's presence was a tower of strength, and his words of loving encouragement lingered long in their memories. As soon as his sermon was ended, a consultation was held, in order that the enterprise might be put into a practical shape. About two hundred persons were present, and of this number nearly half were willing to take part in the undertaking. The rest, including Robinson himself, were prevented by various causes from leaving Holland, though there were few who did not express a wish that they might be able ultimately to find their way to America. Even with their numbers thus reduced they were forced to ask assistance, and to mortgage their future prospects in order to secure a passage across the Atlantic. With the necessity of borrowing came the necessity of yielding to the terms of those who were willing to lend. The firm and steadfast step with which they had hitherto walked straight towards their goal was now to be exchanged for uncertainty and delay.

The adventurers.

They had applied for money to Thomas Weston, a London merchant, who had visited them at Leyden. He assured them that they should want for nothing. He would form a company to bear the risks of the undertaking, upon the security of a certain share of the profits.

With the company thus formed an agreement was duly signed; but difficulties in its interpretation were not slow to arise. Looking to the past history of colonisation, the shareholders may well have felt that they were taking part in a scheme of which the chances of failure were far greater than those of success. The Leyden congregation had determined that they would not fail, and the resolute purpose which was to ensure success made them impatient of the doubts of others. It was sadly against their will that they finally yielded to the stringent conditions on which alone the money was to be had.*

Narrative, in *Young's Chronicle*, 382. The patent itself has not been preserved.
* Bradford. *History of Plymouth Plantation*, 42—54.

THE EMIGRANTS AT DELFT HAVEN.

In these negotiations, time, always precious to the poor, was lost. The autumn and the winter of 1619 passed slowly away. The spring of 1620 came, and there was yet a possibility that they might reach America before the summer was at an end. But the months were suffered to slip away, and it was not till July that the preparations were complete. At last, however, everything was ready. The Mayflower, a little vessel of 180 tons, had been hired for the voyage, and was lying in Southampton Water. The Speedwell, of sixty tons, had been purchased, and it was intended that she should be used as a fishing vessel on the other side of the Atlantic. She was now despatched to bring over the emigrants from Holland.

Many precious lives would have been saved if the time of departure could have been delayed till a more favourable season; but money was running short, and the poor men could not afford to wait. The day was fixed, a day sad both for those who were to go and for those who were to remain. Yet their sorrows were not unmixed with such hopes as befitted their devout and sober piety. "So being ready to depart," wrote one who set his face towards the wilderness, "they had a day of solemn humiliation, their pastor taking his text from Ezra viii. 21: 'And there at the river by Ahava I proclaimed a fast, that we might humble ourselves before our God, and seek of Him a right way for us, and for our children, and for all our substance,' upon which he spent a good part of the day very profitably and suitably to the present occasion. The rest of the time was spent in pouring out prayers to the Lord with great fervency, mixed with abundance of tears. And the time being come that they must depart, they were accompanied with most of their brethren out of the city unto a town sundry miles off called Delft Haven, where the ship lay ready to receive them. So they left that goodly and pleasant city which had been their resting-place near twelve years; but they knew they were pilgrims and looked not much on those things, but lift up their eyes to the heavens, their dearest country, and quieted their spirits. When they came to the place, they found the ship and all things ready; and such

Marginal notes: Ch. VII. 1620. The Mayflower at Southampton. Departure from Leyden.

Ch. VII.
1620.

of their friends as could not come with them followed after them; and sundry also came from Amsterdam to see them shipped and to take their leave of them. That night was spent with little sleep by the most, but with friendly entertainment and Christian discourse and other real expression of true Christian love. The next day, the wind being fair, they went aboard and their friends with them, where truly doleful was the sight of that sad and mournful parting, to see what sighs, what sobs and prayers did sound amongst them, what tears did gush from every eye, and pithy speeches pierced every heart; that sundry Dutch strangers that stood on the quay as spectators could not refrain from tears. Yet comfortable and sweet it was to see such lively and true expressions of clear and unfeigned love. But the tide, which stays for no man, calling them away that were thus loathe to depart, their reverend pastor falling on his knees, and they all with him, with watery cheeks commended them with most fervent prayers to the Lord and His blessing. And then, with mutual embraces and many tears, they took their leaves one of another, which proved to be the last leave to many of them." *

Passage to Southampton.

And so, "lifting up their eyes to the heavens, their dearest country," they parted one from another. Of those who returned to Leyden, there were some who were, in due time, to follow in the footsteps of the emigrants. There were others who, like Robinson himself, were to leave their bones in the city which had sheltered them so long. The Speedwell, laden with its precious freight, bore the emigrants to Southampton, where they were joined by their companions who had been sent before to complete the preparations for the voyage, and to collect such recruits as were willing to join them.

About one hundred and twenty persons, men, women, and children, embarked as passengers on board the two vessels. Brewster and Bradford were there to represent the old Scrooby congregation. Edward Winslow, a

---

* Bradford. *History of Plymouth Plantation*, 58. It is a pity that in the fresco which adorns the Houses of Parliament, the realities of this scene should have been neglected for an imaginary parting on a beach which never existed.

gentleman by birth, happening to pass through Leyden on his travels, had been attracted by Robinson's preaching, and had thrown in his lot with the despised Separatists. More peculiar was the position of Miles Standish. He was not, nor did he ever become, a member of their Church; but he had willingly offered to share their exile, and he brought with him the military skill of which they were not unlikely to stand in need. He had, in all probability, served some years as a soldier in the garrison of one of the cautionary towns. He may have been actuated in his wish to join the exiles partly by a daring spirit and a love of adventure. But he was a man of sober worth, and he may well have clung to the society of those of whom the congregation was composed, even if he could not altogether adopt their tenets.

CH. VII.
1620.

Precious time was again lost at Southampton in a vain attempt to obtain better terms from the company. After a delay of seven days, the two vessels dropped down past Calshot and the Needles into the Channel. It was soon discovered that the Speedwell had sprung a leak, and the exiles were forced to put into Dartmouth for repairs. Once more, as soon as the mischief had been remedied, they weighed anchor with renewed hope. This time they were out of sight of land before any complaint was heard; but the smaller vessel was overmasted, and the leak was soon as bad as ever. With heavy hearts they put back to Plymouth, where it was resolved to leave the Speedwell behind, and to get rid of those of their fellow-passengers who were already growing sick of the hardships of the voyage.

The two vessels leave Southampton.

The Speedwell left behind.

On the 6th of September, just as the couriers were speeding to England with the news of Spinola's attack upon the Palatinate, the emigrants bade farewell to that lovely harbour from which, three years before, Raleigh had started in pursuit of his phantom of the golden mine. Râme Head, and the Lizard, and the Land's End, the cold grey bulwarks of unsympathizing England, one after another dropped out of sight. At last they were alone upon the Atlantic. Behind them, save in a few distant Leyden garrets, there were none to whom their failure or their success would furnish more than a few hours' scornful

Sept. The voyage of the Mayflower.

E 2

gossip. Before them was the stormy sea, and in the far West lay that wilderness which was only waiting for their approach to stiffen under its winter frosts. Yet there was no sign of blenching. If God were on their side, what mattered the coldness of the world, the jeers of the sailors, or the howling of the Atlantic storms?*

The voyage was chequered with but few incidents. But there is one passage in the narrative in which Bradford has embalmed the story of those days of trial, which is too characteristic of the writer and his companions to be passed over in silence. "I may not," he wrote, "omit here a special work of God's providence. There was a proud and very profane young man, one of the seamen. He would alway be contemning the poor people in their sickness, or cursing them daily with grievous execrations, and did not let to tell them that he hoped to cast half of them overboard before they came to their journey's end, and to make merry with what they had; and, if he were by any quietly reproved, he would curse and swear most bitterly. But it pleased God before they came half seas over to smite this young man with a grievous disease, of which he died in a desperate manner, and so was himself the first that was thrown overboard. Thus his curses lighted on his own head, and it was an astonishment to all his fellows, for they noted it to be the hand of God upon him."

It was on the 9th of November that the emigrants caught sight of land. The low shore of Cape Cod stretched away for miles in front of them. From the spot at which they had struck the coast, a short voyage of less than seventy miles would bring them to the place which they had marked out for their settlement. The ship's course was accordingly altered in a southerly direction, and an attempt was made to reach the mouth of the Hudson. They had not gone far before they found themselves off Sandy Point, amongst shoals and breakers white with foam. The captain declared that the danger was too great to be faced, and altering the ship's course once more he steered to the northward along the coast.

* Bradford. *History of Plymouth Plantation*, 68—74.

On the 11th, the Mayflower rounded the extreme point of the peninsula of Cape Cod, and dropped anchor in the smooth water inside. Of the emigrants, one had died during the passage, but their numbers were still the same as when they left Plymouth harbour, a child, Oceanus Hopkins, having been born on board. One hundred and two persons, of whom about fifty only were full grown men, looked out under the bleak November sky upon the desolate shore, on which they were, with as little loss of time as possible, to search for a home.

Before anyone was allowed to leave the ship, a meeting was called, to take steps for the prevention of a danger which threatened to sap the foundations of the infant colony. In one respect the breakers off Sandy Point had made a great alteration in their position. At the mouth of the Hudson they would have been within the limits of the Virginia Company's authority. At Cape Cod those limits were passed, and the patent which had been obtained with so much difficulty had suddenly been rendered useless. For many months it would be impossible to communicate with the northern company in whose territories they now were, and it would be hazardous to establish a colony without any recognised government to preserve order in its ranks; for already it had been discovered that among the recruits who had joined them at Southampton, there were those who were muttering that they might do as they pleased, since there was no longer any legal authority which could call them to account for their actions. It was to meet this difficulty that a document framed in the following terms was laid before the meeting for signature:—

"In the name of God, Amen. We, whose names are underwritten, the loyal subjects of our dread Sovereign, King James .... having undertaken for the glory of God and the advancement of the Christian faith, in honour of our King and country, a voyage to plant the first colony in the northern parts of Virginia, do by these presents solemnly and mutually, in the presence of God and one another, covenant to combine ourselves into a civil body politic, for our better ordering and preservation, and furtherance of the ends aforesaid; and by virtue hereof,

Ch. VII.
1620.

Agreement to form a Government.

The instrument of government.

CH. VII.
1620.

November. Carver chosen governor.

to enact, constitute, and frame such just and equal laws, ordinances, acts, constitutions and offices from time to time as shall be thought most meet and convenient for the general good of the colony; unto which we promise all due submission and obedience."

To this declaration not one of the emigrants refused to set his hand. The meeting next proceeded to choose as their first Governor, John Carver, who had taken an active part in the negotiations with the Company in England.*

In all this there was nothing new. The election of administrative functionaries took place in every borough town in England. What was really new was that whilst in England each corporation was exposed to the action of the other forces of the social system, in America the new corporation was practically left to itself. It was as if Exeter or York had drifted away from the rest of England, and had been left to its own resources on the other side of the Atlantic. The accident which had deprived the colony for a time of all legal connexion with the home Government, was only a foreshadowing of its future fortunes. Sooner or later the colonists would have a social and political history of their own, which would not be a repetition of the social and political history of England. When once the first difficulties were at an end, there would be a society in which no one was very poor, and no one was very rich, and it was evident that to such a society many of the provisions of the English constitution would be altogether inapplicable.

Nov 11. Exploration of Cape Cod.

For the present, however, there was work before the emigrants which left no time for the discussion of political principles. Immediately after Carver's election, fifteen or sixteen of their number who were sent on shore for wood, returned with a report that they had

---

* "After this," writes Bradford, "they chose, or rather confirmed, Mr. John Carver for that year." *History of Plymouth Plantation,* 90. Mr. Deane, the editor of Bradford's *History,* suggests that "or rather confirmed," was written inadvertently. This is very unlikely. I have no doubt that Carver was named to the office in the lost patent from the Virginia Company. It will be remembered, that the first Council of Virginia was nominated in England. That it was intended that the New England colonists should elect their governor after the first year, appears from Robinson's letter in Bradford's *History,* 66.

found soil of rich black earth behind the sandhills. The next day they kept their Sabbath, the first Sabbath in the new world which was opening before them. On Monday morning they were anxious to commence the exploration of the country, but the shallop which they had brought with them for that purpose, was found to have been injured on the voyage. Whilst it was being repaired, a party, under the command of Standish, was set on shore to explore the immediate neighbourhood. They returned on Friday, bringing with them some Indian corn, which they had found in a deserted native village. This little stock was invaluable to the settlers, as, by some extraordinary mismanagement, they had left all their seed corn behind them in England.

Standish had hoped to find the shallop ready on his return; but the carpenter was lazy or careless, and contrived to consume fourteen days upon what should have been at most the work of six. It was not till the 27th that the exploring party was able to start. The weather had now become very bad. Winter had come down upon them in all its rigour. The cold blasts pierced to the skin, and the snow fell thick upon the houseless wanderers. The water near the shore was so shallow, that it was impossible to land, except by wading. Time and means to dry their dripping garments were alike wanting. Not a few owed their deaths to diseases, the seeds of which were implanted in the constitution during these melancholy days. Yet they struggled on bravely. They made their way to the southward along the inner shore of the peninsula, sometimes in an open boat, sometimes on foot, over hills and valleys, wrapped in a deep covering of snow. On the evening of the 30th, they returned on board, footsore and weary, and reported in favour of a spot near the mouth of the Pamet River, not far from the place where the Indian corn had been found.

Long and earnest was the consultation that evening on board the Mayflower. Many reasons concurred in recommending the spot which had been selected by the pioneers; but the coast was shallow, and there was no running stream of fresh water in the immediate neighbourhood. In the midst of the discussion, they were told

Ch. VII.
1620.
Nov. 12.
Nov. 13.

Nov. 17.

Nov. 27.

Nov. 30.

December. Exploration of the mainland.

Ch. VII.
1620.

by the pilot of the ship that he remembered that, when he was last on the coast, he had seen a good harbour on the mainland opposite. Upon this, they resolved not to come to a final resolution till a fresh exploring party had visited the spot.

Accordingly, on the 6th of December, ten of the emigrants, accompanied by six of the crew, set out to face the hardships of another search. The weather had not improved. Their clothes stiffened under the freezing spray, till they were like coats of iron. Here and there as they coasted along, they stopped to examine the nature of the soil. On the morning of the third day, as they were rising from their bivouac, they were attacked by Indians. With difficulty they regained their boat; but they had scarcely put off from the land, when the wind rose to a hurricane. Fortunately it blew in the direction of their course; but, as they swept along amidst the blinding snow, they began to feel anxious lest they should be dashed against the coast, which, as they knew, was not far in front. A huge wave dashed over them, carrying away the rudder as it passed. As they were steadying the boat with the oars, the pilot, peering through the driving snow, caught sight of land, and cheered them by announcing that he recognised the harbour of which he had told them. He had scarcely uttered the words, when the mast was broken short off by a sudden gust, and the fallen sail, flapping as it lay against the side of the boat, so impeded their movements, that, but for the flood tide which was running strongly into the harbour, they would have been dashed to pieces amongst the breakers. Yet even then the danger was not over. The pilot fancied that he had mistaken the place, and lost his presence of mind. With a wild cry of, "The Lord be merciful! my eyes never saw this place before," he attempted to beach the boat amongst the tumbling surf. Happily, the other seamen interfered, and smooth water was gained at last. As the shadows of night closed in, the wanderers, wet to the skin, and faint with watching, stepped on shore.

The landing at Plymouth.

At midnight the wind shifted, and the stars shone clearly out through the frosty air. When the morning dawned, the emigrants discovered that they were on an island in the midst of the spacious and landlocked bay, to which Smith had given the name of Plymouth, a name which they gladly retained in memory of the last spot upon English soil on which their feet had trodden. Here they remained for two days to recruit their exhausted frames. On the morning of the 11th of December, a day never to be forgotten in the annals of America, they made their way to the mainland. The granite boulder on which they stepped as they landed became an object of veneration to their descendants. Fragments of it were treasured up in the homes of New England, with a reverence scarcely less than that which in Catholic countries is bestowed upon the relics of the saints. The Pilgrim Fathers, as their children loved to call them, hold a place in the annals of a mighty nation which can never be displaced. But it is not merely because they were the founders of a great people that this tribute has been willingly offered to their memories. It is because they sought first the Kingdom of God, and His righteousness, that honour and reverence has been freely paid to them by a people whose heart has warmed to the tale of spiritual heroism, all the more, it may be, because its own life had assumed, in its long struggle with physical difficulties, a less ideal character.

The honours which were to be paid them in future times were far from the thoughts of the exiles. With pleased eyes they looked upon the clearings in the forest, and upon the blades of Indian corn, which gave tokens of human presence. They marked the rattling brooks which promised a perennial supply of water, very different from that which they had drunk from the ponds of Cape Cod: and they noted that the harbour was safe and deep. A hasty glance was sufficient to satisfy them, and they hurried back to bear the good tidings to their companions in the Mayflower. To one at least of their number the day on which he rejoined his comrades must have been ever remembered as a day of bitter sorrow. As Bradford stepped on board, he was met by the news that his wife had fallen overboard, and had perished before help could reach her.

On the 16th, the Mayflower cast anchor in Plymouth

Bay. Two or three days were spent in further exploration. On the 19th, "calling upon God for direction," the whole company decided in favour of the spot at which the pioneers had landed. It was no holiday employment which they had undertaken. On the 20th, they began to work. The next day it was blowing a hurricane. Those who were on shore were drenched to the skin, and those who had remained on board were unable to join their companions. For two days the storm raged without intermission. On the 23rd, the weather moderated, and they were able to fell and carry timber. Then came the Sabbath rest, the day on which their trials were all forgotten—a rest which was this time to be disturbed by an alarm, happily false, of approaching Indians. The next day was the 25th, Christmas-day in England. "That day," says the journal of the exiles, with grim brevity, "we went on shore, some to fell timber, some to saw, some to rive, and some to carry. So no man rested all that day." And so the narrative of their labours proceeds. The work was often interrupted by the terrible weather, but they struggled manfully on, and by the middle of February, sixteen log huts were ready for the reception of the families of the builders.

It would have been well if these hardships had been the worst against which they had to contend. But fatigue and exposure had told heavily upon them. Before the summer came, fifty-one persons, a full half of their scanty number, had been struck down by disease. Yet it was in the very depth of their suffering that the power of Christian charity was seen. "In the time of most distress," wrote one who passed through that gloomy winter, "there was but six or seven sound persons who, to their great commendation be it spoken, spared no pains night nor day, but with abundance of toil and hazard of their own health, fetched them wood, made them fires, dressed them meat, made their beds, washed their loathsome clothes, clothed and unclothed them—in a word, did all the homely and necessary offices for them which the dainty and queasy cannot endure to hear named—and all this willingly and cheerfully, without any grudging in the least, shewing herein their true love unto their friends and brethren. A rare example, and worthy to be remembered. Two of these seven were Mr. William Brewster, their reverend elder, and Miles Standish, their captain and military commander, unto whom myself and many others were much beholden in our low and sad condition."

<small>Ch. VII.
1621.</small>

Nor was it only to one another that they were ready to show kindness. The sailors of the Mayflower had been rude and scornful. When the disease was raging at Plymouth, the captain had refused to send on shore even a little beer for the sick. At last his own men were struck down, and, as he saw them dying around him, he repented of his harshness. The settlers, he now said, might have as much beer as they wanted, if he had to drink water on his voyage home. A few of the passengers who were still on board devoted themselves to nursing the sick. One of the sailors was heard expressing his gratitude for the kindness he received. "You," he said, "show your love like Christians indeed to one another; but we let one another lie and die like dogs."*

<small>And on board the Mayflower.</small>

At last the remnant of the emigrants was sufficiently established to dispense with the Mayflower. On the 5th of April, the vessel which had been their home for so many months, sailed away for England. The blue waves of Plymouth Bay rolled in once more unbroken to the beach. The settlers were alone. Some twenty full-grown men remained to encounter, as best they might, the dangers of the wilderness. By their side were a few true-hearted women, with their tender little ones clinging round them. At the end of the short street were the graves of those they loved, who had fallen before the blasts of that terrible winter, and beyond was the illimitable forest, with its unknown perils. Yet were they full of hope. One danger at least proved less than they had expected. From a few straggling Indians who found their way to the village, they learned that the whole country had recently been depopulated by an epidemic, and that they had only to deal with the shattered remnants of the populous and warlike tribes which had once

<small>April.
Return of the Mayflower.</small>

---

* Bradford. *History of Plymouth Plantation*, 81—93. Mourt's Relation, in *Young's Chronicles*. The latter account is generally ascribed to Bradford and Winslow.

Ch. VII.
1621.
April.

Bradford elected governor.

been masters of the soil. As for themselves, a turn seemed to have taken place in the tide of their fortunes. The warm summer was coming on, and though deaths still occurred, the mortality was rapidly diminishing.
Amongst those who died after the departure of the Mayflower, was Carver. The colonists instantly elected Bradford to the vacant post of governor. So well did he perform the duties of the office, that he was chosen year after year with scarcely an interruption, till age unfitted him for further service. By his side, ever ready to support his authority, were Standish, now formally installed as military commander, and Winslow, not as yet holding any official position, but recognised as the man whose tongue and pen could be reckoned on if ever the infant colony should be menaced with interference from the mother country. In the absence of a regular minister, the services of the Church were conducted under the presidency of Brewster.

For the present at least the exiles had gained the object of their double emigration. With the exception of a few of their number who had joined them at Southampton, they were, to all appearance, men who were likely to keep at bay the temptations of the world. Peaceful and God-fearing, they had sought to found a society, from which evil should, as far as possible, be excluded. How their hopes were disappointed:—how the world, attracted by their success, came pouring in upon the shores which they had marked as their own; how they rose above temptation, and showed that by sheer force of goodness they could win the submission of the very men who had wronged them most bitterly, as easily as they could resist with brave endurance the famine and its attendant miseries which burst in upon them once more through the ill-doing of the new comers; this, and more than this, is written in the first pages of the history of New England. But from all this we are bound to turn away. It is enough for us to ask how England itself was likely to be affected by the principles which had conducted the emigrants across the Atlantic.

Prospects of toleration in England.

That a country like England, with its old social distinctions, and the many-sided life of its redundant population, should ever permanently transform itself after the form which commended itself to the devout hearts of the Separatists, was manifestly impossible; and, but for the extraordinary blunders of the Government in the next generation, it would have been no less impossible for men possessed by the spirit of Bradford and Brewster to rise even temporarily to authority in the land. But it was no slight indication of the tendency of the age, that at a time when the question of religious toleration lay at the root of so many difficulties, two men, so opposite in every respect as Robinson and Selden, should have arrived independently at the conclusion, that the clergy had no right to require the State to exercise coercive jurisdiction in support of their opinions.* No doubt this concurrence was brought about by arguments of a very different kind. Selden would have restricted the clergy to the use of moral suasion, because he dreaded their encroachments upon the rights of the laity. Robinson would have asked for the same change because he dreaded lest they should interfere with the free exercise of religious zeal. If Selden had had his way, there would have been very little religious zeal left to interfere with. To such a man the one-sidedness, the violence, the very excitement of theological partizanship were eminently distasteful. He looked upon the enthusiasm of Laud, and the enthusiasm of Robinson, as equal nuisances to society. He never forgot that strong feeling contains the germs of possible tyranny over the opinions of others, and, in his heart, he fixed his hopes upon a calm and philosophical religion in which,

CH. VII.
1621.

Robinson and Selden.

---

* Amongst the articles presented by the emigrants to the King before they obtained leave to sail, and signed by Robinson and Brewster, were some in which they agreed to respect and obey the bishops, but only on account of their position as officers of the Crown.

"We judge it lawful," they say, "for his Majesty to appoint bishops, civil overseers, or officers in authority under him, in the several provinces, dioceses, congregations, or parishes, to oversee the churches and govern them civilly according to the laws of the land, unto whom they are in all things to give an account, and by them to be ordered according to godliness."

"The authority of the present bishops in the land we do acknowledge, so far forth as the same is indeed derived from his Majesty unto them, and as they proceed in his name, whom we will also therein honour in all things, and lie in them."

"We believe that no synod, classes, convocation, or assembly of ecclesiastical officers hath any power or authority at all, but as the same by the magistrate is given unto them." *S. P. Colonial,* i. 43.

though there might be no fanaticism, there would be but little life. If Robinson, on the other hand, had had his way, the English Church would have been parcelled out into a number of independent congregations, the members of which would have treated the mass of their countrymen as unworthy of the very name of Christians. Piety and devotion would have been found accompanied by much narrowness of mind and intolerance of spirit.

<small>The liberal statesmen and the Puritans.</small>
Fortunately for England, men like Selden and men like Robinson were able to work together towards a common end. In the great revolution which was approaching, it was Puritanism which was to play the part of the motive power. It was not enough that men should hold theories about liberty. What was needed was that there should be found men who were ready to dare anything and to suffer anything on behalf of Him whom they called their Lord; men who could confront kings as being themselves the servants of the King of Kings. When such as these had done their work, then would come the part of the calm philosophic statesmen, of the men whose minds were directed to the study of the natural creation, rather than to the contemplation of the perfections of the Creator, and who were quick to mark the moment at which the enthusiasm of their allies blinded them to the laws of nature, or hurried them on to demand the realisation of an ideal to which the world would be unwilling to submit.

CHAPTER VIII.

LORD DIGBY'S EMBASSY TO VIENNA.

By the declaration which had been voted so enthusiastically on the 4th of June, the Commons had left to the King that full liberty of action which he loved so dearly. They had also left him that of which he was less desirous—the responsibility of acting wisely—and, unfortunately, partly through his own fault, but still more through the faults of others, the chance that he would be able to act wisely had been considerably lessened by the events of the seven months which had elapsed since the battle of Prague.

Ch. VIII. 1620. Nov. Germany after the battle of Prague.

Between Ferdinand and Frederick nothing but distrust was now possible. In the eyes of the Emperor his fugitive enemy was a mere disturber of the peace whose flagitious intrigues must be baffled at any cost. In the eyes of Frederick, Ferdinand was himself a pretender who had been lawfully dethroned, and who now owed his success to the armies and the gold of the King of Spain. Nor were the views with which the rivals regarded their obligations as members of the empire less opposite to one another. Ferdinand held that in virtue of his office, he was the guardian of the peace of the empire, and that this peace had been broken by the invasion of his dominions, and by the illegal assumption of one of the seven Electorates. Frederick, on the other hand, held that he had no quarrel with the Emperor as such. He had merely defended against an Archduke of Austria the throne which he held by legitimate election.

Ferdinand and Frederick.

For years political controversy raged around these simple points in an interminable circle. Masses of paper wearisome to read, wearisome even to look at, were piled up by learned controversialists on either side. Each party started from premises which were rejected by the other,

Ch. VIII.
1620.
Nov.

Views prevalent in Germany.

and they naturally failed either in conv
temporaries, or in instructing posterity.
Regardless of such technicalities, the
German Protestants had maintained an a
during the Bohemian war. For they
Frederick's theories involved the perman
of anarchy. If the Emperor was to be n
the nominal head of a federation, ber
authority needed for the repression of priv
its members, order could never be preserv
who coveted his neighbour's lands woul
excuse for invading them, whilst the only
to the constitution would be powerless to

Yet strong as the disposition was to
Emperor, there were not wanting other
lead thinking men in an opposite direct
law of which Ferdinand had constitu
champion, was almost certain to be rui
existence of Protestantism itself in Gern
claring Frederick to be a traitor, it was
forfeiture of his lands and dignities. If i
and such as Frederick, had been alone ex
the world would easily have borne the r
presence of a new Catholic Elector at
Assemblies of the Empire, could hardly fa
with undesirable consequences, and it w
new Catholic Lord of the Palatinate w
work with the conscientious convictions
The next step would be to demand the r
ecclesiastical lands which had been seize
of Augsburg, and to convert each rega
bishopric into an outpost of Jesuitism.
spect for the letter of the law, the triu
stopped here, every Protestant knew full we
religious aggression would not thus be stay
tant prince would learn that power had p
and that favour was to be obtained there
If he would only consent to abandon
restored ecclesiastical estates would offer
canonries for his younger sons. Partial
ready to listen with open ear to the cor

Catholic who had quarrelled with his neighbours. One by one, it was to be feared, they would drop off into the seductive arms of the Church of Rome, as the Protestant aristocracy were dropping off in France; and as Wolfgang William of Neuburg had dropped off in Germany, at the time when his claims upon the Duchy of Cleves stood in need of Catholic assistance. Each apostate in turn would carry with him the legal right of proscribing the religion which his subjects had learned to cherish, and each defection would have closed in more tightly the ever narrowing circle within which Protestantism could live, and within which alone the free moral and intellectual life of the Germany of the future would be able to develope itself.

Ch. VIII. 1620. Nov.

Such were the thoughts, dimly and confusedly penetrating the minds of the great majority of German Protestants. If only John George of Saxony had been capable of translating their inarticulate feelings into prompt and decisive action, he might have won himself a name second to none in the annals of his country. If he could have stood forward at the head of the Princes and people of Northern Germany, to tell the Emperor that he might deal as he pleased with Frederick, but that the frontier of Protestantism must not recede, he would have found no want of support. Unhappily he did nothing of the kind. Knowing full well the double danger of civil anarchy and ecclesiastical tyranny with which the empire was threatened, he wavered between the two. At one time he was eager for Frederick's complete restitution. At another time he was eager to see him completely crushed, and after every disappointment, he was ready to take refuge in the solace of the hunting-field and the bottle.

Weakness of the Elector of Saxony.

That which John George might have accomplished with comparative ease, presented far greater difficulties to James. Of course, if he pleased, he might spend any subsidies which Parliament might be willing to grant him in increasing the confusion which already weighed so heavily upon that distracted land. But if he wished to do more than this; if he intended to interfere in the quarrel in the only way in which a foreign power can

Difficulties in the way of James.

VOL. II. F

CH. VIII.
1620.
Nov.

hope to interfere to any purpose, namely, by giving strength and solidity to the national will, he would have a hard task before him; a task of which more than half the difficulty arose from the impracticable temper of his son-in-law.

Frederick persistently renews his claims.

For unhappily, for himself and for his country, Frederick was still living in that dream-land which had so long usurped the place of reality in his mind. To him the defeat on the White Hill was not the final result of years of anarchy. It was a mere accident of fortune, a military check with which a little perseverance might easily be repaired. His confident belief was still that others would be ready to do that for him which he had made no serious effort to accomplish for himself. "The hopes of the King and Queen," wrote Conway, a few days after the battle, "are that their father will do for them now, and not treat." *

On the 7th of November the cavalcade of fugitives took refuge in Breslau. On the 11th Frederick issued a manifesto in the form of a letter to the Princes of the Union. Silesia and Moravia, he wrote, were still true to him. Bethlen Gabor was ready to assist him to recover all that had been lost. Let them see that they too were ready to join heart and hand in his cause. If they now refused, the Emperor would soon reoccupy the ecclesiastical domains by force of arms.† To James he was less explicit. With English aid, he said, his affairs would soon mend. Elizabeth, as was her wont, spoke out her mind, and asked that the help promised for the Palatinate might be extended to Bohemia.‡ "I am not yet so out of heart," she wrote a fortnight afterwards to her old friend Carleton, "though I confess we are in an evil estate, but that, as I hope, God will give us again the victory; for the wars are not ended with one battle, and I hope we shall have better luck in the next. The good news you write of the King my father's declaring himself

---

* Conway to Buckingham, Nov. 18. *Harl. MSS.* 1580, fol. 281.
† Frederick to the Princes of the Union, Nov. 11. *Theatrum Europæum*, i. 454.
‡ Frederick to the King. Elizabeth to the King, Nov. 13. Ellis, Ser. i. 3, 111, 112.

for the Palatinate, I pray God they may be seconded with the same for Bohemia."*

Ch. VIII.
1620.

Ruinous as her counsel was, it was well for her that her brave woman's heart could beat so cheerily in the midst of trouble. She was herself sent away to seek a refuge at Cüstrin to give birth to a child, the little Maurice, who was doubtless loved all the more tenderly for the gloom amidst which his stormy life began.† Bad news was coming in almost every day. The Moravians, it seemed, were ready to make their peace with Ferdinand. Frederick, blind to much, could see that the ground was slipping from beneath his feet. There were those in Breslau who were already muttering that it would be better to come to terms with the Elector of Saxony. Frederick's fears got the better of him. He told the Estates of Silesia that he would leave them for the present; but he would soon be back with powerful allies to support his cause. If they wished to send commissioners to treat with the Saxons, he would make no objection. Such a negotiation, he privately added to those who were in his confidence, would serve to gain time till he was able to return with an army at his back.‡ On the 23rd of December he left Breslau for ever, not forgetting to despatch an embassy to John George to demand a cessation of arms, and to ask for assistance to drive the Emperor out of Bohemia. To this impertinence the Elector replied by a solemn lecture on the recognition which his adversary's right had received from Providence, and by a well-timed admonition to make his submission to the Emperor before it was too late.§

December. He leaves Silesia.

On the 12th of January, the day before this answer was given at Dresden, the ban of the empire was pronounced at Vienna against Frederick and his principal followers. They were declared to have forfeited their lands and dignities, whilst the execution of the sentence was significantly entrusted to the Duke of Bavaria,

1621.
January.
The ban pronounced against him.

* Elizabeth to Carleton, Nov. 27. *S. P. Holland.*
† Nethersole to Naunton, Dec. 4. *S. P. Germany.*
‡ Frederick to the Estates of Silesia, Dec. 12, Dec. 23. *Londorp,* ii. 237. Nethersole to Naunton, March 19, 1621. *S. P. Germany.*
§ *Theatrum Europæum,* i. 462.

F 2

Ch. VIII.
1621.
January.

Rusdorf's advice.

who was eager to put himself, if possible, in possession of both.

As soon as the news was published, a shriek of horror arose from the whole circle of Frederick's partisans. It was only after a legal trial, they said, that the ban could lawfully be proclaimed. Ferdinand's reply was that this might well be the case in time of peace; but it was notorious that Frederick had levied war against the Emperor, and it was no less notorious that he had not the slightest intention of submitting to any form of trial whatever. Whether Ferdinand were technically in the right or not, it is certain that legal formalities had been too often unblushingly disregarded by Frederick and his supporters to justify them in interpreting them very strictly in their own favour.*

On the day on which the ban was pronounced Frederick was riding out of Cüstrin to urge the princes of Lower Saxony to take arms on his behalf.† Yet he had not been left altogether without a warning. Rusdorf, one of his ablest councillors, had written earnestly to dissuade him from his imprudence. The foreign powers in which he trusted, he told him, would be sure to fail him in the end. The wound in Bohemia was mortal, and no recovery was possible there. Of the Palatinate he could speak from personal experience. Soldiers and officers were alike intent upon their own private aims. There was not one amongst them who believed in the goodness of the cause for which he was fighting. The country was laid desolate by its own defenders. It was to be feared that the inhabitants would, in sheer self-defence, break out into open sedition. The Union, at all events, would

---

* The clause in the Capitulation which Ferdinand was said to have broken is the following one:—" Wir sollen und wollen auch fürkommen und keines Wegs gestatten dasz nun hinfüro jemand hohes oder niedriges Stands Churfürst, Fürst, oder anderer, Ursach auch unverhört, in die Acht und Oberacht gethan, bracht, oder erklart werde; sondern in solchem ordentlichen Procesz, und des H. R. R. in gemeldetem 55ter Jahr reformirten Cammergerichtsordnung, und darauff erfolgter Reichs Abschied in dem gehalten und vollzogen werde, jedoch dem Beschädigten seine Gegenwehr vermög des Landfriedens unabruchig." Linnæus, *Capitulationes*, 591. See for Ferdinand's view of the case, his reply to the Danish Ambassadors. *Londorp*, ii. 392.

† Nethersole to Naunton, Jan. 19. *S. P. Germany.*

certainly break down as soon as it was exposed to real danger.*

To the truth coming from one of his own ministers Frederick could refuse to listen. To Sir Edward Villiers, who met him at Wolfenbüttel with a message from the King of England, he was unable to close his ears; for he knew well that, unless James took up his cause, there would be few indeed amongst the princes of Germany who would venture to declare in his favour.

Frederick listened to Villiers, and announced in a letter to his father-in-law the result of his conversation. "Whatever has been done," he wrote, "proceeded from a good intention. If it had pleased God to grant me success, the whole party of the religion would have been relieved; but since this has not been the will of God, it is for me to take the good and the evil at His hand; and although I hoped, with His aid, and with the assistance of your Majesty and the other princes and states of the religion, to regain what I had lost, holding still, as I do, Silesia and several towns in Bohemia, yet, seeing by your letter that you incline rather to an accommodation, I am ready to follow your good counsels and commands." †

Even if Frederick had meant what he said, there was a studied vagueness about his language which augured ill for the success of James's negotiations. But the truth was, that the engagement thus wrung from him was no indication of his real intentions. Two days after his promise was thus given to his father-in-law he wrote to Mansfeld to assure him that he would never surrender his kingdom of Bohemia. He had justice on his side, and he would soon win back all that he had lost.‡

Frederick was, within the limitations of his own narrow mind, thoroughly consistent with himself. Utterly to destroy the German branch of the House of Austria: to convert the empire into a federation of independent princes, amongst which the stronger would find no restrictions upon their desire to prey upon their weaker

---

* Rusdorf. *Consilia et Negotia*, 8. The same desponding feeling is to be traced in the letters of Camerarius. Söltl. *Religionskrieg*, iii. 105—115.
† Frederick to the King, Jan. 31. *Harl. MSS.* 1583, fol. 219.
‡ Frederick to Mansfield, Feb. 2. *Londorp*, ii. 377.

neighbours, and to establish the supremacy of Protestantism, and especially of its Calvinistic form, by force of arms, were the objects at which his father had aimed, and to the attainment of which, with such reserves as sufficed to conceal from his own mind the iniquity of his proceedings, he had himself directed his course.

No doubt there are higher rights than those of kings and emperors. No doubt injustice receives no consecration from the successful efforts of pikemen and musketeers. But what Frederick forgot was that his enemies were not confined to those who looked for inspiration to Munich or Vienna. He had alienated his own allies; he had converted the lukewarm into hostile antagonists; he had dragged in the dust the great cause of German Protestantism. Prudent politicians stood aloof from his rash and impatient violence; sober and religious men shrunk from accepting the advocacy of a champion whose victory would have destroyed much and founded nothing. Whilst Frederick was imagining that he had only to contend with the armies of Ferdinand and Maximilian he had in reality a far harder battle to fight; for he had to convince his fellow Protestants that he could protect their religious independence without converting Germany into a den of thieves.

The Assembly of Segeberg. Meanwhile the King of Denmark and the other princes of the Lower Saxon Circle were assembled at Segeberg to listen to Frederick's proposals. The selfish and unprincipled Christian IV. thought of little else than the retention of the secularised Church property which he had got into his possession, but he was shrewd enough to perceive how the settlement of that question had been retarded by Frederick's proceedings in Bohemia. "Who advised you," he called out savagely to the fugitive Prince, "to drive out kings and to seize kingdoms. If your councillors did so, they were scoundrels." He then told him plainly, as Villiers had told him before, that, if he wanted help, he must submit to the Emperor. When he had done that, he might expect aid to drive Spinola from the Palatinate.

A day or two after this scene, Christian had cooled down. Frederick, ostensibly at least, consented to give up his claims to Bohemia, and was informed in return that a Danish embassy would be sent to ask for peace at Vienna. If that failed, the princes of Lower Saxony would not desert him.*

<small>Ch. VIII.
1621.
February.</small>

Before the assembly broke up, Sir Robert Anstruther arrived from England. He had come to ask Christian for a fresh loan of 25,000*l*., of which 5000*l*. were to be at once repaid as interest due upon the loan of the preceding summer, whilst the remainder was to be made over to Elizabeth as a present from her father. Anstruther found that the King of Denmark had little faith in the success of the proposed embassy to Vienna, and that he was looking forward to a campaign on the Rhine in conjunction with England and the Netherlands. "By God," he said, laying his hand familiarly on the Ambassador's shoulder as he spoke, "this business is gone too far to think it can be redressed with words only. I thank God we hope, with the help of his Majesty of Great Britain and the rest of our friends, to give unto the Count Palatine good conditions. If ever we do any good for the liberty of Germany and religion it is now time."†

<small>Anstruther's mission.</small>

After some weeks' delay Anstruther obtained his money,‡ and the 20,000*l*. was duly paid over to Elizabeth.

From Segeberg Frederick set out for the Hague,§ where the Prince of Orange was waiting to receive him with open arms. It was not what his father-in-law would have wished. He had charged Villiers to recommend him to betake himself at once to the Palatinate, and he had sent orders to Carleton to prevent him from coming to England.‖ Such advice, though doubtless in part inspired by fear lest Frederick should place himself at the head of the Parliamentary opposition, was probably, but for Frederick's own weakness of character, the best that could be given. In Holland the exile would be breathing an

<small>March.
Villiers advises Frederick to go to the Palatinate.</small>

---

* Müller. *Forschungen*, iii. 468.
† Anstruther to Calvert, March 10. *S. P. Denmark.* The expressions given are taken from different parts of a long harangue.
‡ Slange. *Gesch. Christians IV.* iii. 170.
§ Carleton to Nethersole, March 5. Carleton to Calvert, March 8. *S. P. Holland.*
‖ The King to Carleton, Jan. 25. Calvert to Carleton, March 1. *S. P. Holland.*

Ch. VIII.
1621.
March.

atmosphere of war; in England he would be far removed from the scene of action. At Heidelberg his presence would have served to keep his subjects in heart in their hour of trial, and it would have given emphasis to his assertions that he had ceased to seek for anything beyond the preservation of his own domains.*

Frederick's reply.

Frederick's reply to Villiers' proposition was not encouraging to those who wished well to his cause. He must first, he said, go to the Hague, that he might place his wife and children in a place of safety. He would then be ready to return to the Palatinate, "so that his Majesty may be speedily assisted with a good army either of his Majesty of Great Britain or of the States, that he may be able to bring with him some comfort and ease to his subjects who languish in expectation thereof. For, if he should go otherwise, and in his own person only, that would get his Majesty very little reputation, and would encourage the Marquis Spinola to assail the Palatinate so much the more earnestly, and to send his Majesty back thither whence he came with shame enough to himself and to all them to whom his Majesty hath the honour to be so nearly allied. And withal, if his Majesty should go in that manner, the Princes of the Union would retire themselves every one to his own house, leaving the defence of the Palatinate, and the charge of the army, upon his Majesty's hands, which would undoubtedly cause the total ruin and subversion of all his Majesty's estates and of his person, and would make him at once lose all his friends and allies. Which considerations being of consequence, his Majesty doth promise himself that his Majesty of Great Britain, examining them maturely, will not only approve them, but also esteem this his retreat into the Low Countries to be good and necessary; and favour him so much with his forces that he may return into the Palatinate, not only with reputation, but with some good effect, by God's help, as he doth most humbly beseech his Majesty, promising himself that such a resolution would serve

---

* It is curious that the Dutch for opposite reasons did not wish him to visit England. "We do not think," wrote Carleton, "the King will discountenance his affairs in Germany by crossing the seas."

for an example, not only to the Union, but also to the King of Denmark, the States, and others, to take a good and a vigorous resolution together, which is very necessary for all those that have made a separation from the Papacy."*

Frederick, it would seem, was Frederick still. No man could be more eager to summon armies from the ends of the earth to fight in his cause. No man could be more unable to define satisfactorily what the cause was for which he wanted them to fight. From a proposal that he should place himself at the head of the troops of the Union, he shrunk as he would have shrunk from the plague. It would endanger his reputation. It would encourage his enemies to assail him more bitterly. If Ferdinand had reasoned so when Thurn was thundering at the gates of Vienna, Frederick would still have been in comfortable enjoyment of the delights of Bohemian royalty.

Whatever may be thought of the advice given by James to Frederick, nothing but sheer timidity can account for his behaviour to Elizabeth. During her journey from Cüstrin she had allowed it to be understood that she wished to take refuge with her father.† James was struck with alarm. He had enough to do to keep the war party in check, and he could not bear to think that his daughter's winning smiles would be placed in the balance against him.‡ Carleton was therefore told that the journey must be stopped at all hazards.§ It is probable that some intimation of her father's repugnance to her visit was conveyed to Elizabeth by her friends; for her language suddenly changed, and she now declared positively that nothing on earth would induce her to cross the sea to England.‖

Elizabeth forbidden to visit England.

---

* The paper is at the end of the February bundle of the Holland State Papers. It is without a date, but is in Nethersole's hand. As Nethersole was in the train of Elizabeth, I suppose the answer must have been given about the middle of March.

† Carleton to Calvert, March 8. *S. P. Holland.*

‡ Tillière's Despatch, March $\frac{10}{20}$. *Raumer,* ii. 308.

§ The King to Carleton, March 13. *S. P. Holland.*

‖ Nethersole to Carleton, March 24. *S. P. Holland.* Amongst these State Papers, there is a note in the handwriting of one of Sir J. Williamson's clerks stating that James had invited her and her husband to

CH. VIII.
1621.
March.
Frederick at the Hague.

On the 4th of April, escorted by a convoy of Dutch soldiers, the King of Bohemia, as he still persisted in calling himself, rode into the Hague. He was received with all honour. The Prince of Orange placed his own house at Breda at his disposal; and in the town itself, the mansion of Count Frederick Henry was assigned to him as a residence.*

Policy of James.

Wise intervention in German affairs was evidently not so easy as the majority of Englishmen supposed. But, in the main, James's policy was undoubtedly the right one. To compel Frederick to renounce the crown of Bohemia, and at the same time to form an alliance strong enough to defend the Palatinate, was the only combination which offered a prospect of success. As usual, it was in the execution rather than in the conception that James's arrangements broke down utterly. He ought to have forced his son-in-law to notify to the world by a renunciation of the Bohemian crown that he was ready to conform to the conditions under which alone he could hope to maintain his hereditary domains. He ought to have made such preparations for war as would have convinced friends and enemies that now at last he was in earnest. Instead of this, he allowed the weeks to slip away, leaving everything to chance, and to the evil designs of men who wished for their own selfish purposes to see the prolongation of the war.

Desire of Spain for peace.

Amongst these, contrary to the general belief in England, the Spanish Government was not to be reckoned. Early in January, Philip, or those who acted in his name, had expressed to the Archduke Albert the anxiety with which the continuance of hostilities was regarded at Madrid. Perhaps, wrote Philip, he might obtain repayment of his expenses by means of the confiscations in Bohemia. Perhaps a contribution might be levied in the Palatinate itself. At any rate, it would be impossible for him long to continue to bear this intolerable burden. As for the Elector Palatine, if he was to

England. This may have been taken from some letter now lost, but in the face of the despatches just quoted, I cannot accept it as a true account of the case, unless, indeed, on the unlikely supposition that an invitation was given earlier and then retracted.

* *Theatrum Europæum*, i. 508.

be restored, he must renounce the crown of Bohemia, and must forsake the Protestant Union. Care must be taken to restrain the Duke of Bavaria from pressing his claims to the Electorate. Perhaps the difficulty might be arranged by allowing the two families an alternative voice in the College.* When such were the opinions of the King of Spain, expressed not in formal diplomatic language, but in private and confidential intercourse, it can hardly admit of a doubt that if Frederick had really given up the shadow of the Bohemian crown, and had offered guarantees for his peaceable behaviour in future, he might have had anything else that he could reasonably ask for. Philip's poverty, if not his will, would have given consent.

The burden of James's inertness fell heavily upon Morton, who presented himself in the beginning of February before the Assembly of the Union at Heilbronn, having brought with him 30,000l., and a few vague promises. He was told that the struggle could not be continued on these conditions. It was true that the ban against Frederick was illegal, and they had sent an ambassador to Vienna to remonstrate against it. But they had no money left. The towns were falling off from the cause. The troops were melting away, and no more than 11,000 men were still under arms. They hoped, therefore, that the States would send them a force of 6000 men, and James would allow them 30,000l. a month till he was prepared to do something more.†

By James the demand thus made was received with complete indifference. His preparations for war had been limited to an order to increase the stock of arms in the Tower, and to an inquiry made through Carleton as to the possibility of procuring in Holland the equipments of an army of 10,000 or 12,000 men.‡

Very different were the feelings of the Dutch Statesmen, by whom the whole chart of continental politics

CH. VIII.
1621.
January.

February.
Morton at Heilbronn.

January.
Dutch Commis-

* Philip III. to the Archduke, Jan. $\frac{9}{19}$. Philip III. to Oñate, Jan. $\frac{9}{19}$, $\frac{\text{Feb. 26}}{\text{March 8}}$. *Brussels MSS.*
† Morton's Proposition. Memorial delivered to Morton. *S. P. Germany.*
‡ Caron to the States General, Jan. 11. *Add. MSS.* 17,677 K, fol. 91. Calvert to Carleton, Feb. 17. *S. P. Holland.*

was not unnaturally regarded through the medium of their own quarrel with Spain. In January, the States-General had sent over to England a body of Commissioners charged to express their views. The truce with Spain, they said, would be at an end in April, and for them at least war was inevitable. Germany and the Protestant religion were in the utmost danger, and they wished to know what were the intentions of the King of England.

From such categorical demands James was always anxious to escape. In his distress he caught at the excuse which was afforded him by the state of affairs in the East. Though the treaty of 1619 had been accepted by the Dutch authorities in those seas, differences of opinion had arisen upon the interpretation of some of its clauses. There was one dispute as to the right of the Dutch to erect a fort at Batavia. There was another dispute about the value of the captured goods to be restored. The English company had sent Commissioners to Amsterdam, but no satisfaction could be had. James, accordingly, instead of giving a plain answer to the plain question which had been put to him, rated the Dutchmen soundly for having nothing to say upon these points, or upon the equally difficult question of the herring fishery.

In despair, the Commissioners applied to Buckingham. He listened to their complaints, but, according to their report, he did not seem to know much about the affairs of Germany. The King, he said, was ready to risk his own life, and the life of his son, in the defence of the Palatinate; but there was no hurry about the matter. "In fact," he concluded by saying, "the Palatinate is by this time pretty well lost. When a good opportunity arrives, the King will try to recover it." Such was the tone in which Buckingham allowed himself to speak of a question upon which depended the peace of Europe for a generation.

Once more the Commissioners turned to the King. They assured him that the States were ready to do their utmost in the defence of the Palatinate, and they begged James to support them by a diversion in Flanders, an operation which they represented as certain to be followed by the recall of Spinola from Germany.* The same advice was repeated at the Hague with even more distinct emphasis by the Prince of Orange in a conversation with Carleton.†

<small>Ch. VIII.
1621.
February.</small>

To Maurice, James did not vouchsafe an answer. To the Commissioners he replied with studied rudeness. He informed them that he had nothing to say to them about the truce, as they understood their own affairs better than he did. As soon as they had obtained full powers to treat about the herring fishery, and other matters of the kind, he would be ready to give them information as to his intentions respecting the Palatinate.‡

It was not right that such a question should have been shuffled out of sight by so palpable a subterfuge. But James was probably justified in regarding with suspicion the councils of men who had so deep an interest in the prolongation of the war. In April the truce of Antwerp would have run its course, and it was no secret that the Spaniards intended, if possible, to wring from the Dutch the abandonment of the East India trade, the opening of the Scheldt, and a guarantee of liberty of worship to the Roman Catholics, as the price of its renewal. In the meanwhile, Maurice, fearing lest the inland provinces, which had less immediate interest than Holland and Zealand in the commerce of the Republic, might prove lukewarm when the time of temptation came, was casting about for the best means of defeating the machinations of his ancient enemy, when the very opportunity which he sought was brought within his reach.

<small>The expiration of the truce in the Netherlands.</small>

There was a certain Madame Tserclaes, an elderly lady, living at Brussels, who had been frequently employed in conveying secret political messages across the frontier. This time she was directed to seek out Maurice himself, and to win him over, if possible, to second the designs of the King of Spain. In the proposal Maurice saw nothing but an attempt upon his fidelity to the Republic,

<small>Intrigues of the Prince of Orange.</small>

---

* Report of the Dutch Commissioners. *Add. MSS.* 22,863, fol. 1—88.
† Carleton to Calvert, Feb. 26. *S. P. Holland.*
‡ Answer of the Privy Council, $\frac{\text{Feb. 21}}{\text{March 3}}$. *Add. MSS.* 22,863, fol. 103.

and determining to meet guile with guile, he assured his visitor that he longed for nothing more than a complete reconciliation with Philip. The unexpected news was at once carried to Brussels, and was transmitted without delay to Madrid. The bait was eagerly taken. Madame Tserclaes spent her whole time during the winter months in passing backwards and forwards between Brussels and the Hague. Maurice redoubled his professions of devotion to the King of Spain, and engaged to do all in his power to induce the States to return to their allegiance. Under other circumstances, it is possible that his language might have been regarded with suspicion even by Spaniards, slow as they usually were to detect imposture when it was covered by profuse declarations of devotion to the puppet sovereign who nominally ruled them. But since the Arminian troubles they had been accustomed to take for granted the extreme weakness of the Republic, and they seem to have imagined that Maurice was only using common prudence in attempting to escape from the ruin of a falling house.*

The consequences of the implicit faith now placed at Madrid in the Prince of Orange were not long in showing themselves. On the 8th of March, it was announced that Pecquius, the Chancellor of Brabant, would shortly arrive at the Hague with a proposition from the Archdukes. Immediately it was seen that Maurice was right in foreseeing a division in the counsels of the Republic. The Deputies of Holland and Zealand urged that not even bare civility should be shown to the ambassador. The other five provinces were in favour of exhausting all honourable means before the prospect of a renewal of the truce was finally abandoned. Maurice, whose word on such a question was law, gave his voice in favour of the reception of the ambassador with all due respect. At the same time he took care to raise expectation, by spreading the most favourable rumours of the probable issue of the negotiation. Madame Tserclaes, he gave out, had assured him that not only would peace be secured

* The evidence of all this is contained in a series of letters, too numerous to quote separately, in the Spanish correspondence of the Archduke with Philip III. in the Brussels Archives. They are spread over the whole of the winter months.

to the Netherlands, but that all reasonable satisfaction would be given with regard to the Palatinate.*

On the 12th Pecquius arrived. The next day he was admitted to the Assembly of the States General. To the utter consternation of all but the one man who held the thread of the intrigue, the Ambassador made a formal demand that the provinces should return to their allegiance. To such words there could be but one reply. Pecquius was ordered to leave the territory of the Republic without delay.†

Maurice had gained his end. Such an insult was resented equally by Calvinist and Arminian; by the seamen of Holland, and the farmers of Utrecht. The Archduke had supposed that if his first proposition were rejected, there would be time to negotiate upon a fresh basis.‡ He now found that he had roused a spirit which made all negotiation impossible.

Thoroughly as the Spanish ministers had been duped, it was not for men whose whole diplomacy was one vast network of intrigue, to complain of the wrong which they had received. Nor, to do them justice, did they show any signs of vexation. When, on the 7th of March, just as Pecquius was starting for the Hague, Digby arrived at Brussels on a preliminary mission before setting off to negotiate peace at Vienna, he was received with open arms. He came to ask for a suspension of arms in the Palatinate. The King of Spain, he was told, would not be unwilling to restore the Palatinate, if he could be assured that James would "contribute all good offices of perfect amity and alliance, and particularly not more to esteem the friendship of the Hollanders than his."§ To this Digby, who wanted to bring the Dutch to commercial concessions through fear of Spain, and the Spaniards to political concessions through fear of Holland, raised no objection. He was then informed that the Archduke would give his good word on behalf of Frederick's re-establishment in the Palatinate, and would order

---
* Carleton to Calvert, March 8, 10, 13. *S. P. Holland.*
† Aitzema. *Saken van Staet en Oorlog*, i. 36.
‡ The Archduke Albert to Philip III. $\frac{\text{Feb. 20}}{\text{March 2}}$. *Brussels MSS.*
§ Digby to Buckingham, March 14. *Clarendon State Papers,* i. App. i.

Ch. VIII.
1621.
March.

Spinola to make arrangements for a suspension of arms. Digby accordingly returned to London under the impression that the Court of Brussels was "very desirous and ready to give satisfaction.* Nor was he mistaken. For the Archduke had just written to assure Philip that he had been well satisfied with the prospect of a pacification opened by Digby, as Spinola's troops would now be wanted nearer home.†

Death of Philip III.

On the 21st of March, the very day on which this letter was written, the sovereign to whom it was addressed, breathed his last at Madrid.‡ Soon it was rumoured that whilst he was on his deathbed, words of no light import had fallen from his lips. The Infanta had been summoned to her father's presence. "Maria," he said, "I am sorry that I must die before I have married you; but your brother will take care of that." He then turned to his son. "Prince," he added, "do not forsake her till you have made her an empress."§ The calculations and intrigues of so many years had been wiped away by the approach of death. The promise which he had given, six months before, to Khevenhüller, that his daughter should become the wife of the Archduke Ferdinand, the future Emperor Ferdinand III., had alone branded itself upon his memory.‖

Philip IV.

The new king, Philip IV., was a mere lad. Unlike his father, he took delight in bodily exercises. His chief pleasure was in the hunting-field. For politics he cared little or nothing, leaving all matters of state to those who understood them, whilst he was intent upon the higher work of keeping himself amused. The favourite companion of his pleasures was the Count of Olivares, and it was soon known that the whole stream of honours and promotions would flow through that channel. Affairs of state were committed to Balthazar de Zuñiga, the uncle of the new favourite, a man of ability and integrity, who

---

* Digby to Carleton, March 23. Answer of the Archdukes, $\frac{March\ 24}{April\ 3}$. S. P. Flanders.

† The Archduke Albert to Philip III., March $\frac{21}{31}$. Brussels MSS.

‡ Aston to Calvert, March $\frac{21}{31}$. S. P. Spain.

§ Cabala, 223.

‖ Vol. i. p. 351.

had formerly served as ambassador at the Imperial Court, and who was inclined from principle to do all that could safely be done to advance the power of the House of Austria and the Church of Rome.

CH. VIII.
1621.
March.

Under these circumstances James naturally conceived some anxiety, and directed Aston to inquire what were the intentions of the young king. The ambassador was met with overwhelming assurances of goodwill, and was told that whatever the late sovereign might have said, Philip IV. was most anxious to go on vigorously with the marriage treaty.*

April.
Aston receives friendly assurances.

Undoubtedly no one but James would have been likely to accept these profuse expressions of goodwill as conveying the real feeling of the Spanish ministers. But even to a more cautious politician, they would not have been without their use. For taken in connection with the circumstances in which the Spanish monarchy was placed, they would at least have served as indications of the value which was placed at Madrid upon the friendship of the King of England. In truth it was in Protestant Germany far more than in Spain that the dangers were to be found upon which James's mediation was likely to be wrecked. Frederick's obstinate retention of the Royal title on the one hand, and the menaces of Spinola on the other, were beginning to produce their natural effect upon the Union. The ardent Landgrave of Hesse Cassel had been compelled to keep the peace by his own subjects, who would not hear of his making war against the Emperor. The cities were the next to give way. They had entered the Union in order to defend themselves and their religion against aggression, and they had no idea of following Frederick in a crusade against the Emperor, in which, to them at least, success or defeat would be equally ruinous. Without the money and supplies which the towns alone were able to furnish, the Princes saw no prospect of being able to carry on the war, and on the 2nd of April, a treaty was signed at Mentz, by which they engaged to withdraw their troops from the Palatinate, and to dissolve the tie by which their Union had

The dissolution of the Union.

* Aston to the King, April 14. *Harl. MSS.* 1580, fol. 8. Francisco de Jesus, 32.

VOL. II.   G

Ch. VIII.
1621.
April.

been formed. On the other hand, Spinola agreed to suspend hostilities till the 4th of May, and this concession was expressly declared to have been granted at the request of the King of England.*

Such was the ignominious end of the alliance which, under better guidance, might have served as the advanced guard of Protestantism in Germany. Many were the gibes, written and spoken, which were circulated at the expense of that now contemptible body. Yet, if all that is known to us had been known to contemporaries, it would have been upon the early rather than upon the later history of the confederacy, that contempt would have been poured. Diverted from its ostensible objects to extract from the pockets of peace-loving and orderly citizens the means of carrying on an aggressive and revolutionary policy, it broke up into its original fragments, as soon as men learned from experience to understand something of the deceit which had been practised upon them.

May.
Frederick persists in opposition.

The dissolution of the Union would not have been without its good effects if Frederick had been induced by it to reconsider his own position. No doubt as long as he contented himself with fixing his eyes merely upon the enemy's proceedings, there was every reason to induce him to persist in his opposition; for we may well believe that it was something more than personal vanity which made him loath to surrender the crown of Bohemia. The cause of his fellow Protestants, whose interests he had striven to serve after his blind, ignorant fashion, was still at stake. If he did not re-appear to save them, his trustiest supporters would soon be hurried to the scaffold, and the clergy who had besieged the gates of heaven with prayers for his success would be thrust forth into poverty and exile. Nor was the position of Protestantism in the Empire free from danger. It was now well known that the Emperor intended to convoke an assembly of German princes to meet at Ratisbon, and it was generally believed that he would ask them to sanction the transference of Frederick's Electorate to the Duke of Bavaria. Yet if Frederick really wished to prevent this unhappy consummation, he ought to have known that, without assistance from his

* *Häberlin*, xxv. 32. *Londorp*, ii. 382.

countrymen, he was powerless to effect his purposes. From one end of Germany to another, wherever public opinion had found a voice to express it, a steady determination had been manifested to remain faithful to the Emperor. On this point, the burghers of Strasburg and Ulm were of one mind with the Elector of Saxony, and with the knightly vassals of the Landgrave of Hesse Cassel. For in the institutions of the Empire, they all saw the only remaining barrier against anarchy, the only possible guarantee that disputes between the States would be decided by some sort of law, and not by the sword.* If Frederick could satisfy this feeling, he might yet hope to stand at the head of a powerful party of his countrymen. If he could not, there was nothing left for him but to become the tool of foreign nations, who saw with delight whatever misery afforded them a prospect of weakening the strength of Germany.

How ready the nation would have been to rally round him, is nowhere more apparent than in the reception which was accorded by members of the Imperial party to Ferdinand's proposition for the transference of the Electorate by members of his own party. Amongst the Catholic prelates, there was none who had stronger personal reasons for desiring the overthrow of the great Calvinist prince, whose territories bordered so closely on his own, than the Elector of Mentz. Yet the first hint that the scheme had been seriously entertained at Vienna, was sufficient to fill him with alarm. He wrote at once to Ferdinand to implore him to desist from so rash an enterprise. It would, he said, be certain to throw into the arms of Frederick many of those who had hitherto held aloof. The Elector of Treves expressed himself in almost similar terms. Oñate, speaking on behalf of the King of Spain, was as decided in his opposition; and John George of Saxony began to talk of the infringement of the Golden Bull, which would be the result if the Emperor's intentions were carried out. Even Ferdinand's own council recommended at least the postponement of the mea-

---

* Watchwords are not worth much as an indication of purpose; but they point to the state of feeling in the public to which the appeal is made. It is, therefore, worth noticing that whereas "Die Deutsche Libertat" is the often recurring formula in the State papers of one party; "Die Liebe Justitia," is its correlative on the other side.

sure.* It needed two years of bitter experience to convince these men that Frederick was indeed incorrigible, and that neither peace nor order was possible so long as he was allowed to set foot within the limits of the Empire.

Meanwhile, a few weeks after his arrival at the Hague, Frederick issued a manifesto, in which he made known his intentions to his countrymen, and demanded that a general amnesty should precede the meeting of the Assembly at Ratisbon. The difference between the amnesty which he thus demanded, and the submission for which the Emperor asked, may seem but slight. Yet in reality it contained within its limits the whole matter in dispute. For submission implied that civil war between the states was a wrong done to the Emperor, whilst an amnesty implied simply that peace had been made between contending parties. In other words, Ferdinand and Frederick were divided on the important question, whether the Empire were a reality or a fiction.†

Of any readiness to sacrifice himself for the public good, not a trace is to be found in Frederick's manifesto. Nor is this to be wondered at; for he had recently sent Nethersole to England, to beg for speedy aid for the defence of the Palatinate, and he had directed him to suggest that when he renounced his own claims to Bohemia, he should be allowed to reserve those of his son, who had been elected as his successor during his occupation of the throne, and to ask that he might not be required to promise to abstain from fresh attacks upon the House of Austria.‡

Infatuated as was Frederick's notion of fighting his battle without winning the moral sympathies of his countrymen, there was equal infatuation in James's belief that the conflict could be allayed by words alone. He had already obtained from the Archduke a prolongation of

* Hurter. *Gesch. Ferdinands II.*, ix. 155.

† Frederick to the Electors, May $\frac{1}{11}$. *Londorp*, ii. 444.

‡ "His Majesty of Bohemia may happily find it strange, that, in setting down the heads of my proposition, I have wholly omitted a very principal part of one of them, and maimed another; to wit, the demanding whether his Majesty should renounce the crown of Bohemia in the name of his children as well as his own, and his desiring not to be obliged never hereafter to attempt anything against the House of Austria." Nethersole to Carleton, May 2. *S. P. Holland.*

the truce in the Palatinate, and, in addition to the money which he had borrowed from the King of Denmark, he now sent to his son-in-law a present of 20,000*l*.* But here his active interference stopped. Long afterwards, Christian IV. bitterly complained that James had blamed his warlike preparations as a hindrance to the success of the English negotiations, and that he had been driven to disband his forces by the coldness with which his overtures had been received in London.† In the meantime not the slightest effort was made to secure the co-operation of the Elector of Saxony, though his policy was almost identical with that which James was now pursuing.

Yet sluggish as he was, so clearly were James's ideas in accordance with the public opinion of Germany, that it is not improbable that if he had had to deal with nothing more dangerous than the intemperate language of his son-in-law, he would have been able to effect something by his mediation. Unfortunately this was not the case. In his obstinate belief that nothing could be done excepting by the sword, Frederick had been drawing more closely the bonds which united him to the man who was certain to bring his cause into greater disrepute than any folly of which he was himself capable.

Ernest Count of Mansfeld was a soldier of fortune. Utterly deficient in those moral qualities which contribute so much to the character of a great general, he was never willing to subordinate his own interests to the public good. For there is nothing which goes so far to make a commander of the first class as the power of self-abnegation. He must bear to be misrepresented and traduced. He must be ready to work in harmony with, or even in subordination to, men whose behaviour is most distasteful to him. He must form no schemes, however glorious, which he does not believe himself capable of carrying into execution. He must be ready to relinquish the most assured success, if he sees that it will stand in the way of the ultimate interests of the cause for which he is fighting. Of all this Mansfeld knew nothing. He was capable of

---

* The King to Frederick, April 16 [?]. *Add. MSS.* 12,485. fol. 69.
† Answer of Christian IV. to Dohna. *Londorp*, ii. 608. Christian IV. to Frederick, May 2. *S. P. Germany.*

Ch. VIII.
1621.
May.

forming the most brilliant conceptions, but he was equally capable of forgetting all about them before a week was over. In the field, he was fertile in resources and daring in action. But personal animosities easily turned him aside, and the mere lack of an intelligent interest in the cause to which he had given his adhesion, made him blindly pass over opportunities which would at once have been appreciated by a general whose heart was in his work.

His behaviour in the Bohemian war.

During the first months of his career in Bohemia, indeed, he had shown the qualities of an active and serviceable officer. His capture of the strong fortress of Pilsen was the only real success of the Bohemian armies, and so long as his troops were paid, he had maintained tolerable discipline. But the time soon came when all attempts on the part of the Bohemian Directors to find money and provisions for their armies ceased entirely, and Mansfeld's men were driven to supply themselves by plunder.

Soldiers of the Thirty Years' War.

If, indeed, nothing more could be said against Mansfeld than that his men were guilty of abominable excesses, it would be unjust to blame him for evils which he was unable to prevent. For, in those terrible years, no army marched into the field without perpetrating horrors which in our day even the most depraved outcasts could not look upon without a shudder. Liable to dismissal at any moment, the soldier thought it no shame to transfer his services from one side to the other with reckless impartiality. No tie of nationality kept him faithful to the cause which he happened to be serving for the moment, and against which he might be fighting to-morrow. Even military pride, which has sometimes been known almost to replace that lofty and patriotic feeling, was wanting to him. He knew that he had sold himself, body and soul, to his hirer for the time being, and according to the law of our nature all other vices followed in the train of that last degradation of which man is capable. In those camps robbery, cruelty, and lust reigned supreme. Smiling fields and pleasant villages were made hideous by their presence. Blazing farmsteads marked the track of their march, and the air was tainted by the mouldering corpses, not of armed men, but of helpless peasants—of tender babes and of delicate women, fortunate if they had escaped by the sharp remedy of the sword a fate more horrible still.

With an army composed of such materials, the only chance of maintaining even a shadow of discipline, lay in the power of furnishing the troops with regular pay and regular supplies. But this had long been out of Mansfeld's power. After his defeat by Bucquoi, in the summer of 1619, he had been at bitter feud with the Bohemian magnates, whom he accused of deserting him in the hour of danger. The revolutionary leaders had little money to spare for their own troops, and none at all for Mansfeld's. He had consequently held aloof at Pilsen during the campaign of 1620, had entered into separate negotiations with the Imperialists, and had probably by his inaction contributed more than any one else to the disaster of the White Hill. Since the great defeat he had offered his sword to the highest bidder. Whilst he was imposing upon Frederick by solemn speeches about his loyalty to his king, and his fidelity to the Protestant religion, he was offering to transfer his services to his old master, the Duke of Savoy,* and was assuring the Elector of Saxony that if he still held some towns in Bohemia in Frederick's name, it was merely that he might have in his hands a pledge for the payment of the arrears due to himself and his men.† At the same time he was attracting fresh troops to his standard by promising to allow them free liberty of plunder to their hearts' content. ‡

The difference, then, between Mansfeld and other generals of the time was, not that his troops were more degraded than theirs, but that he erected into a system that which, with them, was an evil which they were powerless altogether to control. It would be difficult to say whether the wretched Bohemian peasants suffered most from Bucquoi's Hungarians, or from Mansfeld's troopers. But there was no doubt that Bucquoi, serving

Ch. VIII.
1621.
May.

Mansfeld's subsequent conduct.

Comparison between him and other generals.

---

* Mansfeld's proposal. S. P. Savoy.
† Mansfeld to the Elector of Saxony. Müller. Forschungen, ii. 60.
‡ Müller. Forschungen, ii. 43.

a regular government, and acting with a distinct military object, would disband his troops as soon as that object was attained. But with Mansfeld there was no such hope. To him it mattered little whether he were victorious or defeated. All he needed was to roam about from one district to another, plundering and destroying as he went. Every German territory would have to learn that it was liable to attack, not in proportion to the good or evil which it had done to one side or the other, but in proportion to the fatness of its pastures, the comfort of its peasants, and the wealth of its citizens.

Such was the man who was formally appointed by Frederick to the command of his armies in Bohemia. But Bohemia had been already pillaged too thoroughly to make it a safe basis of operations for an army led on these principles. One post after another surrendered to the enemy. Pilsen itself was sold by its own garrison during the temporary absence of Mansfeld.* By the end of April, Tabor and Wittingau alone remained in his hands; and he was himself driven to take refuge in the Upper Palatinate.

The question of Frederick's immediate abdication of the Bohemian crown was therefore no mere point of diplomatic propriety. With such a commander still holding two fortified positions in the country, every day that he retained his claim brought with it a fresh provocation to war. It was impossible for Ferdinand, in spite of his past successes, to feel any confidence for the future. The standard raised in Frederick's name was, in reality, a standard of brigandage. The dissolution of the army of the Union had come in time to supply Mansfeld with throngs of fresh recruits, and, before the end of May, a force of sixteen thousand men, without a country or resources of their own, hung like a dark cloud amongst the forest-clad defiles which command the passes from the Upper Palatinate into Bohemia.

To Frederick, Mansfeld represented himself as only anxious to stand on the defensive. But there were few who believed in the sincerity of his professions. Even

* *Khevenhüller*, ix. 1304.

in Protestant lands it was looked upon as certain that he was meditating a vast aggressive movement. The only doubt expressed was, whether the blow would fall upon Bavaria or Bohemia.* Nor did he himself make any secret that he did not consider himself bound to remain within the hereditary dominions of his master. In forwarding to the Bavarian commander an extract from a letter in which Frederick had directed him to conclude, if possible, a suspension of arms in the Upper Palatinate, he requested that the towns which still held out in Bohemia might be included in the armistice, and threatened that in case of refusal he should proceed to relieve them by force of arms.† Such a demand was of course regarded as totally inadmissible, and both sides prepared for war.‡ In the meanwhile the unhappy inhabitants of the Upper Palatinate had to suffer from the unwelcome presence of their protectors.§

Such were the circumstances under which, after a ruinous delay of months, Digby was at last preparing to leave England. The instructions which he carried with him were drawn up in a manly and self-reliant strain, which stood in marked contrast with the pettish ignorance which was stamped on every line of those which had been prepared two years before for the guidance of Doncaster, and which, if internal evidence be worth anything, would lead to the conclusion that the paper had been prepared under the eye of the ambassador himself.

Digby was first to demand of the Emperor the complete restitution of all that Frederick had possessed before he thought of meddling with Bohemia. "But," James went on to say, "for that it is not likely that

Ch. VIII.
1621.
May.

May 23. Digby's instructions.

The restitution of Frederick's lands and dignities demanded.

---

* Carpenter to Calvert, June 10, 17, 23, July 1. *S. P. Germany.*
† Extract from a letter from Frederick to Mansfeld. Mansfeld to Tilly, May $\frac{16}{26}$. Uetterodt, *Graf Ernst zu Mansfeld*, 746.
‡ This refusal is perpetually referred to in Frederick's letters as a grievous wrong.
§ "Der üble Zustand in der Oberpfalz ist nicht zu schildern. Das Mansfeldische Kriegsvolk haust übel." Camerarius to Solms, May $\frac{17}{27}$. Söltl. *Religionskrieg*, iii. 129. Printed "Unterpfalz," by an evident error, as Onno Klopp has already pointed out.

CH. VIII. fortune, having so much favoured the Emperor's party
1621. this last year in Bohemia, and that he, being actually in
May 23. possession of a great part of the Palatinate, will be drawn
to restore it simply for our respect and friendship, but
likewise that he may be assured of the respect, amity,
and due observance of our son-in-law for the future,—
we would have you, forasmuch as concerneth us, to let
him know our great propension and desire of entertaining
all friendship and amity with the House of Austria, and
more particularly by uniting ourselves strictly by a match
which we hope will take effect between the Prince our
son and the Infanta of Spain; and, forasmuch as concerneth our son-in-law, we will undertake on his behalf
that, upon the Emperor's revoking or disannulling of the
ban imperial against him, and the restoring of him in
such sort as it is above desired, he shall do all things
that can justly be required by the Emperor, and may
stand with the honour of a prince of his quality and
birth. And for that it will be necessary to fall from
these generals unto particulars, we will engage ourselves
that he shall decline and depart from all pretensions to
the Crown of Bohemia and the annexed provinces both
for himself and his son; and shall make unto the Emperor all fitting and due recognition and acknowledgment,
so that he be not pressed to any such deprecation as
shall be dishonourable or unworthy of his blood and
rank."

Terms offered.

If they are rejected, Digby is to go to Spain.

If Ferdinand accepted these terms it would be well.
But James proceeded to say, "In case you shall find
the Emperor resolved not to condescend to these our
demands in any real point either of our son's honour or
inheritance, you shall then let him know that, as we
should have been glad that he would have laid hold of
this occasion of obliging us, so, by the contrary, he
embarketh himself in a business which must make an
immortal and irreconcilable quarrel both betwixt us and
our posterities, which we shall be heartily sorry for;
but, in a case which toucheth us so nearly both in honour
and blood, and wherein we have not omitted to essay all
courses of friendship and amity, if they may not prevail,
we must betake ourselves to all other lawful means which

God shall give us for the righting of ourselves and our children. And then you shall use all possible speed for the transferring of yourself into Spain, where you shall insist upon the same propositions unto that King, urging the hopeful promises given by the King his father and his ministers to our ambassador and agent there, both by word and writing. And, in case you shall find them desirous to evade by transferring the authority and power in this business unto the Emperor, you shall then let that King know that the inheritances of our children have been invaded, and remain yet possessed by his army and under his pay, and no way but titularly belonging unto the Emperor; and therefore you shall in our name earnestly move him that he presently withdraw his army out of the Palatinate, and leave the Emperor to himself, which, if he shall refuse to do, you shall then make it known that we shall be little satisfied with that pretended evasion of having our children dispossessed of their inheritance by his army under the commission of the Emperor, but must desire to be excused if we address ourselves directly for reparation to the hand that really and immediately hurt us. Our meaning briefly and plainly is, that in case herein satisfaction shall be denied us, you endeavour to fix the quarrel as well upon the King of Spain as upon the Emperor. But this we would have you do rather solidly than by any words of threatening or menace, and rather to give us a just and good ground, when we shall see occasion, to enter into a war than suddenly to embark us in it."

Finally, the ambassador was directed, if he found the King of Spain unwilling to listen to reason, "without any further treating of the match or anything else, fairly to take his leave."

The terms which Digby was thus authorised to propose were such as to be equally distasteful to the zealots, who think that a Protestant nation ought at all times and under all circumstances to cast its sword into the scale on behalf of a Protestant population, and to the theorists who hold that interference in the affairs of foreigners is at no time either lawful or desirable. But they will commend themselves to those who think that

James's intervention in Germany.

it is the duty of a great nation to incur some risk in order to avert great evils, and who believe that such intervention can only be attended with success when it comes to give weight to a strong national feeling which is smothered under the overwhelming brute force of a foreign conqueror, or of a domestic faction in league with the armies of a foreign Sovereign. Such was the intervention of William of Orange in England in 1688, and of Napoleon III. in Italy in 1859. Such, as far as words went, was the intervention undertaken by James in Germany in 1621.*

Unfortunately it went no further than words. Backed by a compact and disciplined army well enough paid to enable it to dispense with the necessity of plunder, Digby might have laid down the law in the Empire. As it was, he had to sooth as he could, by the mere persuasiveness of his voice, two armies which were ready to fly at each other's throats. On the one side was Maximilian impatient to add the Upper Palatinate to his hereditary dominions; on the other side was Mansfeld, whose disorganized forces combined the least possible power of resistance with the greatest possible amount of provocation.

Even whilst Digby was on his way to Vienna, the danger of an immediate collision was increasing. Mansfeld, now at the head of 20,000 men, had seized and fortified Rosshaupt, a strong post within the Bohemian frontier. The Margrave of Jägerndorf, a kindred spirit, was at the head of 7000 men in Silesia, and was threatening, after levying contributions from the territories of the Catholics, to cross the mountains and to join forces with Mansfeld before the gates of Prague. In Hungary, Bethlen Gabor was making head against Bucquoi. On every side the wild terrors of the storm which had been quelled for a moment threatened to burst forth with redoubled violence.†

The seizure of Rosshaupt filled, in Maximilian's eyes, the cup of Mansfeld's offences to the brim. It might now be seen, he wrote to the Emperor, what was the

---

* Digby's instructions, May 25. *S. P. Germany.*
† See especially for Mansfeld's proceedings the letters printed by Uetterodt. *Ernest Graf zu Mansfeld,* 328—353.

real value of the adventurer's protestations that he was only standing on the defensive. Ferdinand replied by authorising him to put his troops in motion, whilst messengers were hastily despatched to Brussels and Madrid to ask for Spinola's co-operation on the Rhine.*

Mansfeld, at least, was determined to show his disregard of all diplomatic attempts to bring about a peace. He turned sharply upon the Bishop of Bamberg and Würzburg, who was guilty of the offence of having sent his troops into Bohemia in common with the other members of the League, and threatened to devastate his territories with fire and sword.† A sudden attack was also made upon the Landgrave of Leuchtenberg, who had admitted a Bavarian garrison into his dominions; and the Landgrave himself was dragged away as a prisoner to Mansfeld's camp.‡

Such was the crisis at which affairs had arrived when Digby entered Vienna. If any man living was capable of pouring oil upon the troubled waters it was he. For he possessed, to a very great degree, the power of penetrating the thoughts and intentions of others, and, in a still higher degree, the power of instant decision in the midst of conflicting perils.

Four months earlier the presence of such a man would have been invaluable. He could now hardly flatter himself that success was otherwise than very dubious. Ferdinand had been confirmed, by recent events, in his belief that it was hopeless to expect peace from Frederick, even if Frederick had the power to control the army which had been created in his name. He had turned a deaf ear to the entreaties of the ambassadors from Denmark and the late Union, though they had asked to negotiate on the basis of Frederick's abdication. It

---

* Menzel. *Neuere Gesch der Deutschen*, vii. 531. Zuñiga's Consulta on Oñate's Despatches, Aug. [1]. *Simancas MSS.* Est. 2506. The Duke of Bavaria to Ferdinand II., June $\frac{18}{28}$. Ferdinand II. to the Archduke $\frac{June\ 25}{July\ 5}$. *Brussels MSS.*

† Mansfeld to the Chapters of Bamberg and Würzburg, July $\frac{4}{14}$. *S. P. Germany.*

‡ The Duke of Bavaria to Ferdinand II., July $\frac{10}{20}$. *S. P. Germany.*

was no wonder if the Emperor was incredulous; for Frederick's secret papers, which had fallen into the hands of the victors after his defeat at Prague, had recently been published, and his intrigues with Mansfeld and Savoy for the partition of the territories of the House of Austria had thus been laid open to the world.*

Digby saw that he had no time to lose. His only chance was, that as he could speak with the authority of the King of England, his engagements on behalf of his master's son-in-law might be accepted, though the promises of others had been rejected with disdain. On the very day after his arrival, therefore, he asked the Emperor for a declaration of his intention to restore Frederick to his lands and dignities. The King of England would then obtain from the Elector Palatine a recognition of his obedience. Upon these terms he hoped that the further execution of the ban would be suspended, and the truce in the Lower Palatinate prolonged.

In three days he received his answer. The Emperor, he was told, could decide nothing without consulting the Princes of the Empire, who had been already summoned to Ratisbon. It was impossible to suspend hostilities any longer. Mansfeld had assailed Bohemia. Jägerndorf had published a commission signed by Frederick at the very moment when he professed to be treating. Yet, even now, if Frederick showed real signs of repentance, the execution of the ban should be stopped.†

The concluding words were a symptom of the hesitation which was gaining ground in the Emperor's mind. During the last few days bad news had been pouring in from every side. Bucquoi had been slain in Hungary, and his troops were in full retreat. The first days of the campaign in the Upper Palatinate had not turned out well for the Bavarians. The Elector of Saxony had refused to attend the assembly at Ratisbon, and his refusal was, with great probability, ascribed to his dislike

---

* The publication of the Anhaltische Canzlei, as it was called, is mentioned in Digby's letter of the 19th of June. Compare, on this subject, Wotton to Calvert, July 8. *S. P. Venice.*

† Digby to the Commissioners for German affairs, July 26. Digby's Propositions, with the Emperor's reply. *Clarendon State Papers*, i. App. 2.

of the plan of depriving Frederick of his Electorate.* Upon Maximilian the effect of the intelligence was merely irritating. He at once concluded a short truce with Mansfeld, which he hoped to turn to his own purposes, and hurried off a courier to Brussels with an urgent demand that Spinola might be ordered at once to take the field.† Ferdinand, whose territories were more immediately exposed to danger, and who was at all times more single-minded than Maximilian, began to hesitate. Was it wise, he wrote to the Duke, to let the opportunity slip? The King of Spain was fully occupied with the Dutch war. If Digby were dismissed without a satisfactory answer, it would not be long before the Elector of Saxony, with the whole of the North of Germany at his back, would be found fighting on Frederick's side.‡

Ferdinand's suggestion was not likely to meet with a favourable reception. Maximilian was indignant that Digby had been listened to for an instant. The Emperor, he said, had solemnly promised that the Electorate should be his. He had come to his assistance when he was in distress, and, if his wishes were now to be disregarded, he would take no further trouble to preserve the Austrian territories from their present danger. Such language did not fail in finding influential supporters at Vienna. The Pope's Nuncio, and Hyacintho, a Capuchin friar, who had lately arrived on a special mission from Rome, put forth all their eloquence in the hope of persuading Ferdinand to break off the negotiations, and to effect an immediate transference of the Electorate to Maximilian.

The Emperor was not usually inaccessible to spiritual influences, and he was bound by every tie of interest and gratitude to Maximilian. But his better nature shrunk

CH. VIII
1621.
July.

Maximilian protests against Digby's offers.

Ferdinand determines to treat.

---

* The Elector of Saxony to Ferdinand II., $\frac{\text{June } 27}{\text{July } 7}$. Ferdinand II. to the Archduke Albert, July $\frac{14}{24}$. *Brussels MSS.*

† Minutes of the Duke of Bavaria's letter to the Archduke Albert, July $\frac{8}{18}$. *Brussels MSS.*

‡ Ferdinand II. to the Duke of Bavaria, July $\frac{8}{18}$. *Brussels MSS.*

Ch. VIII.
1621.
July.

from the prospect of interminable and perhaps hopeless war which was opening before him. After some days' hesitation, he told the Nuncio that he had made up his mind to treat with Digby. "If the Pope," he said, "knew what the position of affairs really is, he would be of the same opinion with myself."

July 21.

On the 21st of July, therefore, Digby was informed of the Emperor's determination. The blame of the recent outbreak of hostilities was thrown upon Mansfeld and Jägerndorf. Let Frederick relieve the Catholic Powers from all fear of future aggression, and no difficulty would be thrown in the way of the proposed negotiation. Letters should be despatched to Maximilian and Spinola, requesting them to abstain from hostilities, if only they had reason to believe that they were themselves safe from injury. It was for Frederick to revoke any commission which he might have issued for an attack upon the Emperor's dominions, and to prove to the world that his lieutenants had acted without his authority. If he could do this, all risk of war would be at an end.*

Digby satisfied.

With this answer Digby was well satisfied. He had gained, he said, in the despatch in which he recounted his proceedings, all that could reasonably be expected. He had hardly hoped that the Emperor would consent to treat the transference of the Electorate as an open question. Yet he was too clear-sighted not to be aware how many difficulties were still to be surmounted. Everything, he said, depended on the part taken by Spain. Yet if, like James, he was inclined to hope for the best from the Court of Madrid, he knew far better than James how unwise it would be to trust to unsupported argument for success. "I must earnestly recommend," he wrote, "the continuing abroad yet for some small time Sir Robert Mansell's fleet upon the coast of Spain, which, in case his Majesty should be ill used, will prove

* The Emperor's second answer, July $\frac{21}{31}$. Londorp. *Acta Publica*, ii. 486. Digby to the Commissioners for German affairs, July 26. *Clarendon State Papers*, i. App. 6. Gritti to the Doge $\frac{\text{July 28}}{\text{Aug. 7}}$. *Venice MSS*. Desp. Germania. Extract from a letter from Vienna, July 30. *S. P. Germany*.

the best argument he can use for the restitution of the Palatinate."*

Yet, in truth, if Digby had been able to speak with confidence of Frederick's intentions, there would have been little need of such arguments as these. The reception by the new Spanish Government of the first hint of the Emperor's proposal to transfer the Electorate to Maximilian had been most unfavourable. Letters were at once despatched in the name of the young King to the Archduke Albert at Brussels, and to Oñate at Vienna. The House of Austria, wrote Philip, owed much to the Duke of Bavaria; but it would be unreasonable to continue the war solely for his personal advantage. It was to be hoped, therefore, that the Assembly of Ratisbon would lead to a speedy pacification.†

By the time that these despatches reached their destination much had changed. Mansfeld's army was daily increasing in numbers, and Maximilian, by the Emperor's orders, was preparing to expel him from the threatening position which he occupied. To an inquiry whether he would desert his allies at such a conjuncture, the Archduke Albert could hardly reply otherwise than he did. He should much prefer, he said, a general pacification; but if the proceedings of Mansfeld made war necessary, he could not leave the Duke of Bavaria to be crushed. The

---

* Digby to the Commissioners for German Affairs, July 26. *Clarendon State Papers*, ii. App. 6.

† It would be well, writes Philip to the Archduke Albert on the $\frac{17\text{th}}{27\text{th}}$ of June, to come to a settlement at Ratisbon, "para cuyo cumplimiento pareze que la dificultad que ocurre es el haver pasado el Emperador tan adelante con el Duque de Baviera en la promesa de la dignidad electoral Palatina, pues es sin duda que el Duque dificultará contentarse con menos, y el Rey de Inglaterra y los demas adjuntos del Palatino es de creer estribarán en que permanezca en su persona la dignidad, y que no se quietarán sin esto; y si bien es muy devido que se tenga con el Duque de Baviera bonissima correspondencia . . . si para esto effecto se huviesse de renovar una guerra perpetua en Alemaña, no será possible que lo que el Rey mi Señor y padre, que está en el cielo, hizo por restaurar la religion, y el Imperio, y los Reynos de Bohemia y Hungria, y provincias patrimoniales se pueda continuar por sola una circumstancia de acrescentamiento del dicho Duque; pues, aunque es mucho lo que ha hecho, y justo el reconocerselo, tambien es de considerar que hera caussa de todos, y que si la religion y el estado se perderán en nuestra cassa, no quedará en pie lo uno ni lo otro en la Baviera; y no es razon que el Duque quiera poner lo todo en compromisso por su fin particular." Compare the King's letter to Oñate of the same date. *Brussels MSS.*

Ch. VIII.
1621.
July.

suspension of hostilities would come to an end on the 22nd of July, and Spinola should receive orders to recommence the war in the Lower Palatinate as soon as he heard that the Bavarians had actually taken the field.*

July 3.
Death of the Archduke Albert.

This order was the last public act of the Archduke. On the 3rd of July he died, after a long and painful illness.† With him the nominal independence of the country came to an end. He left no children to succeed him, and his widow, the aunt of the young King of Spain, was now again the Infanta Isabella, the Spanish Governor of the Spanish Netherlands. But, excepting that perhaps the Infanta was rather more reluctant to embark in hazardous enterprises than her husband had been, no change in the system of government was observable.

The Spanish operations suspended.

She had not been long in possession of authority, when she learned that Mansfeld had attacked the Catholic States in his neighbourhood, and that Maximilian's worst fears were already realised. When Trumbull saw Spinola, who had been recalled to Brussels to conduct the preparations against the Dutch, he found him greatly excited. "What," he said, "will the world think of us, if we make a truce in the Palatinate whilst the throats of our confederates are being cut?"‡ A few days afterwards, however, Cordova, who had been left in command of the troops in Germany, contrived to intimate to Frederick's officers that, though the truce would not formally be renewed, he should not take the field without special orders from Brussels;§ and it was not long before a letter arrived from Ferdinand conveying the intelligence that negotiations had been opened with Digby, and expressing a wish that, unless there were grave military reasons to the contrary, hostilities should continue in suspense till it was seen whether Frederick's assent could be obtained to the terms proposed by the English

---

* The Infanta Isabella to Philip IV. July $\frac{16}{26}$. *Brussels MSS.*
† Trumbull to Calvert, July ?. *S. P. Flanders.*
‡ Trumbull to Calvert, July 21. *S. P. Flanders.*
§ Cordova to the Landgrave of Hesse-Darmstadt, $\frac{July\ 24}{Aug.\ 3}$. *S. P. Germany.*

Ambassador.* Trumbull was accordingly assured by Spinola, that if Frederick were really in earnest he might have a truce for six months.†   *Ch. VIII. 1621. July.*

It is therefore beyond all reasonable doubt, that at the beginning of August the Duke of Bavaria stood alone in his desire to proceed to extremities. The Courts of Spain, of Brussels, of Vienna, and of Dresden might, from various causes, and with different degrees of earnestness, be counted amongst the supporters of Digby's pacificatory negotiation. Unhappily Maximilian found one man who was doing everything in his power to give effect to his warlike policy. That one man was no other than Frederick himself.   *Frederick's proceedings.*

That unhappy prince could see plainly enough that Maximilian wanted to possess himself of the Upper Palatinate; but he could see nothing else. That his retention of the Bohemian crown was a gage of battle flung down at the feet of the Catholic Powers, and that it alienated from him the sympathies of three-fourths of the Protestant Powers, was a truth which he was incapable of comprehending. His language when he heard of the violent proceedings of Mansfeld and Jägerndorf, was the language of hopeless incapacity. He had given them no orders; but he could not blame them. It was all the fault of Ferdinand and Maximilian. His lieutenants had been in the service of the Bohemian Estates before they entered his. No doubt they had pretensions of their own in Bohemia; if so, he could not hold them back. He could not even say that they were in the wrong in offering a helping hand to the oppressed Protestants.‡

It was quite true that the Bohemian Protestants were in evil case, and it was impossible to blame Frederick for his sympathy with his late subjects. But it is certain that a

---

* Ferdinand II. to Spinola, $\frac{\text{July 26}}{\text{Aug. 5}}$, *Londorp*, ii. 487.

† Trumbull to Calvert, Aug. 13. *S. P. Flanders.* Spinola said that the Emperor's letter had not arrived. Judging from the similarity of his language with that held by Ferdinand, I doubt this. But if so, it shows that the same conclusion was independently adopted at Brussels and Vienna.

‡ Carleton to Calvert, July 19. Frederick to the King, July 28. Frederick to Digby, Aug. 13. *S. P. Holland.*

Ch. VIII.
1621.
July.

August.
Frederick in the Dutch camp.

He is resolved to prosecute the war.

wise man would have attempted to help them in a very different way. If Bohemian Protestantism was to be saved, it would only be because German Protestantism was strong. Still, as three years before, the only hope of strengthening German Protestantism lay in a close union between Heidelberg and Dresden, and it was notorious that it was mainly by Frederick's aggressive ambition that such a union had hitherto been rendered impossible. It was therefore only by abdicating the throne of Bohemia, that he could hope to help the Bohemians.

In the mood in which Frederick was, it was inevitable that he would do something foolish. But even those who thought most meanly of his understanding, can hardly have been prepared for the gratuitous act of folly of which he was now guilty. If he had made his way to Mansfeld's camp, had placed himself at the head of his troops, and had given orders to march upon Prague, there would at least have been some method in his madness. But what was to be said when he gravely proposed to join the camp which the Prince of Orange was forming at Emmerich for operations against the Spaniards? Such a proceeding could do him no possible good, whilst it was certain to be regarded at Brussels and Vienna as an act of defiance. Carleton and Nethersole were at their wit's end. Even Elizabeth, ready as she invariably was to encourage her husband in any rational act of manliness, joined in protesting against the step. It was some time before the English envoys were able to discover what Frederick's motive could be. At last it came out that he was ashamed of the part which he had played at Prague, and that he hoped, under Maurice's tuition, to learn enough of war to qualify him for taking command of his own troops at some future time. On the 16th of August, he set out from the Hague, with this childish fancy in his head.*

The real cause of Frederick's headstrong conduct, however, lay far deeper. The news of Bucquoi's defeat, which had alarmed Ferdinand, restored the confidence of his rival. Once more the fugitive prince was dreaming of

---

* Nethersole to Calvert, Aug. 13. *S. P. Germany.* Carleton to Calvert, Aug. 13. *S. P. Holland.* Nethersole to Calvert, Aug. 22. *S. P. Germany.*

entering Prague as a conqueror. "Our affairs," wrote Elizabeth to a confidential friend in England, "begin to mend. The king of Hungary is master of the field. Mansfeld and Jägerndorf do daily prosper."* Carleton complained bitterly that Frederick was now "less tractable than before." In fact, he was now possessed by the most extraordinary delusion. Ferdinand's cause he believed to be hopeless. The only question was, whether Bohemia should belong to himself or to Bethlen Gabor, and he came to the conclusion that it was his duty to prevent the surrender of Prague to an ally who was, after all, a mere creature of the Turks. In this absurdity he was encouraged by Mansfeld, in whose busy brain the idea in all probability originated.†

Already Digby, at Vienna, had been made to feel the change. On the 4th of August, Andrew Pawel, one of Frederick's councillors, arrived to assist him in his negotiation. He found that the English Ambassador had resolved upon striking the iron whilst it was hot, by presenting for Ferdinand's approval a form of submission which Frederick should be required to make, and that he proposed that in proof of Frederick's sincerity he should surrender the two towns which he held in Bohemia, on receiving a guarantee that the religion of their inhabitants would be respected. To both these proposals Pawel offered a determined opposition. For the present, at least, he said, his master would not hear of the surrender of the towns. Still less would he agree to make any kind of submission to the Emperor. By so doing he would acknowledge that he had committed a fault. The truth was, that the ban was a nullity, and he would never bring himself even to ask for its revocation. "I think," wrote Digby to Calvert, "they would have the Emperor ask them forgiveness for having wronged them with so injurious a ban."‡ Almost at the same time Frederick was writing a despatch to Digby, in which he adopted these extravagant pretensions. He would be ready, he

---

* Elizabeth to Roe, Aug. 21. *S. P. Germany.*
† Mansfeld to Frederick, Aug. 2. Nethersole to Calvert, Aug. 13. *S. P. Germany.*
‡ Digby to Calvert, Aug. 12. *Clarendon State Papers,* i. App. 17.

Ch. VIII.
1621.
August.
Digby's opinion of the crisis.

said, to pay all due respect to the Emperor, but he would make no submission.*

Deeply mortified as Digby must have been by Frederick's unreasonableness, he knew that it was from another quarter that the immediate danger was to be apprehended. "As for the main business," he wrote to James, "I am in great hope that in convenient time it may be affected to your Majesty's good satisfaction; and, in the interim, a general cessation of arms both in the Lower and Upper Palatinates might have been procured, were it not in respect of the Count Mansfeld, whose present condition is such that it hindereth and overthroweth all I have in hand; neither know I what course to take for the redress of it, for when I proposed here a cessation of arms in the Palatinate, until by treaty all things may be finally and conveniently ended, it is answered me that the Emperor is not averse thereunto; so that it may be general as well in the Upper as the Lower Palatinate, and that the Emperor's territories may not be assailed, for which I am very doubtful whether the Prince Elector himself can do it. For, although the Count Mansfeld shelter himself under the name and authority of the King of Bohemia, yet I doubt much, in case he should command him absolutely to disarm, or in the interim to stand upon a pure defensive, whether therein he would obey him; neither see I, indeed, well how he could, for he hath now with him above twenty thousand men, most of them adventurers, and in case he should yield unto a cessation of arms, most of them must either disband or starve. For the Upper Palatinate is absolutely ruined and wasted, so that his army can no way remain there, and if he shall attempt the living upon any other neighbour country, it will be esteemed a public act of hostility; and as for the dismissing of his army, it is a thing impracticable until the business shall be well settled, and there must be means found for his payment before he will out of the Upper Palatinate. Besides, he pretendeth great sums of money to be due unto him by the estates of Bohemia, and for that debt pretendeth to hold Tabor and Wittingau. So that, whereas it is said that those towns hold for the Prince

* Frederick to Digby, Aug. 13. *S. P. Holland.*

Palatine, I conceive they are very willing to advantage themselves with that pretext. But, in case upon any composition he should command them to be restored to the Emperor, I have just cause to doubt he would not therein be obeyed. Insomuch that his name and authority is used in that which is prejudicial to him. But wherein it may be for his good and advantage, I fear he will find his authority very limited." *

Such were the unpromising elements of the problem which Digby had undertaken to solve. Yet, strange to say, it was not on the Bavarian frontier that the first blow was struck. Since the dissolution of the Union, the command in the Lower Palatinate had been entrusted by Frederick to Vere, and Vere was beginning to experience the same difficulties as those by which Mansfeld was beset. His troops were ill-paid and ill-provided. The land was exhausted. In the presence of the spectre of war, the peasants had not ventured to sow their fields, in order to prepare a harvest which they would not be allowed to gather into their barns. It was with famine staring him in the face, that Vere read the letters which reached him from Digby, from Trumbull, and from Calvert, urging him to keep the peace at all hazards. But, though he was an Englishman, he was not in the King of England's service. James had plenty of advice to give, but he sent no money with which to alleviate the distress of the army. Frederick was equally unable to supply him, and whatever advice he had to give was very bad. His representative, the Duke of Deux Ponts, joined the council of Heidelberg in urging that something should be done. Vere was a good soldier, but he was not a statesman; and, in his desperation, he weakly consented to a middle course from which no good could possibly come.†

The lands of the Bishop of Spires had been untouched by the war, and Vere knew that it would be a great relief

---

* Digby to the King, Aug. 12. *S. P. Germany*. "Cependant" wrote Mansfeld, a few days later, " nous tascherons de fayre nos recrues, et voir si vous pourrons avoir de Hongrie le secours demandé ; que, si cela est, nous sommes bastans pour tirer raison de nos ennemys de la pointe de l'espée, et fayre nos affayres a la ruine de leurs." Mansfeld to Frederick. *S. P. Germany*.

† Vere to Carleton, Aug. 9. *S. P. Holland*.

Ch. VIII.
1621.
August.

to his own men, if he could quarter one or two regiments upon the inhabitants. His soldiers, he believed, were well under control. They would take nothing from the people but provisions. No pillage should be allowed. In all courtesy, he would first ask the bishop for his consent. Upon this scheme he acted. Making a virtue of necessity, the bishop gave the required permission, and sent a commissary to watch the proceedings. But the peasants who were to find quarters for the men, did not take the matter quite so easily. They had a strong suspicion that the soldiers would not prove quite as lamblike as their commander reported. In one village, resistance was offered, and shots were fired. The troops forced their way into the place, striking down in the fray those who attempted to bar their path.*

Stein seized by Cordova.

In a moment the whole Catholic party was roused to indignation. This, then, was what Frederick meant by peace. Cordova at once declared that the truce was at an end, seized the strong castle of Stein, which commanded the passage of the Rhine, and threatened Vere's weak battalions with his superior force.

James expostulates with Frederick.

At last James was roused from his apathy. Upon his son-in-law he bestowed a severe but not unmerited rebuke. If he wished for any further aid from England he must leave the Dutch camp; he must recall all commissions by which his officers were empowered to take any measures not needed for the defence of his own dominions, and a copy of this revocation must be sent at once to Digby. Above all, he must consent to make due submission to the Emperor, and must leave it to the English Ambassador to see that it was not couched in degrading terms.† At the same time Calvert was directed to expostulate with Gondomar on Cordova's precipitation.

Sept.
Digby's complaints.

It was somewhat of the latest. Digby felt deeply the want of that support upon which he might fairly have counted. To Calvert he poured out his sorrows. Every-

---

* Vere to Carleton, Aug. 7. *S. P. Holland.* Vere to Calvert, Sept. 14 (?). *S. P. Germany.*
† The King to Frederick, Aug. 28, 30. *S. P. Germany.* There are two letters of the latter date.

where Frederick's commanders had been the first aggressors. "I will make no complaint," he wrote, in the bitterness of his heart, "but I must needs confess it hath been a strange unluckiness." For every one of Frederick's servants who desired peace, there were five who wished to drag England into a war with Spain.* If the King intended to carry out his plans, "he must first reduce the business to such a conformity that that which his faithful ministers shall have established in one part be not overthrown by the malice or artifice of the attempts of others in other parts, as hitherto hath happened.†

CH. VIII.
1621.
Sept.

Whatever man could do was done by Digby. To the Emperor's reasoning that he could not be expected to grant an armistice unless it were to include the whole theatre of the war he had nothing to reply. But neither Mansfeld nor Jägerndorf were under his orders, and it was more than doubtful whether they would obey Frederick himself. Yet, unless he took some responsibility upon himself, all chance of peace was at an end. Accordingly he concerted with the Emperor a plan for a pacification, and trusted to accident to enable him to realise it.

Ferdinand, according to this scheme, engaged to write once more to the Infanta Isabella and the Duke of Bavaria, urging them to suspend hostilities unless they could show good reason to the contrary. Mansfeld would be bound to respect the armistice which, it was hoped, would then be signed, on pain of being treated by James and Frederick as a common enemy. Frederick was to be induced to revoke his commission to Jägerndorf, and to surrender the towns in Bohemia. Negotiations for a peace were then to be opened, and, as soon as the execution of the ban had been suspended, Mansfeld's troops were to be disbanded on a promise from the Emperor that he would give three months' notice before renewing the war.‡

Sept. 3.
Digby's new plan.

* Calvert to Buckingham, Aug. 27. *Harl. MSS.* 1580, fol. 160.
† Digby to Calvert, Sept. 5. *S. P. Germany.*
‡ Ferdinand II. to the Infanta Isabella, Sept. $\frac{1}{11}$. *S. P. Germany.* Answer given to Digby, Sept. $\frac{3}{13}$. Digby to the Commissioners for German Affairs, Sept. 5. *Clarendon State Papers*, i. App. 4, 10, 14.

CH. VIII.
1621.
Sept.
He leaves Vienna.

Digby's hopes of the success of his endeavours were not high. He knew that he had not a single line under Frederick's hand to authorise him to make the concessions which he regarded as indispensable, and he could hardly suppose that the last arrangement, depending as it did upon the consent of the Duke of Bavaria, would really take effect. He was now leaving Vienna, anxious to visit Maximilian on his way home. "Of my proceedings here," he wrote to the Prince of Wales before he started on his journey, "I will only say this, that things have been so carried as if the chief care and study had been to overthrow the treaty I had in hand, and to renew the war; which I doubt not we shall find by experience will turn infinitely to the prejudice of the King's son-in-law."*

Invasion of the Upper Palatinate.

In a few days after these words were written, Digby's worst fears were realised. Unsupported by Frederick, no engagement which he could enter into could offer any solid guarantee to the Imperialists. In recommending the scheme of the English Ambassador to Maximilian, Ferdinand acknowledged that he was mainly influenced by the despondent view which he took of his military position.† Such an argument was not likely to weigh much with Maximilian. He had made up his mind to cut the knot with the sword, and without waiting for any further instructions from Vienna, he threw himself with all his forces upon the Upper Palatinate.

Then was seen on what a broken reed Frederick had placed his confidence. The great adventurer, the would-be conqueror of Austria and Bohemia, was not even in a condition to defend the country which had been trusted to his care. Unpaid and unprovided with supplies, Mansfeld's troops had reimbursed themselves at the expense of those whom they had been charged to defend. Rapine and violence had done their work. The heart of the population was alienated from the prince who had

* Digby to the Prince of Wales, Sept. 5. *Clarendon State Papers*, i App. 8. Wrongly dated Aug. 5.
† Hurter. *Gesch. Ferdinands II.* ix. 40. His narrative is based upon documents in the Vienna Archives, which I have not seen.

entrusted his subjects to the care of such a pack of wolves. The magistrates refused to provide for the defence of the country. It was better, men were heard to say, that the Duke of Bavaria should take the land than that Mansfeld should remain in it a moment longer.*

As usual, Mansfeld sought to escape from his difficulties by trickery. In the spring he had invited his nephew René de Chalon to come to him from Flanders in order that he might be the medium of an arrangement by which he then hoped to sell his services to the Emperor. When Chalon arrived Mansfeld had reinforced his army, and was looking forward to the reconquest of Bohemia. He did not, however, let go the thread of the intrigue, and while continuing to hold out hopes to the Imperialists, he took credit with Frederick for the firmness with which he had resisted their seductions. He now intimated to Maximilian that he was ready to sell his master's interests. A treaty was drawn up by which he engaged, in consideration of a large sum of money, either to disband his army or to carry it into the service of the Emperor.†

As chance would have it, Mansfeld, riding into Neumarkt for the purpose of signing this infamous treaty, met Digby's train on its way to Nuremberg. Putting a bold face on the matter, he asked the ambassador to accompany him and to assist him with his advice. Digby answered coldly that he had no authority to treat with the Duke of Bavaria. Upon this Mansfeld began to defend his conduct. His wants, he said, were great; his forces were too weak to hold head against the enemy; the people of the country were traitors; all that he meant in treating with Maximilian was to gain time in order to transfer his army to the Lower Palatinate. To Digby such language was intolerable. He had seen, he told him, the articles of the treaty by which he had bound himself not to serve against the House of Austria. He knew what was the exact sum of money for which he had sold his master. "When I replied unto him thus,"

---

* Mansfeld to Frederick, Oct. 1. *S. P. Germany.*
† Hurter. *Gesch. Ferdinands II.* ix. 58. Villermont. *Mansfeld,* i. 304. Uetterodt. *Ernest Graf zu Mansfeld,* 369.

CH. VIII.
1621.
Sept.

was Digby's account of the scene, "I never saw so disturbed or distracted a man, and he would have recalled many things he had said, and began to swear nothing was concluded, but that things were to be ended now with the Commissioners, and that he would do nothing but with the consent of the Council of Amberg, who he had likewise appointed to be there, and desired that Monsieur Andreas Pawel might return with him to be present at their meeting. Much passed betwixt us, for we were together almost two hours. I concluded by telling him freely my opinion, that the defence of the Palatinate being committed to him, and being now only invaded for his cause in regard of his assailing Bohemia, if he should now, with so great and flourishing an army, abandon to the enemy a country for the defence whereof his honour was answerable, especially for a mercenary reward of money, I conceived that the Count Mansfeld would, from one of the most renowned cavaliers of Christendom, become the most vile and infamous; and on these terms we parted, he swearing he would do nothing but what would stand with his honour; but, my lords, I must confess that so perturbed a man I never saw."*

So the two men separated: the one to his duty, the other to his treason.

Conquest of the Upper Palatinate.

Under such circumstances the fate of the Upper Palatinate could not remain long undecided. On the 15th of September the strong military post of Cham had surrendered to the Bavarians. Before the end of the month Maximilian's troops were welcomed by the whole country as deliverers from the tyranny of Mansfeld. Frederick's general retained nothing more than the ground on which his troops were encamped.†

The Electorate secretly conferred upon Maximilian.

It was not in the field alone that Maximilian was victorious. The first news of his determination to appeal to the sword had been followed by a total change of policy at Vienna. Ferdinand's hesitation was at an end. Whatever the prospects of the two armies might be, he had no intention of deserting his old and tried friend for

* Digby to the Commissioners for German Affairs, Oct. 2. *S. P. Germany.*
† Nethersole to Calvert, Oct. 9. *S. P. Germany.*

such a will-of-the-wisp as the mere chance that Frederick, who had never done a wise thing in his life, would now at last be wise enough to adopt the terms to which Digby had consented in his name. On the 12th of September he sent for the Friar Hyacintho, and placed in his hands, in the strictest secrecy, an act by which he conferred the Electorate upon Maximilian. The Archduke Charles, the Emperor's brother, was despatched to Dresden to gain over John George. Hyacintho himself was to go to Madrid to wring, if possible, an assent from the King of Spain.*

For whatever Englishmen might think about the matter, it was from Spain that the most strenuous opposition was to be expected. If the Spanish Government continued to take part in the war at all, it was only because Frederick's folly made it impossible for them to withdraw with honour. In June the Council of State at Madrid was looking forward with hope to a general pacification. Then had come the news of Mansfeld's excesses in Würzburg and Leuchtenberg, and it was necessary to take the change of circumstances into consideration. Zuñiga was consulted, and his advice was embodied in a despatch written by Philip to his ambassador at Vienna. "By all means," such was the substance of the letter, "take care to oppose the pretensions of the Duke of Bavaria to the Electorate. Induce the Emperor, if possible, to satisfy him by the cession of the Margravate of Burgau, or of some other Austrian territory. Every day increases the necessity for obtaining a settlement to which the Palatine will agree. Probably the best solution is that which has been indicated by a councillor of the Elector of Saxony. If Frederick would abdicate the Electorate, his son might at once be accepted as his successor, and educated at the Emperor's Court." † A few days later Philip wrote again approving the support which Oñate had given to Digby. It was necessary, he said, that the troops in the Lower Palatinate should come to

---

* Hurter. *Gesch. Ferdinands II.* ix. 158.
† Consulta by Zuñiga, Aug. (?). *Simancas MSS.* Est. 2506. Philip IV. to Oñate, Aug. $\frac{20}{30}$. *Brussels MSS.*

Ch. VIII.
1621.
Sept.

Recommendation of Frederick's abdication.

the assistance of the Bavarians, but he hoped that the negotiations for a general pacification would not be postponed.*

The plan thus put forward by the Spanish Government is the more noteworthy, because it continued to be the object of its desires till the course of events made its position altogether untenable. It sprung from a profound conviction that with Frederick no peace was possible. It had the advantage of offering a middle ground upon which both parties might agree. But it had the disadvantage with which all the schemes which proceeded from the Catholic side were attended. It dealt only with the wrongs of the Princes, and forgot the wrongs of the people. That education at the Emperor's Court involved a change of religion it was impossible to doubt; and as matters stood in Germany, the voluntary conversion of a prince carried with it the forcible conversion of his subjects. Perhaps if some neutral Protestant Court had been substituted for Vienna as the place of education, the plan might ultimately have been found to promise the most satisfactory solution. But it was evidently premature to expect that it would as yet be acceptable to anyone.

Mission of Villiers to the Hague.

Yet if any better terms were to be obtained, it was indispensable that Frederick should be brought to his senses. Accordingly James, finding that his son-in-law paid no attention whatever to his letters, despatched Sir Edward Villiers to Holland with orders to insist upon his return from the Dutch camp. Frederick saw the necessity of obeying, and whilst Sir Edward was journeying towards him by one road to the camp, he hurried back to the Hague like a truant schoolboy by another. But it was more difficult to extract from him a promise that he would make the required submission to the Emperor. He placed in Villiers' hands a lengthy argument by which he proved, to his own satisfaction, that such a step would be ruinous to his country and dishonourable to himself.† At last however he

* Philip IV. to Oñate, Sept. $\frac{1}{11}$. *Brussels MSS.*

† Brieve déduction des Causes, &c. Sept. 29. *S. P. Germany.*

yielded, and protested that he would do as he was bidden.*

Nor did James stand alone in urging upon Frederick the necessity of submitting. In a letter written to him about this time by the Princes of Lower Saxony, the blame of all that had occurred is distinctly ascribed to his own restlessness; and his obstinacy is characterised as the chief impediment to the peace of Germany.† Even Frederick's own subjects in the Palatinate were of the same opinion. Men openly said that if he had but written a few lines to the Emperor, all would have been well.‡

Experience was not very favourable to the hope that Frederick would take these admonitions to heart. Yet, considering the interests that were at stake, Digby was no doubt right in refusing to throw up the game. He had been summoned in haste to Heidelberg to assist in providing for the defence of the Lower Palatinate.§ He found the troops in a pitiable condition. The Spaniards were masters of the open country on both sides of the Rhine. Vere's little force of three or four thousand men were fully employed in garrisoning Heidelberg, Mannheim, and Frankenthal. The troops at Frankenthal, which was soon actually besieged by Cordova, were under the command of Sir John Burroughs, a brave and skilful veteran, who was supported by the ardour of the town's people, who mainly consisted of Protestant emigrants from the Spanish Netherlands. Yet it was evident that, unless succour came, he could not hold out long. Nor was this the worst. There were symptoms that the same causes which had produced the defection of the inhabitants of the Upper Palatinate, were operating in the Lower. "The gentry of the country were using means to be preserved in their estates and goods." The people were groaning under their hardships, and were seeking to accommodate themselves with the enemy. Vere's men

---

* Frederick to the King, Oct. 3. *S. P. Germany.* Carleton to Trumbull, Oct. 4. Villiers to Carleton, Oct. 10. *S. P. Holland.*
† The Princes and States of Lower Saxony to Frederick, Oct. 20. *S. P. Germany.*
‡ Camerarius to Solms, Sept. $\frac{18}{18}, \frac{18}{28}$. Söltl. *Religionskrieg,* iii. 133, 135.
§ The Council of Heidelberg to Digby, Sept. 21. *Sherborne MSS.*

Ch. VIII.
1621.
Sept.
He supplies the Council with money.

were almost in open mutiny for want of pay, and food to satisfy them was not to be had.

Such was the position of affairs when Digby arrived. He was not the man to shrink from responsibility. Though without orders, he would supply what was needed to carry on the defence of the country. He borrowed money on his own credit from the Nuremberg bankers. He sent his plate to the melting pot. In this way he got together a sum of 10,000*l.*, which he at once placed in the hands of the Heidelberg Council. "If this sum," he wrote to his own Government, "could be made up to 20,000*l.*, the garrisons might still hold out. If not, everything would run a hazard." 20,000*l.* supplied now, would do more than 100,000*l.* afterwards.*

Mansfeld in the Lower Palatinate.

Digby, satisfied that he had done his duty, passed on to Brussels. Strange news awaited him there. After all, Mansfeld had come to the conclusion that Frederick's service was better than the Emperor's, and had made up his mind to continue steadfast to what he was pleased to call his principles. Deceit and trickery cost him nothing. On the 30th of September, he disarmed the suspicion of his enemies by signing the engagement to disband his army.† Before the next sun rose, he slipped away with his whole force, and marched with all speed for Heidelberg.‡

October.
Digby at Brussels.

There was now little to be done at Brussels. Digby had no confidence in Mansfeld. The Bavarians would soon be at his heels, and even if he remained master of the field, it was not likely that he would consult any interests but his own. The Infanta could do nothing. Personally in favour of a general suspension of arms,§ she had been charged by the Emperor to take no steps with-

---

* Digby to the Commissioners for German Affairs, Oct. 2. *S. P. Germany.* An unguarded expression of Lingard has induced many Continental writers to suppose that this money was given to Mansfeld, and Hurter even grounds upon this supposition a thoroughly baseless charge against Digby of connivance in Mansfeld's treachery.

† The agreement in the Vienna Archives is cited by Hurter, *Gesch. Ferdinands II.* ix. 59.

‡ The Council of Heidelberg to Digby, Oct. 8. *Harl. MSS.* 1581. fol. 172.

§ The Duke of Bavaria to the Infanta Isabella, Sept. $\frac{10}{20}$. The Infanta Isabella to Philip IV., Sept. $\frac{14}{24}$, Oct. $\frac{4}{14}$. *Brussels MSS.*

out the consent of Maximilian, and that consent had not been accorded to her. Nor was Digby in a very dissimilar position. He had no authority to speak in Frederick's name. He contented himself, therefore, with using strong language on his own account. "I know not," he wrote to Calvert, "what I may be held in England, but I am sure here I shall hardly ever be held Spanish hereafter; for I assure you I have dealt very plainly with them."* It was in Spain, as he well knew, that, so far as it was possible to do anything whilst Frederick and Mansfeld were masters of the position, his work was to be done. He accordingly hastened back to England, to impart to James the knowledge which he had acquired, hoping to start again from Madrid as soon as possible. Before he left the Continent, he heard that Mansfeld had arrived in the Lower Palatinate, and that Cordova had been forced to raise the siege of Frankenthal.

Ch. VIII. 1621. October.

His return to England.

A short breathing-time was gained. It was just possible that it might yet be used to force reasonable terms on Frederick and Maximilian alike. Perhaps, if Digby had been King of England, it might have been done; for no man knew better than Digby how little words could effect in such a case. The firmness of will and the promptness of action which had saved the Council of Heidelberg from ruin, might perhaps, if they had been allowed free play, have saved Europe from war.

For pacific as were the designs of the Court of Madrid, it would not be wise to trust them too far. Philip's ministers, after all, did not desire peace because they had no wish to encroach in Germany, but because they were afraid of the consequences. Unfortunately, during Digby's absence, James had, as usual, been acting in the way which was most calculated to remove any fear that he would ever take up an independent position in opposition to Spain.

On the 27th of November in the preceding year, Mansell cast anchor with his fleet of twenty ships in the roads of Algiers. He sent a formal demand to the Dey for the restitution of all English vessels and English subjects in

1620. November. Mansell at Algiers.

---

* Digby to Calvert, Oct. 22. *S. P. Flanders.*

Ch. VIII.
1620.
November.

his possession, and for the execution or surrender of the pirates by whom they had been captured. He might have saved himself the trouble. The Algerines pretended extreme eagerness to comply with his wishes, and released some four-and-twenty captives. Mansell was well aware that such a handful of men formed but a small instalment of the crews of the hundred and fifty English vessels which had been taken in the past six years; but though he was ready to remonstrate, he was not prepared to fight. Supplies promised him from England had not reached him; sickness was raging in his fleet, and he sailed away leaving the town untouched. For five months, he did little or nothing. It was not till the 21st of May that he re-appeared at Algiers. Three days afterwards, the wind at nightfall blew towards the shore, and he launched his fire-ships against the pirate shipping. For a moment success smiled upon his attempt. In no less than seven places the flames were seen shooting up amongst the rigging; but the English sailors had been ill-supplied with ammunition, and in a few minutes they had got rid of all their powder. The Algerines were not slow to profit by the opportunity. Hurrying back to the mole, they drove off their assailants, and with the timely assistance of a shower of rain, they succeeded in extinguishing the flames.

1621.
May.
He fails in an attack upon the town.

Not a breath of air was stirring, and, before the wind rose, the harbour was rendered inaccessible by a boom thrown across its mouth. The failure was complete, and there was nothing left for Mansell to do but to sail away to Alicant.*

Recall of part of the fleet.

On his return to harbour he found orders to send back four of his ships to England. To this number he added four others, which had become unserviceable. Twelve only remained in the Mediterranean.†

It does not appear on what grounds the four vessels

---

* Mansell's account of his Proceedings, Dec. 1620. *S. P. Barbary States.* Mansell to Buckingham, Jan. 13, 1621. *Harl. MSS.* 1581, fol. 70. Mansell to the Commissioners for the Expedition, Jan. 16. Mansell to Calvert, Jan. 17. *S. P. Barbary States.* Mansell to Calvert, March 15. *S. P. Spain.* Mansell to Buckingham, June 9. *Cabala,* 297.

† Algiers Voyage. *S. P. Dom.* cxxii. 106.

were recalled; but it was not long before a resolution of a more important character was taken. The outbreak of hostilities between Spain and Holland had been accompanied by a renewal of the dispute about the blockade of the Flemish ports. The Dutch claimed a right of excluding all commerce from the enemy's harbours. James, on the other hand, declared that they were not justified in stopping anything under a neutral flag but contraband of war. To such an assertion as this, the Prince of Orange refused to listen for an instant. "These countries," he said one day to Carleton, "will sooner cast themselves into the hands of the King of Spain, than permit the trade of any nation to enter the ports of Flanders."

Ch. VIII. 1621. The blockade of the Flemish ports.

Even if James's claim had been far better than it was, it would have been unwise to have insisted upon it in the existing state of his relations with the Continent. But with James such considerations were of little weight. Before July was over, the remainder of Mansell's fleet was recalled to maintain the supremacy of the English flag in the Narrow Seas.*

July. The rest of the fleet recalled.

In the course which he was now taking, James received every encouragement from Buckingham. Again, as in the previous summer, the Lord Admiral saw in an injury done to an English ship a personal insult to himself.

Buckingham hostile to the Dutch.

Caron looked upon this state of things with sorrow, for he knew the value of the English alliance to his country, and though he could not recommend the opening of the Flemish ports, he was aware that the long delay in sending the promised commissioners to treat on the East India business was bringing to Buckingham a support which would otherwise have failed him. "I have seen the time," he wrote, "when the friends of Spain were held here as open enemies. But the King's subjects are now so irritated by these East Indian disputes, that they take part against us." Yet there was no lack of hostility to Spain. James, he went on to say, was as certain of the restoration of the Palatinate, as if he held it in his own hand. Gondomar was growing in credit every day, and Buckingham was entirely devoted to him.

* Chamberlain to Carleton, July 28. *S. P. Dom.* cxxii. 46. Calvert to Carleton, Aug. 11. *S. P. Holland.*

Ch. VIII.
1621.
July.

Sept. Destination of Mansell's fleet.

Mandeville's enforced resignation.

A few days ago, the favourite had accompanied the Spaniard to his house in a litter. As they passed through the streets, no man took off his hat, and not a few muttered a wish that they might both be hanged.*
It was not without reason, that Caron spoke of the growth of Gondomar's credit. It was at his request that the decision had been taken to recall the fleet.† In September, however, he intimated that his master would prefer a different arrangement, and that he wished twelve ships to remain in the Mediterranean, whilst twelve others were employed against the Dutch. What may have been the motives of the King of Spain we do not know. But we do know that James made no objection to changing his plans at the bidding of a foreign ambassador, that he bore down all opposition in the Council, and that, but for the sudden arrival of Mansell in the Downs, in obedience to previous orders, Gondomar's plan would have been carried out to the letter.‡

The opposition in the Council had been headed by the Lord Treasurer. Mandeville may have been a bad financier, but he was a good Protestant, and he had a deeply rooted aversion to the Spanish alliance. It was now intimated to him that he must resign his office. If he gave way without difficulty, his fall would be softened. The post of Lord President of the Council, long disused, should be revived in his favour, though, as Gondomar remarked, no one knew what its duties were. At the same time, the 20,000*l*. which he had given to the King for his appointment would be acknowledged as a debt, for which Buckingham was ready to become security. Mandeville was not the man to struggle against such pressure as this. He accepted the terms without difficulty. "My lord," said Bacon, when next they met, " they have made me an example, and you a president." The jest was made more

---

* Caron to the States General, July $\frac{2}{12}$. *Add. MSS.* 17,677 K, fol. 140.

† Philip IV. to Ciriza, $\frac{\text{May 27}}{\text{June 6}}$. Gondomar to Philip IV., July $\frac{11}{21}$.—*Simancas MSS.* Est. 2518, 2602.

‡ Gondomar to Philip IV. Sept. $\frac{12}{22}$, $\frac{20}{30}$. Calvert to Gondomar, Sept. $\frac{17}{27}$. *Simancas MSS.* Est. 2602. Order in Council, Sept. 15. *S. P. Dom.* cxxii. 126.

tolerable by the spelling of the day, than it could possibly be considered now.*

Almost as a matter of course, the white staff was placed in Cranfield's hands. A few weeks later the Chancellorship of the Exchequer, vacant by the resignation of Greville, who had recently been raised to the peerage as Lord Brooke,† was committed to Sir Richard Weston.‡

<small>Ch. VIII.
1621.
Sept.
Cranfield Lord Treasurer, and Weston Chancellor of the Exchequer.</small>

As far as the administration of the finances was concerned, it was a happy change. If any one living could restore order and economy it was Cranfield. But the manner of his appointment was of evil augury. The nation was thinking far more of its religious sympathies with the German Protestants than of its commercial rivalry with the Dutch, and it was well known that, though Cranfield cared a great deal about the prosperity of trade, he cared very little about the ruin of the Protestant Churches on the Continent.

In the meanwhile Buckingham was hounding on the King to an open declaration of war against the Dutch. Nor was he less inclined to speak evil of Frederick. Sharp tongues had been busy at the Hague, and it was rumoured that, at the little Court of the exiles, he had been spoken of as a Papist and a traitor. In revenge he placed in Gondomar's hands the letters which Frederick and Elizabeth had written to the King, and assured the pleased ambassador that not a penny should be sent from England for the defence of the Palatinate.§

<small>Buckingham eager for war with the Dutch.</small>

Such was the direction in which James, carried away as usual by the feeling which happened to be uppermost for the moment, had been tending during Digby's absence. Yet when the news reached him of the danger of the Lower Palatinate, he roused himself to unwonted activity. He not only promised to repay the money which had been advanced by Digby to the Heidelberg

<small>Digby in England.</small>

---

* Locke to Carleton, Sept. 29. *S. P. Dom.* cxxii. 152. Gondomar to Philip IV., Sept. 28/Oct. 8. *Simancas MSS.* Est. 2602. *Bacon's Apothegms; Works,* vii. 181.
† Jan. 29, Pat. 18 Jac. I., Part 2.
‡ Nov. 13, Pat. 19 Jac. I., Part 1.
§ Gondomar to Philip IV., Sept. 28/Oct. 8. *Simancas MSS.* Est. 2602.

Ch. VIII.
1621.

Council, but he engaged to add another 10,000*l*.* On the 31st of October Digby himself returned to tell his story. James was moved at least to momentary indignation. The next day the Privy Council was summoned to listen to the narrative. The cry for immediate action was loud.† On the 3rd of November a proclamation appeared summoning Parliament, which had lately been adjourned once more by the King's orders, to meet on the 20th of the same month.‡

Nov. 3.
Parliament summoned.

Terms offered by James.

This time there was to be no hesitation. Steps were taken which should have been taken at least ten months before. Money was borrowed, and the promised 10,000*l*. swelled into 30,000*l*., which were immediately§ despatched to Frederick at the Hague. More was to follow as soon as supplies had been voted by the Commons. Frederick was again urged to put himself at the head of his troops in the Palatinate. At the same time James wrote to the Emperor, renewing his original demand for the restitution of the lands and dignities of which his son-in-law had been deprived, and engaging that he would relinquish the crown of Bohemia, and, after making such full submission as might be consistent with his honour, would renounce any confederacy by which the peace of the Empire might be endangered. A copy of this letter was sent to Frederick, in order that he might signify, in writing, his consent to negotiate on the proposed terms. If he did so, he was told, James would put forth his whole strength on his behalf.||

Popular enthusiasm.

For a few days Digby was the most popular man in England. There may have been some who wondered why all this had not been done long ago; but such thoughts were drowned in the general enthusiasm. At last, men said, the weary time of weakness and vacillation

---

* Digby to the Council of the Palatinate, Oct. 24. *S. P. Germany.*

† Gondomar to the Infanta Isabella, Nov. $\frac{1}{11}$. *Simancas MSS.* Est. 2602. Locke to Carleton, Nov. 3. *S. P. Dom.* cxxiii. 84. Salvetti's *News-Letter*, Nov. $\frac{8}{18}$.

‡ Proclamation, Nov. 3. *S. P. Dom.* clxxxvii. 98*.

§ The King to Carleton, Nov. 12. *S. P. Holland.*

|| Calvert to Carleton, Nov. 5, 10. *S. P. Holland.* The King to Ferdinand II., Nov. 12. *Cabala*, 239. The King to Frederick, Nov. 12 (?). *Add. MSS.* 12,485, fol. 99 b.

was at an end. "God grant," wrote the Earl of Bedford, "that the King's resolutions may be so propounded to the Parliament, as they may with a general applause be seconded, and not disputed, and that no past distastes breed such variance at home as may hinder the speedy execution requisite for the good success of what is to be done by us abroad."*

Even now, however, James unhappily did not know how serious the crisis was. If everything else failed, the King of Spain, he fancied, was certain to see him righted. His words had been for the moment the words of Digby, manly, self-reliant, and far-sighted. His thoughts were his own. Still, as ever, he hated trouble and responsibility. He was the more disposed to confidence in Spain because good news, or what he held to be good news, had lately reached him of the progress of that foolish marriage treaty of which he was so deeply enamoured. Early in the year Lafuente had arrived at Rome, and had soon been joined by George Gage, Conway's Roman Catholic cousin, who had been sent to watch the negotiation on the part of the English Government. There had been a delay at first in consequence of the death of Paul V., and a further delay in consequence of the death of Philip III. But these obstacles were now surmounted. A congregation of cardinals was appointed by the new Pope, Gregory XV., to consider the propriety of granting the dispensation asked for. Nor was it long before Gage was able to report that, if only James could make up his mind to make concessions to the English Catholics, no difficulties would be thrown in the way of the marriage by the Pope.†

It was in the frame of mind resulting from his knowledge of the progress which had been made in this affair, that James prepared to meet his Parliament. At a moment when he ought to have done his utmost to impress Gondomar with a sense of the firmness of his attitude, he sent him a message, bidding him not to care for anything that might be said in Parliament, as he

---

* Bedford to Carleton, Nov. 5. *S. P. Holland.*
† Gage to Digby, Sept. 1. *S. P. Spain.* Francisco de Jesus, 32—35.

CH. VIII. 1621.

Nov. 20. Meeting of the Houses.

Nov. 21. Speech of Williams;

of Digby;

would take good care that nothing was done which would be displeasing to his Catholic Majesty.* With the dice thus loaded against him, Digby had a hard game to play.

On the appointed day the Houses met. On the 21st, the Commons were called up to the House of Lords, to hear a statement on behalf of the King, who was detained at Newmarket by real or affected illness. The proceedings were opened by Williams. He spoke, men said, "more like a divine than a statesman or orator."† He recommended the Commons "to avoid all long harangues, malicious and cunning diversions," and to postpone all business, except the grant of a supply for the Palatinate, till their next meeting in February.‡

Then Digby rose: the one man in England who could avert, if yet it were possible, the evil to come. Of no party, he shared in all that was best in every party. With the Puritans, he would have resisted the encroachments of the Catholic Powers at home and abroad. With the King he was anxious to put an end to religious war, and to grant religious liberty to the English Catholics. On the Continent he would have done that unselfishly, and in the interest of the world, which Richelieu afterwards accomplished selfishly, and in the interest of France. Such designs, so vast and so far reaching, might easily take root in the brain of a dreamer. But Digby was no dreamer. He knew that there were times when the road to peace lay through the gates of war, and that that time had almost come. Now or never Spain must be made to understand that she must choose her side.

Digby's statement was a very simple one. He spoke of the King's efforts to maintain peace, of the hopes of success which had attended his own embassy at Vienna, of the terror inspired by Mansfeld's army, of the change which, at the instigation of the Duke of Bavaria, had come over the Emperor's intentions, and of the consequent renewal of the war. The King, he said, must now

---

* Gondomar to the Infanta Isabella, $\frac{\text{Nov. 21}}{\text{Dec. 1}}$. *Simancas MSS.* Est. 2518.

† Chamberlain to Carleton, Nov. 24. *S. P. Dom.* cxxiii. 122.

‡ *Proceedings and Debates,* ii. 183.

"either abandon his children, or declare himself by a war." The King of Spain had written "to the Emperor effectually for peace," and it was "the fault of the Emperor that it was not effected." It remained, therefore, to be considered what course was to be now pursued. The force of twenty thousand men under Vere and Mansfeld, would be sufficient to hold the Lower Palatinate during the winter. But if this were to be done, money must at once be sent. Mansfeld's soldiers were mere mercenaries, and if they were left any longer without their pay, they would soon be in open mutiny. An additional army must be sent in the spring, and the cost of maintaining such an army for a year would not be less than 900,000l.*

Cranfield followed, urging a liberal supply, without naming any precise amount.

The next morning, it was arranged by the Commons that the King's message should be taken into consideration on the 26th. In the meanwhile an objection was not unnaturally raised to some expressions which had been let fall by Williams. They had been directed, said Alford, to meddle with nothing but the supply for the Palatinate. It would be an evil precedent if the King were permitted to assume the right of prescribing the subject of their debates.† In the same spirit Digges, whose facile and impressionable nature made him ever ready to adopt the prevalent feeling of those with whom he was acting, drew attention to the late imprisonment of Sandys. He hoped, he said, that in the great debate to which they were looking forward, no exception would be taken to anything which they might say in discharge of their consciences.

Sandys himself was not present, having been detained by illness. Calvert, however, rose to explain that he had not been imprisoned for anything that he had said or done in the House. The statement, though literally true, was received with general incredulity, and murmurs of dissatisfaction were heard on every side. It was only upon Calvert's agreeing that his words should be entered

Ch. VIII.
1621.
Nov.

and of Cranfield.

Freedom of debate.

Sandys' imprisonment.

---
* *Proceedings and Debates*, ii. 186. *Lords' Journals*, iii. 167.
† *Proceedings and Debates*, ii. 197.

<small>Ch. VIII.
1621.
June.</small> upon the clerk's book, that calm was restored. It was evident, however, that a question had been raised which, unless it were speedily settled, would give rise to serious perplexities in the future.*

<small>Nov. 26.
Debate on the demand for a supply.</small> On the 26th of November, a full House met to take part in the great debate which was to decide the Continental policy of England for years to come. The zeal of the Commons, it is true, may sometimes have outrun discretion. Their knowledge of the policy and designs of the Courts of Europe was defective. But their single-mindedness was undoubted. In their deliberations, that narrow patriotism which is only a larger selfishness, had no place. All that they asked was to devote themselves to that cause which, as they honestly believed, was the cause of God and man.

The House, it must be acknowledged, approached the question under peculiar difficulties. Digby had told them the truth, but not the whole truth. It is no wonder that there were many amongst his hearers who were incredulous when they heard of the efforts of the King of Spain in favour of peace. What they knew was that it was only by the aid of Spanish troops that the war had been possible. And yet how could Digby offer them the key by which alone the mystery could be unlocked? Even if he had thought it wise to publish to the world the follies of his master's son-in-law, would not the blame which would deservedly be attributed to Frederick, fall in part upon his master himself?

<small>Speech of Digges;</small> The debate was opened by Digges. He hoped that the House would support the Crown. Yet they must not forget that it was the King of Spain who was seeking to bring all Europe into subjection. Without a war of <small>of Rudyard;</small> diversion no good would be done. Sir Benjamin Rudyard rose next. Lately appointed, by Doncaster's influence, Surveyor of the Court of Wards, he was at this time attached to that band of politicians who, with Pembroke at their head, hoped to reconcile a stirring foreign policy with the fullest devotion to the Crown. He took no notice of Digges's proposal for a war of diversion, but

---

* *Proceedings and Debates*, ii. 198.

contented himself with urging the House to grant the supply at once. In the same strain Sir Miles Fleetwood followed, adding a recommendation that the advice of the Lords should be asked not only upon the amount required, but on the manner in which it should be expended.

Ch. VIII. 1621. Nov. 26. of Fleetwood;

Perrot came next. He was for a war on a large scale, a war of diversion, as Digges had expressed it; a war, that is to say, which would have sought out the sources of the strength of Spain in the Indies. Let them give what was needed now, and increase their supply as soon as war had been really declared. So far he had said nothing which was in marked opposition with Digby's proposal. The question of the mode of carrying on the war might well be left for future consideration when war was actually commenced. But in the eyes of the author of the declaration with which the House had separated in June, the crisis was fully as much religious as political. He ended, therefore, by reminding his hearers that there were those at home whose hearts were at the service of the King of Spain, and that it was necessary to take precautions against their machinations.

of Perrot;

Sackville saw that the discussion was getting upon dangerous ground. Like Rudyard, he had thrown himself heart and soul into the cause of the German Protestants, and like Rudyard he knew that, excepting with the good-will of James, it was impossible to put the forces of England in motion to their assistance. The passing bell, he said, was now tolling for religion. It was not dead, but it was dying. Let them consider two things: first, what was fit to be done at this time; secondly, what was unfit to be now talked of. Let them give at once what was needed for the present supply of the troops. But for the present let them dismiss from their minds all consideration of the larger grant which, as the Lord Treasurer had told them, would be needed in the spring, if war were then declared.

of Sackville.

The House would probably have been wise if it had closed with this suggestion. It is true that little confidence could be placed in the King. But unless the

Feeling about the Spanish match.

Ch. VIII.
1621.
Nov. 26.

Commons were prepared to leave the Continent to its fate, it was necessary to trust him at least to the extent of Sackville's proposal.

Such would no doubt have been the view which a consummate political tactician would have taken of the situation. But it is seldom that such considerations have much weight with a popular assembly, and, least of all, with an assembly with no definite leadership. There was scarcely a member there who did not sympathize from the bottom of his heart with the thoughts which had found utterance in the speeches of Digges and Perrot. No doubt their belief that the King of Spain was aiming at universal monarchy was a gross exaggeration. But it was perfectly true that he was exercising an influence over the King of England which was justly intolerable to every true-hearted English subject, and they knew that, unless a remedy were found for the mischief, it would not be long before Philip would find in the wife of the future King a representative whose soft accents would be even more persuasive than the loud tones which were so readily at Gondomar's command.

Of Phelips.

A feeling so universal and so deeply seated could hardly fail to find expression in the debate. Gifted with an eloquent tongue, and with every virtue except discretion, Phelips, at least, was not the man to leave unuttered the opinions which he shared with those around him. Their enemies, he reminded his hearers, were the Catholic States. There was the great wheel of Spain, and the little wheel of the German Princes. Their own natural allies were the Protestants of Europe. It had been said that the King of Spain was their friend. But did not everyone know that he was the President of that Council of war by which the Palatinate had been invaded. It was from his treasure that the attacking forces had been paid. The Duke of Bavaria was but a petty Prince. God, he believed, was angry with them because they had not kept the crown on the head of the King of Bohemia. Phelips then turned to home affairs. Trade, he said, was ruined, and the hearts and affections of the Papists were at the disposition of the King of Spain. They had lately grown so insolent as to talk of Protestants as a faction.

They had begun to dispute openly on their religion. Against such dangers the Commons were bound to guard the country. Let the bills before the House be proceeded with. Let them refuse to grant any supply for the present. At their next meeting they might grant subsidies, and prepare for a thorough war. Till that time the defence of the Palatinate might be otherwise provided for. A small sum would be sufficient to support Mansfeld during the winter.

After a short speech in the same strain from Sir Edward Giles, Calvert saw that it was time to interfere. In a few weighty words he explained the policy of the Government. "The friendship amongst princes," he said, "is as their strength and interest is, and he would not have our King to trust to the King of Spain's affection. As for the delaying of a supply any longer, if we do it, our supply will come too late. It is said our King's sword hath been too long sheathed; but they who shall speak to defer a supply, seek to keep it longer in the scabbard." It was impossible to declare more plainly that, in case of necessity, the proposed armaments would be directed against Spain. If James, instead of loitering at Newmarket, had been there to confirm his Secretary's words, he would have carried everything before him.

For a short time it seemed as if Calvert's words had not been without their effect. Of the three speakers who rose after him, not one recurred to Phelips' proposal to withhold supplies. But the distrust was too deeply-seated to be easily removed. Phelips found a supporter in Thomas Crew, a lawyer of reputation for ability and honesty. "Before they gave anything," he said, "they ought to know who was their enemy. If at their next meeting they could be assured that their money was to be used against Spain, and if hope was given them that the Prince would marry one of his own religion, they might then grant a liberal supply."

Amongst the few who listened with dissatisfaction to the introduction of this irritating topic was Sir Thomas Wentworth, Calvert's youthful colleague in the representation of Yorkshire. Gifted with a clear and commanding intellect, he looked with apprehension upon the

Ch. VIII.
1624.
Nov. 26.

His character and policy.

renewal of the religious wars of the past century, and he believed with Digby that, if the King could make it clear that the nation was at his back, Spain would be certain to give way to any reasonable demand.* Yet there were many reasons why, at this juncture, Wentworth should have carried but little weight in the House. He would, it is true, have gone as far as Phelips or Perrot in opposing the miserable system by which the first place in the councils of an English Sovereign was held by the ambassador of a foreign Prince. But in the wide European sympathies of the leading members he had no share. His policy was purely English, and it was nothing more. In matters of domestic legislation he took the deepest interest. He seldom rose without urging the importance of pushing on the Bills before the House without loss of time. But Puritanism, and everything that savoured of Puritanism, he regarded with loathing. For him religion must be decorous and stately. Yet if he bitterly hated the restlessness of the champions of liberty, he hated still more bitterly opposition to his own will. Proud of his ancient lineage, and of the princely fortune which had descended to him from his ancestors, his fierce resolute spirit brooked no resistance. The clash of thought, the conflict of opinion out of which lasting progress springs, was to him an object of detestation. Even when, a few years later, he was throwing in his lot with the Commons in their struggle against Buckingham, he was never one in feeling with those with whom he was, for the time, politically associated. The value which he set upon Parliamentary discussion may be gathered from a curious passage in a letter to a friend. He had just seen, he said, a statue representing Samson in the act of killing a Philistine with the jaw-bone of an ass. " The moral and meaning whereof," he adds, " may be yourself standing at the bar, and there, with all your weighty, curiously-spun arguments, beaten down by some such silly instrument as that ; and so the bill, in conclusion, passed, sir, in spite of your nose." †

* Wentworth to Darcy, Jan. 9, 1622. *Strafford Letters*, i. 15.
† Wentford to Wandesford, June 17, 1624. *Strafford Letters*, i. 21. The characteristic story of the Yorkshire election petition will be well known to every reader of Mr. Forster's *Life of Sir J. Eliot*.

Such was the man who now attempted to stem the tide which was running strongly against the Government. He proposed, with the evident intention of giving time to communicate with the King, that the debate should be adjourned for some days. It was not an unwise suggestion, and if it had come from one with whom the House could sympathize, it might perhaps have been adopted. As it was, its rejection was certain. The renewal of the discussion was fixed for the following morning.

He proposes an adjournment.

The next day, therefore, the debate was resumed. Member after member rose to urge the necessity of engaging in war with Spain, and of putting in force the laws against the Papists, who were the chief supporters of Spanish influence in England. Once more Sackville rose to advocate compliance with the King's demands. "The King of Spain," he said, "hath laid out his money to gain from us the Palatinate. Let us, therefore, give some present supply towards the keeping of that which is left us in the Palatinate; and it will not be long before we discover plainly whether the King of Spain be our enemy or no; which if he be, then will the King, without question, understanding of our affections and inclinations, proclaim a general war against him, and then shall we have our desires."

Nov. 27. Sackville's argument.

Every hour the question was becoming more evidently than before a question of confidence in the King. James had placed his supporters at a terrible disadvantage. He had asked for a supply, but he had not disclosed his policy. Was there any reason to believe, it might well be argued, that it was worth while to make a fresh application to Spain? And if such a reason existed, why had it not been communicated to the House? James could hardly indeed have been brought to set forth in detail to his own condemnation all the blunders of the past year. But it can hardly be doubted that if he had produced in substance the terms which he had submitted to Frederick for his acceptance, and had declared that the refusal of those terms, whether by Spain or by any other power, would be followed by an immediate declaration of war, he would have carried the House with him, and would have given a support to his diplomacy which could be obtained in no other quarter.

But James was far away at Newmarket, and, whatever his partisans might say, it was plain that they were speaking without authority. For a time, indeed, Sackville seemed to have made an impression. He was seconded by Wentworth, who recommended an immediate grant, leaving to the King the choice of a fit time for declaring war. Weston and Heath followed on the same side.

The speeches which had hitherto been made in opposition to the Crown may, in some particulars, have been indiscreet and exaggerated; but they struck at real evils, and they had been expressed in language which it became the leaders of the English Commons to utter. Very different was the tone assumed by the speaker, who now rose to address the House. On ordinary occasions Coke's rugged independence was apt to degenerate into coarseness of thought and language, and he had been too long accustomed to pour out the vials of his wrath, amidst popular applause, upon Jesuits and Papists, to approach the subject under discussion with any degree of calmness. Nor were special causes of irritation wanting. During the recess an attempt had been made to punish him indirectly for the uncourtly part which he had taken in the House. Two men, named Lepton and Goldsmith, considered themselves to have been wronged by the decision of a committee of which Coke had been the chairman. They applied to Lady Hatton for advice as to the best mode of revenging themselves upon her husband. The result of their machinations was that a bill was filed in the Star-Chamber containing numerous charges against him for misconduct in the days long past when he was still upon the Bench. The affair had recently been brought before the notice of the Commons, and a committee had been appointed to inquire into what looked very like a conspiracy to inflict punishment upon a member of the House for the discharge of his duty.*

It was therefore under the influence of a not unnatural feeling of indignation that Coke now rose. He went at

* *Proceedings and Debates,* ii. 201, 248.

length over the old quarrel between Elizabeth and the Pope. The Pope, he said, had discharged the Queen's subjects from their allegiance. The Jesuits had never ceased to provoke her by their conspiracies. They had practised to kill her; they had attempted to poison her. At the moment when English commissioners were treating for peace, Spain had sent the Armada. The scab which was so destructive to sheep in England came from Spain. The foulest disease by which mankind was afflicted spread over Europe from Naples, and Naples belonged to the King of Spain. From Spain nothing but evil was to be expected. The Papists flocked to the house of the Spanish Ambassador, and England was in danger as long as she nourished Papists in her bosom. Let the House, therefore, turn its attention to the legislation before it. The sudden grant of supply would do no good. He had heard nothing to make him think that there was any necessity for giving money at present.

Resolution of the House.

Overjoyed at finding so thoroughgoing a supporter, Phelips rose once more to reiterate the arguments which he had used on the preceding day. But neither Phelips nor Coke could lead the House astray from the point at issue. Still, as before the adjournment, the vast majority were determined that, if by any means it could be avoided, there should be no breach with the King. It was resolved that the supply for which James had asked should be granted.* The precise amount to be given, and the manner in which it was to be raised, should be

---

* "The Commons," says Mr. Hallam, (*Const. Hist. of England*, ed. 1854, i. 364,) "had no reason, perhaps, to suspect that the charge of keeping 30,000 men in the heart of Germany would fall much short of the estimate. Yet, after long haggling, they voted only one subsidy, amounting to 70,000*l.* a sum manifestly insufficient for the first equipment of such a force. This parsimony could hardly be excused by their suspicion of the King's unwillingness to undertake the war, for which it afforded the best justification." That such a sentence should have been penned by such a writer, would be truly astonishing, if it related to any other period of history than one which has never hitherto been thoroughly investigated. Every word is altogether at variance with the facts of the case. The subsidy was not meant to have anything to do with the army of 30,000 men. When the answer had come from Spain and the Emperor, it would be time enough to provide for that force which might never be levied after all. What was now needed was to provide a special fund for the pay of Mansfeld's men for one or two months, in addition to the money which Frederick drew from the Dutch.

considered in Committee. But to this resolution, which in itself was everything which the King could desire, two instructions to the Committee were appended at which he might possibly take umbrage. It was to prepare a petition asking him to end the session at Christmas, by passing the bills to which, in spite of the Lord Keeper's intimation, they intended to devote their attention. It was also to take into consideration the state of religion, and to draw up a petition for the due execution of the laws against the Papists.*

Nov. 28. Pym's speech in the Committee on religion.

The next morning, accordingly, the House went into Committee. The debate which ensued is memorable for the speech in which John Pym placed himself beyond question in the first rank amongst the leaders of the House. Of the King he spoke with the utmost respect; but he feared lest his goodness had been abused by the Papists. It was his Majesty's piety which had led him to be tender of other men's consciences. Yet it must not be forgotten that whilst there were errors "seated in the understanding," misguiding "practice and devotion in the manner of worshipping God," there were others which produced effects "to the distemper of the State." It was for this reason that it had always "belonged to the outward and coercive power of magistrates to restrain not only the fruit but even the seeds of sedition, though buried under the pretences of religion." By "the same rules of faith from whence the Papists received the superstitious part of their religion," they were bound to "opinions and practices dangerous to all princes and states which" did "not allow of their superstitions." It was therefore to be understood that "the aim of the laws in the penalties and restraint of Papists, was not to punish them for believing and thinking, but that they might be disabled to do that which they think and believe they ought to do."

The speaker then proceeded to enumerate the dangers which were impending over the country. "If the Papists," he said, "once obtain a connivance, they will press for a toleration; from thence to an equality; from an

---

* *Proceedings and Debates,* ii. 206—226. *Commons' Journals,* i. 644—649.

equality to a superiority; from a superiority to an extirpation of all contrary religions." He therefore advised that an oath of association for the defence of his Majesty's person, and for the execution of the laws made for the establishing of religion, should be taken by all loyal subjects; and that the King should be asked to issue a special commission for the suppression of recusancy.*

Such was the language which, as we can well believe, "had great attention, and was exceedingly commended, both in matter and manner." † Even we who are unable to find much to commend in its conclusions, may well find in it grounds upon which we may base our respect for the speaker.

For it is evident that such a speech as this stands in striking contrast with the gushing impetuosity of Phelips and with the snarl of Coke. He who spoke these words was born to be a leader of men. He was not a philosopher like Bacon, with anticipations crowding upon his brain of a world which would not come into existence for generations. His mind teemed with the thoughts, the beliefs, the prejudices of his age. He was strong with the strength, and weak with the weakness of the generation around him. But if his ideas were the ideas of ordinary men, he gave to them a brighter lustre as they passed through his calm and thoughtful intellect. Men learned to hang upon his lips with delight, as they heard him converting their crudities into well-reasoned arguments. It was by listening to him that they made the discovery that their own opinions, the result of passion or of unintelligent feeling, were better and wiser than they had ever dreamed. Nor was it by a mere dry intellectual logic that he touched his hearers. For if there is little trace in his speeches of that fertility of imagination which in a great orator charms and enthrals the most careless of listeners, they were all a-glow with that sacred fire which changes the roughest ore into gold, which springs from the highest faith in the Divine laws by which earthly life is guided, and from the profoundest sense of man's

---

* *Proceedings and Debates*. ii. 210.
† Chamberlain to Carleton, Dec. 1. *S. P. Dom.* cxxiv. 2.

Ch. VIII.
1621.
Nov. 28.

duty to choose good and to eschew evil. And so it came about that between this man and that great assembly a strong sympathy grew up, a sympathy which it refuses to original genius and to flashes of wisdom which are beyond its comprehension, but which it grants ungrudgingly to him who can lead it worthily, by reflecting its thoughts with increased nobility of expression, and by shaping to practical ends its fluctuating and unformed desires.

Tolerance and intolerance.

In the speech which he had just concluded, Pym had placed the duty of persecution upon a plain and intelligible basis. No one had ever expressed so clearly the idea which had vaguely taken possession of his generation, and which was common to men whose minds were so differently constituted as were those of James of England and Ferdinand of Austria; the idea, namely, that religious error was not so much to be attacked because it was hurtful to the soul and conscience, as because it undermined the constitution of the State. It is true, that, except as an indication of the direction in which the current was setting, there was very little importance in the distinction. To a man who was led to the scaffold, or immured in a prison, it was a matter of supreme indifference whether he was told that he was suffering for an offence against religion or for an offence against civil order. But there can be no doubt, that, unsatisfactory as it was in itself, the indirect results of the new phase thus taken by persecution were most salutary. It served to impress upon men the truth, that religious persecution was a bad thing, and it would not be long before they opened their eyes to the further truth, that the recusancy laws were only religious persecution under a more subtle form.

The Spanish match.

If, indeed, Pym's lot had been cast in ordinary times, he might have learned to oppose the precautions which he was now advocating. But, in truth, the times were not ordinary. It was indeed certain that a nation like England, in which Protestantism had taken deep root, would never voluntarily throw itself back into the stifling embraces of the Church of Rome. The human mind does not work at random, and no such backward course is possible so long as liberty of choice remains. But how long would such liberty be left? If no European people which had once heartily embraced Protestantism had ever abandoned it but by compulsion, there had been many examples in which a forcible conversion had been effected by the power of the sword. When the leading minds of a people had been silenced, when thought and speech were no longer free, it would be impossible to answer for the constancy of those who were left desolate in the face of temptation.

Who could tell how soon England might be exposed to such a fate? We are perhaps inclined to think hardly of Pym and the House of Commons for seeking, as Wentworth once expressed it, to put a "ring in the nose of Leviathan,"* by fining the Catholic laity for their religion, by dragging their children from the care of their parents, and by mewing up within prison walls the devotion of the Catholic missionaries. But let us remember that it was James who was encumbering the path of tolerance with obstacles. It may be that at times the gleams of a higher wisdom than had been revealed to his contemporaries, were fitfully playing, like flashes of summer lightning, over his darkened mind. But it was not on any well-grounded conception of religious liberty that he was acting. If he favoured the Catholics, it was not because opinion ought to be free; but because the King of Spain was ready to give a large portion with his daughter, because the Puritans were dangerous, or because parliaments were unruly.

And now, as if it were a light thing that the Spanish Ambassador was consulted and trusted above all other men, a Spanish Infanta was to become the future Queen of England, and the mother of a stock of English Kings. In the course of nature, her child would within forty or fifty years be seated on the throne of Henry and Elizabeth. A Roman Catholic sovereign—for what else could he be?—would have the power of loosing the tongues of the Jesuits, of stopping the mouths of the defenders of the faith. All Court favour, all power of lulling men's consciences to sleep by the soporific potion of place or

* Wentworth to Wandesford, June 17, 1624. *Strafford Letters*, i. 21.

<small>Ch. VIII.
1621.
Nov. 29.</small>

pension, would be in his hands. It was he who would make the judges; it was he who would make the bishops; and who might, therefore, in the language which has sometimes been attributed to James, make both law and gospel. If all other means failed, he would have at his disposal the arms of his Spanish kinsman, the lord, it might be feared, by right of England's cowardice, of half of Germany, and of the territory that had once been held by the Dutch Republic.

<small>A petition on religion.</small>

Such must have been the thoughts which strove for utterance in the hearts of the men who looked to Pym with such visible tokens of approbation. They ordered that a petition should be drawn up for presentation to the King, and at the same time they resolved, without a dissentient voice, that a subsidy should be granted for the support of the troops in the Palatinate. To this subsidy recusants were to be assessed at double rates, as if they had been aliens.*

<small>Dec. 1.
Mischiefs complained of.</small>

On the 1st of December the petition was brought in by the sub-committee which had been directed to prepare it. It began by representing the causes of the apprehended danger. Abroad, the King of Spain was aiming at an exclusive temporal monarchy; the Pope at an exclusive spiritual supremacy. Popery was built upon devilish positions and doctrines. The professors of the Protestant religion were in a miserable plight. His Majesty's children were treated with contempt, and the confederacy of their Popish enemies was backed by all the armies of the King of Spain. At home, matters were as bad. The expectation of the Spanish marriage and the favour of the Spanish Ambassador had elated the spirits of the recusants. They resorted openly to the chapels of foreign ambassadors; they were thronging up in large numbers to London; they sent their children to the Continent to be educated in Popish seminaries. The property which had been forfeited by law was frequently restored to them; their licentious and seditious books were allowed to circulate freely; their priests were to be found in every part of the kingdom. If something were not done they would soon place themselves in oppo-

---

* *Proceedings and Debates*, ii. 241. *Commons' Journals*, i. 650.

sition to the laws, and strong in the support of foreign princes, they would carry all before them till they had succeeded in the utter subversion of the true religion.

Let his Majesty then take his sword in his hand; let him gather round him the Protestant States upon the Continent; let him direct the operations of war by diversion or otherwise, as to his deep wisdom should seem fittest, and not rest upon a war in those parts only which would consume his treasure and discourage the hearts of his subjects. Let the point of his sword be against that prince who first diverted and hath since maintained the war in the Palatinate; let a commission be appointed to see to the execution of the laws against the recusants; and for the frustration of their hopes, and for the security of succeeding ages, let the Prince be timely and happily married to one of his own religion. Let the Papists' children be educated by Protestant schoolmasters, and prohibited from crossing the seas; let the restoration of their forfeited lands be absolutely prohibited.*

The petition accepted by the Committee was taken into consideration by the House on the 3rd. The debate turned almost entirely upon the clause relating to the Prince's marriage. It was opened by Sackville, whose hatred of Rome was undoubted. Yet he urged that any interference with the King's prerogative on a point so delicate as this would give offence. As a matter of parliamentary tactics, Sackville was undoubtedly in the right. If James could be brought to declare war with Spain, the marriage treaty would give no further trouble. It would be far better, therefore, to avoid for two or three months longer a topic by the introduction of which the King's touchy nature would be wounded to the quick. But it was hardly likely that the House would allow its course to be determined on these grounds. A great evil was impending over the nation, and it was the duty of its representatives to discharge their consciences by protesting against it. They had granted a subsidy unconditionally. Even now they had no wish to impose terms on the King. One member after another rose to point out that their petition did not even require an answer.

* *Proceedings and Debates*, ii. 261.

Ch. VIII.
1621.
Dec. 3.
It is adopted with an additional clause.

No man, during the whole course of a long and active life, showed himself a stouter champion of the prerogative than Heath, the Solicitor-General. Yet Heath expressed his approval of the petition on this very ground. He contented himself with moving that an explanatory clause should be added to convey what was evidently the general sense of the House. Phelips and Digges rose to support the proposal, and it was at once adopted without a dissentient voice.

"This," such were the phrases with which the Commons fondly hoped to sweeten the bitter medicine which they were offering, "this is the sum and effect of our humble declaration, which,—no ways intending to press on your Majesty's most undoubted and regal prerogative,—we do with the fulness of all duty and obedience humbly submit to your princely consideration."*

Gondomar's letter to the King.

Already, before the petition had been actually adopted, some one had placed a copy in the hands of Gondomar. The astute Spaniard had been invited by the King to Newmarket,† but had preferred to watch events in London. He now saw that his time was come. Long experience had taught him how to deal with James. The letter which he wrote was one the like of which had never before been placed in the hands of an English sovereign. Incredible as it might seem, even his own past audacity was now outdone.

If it were not, he said, that he depended upon the King's goodness to punish the seditious insolence of the House of Commons, he would have left the kingdom already. "This," he added, "it would have been my duty to do, as you would have ceased to be a king here, and as I have no army to punish these people myself." ‡

---

* *Commons' Journals,* i. 655. *Proceedings and Debates,* ii. 265, 269.

† Gondomar to the Infanta Isabella, Dec. $\frac{6}{16}$. *Simancas MSS.* Est. 2538.

‡ "Yo avia escrito al Rey y al Marques de Boquinguam, quatro dias antes, la sedicion y maldad que pasaba en este Parlamento, y que, sino estuviera tan seguro de la palabra y bondad del Rey que lo castigaria y remediaria con la brevedad y exemplo que convenia, me huviera salido de sus Reynos sin aguardar á tercero dia; deviendo hazello assí cumpliendo con mi obligacion, si el no fuera Rey de estas gentes, pues al presente yo no tenia aquí exercito con que castigarlos." Gondomar to the Infanta Isabella, Dec. $\frac{6}{16}$. *Simancas MSS.* Est. 2538.

For such insolence as this James had no sensitiveness. But his annoyance with the Commons had for some days been on the increase. He had already heard with displeasure that they had resumed their investigation into the affair of Lepton and Goldsmith, and had ordered Sandys to be questioned on the reasons of his imprisonment.* He now burst out into paroxysms of impotent rage. Without waiting for the formal presentation of the petition, he dashed off at once an angry letter to the Speaker.

Ch. VIII. 1621. Dec. 3. The King's displeasure.

He had heard, he said, that his absence from his Parliament had "emboldened some fiery and popular spirits to debate and argue publicly in matters far beyond their reach or capacity, and so tending to" his "high dishonour and to the trenching upon" his "prerogative royal." The House was, therefore, to be informed that its members were not to be permitted to meddle with matters of Government or "with mysteries of state." There was to be no speech of the Prince's "match with the daughter of Spain," or anything said against "the honour of that king." They must also forbear from interfering in private suits "which have their due motion in the ordinary courts of justice." As for Sandys, he would inform them himself that his imprisonment had not been caused by any misdemeanour in Parliament. He would have them, however, to understand that he thought himself "very free and able to punish any man's misdemeanours in Parliament, as well during their sitting as after," and that hereafter he should not be sparing in his use of this power "upon any occasion of any man's insolent behaviour there." If they had touched in their petition upon any of the topics which he had forbidden they were to be told that, "except they reform it," he would "not deign the hearing of the answering it." Finally, he was willing to end the session at Christmas, and to give his assent to any bills which were really for the good of the commonwealth. If the bills were not good, it would be their fault and not his.†

His letter to the Speaker.

---

* *Proceedings and Debates*, ii. 248, 259.
† The King to the Speaker, Dec. 3. *Proceedings and Debates*, ii. 277. There is a letter from the Prince of Wales to Buckingham amongst

Ch. VIII.
1621.
Dec. 4.
It is read in the House.

On the morning of the 4th of December this extraordinary letter was read in the House. A peremptory refusal to accept the advice tendered would have created incomparably less consternation. Even the denial of the right of the Commons to meddle with matters of foreign policy, unless their attention had been specially directed to them, might perhaps have been passed over in silence. But it was intolerable that the question of immunity from punishment for speeches uttered in the House should be thus reopened. Practically, it was a point of far greater importance than the other. If the King were in need of money, he would always be obliged to listen to anything that they might choose to say to him. If he were not in need of money, he could always close their mouths by a prorogation or a dissolution. But it was not to be borne that they should have the semblance of freedom without its reality, and that each member as he rose to speak should be weighted with the knowledge that he might soon be called upon to expiate in the Tower any uncourtly phrase which might fall from his lips.

Adjournment of the House.

Such a letter, it was at once felt, must not be answered in haste in a moment of irritation. Never, said Phelips, had any matter of such consequence been before them. The members who had been despatched to lay the petition before the King were at once recalled, and the House rose for the day, in order that full consideration might be

the Tanner MSS. printed in Goodman's *Court of King James*, (ii. 209,) which seems to show that Charles went even beyond his father in his dislike of the proceedings of the Commons.

" The Lower House this day," he wrote, " has been a little unruly, but I hope it will turn to the best, for before they rose they began to be ashamed of it ; yet I could wish that the King would send down a commissioner for that, if need were, such seditious fellows might be made an example to others by Monday next, and till then I would let them alone ; it will be seen whether they mean to do good or persist in their follies, so that the King needs to be patient but a little while. I have spoken with so many of the Council as the King trusts most, and they [are] all of this mind ; only the sending of authority to set seditious fellows fast is of my adding." The letter is plainly dated, " Fryday 3 No. 1621," without erasure or tear, as I am informed, by the kindness of Mr. Hackman, to whom I applied in order that I might be quite sure that there was no mistake. The date is of course impossible, as Parliament was not sitting at the time, and I do not find any Friday during the debates to which the Prince's remarks apply. The most likely day would be Dec. 3. But that was a Monday.

given in private to the King's demands. "Let us rise," said Digges, "but not as in discontent. Rather let us resort to our prayers, and then to consider of this great business."*

The next morning after a long debate a committee was appointed to draw up an explanatory petition, and the House again adjourned, refusing to enter upon any further business till their privileges had been defended from further attack.

On the 8th, a second petition was ready to be despatched to the King. It presented a marvellous contrast with the imperious tones of the royal rescript. It pushed concession to the verge of imprudence. It touched but lightly upon the claim put forward by the House to discuss matters of general interest, and offered James a loophole of escape from the position which he had rashly assumed, by resting their right to enter upon questions connected with the penal laws and the Spanish marriage upon the simple ground that they were involved in the question of the defence of the Palatinate which he had himself commended to their consideration. They acknowledged distinctly that it was the King's business and not theirs to resolve on peace and war, and to choose a wife for his son. They merely asked him to read their petition. It was only to the clauses which related to the recusancy laws and to the passing of bills that they expected an answer. "And whereas," they added, touching at last, as if with reluctance, upon the burning point of their own privileges, "your Majesty, by the general words of your letter, seemeth to restrain us from intermeddling with matters of government, or particulars which have their motion in courts of justice, the generality of which words in the largeness of the extent thereof,—as we hope beyond your Majesty's intentions,—might involve those things which are the proper subjects of parliamentary action and discourse; and whereas, your Majesty's letter doth seem to abridge us of the ancient liberty of parliament for freedom of speech, jurisdiction, and just censure of the House, and other proceedings there; wherein, we trust in God, we shall never transgress the bounds of

* *Proceedings and Debates*, ii. 278.

loyal and dutiful subjects; a liberty which we assure ourselves so wise and just a King will not infringe, the same being our undoubted right and inheritance received from our ancestors, and without which we cannot freely debate nor clearly discern of things in question before us, nor truly inform your Majesty, wherein we have been confirmed by your Majesty's former gracious speeches and messages; we are, therefore, now again enforced humbly to beseech your Majesty to renew and allow the same, and thereby take away the doubts and scruples your Majesty's late letter to our Speaker hath brought upon us." *

The reception accorded to the members of the deputation which carried this petition to Newmarket was far better than they had expected. The King, they found, had recovered his temper, and it was only by a jest that he showed his deeply-rooted suspicion of the claims put forward by the House. "Bring stools for the ambassadors," he cried out to the attendants as soon as the members were introduced, so as to give them to understand that he looked upon the body from which they had come as asserting nothing less than a right to sovereign power.† He treated them with great familiarity, and sent them away with a long rambling letter, which he probably supposed to be sufficient to settle the question at issue.

On the 14th the King's letter was read in the House. He had expected, he said, to hear nothing but thanks for all his care to meet their wishes; but he must tell them that the clause which they had added to their petition was contrary to the facts of the case. For, whatever they might say, there could be no doubt that they had usurped upon his prerogative, and had meddled with matters beyond their reach. Their protestation that they did not intend to do this was like the protest of the

---

* *Proceedings and Debates*, ii. 289—300.
† " It seems they had a favourable reception, and the King played with them, calling for stools for the ambassadors to sit down." Chamberlain to Carleton, Dec. 15. *S. P. Dom.* cxxiv. 40. Wilson makes James say, " Here are twelve kings come to me ;" and, as usual, the joke thus spoiled has been repeated again and again by historians. James was shrewd enough to ascribe the claim of royal power to the collective body, not to individual members.

robber who took a man's purse, and then said that he did not mean to rob him. Their excuse that he had virtually invited them to discuss all questions bearing upon a war in the Palatinate was ridiculous. Because he had asked for money to keep up an army at present, and to raise another army in the spring, it no more followed that he was bound at once to declare war against Spain, and to break off the marriage treaty, than it followed that, if he borrowed money from a merchant to pay his troops, he was bound to take his advice on the conduct of the war. It was all very well for them to say that the welfare of religion and the state of the kingdom were matters not unfit for consideration in Parliament; but to allow this would be to invest them with all power on earth, and they would want nothing but the Pope's authority to give them the keys of heaven and purgatory as well.

Having thus disposed of the pretensions of the House, James proceeded to give his own account of the crisis on the Continent, an account in which, to say the least of it, there was as much truth as in that which had been accepted by the Commons. It was Frederick, he said, who, by usurping the Bohemian crown, had given too fair an excuse to the Emperor and the Pope to ill-treat the Protestants. He denied that it was true that the King of Spain was aiming at universal monarchy. As to the Spanish marriage, he would take care that the Protestant religion received no prejudice. But he was so far engaged in it, that he could not in honour go back, unless Spain refused to fulfil its obligations. It was a calumny to say that he was cold in religion. It was impossible for them to handle such high matters. Of the details of his diplomacy, and of the intentions of the various Courts of Europe they were necessarily ignorant. If he were hampered by their interference, foreign princes would cease to put any confidence in his word. They must therefore be satisfied with his engagement that he would do everything in his power to propagate his own religion, and to repress Popery. The manner and form must be left to him. If he accepted their advice, and began a hot persecution of the Catholics, they would soon hear of

Ch. VIII.
1621.
Dec. 14.

reprisals upon the Protestants abroad. But no Papist who was insolent should escape punishment, and he would do all that was in his power to prevent the education of the children of the English Catholics in foreign seminaries. Let them, therefore, betake themselves to the consideration of the bills before them. As to their privileges, he added, although he could not allow of their speaking of them as "their ancient and undoubted right and inheritance," but had rather that they had said that they were derived from the grace and permission of his ancestors and himself; "for most of them grew from precedents, which shows rather a toleration than inheritance; yet" as long as they contained themselves within the bounds of their duty, he would be as careful as any of his predecessors to protect their lawful liberties and privileges. All that they needed, therefore, was to beware how they trenched on his prerogative, so as to enforce him to retrench of their privileges, those "that would pare his prerogative and flowers of the Crown." "But of this," he concluded by saying, "we hope there shall never be cause given."*

Reception of the King's answer.

It was indeed a hard matter to alienate the loyalty of the Commons. "If the King's answer," said Phelips, "doth not strike the affection and soul of every member of this House, I know not what will." "If any one," exclaimed Digges, "be of opinion that our privileges are yet touched, let us first clear that; but my own opinion is that our privileges are not touched." It was finally resolved to take the King's answer into consideration on the following morning.

Dec. 15.
Debate upon it.

Night, however, brought to many the belief that the crisis was more serious than had been at first supposed. In the debate which ensued, indeed, all opposition to James's foreign policy was deliberately abandoned. His declaration that he would maintain the Protestant religion was singled out for special praise. Perrot's suggestion that the King should be asked for fresh guarantees against Popery, found no echo in the House. "If we had known sooner," said Phelips, "how far his Majesty had

---

* The King to the House of Commons, Dec. 11. *Proceedings and Debates*, ii. 317.

proceeded in the match of Spain, we should not, as I think, have touched that string." But if the House was of one mind in its resolution to trust the King to the end as far as actual questions of policy were concerned, it was no less unanimous in its feeling that to acknowledge his theory about their privileges would be to surrender everything which made them worthy of the name of a parliament. Henceforth they would be, as James had roughly expressed it, like merchants who were asked for money, but who had no voice in its disposal. The more moderate their wishes were, the more intolerable was the King's interference; for they did not ask him even to explain his policy to them, unless he chose, much less to become in any way responsible to them for his actions. All they wanted was that he should recognise their right to lay their opinions humbly at the foot of the throne, leaving him to deal with them as he pleased, and that he should acknowledge the right of individual members to freedom of speech, without which it would be impossible for them as a body to come to an unbiassed conclusion as to the advice which they were to tender.

Ch. VIII. 1621. Dec. 15.

The points that were thus at issue were, like so many other difficulties, a legacy bequeathed by Elizabeth to her successor. In the Middle Ages the Commons had never carried with them sufficient weight to make the sovereign think of imposing restrictions upon debates which he had no reason to fear. With one exception in the distracted times of Richard II., and another in the equally distracted times of Henry VI.,* no attack had been made upon the House's right of free speech in political affairs. The object at which the Commons were aiming was freedom from arrest upon civil process before the ordinary courts; and it was this that was finally conceded to them in the reign of Henry VIII.†

Precedents on the question.

If, however, the question of freedom of speech in affairs of state was not openly discussed at the same time, it was simply because the members of the House did not venture to enter into a contest with the self-willed

---

* Cases of Haxey and Young. Hallam. *Middle Ages* (1853), iii. 75, 102.
† 4 Henry VIII. cap. 8.

Ch. VIII.
1621.
Dec. 15.

monarch. "Tell that varlet, Gostwick," he was once heard to say of a member who had ventured to criticize the conduct of Cranmer, "that if he do not acknowledge his fault unto my Lord of Canterbury, and so reconcile himself towards him that he may become his good lord, I will sure both make him a poor Gostwick, and otherwise punish him to the example of others." The threatened member trembled and obeyed.*

Elizabeth's proceedings.

It was by Elizabeth, however, that the first serious attempt was made to restrain liberty of debate upon principle. In 1562 she contented herself with intimating her dislike of a proposal to settle the succession. In 1566 she sent a message directing the House to lay aside an address on the subject of her marriage. On this occasion, however, she thought it prudent to give way, and the debate was suffered to proceed. In 1571, she made use of fresh tactics. Instead of issuing her commands to the House itself, she ordered a member who had brought in an obnoxious bill, to refrain from attending the sittings. Again the House protested, and again the Queen gave way. But in 1588, the tide had turned. Two members were committed to the Tower, where they remained till after the dissolution, and in 1593 the same measure was dealt out to a larger number.†

To an historian, the dates of these transactions speak for themselves. In ordinary times the House had protested against the Queen's assumptions, and the protestation had not remained without effect. But in 1588, when the ports of Spain were swarming with the vessels of which the armada was to be composed, and in 1593, when the shouts of triumph were still ringing in the ears of her subjects, she had had her way. Such a view of the case, however, was not likely to be taken by James. The right to interfere had been maintained by his predecessor. His dignity would suffer if he abandoned it on any pretext whatever. The Commons, on the other hand, fell back on the necessities of their position, and the almost uninterrupted practice of earlier generations.

* Morice's *Anecdotes of Cranmer*. *Narratives of the Reformation*. Camden Society, 254.
† Hallam, *Const. Hist. of England*, i. ch. 5.

During the debates on the vote of supply, and on the petition for the execution of the recusancy laws, differences of opinion had not failed to show themselves in the House; but on the question which James had now unwisely raised, there was no difference of opinion whatever. It was no longer left to Phelips and Perrot to point out the weak points in the policy of the Crown. The staunchest supporters of the Government were of one mind with the popular majority. During the whole of the session, Wentworth and Sackville had distinguished themselves by the ability with which they had enforced the necessity of keeping on good terms with the King. Yet Wentworth and Sackville now stood forth to declare that the liberties of Parliament were the inheritance of Parliament; and so strong was the current, that even a mere courtier like Sir Henry Vane was carried away by it. He had no doubt, he said, that their liberties were their inheritance. Even Heath declared himself to be of the same opinion. But if the House was of one mind in its refusal to sacrifice its own independence, and the independence of future generations, it was no less of one mind in its desire that a quarrel with the King should, if it were still possible, be avoided. Wentworth threw out a suggestion that instead of carrying on an endless controversy with James, the House should content itself with entering a protestation upon its own journals.* Coke said that perhaps the offensive words were a mere slip of the pen, excusable at the end of so long a letter, and the explanation thus offered was thankfully accepted by Calvert. It was finally resolved that the House should go into Committee at its next sitting, in order to take its privileges into consideration.†

The following day was a Sunday, and James had thus sufficient time to consider his position calmly. From his present difficulties Williams's ready tact might even now have saved him, if he would have listened to reason. The

Ch. VIII.
1621.
Dec. 15.
Unanimity of the House.

Dec. 16.
Advice of Williams.

---

* So I understand the Notes in the Commons' Journals, and this interpretation would be placed beyond doubt if a speech, which has been preserved in Edmondes's handwriting (*S. P. Dom.* cxxiv. 22) be, as I suppose, the one which Wentworth uttered on this occasion.

† *Commons' Journals,* i. 664. *Proceedings and Debates,* ii. 330.

privileges of the House, wrote the Lord Keeper, were originally granted by the favour of princes. But they were now inherent in the persons of its members. Let his Majesty declare as much, and let him add that he had no wish to impair or diminish them, and all controversy would be at an end.*

It was too late. Far away from such counsellors as Williams and Digby, with Buckingham ever pouring poison into his ear,† James was incapable of adopting frankly the good advice which had been offered.‡ It was not in his nature to look a difficulty fairly in the face, and though he had no wish to enter upon a quarrel with the Commons, he could not make up his mind either to define distinctly the rights which he claimed, or to abandon a phraseology which, in some hazy way, he considered to contribute to his dignity.

He had heard, he wrote to Calvert, of the intention of the Commons to appoint a Committee. He was to tell them not to misspend their time. He was quite ready to give them an explanation of his words. The plain truth was that he could not endure to hear his subjects using such an anti-monarchical expression as when they called their liberties their ancient right and inheritance, without adding that they had been granted by the grace and favour of his ancestors. "But as for our intention therein," he went on to say, "God knows we never meant to deny them any lawful privileges that ever that

---

* Williams to Buckingham, Dec. 16. *Cabala*, 263.

† Gondomar to the Infanta Isabella, $\frac{\text{Dec. 22}}{\text{Jan. 1}}$. *Simancas MSS.*

‡ "Miss Aikin," says Mr. Forster (*Life of Pym*, 24, Note 2), is in error in supposing that this was written before the dispatch of the King's letter." It is not a point of any great importance, but the internal evidence is in favour of the supposition that the King, in writing to the House, had Williams's letter before his eyes. Nor is there any difficulty in supposing that this was the case, excepting that Williams refers to something which had passed in the afternoon. But the King was now at Royston, only thirty-eight miles from London, and if Williams dispatched his messenger at three o'clock the letter would be delivered at least by nine. That the King's letter was written late, there is a piece of evidence which Mr. Forster appears not to have seen. In a letter to Buckingham written on the following day, (*Harl. MSS.* 1580, fol. 120,) Calvert speaks of it as "that gracious letter which I received from his Majesty this morning," and which was therefore, without doubt, written late in the preceding evening.

House enjoyed in our predecessors' times, as we expected our said answer should have sufficiently cleared them; neither, in justice, whatever they have undoubted right unto, nor, in grace, whatever our predecessors or we have graciously permitted unto them. And therefore we made that distinction of the most part; for whatsoever liberties or privileges they enjoy by any law or statute shall be ever inviolably preserved by us; and we hope our posterity will imitate our footsteps therein. And whatsoever privileges they enjoy by long custom and uncontrolled and lawful precedents, we will likewise be as careful to preserve them, and transmit the care thereof to our posterity; neither was it any way in our mind to think of any particular point wherein we meant to disallow of their liberties, so as in justice we confess ourselves to be bound to maintain them in their rights; and in grace we are rather minded to increase than infringe any of them, if they shall so deserve at our hands."*

CH. VIII.
1621.
Dec. 16.

Evidently, James fancied that he had made every reasonable concession. He had, at Williams's suggestion, lowered his demands till he asked for nothing more than a mere polite acknowledgment of a historical fact. But he had not adopted Williams's suggestion that he should himself acknowledge that time had converted privileges which were once precarious into rights inherent in the persons of the members of the House. Through the veil of language as vague and unintelligible as his own logic, he allowed it to be seen that, though he had no intention of putting forth his powers of interference with the present House, he utterly refused to abandon the rights which he supposed himself to possess. What those rights precisely were he did not think fit to state. With every desire to make their peace with the King, the Commons were driven to ask for more than this.

No sooner, therefore, was the letter read in the House on Monday morning, than Coke rose. Rugged and irascible as he was, he had an ingrained reverence for his Sovereign, and from the very commencement of the session he had aimed at bringing about a close union be-

Dec. 17.
Coke's proposal.

---

* The King to Calvert, Dec. 16. *Proceedings and Debates*, ii. 339.

tween the King and the Houses, by the simple process of inducing both to accept the doctrines which he himself pronounced to be right. He now stood forth as a peacemaker, by giving his support to the proposition which had been made by Wentworth at the last meeting. The King's message, he said, contained an allowance of all their privileges. For they claimed nothing but what was theirs already by law, by precedent, and by Act of Parliament. What was needed now was to know precisely what those privileges were. If they were to set them down in writing, it would clear them of all these rubs.*

The next morning, just as the members were preparing to take Coke's proposal into consideration, they were met by one more letter from the King. If they wished, he said, to have the session ended at Christmas, they must go to business at once. If they did that, he would be willing to postpone the passing of the Subsidy Bill till the next session.†

Such a letter was a direct insult to the Commons. James, it seemed, was prepared to bribe them into a surrender of their privileges by relinquishing a grant of money which his ministers, speaking again and again in his name, had declared to be absolutely needed for the defence of the Palatinate. Yet such was the temper of these loyal subjects, that they refused to see what the King meant. They sent a deputation to thank him for his gracious letter, and intimating that they would prefer a simple adjournment, proceeded to appoint a sub-committee to draw up the protestation which had been suggested by Wentworth and Coke.

Those who were intrusted with the duty knew that their time was short. The next morning the Parliament might be adjourned or prorogued, and the opportunity would be gone. It was, therefore, ordered that the House should meet in the afternoon to receive the protestation.

And so by the dim candle-light in the gloom of that December afternoon, the Commons resolving, in the

---

* *Proceedings and Debates*, ii. 341.
† The King to the Speaker, Dec. 17. *Proceedings and Debates*, ii. 350.

warmth of their inflexible loyalty, to trust their King with everything but with those liberties, which, handed down to them from generations, had been sometimes infringed, but never, save in a moment of thoughtlessness, relinquished, laid claim to the rights which, for the sake of themselves and their posterity they dared not abandon.

Ch. VIII.
1621.
Dec. 18.

"The Commons now assembled in Parliament," so ran this memorable protest, "being justly occasioned thereunto, concerning sundry liberties, franchises, and privileges of Parliament, amongst others not herein mentioned, do make this protestation following:"—

The protestation.

"That the liberties, franchises, privileges, and jurisdictions of Parliament are the ancient and undoubted birthright and inheritance of the subjects of England; and that the arduous and urgent affairs concerning the King, state, and defence of the realm and of the Church of England, and the making and maintenance of laws, and redress of grievances, which daily happen within this realm, are proper subjects and matter of counsel and debate in Parliament; and that in the handling and proceeding of those businesses every member of the House hath and of right ought to have freedom of speech, to propound, treat, reason, and bring to conclusion the same:"—

"That the Commons in Parliament have like liberty and freedom to treat of those matters, in such order as in their judgments shall seem fittest, and that every such member of the said House hath like freedom from all impeachment, imprisonment, and molestation other than by the censure of the House itself, for or concerning any bill, speaking, reasoning, or declaring of any matter or matters, touching the Parliament or Parliament business; and that, if any of the said members be complained of and questioned for anything said or done in Parliament, the same is to be shewed to the King by the advice and assent of all the Commons assembled in Parliament, before the King give credence to any private information."*

In the preceding debates, it had been suggested by some speakers that the protestation should be laid before

It is entered on the journals.

---

* *Proceedings and Debates,* ii. 359.

Ch. VIII.
1621.
Dec. 18.

the King. But the House would not hear of it. There was to be no attempt to bandy words with their Sovereign any further. He might, if he pleased, consider that nothing more had been done than to fill up the details which had been left open by his own letter. They would not ask him to retract or to explain away his words. Their protestation was simply to be entered on their Journals, " there to remain as of record."*

Its value. The House by which this protestation was adopted was, as James afterwards contemptuously asserted, not a full one. Some may have stayed away through fear of offending the Court; but there may well have been others whose minds were distracted by opposing duties. For there can have been few who really expected anything else than a rupture with the King after the step which was being taken, and it was certain that a rupture with the King would cloud the prospects of an English intervention in the Palatinate. Yet much as we must sympathize with the feeling which urged these men to risk the loss of their own privileges in the defence of the Continental Protestants, it is indubitable that those who saw their first duty in the needs of their own country, chose the better part. For even if there had been more chance than there was that anything worthy of England would be effected by James upon the Continent, the cause of political liberty at home was at least as worth struggling for as the cause of such religious liberty as was represented by Frederick abroad. It is, indeed, true, that to us who look upon the dispute with the assistance of a long series of historical investigations, there is something unreal in the weapons which were used on both sides. The privileges of the House, growing up as they did in the midst of the living forces by which the constitution was moulded, and swaying backwards and forwards with the fortunes of contending parties, were certainly not acquired, as James asserted, by the mere grace and permission of the Crown. Nor can they be said, at least so far as they were claimed by the House of Commons, to be the ancient and undoubted inherit-

* *Proceedings and Debates*, ii. 360.

ance of Englishmen. There had been times when the Lower House had been far too weak to take up the prominent position to which it was now entitled. But in its spirit, at least, the assertion made by the House of Commons was true to the fullest extent. By the old constitution of England, long before the Norman Conquest placed its mark for good and for evil upon our polity, the burden of government had been shared between the kings of English race and that free assembly which was formed promiscuously, and as it were by hazard, out of all classes of the community. Nor had the change which followed upon the defeat of Hastings effected any permanent alteration. If the voice of the ordinary freeman was no longer to be heard, still the Great Council gathered round the Sovereign, ready to vindicate, sword in hand, any attempt to crush down into silence the voice of the Norman Baronage. And when once more the Commons appeared by representation on the scene, it was not at first to take the government of the nation into their hands, but to add weight by their voices either to the Crown or to the nobility in turn. That the position which they now claimed was in some respects new it is impossible to deny. They, and not the Lords, stepped forth as the representatives and the leaders of the English nation. All precedents of ancient freedom and right centred in them. It was nothing to them that their predecessors in the Plantagenet reigns had sometimes spoken with bated breath, and had been often reluctant to meddle with affairs of state. It was for them to take up the part which had been played by the barons who had resisted John, and by the earls who had resisted Edward. Here and there, it might be, their case was not without a flaw; but the spirit of the old constitution was upon their side. The rights which they demanded had been sometimes in abeyance, but had never been formally abandoned. What was more to the purpose, it was absolutely necessary that they should be vindicated if England was any longer to be a land of freemen. If these were lost, the last refuge of free speech was gone. At the will of the King the clergy could be disciplined, and the judges could be dismissed. At the will of the King, books could be suppressed, and their authors imprisoned. Within the walls of Parliament alone could words be spoken which must reach his ears, and not only did he refuse to listen to those words, but he claimed the right of punishing those by whom they were uttered. If this claim were allowed, all other liberties were for ever impossible. If it were successfully resisted, all other liberties, civil and religious, would live together with this.

To lead a nation, or to be thrust aside, is the choice set before every man who attempts to govern men. James, at his very best, and in listening to Digby's counsel he was at his very best, could never govern England. All that he could do was to set up barricades, by which to thwart and hamper the onward march of those who were stepping into his place.

The last sitting of the House on the morning of the 19th passed off quietly. The Commons were told that in compliance with their request, Parliament would be adjourned till February. They were able to separate, with a dim hope that their efforts to serve both their King and their country had not been thrown away.*

James took some days to consider what he would do. At last, when the Christmas festivities were over, he made up his mind. He would be every inch a king. No tongue should move in England but by his permission. On the 30th of December he came to Whitehall, sent for the journals of the House, and in the presence of the Council and of the Judges, tore out with his own hands the obnoxious page on which the protestation was written.† Seven years before he had presided over the operation of burning the written arguments with which the leaders of the Commons were prepared to assail his claim to levy impositions without consent of Parliament, and he had heard no more about the impositions. He hoped now that he would hear no more about liberty of speech.

After such an act as this there could hardly be any further question whether Parliament should be dissolved or no. Yet it was upon this that James affected to seek

---

* *Proceedings and Debates,* ii. 361.
† *Parliamentary History,* i. 1362.

the advice of his Council. There was, indeed, one argument against a dissolution by which the King was touched most nearly. The Subsidy Bill had not passed, and the Exchequer would be the poorer by 80,000*l*. Yet so decidedly had James declared his wishes, that no one ventured openly to oppose them. For some time the Councillors sat gloomily regarding one another in silence. At last Pembroke's voice was heard. "The King," he said, "has declared his will; it is therefore our business not to dispute but to vote." "If you wish to contradict the King," replied Buckingham, tauntingly, "you are at liberty to do so, and to give your reasons. If I could find any reasons I would do so myself, even though the King is present." Pembroke held his tongue. The assent of the Council was given in silence to a measure which they justly felt to be now inevitable. As soon as the decision had been taken, Buckingham hurried to Gondomar to congratulate him on the result.*

CH. VIII.
1621.
Dec. 30.

With a sardonic smile, in which scorn and exultation were combined, the Spaniard had been watching day by day this pitiable exhibition. "It is certain," he wrote, a day or two after the adjournment, "that the King will never summon another Parliament as long as he lives, or at least not another composed as this one was. It is the best thing that has happened in the interests of Spain and the Catholic religion since Luther began to preach heresy a hundred years ago. The King will no longer be able to succour his son-in-law, or to hinder the advance of the Catholics. It is true that this wretched people are desperately offended against him; but they are without union amongst themselves, and have neither

Gondomar's triumph.

---

* After the King had declared his intention, "ninguno se atrebió á contradizelle, mas de que el Conde de Pembrue, Conerero Mayor, gran Puritano, dijo que havia que votar no disputar, pues el Rey havia declarado su voluntad, á que el Marques de Boquinguam replicó que, si queria contradezir á la voluntad del Rey, lo hiziese, y diese razones para ello;—que él hiziera lo mismo si las hallara, aunque su Magestad se hallava ally presente; con que el Conde calló, y lo aprobó, y los demas; y luego vino el Marques a darme quenta de todo con gran gozo del subceso, y con razon, porque a sido la llave para abrir y obrar todo lo bueno que de aqui se puede esperar en servicio de Dios y de Vuestra Majestad sin oposicion, en que el Marques de Boquinguam á tenido gran parte, y merece muchas gracias."—Gondomar to Philip IV., Jan. 21/31. *Simancas MSS.* Est. 2518.

leaders nor strong places to lean upon. Besides, they are rich and live comfortably in their houses; so that it is not likely that there will be any disturbance." "The King," he wrote, a day or two later, " seems at times deeply distressed at the resolution which he has taken to leave all and to attach himself to Spain. Yet he sighs deeply, and says that if he acts otherwise these Puritan malcontents will cause him to die miserably." *

Even now James could not make up his mind to issue the proclamation dissolving Parliament. As the critical moment approached, he himself perhaps felt more keenly the importance of the step which he was about to take. Gondomar took good care to widen the breach between the King and the leaders of the House.† He had lost no opportunity of urging James to punish them for their insolence, and his efforts were unhappily crowned with success.

Coke was the first to be sent for. His position as a Councillor was regarded as a special cause for irritation. On the 27th of December he was committed close prisoner to the Tower, and Sir Robert Cotton and two other persons were commissioned to search his papers. It was given out at first that he was not questioned for anything that he had done in Parliament; but it was impossible long to keep up such a deception. In a few days two other members of the House, Phelips, who had been foremost in the onslaught upon Spain, and Mallory, of whose special offence we are ignorant, followed Coke to the Tower.‡ Pym was also ordered to place himself in confinement in his own house in London. Three months later he was allowed, on the plea of ill health, to exchange the place of his restraint for his country-house in Somersetshire.§

For Sir Dudley Digges and one or two others a punish-

* Gondomar to the Infanta Isabella, $\frac{\text{Dec. 22, 23}}{\text{Jan. 1, 2}}$, 162$\frac{1}{2}$. *Simancas MSS.* Est. 2558.

† Gondomar to Philip IV., Jan $\frac{21}{31}$, 1622. *Simancas MSS.* Est. 2518.

‡ Chamberlain to Carleton, Jan. 4, 1622. Locke to Carleton, Jan. 12. *S. P. Dom.* cxxvii. 8, 26. The three prisoners, as will be seen, were released in the following August.

§ *Council Register*, April 20, 1622.

ment was invented against which they would find it difficult to complain. They were named members of a commission which was about to be sent over to investigate the grievances of Ireland. It is true that their expenses were to be paid; but James judged rightly that they would prefer keeping Christmas amongst their families at their own expense to a compulsory tour in the depth of winter amongst the Irish bogs.

With the imprisonment of Phelips and Mallory all James's hesitation was at an end. In spite of Pembroke's renewed entreaties, the proclamation dissolving Parliament appeared on the 6th of January. That day had almost been the last of James's reign. Riding in Theobalds Park in the afternoon, his horse threw him into the New River, so that "nothing but his boots were seen." Sir Richard Young jumped into the water and pulled him out. He was well enough to ride home, was put into a warm bed, and got up the next day none the worse for the accident.

In the proclamation which was now issued, James attempted to throw the blame of what had happened on a few of the leaders of the Commons. "Some particular members," he said, "took such inordinate liberty not only to treat of our high prerogative, and of sundry things that without our special direction were no fit subjects to be treated of in Parliament, but also to speak with less respect of foreign princes, our allies, than was fit for any subject to do of any anointed king though in enmity and hostility with us." They had disputed on "words and syllables of" his letters, and they had claimed, "in ambiguous and general words," privileges which derogated from the rights of the Crown, possessed not only in the times of earlier kings, "but in the blessed reign of" his "late predecessor, that renowned Queen Elizabeth."*

This at least must be conceded to James, that the rights which he claimed were rights of which, as he said, "he found his crown actually possessed." Unfortunately for him, he could not see that the legacy which Elizabeth

* Mead to Stuteville, Jan. 10. Meddus to Mead, Jan. 11. *Harl. MSS.* 389, fol. 127, 129.

Cʜ. VIII.
1622.
January.
Digby's policy.

had left him was one of a nature to do him more harm than good.

Of all to whom the dissolution of Parliament brought anxiety and grief, there was not one who was more competent to estimate the ruinous consequences of James's blunder than Digby. When he first returned from the Continent he soon discovered that his great designs would find no favour with Buckingham. One day, it is said, as he was speaking in the Council of the courtesy which he had received from the Emperor, the favourite expressed his astonishment that he had repaid them so ill. "When I receive courtesy as a private man," answered Digby, with that quiet dignity which never left him, "I strive to repay it by personal services; but, as a man of honour, I will never repay them at my master's cost." *

One attempt he had made to avert the catastrophe which he dreaded. On the 14th of December he had entreated the Lords to demand a conference with the Commons, with the object of pleading once more the imminence of the danger in Germany. If money, he said, had been sent liberally to the Palatinate, immediately upon his return, the whole face of affairs would have been changed. The Princes of the late Union, the Elector of Saxony, the Kings of Denmark and Sweden would have rallied to the standard set up in opposition to the encroachments of the Emperor. In the request thus urged the Lords at once acquiesced. But it was too late. The Houses were adjourned before Digby could find an opportunity of stating his case to the Lower House.†

His vexation.

The dissolution of Parliament was a crushing blow to Digby. He at least knew better than to cherish the delusion which had imposed upon the feeble mind of James. In conversation with those friends in whose secresy he could confide, his language was most desponding. It had pleased the King, he said, to quarrel with

* Tillière's Despatch, Nov. $\frac{15}{25}$, 1621. *Raumer*, ii. 319.

† *Parliamentary History*, i. 1365. Gondomar to the Infanta Isabella, $\frac{\text{Dec. 22}}{\text{Jan. 1}}$, 1621. *Simancas MSS.* Est. 2558.

his subjects, and not even to argue with them on the offers which they made with the intention of doing him all the service that he could desire. If he had listened to his Parliament, he might have laid down the law in Europe. As it was, he would have to obey the King of Spain; and he must not be surprised if, now that he had no other arms in his hands than supplications, his diplomacy turned out as badly at Madrid as it had done in Vienna. To James himself Digby conveyed the same lesson in a more courtly form. As long as there had been any doubt, he said, of the turn which affairs would take, he had recommended that England should remain on good terms with the enemies of Spain. Now, however, he must tell him that he would ruin himself if he did not place himself altogether in the hands of the Spanish Government.*

<small>Ch. VIII. 1622. January.</small>

Whatever face he might put upon the matter in public, Digby knew that he had failed, and that the victory had been won by his Spanish rival. So signal, indeed, was his defeat, that, but for the credit which he subsequently acquired by his resistance to the arrogance of an unpopular favourite, his name would probably have passed out of the memory of all but a few diligent students of the bye-paths of history. Yet if the worth of a statesman be judged rather by that which he is than by that which he is permitted by circumstances to accomplish, it is absurd to think of a man like Gondomar as entering into competition with him for a moment. For, if it be the true test of statesmanship to know the wants of the age, and to remove gently and firmly the impediments which stand in the way of their satisfaction, then are all Gondomar's momentary triumphs beneath contempt. With great knowledge of human nature, and with a transcendent power of playing upon the hopes and passions of his instruments, he gained from fortune the fatal boon of success. He wrested the solution of the great European problem from the hands of the King of England to transfer it to the hands of his own master.

<small>Comparison between Digby and Gondomar.</small>

* Gondomar to the Infanta Isabella, $\frac{\text{Dec. 22}}{\text{Jan. 1}}$, 1621. *Simancas MSS.* Est. 2558.

Ch. VIII.
1622.
January.

But that was all. In the unreal atmosphere in which he lived, in his utter blindness, not merely to the religious strength of Protestantism, but to the physical forces which it could command, he did his best to urge on the Spanish Government and nation to an impossible enterprise—to the conversion, half by force and half by cajolery, of all that remained Protestant in Europe. With what results to Spain the effort was attended it is unnecessary to say.

To Digby's clear eye and resolute will such a blunder was impossible. Weighing each element in the European crisis at its just value, detecting the strength and the weakness alike of friend and foe at a glance with singular impartiality, he turned neither to the right nor to the left from love of popular sympathy or from the hope of royal favour. No statesman of his age held opinions which were so little in harmony with the theories which prevailed in the House of Commons. No minister of James refused so utterly to compromise his dignity by stooping to flatter Buckingham. And now, in 1621, the chance had been offered him, a chance which was never to return, of settling European society upon a permanent basis, whilst it was still unexhausted by the prolonged agony of the impending conflict. By fixing a territorial limitation to the two religions, he would have removed the causes of religious war. That he would have placed his own country at the head of European nations is indubitable. But he would have done more than that. He would have woven closely the bonds which still attached the hearts of the people to the throne of the Stuarts. James's love of peace, and the warlike zeal of the Lower House, would equally have served his purpose; for he would have taught the Sovereign and his subjects to work together for a common end, and to learn to bear each with the other's weakness, and to understand each the other's strength.

It may be that in any case all this would have been but a dream. Even Digby could hardly have hoped to bend all the opposing elements of the strife to his will. It was, perhaps, not merely James's petulant vanity which ruined his hopes. But at least he deserved success as few have ever done. When England looks around her for guides in the thorny path of foreign policy, it would be well for her to think for a moment of the forgotten statesman who, in more propitious times, would have graven his name upon the tablets of history in lines as firm as any which have been drawn by the Pitts and the Cannings whose deeds have become amongst us as household words.

CHAPTER IX.

THE CONFERENCE AT BRUSSELS.

<small>Ch. IX.
1622.
January.
The new year.</small>

THE new year opened under unpropitious auspices. There were few who did not acknowledge with a sigh that the times were evil, and that reformation was slow in coming. "I am ready to depart," said the dying Sir Henry Saville, "the rather that having lived in good times, I foresee worse."* The dissolution of Parliament fell like a blight upon all who had fancied that England was to be an instrument for good in Europe. Buckingham's passionate self-will, it seemed, was to rule supreme, so far at least as he was anything more than an unsuspecting tool in the hands of Gondomar.

<small>Gondomar's plan for breaking the blockade of the Flemish ports.</small>

One success alone was wanting to crown the diplomatic career of the Spanish Ambassador. He had, as everyone but James knew, made active interference in the Palatinate impossible. It would be a master-stroke of policy if he could embroil England with the Republic of the Netherlands. He had watched with pleasure the preparations which James was making in defence of what he called his honour in the narrow seas, and had constantly urged him to lose no time in breaking the Dutch blockade of the Flemish harbours. Nor was he content with trusting to the uncertain activity of James. Some English merchants, careless of public opinion, had proposed to allow him to hire from them eight or ten ships ready manned, to be employed in opening the ports. James at once gave his consent; and Gondomar, to whom anything was acceptable which would bring Englishmen into collision with the Dutch, threw himself heartily into the scheme. But he had forgotten to ask the consent of the English people. Not a sailor would

* Chamberlain to Carleton, Feb. 16, 1622. *S. P. Dom.* cxxvii. 101.

agree to serve on board his vessels, and in the end he was compelled to abandon the design.*

Yet, if he was baffled here, he had still reason to hope that his work would be done by James. The Dutch Commissioners, whose coming had been so long expected, arrived at last in November. After some delay, a negotiation was opened for the restitution of the value of the English goods which had been seized in the East. The Commissioners professed their readiness to make good the losses of the East India Company. But as the articles in question had been brought to Europe by Dutch vessels, they claimed to make a deduction of 130*l.* per last for freight. By the English negotiators the justice of the demand was acknowledged in principle; but its amount was pronounced to be exorbitant: 25*l.*, or at most 28*l.*, it was said, was the usual payment. They were however ready, for the sake of peace, to go as far as 35*l.* The Dutch refused to abate a penny of their original demand, and, for the time at least, the negotiations were broken off.†

That James should have been deeply annoyed by the exorbitant pretensions of the Dutch, was only natural. But it showed but little perception of the relative value of the objects for which he was striving, that he should, at this critical moment, have revived the project for a joint attack by England and Spain upon the territories of the Republic. Yet there can be no doubt that before the month of January was at an end, Digby had received instructions to bring forward such a proposal at Madrid as soon as the marriage treaty was concluded.‡

It would however be long before that period arrived;

---

* Philip IV. to the Infanta Isabella, $\frac{\text{Nov. 23}}{\text{Dec. 3}}$, 1621. *Brussels MSS.* Salvetti's *News-Letters*, $\frac{\text{Jan. 25}}{\text{Feb. 4}}$, Feb. $\frac{}{11}$. Gondomar to Philip IV., Jan. $\frac{21}{31}$. *Simancas MSS.* Est. 2518. The Dutch Commissioners to the States General, Feb. $\frac{11}{21}$. *Add. MSS.* 17,677 K, fol. 192.

† The Dutch Commissioners to the States General, Feb. $\frac{11}{21}$. *Add. MSS.* 17,677 K, fol. 192. Council Register, Feb. 9.

‡ The fourth point of his instructions, wrote Gondomar to Philip IV. on the $\frac{21 \cdot t}{31 st}$ of January, "es tratar con V. Mag.ᵈ de la reducion de las provincias de Olanda, y hazer para esto muy estrecha liga offensiva y deffensiva, dandole V. Mag.ᵈ algo á este Rey desta empeñada." The

Ch. IX.
1622.
February.
Attempt to seize two Dutch ships.

and in the meanwhile more legitimate efforts might be made to obtain redress. In the midst of these disputes, news came that two Dutch ships returning from the East had been seen passing Plymouth. Orders were accordingly given to Oxford, who had been appointed to the command of the fleet in the narrow seas, and who had hurried down to Dover to take the command, charging him to do his best to intercept them. But Oxford was either unlucky, or had no heart in the business, and the vessels found their way safely into a Dutch port.*

Capture of a third ship.

March.

Unsuccessful as the attempt had been, it was not without effect upon the Commissioners. They had no wish to see their East India ships running the gauntlet of a hostile squadron, and they wrote to the Hague, asking permission to yield the point at issue. Their request was at once granted. No sooner had the answer arrived, than they went through the form of demanding an audience of James, and of assuring him that they withdrew their pretensions in deference to his superior wisdom. They were just in time. Scarcely had the concession been made, when news arrived that a Dutch East Indiaman had been captured in the Channel by two ships of the royal navy. Fortunately, James was now again in a good humour. He told the Commissioners that their ship had been taken by mistake; that it should be immediately restored; that he had recalled the Earl of Oxford; and that he wished for nothing better than to be on good terms with the Republic.†

Oxford recalled.

The negotiations with the Dutch were at once resumed. The recall of Oxford, regarded by all who hated Spain as a signal that James would desist from any further intention of coming to blows with the Dutch,

statement is corroborated by frequent cautious allusions in Digby's despatches, and by a paper of instructions to him and to Buckingham, which will be mentioned in its proper place.

* Salvetti's News-Letters, Feb. $\frac{1}{11}$, $\frac{15}{25}$.

† The Dutch Commissioners to the States General, Feb. $\frac{11}{21}$, March $\frac{19}{29}$, $\frac{\text{March } 29}{\text{April } 8}$. Add. MSS. 17,677 K, fol. 192, 195, 204. Calvert to Carleton, Feb. 7, March 6, 24, April 3. Carleton to Calvert, March 9. S. P. Holland. Salvetti's News-Letter, March $\frac{15}{25}$.

was received with enthusiastic demonstrations of joy; and so deeply had the hatred of Spain penetrated, that amongst those whose faces were beaming with delight were to be seen merchants who had suffered considerably from the unprovoked attacks of the Dutch in the East.*

And yet it was from no friendly feeling towards the Netherlands that James had decided upon recalling Oxford. Gondomar had long been pleading for the removal of a commander whom he had represented as a great Puritan, and a pensioner of Holland.

Oxford was probably not a pensioner of Holland, and it is certain that, excepting in the political sense of the word, he was not a Puritan. But he detested Spain from the bottom of his heart, and he, at least, knew well to whose influence his recall was to be ascribed. He was not a man to measure his words. England, he was heard to say, was altogether ruined. They had a King who had placed his ecclesiastical supremacy in the hands of the Pope, and his temporal supremacy in the hands of the King of Spain. James was now nothing better than Philip's viceroy. This violent language was soon reported at Whitehall. The Earl was immediately sent to the Tower, and James talked of bringing him to trial for high treason, and of cutting off his head.†

Whilst he was still at large, Oxford had found an opportunity of showing that his contempt for the King extended to the favourite. Early in the preceding year it had been rumoured that a bargain had been struck, in accordance with which a young gentleman of the bedchamber named Wray, who had managed to secure the good will of Buckingham, was to marry Elizabeth Norris, the daughter and heiress of the newly created Earl of Berkshire.‡ Time passed away, and a new arrangement was made. The young lady was now to be the wife of Christopher Villiers, whose previous wooing had ended in grievous disappointment. The match appeared to be the more advantageous, as her father had

---

* Salvetti's *News-Letter*, March 22 / April 1.
† Gondomar to Philip IV., May 6/16. *Simancas MSS.* Est. 2603.
‡ Vol. i. p. 408.

Ch. IX.
1622.
March.

recently committed suicide, and had left her in actual possession of his estates. But, as usual, the very name of Buckingham's brother as a suitor was received with every mark of disapprobation by the lady to whom his addresses were paid. Elizabeth Norris, it would seem, had not cared much for Wray; but anything was better than to become the wife of Christopher Villiers. One morning she slipped away from the house of the Earl of Montgomery, under whose charge she was living, and before any one had time to interfere, was married to her last year's lover. Oxford, it was said, was privy to the plot; and it was in his house that the young couple took refuge as soon as the wedding was over.

James was very angry; but all that he could do was to turn Wray out of his place in the bedchamber, and to leave the unlucky wooer to console himself as best he might. Another member of the great house, Sir William Fielding, the plain country gentleman, who had had the good luck to marry Buckingham's sister in the days of her poverty, had been raised to the peerage as Baron Fielding, in 1620. He was now to be known by the higher title of Viscount Fielding, and had lately, by Cranfield's resignation, become Master of the Wardrobe.

1621.
Bacon at Gorhambury.

October.
Question of the sale of York House.

Whilst the doors of the peerage were thus flung widely open to Buckingham's relations, the favourite continued to measure all public business by the scale of his personal interests and antipathies. Not long after Bacon's return to Gorhambury, in the preceding summer, he had received an intimation that his great patron was desirous of purchasing the remainder of his lease of York House. The proposal, Buckingham may well have thought, was not likely to meet with a refusal; for the house was too large to be any longer suitable for Bacon in his straitened circumstances, and any other man in his position would have been only too glad to rid himself of the incumbrance. But Bacon, as was so often the case when any question of expenditure was mooted, allowed his feelings to get the better of his reason. The house had been his father's; there he had been born, and there he

* Chamberlain to Carleton, March 30. Locke to Carleton, March 30. *S. P. Dom.* cxxviii. 96, 97.

wished to die. His wife liked the place, and he could not turn her out of doors.* Buckingham was highly incensed at the rebuff; yet he did not break out openly into a passion. He preferred putting himself ostentatiously forward as Bacon's protector. At his intercession the heavy parliamentary fine of 40,000*l.* was made over to trustees of Bacon's own nomination.† A few days later, the virtual remission of the fine was followed by a general pardon, which, though the penalties imposed by Parliament were excepted from its operation, left him free from any further molestation on account of irregularities committed during his official career;‡ and this pardon he obtained in spite of the opposition of Williams, who was naturally anxious, on the eve of the reassembling of Parliament, not to give offence to the House of Commons.§

Buckingham probably still hoped to carry his point by a mixture of friendliness and severity. He knew well that the clause in Bacon's sentence which prohibited him from coming within twelve miles of the Court was most distasteful to him. At Gorhambury the cold blasts of winter were far too keen for his enfeebled constitution, and he was now earnestly pleading for the extension of a temporary permission to visit London which had been recently accorded to him. In this, however, Buckingham, as he soon found, would give him no help. He would not even see him. Bacon might keep the lease of York House in his hands, if he pleased, but he should not live under its roof.‖

For the time, indeed, there were special reasons for refusing Bacon's request. Whilst Parliament was sitting, James might well fear that the late Chancellor's presence in London would "be a general distaste to the whole

---

* Buckingham to Bacon, Oct. 1, 1621. Bacon to Lennox, Jan. 30 (?), 1622. *Works,* ed. Montagu, xiii. 33 ; xii. 420.
† Grant to Hutton and others, Oct. 14, 1621. *Patent Rolls,* 19 Jac. I., Part 16.
‡ Pardon, Oct. 17, 1621. *Patent Rolls,* 19 Jac. I., Part 16.
§ Williams to Bacon, Oct. 18. Bacon to Williams, Oct. 18. Bacon to Buckingham, Oct. 18. Buckingham to Bacon, Oct. 20. *Bacon's Works,* ed. Montagu, xii. 412; xiii. 34. Williams to Buckingham, Oct. 27. *Cabala,* 263.
‖ Bacon to Buckingham, Oct. 1621. *Bacon's Works,* ed. Montagu, xii. 272.

Ch. IX.
1622.
January.

The bargain for York House.

February.

March.

state."* But with the dissolution, the objection fell to the ground, without affecting Buckingham's resolution in the slightest degree.

Luckily for Bacon, an opportunity presented itself, which enabled him, in some measure, to soothe the wounded vanity of the favourite. Lennox wrote to ask for the house. Bacon replied that he was determined not to part with it to any one; and that if there were no other obstacle in the way, he owed it to Buckingham not to dispose of it to any other than himself.†

The compliment was well aimed. Buckingham wrote at once to say that he should be sorry to prevent him from dealing as he pleased with his own property. As soon as it was possible, he would move his Majesty to relax the restriction upon his place of abode. As for himself, he was already provided with another house.‡

Still, however, Bacon was left without the permission to return to London, which he so anxiously expected. At last, after some weeks, he was told that he might come as far as Highgate. Sackville, who was acting in the matter as Bacon's friend, expostulated with Buckingham on the restriction. "Sir Edward," was the answer, "however you play a good friend's part for my Lord St. Alban, yet I must tell you I have not been well used by him." It finally came out that Cranfield wanted the house, and that Buckingham intended him to have it. "If York House were gone," wrote Sackville to Bacon, "the town were yours." Bacon bowed to necessity, gave up the lease, and obtained in return permission to come to London as soon as he pleased.§ It was not to Cranfield, however, that the house was surrendered. Buckingham did not lose much time in getting it into his own possession, and he continued to occupy it during the remainder

---

* Buckingham to Bacon, Oct. *Bacon's Works*, ed. Montagu, xiii. 33.
† Lennox to Bacon, Jan. 29. Bacon to Lennox, Jan. 30 (?). *Bacon's Works*, ed. Montagu, xii. 419, 420.
‡ Buckingham to Bacon, Feb. 4 (?). Sackville to Bacon, March 11 (?), (not May 11, as printed). *Bacon's Works*, ed. Montagu, xii. 35, 431.
§ Meautys to Bacon, March 10 (?). Sackville to Bacon, March 10 (?). Bacon to Cranfield, March 12. Meautys to Bacon, March. Bacon to Buckingham, March 20. *Bacon's Works*, ed. Montagu, xii. 425, 431, 427; xiii. 36.

of his life. Already, however, before the bargain was struck, the favourite had taken up his quarters at Wallingford House, which he had purchased from Lord Wallingford.* He was now again on thoroughly good terms with the Howards. Suffolk's second son was created Viscount Andover; and, after an imprisonment of six years, Somerset and his wife were released from the Tower, and allowed to come forth into a world which had almost forgotten their former greatness.†

Ch. IX. 1622. March. Buckingham's reconciliation with the Howards.

There was something more than a personal reconciliation in these advances made by the favourite to the family which, three years before, he had crushed down with an unsparing hand. The Howards were all, more or less, in close connection with the Catholics, and in his vexation with the House of Commons and with the Court of the exiled Frederick, Buckingham with his usual impetuosity was, for the time being, a zealous protector of the Catholics. Nor was this all. For those who were admitted to his confidence were well aware that it was by no means impossible that before many months elapsed he would himself be a declared member of the Church of Rome. For the moment he was peculiarly susceptible to domestic influences. His wife's conversion, in spite of the eloquence of Williams, had been merely nominal, and his mother had recently been giving ear to the persuasions of a Jesuit, who was generally known by the assumed name of Fisher.‡ Lady Buckingham, in truth, was made of the very stuff to be easily moulded by a Jesuit's hand. Without the slightest wish to become either wiser or better, she was looking about for a religion to make her comfortable, and in an infallible Church which would save her the trouble of thinking she found exactly what she wanted.

At what time this selfish and unprincipled woman first gave ear to Fisher's soothing strains is uncertain: but on the 3rd of January a comedy was played which we shall hardly be wrong in ascribing to the King's remonstrances.

Confirmation of Buckingham and his family.

---

* Chamberlain to Carleton, Jan. 19. *S. P. Dom.* cxxvii. 35. Indenture between Wallingford and Buckingham, May 27. *Close Rolls,* 20 Jac. I., Part 27. The price given was 3000*l.*
† Commission to Sir A. Apsley, Jan. 17. *S. P. Grant Book,* p. 340.
‡ His real name was Percy.

Ch. IX.
1622.
January.

Accompanied by two or three courtiers, by his wife and mother, by his sister, Lady Fielding, and his sister-in-law, Lady Purbeck, by one kinswoman whom Lady Buckingham had just married to Serjeant Ashley, and by another kinswoman whom she was anxious to marry to any one who might present himself with a long purse, Buckingham went in state to dine with the Bishop of London. Before dinner was served, the whole party betook themselves to the chapel, to receive the rite of confirmation.* Such a demonstration could have but little influence on the waverers, and, as a last resource it was suggested that it would be well to invite the Jesuit to discuss with some Protestant divine the main questions at issue between the Churches. Dr. White, one of the Royal chaplains, was accordingly selected for the purpose, and conferences were held on two several occasions, in the presence of the King, the Lord Keeper, the Marquis, the Marchioness, and the Countess of Buckingham. James himself entered into the strife, and produced nine questions, which he called upon the Jesuit to answer.

Conference between Fisher and White.

As far as Buckingham's mother was concerned, it was soon evident that any discussion of particular doctrines would be absolutely thrown away. She considered, she said, "that it was not for her, or any other unlearned person, to take upon them to judge of particulars." She wished to depend "upon the judgment of the true Church." All that she required was to be informed in which direction to look for the "continual, infallible, visible Church."†

May 24.
Conference between Fisher and Laud.

To the issue thus taken, Laud was called upon to reply instead of White. It was not without reason that, in after years, he recurred with satisfaction to the part which he took on this occasion.‡ For a moment we may well forget the harsh and rugged disciplinarian in the argument which he that day poured forth. He pointed those who were seeking for truth to the scriptures and creeds. Beyond these, he would admit of no infallibility,

---

* Chamberlain to Carleton, Jan. 4. *S. P. Dom.* cxxvii. 8.
† Conference with Fisher. *Laud's Works*, ii. 2. See also Preface, ix.—xii.
‡ Conference with Fisher. *Laud's Works*, ii. 359.

of no irreversible decision. To him declarations of general councils were like Acts of Parliament. They were to be accepted for the sake of order, but they were to be always open to further investigation, always liable to be repealed, if proved by argument to be faulty. Upon Lady Buckingham such reasoning was utterly thrown away. Could she be saved in the Church of Rome? was the question which rose to her lips as the disputants closed the discussion. Laud could not say that it was impossible. Could she be saved, she then demanded, in the Protestant faith. "Upon my soul," replied Fisher, "there is but one saving faith, and that is the Roman."* Such an answer was decisive with one who was seeking not for truth but for safety. For some time she continued to conceal her resolution, and even received the Sacrament publicly in the Royal Chapel; but before the summer was at an end, she announced that she had changed her religion, and was in consequence ordered to abstain from presenting herself at Court.†

<small>Ch. IX.
1622.
May.</small>

Buckingham himself was more tractable. Thirty years later, if he had lived so long, he might perhaps have followed his mother's example. But he had not yet reached the age when men of his stamp become seriously alarmed for the safety of that soul, the purity of which they have done so little to guard. His choice was soon made. He professed his satisfaction with Laud's arguments. He even went so far as to offer to lay bare before him the secrets of his heart, and to look to him on all occasions of difficulty for that assistance which in Catholic lands a penitent is accustomed to expect from his confessor.‡ No doubt amidst much bad advice, Laud may frequently have whispered good counsel into the favourite's ear; but of what avail would be the wisest admonitions so long as the man remained the same giddy, self-seeking, passionate upstart that he had ever been?

<small>Laud and Buckingham.</small>

The religious opinions of Buckingham and his mother were of no importance to any one but themselves: but Laud's reasoning cannot be safely passed over by any

<small>Laud's opinions on religious liberty.</small>

---

* Conference with Fisher. *Laud's Works,* ii. 359.
† Conference with Fisher. *Laud's Works,* ii. 413. Chamberlain to Carleton, June 8, 22, Sept. 25. *S. P. Dom.* cxxxi. 24, 53, cxxxii. 24.
‡ Laud's Diary, June 15, 16. *Works,* iii. 139.

one who desires to trace the progress of opinion. It is true that he had no thought of conceding to individuals the right to promulgate independent doctrines, and that the liberty of which he was the champion was not likely to be of much practical use. The notion that truth would be advanced by men who, for the sake of order, were ready to acquiesce in the decrees of the last general council, and who were contented to urge their objections in a quiet, respectful way, in the mere hope that some day or other another general council, better informed than the last, would meet to adopt their suggestions, was an idea which could only have commended itself to one who was better acquainted with books than with men. From the fierce revolt against falsehood and wrong doing which arms the champions of truth against the overlying weight of prejudice, and from the dust and din which accompany the hammers clanging upon the anvil on which the pure gold of a new thought is beaten out into forms of usefulness and beauty, Laud instinctively recoiled. Yet it was no light thing that one to whom disorder was so hateful, should have raised his voice so strenuously against the doctrine which declares that it is the duty of the individual to submit his conscience without question to the authoritative decrees of an ecclesiastical organization.

In no better way can justice be done to Laud's intellectual position, than by comparing it with that which had been assumed by a man whose actions were, about this time, attracting considerable attention in England. Marco Antonio De Dominis, was a native of Dalmatia. He had been educated by the Jesuits at Padua; but his active mind was little suited for the unreasoning submission required by the statutes of his order, and he quickly turned aside in search of a more independent life. His abilities and industry soon brought him preferment, and in 1602, he became Archbishop of Spalatro, and primate of his native province. Three years afterwards, when the dispute between Paul V. and the Venetian Republic broke out, he took the warmest interest in the resistance made to the Pope's attack upon the criminal jurisdiction of the state over the clergy. With the miserable compromise by which Venice virtually surrendered its rights, he was, no doubt, deeply dissatisfied, for it was not in his nature to be swayed by mere considerations of policy. Plunging deep into the foundations of the controversy, he set himself to master the history and the constitution of the early church; and, after long and anxious study, he came to the conclusion that successive Popes had been guilty not merely of encroaching upon the temporal jurisdiction of the states of Europe, but of the far more heinous crime of adding new and unwarrantable articles to the creed of the Church. Before him, as he pursued his investigations, arose that splendid vision which has dazzled the eyes of so many well-meaning and pious inquirers, the vision of a Church without either a visible head or internal disputes, of a Church governed by an aristocracy of virtuous and learned prelates, welcoming free discussion, but never coming to a wrong conclusion, and repressing the vagaries of error, not by the dungeon or the stake, but by the solemn force of unanswerable reasoning.

At last, in 1616, De Dominis had prepared for publication at least a part of the great work in which his principles were to be set forth; but he soon found that he could never hope to obtain a hearing in any corner of Catholic Europe. In England he knew that an episcopal Church was to be found, which, at least in its external organization, answered to the ideal which he had formed; and he had learned, from his conversations with Wotton's chaplain, the large-hearted and gentle Bedell, to hope that he would there find a welcome for his ideas. He therefore made up his mind to seek a refuge in England.

It was in no spirit of humility that the Archbishop of Spalatro set foot upon our shores. To an abundant measure of learning, he added all a scholar's vanity and ignorance of the world. Where popes and churches had missed the road, he alone saw clearly. To him England was no more than the fulcrum which would enable him to overturn the whole system of Papal religion. Let his book once be published, and Christendom, recognising its errors, would bow its head before his teaching. Once more would be seen upon earth the spectacle of an undivided Church, in which the Pope would find no place.

As far as his personal reception was concerned, his highest expectations can hardly fail to have been satisfied. Never before had an archbishop sought refuge in England after forswearing the errors of the Church of Rome. Crowds flocked round him, eager to catch a sight of the illustrious convert. Court was paid to him by the highest in the land. Prelates and peers vied in offering him costly gifts. The Archbishop of Canterbury received him into his house till he was otherwise provided for. James gave him a hearty welcome, and presented him to the Mastership of the Savoy and the Deanery of Windsor, two preferments which brought him in an income of 400*l*. a-year.*

In a short time, however, the popular enthusiasm died away. De Dominis was at liberty to prosecute his studies without impediment, and to publish successive volumes amidst the compliments of the learned ; but it was in vain that he looked for the slightest sign of readiness on the part either of the Church of England or of the Church of Rome to submit to his arbitration. Equally displeasing to his personal vanity was the dissatisfaction which was aroused by his ignorance of English habits. His income, though it was quite sufficient in those days to maintain an unmarried man in luxury, did not equal his desires. One day, therefore, he took the unusual course of presenting himself to a living in the gift of the Dean and Chapter of Windsor. At another time he attempted to take advantage of a flaw in a lease, so as to get a tenant's house into his own hands. He next made the discovery that the leases of the Savoy lands were legally forfeited to the King, and he proposed to James to proceed against the tenants, and to restore the institution to its original purpose as a hospital for travellers. James, who knew well enough what the English feeling was on the subject of ecclesiastical property in lay hands, refused

---

* Goodman's Statement (*Court of King James*, i. 340) is confirmed by the allegation of De Dominis himself, in a letter to the King (Feb. 16, 1622. *S. P. Dom.* cxxviii. 103, xiii.), and must therefore be accepted in preference to Hacket's calculation of 800*l*.

to listen to him for an instant. "You are a stranger here," was his curt reply; "leave things as you found them."

Such stories as these, told with considerable exaggeration,* were certain to detract from whatever popularity he yet retained. At last he fancied that an opportunity had arrived of gaining the position to which he believed himself entitled. He heard that the Archbishopric of York was vacant, and he hastened down to Theobalds to beg James to give him the second dignity in the English Church. To his mortification, he was told that Archbishop Mathews was still living, and that no foreigner would be permitted to occupy an English bishopric. De Dominis was not long in learning that his failure had been such as to bring upon him special ridicule; for it was well known to everyone but himself that the old archbishop was accustomed from time to time to spread rumours of his own death, in order to enjoy the excitement caused amongst the crowd of suitors who were eager to step into his place.

Bitterly as these disappointments must have been felt by a man so convinced of his own importance, there were causes of a very different nature at work to render his position irksome. The English Church was by no means that which his imagination had depicted. Upon his arrival he had been warmly welcomed by Abbot and by those amongst the clergy who shared his admiration for the Calvinistic theology. When they heard him denouncing the Romish Babylon, and comparing the Pope to Pharaoh, they were ready to applaud him to the echo; but with these men he had nothing in common excepting his dislike of the Papal supremacy. His ideas were, in the main, those of Laud; yet between him and Laud there was a great gulf which neither could pass over. Both believed that the Church of England and the Church of Rome were branches of one Catholic Church. Both looked hopefully to the power of argument, and appealed to the decision of a general council. But Laud, the child

His views of the Church of England.

---

* The original story about the Savoy, for instance, is evidently the one which I have adopted from Goodman (i. 344). In Fuller it assumes a much worse character.

of the English Reformation, was contented if he could persuade himself that he was living in a society which held the doctrines current in the primitive Church, whilst his desire for the reunion of a general council was little more than a pious wish entertained because it was necessary for the completion of his intellectual conception, but not likely to exercise any practical effect upon his conduct. In the mind of De Dominis, the pupil of the Jesuits, the necessity of a visible Church unity was foremost. And so, in despair of effecting his object in England, he once more turned his eyes to Rome. Paul V. was dead, and the new Pope, Gregory XV., had been his friend in youth. Perhaps he might be induced to reform the Church, and to allow free discussion on controverted points. He might even be brought to acknowledge that the Churches of Rome and England were already portions of one undivided Church. It would then be easy for him to give his approbation to the Book of Common Prayer, and to explain satisfactorily those practices which were most repulsive to Protestants.

In the midst of these meditations he heard that Gregory had expressed his readiness to welcome him at Rome. He at once made up his mind to accept the offer. On the 16th of January, 1622, he announced his intention to the King. James was exceedingly angry, especially as a rumour had sprung up that De Dominis was to go on a special mission from himself, in order to reconcile England with the Pope. Yet he contented himself with sending to inquire the motives of his conduct. He himself refused to see him, and, after allowing him time to make any explanations he wished, ordered him to leave the kingdom within twenty days.*

Before he left England he received a visit from Bishop Morton, who did what he could to dissuade him from his

---

* The account given by Fuller (v. 504—530) is evidently prejudiced. See testimony of Cosin (*De Transubstantiatione*, cap 2, § 7), and Goodman as cited above. His own words are the best indication of his character, and the narrative of the transactions immediately preceding his departure (S. P. Dom. cxxviii. 103) is especially useful as indicative of his opinions. That Gondomar had anything to do with the Archbishop's return to Rome, is very doubtful. It is hardly compatable with the narrative above referred to.

design. "Do you think," said De Dominis, "that the Pope and the Cardinals are devils, so that they cannot be converted?" "No," replied Morton; "neither do I think that you are God, to be able to convert them."*

On his return, the stray sheep was welcomed back into the fold with every mark of respect. At Brussels he was received by the Papal Nuncio into the bosom of the Church. In his journey through Italy his vanity, for some time unused to adulation, was tickled by the long train of horses and carriages placed at his disposal by the Pope, and by the friendly greetings which met him on every side.†

Again the scene changed. Within a few months after his arrival at Rome, the death of Gregory left him without a protector. The new Pope handed him over to the tender mercies of the Inquisition. The man who had started from England buoyant with hope and confidence was thrown into prison, and condemned to the uncongenial task of refuting his own arguments. On the whole, he appears to have behaved with honesty. Where his own opinions had changed he made no difficulty in stating, for the use of others, the considerations by which he had been influenced; but nothing would induce him to sign the decrees of the Council of Trent, or to surrender his favourite doctrine of the essential unity of the Churches of Rome and England. After his death he was declared guilty of heresy, and his body was burned by order of the Inquisition.‡

Such a man was not likely to meet with anything but obloquy. Men who could agree upon nothing else, combined to speak of him as being utterly without any religious principles whatever. Two years after he left England, Sir Edward Sackville visited him in his dark and confined prison. "My Lord of Spalatro," he said tauntingly, "you have a dark lodging; it was not so with you in England. There you had at Windsor as good a prospect by land as was in all the country; and at the

---

* Hacket's *Life of Williams*, 102.
† *Dalrymple*, 145.
‡ Hacket, 103. Cosin, *De Transubstantiatione*, cap. 2, § 7.

Savoy you had the best prospect upon the water that was in all the city." "I have forgot those things," was the calm reply; "here I can best contemplate the Kingdom of Heaven." "Do you think," said Sackville, after he had left the prison, to the Rector of the English College, "that this man is employed in the contemplation of heaven?" "I think nothing less," answered the priest, "for he was a malcontent knave when he fled from us, a railing knave while he lived with you, and a motly particoloured knave now he is come again."*

His character.

More pertinent still was an answer given by Andrewes, soon after De Dominis arrived in England, to some one who asked whether he were a Protestant or no. "I know not," said the Bishop, "but he is a detestant of divers opinions of the Church of Rome." † Ignorant how small a part of religious life is to be found in the logical scaffolding on which it rests, and how thoroughly masses of men are moulded by popular feeling, he thought that it was possible by softening asperities of opinion, and by explaining away the harshness of doctrine, to form a common belief which all Christian men might agree to hold. As Rome and England alternately repelled his presumption, his mind was filled with detestation at their refusal to settle down upon the Procrustean bed which his own imagination had fashioned. His vacillations and inconsistencies were more apparent than real. In the main, his opinions remained unchanged, and he died impressed with the same delusion which had led him astray in life.

Question of toleration.

The fate of De Dominis is a standing warning to those dreamers who count a union between the Churches of Rome and of England to be amongst the possibilities of the future; but that such a dream should have been entertained at all was one amongst many symptoms that a new mode of regarding religious questions was taking possession of the minds of men. The age did not need a restoration of unity either by explaining away the distinctive differences of the two creeds, or by the forcible conversion or extermination of the members of either.

---

* Hacket, 104.
† Bacon's Apothegms. *Works*, vii. 159.

But it did need a change of system which would enable Catholic and Protestant to live together in peace, and to trust to argument and not to the sword for the extension of their opinions.

Such a change was yet far distant; but much had been already done to limit the difficulties of the future. In spite of what was passing in Germany, one half of Europe was no longer banded together in confederacy against the other. Catholic states and Protestant states had found it possible to exist side by side without mutual recrimination. The question now was narrowed to the amelioration of the position of religious minorities in the various countries. Of still greater importance was the change in the point of view from which such difficulties were regarded. Every year there was an increase in the number of those who, if they desired the suppression of the adverse religion, desired it not because its opinions were untrue, but because its existence was incompatible with civil government.

It was in this light that the position of the English Catholics had been viewed by Pym. If only they could keep aloof a few years from political combinations which were distasteful to the English nation, and, above all, if they could resist the compromising assistance of the Spanish Ambassador, they might look forward with assurance to a speedy alleviation of the pressure which weighed so heavily upon them.

The condition of the French Protestants, far better in appearance, was in reality less hopeful than that of the English Catholics. By the Edict of Nantes, liberty of conscience was accorded to them in every part of France. Liberty of worship was permitted in the houses of 3500 gentlemen, and in a large number of towns, whilst the right of maintaining Protestant garrisons in certain strong places was conceded to them as a security against the encroachments of the Catholic nobility.

The last clause was perhaps necessary, but it was full of danger for the future; for it offered a strong temptation to the Protestant body to form themselves into an independent community, and to throw themselves in the way of the organization of the monarchy. At last, in the

Ch. IX.
1621.

Quarrel between Herbert and Luynes.

Doncaster's mission.

Oct. 17.

spring of 1621, a civil war, long expected, broke out once more. Whilst the most trusted leaders of the Reformed Churches were proclaiming the necessity of submission to the Crown, in spite of present grievances and future fears, the Protestants of the towns, with their clergy at their head, had persisted in maintaining, in the face of the Government, the right of holding an illegal assembly at Rochelle. They had sadly miscalculated their power. Taking the King with him, Luynes swept down upon Protestant France. One town after another fell before him, and he was in the full career of conquest when Sir Edward Herbert presented himself with an offer of mediation in his master's name. He was treated with studied insolence. "What," said Luynes, "has the King your master to do with our actions? Why does he meddle with our affairs?" After some altercation, Luynes burst out into a passion. "By God," he said, "if you were not an ambassador I would treat you in another fashion." Herbert, who was one of the most noted duellists in Europe, laid his hand upon his sword. "If I am an ambassador," he replied, "I am also a gentleman, and there is that here which would make you an answer." After such a scene as this, James had hardly any choice but to recall his ambassador.* It would have been well if he had also desisted from any further attempt to mediate in the quarrel, and had opened his eyes to the fact that by rousing the national susceptibilities of the French, he was doing the greatest possible injury to the cause which he meant to serve.

Such, however, was not James's opinion. Laying all the blame upon Herbert's personal conduct, he despatched Doncaster upon a special mission to plead the cause of peace. Personally the selection was a good one. Always a warm partizan of France, Doncaster was more likely than anyone else to obtain a courteous answer to his propositions. Yet it was probably fortunate for him that, shortly after his arrival in France, he was prevented by an attack of fever from demanding an audience. When at last he was sufficiently recovered to carry on the negotia-

* *Life of Lord Herbert of Cherbury.* Herbert to the King, July, 31. Doncaster to the King, Aug. 1, 1621. *S. P. France.*

tion, the Royal forces had been checked in their career of victory. The old Huguenot spirit had been roused at last, and the southern Protestants were standing at bay behind the walls of Montauban. Doncaster was accordingly told that the King was ready to show mercy to the rebels, and to give assurance that no attack should be made upon their religious liberties, if they would only consent to make submission to him as their Sovereign.*

<small>Ch. IX. 1621.</small>

Five days after this reply was given the siege of Montauban was raised. In less than six weeks Luynes was dead, and whatever hopes of peace had been entertained were suddenly blasted. Lewis fell for the time into the hands of the party which was bent upon continuing the war, and Doncaster, finding his efforts thwarted on every side, returned to England to give an account of his failure.

<small>Death of Luynes.</small>

<small>1622. Doncaster's return.</small>

Yet even this amount of humiliation was not sufficient for James. Doncaster, he resolved, must go back, to be flouted yet more by the French. It was, indeed, a thankless task. By the French ministers he was received with all courtesy; but he was plainly told that it did not stand with their master's honour to allow a foreign sovereign to mediate in their internal disputes. On the 22nd of June, therefore, he took his leave without having effected anything whatever.† Sir Edward Herbert was ordered to go back to his post, the death of Luynes having removed the obstacle in the way of his career.

<small>April. He goes back to France.</small>

<small>June. He returns a second time.</small>

There still remained a practical question awaiting the decision of James. During the winter, commissioners from Rochelle had been received by him with civility. He had given them permission to export provisions and munitions of war, and he had authorised the Bishops to order a collection in all the churches in aid of the French Protestants who had taken refuge in England.‡ But the Rochellese were not content with assistance of this moderate kind. The Channel swarmed with their pri-

<small>Deputies from Rochelle.</small>

---

* Doncaster to Calvert, Oct. 26, 1621. *S. P. France.*
† Doncaster to Calvert, June 26, 1622. *S. P. France.*
‡ The Deputies to Calvert, $\frac{\text{Aug. 24}}{\text{Sept. 3}}$. Doncaster to Calvert, Oct. 26. Order in council, Oct. 12. *S. P. France.*

N 2

vateers, and every week some fresh prize belonging to French owners was brought into the English ports. For some time the French Ambassador, Tillieres, remonstrated in vain. The Council received his complaints, and promised that redress should be given.* Orders were issued to seize the prizes which had been brought into English harbours, and to restore them to their owners. Such orders, however, were not always executed with punctuality. The sympathies of the inhabitants of the ports were all on the side of the privateers, and it not unfrequently happened that a Rochellese captain was able to sell his booty at Plymouth or Dover, before the magistrates chose to open their eyes to his presence.†

Affairs of Germany. By the mere force of inertness James had come to the wise conclusion that it would be better not to interfere in France. Unhappily it needed very different qualities to bring him to a right judgment with respect to the war in Germany. For in no sense could the German quarrel be considered as a merely internal dispute. Not only were the various states of which the Empire was composed possessed of rights which almost elevated them to the position of independent sovereignties, but the interference of Spain had raised a question which all European governments were interested in solving.

Interference and non-interference. Yet, after all, different as might be the mode in which a wise statesman would have dealt with the two countries, his principles of action would have been identical. For in both France and Germany it would be necessary to avoid the slightest appearance of compromising civil order by the protection given to religious liberty. In France interference was unwise because it would only serve to perpetuate anarchy. In Germany it would be wise in so far as it could be made use of to make anarchy impossible.

Digby's policy. It was this thought by which Digby's policy had been inspired. What difficulties he had met with from Maxi-

---

* Remonstrances of Tillieres. *S. P. France*, 1621, 1622, *passim*.
† Mayor of Rye to Calvert, May 1. The Council to Zouch, May 4. Vivian to the Council, May 17. Fulnetby to Zouch, May 17. Petition of R. Dure, May (?). The Council to Zouch, July 11. *S. P. Dom.* cxxx. 1, 16, 91, 92, 134, cxxxii. 28.

milian's ambition and from Frederick's selfwill have been already told. When he returned to England in the autumn his game was all but ruined. One chance yet remained. If James, putting himself at the head of the nation, could force Spain and the League to respect his power, and could at the same time compel his son-in-law to offer solid guarantees that he would from henceforth refrain from breaking the peace of the Empire, all might yet be well.

With the dissolution of Parliament this last chance was thrown away. Mere words would not go far to reassure the peaceful populations of Germany, to inspire Ferdinand with the belief that his enemy could be safely entrusted with power, or to crush in Frederick's bosom that ill-timed elation which the slightest breath of success was certain to quicken into life.

How completely his cause was lost was the last thing which James was likely to perceive. "I will govern," he said triumphantly, "according to the good of the commonweal, but not according to the common will."* Yet, as he looked upon Germany, he might well have despaired; everything there was in confusion. Mansfeld had hardly reached the Palatinate, when Tilly and the Bavarians, following hard upon his heels, planted themselves securely in that fertile plain which stretches from the forest-clad slopes of the Odenwald to the banks of the Rhine. Mansfeld was in want of money and supplies, but he had never far to look for plunder. The Bishopric of Strasburg, and the Austrian lands in Alsace, provided quarters for his famished troops.† Next spring, he gave out, he would not stand alone. The air was full of rumours. The Margrave of Baden, it was said, was arming, and would soon have more than 20,000 men under arms. The Duke of Wirtemberg would bring 8000 into the field. Christian of Brunswick, with 5000 horse, was harrying the lands of the Bishop of Paderborn, and would swoop down upon the Palatinate as soon as the fine weather appeared.‡ Such numbers

---

* Meade to Stuteville, Feb. 2. *Harl. MSS.* 389, fol. 140.
† Vere to Carleton, Dec. 20, 1621. *S. P. Holland.*
‡ Vere to Carleton, Dec. 27, 1621. *S. P. Holland.*

would far exceed any force that Tilly could bring against them, and James was easily persuaded that no great effort on his part was needed.

Yet at least he would do something. Immediately upon the adjournment of the Houses, he had announced his intention of sending 8000 foot, and 1600 horse, to take part in the war. The Commons, he thought, would be willing to grant the necessary supplies, when they met again in February.*

The dissolution followed, and all hope of a Parliamentary grant was laid aside. By a fresh stretch of the prerogative the imposition on wine was doubled, and an extraordinary payment of ninepence in the pound was laid upon all commodities imported by aliens.† Recourse, too, was once more had to a Benevolence. Wealthy men were again summoned, as they had been summoned in 1614, from every part of England, and were ordered, in the presence of the Council, to name the sum at which they were willing to be rated. The justices of assize, the magistrates of the counties and the boroughs, were ordered to push on the contribution, and to certify to the Government the names of those who were hanging back. One nobleman, Lord Say, who in the late Parliament had begun his long career of pertinacious opposition to arbitrary power, was committed to the Fleet for daring to advise his neighbours to keep their money in their pockets.‡ Yet the result of the appeal was far from equalling the expectations which had been formed. At Court it had been supposed that 200,000*l*. would be obtained with ease.§ Nine months passed away, and little more than 77,000*l*. had been paid into the Exchequer, a sum which, in the course of the winter, was raised to 88,000*l*., and which, even then, scarcely exceeded

* Nethersole to Carleton, Dec. 20. *S. P. Holland.* Digby to Frederick, Dec. 30. *Collectio Camerariana,* xlviii. 92. Royal Library, Munich.

† Council Register, Jan. 12. Locke to Carleton, Jan. 23. *S. P. Dom.* cxxvii. 40.

‡ Council Register, June 6. Salvetti's *News-Letter,* June 7. Southampton, on the other hand, urged on the payment. Southampton to the Council, May 5. *S. P. Dom.* cxxx. 19.

§ Council Register, Feb. 4, March 31. Chamberlain to Carleton, Jan. 19. Locke to Carleton, Feb. 16, March 2. *S. P. Dom.* cxxvii. 35, 102; cxxviii. 9. Salvetti's *News-Letters,* Jan. $\frac{18}{28}$, $\frac{\text{Jan. 25}}{\text{Feb. 4}}$, Feb. $\frac{15}{25}$, $\frac{\text{Feb. 26}}{\text{March 8}}$.

in amount the single subsidy which the Commons had been ready to vote for the mere maintenance of Mansfeld's army for two or three months.*

Nor was it only amongst those who were called upon to pay heavily towards the Benevolence that maledictions were pronounced against James. Here and there angry words bubbling up to the surface testified to the suppressed feeling of indignation which was seething below. A year before, the prevailing dissatisfaction had vented itself upon Gondomar. It was now directed against the King. In January, "a servant to one Mr. Byng, a counsellor," was stretched upon the rack "for saying that there would be a rebellion."† In February, "a simple fellow" was condemned to a traitor's death for declaring that, though he was ready to spill his blood for the King, if he maintained religion, he would be the first to cut his throat if he failed therein.‡ A week later, James was driven to the necessity of summoning the bishops, in order to protest in their presence that he was sincere in his desire to maintain the established religion. §

Nowhere is the change, which had in three short years come over the popular feeling, portrayed more vividly than in a coarse and scurrilous libel which, under the name of "Tom Tell-Truth," was passed in manuscript from hand to hand. James, said the writer, might, if he pleased, style himself Defender of the Faith; but it was the faith of the Papists, not the true faith, that was defended by him. He might be head of the Church, but it was of the Church dormant, certainly not of the Church militant or triumphant. For one health drunk to the King there were ten glasses emptied to the success of his daughter and her husband. It was well known that he allowed Gondomar to become master of the secrets of his cabinet with the help of a golden key. Whilst he was calmly looking on, Spain had become undisputed master of the West Indies, whilst the Dutch, "the very pedlars whom we ourselves set up for our own use," had

---

* Receipt Books of the Exchequer.
† Locke to Carleton, Jan. 12. *S. P. Dom.* cxxvii. 136.
‡ J. Nicholas to E. Nicholas, Feb. 26. *S. P. Dom.* cxxvii. 133.
§ Inclosure dated March 8, in a letter from Mead to Stuteville, March 16. *Harl. MSS.* 389, fol. 157.

Ch. IX.
1622.

become masters of the East Indies. The Protestants of the Continent had been left without a protector. The Deputies of Rochelle had been neglected. Nothing had been done for the Palatinate. The Papists were supreme in Europe. In the meanwhile, the writer broadly hinted, James was frittering away his time, not merely in reckless jollity, but even in the indulgence of the most hideous vices of which human nature in its utmost depravity is capable.

Such was the explanation which men were now ready to give to that which they had hitherto passed by as mere folly. The coarseness of James's language, the rudeness of his merriment, the indecency of his doting fondness for Buckingham, were readily interpreted in the worst sense by men who were only too glad to believe the foulest charges against the Sovereign whom they despised.*

April. Knight's sermon.

Less startling from the nature of the utterance, but even more alarming, on account of the quarter from which the attack proceeded, was a sermon preached on the 14th of April, in the very midst of the loyal University of Oxford. The preacher, a young man named Knight, took for his subject the persecutions of Elijah by Ahab, and declared it to be his opinion that it was "lawful for subjects when harassed on the score of religion to take arms against their Prince in their own defence." When called to account by the Vice-Chancellor for the language which he had used, he replied that he had derived his opinions from a book written by Pareus, the Professor of Divinity at Heidelberg, and that he had also on his side the still higher authority of his Majesty, who, if he was rightly informed, was about to assist the French Protestants against their Sovereign. Knight was accordingly sent up to London, where he repeated his defence before the Council. He was by them committed to the Gatehouse, where he remained for two years, and was at last released on the score of his

* Tillières' Letters given by Raumer are frequently appealed to as conveying evidence against James; but the letter of Jan. $\frac{14}{24}$, shows that no fact could be proved against him.

youth at the intercession of Williams, whose voice was always raised on the side of mercy.

James next proceeded, as he fancied, to strike at the root of the evil. The libraries and the booksellers' shops were searched for Pareus's Commentaries on the Epistle to the Romans. One heap of the books thus collected was consumed at Oxford. At Cambridge and in London the curiosity of the multitude was amused by similar bonfires. A few days later the obnoxious opinions were solemnly repudiated by the University of Oxford. For the future, none were to be allowed to take a degree who refused to swear "that they do not only at present condemn and detest the proposition above mentioned, but that they shall always continue of the same opinion."*

In the original work of Pareus, the passage from which the condemned propositions were taken, followed upon a long and sustained argument against the Pope's jurisdiction over princes. Such an argument, however, if left to stand alone, would have exposed the writer to a crushing retort. "What!" some Jesuit might well have answered, "do you mean to say that kings and princes are to be subjected to no control whatever? May they change the laws and religion of their subjects at their pleasure? May they commit murder with impunity?" The answer of Pareus to this objection was singularly moderate. If a king, he said, should with his own hands make an attack like a common robber upon one of his subjects, he who is so treated may lawfully defend his own person from injury. Against religious and political tyranny only two remedies may be adopted. The clergy may point out to a notorious tyrant that he is breaking the laws of God and man, and, if he refuses to change his conduct, may cut him off by excommunication from the communion of the Church. Neither the clergy, however, nor private persons may draw the sword against their Prince. But subordinate magistrates may take such measures as are necessary to defend the country against horrible oppression, and if security cannot other-

---

* Collier's *Ecclesiastical History*, vii. 434. Hacket, 88. Wood, *Hist. et Ant. Univ. Ox.* i. 327.

Ch. IX.
1622.
June.

Interference with Oxford studies.

Terms offered and accepted by Frederick.

wise be obtained, may even resist and depose their Sovereign.

Such language, translated into the equivalent phrases of modern times, would not now be considered very appalling. The liberty of the press and the legality of national resistance have, in England at least, long been counted amongst the common-places of politics. But in the beginning of the seventeenth century, they had a dangerous sound, and it is no wonder that the King, who had just dismissed his Parliament in anger, and was scheming for a marriage which would, in all probability, give him a Roman Catholic grandson, should have been unwilling to listen to such reasoning with patience. If the University of Oxford had contented itself with answering the argument of Pareus, it would have been well enough. But to present four propositions in a garbled form* to her students, and to require them to swear that they would never adopt them at any future time, was an act as injudicious as it was tyrannical.

If men were to swear that they would disbelieve the arguments of Pareus, it was, perhaps, as well that they should not read them. James, accordingly, wrote to the Vice-Chancellor, when he first heard of Knight's sermon, directing him to take care, " that those who designed to make divinity their profession, should chiefly apply themselves to the study of the Holy Scriptures, of the Councils and Fathers, and the ancient schoolmen ; but, as for the moderns, whether Jesuits or Puritans, they should wholly decline reading their works."†

If James could have succeeded in putting an end to the war in Germany, he would have had little need to trouble himself with the attacks to libellers or reasoners at home. As far as he was concerned, indeed, there were no signs of

---

* The first proposition as condemned at Oxford is as follows :—" Episcopi et pastores magistratus suos impios aut injustos, si contumaces sint, possunt et debent de consensu Ecclesiæ Satanæ tradere donec resipiscant." Wood, *Hist. et Ant. Univ. Ox.* i. 327. In Pareus's *Commentary* 1349, it stands thus :—Episcopi et pastores magistratibus suis impiis aut injustis possunt ac debent resistere, non vi aut gladio, sed verbo Dei, arguendo eorum notoriam impietatem aut injustitiam, et ad officium juxta verbum Dei et juxta leges faciendum eos cohortando, contumaces vero de consensu Ecclesiæ etiam Satanæ tradendo, donec resipiscant.

† Extract from the King's letter, April 24. Collier's *Eccl. Hist.* vii. 435.

despondency. In the preceding November he had at last laid before Frederick categorically the terms on which he was willing to render him assistance. "The Count Palatine," he had demanded, "shall, for himself and his son, wholly renounce and acquit all pretence of right and claim unto the Crown of Bohemia, and the incorporated countries thereof. He shall from henceforward yield all constant due devotion unto the Imperial Majesty, as do other obedient Princes, Electors of the Empire. He shall, upon his knee, crave pardon of the Imperial Majesty. He shall not hereafter, any manner of way, either unfittingly carry or demean himself towards the Imperial Majesty, or disturb his kingdoms or countries. He shall upon reasonable conditions reconcile himself with other his neighbour princes and states of the Empire, and hold good friendship with them; and shall really do all other like things as is above contained, and that shall be reasonable or necessary."*

The terms thus laid down contained, indeed, all that the most impartial arbitrator could suggest. On the one hand, they denied to Frederick the right of private war, and they placed him in a position of inferiority towards the Chief of the Empire, to which the Princes of Germany had long been unaccustomed. On the other hand, they placed a decided barrier to the encroachments of the Roman Catholic Church upon Protestant soil. But unhappily it was something more than wise suggestions that were needed to quench the flames of the German conflagration. In his heart, Frederick would be contented with nothing short of the position of an independent sovereign. In his heart, Ferdinand would be contented with nothing short of the predominance of his Church. It was true that Frederick, not without allowing his dissatisfaction to be plainly seen, accepted his father-in-law's terms,† and that the Emperor expressed his determination to send an ambassador to Brussels, in order to treat with James for a suspension of arms, to be followed by negotiations for a general pacification.‡

* The King to Ferdinand II., Nov. 12, 1621. *Cabala*, 239.
† Frederick to the King, Nov. 25. *S. P. Germany.*
‡ Ferdinand II. to the King, Jan. 4, 1627. *Cabala*, 241. Ferdinand II. to the Infanta Isabella, Jan. 3. *Brussels MSS.*

Ch. IX.
1622.
The intercepted despatches.

Unhappily James was encouraged to take too favourable a view of the prospects of his mediation, by the sight of a bundle of despatches from Vienna to Madrid, which had not many weeks before fallen into the hands of Mansfeld. From these letters it appeared, indeed, that there could be no longer the slightest doubt of Ferdinand's resolution to transfer the Electorate. But it also appeared that he anticipated the resistance of the Spanish Government to his scheme. James was, therefore, right in calculating on the help which it was possible for him to derive from Spain. Where he was wrong was in supposing that he could count upon Spanish aid one moment after he had ceased to inspire the Court of Madrid with a belief in his strength.

With the assurances which reached him from Spain, therefore, James was perfectly content. What mattered it, he thought, if Frederick and Ferdinand should prove recalcitrant, if only Philip were on his side. He accordingly ordered Weston to repair to Brussels as soon as the conference was opened by the Infanta, in order to settle the conditions for the suspension of arms. At the same time he fancied that he was giving a great proof of his vigour by authorising Vere to take the command of the royal troops in the Palatinate, as soon as he should be able to find money to pay them.*

Frederick's troops.

In truth, it was the want of money, far more than the want of men, which was likely to be the stumbling block in his path. For Frederick's troops, even if they would, could not now carry on the war otherwise than as brigands. Without any basis of operations other than the ruined and exhausted Palatinate—without money and without supplies—what could they do but throw themselves in search of livelihood upon one Catholic district after another? War in those days was terrible enough, at its best, and deeds of blood and shame weigh heavily upon the memory of the Catholic armies. But neither Spaniards nor Bavarians were forced to order their movements in accordance with the sheer necessity of plundering. They were tolerably paid, and their commissariat was, at least to some extent, provided for. To their

* Commission to Vere, Feb. 16. *S. P. Germany.*

leaders war was not a necessity, and if the order for recall was given, there would be no difficulty in enforcing its execution.

Of the sentiments which prevailed in Mansfeld's camp, we happen to possess evidence in a letter which was at this time written by one of his officers. "The Bishopric of Spires," he says, "is ours. We are plundering at our ease. Our general does not wish for a treaty, or for peace. He laughs at the enemy. All his thoughts are fixed upon the collection of money, of soldiers, and of provisions. When the spring comes, he hopes to have fifty thousand men under arms. With this object he employs the strangest means of levying money. The Union has promised to bring into the field a force equal to ours. Knyphausen and the nobility of the Palatinate are proposing, with the aid of the Landgrave of Hesse, to attack the territories of the priests, and to pillage them thoroughly before they retire. By this diversion the enemy will be compelled to divide his forces. If we come across a great square cap, we will take care to make it pay a wonderful ransom." The letter ended by pointing out the ease with which the territories of Spires, Worms, Mentz, and Alsace, might be cut up into principalities for the conquerors.*

Whilst Mansfeld was thus plundering the lands upon the Upper Rhine, another adventurer was making havoc of the Westphalian Bishoprics. Christian, the brother of the Duke of Brunswick-Wolfenbüttel, was the nephew of the late Queen Anne. At the age of seventeen he had been appointed Bishop or Administrator of Halberstadt, by one of those arrangements which were frequently employed by the heads of Protestant Houses, whenever they wished to provide for their relations at the expense of the ecclesiastical domains in their neighbourhood. The title assumed by him was purely nominal, and there was nothing episcopal about him, excepting his claim to enjoy the revenues of the see—a claim which, as it was not under the guarantee of the Peace of Augsburg, he would hardly be able to maintain in the face of a decisive victory

* I have omitted portions of the letter. The whole will be found in Villermont. *Tilly,* i. 160.

of the Imperialists in the Palatinate. As the cousin of the exiled Queen of Bohemia, he affected to put himself forward as her special champion. He carried in his cap a glove, which she had once dropped, under which he bore the motto, "All for God and her." Against the ecclesiastical principalities he vowed a special hatred. Wherever he came the churches were sacked, and the silver images were coined into pieces bearing the inscription, "God's friend, and the enemy of the priests." Fire and desolation marked his track, and the hovel of the peasant and the home of the citizen were regarded as lawful prey by the bands of ruffians whose commander counted it as the worst of crimes to live under a bishop's rule.

Such were the commanders into whose hands the fortunes of German Protestantism had fallen. Ferdinand and Maximilian were not so far wrong when they spoke of peace as hopeless, excepting by a vigorous prosecution of the war. "I understand," wrote Vere, in language which might well have startled James out of the fool's paradise in which he was living, "by a chief officer of the Count Mansfeld, that he believes that there will be a truce, and is so much troubled at it, that he says it is intended to undo him, and is, therefore, resolved withal not to lay down his arms."* About the same time a letter reached James from Mansfeld himself. He was ready, he said, to be included in the negotiations for peace; but it must be remembered that his master owed him no less than four million florins, and that there was not the slightest chance that he would ever be able to pay him. He therefore expected that Haguenau, an Austrian town in Alsace, which he had lately taken, should be made over to him in full possession.†

It was evident that the time had passed when James could interfere with advantage. With his exchequer filled with parliamentary subsidies, he might have exercised some influence over Mansfeld and Christian. But who was the King of England, that his mere word should check the career of these needy adventurers? The deadly

---

* Vere to Calvert, March 15. *S. P. Germany.*
† Mansfeld to the King, March. *S. P. Germany.* Misplaced amongst the papers of 1623.

combat between anarchy and despotism must be fought out now to its bitter end. James's attempts to carry on war were as futile as his attempts at diplomatic success. Already the ten thousand men whom he had proposed to levy for the Palatinate, were melting into air. Chichester, indeed, whose splendid services in Ireland, deserved a better fate, had been dragged from his retirement, and ordered to betake himself to Heidelberg, that he might exercise a general supervision over his master's interests.* It was with no goodwill that he prepared for the bootless errand. He would rather, he said, give 500*l.* to the Benevolence than go.† But his excuses were not admitted. The 20th of March, the day on which Digby left London for Madrid, was fixed for him to set out, carrying with him the sum which would be needed for the supply of the intended army. The 20th of March arrived, but Chichester was still detained. The Benevolence came in slowly, and the money was not to be had.‡ To hasten the payment, recourse was had to harsh and extreme measures. Several persons who had refused to contribute were told that they must make up their minds to accompany Chichester to the Palatinate. Amongst these, an aged citizen, who had formerly been a cheesemonger, was informed that his services would be needed to supply the army with cheese.§ Yet so little did the threats of the Council effect, that March and April passed away before Chichester was enabled to set out.

On the 3rd of April, Ferdinand's ambassador, the Count of Schwarzenberg, arrived in England.∥ James was overjoyed at seeing him. The Palatinate, he declared, would soon be restored. Spain was putting forth all its influence in favour of peace; and, in spite of the Duke of Bavaria, the Emperor would be forced to submit.¶

Cn. IX.
1622.
March.

April.
Schwarzenberg in England.

---

* Locke to Carleton, Jan. 19. *S. P. Dom.* cxxvii. 36.
† Locke to Carleton, Feb. 4. *S. P. Dom.* cxxvii. 67.
‡ Salvetti's *News-Letters*, Feb. $\frac{15}{25}$, March $\frac{8}{18}$. Calvert to Carleton, March 24. *S. P. Holland.*
§ Meade to Stuteville, Feb. 2. *Harl. MSS.* 389, fol. 110. Chamberlain to Carleton, March 30. *S. P. Dom.* cxxviii. 96.
∥ Calvert to Carleton, April 3. *S. P. Holland.*
¶ Salvetti's *News-Letter*, April $\frac{5}{15}$.

Ch. IX.
1622.

Winniffe's sermon.

English regiments for Spain.

Schwarzenberg's immediate mission was however one of mere compliment. He had to inform James that after the suspension of arms had been concluded, the Emperor would open negotiations for a general peace at Brussels, Cologne, or Frankfort. After remaining a few days in London, he proceeded to Brussels in order to take part in the conference which was soon to commence.

Yet, short as his visit was, he was not left in ignorance of the light in which his master's proceedings were popularly regarded in England. Dr. Winniffe, one of the Prince's chaplains, preaching on the "lusts which war against the soul," took the opportunity of illustrating the attack of the devil upon the soul, by the attack of Spinola upon the Palatinate. The bold preacher was at once committed to the Tower, from which he was soon afterwards set free at Schwarzenberg's request.*

So well satisfied was James with the position of affairs, that he ostentatiously granted permission to Gondomar to levy one regiment in England, and another in Scotland, for the Spanish service, under the command of Lord Vaux and the Earl of Argyll. So popular was the employment amongst the Catholics, that in a few days the whole number required was ready to cross the seas.†

Both at this time, and at a later period, it was the settled conviction of the English people that Ferdinand was not in earnest in his desire for peace, and if it is meant by this, that he had no desire for such a peace as Frederick would have been willing to submit to, the charge is undoubtedly correct. He had made up his mind to the transference of the Electorate as an act to which he was bound by this promise to Maximilian, and by his duty to the interests of the Catholic Church. He therefore took good care to warn the Infanta that she was by no means to allow any question upon this point to be raised at Brussels. But, as far as the restitution of Frederick's hereditary dominions went, he had, in all

---

* —— to Mead, April 12. *Harl. MSS.* 389, fol. 168.
† Locke to Carleton, April 6, 20. *S. P. Dom.* cxxix. 7, 50. Salvetti's *News-Letters,* April $\frac{5}{15}, \frac{12}{22}$.

probability, not come to any definite conclusion. As far as it is possible to discover his intentions from his private correspondence, it would seem that if Frederick had been willing to submit to his terms, to engage to give guarantees that he would abstain from hostilities for the future, and to accept the subordinate position which the old constitutional theory allotted to the princes of the Empire, he would willingly have given way. But on the other hand, in common with all reasonable men, he had a strong opinion that Frederick would do nothing of the sort, and he sometimes expressed himself as if he was resolved upon continuing the war whatever might happen.

<small>Ch. IX.
1622.
March.</small>

In the meanwhile, however, Mansfeld was playing his old game in Alsace. With all gravity he was negotiating with Raville, an emissary from Brussels, an engagement by which he promised to change sides for the consideration of a large sum of money for his troops, and of high honours for himself; purposing all the while, as he informed Vere, "to keep off that side from further levies by the hope they have of his turning unto them."*

<small>Mansfeld's intrigues.</small>

From Mansfeld's mode of carrying on war, Vere at least expected but little good. "His means," he wrote, on the 1st of April, "grow here so short, that he can subsist very little longer in these parts. Whither he will direct himself is to himself, I believe, most uncertain; but most conceive it must be where he may find least opposition."†

<small>Military prospects.</small>

It was a dangerous policy in the face of the enemy whom he was now to confront. Tilly's soldiers, indeed, were not the orderly and inoffensive warriors which it has pleased partizan writers to represent them. They, too, knew full well how to burn villages, and to cut the throats of innocent peasants. But in comparison with the hordes who followed Mansfeld's banner, their discipline was perfect. Tolerably paid, and with supplies from the rear at their disposal, the Bavarian army was under no necessity of roaming about in search of plunder. Nor was its commander a man who was likely to march "where there was least opposition." Thoroughly con-

<small>Tilly in the Palatinate.</small>

---

* Vere to Calvert, March 15. *S. P. Germany.*
† Vere to Calvert, April 1. *S. P. Germany.*

VOL. II. O

Ch. IX.
1622.
April.

vinced of the goodness of the cause for which he was fighting, Tilly united to those military qualities which raised him to a place amongst the most consummate generals of the age a rare single-mindedness and honesty of purpose. Believing that the cause of order and peace was entrusted to his keeping, he had devoted his life to the suppression of that anarchy which was in his eyes the worst of crimes. Yet if his bearing was firm, he did not underrate the strength of his opponents.

His military position.

To the south of the post which he had taken up between the Odenwald and the Rhine, lay the two strong fortresses of Heidelberg and Mannheim, whilst the western side of the great river was guarded by Frankenthal. Behind these positions, Mansfeld could operate in security, having the bishopric of Spires, and the Austrian lands in Alsace at his mercy. Beyond the Main again, Christian of Brunswick, who had been repulsed in the winter, was again gathering his forces, and hanging upon his rear. If the states of the dissolved Union should listen, as was by no means unlikely, to Mansfeld's voice, —if Baden, Wirtemberg, Hesse-Cassel, and the Protestant towns should spring to arms, the forces which could be brought against him would be overwhelming.* To make matters worse, he was by no means certain of the cordial co-operation of his Spanish allies. Ever since the prospect of a suspension of arms had been opened, Cordova, acting no doubt by instructions from Brussels, had been turning a deaf ear to the demands for aid which had been addressed to him by the Bavarian commander.

Moral and political question at issue.

Against these dangers, Tilly was able to oppose his own military skill, a well-disciplined army, and the advantages of a central position. But all this would have availed him nothing, but for the moral superiority of his cause. Nowhere in Germany could the slightest enthusiasm for Frederick be discovered. In the Protestant States men might fear the consequences of a Catholic victory, but they feared disorder and organized plunder

* See the calculations of Maximilian in his letter to the Emperor, Jan. $\frac{16}{26}$. Hurter. *Gesch. Ferdinands II.* ix. 633.

more. The authority which Ferdinand would exercise might be a stern one; the religion which would follow in its train might be utterly unacceptable. But the immediate danger did not lie there. The pretensions of Frederick to meddle with Bohemia had never yet been publicly renounced, and it was felt that those pretensions carried with them the germs of an interminable war. Protestants who had long grumbled against the interference of the Emperor in religious disputes, shrunk from giving support to an opposition which proclaimed no law but that of the strongest, and to a prince who had collected round his standard a band of hungry adventurers, who were utterly unable to support themselves except by pillaging their neighbours. The price which Germany was called upon to pay for ridding itself of the Imperial authority, may well have seemed too high. From henceforth, if Frederick were victorious, every petty prince would know that if he wished for honour and distinction, he had nothing to do but to gather round him a band of hardy ruffians, and to live at his ease amidst the despair of plundered citizens, and the agony of burning towns.

CH. IX.
1622.
April.

Yet to all this, Frederick was as blind as ever. He could not see that the one hope for his cause lay in the possibility of disentangling the prospects of Protestantism from the progress of anarchy. If he could do this, then would a mightier Union than that which had sunk ingloriously the year before, arise to support him. Then would the great Protestant States of the North stand forward as one man to defend the cause of religious independence and political order. But with a war such as that which was being waged by Mansfeld and Christian, they would have nothing to do.

To the hopeful predictions which reached him from time to time from Mansfeld's camp, Frederick's ears were ever open. Now that such an army was gathered round his standard, he thought it was time to show himself in the field. Issuing a manifesto calling the princes of Germany to arms,* he suddenly left the Hague. Making his way across France in disguise, he unexpectedly

Frederick goes to the Palatinate.

* *Theatrum Europæum*, i. 622.

appeared on the 2nd of April in Mansfeld's camp at Germersheim. He found the commander in earnest conversation with Raville, and apparently about to conclude a convention which would have placed his whole army at the Infanta's disposal. Mansfeld, as he had probably intended from the beginning, announced to the astonished emissary that all negotiations must now be at an end.

James had given a hearty consent to the journey of his son-in-law, under the impression that he would be able to exercise authority over Mansfeld, and to forbid him from hindering the prospects of the conference by any attack upon the neighbouring States. Yet to suppose that Frederick could do anything of the sort was to misunderstand utterly the character of the man, and the conditions under which such an army as Mansfeld's could be maintained. Frederick's first words upon his arrival at Germersheim, had shown how little he thought of anything but war. "I will have nothing to do with a suspension of arms," he said, turning to Raville as he spoke, " for that will be my ruin. I must have either a good peace, or a good war."* Nor did he want allies. The Margrave of Baden rose at his summons, and the combined forces marched to attack Tilly, who had already opened the campaign by a series of assaults upon the smaller posts by which Heidelberg was surrounded.

If Frederick had been at the head of a well-disciplined and well-commanded force, such a step would have been the best for him to take. His subjects were being butchered almost before his eyes,† and it was certain that he would have a better chance of being listened to in the approaching negotiations, if he could present himself as undisputed master in his own dominions. But it was not long before the unhappy Prince was taught by bitter experience what was the meaning of making war with Mansfeld in command.

---

* The Infanta Isabella to Philip IV., $\frac{\text{April 21}}{\text{May 1}}$. *Brussels MSS.*

† *Theatrum Europæum*, i. 621. " At one place taken by Tilly, we hear that half the citizens were also slain ; the rest for the most part wounded to death. Many women and children were also slain. The women did great hurt by throwing of hot scalding water." Advertisement, April 19. *S. P. Germany.*

His first operations, indeed, were crowned with success. Near Wiesloch the united Protestant army fell upon the Bavarians, and inflicted a severe loss upon the enemy. Tilly retreating to Wimpfen on the Neckar, called upon Cordova for assistance, and in the face of so imminent a danger, he did not call in vain. Yet, in spite of the junction of the Imperialist commanders, their forces were outnumbered by those at Frederick's disposal. But there was no unity of action in his camp. The Margrave proposed that the whole force of the enemy should be kept in check, till the arrival of Christian enabled them to overwhelm him by sheer force of numbers. To this plan Mansfeld was unwilling or unable to accede. For an army such as his it was a physical impossibility to occupy the same position for more than one or two days without starvation. In spite of all remonstrances, he marched away with the intention of seizing the passage over the Neckar at Ladenburg, after which he would make a sudden swoop upon Cordova's bridge over the Rhine at Oppenheim. The Margrave remained at Wimpfen, to make head against the enemy as best he might.

As might have been expected, Tilly profited by the opportunity. Gathering all his strength, he fell upon the troops which had been deserted by Mansfeld. On the evening of the 26th of April, the Margrave of Baden was flying in headlong rout from the battle-field of Wimpfen.

In the meanwhile Mansfeld had taken Ladenburg, but he had done nothing more. Cordova, he heard, had, immediately after the battle, marched straight for Oppenheim, and in that quarter nothing was to be effected. On the day of the battle, there had been no more than two days' provisions in Mansfeld's army. He had, therefore, now no choice before him but to beat a hasty retreat from the Palatinate, even if he had not been desirous to transfer his army to Alsace for reasons of his own. For he already looked upon Haguenau as a place destined to be the capital of the principality, to which he hoped to entitle himself by the sword, and he knew that siege had been laid to it by the Emperor's brother, the

Archduke Leopold, who, rash and incompetent as he was, was always better pleased to be at the head of an army than to preside in episcopal vestments in the cathedrals of Strasburg or Passau, of which an unwelcome fate had condemned him to call himself the Bishop. It was seldom, however, that his military efforts were crowned with success, and this time he was only just in time to fly in hot haste before Mansfeld's superior forces.*

On the 23rd of April, three days before the rout at Wimpfen, Weston set out for Brussels. The temper in which he entered upon his embassy was only too likely to bring with it grievous disappointment; for he seems to have expected that because he was himself sincerely desirous of peace, all difficulties would give way before him. Yet he ought to have known that the position of the Infanta was by no means an easy one. Fully empowered by the Emperor to negotiate the suspension of arms, she was herself, whatever her ulterior objects might be, enlisted in favour of the success of the negotiations. But she was unable to conceal from herself that the news from the Palatinate was not favourable to peace. She had just heard of Frederick's arrival, of the rash words in which he had explained to Raville, that he would not hear of a suspension of arms, and of his junction with the Margrave of Baden. She wrote despairingly to Philip, that before the negotiations could come to an agreement a whole year would have passed away.†

A preliminary difficulty about the form in which the Emperor's authority to treat was couched, was soon got over, upon a promise made by the Infanta's ministers that a document, drawn up in proper form, should be forthcoming before the consultations were brought to an end. But when it came to Weston's turn to produce his powers, a more formidable obstacle presented itself. He had brought with him an assurance from James that he would take care that his son-in-law conformed to his wishes; but from Frederick himself he could not produce

---

* Nethersole to Calvert, April 26, 29, May 5. Narrative by the Margrave of Baden, April. Wrenham to ——, May 6. *S. P. Germany*.

† The Infanta Isabella to Philip IV., $\frac{\text{April 21}}{\text{May 1}}$. *Brussels MSS*.

a line; still less could he show that he had authority to make any engagement on behalf of either Mansfeld or Christian; and whatever might be the nominal position of those commanders, no one at Brussels doubted for an instant that they were practically their own masters.* At last, on the 16th of May, Weston was allowed to despatch a courier to the Palatinate, to request that Frederick and his generals would send representatives, to give him their advice at the Conference. By this means he fondly hoped all obstacles would be overcome.†

Whilst Weston was struggling to disentangle the diplomatic web, Frederick had gone through many changes of opinion. In truth, the dilemma into which he had brought himself, was one which admitted of no escape. Without either money or supplies, it was impossible for him to keep together an army in sufficient numbers to defeat the enemy. It was equally impossible for him to support his army without ravaging the neighbouring territories. It would be well with him if he could drive Tilly back to Bavaria. It would also be well with him if he could sign a peace which would enable him to disband his troops. But a suspension of arms which would oblige him to keep his forces together, but which would not enable him to feed them, was fraught with disaster. "A truce," he wrote to James, before he heard of the defeat of his ally at Wimpfen, "will be my utter ruin. The enemy will supply his army with food and money. We are in a ruined country, and we have no mines in the West Indies to fall back upon." ‡ Even the bad news that followed, did not alter his opinion.§ But a sharp letter from James, coming simultaneously with Mansfeld's determination to abandon the attack upon Oppenheim, shook his resolution. On the 3rd of May he wrote to assure his father-in-law that he was now ready to consent to a truce for a month.∥

<small>Frederick's difficulties.</small>

---

* Weston to Calvert, May 15. *S. P. Flanders.*
† Weston to Nethersole, May 16. *S. P. Germany.* Weston's Report, fol. 2. *Inner Temple MSS.* Vol. 48.
‡ Frederick to the King, $\frac{\text{April 26}}{\text{May 5}}$. *S. P. Germany.*
§ Vere and Nethersole to Calvert, June 11. *S. P. Germany.*
∥ Nethersole to Carleton, May 2. Frederick to the King, May $\frac{3}{13}$. *S. P. Germany.*

Yet this mood did not last long. On the 18th, he met the Margrave of Baden at Spires, who assured him that in spite of his defeat he was still able to bring 7000 men into the field. A fresh bargain was struck between them, and Frederick promised to agree to no terms without the consent of the Margrave. Christian was known to be at last approaching the Main, and it was settled that the two armies should again combine in order to effect a junction with the new comers.

The day after this agreement had been made Weston's despatch arrived. Frederick coolly answered that he was now under an engagement to the Margrave, and that till the opinion of his ally had been taken, he could say nothing about the Conference at Brussels.*

On the evening of the 22nd, the whole force marched out of Mannheim. The next morning the troops were before the gates of Darmstadt. Unable to resist, the Landgrave Lewis invited the leaders into the town, where he entertained them hospitably, whilst the soldiers without were driving off the cattle from the fields, and plundering the houses of his subjects. As a Lutheran, who had warmly taken the Emperor's part, he was especially obnoxious to Frederick. The Landgrave now tendered his advice that it would be well for him to submit to the Emperor; but Frederick was in no humour to think of yielding. He was now, he said, at the head of a powerful army. He would have nothing to do with submission. His quarrel was not with the Emperor in his imperial capacity. He had only to do with an Archduke of Austria. If he was to have a peace, the arrears of his soldiers' pay must be satisfied. The Electoral dignity and the whole of the Palatinate must be restored. The privileges and religion of the Bohemians must be guaranteed afresh.†

Such words proceeding from a conqueror thundering at the gates of Munich or Vienna would have been in their place. Coming from Frederick, they were most

---

* Nethersole to Weston, May 22. Nethersole to Calvert, May 22. *S. P. Germany.*

† The Landgrave of Hesse-Darmstadt to the Elector of Mentz, May 29. *S. P. Germany.*

disastrous to the cause of which he had made himself the champion. We can fancy the grim smile of scorn with which they would be received in every Catholic town in Europe. The proscribed prince, it would be said, was incorrigible. This, then, was the meaning of the negotiation opened at Brussels, and of the promise to accept the decision of his father-in-law. If he was so elated by the capture of an undefended town, as to talk of re-opening the question of the government of Bohemia, what security could there possibly be that, if he were re-instated in his hereditary dominions, he would not use the power thus conceded to him for a renewed aggression upon his neighbours?

<small>Ch. IX. 1622. May.</small>

Yet Frederick did not stop here. The Landgrave of Darmstadt had a fortified post at Russelheim, which commanded a passage over the Main. He was now ordered to place it in the hands of his importunate guest. Unable to resist, Lewis sought safety in flight. His movements were discovered. He was captured, and brought back to the town. But Frederick, and his instigator, Mansfeld, soon found that they had gained but little by their violence. Turning to bay, the Landgrave refused to comply with their demands, and was carried off as a prisoner when the army marched towards the Main.

<small>Imprisonment of the Landgrave.</small>

In spite of Lewis's refusal, Mansfeld directed his course towards Russelheim, hoping to overawe the commander of so small a post. The man, however, proved staunch to his duty, and Mansfeld turned aside towards Aschaffenburg, searching for a passage across the broad river which divided him from Christian. He had not gone far before bitter news was brought. Tilly had received a strong reinforcement, and was on the watch to intercept him. The next moment the great army of which Frederick had spoken so boastfully was in full retreat. Its rearguard was attacked near Lorsch, and suffered some loss; but the remainder of the force contrived to find an inglorious shelter behind the walls of Mannheim.*

<small>Mansfeld's retreat.</small>

Anything more disastrous it is impossible to conceive.

---

* Nethersole to Calvert, May 27, June 2. *S. P. Germany.* Vere to Carleton, June 2. *S. P. Holland.*

CH. IX.
1622.
May 30.
Ruin of Frederick's cause.

At the moment of that fatal raid, what little chance of an accommodation remained melted into the air. After all that had passed, it was perhaps a light thing for Frederick that the Emperor or the Duke of Bavaria should steel their hearts against him. It was the last hope of summoning Protestant Germany to his aid, which he had dashed aside. In the beginning of May, there had been signs that the neutral states were alarmed at the progress of the Imperialists. The Duke of Wirtemberg had offered his mediation; the King of Denmark had sent a fresh embassy to plead the cause of the proscribed Elector; and, what was more significant still, the Elector of Saxony himself had written to Ferdinand, to urge him to a complete restitution of all that Frederick had ever possessed.* The imprisonment of the Landgrave of Darmstadt, and the rash words which Frederick had uttered about Bohemia, put an end to these well meant efforts. The King of Denmark and the Duke of Wirtemberg submitted to the rebuff which had become inevitable; and, before two months were over, John George was giving his warmest approval to the Emperor's scheme of transferring the Electorate to Maximilian.†

Chichester's arrival.

The day before Frederick's return to Mannheim, Chichester arrived from England.‡ He brought with him such money as the Benevolence had, after long waiting, afforded; and he had instructions to require Frederick to remain within the Palatinate, and to abstain for the future from any aggression upon the territories of his neighbours.

To Chichester's military eye nothing could be more deplorable than the aspect of the troops which he saw defiling past. The long train of baggage, and the crowds of wretched women who had been dragged or enticed from their devastated homes, did not bode well for the future operations of the army. It was "ill disciplined," he wrote, "and ill armed." As for the skirmish at Lorsch,

---

* The Elector of Saxony to the Emperor, May 4. *Londorp,* ii. 605.
† Hohenzollern to the Emperor, July $\frac{8}{18}$. *Khevenhüller,* ix. 1763.
‡ Vere to Carleton, June 2. *S. P. Holland.*

"considering the advantages which the enemy had, and the assurance which they had to give an absolute defeat, I hold it for a very happy and honourable day for the King."*

For some time Chichester pleaded in vain with Frederick. The army was again about to retire into Alsace, and he refused to remain in the Palatinate alone. A letter from Weston, however, changed the current of his thoughts. The Infanta, it seemed, had consented to request Chichester to negotiate a short armistice, in order to give time for the discussion of the arrangements for a permanent suspension of hostilities, and had written to Cordova and Tilly, asking them to accept the terms proposed by him. To an armistice thus demanded, Mansfeld was willing to agree; for he had no longer any hope of beating Tilly in the field, and he supposed that the Infanta would still be ready to buy off his opposition at his own price. Frederick, who was now entirely in Mansfeld's hands, turned round once more. He was ready, he said, to consent to an armistice for three weeks. The troops would be able, for so short a time, to shift for themselves, without leaving the Palatinate. He would himself send an agent to Brussels, and his allies would do the same.†

Chichester next turned to the Imperial commanders. But the moment was ill chosen to talk of an armistice. Provoked by the attack upon Darmstadt, they were little inclined to halt in their career of victory. Nor were better reasons wanting to hold them back from accepting the proposal of the English Ambassador. At last Christian, laden with the plunder of the Westphalian Bishoprics, was drawing near. It was not even pretended that he had agreed to suspend hostilities, and they had no wish to see him effecting a successful junction with Mansfeld. Cordova accordingly, taking advantage of a phrase in the Infanta's letter by which the granting of the armistice was made conditional on the military situation, answered that he could do nothing without the consent of the

Ch. IX. 1622.

June. He attempts to negotiate an armistice.

Its rejection by Tilly.

---
* Chichester to the King. Chichester to Carleton, June 2. *S. P. Germany.*
† Chichester to Weston, June 5. Chichester to the King, June 6. *S. P.*

CH. IX.
1622.
June.

Chichester's opinion of Frederick's forces.

other commanders, and prudently omitted to forward the letter which was intended for Tilly.* Tilly's course was thus made plain before him. He had heard nothing, he said, from the Infanta; and without an express order from the Emperor he could do nothing. But he should be glad to be informed where the troops of Mansfeld and Christian could take up their quarters, so as to be able to abstain from attacking the Emperor's allies, and what assurance could be given that they would observe an armistice if it were agreed upon.†

Of the treatment to which he was subjected, Chichester complained bitterly. But in his calmer moments he could not deny that Tilly's doubts were not unreasonable. "I observe," he wrote to Calvert, on the 11th of June, "so much of the armies of the Margrave of Baden, and of the Count Mansfeld, which I have seen, and of their ill-discipline and order, that I must conceive that kingdom and principality for which they shall fight to be in great danger and hazard. The Duke of Brunswick's, it is said, is not much better governed, and how can it be better, or otherwise, where men are raised out of the scum of the people, by princes who have no dominion over them, nor power, for want of pay, to punish them, nor means to reward them, living only upon rapine and spoil, as they do? I pray God to preserve the Duke of Brunswick and his forces; for if they receive a blow, as I have cause to doubt, all that is left to the Prince within the Palatinate will be in danger. His towns are ill-victualled, his garrisons weak, and the soldier discontented, his weekly pay being so small, by raising of the value of money, that it can hardly buy him bread to sustain nature. These and other miseries which I daily behold with grief, together with the strange carriage of the Emperor's chiefs since the receipt of the Infanta's letters, make me to doubt the good success of our part by arms. I pray God it was otherwise."‡

---

* Weston's Report, fol. 4 b. *Inner Temp. MSS.* Vol. 48. Weston to Calvert, June 22. *S. P. Germany.*

† Tilly to Chichester, June $\frac{8}{18}$. Chichester to the King, June 11. *S. P. Germany.*

‡ Chichester to Calvert, June 11, *S. P. Germany.*

Already, the day before these prescient words were written, the blow which Chichester feared had fallen upon Christian. Rapidly marching upon Aschaffenburg, the combined forces of Tilly and Cordova had crossed the Main, at the very spot at which Mansfeld had hoped to pass the river a few days before. Wheeling to the left, they took their way with all speed towards the further bank. At Höchst they found Christian utterly unprepared for the attack. After a short struggle, his troops were driven in headlong rout across the stream. Gathering together the scattered remnants of his beaten army, he contrived to make his way to Mannheim.*

Ch. IX.
1622.
June 10.
Battle of Höchst.

Frederick was in evil plight. Twenty-five thousand men were still collected round him; but with such an army he could neither wage war, nor make peace. The Margrave of Baden was the first to slink away without a word, leaving his troops to extricate themselves from their difficulties as best they could.† Mansfeld and Christian were in haste to be gone far away from the terrible sword of Tilly. Whilst they remained at Mannheim, their troops had consumed the provisions which had been laid up for the garrison, and there was nothing but starvation before them if they remained.

Frederick disheartened.

Chichester saw clearly that if peace was to be had at all, Frederick must be separated from the adventurers into whose hands he had fallen. He begged him, therefore, to stay behind at Mannheim. Finding that his reasoning was without effect, he produced an indignant letter which James had written on the first news of his son-in-law's refusal to take part in the conference at Brussels.‡ It was all to no purpose. Frederick was resolved to go. If his father-in-law, he said, knew the state in which he was, he would not press him to remain. He was ready to submit to the treaty. He would do no hostile act; but his person was not safe at Mannheim. If the King did not like him to accompany the army he would go to Switzerland. On the 13th, he rode out of

He determines to leave the Palatinate.

---

* Vere to Calvert, June 11. Nethersole to Calvert, June 18. *S. P. Germany.*
† Chichester to Weston, June 22. *S. P. Germany.*
‡ The King to Frederick, June 3. *Add. MSS.* 12,485, fol. 133 b. The King to Chichester, June 3. *Sherborne MSS.*

Ch. IX.
1622.
June.

Mannheim with the troops on their retreat to Alsace.* Never again was Frederick to look upon his native soil till he returned in the train of a mightier deliverer, to find himself in victory, as in defeat, a mere helpless waif upon the current. He was not wholly selfish or unprincipled. His weak and unstable nature had been stirred to its shallow depths by the passions of his age; but his mind was of that temper that everything seemed easy to him which was yet to be undertaken, and every obstacle seemed insuperable when he was brought face to face with its difficulties. It was his sad destiny never to see anything as it really was, and never to count any enterprise impossible till he was called upon to engage in it. The popular common-places about German liberty and religious freedom were ever on his lips, whilst he never for a moment thought it worth his while to test their meaning, or to ask himself how far they represented valuable ideas, or how far they had been encrusted with notions and opinions which were altogether destructive and indefensible. Even now, after all that he had seen, he could not discern that, whatever his countrymen might be ready to do in future days after they had gained full experience of the weight of the Emperor's yoke, they were not yet prepared to cast down the imperial edifice which, time-worn and shattered as it was, was yet their only shelter against high-handed injustice and never-ending strife. The strength of Ferdinand and Maximilian lay in the position which they occupied as supporters of order, and as champions of national unity. The rash appropriation of the Bohemian crown, the refusal to acknowledge the consequences of defeat, and above all, the employment of Mansfeld and his freebooters, had left Frederick without a reputable friend in the empire.

Vere's position.

From such a spectacle as this it is well to turn for a moment to the calm devotion of the English commander. No man knew better than Vere how hopeless his military position was. Yet it was not of the overwhelming forces of the enemy that he complained the most. During the days which Frederick had spent at Mannheim, that un-

* Chichester to the King, June 23. *S. P. Germany.*

happy prince had learned to see with Mansfeld's eyes, and to hear with Mansfeld's ears. To Vere, who was ready to sacrifice everything in his cause, he refused even the courtesy of a seat in the Council of War.* Of his plans and desires he left him in as complete ignorance as the meanest soldier in the camp. And now when, with the help of the money which Chichester had brought, Vere was able to fill up the ranks of his garrisons, the same evil influence met him at every turn. Mansfeld's men had consumed the provisions on which he had depended to carry him through the siege. "If we be attempted," he wrote despairingly to Carleton, "I shall doubt very much of the event. Besides, Count Mansfeld hath taken a great part of our serviceable men from us, and put the most poor in their places that ever I saw."† It could not well be otherwise in such a war. Licence to rove unheeded in quest of fresh stores of plunder, was the bait by which Mansfeld attracted round him his demoralised soldiery. Hard blows for the sake of a prince who had himself refused to share the dangers to which his followers were exposed, were all that Vere could offer.

The crisis seemed to be rapidly approaching. On the 20th of June, seven days after Frederick turned his back upon Mannheim, Tilly appeared before Heidelberg, and shots were exchanged with the garrison. To Chichester's demand that he should refrain from attacking a town held by the troops of the King of Great Britain, he returned a curt answer that he should not change his plans without an express order from the Emperor. This time, however, the danger passed away. The Imperialist commanders came to the conclusion that as long as Mansfeld was at large, it would be dangerous to undertake the siege. It was always possible that the adventurer might recross the Rhine, and make a dash at the unplundered homesteads of the great Bavarian plain. Tilly, therefore, marched southwards to bar the way, leaving Cordova to make the return of the enemy into the Palatinate impossible. The Spaniard did his work with pitiless severity.

* Vere to Carleton, June 11. *S. P. Holland.*
† Vere to Carleton, June 24. *S. P. Germany.*

CH. IX.
1622.
June.

From behind the walls of Mannheim, Chichester, fretting under the enforced inaction, was able to trace his progress by the rolling flames which sprung aloft from the villages which had once been the happy homes of a contented peasantry. If Mansfeld should attempt to return he would find nothing but a blackened wilderness, unable to supply food to his army for a single day.*

Discussion at Brussels about the powers.

To the peasant, who saw the result of his life-long toil drifting away amidst smoke and flame, it mattered little whether his ruin was to be ascribed to Cordova or to Mansfeld. But to all who were looking anxiously into the future, it made a great difference whether these atrocities were committed with a definite military object or not. When that object was attained, Cordova's ravages would cease, whilst the evil deeds of Mansfeld's bands would never come to an end, as long as his army remained in existence. When, therefore, on the 15th of June, the conferences were reopened at Brussels, Weston soon discovered that his position was changed for the worse. The letter of credence which he now produced from Frederick was at once rejected, and formal powers as binding as those which had by this time been received from the Emperor, were demanded by the Infanta's Commissioners. It was in vain that Weston stood up for the sufficiency of his master's guarantee. Such arguments, he found, had little weight with men who knew that, in his conversation at Darmstadt, Frederick had flung his promises to the winds, and had positively declared that he had no intention of submitting to the Emperor at all. A fresh difficulty, which arose from the probability that if Frederick consented to sign the powers required, he would insist upon styling himself King of Bohemia, was got over by an agreement that James should issue a fresh commission in plainer terms, and that it should be sent to his son-in-law, to be confirmed by the simple signature—Frederick. At the same time it was agreed that Mansfeld and Christian should be asked to send special powers, binding themselves to submit to the arrangements made

* Chichester to Carleton, June 26, July 10, 22. Tilly to Chichester, $\frac{\text{June 25}}{\text{July 5}}$. *S. P. Germany.*

at Brussels.* As there would be some delay in obtaining the fresh commission from England, Weston took advantage of the courier who carried these demands, to ask Frederick to send full powers at once, which, even if they were rejected on account of the title used by him, would at least serve to show that he was in earnest in submitting to the negotiation in progress.

The next few days only served to bring out more clearly the real difficulties of the case. Christian of Brunswick had held back from taking any part in the conferences whatever. Mansfeld had sent a Captain Weiss to consult with Weston, with instructions to ask not only for a pardon for himself and his followers, and for permission to retain the places which he held in the empire till the conclusion of the final treaty of peace, but also for a considerable sum of money to pay and disband his troops. It was this last request which was justly considered as exorbitant by Pecquius. "They who have employed the Count," he said to Weston, "ought to satisfy his demand for money." Nor was it only from the difficulty of treating with such a commander as Mansfeld that the Infanta began to despair of the success of her efforts at mediation. Every letter which reached her from Vienna, conveyed a fresh assurance of Ferdinand's resolution to deprive Frederick of the Electorate, whatever he might do about the territory; and an objection made, at the request of the Imperial ambassador, to the use of the word "Elector" in James's commission, had been met by an announcement from Weston, that his master required the restitution of his son-in-law's honours as well as of his patrimony.†

To no one did the pretensions advanced on both sides give greater disquietude than to the Infanta. On the one hand, she insisted on rejecting Mansfeld's demand for money; on the other hand, she wrote to Oñate, begging him to urge the Emperor to desist from his design, and

---

* Weston to Calvert, June 22. *S. P. Germany.* Narrative of the Conference, $\frac{\text{June 24}}{\text{July 4}}$. *Brusse's MSS.*

† Weston to Calvert, June 30. *S. P. Germany.* The Infanta Isabella to Philip IV., $\frac{\text{June 24}}{\text{July 4}}$. *Brussels MSS.*

CH. IX.
1622.
June.
Frederick in Alsace.

His complaints of the army.

July.
He dismisses it from his service.

to tell him plainly that if he refused to do so, he must give up all hope of peace.

It was in the midst of this entanglement that news arrived from Alsace, which, for a time, seemed likely to extricate the English negotiator from his difficulty. A few weeks' experience in Mansfeld's camp was beginning to tell even upon Frederick. It was evidently not by aimless wandering in pursuit of booty that the Palatinate would be recovered. When Weston's demand for powers reached him on the 28th of June, he was in no mood to raise any further obstacle. The next day he forwarded to Brussels two copies of the document required, one with, and the other without the only seal which he possessed—the seal of the Kingdom of Bohemia. In a letter to Chichester, which was written on the same day, he bitterly complained of his position. "I hope," he wrote, "that the excesses committed here will not be imputed to me. I am very sorry to see them, and I wish for nothing better than to be away from them." The day before he had expressed himself in stronger terms. "As for this army," he said, "it has committed great disorders. I think there are men in it who are possessed of the devil, and who take a pleasure in setting fire to everything. I should be very glad to leave them. There ought to be some difference made between friend and enemy; but these people ruin both alike.* Yet what to do, Frederick hardly knew. At first he talked of returning to Mannheim. But this plan he surrendered in the face of Mansfeld's objections, and he finally deter-

* Frederick to Chichester, June 28. *S. P. Germany.* The following extract from a letter from Frederick to his wife will be found misplaced amongst the Holland State Papers of December, 1622. It is evidently the decypher of part of a paragraph in cypher from a letter written about this time, the first clause being imperfect :—"Le desordre parmy la soldatesque qui pilloit tout sans respect ny difference avec autres inormitez, il estoit a craindre que l'ennemie le poursuivant il serait forcé a se retirer en Lorain, et nos soldats y faire autant d'insolences commes ils ont accoutumé, ainsois je ferois sans nulle utilité plus d'ennemis, et estoit à craindre une mutination, a faute d'argent et vivres. Mansfeld a desiré que le Roi de Boheme le licentia et donnast permission de chercher autre part condition, menant toutes les officiers. Je luy ay donné cela par escrit, n'ayant aucun moyen de les entretenir. Il dit me pouvoir plus servir par diversion; le Duc de Brunswic a bien bonne intention, si le Prince d'Orange luy pouvoit envoyer quelqu'un pour l'assister de bon conseil."

mined to take refuge with the Duke of Bouillon at Sedan. On the 3rd of July, therefore, he left the army, after issuing a proclamation by which he dismissed the troops from his service, assigning as a motive his inability to find means to pay them.

In the separation thus effected between Frederick and Mansfeld, Weston saw a door of escape from his difficulties. He had lately asked in vain for a suspension of arms in the Palatinate alone, and had been told that unless he could engage that the whole of the forces on his side would remain quiet, the Infanta was utterly without power to restrain the armies of the Emperor.* As soon, therefore, as the news reached him, he hurried to Spinola, and told him what had happened. To his surprise, Spinola did not seem to think the intelligence of any great importance. The army, he said, was less by one man only, the same commanders and the same enemy were still in the field. Most likely the whole affair was a trick. Against this insinuation Weston protested loudly. His master's son-in-law, he said, was now ready to conform to anything. The King of England had no command over those who were not his subjects nor in his pay. If they wished it, he would join his arms with those of the Emperor against the perturbers of the public peace. If a suspension of arms were not granted in the Palatinate without reference to Mansfeld, and if Heidelberg and the other towns were assaulted, his Majesty would take it as a declaration of war against himself. "The treaty," Spinola replied, "were it not for the point of the auxiliaries, might be most easily and speedily concluded; but if, while these men spoil our countries, we shall stand with our hands tied, all the world will deride us." †

Nor was it only from the language addressed to his representative at Brussels that James learned that he would not be allowed to have everything his own way. For he had already received a letter from the Emperor, announcing that he intended to hold at Ratisbon, on the 22nd of August, an assembly composed of the five loyal

Ch. IX.
1622.
July.

Weston presses for a suspension in the Palatinate.

July 12.

Projected assembly at Ratisbon.

Aug. 22.
Sept. 1.

* Weston to Calvert, July 6. *S. P. Flanders.*
† Weston to Calvert, July 13. *S. P. Flanders.*

Ch. IX.
1622.
July.

Electors, together with three Protestant and three Catholic Princes, for the purpose of settling the conditions of a permanent peace; and this announcement was coupled with an invitation to send an English ambassador to take part in the negotiations.*

That James should have been startled by this letter was only natural. Of the eleven members of whom the assembly would be composed, the three Ecclesiastical Electors, with the Duke of Bavaria, the Archbishop of Salzburg, and the Bishop of the two sees of Bamberg and Würzburg, were hardly likely to take a lenient view of Frederick's proceedings. Nor were the names of the Protestant minority more reassuring. The Elector of Saxony, the Elector of Brandenburg, the Landgrave of Hesse-Darmstadt, and the Dukes of Brunswick and Pomerania, were all either hostile or indifferent to the fugitive Elector Palatine. Yet, if the announcement could not be otherwise than unsatisfactory to James, it ought surely to have driven him to reconsider his position. If it was true, as rumour said, that the first proposition submitted to the meeting would be one for the transference of the Electorate, it would be well for James to ask himself how it was that it had become possible for Ferdinand to expect support in such a policy from a body in which Protestant Germany was so largely represented. The answer was, in truth, not difficult to be found by any one who knew how to look for it. That Mansfeld, and such as Mansfeld, should have the free range of the Empire to burn and plunder where they would was an intolerable evil. In the face of danger the nation was clinging to the Imperial organization as the only centre of unity which it possessed. No foreign Prince who tried to break up this unity, loose as it was, would have a chance of being heard, unless he could provide for the restoration of civil order. For the moment, the religious question was in abeyance. These, however, were not the thoughts with which James's mind was occupied. In the Emperor's letter he saw nothing more than a gross personal insult to himself. Ferdinand, he

* Ferdinand II. to the King, June $\frac{8}{18}$. *S. P. Germany.*

declared, had promised to treat with him on equal terms. What right had he to make his decisions in any way dependent upon the wishes of the Princes of the Empire? It was derogatory to the honour of a King of England that his ambassador should be summoned to dance attendance upon an assembly so composed.*

Nor was it only on this point that James failed to comprehend the situation of affairs. For it was impossible for any candid mind to dissociate the proceedings of Frederick from the proceedings of Mansfeld. Spinola was, no doubt, in the wrong when he spoke of Frederick's proclamation, by which his troops had been disbanded, as altogether illusory. But the question to be considered was not whether he meant what he said now, but whether he would say the same thing if he found himself restored to his ancient position. If the capture of an undefended town had led him to reject with scorn the suggestion made by the Landgrave of Hesse-Darmstadt, that he should submit to the Emperor, what was to be expected if he found himself once more in the possession of the Palatinate? How long would it be before he took some new offence at one or other of his neighbours. Then would be seen the consequences of Imperial lenity. Fresh hordes of brigands, unpaid and unprovided, would pour forth once more to seek their prey, and the whole work of repression would have to be done over again.

Such was the wide-spread feeling which at this conjuncture led Protestant and Catholic alike to give their support to Ferdinand. As far as Frederick was personally concerned, the argument was unanswerable. Every year his power for doing good had grown less and less. One by one, he had thrown away his chances. In 1619, by refusing the crown of Bohemia, he might probably have secured the religious liberty of that country. At the close of 1620, by renouncing the throne which he had lost, he might have secured the religious liberty of Protestant Germany. In 1621, by cordially accepting Digby's mediation, he might at least have obtained, under very stringent conditions, the restitution of his own states. And

Ch. IX.
1622.
July.

Frederick's cause hopeless.

---

* The King to Ferdinand II. July 8. *S. P. Germany.*

Ch. IX.
1622.
July.

Question of his abdication.

January. Desire of Spain for peace.

now even that hope was gone. From the moment of his attack upon Darmstadt he had nothing left but abdication.

As usual, in James's unhappy reign, the true policy of England is to be found not in the manifestoes of its sovereign, or in the despatches of its ministers, but in the memorials in which Spanish statesmen expressed their apprehensions; for the Council of State at Madrid was still divided between its desire to further the interests of the Catholic Church in Germany and its dread of provoking a war with England. Of the necessity of peace for the best interests of the monarchy, none could be more clearly convinced than the ministers of Philip. "If we go on with the war in the Lower Palatinate," the Infanta Isabella had written towards the close of the preceding year, "we shall have before us a struggle of the greatest difficulty. We shall be assailed by the whole force of the opposite party, and the burden will fall with all its weight upon Spain. It will hardly be possible to bring together sufficient forces to meet the enemy. It will, therefore, be better to agree to a suspension of arms for as long a time as possible, leaving each side in the possession of the territory occupied by it, in the hope that time will show what is best to be done."*

Rejection of a proposed cession of the Lower Palatinate.

In the same spirit the Council of State utterly rejected a suggestion which had been thrown out by one of the Emperor's councillors at Vienna, to the effect that the brother of the King, the Infant Charles, might marry the eldest daughter of the Emperor, receiving a new kingdom to be composed of Franche Comté, Alsace, and the Lower Palatinate.† Oñate was directed to inform Ferdinand that Spain wished for no extension of its territory. It was by positive declarations that nothing of the kind was intended, that the King of England had been induced to refrain from taking part in the war, and the promise

Plan for the settlement of Germany.

thus solemnly made must not be broken. The Council then proceeded to adopt Zuñiga's scheme ‡ in full. Let the Electorate and the two Palatinates be transferred from Frederick to his son. Let the boy be educated as a

---

* The Infanta Isabella to Philip IV., Dec. $\frac{14}{24}$, 1621. *Brussels MSS.*

† Minutes of Oñate's Despatch, Nov. $\frac{7}{17}$, 1621. *Simancas MSS.*

‡ Vol. ii. 109.

Catholic either at Vienna or at Munich, and be married either to the daughter of the Emperor or to the niece of the Duke of Bavaria. The administration of the territories might be confided to Maximilian as long as the young prince was under age, in order that he might be able to pay himself for the expenses of the war. A pension might be assigned to Frederick for his support. His son would be a Catholic, and his states would soon be Catholic also.*

Ch. IX.
1622.
January.

That such a proposal should ever have been made is only one more proof of the ignorance of the Spanish ministers of a world which was not their own. It must however be acknowledged that James at least had done his best to blind them to the difficulties of a scheme which would satisfy the dynastic interests of his family at the expense of the religious independence of the inhabitants of the Palatinate. Yet even thus Zuñiga shrunk from openly proposing the adoption of his plan. It would, he said, be accepted at once by James and his son-in-law, but they would add a stipulation that the boy should be educated at Dresden instead of at Vienna.

That the policy thus indicated was the only sensible policy for James to adopt there can be no reasonable doubt. It would leave the boundary between the two religions untouched, at the same time that it would afford the surest guarantee for the future peace of the empire. Unfortunately, its very wisdom was enough to place it out of the question with James.

Whilst Spain and England were thus both employed in offering impossible compromises, Ferdinand, without making up his mind upon the future disposition of Frederick's territory, was doing his best to obtain the consent of the King of Spain to the transference of the Electorate; and it was not long before the Friar Hyacintho arrived at Madrid bearing with him the despatches of which the copies had been intercepted by Mansfeld. To all outward appearance, he failed in the object of his mission. Fresh despatches were sent to Oñate, directing

Hyacintho at Madrid.

* Consulta of the Council of State, Jan. $\frac{8}{18}$. *Simancas MSS.* Est. 2403. Philip IV. to Oñate, Jan. $\frac{18}{28}$. *Brussels MSS.*

him to support an arrangement which would confirm the son of Frederick in the Electorate. But he was privately assured by Zuñiga that the King had no special predilection for the proposal made in his name, and that if the Emperor could only manage to carry out his wishes without implicating Spain in the affair, he need fear no opposition at Madrid. All that was really wanted was that they should be able to make James believe that the thing had been done against the wish of the King of Spain. So secret was this declaration to be kept that not even the Council of State was acquainted with its purport.*

Such were the circumstances under which Digby set out from London to return to Spain.† The hopes which he had cherished four short months before were gone for ever. The vision of an English army in the Palatinate well disciplined and well paid, strong enough to inspire respect, and unencumbered with the necessity of plundering in order to maintain itself in existence, had melted into air. But it was still possible, he thought, to secure the co-operation of Spain by a strong representation of the evils which would necessarily result from a renewal of the religious struggle of the past century, and by threats of the imminence of war if any support were given to the aggressive designs of the Emperor. Yet it is easy to perceive from the tone of his despatches that he felt that he had come as an ambassador and not as a statesman. In every line is to be traced the fearless independence of a man who is capable of forming his own opinions; but he is no less careful to show that he comes to carry out a policy which has been shaped by others, and the success of which will mainly depend upon measures over which he has no control.

Not only was the mission on which Digby now started an unsuccessful one, but he altogether failed to penetrate the motives and intentions of the Spanish Government. It was not that he did not give himself extraordinary pains to discover the secret intrigues of the ministers.

---

* *Khevenhüller*, ix. 1765—1771. Philip IV. to Oñate, March $\frac{5}{15}$, May $\frac{8}{18}$. *Brussels MSS.*
† Calvert to Carleton, March 24. *S. P. Holland.*

He found means of acquainting himself with the debates in the Council of State, and of getting a sight of the orders which issued from the Royal Cabinet.* Trickery and falsehood he was prepared to meet; but even his long residence at Madrid had not prepared him for the wild hallucinations by which the Spanish statesmen were actuated. It was possible, he thought, that Philip and Zuñiga might embrace the prospect of maintaining that peace of which the monarchy stood so much in need. It was also possible that they might be carried away by religious zeal to throw in their lot with the Emperor. But that they should fancy it possible to convert the Palatinate by force, and at the same time to remain on a friendly footing with a Protestant nation—that they should look forward with satisfaction to the frustration of the hopes of James by the interposition of the Pope's veto upon the marriage treaty, without expecting to wound his susceptibilities, was so utterly ridiculous, that Digby could never bring himself to believe that the policy of a great nation could be moulded on so wild a fancy. And yet it was at nothing less than this that Zuñiga was aiming.

The truth was, that Spanish politicians were walking upon enchanted ground. Nothing seemed in their eyes to be what it really was. The old illusion of Philip II., that Spain could beat down all opposition by force, had only been surrendered to make way for a still stranger illusion that Spain could gain her objects without using force at all; and yet the statesman who now directed the counsels of the monarchy was incomparably superior to any minister who had been known in Spain for many years. With Lerma and Uzeda the first thought had been how to fill their own pockets. With Zuñiga the first thought was how to make his country prosperous at home and respected abroad. Vigorous attempts had been already made to effect at least some improvement in the shattered finances, and to encourage population and industry by every measure which the political knowledge of the day was able to suggest.† Such reforms, indeed,

* Bristol to the King, Aug. 18, 1623. *S. P. Spain.*
† Lafuente. *Hist. Gen. de España*, xvi. 21—28.

Cн. IX.
1622.
March.

were not likely to go far as long as the social and intellectual habits of the people remained unchanged; but they were certain, as Zuñiga was well aware, to be entirely thrown away if Spain engaged in a fresh continental war.

To a certain extent, Zuñiga's opinions were shared by the other members of the Council of State. Like him, they were anxious to maintain peace with England; like him, they thought that peace would not be broken even though Protestantism were stamped out in the Palatinate; but they refused to believe that it would not be broken if the dynastic interests of James were affected by the transference of the Electorate.*

Character of Philip IV.

In this difference of opinion between the Council and the chief minister the judgment of the King was of no weight whatever. Philip IV., at this time a lad of seventeen, had no mind for anything but amusement. He was fond of bull-fights and hunting; he was no less fond of Court festivities and of dissipation of a more degrading kind; but he never could be induced to take a moment's thought for serious business.† Whatever Zuñiga recommended he was ready to say or do. Further trouble than that he utterly refused to take.

Zuñiga and the Council of State.

Yet even with this advantage, Zuñiga did not venture openly to oppose the decisions of the Council of State. Composed, as this body was, of men of high birth, who had many of them taken a share in its deliberations for a long series of years, he seems to have doubted whether even Philip's nonchalance would be proof against an open breach between himself and the Council. At all events, he preferred not to face the storm. The decisions of the Council should be taken to the King to be converted into royal ordinances, or to be recommended to the Spanish Ambassadors at foreign Courts as the basis of their diplomacy, whilst he was all the while watching the current of events which would make the policy which he ostensibly adopted impossible, or was even intriguing to

* The difference of opinion is scarcely indicated by Khevenhüller at this time. But from a later passage which will be afterwards quoted, in which he describes the causes of Zuñiga's death, it is evident that it already existed.
† Relazioni Venete, Spagna, i. 600.

defeat the measures to which he had himself publicly assented.

Such was the strange chaos of wild hopes and incompatible designs across which Digby, strong only in his honesty of purpose and his knowledge of the laws by which the conduct of ordinary men is guided, had come to lay a road firm enough for human beings to walk without danger of being engulfed in the depths beneath. Believing, as he did, that even Spaniards would hardly go on seriously with the marriage treaty unless they meant to give satisfaction to his master in Germany, he made it his first object to discover their intentions on this important point. It was not long, therefore, before he spoke plainly to Zuñiga on the subject. It was now, he said, two years since Lafuente had left England in order to make a demand for the dispensation at Rome. As yet nothing had been done; he therefore wished to know whether the Spanish Government would obtain a decision one way or another, in order that, if the difficulties proved insuperable, his master might bestow his son elsewhere.

margin: June. Digby asks for an assurance about the marriage treaty.

Zuñiga, in truth, would have been glad enough if the cardinals could have been persuaded to continue the discussion of the marriage for twenty years instead of two; but he did not venture to say so, and after giving Digby every assurance of his personal good will, asked him to repeat the question to the King himself.

Philip accordingly, being well tutored, gave the most satisfactory of answers. The proposition, he said, was very grateful to him. He desired the match as much as his father had done, and there should be no want on his part in bringing it to a speedy conclusion. If it had not been begun by his father, he would himself have been the beginner of it. He only hoped that the King of England would be well satisfied with the expected decision of the Pope.*

margin: Philip's answer.

Digby was, however, too well versed in the arts of Courts to put his trust in words alone. The test which he selected of Philip's sincerity was derived from his

margin: Digby's interview with the Infanta.

* Bristol to the King, Aug. 18, 1622. *S. P. Spain.*

intimate knowledge of Spanish manners. In those southern countries it was considered the height of impropriety to allow a lady to receive the addresses of a suitor before her parents or guardians had made up their minds to allow the marriage to take place. The ambassador, therefore, asked leave to visit the Infanta, and stated as his motive that he had a message to deliver from the Prince. His request was immediately granted, and he was allowed to assure the lady "that as there was not the thing in the world which" the Prince "more desired than to see the treaty effected, so he hoped it was agreeable to her, and that she would aid in it." "I thank the Prince of England much for the honour which he does me," replied the Infanta, and the interview was at an end.

Upon this visit Digby laid no little stress in his report of the sentiments of the Court. Yet he was not altogether at his ease. He added a request for positive instructions to come away at once, the moment that he was able to discover the slightest inclination to delay the conclusion of the treaty. If, however, he could believe the assurances that were given him, there was no reason why the Infanta should not be in England in the spring.*

For the moment, however, the Spaniards had a valid excuse for delay. They could not treat about the marriage till a definite decision arrived from Rome; they could not treat about the Palatinate till Gondomar, who had been recalled to Spain as the only man who was fit to cope with Digby,† arrived at Madrid.

Gondomar's departure from London had been accompanied by a general shout of exultation from the English people. No more unpopular ambassador has ever left our shores. In addition to the evils which he undoubtedly caused, his memory was saddled with countless crimes of which he was no less undoubtedly innocent. Yet, after every deduction has been made, enough remains to justify the popular verdict. He had stood in the way of the

---

* Digby to Calvert, June 30. Digby to the Prince of Wales, June 30. S. P. Spain.

† This is the explanation given in a despatch of Philip to the Infanta Isabella, March $\frac{5}{15}$. Brussels MSS.

national resolve; he had induced James, by alternately wheedling him and bullying him, to carry out the behests of the King of Spain. No other ambassador, before or since, succeeded so completely in making a tool of an English king. So thoroughly had he earned the hatred of the people amongst whom he had been living, that his successor, Don Carlos Coloma, was for the moment almost popular in England. An honest soldier who had served in many a hard fight under the flag of his country was, it was thought, not likely to be an adept in those arts of dissimulation which had served Gondomar so well.

Ch. IX. 1622. May.

Meanwhile the course of events was bringing small comfort to Digby. One courier after another brought bad news from Germany. First it was the attack upon Darmstadt; then it was the dismissal of Mansfeld's troops and the isolation of Frederick, lastly, he heard of the threatened siege of Heidelberg. Yet he did not allow himself to be discouraged at the consequence of the neglect of his advice. "For my part," he wrote on the 13th of July, "I have been long of opinion, and so continue still, that this business will never be brought to any good conclusion but by the absolute authority of these two kings, who must agree of such conditions as they shall judge reasonable, and reciprocally oblige themselves to constrain both parties to condescend unto them; for all other particular treaties will still be overthrown either by the inconstancy of the parties who will, from time to time, alter and change upon the advantage of accidents of war, or else be interrupted by continual jealousies and new provocations. This course I hope one day to see set on foot when once the business of the match is fully resolved and concluded; for I esteem that must be the basis and foundation upon which all the good correspondency and mutual exchange of good offices betwixt England and Spain must depend, and, that once taking effect, I shall not much doubt of the other."*

July. Digby urgent for a cessation of hostilities.

A few weeks later Digby was able to give a satisfactory report of his negotiation. Gondomar had arrived and had thrown his whole weight into the scale in his

August. Decision of the Council of State.

---

* Digby to the Prince of Wales, July 13. *S. P. Spain.*

Ch. IX.
1622.
August.

Digby's approval of the Assembly.

favour. The question of the Palatinate had been referred to the Council of State, and it had been decided, after a full discussion, that complete satisfaction should be given to the King of England.

No doubt Digby greatly overestimated the value of this decision. He did not know what was the extraordinary arrangement which was supposed by the members of the Council to be likely to give satisfaction to James, still less did he know what was the wilder scheme which had approved itself to Zuñiga; but, in fact, it mattered very little whether the Spaniards were speaking truth or not. If James and Frederick could win the confidence of Protestant Germany, they might dictate their own terms to the Emperor; if not, they must take whatever the Courts of Vienna and Madrid would be pleased to give. With his master's foolish objections to the assembly at Ratisbon, therefore, Digby had no sympathy whatever. "It is a weakness," he wrote, "to think that this business can be ended without a diet." He felt truly that his part had been done. Sincerely, or not, the Spanish Government had consented to take up Frederick's cause; it was James's business, not his, to make that cause palatable to the German nation.*

James throws all responsibility upon Spain.

Of all this, however, James had simply no conception whatever. That it was necessary for him to take any trouble about the matter, beyond that of writing occasionally a scolding letter to his son-in-law, never entered into his mind. Just as he had dealt with Raleigh five years before, he now proposed to deal with Philip. All responsibility for the restitution of the Electorate and the Palatinate was to be left to the King of Spain. If he succeeded, James would reap the benefit; if he failed, he would declare war upon him, just as he had punished Raleigh's failure by sending him to the scaffold.

July 14.
Proposed sequestration of the towns in the Palatinate.

It was while he was in this temper that he received information from Weston of an important proposal which had been unofficially made to him at Brussels. Let Heidelberg, it was suggested, be neutralised, and assigned to Frederick as a residence, on condition of the surrender of Mannheim and Frankenthal to the Infanta, who would

* Digby to Calvert, Aug. 9. *S. P. Spain.*

engage to restore them to the English garrisons whenever the peace negotiations were brought to a close one way or other. "If peace and restitution be concluded," said Pecquius, in supporting the scheme, "yet, however the Prince Palatine promise, and his Majesty oblige himself, it may be thought there shall be demanded some places of caution at least for a time; and, if it should come to that, I know not in whose hands they could more safely be deposited."*

To the proposal thus made James refused to give even a moment's consideration. It was contrary, he declared, to his honour, and it did not offer sufficient security for the future. No doubt this was true enough; but what better could he do? He had already protested against Ferdinand's invitation to send an ambassador to Ratisbon, as a breach of the Emperor's engagement to enter into direct negotiations with himself.† And if he would neither negotiate with the Emperor nor fight with him, there was nothing left but to throw himself unreservedly into the arms of the King of Spain, and to pick up the crumbs which fell from his table.

In one respect at least Weston was an excellent servant. The absurdity of the position in which he was placed never dawned upon him for an instant. He gravely continued to reiterate his master's demands for a suspension of arms in the Palatinate alone, which would have left Mansfeld free to strike his blows in whatever direction he pleased.

To such a demand as this the Infanta had no power to assent. Ferdinand had commissioned her to come to terms with Frederick, on the supposition that he was able to dispose of the forces which he had raised. The Emperor would never, as she knew full well, ratify any agreement which would leave the roving bands of Mansfeld free to wander at their pleasure in search of booty.

Nor was the danger by any means at an end since Mansfeld's dismissal by his nominal master. While

---

* Weston to Calvert, July 19. *S. P. Spain.*
† The King to Ferdinand II., July 8. *S. P. Germany.*

Weston was wasting his breath at Brussels, that captain of brigands had been offering his services to the highest bidder. If his assurances were to be believed, he was equally ready to serve the Emperor, the Infanta, the King of France, or the Dutch Republic. But answers were slow in coming in, and Alsace, stripped as by a swarm of locusts, no longer sufficed to support his army. The Archduke Leopold, too, who commanded the Emperor's forces in those parts, had received reinforcements from Tilly, and was ready to make head against him. Hastily evacuating that Haguenau which he had hoped to make his own for ever, he flung himself suddenly upon Lorraine. Before crossing the frontier, however, he wrote to the Duke asking permission to pass through his territories on his way to France, in which country he hoped to find entertainment for his troops. It was impossible, however, he added, to keep his men to their duty unless they were fed, and he must therefore request that rations might be provided for twenty-five thousand men. His soldiers, he went on to say, received but little pay, and were accustomed to commit great excesses. For this reason it would be well if the inhabitants were ordered to carry off their property to the fortified towns in which they would be able to defend it.*

Mansfeld's candid avowal was fully justified by the conduct of his men. As he passed the border, they set fire to the town of Pfalzburg. Further on, his march was lighted by the flames of thirty blazing villages. Famine and desolation marked his track. From Lorraine his soldiers spread over the Bishoprics of Metz and Verdun; and even Sedan, the little nook of land where Frederick was cowering under his uncle's protection, was not safe from their devastating tread. "We are here," wrote the Duke of Bouillon, "in the midst of an army, without arms, without leaders, without discipline, or fitness for war. Those who hold out their arms to these men, or attempt to ameliorate their condition, are treated worse than could be expected from the most exasperated enemy."†

* Mansfeld to the Duke of Lorraine, July. *S. P. Holland.*
† The Duke of Bouillon to Carleton (?), Aug. 15. *S. P. Holland.*

Ferdinand's indignation, when he heard of this fresh aggression, was unbounded. Now, at least, he wrote on the 25th of July to the Infanta Isabella, there could no longer be any doubt that the enemy was only talking about a suspension of arms in order to gain time.* His own position was indeed a strong one. Frederick and Mansfeld had been doing his work only too surely. From every side despatches were pouring in, with acceptances of his invitation to the assembly at Ratisbon, which had now been postponed till the 21st of September.† At this moment James's protest against the assembly reached him. He at once replied that he was not to blame. It was Frederick who had caused the failure of the negotiations at Brussels. The basis of those negotiations had been the promise of the deprived Elector to make due submission to the Emperor, and yet he had plainly told the Landgrave of Darmstadt that he had no intention of doing anything of the kind. In the meantime the Empire had been exposed to spoil and pillage, and he had therefore summoned the princes to consult for its safety. To James's request that he would order his troops to abstain from attacking the places in the Palatinate, he returned an evasive answer, referring him to the negotiators at Brussels.‡

In fact, Ferdinand had thoroughly made up his mind as to the course he would pursue. As soon as the assembly met, he would announce the transference of the Electorate with every prospect of obtaining its assent. He would leave it to the princes to decide how the territory was to be disposed of, and how the expenses of the war were to be paid. But he knew that he would have more chance of gaining his object, if the strong towns, which were garrisoned by the King of England's troops, were in his hands before the princes arrived at Ratisbon. On the 13th of August, therefore, two days after he had answered James's letter, he despatched a courier to Tilly,

Ch. IX.
1622.
July.
Ferdinand's indignation.

August.
His reply to James's protest.

His intentions.

---

* Ferdinand II. to the Infanta Isabella, $\frac{\text{July } 25}{\text{Aug. } 4}$. Brussels MSS.

† October 1, N.S.

‡ Ferdinand II. to the King, Aug. $\frac{11}{21}$. Simon Digby to Calvert, Aug. 14. S. P. Germany.

CH. IX. 1622.
August.
Weston's proposition.

ordering him to proceed at once to the siege of Heidelberg.* Whilst Ferdinand's messenger was speeding across Germany, Weston was doing his best at Brussels to separate the cause of Frederick from the cause of Mansfeld. On the 15th of August, he presented to the Infanta's commissioners a proposition for settling the points at issue. Let the towns in the Palatinate, he said, in effect, be allowed to remain in the position in which they are, and the King of England will engage to make war upon Mansfeld and Christian, if they should be so illadvised as to return to that part of Germany; and he will also promise that if, whenever the negotiations for peace are seriously taken in hand, those adventurers still refuse to submit to reasonable conditions, he will "declare himself their enemy, and jointly employ his forces against them, as against the perturbers of the common repose of Christendom."†

Mansfeld's troops.

Such a proposal could hardly be seriously entertained by the Infanta. The time had long passed since either Frederick's engagements to make peace, or James's engagements to make war, had been regarded as having any practical bearing upon the course of events. Rightly or wrongly, every Catholic in Europe was fully persuaded that in Frederick's hands the strong places garrisoned by Vere would be a basis of operations for Mansfeld and his marauders; and, whatever might be the ulterior designs cherished at Brussels and Vienna, there was no hesitation in the resolution formed to hinder him from again taking root in the Palatinate. Nor was there the slightest reason to suppose that Mansfeld was likely to be less dangerous than before. Even Weston acknowledged that it was certain that the adventurers had no intention of submitting to any terms whatever. They had begun, he said, by demanding unreasonable conditions. They had sent him no powers

* Ferdinand II. to Khevenhüller, Aug. $\frac{8}{18}$. Oñate to Philip IV., Aug. $\frac{10}{20}$. *Simancas MSS.* Simon Digby to Calvert, Aug. 14, 15, 22. *S. P. Germany.*

† Weston's Proposition, Aug. 15. Weston's Report. *Inner Temple MSS.* Vol. 48.

to treat, and for some time had not even troubled themselves to answer his letters.*

In fact, it was no longer possible for them to remain where they were. The Duke of Nevers, whilst pretending to negotiate with Mansfeld the terms upon which he was to enter the French service, had rapidly collected a force strong enough to bar the road into France. An attempt to make a dash for the Lower Rhine, made early in August by Christian, had failed, not so much from the resistance offered by the Spanish Governor of Luxemburg, as from the mutinous spirit of his own men.† Under these circumstances an offer which reached Mansfeld from the States-General was eagerly seized. Things had not been going well with the Republic since the reopening of the war. In the winter Juliers had surrendered to the Spanish arms, and Spinola had now sat down before Bergen-op-Zoom, with every prospect of conducting the siege to a successful conclusion. In order to avert such a blow, the States offered to take Mansfeld into their service for three months.

Mansfeld leapt at the offer. Leading his men by a circuitous route, he hoped to slip unperceived across the Spanish Netherlands, and to join the Prince of Orange at Breda. But on the evening of the 18th of August he found that his way was barred by Cordova, whose forces had been recalled in hot haste from the Palatinate. At daybreak on the following morning, he prepared for action; but scarcely was the word given when two of his regiments broke out into mutiny, shouting for money. Of the troops which remained faithful, many had sold their arms for bread, and many had thrown them down in sheer weariness. Yet, deficient as he was in those moral qualities, without which no man can conduct a campaign to a successful issue, Mansfeld showed on this day that he was possessed in an eminent degree of that dogged courage and cool presence of mind which befit a leader of banditti. Riding up to the mutineers, he adjured them, if they would not fight, at least to keep together, so as to impose upon the enemy. Receiving a

* Weston to Calvert, Aug. 15. *S. P. Flanders.*
† Advertisement from Sedan. Aug. 8. *S. P. Holland.*

Ch. IX.
1622.
August.

favourable reply, he placed them in a body amidst a crowd of camp followers, so as to present the appearance of a formidable array. With the rest of his force he dashed at the Spaniards. Three times he was repulsed; but at last Christian, with that impetuous bravery which has blinded half the world to his want of all other virtues, drove the enemy's cavalry before him in headlong rout. But in the midst of his charge, he received a wound in the arm, and his followers, when they saw him led away from the field, made their leader's misfortune an excuse for refusing to take any further part in the battle. The Spanish army was saved from almost certain annihilation. Mansfeld was able to pursue his march, and to join the Dutch camp at Breda.*

The wound in Christian's arm was unskilfully tended, and he was forced to submit to amputation. He ordered the trumpets to be sounded whilst the operation was being performed. Not long afterwards he replaced the lost member with a substitute skilfully constructed of cork and silver. "The arm which is left," he boastfully declared, "shall give my enemies enough to do."

Mansfeld at Breda.

His companions in arms were not yet ready to take the field. The starving wretches needed to be rearmed and reclothed before they could be made available against Spinola. But the garrison of Bergen would be likely to fight the more manfully, now that they knew that relief was at hand.

Weston again asks for a suspension of arms.

The change of Mansfeld's quarters inspired Weston with renewed hopes. Now, at least, he urged, there should be no longer any difficulty in granting the suspension of arms. Mansfeld and Christian had transferred their services to the Dutch, and would no longer stand in the way of an accommodation. The siege of Heidelberg, he had heard, was again opened, and he therefore hoped that the Infanta would give orders for the suspension of hostilities. Yet, in spite of all that Weston could say, the Infanta knew that she had no

* *Theatrum Europæum*, i. 666. Carleton to Buckingham, Aug. 27. S. P. Holland.

power to agree to a cessation of hostilities, in which Mansfeld and Christian were not included. It was notorious that the adventurers had only taken service with the States for three months, and no one at Brussels doubted that they would return to ravage Germany in the winter. Weston was, therefore, obliged to content himself for the present with hearing that fresh letters would be sent to Tilly and the Archduke Leopold; but he was plainly told that it was not likely that they would do any good.* Excepting in the garrisons on the left bank of the Rhine, there were no longer any Spanish troops in the Palatinate,† and there were therefore no forces in the army before Heidelberg under the immediate orders of the Infanta.

Ch. IX.
1622.
Sept.

At last, on the 8th of September, Weston received a formal reply to his proposition. He was told that nothing could be done unless he could obtain an assurance from Mansfeld and Christian that they would not again attack the obedient princes of the Empire; and that it was expected that they would also engage to abstain from assailing the territories of Spain.

The Infanta's reply.

"Likewise," the Infanta proceeded, referring to the Flemish extraction of the adventurer, "seeing the same Mansfeld hath refused to accept the grace and pardon of his Majesty, whereby he might have turned to his royal service, and to his own natural obedience, and hath withal drawn from this city him whom he hath sent hither to treat on this his behalf; seeing also how little he can hope for from the Hollanders, and how his pride will not let him remain in Holland, there being withal particular advertisements that his end and purpose is to trouble the affairs of Germany:—

"Lastly, seeing the Duke Christian will take the same course, as he hath also expressly declared; there is none that seeth not clearly the truth of that which hath been said, and that it is now more necessary than ever to provide for the general assurance."

The Infanta ended by saying that, though she herself

* Weston to Calvert, Sept. 3. *S. P. Flanders.*
† The Infanta Isabella to Cordova, Aug. $\frac{14}{24}$. *Harl. MSS.* 1581. fol. 177.

saw no way out of the difficulty, she would gladly listen to anything that Weston had to propose.*

To the question thus put, Weston had very little to reply. For he was perfectly aware that the adventurers really contemplated a return to Germany as soon as their engagement with the Dutch was at an end. "I must tell you," Mansfeld had written to him a fortnight before, "that you are labouring in vain. For you will never accomplish anything where you are. When those people get a thing between their teeth, they never let it go unless after the loss of a great battle. You ought, therefore, to advise his Majesty to recall you; for I see well enough that there is no remedy unless we begin the war in Germany afresh."†

Weston was therefore obliged to content himself with reiterating his opinion, that Mansfeld had no longer any connection with Frederick, and with renewing his declaration that his master was ready to join the Emperor in opposing his designs. As for the demand that Mansfeld should be prevented from attacking Spain under the orders of the Prince of Orange, he could only say that the King of England was quite ready to mediate a treaty between Philip and the Dutch.‡

Baffled and discontented, Weston had for some time been earnestly pleading for his recall. His denunciations of the Infanta's perfidy were loud enough to please the stoutest Puritan in England. He had gone to Brussels under the impression that he had an easy task before him. He had shared with so many of his countrymen the belief that Spain was everything and Germany was nothing; and he could not conceive it to be possible that the destinies of the Empire were determined at Vienna rather than at Madrid.

On the 15th, Weston had his last audience of the Infanta. He had orders, he said, to return home unless either the siege of Heidelberg were raised, or the sus-

---

* Answer to Weston's Proposition, Sept. 8. Weston's Report, fol. 16. *Inner Temple MSS.* Vol. 48.

† Mansfeld to Weston, $\frac{\text{Aug. 24}}{\text{Sept. 3}}$. *S. P. Germany.*

‡ Weston's Reply, Sept. 12, in his Report, fol. 19. *Inner Temple MSS.* Vol. 48.

pension of arms granted. He was again made to understand that he was asking for that which it was no longer in her power to accord. The King of England, the Infanta said, "had deserved a crown of palm by his royal carriage;" and she would never cease to do all that she could to give him satisfaction.*

And so, at last, this long negotiation was brought to an end. That the Infanta was earnestly desirous to conduct it to a better termination cannot be doubted for an instant. As late as the 27th of August, she had written again to press the Emperor to abandon his design of transferring the Electorate. But James had never been sufficiently alive to the absolute importance of guaranteeing the Empire against anarchy. His own inability to provide pay for his son-in-law's army, Frederick's rash words at Darmstadt, and the ravages of Mansfeld, had by this time thoroughly confirmed Ferdinand's conviction that peace was only to be obtained by the establishment of the absolute supremacy of his own party in the Empire. To this conviction James had nothing to oppose. He had no watchword by which to rally the North German Protestants to his cause. He had no real power over his son-in-law's actions, still less over those of Mansfeld. All that he could do was to bluster about keeping Mansfeld quiet by force; and when he found that no one would listen to his protestations, he had no other resource left but to call upon Spain to help him out of the mire into which he had so hopelessly plunged himself by his blunders.

* Weston to Calvert, Sept. 16. *S. P. Flanders.*

CHAPTER X.

THE MISSION OF ENDYMION PORTER.

*Ch. X.
1622.
August.
English feeling.*

The months during which the comedy was being played out at Brussels had brought increasing exasperation to the English people. Even if the whole truth had been laid before them, there would have been more than enough to cause the most serious disquietude in all with whom the interests of Protestantism were worth a moment's consideration. For it was impossible to deny that, wherever the blame was to be laid, the very existence of Protestantism was seriously endangered over a large part of the Continent. But, in truth, the great mass of Englishmen knew very little of the real facts of the case. Of Frederick's helplessness and vacillation, of Mansfeld's atrocities, of the abominable anarchy which was certain to be the result of the victory of their allies, they were utterly and hopelessly ignorant. What they saw, was only a new phase of the eternal conflict between virtue and vice, between freedom and tyranny; and, imperfect as this view of the case undoubtedly was, they were at least clear-sighted enough in marking the evil which had arisen from their Sovereign's faults. It was only in the pulpit that these feelings, freely expressed in private conversation, could find vent in public, and it is no wonder that a man like James, in his dislike at the free language which was springing up around him, took refuge in sending the obnoxious preachers to prison. Dr. Everard, who had been committed in the preceding year to the Gatehouse for abusing the Spaniards in a sermon, now found his way into the Marshalsea. Another preacher, Mr. Clayton, was sent to prison for reproducing Coke's scurrilous allusion to the introduction of the scab by sheep imported from Spain, and a third, Dr. Sheldon,

Imprisonment of preachers.

was thought lucky to have escaped with a reprimand for some harsh reflections upon the people who worshipped the beast and his image.*

Nor was it only against abuse of Spain that James had decided upon making war. He was now disquieted, as many wiser men than he have often been disquieted, by the bitterness of theological polemics. Arminianism, silenced in Holland, had taken firm root in England, and had been welcomed by those who were most under the influence of the reaction against Puritanism. Of necessity, the new views were received with deep distrust by all who attached value to the Calvinistic theology. In every corner of the land, the pulpits rang with declamations on predestination and the perseverance of the saints. Till lately, at least, James had regarded with favour the doctrine in which he had been educated. But he hated turmoil, and he thought, in spite of Barneveldt's example, that he might succeed in laying the storm by directing Abbot to issue a few well-meant instructions to the preachers. From henceforth, no one under the degree of a bachelor of divinity was to "presume to preach in any popular auditory the deep points of predestination, election, reprobation, or of the universality, efficacy, resistibility or irresistibility of God's grace ; but leave those themes to be handled by learned men, and that moderately and modestly, by way of use and application rather than by way of positive doctrine, as being points fitter for the schools and universities than for simple auditories."†

As mere advice, no exception can be taken against such words as these. But, coming as they did, as an attempt to enforce silence on the great religious question of the day, they only served to embitter the quarrel which they were meant to calm. Left to itself, the tendency of the age was undoubtedly in favour of the Arminians. For whatever may be the theological or philosophical value of their opinions, they were

* Chamberlain to Carleton, Aug. 10. *S. P. Dom.* cxxxii. 91. Mead to Stuteville, Sept. 14. *Harl. MSS.* 389, fol. 228.
† Hacket, 89. The King to Abbot, Aug. 4. Abbot to the Bishops, Aug. 12, Sept. 4. Wilkins's *Concilia,* iv 465

Ch. X.
1622.
August.

doing the same work in the domain of thought which Digby with his doctrine of territorial sovereignty was doing in the domain of practical politics. They were finding a middle course, which might put an end to that violent opposition which existed between the contending churches. It was to the decrease of theological virulence that they owed their existence as a school of thinkers. It was to their habits and modes of thought that the growth of a spirit of toleration would be mainly due. The greatest service that could be done to them was to allow them to win their way by argument. The greatest injury that could be done to them was to enable them to silence their adversaries by force. Men who could preach about nothing but predestination, and who could use no language better than coarse invective, were no doubt a great pest to the community. But, after all, liberty of thought is better in the end than correctness of reasoning, or moderation of expression, and it is impossible for any one external to the modes of a preacher's thoughts to judge of the intimate connection which exists in his mind between the abstract doctrines which he professes and the practical lessons which he desires to enforce. The great battle of the sixteenth century had been waged between Catholicism and Protestantism. The great battle of the seventeenth century, as yet felt rather than understood, was to be waged on behalf of mental and personal liberty. It was the great misfortune of James's character, that, whilst both in his domestic and foreign policy he was far in advance of his age in his desire to put a final end to religious strife, he was utterly unfit to judge what were the proper measures to be taken for the attainment of his object. And unfortunately it lay in his power to a great extent to decide whether the Arminians should range themselves, on the whole, on the side of the advancing or of the retrograde party amongst their countrymen. Laud, disputing with a Jesuit or a Calvinist, was a true Protestant, a genuine successor, according to the altered conditions of the age, of Luther and of Knox. Laud, entrusted with power to silence his opponents, to forbid the study of books which he considered objectionable, and to restrain the preaching of sermons which he held to be mischievous, would be upon the side of the Jesuits and the Pope.

<small>Ch. X.
1622.
New invigoration of Puritanism.</small>

It was thus that James succeeded against his will in giving new life to Puritanism. Invigorated by the restraints under which he placed it, it rose up once more with giant strength to suffer and to dare in the name of law and of religion. It gained the alliance of many a man who had no sympathy with the narrowness of its tenets, but who felt in the lofty and noble spirit by which it was pervaded, the strength which would enable him to shake off the weight which pressed so heavily upon the energies of the nation.

<small>Release of the Catholic prisoners.</small>

For little as the English people knew of what was passing at Rome and at Madrid, they were well aware that James had lowered the dignity of the English crown till the laws of England had been made a subject of treaty with foreign statesmen and foreign priests. He had been guilty in the eyes of his contemporaries of sacrificing the national independence, the great cause of which Henry VIII. and Elizabeth had been the champions. He is guilty in the eyes of posterity, of defiling the sacred cause of religious liberty by making bargains over it for Spanish gold and Spanish aid. Even now an act, with which in itself no one can possibly find fault, had been contaminated by the mode in which it was accomplished. Writs were issued in August to set free from prison crowds of Catholics who were suffering for their religion.* In defence of the act thus done, Williams was able to produce the most admirable arguments, and to plead the wisdom of showing mercy to the Catholics, at a time when the King was demanding mercy to the Protestants abroad.† But all such arguments fell flat on the world, for men knew that the prisoners owed their release to Gondomar's intercession,‡ and that it was likely to be a prelude to a long series of favours to be granted to Spain. Never, wrote the Venetian ambassador about this time, was the Catholic religion

---

* Williams to the Judges, Aug. 2. *S. P. Dom.* cxxxii. 84.
† Williams to Annan. *Cabala*, 269.
‡ Ciriza to Aston, $\frac{\text{June 27}}{\text{July 7}}$. *S. P. Spain*.

more freely exercised in England. But the Spaniards were not content. They wanted to have everything or nothing.*

Liberation of Coke, Phelips, and Mallory.

Nor did James gain any fresh popularity by giving directions, within a week after the Catholics had been set free, for the liberation of Coke, Phelips, and Mallory from the Tower, on condition that they, like Pym, would place themselves under restraint not to travel more than a limited distance from their own houses in the country.† The measure was in all probability dictated by a desire to be prepared to meet a Parliament, if the negotiations at Brussels should prove abortive. But in Coke's case, at least, nothing that now could be done was likely to soothe his exasperation. For an unwise attempt to prosecute him in the Court of Wards upon some private offence which he was supposed to have committed had broken down completely, and he had been declared innocent by the unanimous decision of all the judges to whom the legal question involved in the case had been referred.‡ Nor in the existing state of popular feeling, did it avail the government much, that Sir John Bennett, who had escaped punishment through the dissolution of Parliament, was now prosecuted in the Star-Chamber for the faults which had brought an impeachment upon him, and was, before the year ended, condemned to a fine of 20,000*l.*, to imprisonment during pleasure, and to perpetual disability from office.§

Punishment of Bennett.

Aug. 25. Arrival of Gage.

All through August, the news from Brussels had been growing worse and worse. At last, when the confusion was at its height, James was startled by the unexpected arrival of Gage, the Englishman who had been commissioned to watch the course of the marriage negotiations at Rome, and who had now come to announce that if the Pope was to be satisfied, new and unheard of concessions must be made.‖

---

* Valaresso to the Doge, Aug. $\frac{9}{19}$. *Venice MSS.* Desp. Ingh.
† *Privy Council Register,* Aug. 6.
‡ Chamberlain to Carleton, July 13. *S. P. Dom.* cxxxii. 38.
§ Chamberlain to Carleton, July 1. Locke to Carleton, Nov. 30. *S. P. Dom.* cxxxii. 1; cxxxiv. 39.
‖ Valaresso to the Doge, Aug. $\frac{9}{19}$. *Venice MSS.* Desp. Ingh.

It was now about a year since, on the 11th of August, 1621, a congregation of four cardinals had been formed for the purpose of examining the articles of the marriage treaty. They were not long in coming to the conclusion that the articles were altogether insufficient. Care had been taken for the religion of the Infanta and her household, but nothing was said about the general body of English Catholics. Unless something were done for them, it would be the duty of the Pope to refuse the dispensation. The vague promises which James had given in the preceding year, were flouted as utterly insufficient. The cardinals had set their hearts upon the conversion of England, and it was certain that the conversion of England would never be effected by a mere promise that the Catholic missionaries should for the future escape the scaffold, and that the penal laws should be executed with moderation. Before the end of October, therefore, they had decided that nothing short of complete liberty of worship would suffice, and that for this they must have some stronger guarantee than the mere word of the King of England.

Ch. X. 1621. August. The Cardinals and the marriage treaty.

October.

Before the end of the year, however, the cardinals discovered that their course was not so easy as they had supposed. The news which reached them of the first proceedings in the House of Commons after the adjournment, was not favourable to the supposition that the changes which they contemplated could be accomplished without opposition. It was not till they heard of the dissolution of the Parliament, of the quarrel with the Dutch Commissioners, and of the imprisonment of the Earl of Oxford, that they finally made up their minds to send Gage back to England, with orders to lay the Pope's decision before the King.

Resolution to send Gage to England.

1622.

Accordingly, on the 4th of July, Gage was summoned before the congregation to receive his instructions. The King of England, said Cardinal Bandino, in the name of the others who were present, had read many Catholic books, and he had no doubt discovered that it was impossible for the Pope to grant a dispensation in such a case as this without the hope of some great public good. As, however, nothing of the kind was to be found in the

Instructions given to him.

Ch. X.
1622.
July.

articles which had been sent from Spain, they had determined to ask for a general liberty of worship in all his kingdoms, and for a satisfactory guarantee of its maintenance. They had been informed, that it would be better that this change should proceed from a voluntary act of the King himself, and they therefore hoped that he would inform them what he was willing to do for his Catholic subjects. The Cardinal then proceeded to touch upon a still more delicate subject. It was utterly impossible, he said, to imagine, that one so versed as the King was in controversial theology could be ignorant that the holy and apostolic Roman faith was the only true and ancient faith in which men could be saved. If, therefore, he did not openly profess his belief, it could only be from a fear of incurring disgrace by changing a religion which he had professed so many years, or from a dread of the personal consequences to himself. As for the first, he should remember that Henry IV. had gained honour by his conversion ; and, as to the second, he need not be afraid. God would certainly protect him. Half his subjects, and the majority of his nobility, were Catholics already, and, if more were needed, the forces of the King of Spain, and of all Catholic princes, would be at his service. The Roman see would be ready to load him with honours. If he chose to pay a visit to Rome, a legate should be sent to meet him in Flanders, and the Pope himself would go as far as Bologna to welcome him. But if he could not make up his mind to his own conversion, let the Prince of Wales be encouraged to take the step from which his father shrunk.*

Alteration in the articles.

The articles, as they were returned to Gage, contained several important alterations. All the Infanta's servants were of necessity to be Catholics. Her Church was to be open to all who chose to enter, and not merely to her household. The priests were to be under the control of a bishop, and were to be freed from subjection to all laws excepting those which were imposed by their ecclesiastical superiors. The Infanta must have the education of her children ; of the girls, till the age of twelve, of the boys, till the age of fourteen.

* Francisco de Jesus, 33—40.

The cardinals had, at least, done James one service by this plain spoken declaration. He could no longer be in any doubt as to the views with which the marriage was regarded at Rome. In truth there was something very similar in the attitude taken by the Pope and that taken by the Emperor, on the two great questions of the day. Both Gregory and Ferdinand had definite objects, and from them neither friend nor enemy would have much difficulty in discovering precisely what was to be expected. To deal with them, all that was necessary was to form an equally definite plan of operations, to be ready to give way where it was possible to yield, and to organize opposition where opposition was needed. But all this required thought and trouble, and James preferred the easier course of throwing the burden upon Spain, and of trusting to Philip's friendliness and sagacity, to help him out of his difficulties.*

<small>Ch. X. 1622. August. Reception of Gage.</small>

Gage arrived in England on the 25th of August. On the 9th of September, James poured out his distress in a letter to Digby. Everything was going wrong at Brussels. He now expected, therefore, that as nothing was to be done with the Emperor, the King of Spain would actually give his assistance in the recovery of the Palatinate and of the Electorate. As for the proposals brought from Rome by Gage, the Infanta's servants were to be nominated by the King of Spain, and there was therefore no object in insisting upon the omission of the words obliging them to be Catholics. It was unimportant whether the superior minister were to be a bishop or not. The other demands were of greater consequence. The cardinals ought to have known that it was out of his power to concede a public church, and that the exemption claimed for the ecclesiastics from the law of the land was a strange one, and was not universally allowed, even in Roman Catholic countries. He would bind himself to allow the children to remain under their mother's care till the age of seven, though the time might be extended if it were found necessary for their health. As to the demand made for the general good of Catholics, he had gone as far as he possibly could by his

<small>Sept. James sends his answer to Digby.</small>

* The King to Digby, Sept. 9. Resolutions upon the Marriage Articles [Sept. 9]. Prynne's *Hidden Works of Darkness*, 16, 14.

Ch. X.
1622.
Sept.

letter of the 27th of April, 1620, in which he had promised that no Roman Catholic should again suffer death for his religion, or should be compelled to take any oath to which capital penalties were attached, whilst the existing penal legislation should be mitigated in practice. If these terms were not accepted by Spain within two months, the treaty must be considered at an end.

Buckingham's letter to Gondomar.

James's formal despatches to his ambassador were accompanied by a confidential letter from his favourite to Gondomar, in which the embarrassments of the hour were depicted as in a glass. "As for the news from hence," wrote Buckingham, "I can in a word assure you that they are in all points as your heart could wish. For here is a king, a prince, and a faithful friend and servant unto you, besides a number of your other good friends that long so much for the happy accomplishment of this match, as every day seems a year unto us; and I can assure you, in the word of your honest friend, that we have a Prince here that is so sharp set upon the business, as it would much comfort you to see it, and her there to hear it. Here are all things prepared upon our part; priests and recusants all at liberty; all the Roman Catholics well satisfied; and, which will seem a wonder unto you, our prisons are emptied of priests and recusants and filled with zealous ministers for preaching against the match, for no man can sooner now mutter a word in the pulpit, though indirectly, against it, but he is presently catched, and set in strait prison. We have also published orders, both for the universities and the pulpits, that no man hereafter shall meddle, but to preach Christ crucified. Nay, it shall not be lawful hereafter for them to rail against the Pope, or the doctrine of the Church of Rome, further than for edification of ours; and for proof hereof, you shall, herewith, receive the orders set down and published. But if we could hear as good news from you, we should think ourselves happy men. But, alas! now that we have put the ball at your feet, although we have received a comfortable despatch from his Majesty's Ambassador there, yet from all other parts in the world, the effects appear directly contrary."

Buckingham then went on to recite the causes of his

discontent. The new conditions sent from Rome were such as could "tend to no other end but to bring his master in jealousy with the greatest part of his subjects." At Brussels Weston had been flouted by the Infanta, and the siege of Heidelberg was still going on.

"And now," he continued, "let me, I pray you, in the name of your faithful friend and servant, beseech you to set apart all partiality in this case, and that you would be pleased as well, like a true Englishman, indifferently to consider of the straits we are driven into. If the Emperor shall in this fashion conquer the whole Palatinate, the ancient inheritance of his Majesty's children, what can be expected but a bloody and unreconcilable war between the Emperor and my master, wherein the King of Spain can be an auxiliary to the Emperor against any other party but his Majesty? And, therefore, as my master lately offered to the Infanta for satisfaction of her desire, that in case the auxiliaries would not be contented with reason, but still perturb the treaty, he offered, in that case, to assist the Emperor and her against them; so can he in justice expect no less of the King your master, that, if the Emperor will, contrary to all promises both by his letters and ambassadors, proceed in his conquest and refuse the cessation, that the King your master will in that case, and in so just a quarrel, assist him against the Emperor, in imitation of the King my master's just and real proceedings in this business from the beginning, who never looked, as you can well be witness, to the rising or falling hopes of his son-in-law's fortunes, but constantly kept on that course that was most agreeable to honour and justice, to the peace of Christendom, and for the fastening of a firm and indissoluble knot of amity and alliance betwixt the King your master and him, which was begun at the time of our treaty with France, and then broken at your desire that we might embrace this alliance with you. You are the person that many times before your departure hence besought his Majesty once to suffer himself to be deceived by Spain.* We, therefore, do now expect to find that

---

* Meaning, perhaps, that Gondomar had answered James's complaints

Ch. X.
1622.
Sept.

great respect to honour in your master that he will not take any advantage by the changing of fortune and success of time, so to alter his actions as may put his honour in the terms of interpretation.* You see how all the rest of Christendom envy and malign this match and wished conjunction. How much greater need then hath it of a hasty and happy dispatch? And what comfort can the Prince have in her, when her friends shall have utterly ruined his sister and all her babes? You remember how yourself praised his Majesty's wisdom, in the election of so fit a minister as Sir Richard Weston in this business; but you see what desperate letters he writes from time to time of their cold and unjust treating with him in this business. You could not but wonder that any spark of patience could be left us here. And to conclude this point in a word, we ever received comfortable words from Spain; but find such contrary effects from Brussels, together with our intelligence from all other parts of the world, as all our hopes are not only cold but quite extinguished here."

The writer then returned to the subject of the marriage. Gondomar, he said, could not but remember how, when the match was first moved, he had assured the King "that he should be pressed to nothing in this business that should not be agreeable to his conscience and honour, and stand with the love of his people;" and he then went on to warn the Spaniard that if the match were to be broken off, "his Majesty would be importunately urged by his people, to whose assistance he must have his recourse, to give life and execution to all the penal laws now hanging upon" the heads of the Catholics.

"It only rests now," he concluded, "that as we have put the ball to your foot, you take a good and speedy resolution there to hasten the happy conclusion of this match. The Prince is now two and twenty years of age, and is a year more than full ripe for such a business. The King our master longeth to see an issue proceed

that he had been deceived by the renewal of the war in 1621, by begging him to suffer it for once, and that all would come right in the end.

* That is to say, as may make it necessary for him to explain his actions, his honour having become doubtful and needing interpretation.

from his loins, and I am sure you have reason to expect more friendship from the posterity which shall proceed from him and that little angel, your Infanta, than from his Majesty's daughter's children. Your friends here are all discomforted with this long delay, your enemies are exasperated and irritated thereby, and your neighbours that envy the felicity of both kings, have the more leisure to invent new plots for the cross and hindrance of this happy business; and for the part of your true friend and servant Buckingham, I have become odious already, and counted a betrayer both of King and country.

"To conclude all, I will use a similitude of hawking. I told you already that the Prince is, God be thanked, extremely sharp set upon the match, and you know that a hawk, when she is first dressed and made ready to fly, having a great will upon her, if the falconer do not follow it at that time, she is in danger to be dulled for ever after.

"Take heed, therefore, lest in the fault of your delays there, our Prince and falcon gentle, that you know was thought slow enough to begin to be eager after the feminine prey, become not so dull upon these delays, as in short time hereafter he will not stoop to the lure, though it were thrown out to him.

"And here I will end to you, my sweet friend, as I do in my prayers to God :—'Only in thee is my trust,' and say, as it is written on the outside of the packets,— Haste, haste, post haste."*

Excepting so far as they throw light upon the character of one whose influence was so ruinous to those who trusted him, Buckingham's momentary expressions of opinion during the reign of James are of no importance whatever. For whilst, like his still more versatile son, he was "everything by turns, and nothing long," it was only when the shifting tide of passionate impulses happened to coincide with some turn of his master's thoughts, that he had any chance of moulding the general policy of the Crown in accordance with his wishes. For the time, however, there was a complete

* Buckingham to Gondomar [Sept. 9]. *Cabala*, 224. The holograph draft is in *Harl. MSS.* 1583, fol. 353.

agreement between the two. If the words of the letter were the words of Buckingham, the thoughts were the thoughts of James. And if, amongst the many miseries with which history teems, there is one more sad than another, it is to see so noble a policy as that of which Digby had been the mouthpiece, so utterly discredited and mishandled. For it cannot be but that the historian, who has to tell, almost as a matter of course, of so many windy schemes, and criminal follies, should feel a special regret when he is called upon to recount the failure of a wise and beneficent idea, in something of the same spirit as that which led the early poets to regard with peculiar sorrow the deaths of youthful warriors, the promise of whose lives was for ever to be unfulfilled, whilst they accorded but a few words of perfunctory sympathy to those whose existence had passed through the ordinary fortunes of men. To settle the war in Germany by guaranteeing the independence of the Protestant States in religious matters, at the same time that the civil authority of the Emperor remained intact; and to settle the domestic difficulty by the gradual relaxation of the penal laws, was a policy worthy of the most consummate statesman. But James, unhappily, was never able to appreciate either the greatness of his own projects, nor the magnitude of the obstacles which he would have to surmount. If he ever admitted lofty principles into his mind, it was always by their smallest side that he approached them. If he had judged rightly with respect to the contest for the Bohemian crown, it was simply because the large issues which were involved in it presented to him a narrow, technical idea which he was competent to grasp. If he now struggled for the religious independence of the Palatinate, it was not because he had formed any adequate notion of the requirements of the states of the Empire, but simply because the heirs of that territory happened to be his own grandchildren. In comparison with the claims of his daughter and her sons, all considerations of policy, all considerations for the cause of Protestantism, passed for very little in his eyes. And as it was with his foreign policy, so it was with his domestic policy. The great work of fostering the growth of a more tolerant spirit in the hearts of Englishmen, was thrown into the background in favour of a scheme for getting a richly dowered wife for his son, or for obtaining the co-operation of the King of Spain in a settlement of the German difficulties, to which, excepting under compulsion, Philip could never give his consent without losing every feeling of self-respect.

As far as words could go, no man could be more unbending than James. Whatever might be the feeling of the English nation, it was to accept from him precisely that system of religious toleration which happened for the moment to suit his own personal or political interests. Whatever might be the feeling of the German nation, or of Continental governments, they were to accept, without modification, precisely that arrangement of their disputes which happened to be consonant with the claims of his own family. If indeed he had shared in the beliefs which prevailed in the House of Commons, if he had thought with Phelips and Coke, that Frederick was an innocent martyr to the Protestant faith, he might well have used the language that he did. But nothing was further from the true state of the case; for no one knew better than James how ruinous every act of his son-in-law's had been to the cause which he imagined himself to be serving. All Frederick's headstrong rashness, all his impracticable perversity and despicable incompetence lay before him as in a book. And it was in spite of all this that he saw the solution of the question by which Germany was distracted, not in a mediation between the religious parties, not in a policy shaped in accordance with the public opinion of moderate men of all parties, but simply and solely in the complete restitution of his son-in-law, at whatever hazard to the future interests of the Empire.

But, after all, this fixity of purpose was confined to words alone. Ready at a moment's notice to issue hazy manifestoes in which the most praiseworthy maxims were shrouded in an almost impenetrable veil of loose verbiage, he never ceased to expect that the plans which he had formed should be carried out by others rather than by himself. He resembled no one so much as that unfor-

CH. X.
1622.
Sept.

Sept. 6.

The fall of Heidelberg.

tunate wight in the well-known legend, who, finding a horn suspended by the side of a sword at a castle gate, summoned the warder to admit him by a long blast, and was swept away to destruction by a whirlwind issuing from the opening gates, with the terrible sentence ringing in his ears,—

"Woe to the wretch, that ever he was born,
Who durst not draw the sword before he blew the horn."

Already the stroke which James dreaded had fallen upon the Palatinate. The siege of Heidelberg, interrupted by the necessity of watching Mansfeld's steps, had been recommenced by Tilly on the 15th of August. That commander had, however, underestimated the difficulties of his task, and the artillery of which he could dispose was so weak that, during the first three days of its employment, he only succeeded in killing a cat and two hens. During the succeeding fortnight, the attack made little progress, and the besieged were beginning to speak more hopefully of their prospects. An attempt made on the 5th of September to carry the place by storm, ended in complete failure. But that very evening, the more powerful artillery of which Tilly was in need reached the camp of the besiegers. During the whole of the next morning, the fortifications by which the western suburb was defended were subjected to a crushing fire, and it so happened that on that very day the money with which the garrison was paid had come to an end. The German mercenaries being what they were, the mere offscourings of the armies of Mansfeld and the Margrave of Baden, were mutinous and discontented. When, therefore, the enemy made a rush to storm the walls, it was found that, in many places the defenders, instead of meeting the attack, threw down their arms and cried for quarter. The governor, Van der Merven, seeing that the suburb was lost, attempted to open negotiations with Tilly for the surrender of the town itself; but the keys of the place had been mislaid, and before they could be found, the gate was blown open by the assailants, and the town was in their hands. Collecting such forces as he could, and surrounded by a huddled crowd of citizens and peasants,

Van der Merven took refuge in the castle. Those who remained without, were subjected to all those atrocities which in that age were the lot of a town taken by storm. Women were outraged, men were cut down in the streets, or tortured to force them to reveal the places in which their real or supposed wealth was hidden.

The castle was incapable of prolonged resistance. A strong outwork on the eastern side had been committed to the charge of two English and Dutch Companies under the command of Sir Gerard Herbert, a kinsman of the Earl of Pembroke. Nowhere did the enemy find so stout a resistance; but the little force was terribly outnumbered. Herbert, in whose hands four pikes had been broken, was killed by a shot, and the party, bringing away with them their guns and the bodies of the slain, retreated grimly into the fortress. It was in vain that they attempted to continue the struggle. The frightened citizens, who had fled for refuge to the castle, clung round the remains of Herbert's band, and refused to allow them to exasperate the enemy by firing another shot. Under these circumstances, the Governor replied to Tilly's summons by a request to be allowed to consult with Vere at Mannheim. Vere could give him no hope of support, and on the 9th the castle surrendered to the Bavarian commander. The troops were allowed to march out with the honours of war, on condition that they were not to join their comrades at Mannheim or at Frankenthal. The citizens were left to their fate.*

Tilly marched straight upon Mannheim. Placed at an angle between the Rhine and the Neckar, that renowned fortress was only accessible on its southern side, and was for this reason justly regarded as the strongest post in that part of Germany. But to Vere these advantages were likely to prove of small avail. His provisions and his money were running low; his men, exposed without hope of succour to the fury of the enemy, were showing signs of a thoroughly mutinous spirit. An unusually dry summer had lowered the water in the fosse, and

* *Theatrum Europæum*, i. 647. Van der Merven's Relatio Historica. Verantwortung der . . . Stadt Heidelberg. *Londorp*, ii. 743. Vere to Calvert, Sept. 7. Chichester's relation of the loss of Heidelberg, Sept.14. Burlamachi to Calvert, Sept. 12, 14. *S. P. Germany.*

CH. X.
1622.
Sept.

his soldiers, even if they had been inspired with the confidence which had animated the burghers of Leyden, were far too few to man the vast extent of fortification entrusted to his care. His first thought, therefore, was to call in Sir John Burroughs, with the garrison of Frankenthal, in order that he might oppose to the enemy the utmost possible resistance at the point where resistance was likely to be of most avail. That, as a military man, he had judged correctly, is beyond a doubt; but the citizens of Frankenthal refused to be so abandoned. Sprung from the Protestant refugees who had fled from Alva's cruelties in the Netherlands, they were bound together by a bitter hatred against the foe, which was hardly shared by the German inhabitants of Heidelberg or Mannheim. Every man amongst them had arms in his hands, and they were proud of the part which they had taken in the short siege of the preceding year. The moment, therefore, that Burroughs showed signs of moving, they gave him plainly to understand that not a single soldier should leave the town alive. They were fighting for a common cause, and they must live and die together.

Vere's desperate position.

Under these circumstances, Vere reluctantly abandoned his intention. "I believe," he wrote to Calvert, "no man's estate can be more miserable. I am as careful as may be to smother these my opinions, knowing it a great weakness to suffer them to appear. But to your Honour, to whom it is proper to be informed in a business of this weight, I hold it fit to be rather free than otherwise. I endeavour myself, so far as means will give me leave, to keep the enemy at a far distance; but if he press strongly upon me, as I perceive he goes about, I shall then be forced, to my great, great grief, to draw my small numbers into a straiter room, for such is the vastness of the town and works, in many places unfinished, and by the now dryness of the ditches much weakened, as would require an army to defend them."*

Chichester at Frankfort.

Vere could, at least, find some relief in the punctual performance of his duty. To Chichester, condemned to pass his time in enforced idleness at Frankfort, even this

* Vere to Calvert, Sept. 23. *S. P. Germany.*

solace was denied. Charged with the mission of protesting at Ratisbon against the Emperor's audacity in daring to consult the Princes of the Empire on a German question, instead of making a private arrangement with the King of England, he had been compelled by a taunting message from the Governors of Worms and Spires to leave Frankenthal for the neutral territory of the Imperial city. They wished to know, they said, what he was doing amongst their master's enemies. If he were an ambassador, why did he not deliver his message to the Emperor? He was now subjected to gibes of an opposite description. Men did not shrink from saying to his face that all the misery around had been caused by the King of England's negotiations. If Frederick had not been forced to dismiss Mansfeld, his army might, "by living upon the Bishops' countries and United Catholics, have ruined them, and have been at hand to have succoured and relieved his distressed towns and country." Chichester knew not what to do. There was no certainty whether the Emperor would go to Ratisbon or not. He therefore took the resolution of despatching Nethersole to England, to lay the state of affairs before the King. Nethersole had accompanied Frederick in his ride across France in the spring, and had only left him when he retreated for the last time into Alsace. He was, therefore, in a position to give an accurate account of all that had passed, and he would be certain not to be remiss in the conveyance of Chichester's warning, that vigorous and immediate action was indispensable, if the Palatinate was not to be abandoned altogether. He was to pass through the Hague on his way, and to consult with Elizabeth and the Prince of Orange.*

On the 24th of September, Nethersole landed in England. The bitter tidings of the fall of Heidelberg had preceded him by four days. But James had other things to think of. As if he had foreseen that it would be a long time before the clouds with which the sky was overcast would roll away, he had signalised by a grand creation of peers, the breathing-time whilst the courier

---

* Chichester to Calvert, Sept. 14. *S. P. Germany.*

with the evil news was still on the way. Digby was rewarded for his many services with the Earldom of Bristol. Doncaster was consoled for his late diplomatic failure with the Earldom of Carlisle. Cranfield, snarling like a watchdog over the Treasury, had quarrelled with Digby about his allowances before he started, till the harsh words "traitor's blood," and "pedlar's blood," flashed forth on either side, and had lately made an unprovoked attack upon Williams, bringing against him charges of malversation, which were proved to be utterly without foundation. Yet, cross-grained and ill-tempered as he was, his fidelity to his master's interests was unimpeached, and he now stepped forth with the lofty title of Earl of Middlesex. When such promotions were in the air, the Villiers family could hardly be forgotten, and Buckingham's brother-in-law, Fielding, was entitled to style himself for the future Earl of Denbigh.

Serious as was the aspect of the times to ordinary Englishmen, there was high festivity at Court. Buckingham had just completed the purchase of the splendid mansion of New Hall, in Essex, from the Earl of Sussex, and the King, who had gone down to take part in the revelries with which the new owner entered into possession, had no time to give to the Palatinate. Nethersole was told not to speak of business till the festivities were over.

He had not, however, long to wait. After a day or two, the King removed to Hampton Court; and, on the 27th, Nethersole had an interview with Buckingham which gave him no less pleasure than surprise. The news from Heidelberg had rooted itself painfully, for the moment, in the shifting sands of the favourite's imagination; and his voice was now to be heard amongst those which were raised most loudly for war. He was very confident, he said, that the King would now perform everything that he had promised. As for himself, he would use all the credit he had in hastening matters to a satisfactory conclusion, and it should not be his fault if he did not go in person to the wars. "Tell the Queen your mistress," he added, " that though I cannot undertake to do so much as the Duke of Brunswick hath done for her service, I will show my good will not to be behind him in affection." Nor did Buckingham stand alone in his eager desire for war. Those who had hitherto favoured negotiation, were now of one mind with Pembroke and Abbot in believing that the time for negotiation had passed by; and Weston's arrival was eagerly expected, in order that a vigorous resolution might be taken, with a fuller knowledge of the state of affairs at Brussels.*

Whether Buckingham would now be any more successful in forcing an energetic policy upon James than on those former occasions when he had happened to be in a warlike mood, might well be doubted. But it was certain that he would have on his side the warm support of the Prince of Wales, and with the aid of the son he might not unreasonably hope to have at least a chance of conquering the reluctance of the father.

Yet it was by his position far more than by his character that the Prince was likely to serve him. Charles had now nearly completed his twenty-second year. To a superficial observer he was everything that a young prince should be. His bearing, unlike that of his father, was graceful and dignified. His only blemish was the size of his tongue, which was too large for his mouth, and which, especially when he was excited, gave him a difficulty of expression almost amounting to a stammer. In all bodily exercises, his supremacy was undoubted. He could ride better than any other man in England. His fondness for hunting was such that James was heard to exclaim that by this he recognised him as his true and worthy son.† In the tennis-court and in the tilting-yard he surpassed all competitors. No one had so exquisite an ear for music, could look at a fine picture with greater appreciation of its merits, or could keep time more exactly when called upon to take part in a dance. Yet these, and such as these, were the smallest of his merits. Regular in his habits, his household was a model of economy. His own attire was such as in that age was regarded as a protest against the prevailing

---

* Nethersole to Carleton, Sept. 28. *S. P. Holland*.
† Relazione di G. Lando. *Rel. Ven. Ingh*. 263.

extravagance. His moral conduct was irreproachable; and it was observed that he blushed like a girl whenever an immodest word was uttered in his presence. Designing women, of the class which had preyed upon his brother Henry, found it expedient to pass him by, and laid their nets for more susceptible hearts than his.*

Yet, in spite of all these excellencies, keen-sighted observers who were by no means blind to his merits, were not disposed to prophesy good of his future reign. In truth, his very virtues were a sign of weakness. He was born to be the idol of schoolmasters and the stumbling-block of statesmen. His modesty and decorum were the result of sluggishness rather than of self-restraint. Uncertain in judgment, and hesitating in action, he clung fondly to the small proprieties of life, and to the narrow range of ideas which he had learned to hold with a tenacious grasp; whilst he was ever prone, like his unhappy brother-in-law, to seek refuge from the uncertainties of the present by a sudden plunge into rash and ill-considered action. With such a character, the education which he had received had been the worst possible. From his father he had never had a chance of acquiring a single lesson in the first virtue of a

---

* Lando describes him (*Rel. Ven.* Ingh. 261.) as "O vincendo e domando, o non sentendo li moti del senso, non avendo assaggiati, che si sappia, certi giovanili piaceri, nè scoprendosi che sia stato rapito il suo amore, se non per qualche segno di poesia e ben virtuose apparenze, arrossendo anco come modesta donzella se sente a parlare di materia poco onesta. Onde le donne non lo tentano nè anche, come facevano col fratello, che tanto pregiava le bellezze, ed era seguitato e rubato da ognuna."

In the face of this, it is impossible to pay any further attention to the vague gossip which Tillieres thought worthy of a place in his despatches.

It is, however, well known that it is generally believed that Jeremy Taylor's second wife was a natural daughter of Charles, born before this time. Against this story Lando's evidence is of some weight, and it is certain that his opinion was shared by many others, as in a letter, addressed to Charles by Digby, on the 12th of August, 1621 (*Clarendon State Papers*, i. App. xvi.), there is mention of a wide-spread belief in Germany that the prince was physically incapacitated from ever becoming a father. The story rests upon family tradition, but anyone who reads Heber's *Life of Taylor*, will see that the traditions of that family were often vague, and sometimes incorrect. The lady, it seems, was very like Charles in personal appearance, and it is by no means improbable that some one may have accounted for the chance likeness in this way, and that in due course of time the story was accepted, if not by herself, at least by her children, who, in those days of Royalist enthusiasm, would feel a sort of pride in tracing their descent from the Royal Martyr.

ruler—that love of truth which would keep his ear open to all assertions and to all complaints, in the hope of detecting something which it might be well for him to know. Nor was the injury which his mind thus received merely negative; for James, vague as his political theories were, was intolerant of contradiction, and his impatient dogmatism had early taught his son to conceal his thoughts in sheer diffidence of his own powers. To hold his tongue as long as possible, and then to say, not what he believed to be true, but what was likely to be pleasing, became his daily task, till he ceased to be capable of looking difficulties fully in the face. The next step upon the downward path was but too inviting. As each question rose before him for solution, his first thought was how it might best be evaded, and he usually took refuge either in a studied silence, or in some of those varied forms of equivocation which are usually supposed by weak minds not to be equivalent to falsehood.*

Over such a character, Buckingham had found no difficulty in obtaining a thorough mastery. On the one condition of making a show of regarding his wishes as all-important, he was able to mould those wishes almost as he pleased. To the reticent, hesitating youth it was a relief to find some one who would take the lead in amusement and in action, who could make up his mind for him in a moment when he was himself plunged in hopeless uncertainty, and who possessed a fund of gaiety and light-heartedness which was never at fault.

For the Spanish marriage, or indeed for any other marriage, Charles had long cared but little, though he had openly declared himself well satisfied with the provision made by his father for his future life. One of the feelings which he had retained from his childhood was a warm attachment to his sister, and it is by no means improbable that he had come to regard the match proposed for him mainly as the mode in which, as he was told, the restitution of the Palatinate might most easily be obtained. It was certainly hardly with a lover's feelings that he consented at last to play a lover's part. One day, after he had been paying compliments in public

* *Rel. Ven.* Ingh. 262.

Ch. X.
1622.
Sept.

His promise to visit Madrid.

to a portrait of the Infanta, he turned to one of his confidential attendants as soon as he thought that his words would be unheard. "Were it not for the sin," he said, "it would be well if princes could have two wives; one for reason of state, the other to please themselves."*

At length, however, apparently after the dissolution of Parliament, a change seems to have taken place, partly, perhaps, because his increasing years brought a growing desire for marriage, partly, no doubt, because what he looked upon as the factious proceedings of the House of Commons, threw him, together with his friend Buckingham, more than ever into the arms of Spain.

Accordingly, during the last months of Gondomar's stay in England, the bonds between the Spanish embassy and the Prince of Wales were drawn more closely. It was one of the final triumphs of that ambassador, that he induced Charles not only to admit Sir Thomas Savage, a known Roman Catholic, amongst the commissioners by whom his revenue was managed, but even to take this step after Savage had decidedly refused to take the oath of allegiance.† Before he left London, the ambassador had drawn from the Prince an offer to visit Madrid incognito, with two servants only, if, upon his return, the ambassador should see fit to advise the step.‡

Gondomar's object.

That in angling for this promise Gondomar was influenced by the idea that, when once he was under the spell of the Roman Catholic ceremonial, it would be easy to induce Charles to profess himself a convert to the religion of his bride, there can be no doubt whatever. Years before, when the marriage was first discussed, the suggestion that the Prince's presence at Madrid might in this way be turned to account, had been made by the Spanish theologians.§ But, though it afterwards formed

---

* *Rel. Ven.* Ingh. 265.

† Gondomar to Philip IV., Jan. $\frac{21}{31}$, 1622. *Simancas MSS.* Est. 2518.

‡ Este Principe me ha offrezido en mucha confiança y secreto que, si llegado yo á España le aconsejase que se vaya á poner en las manos de V. Mag^d. y á su disposicion, lo hará y llegará á Madrid yncognito con dos criados." Gondomar to Philip IV., May $\frac{6}{16}$. *Simancas MSS.* Est. 2603.

§ Vol. i. p. 108.

the groundwork of the complaint against Buckingham that he had been a fellow-conspirator with the Spaniard in an attempt to turn away his master's son from the Protestant faith, it is almost inconceivable that he can seriously have entertained any such notion, though it is not impossible that just at that moment when what faith he had was trembling in the balance, when he was listening with one ear to his wife and his mother, and with his other ear to Laud, he may have uttered some rash words which cannot fairly be taken as affording a safe clue to his subsequent conduct. It can hardly be doubted that he looked upon the expedition as a bold dashing exploit, and that as such he represented it to Charles, who would naturally be captivated by the part which he would himself be called upon to play.

Since that conversation with Gondomar, however, much had passed. As bad news came in from Brussels and from Heidelberg, Charles began to doubt whether his sister's inheritance was to be regained by the aid of Spain, and he was heard complaining loudly of the tricks which the Spaniards had been playing.* It was under this impression of uncertainty that Buckingham's last letter to Gondomar had been written,† and it was with the same feeling that the two young men determined, as soon as the fall of Heidelberg was known, that the next despatch should be carried by a confidential person who might be trusted with the delicate task of reminding Gondomar of the Prince's promised journey, and of bringing back a faithful report of the language of the Spanish ministers.

The messenger selected for this purpose was Endymion Porter. By a strange destiny he had passed the early years of his life in Spain, in the service of Olivares.‡ He had afterwards returned to England, where he had attached himself to Buckingham, and had risen high in his favour. Report said that he had amassed a large

---

* Valaresso to the Doge, Sept. $\frac{20}{30}$. *Venice MSS. Desp. Ingh.*
† P. 240.
‡ Interrogatories to be administered to Porter, 1627. *Sherborne MSS.* As these questions proceeded from Bristol, I can hardly be wrong in taking them as equivalent to assertions of fact.

fortune by the bribes for which he had sold his master's goodwill.* He was now a gentleman of the Prince's bedchamber, and was occasionally employed by Buckingham to conduct his Spanish correspondence.

This man had already, on the 18th of September, written by Buckingham's direction to Gondomar, to assure him that the Lord Admiral was getting a fleet ready, and that " he intended to take his friend with him in secret, to bring back that beautiful angel."† These words, almost the only ones in the letter which have been preserved, show that the original intention of the Prince to visit Madrid alone had been for the time abandoned. If the proposal thus made was not without elements of rashness, it was wisdom itself as compared with the wild scheme which was ultimately adopted. For if, as was evidently pre-supposed,‡ Buckingham was to sail in command of the fleet which was to bring the Infanta home, he would certainly not leave England till the marriage articles had been finally agreed upon, and there would therefore be no danger that the Spaniards would be emboldened to raise their terms by the Prince's presence at Madrid.

Whether James was at this time informed of the project or not, it is impossible to say.§ It is at all events certain that the Privy Council knew nothing about the matter. On the 29th of September, that body met to receive from Weston the report of his mission. After a long and anxious deliberation, extending over four days, it was decided that a direct summons should be addressed to the King of Spain. Seventy days were to be allowed him to obtain from the Emperor the restitution of Heidelberg, and if it should happen that either Mannheim or Frankenthal had also been taken, it was to be restored as well. Philip was also to engage that the negotiations for a general peace should be resumed on the basis laid down in the preceding winter, and to bind himself by an express stipulation that, if the Emperor

---

* *Rel. Ven.* Ingh. 244.
† Interrogatories administered to Porter, 1627. *Sherborne MSS.*
‡ The plan was adopted immediately upon Porter's return.
§ The reasons for setting aside Clarendon's story, at least in part, will be given later.

refused to consent to these terms, he would order a Spanish army to take the field against him, or, at least, would give permission to an English force to march through Flanders into the Palatinate. If, within ten days after this resolution was laid before Philip, he had not given a favourable answer under his hand and seal, Bristol was to leave Madrid at once, and to declare the marriage treaty broken off.

The despatch* which contained the demands thus put forward by the Council was entrusted to Porter,† and served well enough to cover the secret mission with which he was charged. In a few weeks, therefore, James, unless he were sadly disappointed, would know what his position really was. Yet it is hardly likely that any one except the King looked upon an armed alliance with Spain against the Emperor as coming within the bounds of possibility. The language used in the Council breathed of war, and of war alone. An army of 30,000 or 40,000 men was to be ready in the spring to march into the Palatinate under the command of the Prince of Wales. Parliament was to be summoned to meet in January to vote the necessary supplies. Even Charles's head was for the moment full of dreams of military glory. He would be the ruin of anyone, he was heard to say, who attempted to hinder the enterprise.‡

Yet, in spite of the warlike din which was sounding in his ears, and in spite of the extravagant demands of the Pope and the cardinals, James could not bear to relinquish his hopes of peace. Gage, he resolved, should at once return to Rome, bearing a letter in which, passing by in silence the foolish language which had been used about his own conversion, he adjured the Pope to use his undoubted influence with the Catholic sovereigns to put a stop to the bloodshed by which Christendom was being desolated. "Your Holiness," he wrote, "will perhaps marvel that we, differing from you

---

* The King to Bristol, Oct. 3. *Cabala*, 238.

† The Dutch Commissioners to the States General, Oct. $\frac{4}{14}$. *Add. MSS.* 17,677 K, fol. 229.

‡ Nethersole to Elizabeth, Oct. 3. *S. P. Holland.* Salvetti's *News-Letter*, Oct. $\frac{11}{21}$. Message sent by Porter. *Simancas MSS. Est.* 2849.

in point of religion, should now first salute you with our letters. Howbeit, such is the trouble of our mind for these calamitous discords and bloodsheds, which for these late years by-past have so miserably rent the Christian world; and so great is our care and daily solicitude to stop the course of these growing evils betimes, so much as in us lies; as we could no longer abstain, considering that we all worship the same most blessed Trinity, nor hope for salvation by any other means than by the blood and merits of Our Lord and Saviour Christ Jesus, but breaking this silence to move your Holiness by these our letters, friendly and seriously, that you would be pleased together with us to put your hand to so pious a work, and so worthy of a Christian Prince."*

If James's nerve and judgment had only equalled the excellence of his intentions, he would indeed have carved out for himself an enduring monument amongst those of the benefactors of humanity. Yet, even as it was, it was well that amidst the turmoil of the strife a voice should be heard from England, calling, however vainly, upon the Head of that Church which styles itself Catholic to warn him not to debase his high office to the miserable work of stirring up the elements which fed the lurid flames of religious war.

On the 3rd of October the despatch which Porter was to carry was placed in his hands, and he would have started on the following day if he had not been delayed by the unexpected arrival of Cottington, who had been recalled from his attendance upon the embassy at Madrid to enter upon his new duties as secretary to the Prince of Wales. As he had been specially detained in Spain till Bristol was able to obtain some certain intelligence of the progress of the marriage treaty, every one was naturally eager to hear what he had to say.

It was not much that he was able to tell. Commissioners, amongst whom were Zuñiga and Gondomar, had been appointed to treat with Bristol, and they had loudly expressed their warm disapproval of the additions which

---

* The King to Gregory XV., Sept. 30. *Cabala*, 376.

had been made at Rome to the Articles, and had declared that the King of Spain would, without doubt, reduce his Holiness to reason.* In addition to the news which he brought, Cottington had with him a letter from Gondomar to the King. He hoped, he wrote, to bring the Infanta with him in the spring, by which time all difficulties would be overcome. If it proved otherwise, he would come himself to England to confess his fault in having deceived his Majesty, and to offer himself as a sacrifice for the wrong which he had done.†

Ch. X.
1622.
October.

The Council, however, were unanimous in declaring that there was no ground for changing its resolution. James indeed was, as usual, inclined to hope for the best, and expressed an opinion that good might yet be expected from the Spanish overtures. But he soon found that he stood alone. Buckingham and the Prince led the cry for active measures, and the Council voted as one man upon their side.‡

Charles and Buckingham opposed to the King.

It was a new position for James. Parliamentary opposition he could silence by a dissolution. The Council he could refuse to listen to. But never before had his son and his favourite combined against him. For the present, however, he was able to maintain his tranquillity; for he had contrived to postpone the immediate solution of the difficulty as long as possible, by despatching a second courier on the 4th, with orders to Bristol not to come home in case of receiving an unsatisfactory reply, but simply to report the fact to England.§ At the same time he told Porter to inform his ambassador that if he were hard pressed he might secretly consent to the extension of the age of the children's education to nine years, though the limit was still to be stated in the public articles as having been fixed at seven.‖ In the

Oct. 4.
Bristol ordered to report his answer.

* Bristol to the King, Sept. 13. *S. P. Spain.*
† Salvetti's *News-Letter*, Oct. $\frac{11}{21}$.
‡ The Dutch Commissioners to the States General, Oct. $\frac{10}{21}$. *Add. MSS.* 17,677 K, fol. 234. Valaresso to the Doge, Oct. $\frac{11}{21}$. *Venice MSS. Desp. Ingh.*
§ The King to Bristol, Oct. 4. Prynne's *Hidden Works of Darkness*, 20.
‖ Calvert to Bristol, Oct. 14. Prynne's *Hidden Works of Darkness*, 21.

Ch. X. 1622. October.	meanwhile he took care to inform the Council that, till Porter's return, no active steps were to be taken to form any alliance with the Continental Protestants.*
Porter leaves England.	At last, on the 7th of October, Porter was ready to start on the mission which, as was fondly hoped, would settle the question one way or another. As he left the royal presence, all the bystanders cried out with one voice, "Bring us war; bring us war." †
He is delayed at Calais.	Porter had not been long gone when news arrived that the vessel in which he crossed the Straits had been driven on shore in an attempt to enter Calais harbour in a storm, and that he had himself slipped as he was leaping into a boat, and had seriously injured his shoulder. It would, therefore, be some days before he was able to continue his journey to Madrid.‡
Buckingham's eagerness for action.	Immediately after Porter's departure the King had returned to Royston, happy enough to be set free from the anxieties of business. To a request from the Council that he would at once give orders for the issuing of writs for a parliament, he returned a distinct refusal. He would do nothing, he said, till he heard again from Spain. Buckingham, as eager now for war as ten months before he had been eager to make war impossible, chafed under the delay. Why, he asked of his fellow councillors, should not a fresh benevolence be raised? Then it would be easy to lay in a store of arms and munition, and to make all necessary preparations for the expected campaign. But the Councillors shook their heads at the proposal.§ They all felt that in the present temper of the nation a benevolence was impossible. In the autumn of 1620, and in the autumn of 1621, the King's declarations had been received with universal enthusiasm; but no one believed in such declarations any longer. Rumours were abroad that Porter had been entrusted with

* The Dutch Commissioners to the States General, Oct. $\frac{10}{20}$. *Add. MSS.* 17,677 K, fol. 234.
† "Quando el Don Antonio Porter salia por el lugar, todos le gritaban —Traiganos guerra,—Traiganos guerra." Message brought by Porter. *Simancas MSS.* Est. 2849.
‡ Mead to Stuteville, Oct. 19. *Harl. MSS.* 389, fol. 243. Nethersole to Carleton, Oct. 18. *S. P. Germany.*
§ Nethersole to Carleton, Oct. 24. *S. P. Holland.*

some special message, and no one doubted for an instant that the result of that message would be to prolong the existing suspense. If the King's object had been merely to send an ordinary despatch into Spain, why should he have selected Porter, of all other men, to perform the work of a common courier." *

<small>Ch. X.
1622.
October.</small>

Yet, if war there was to be, it was of evil omen that the thoughts of those who were likely to be entrusted with its management turned once more in the direction of Mansfeld. According to his habitual practice, James was anxious to carry out his plans at the expense of others, and he actually had the effrontery to ask the Prince of Orange to keep Mansfeld and his troops in the pay of the States for a month after their engagement was at an end, in order that, if Porter brought back an unsatisfactory reply, they might then be ready to enter the English service.†

<small>Negotiation with Mansfeld.</small>

This amazing request was, of course, met by a courteous but distinct refusal. The finances of the States General were by no means prosperous, and they had just succeeded in achieving the object for the sake of which they had secured the adventurer's services. At the approach of Maurice, with Mansfeld in his train, Spinola had suddenly raised the siege of Bergen-op-Zoom, and all further danger from the Spanish armies was at an end for the year. Nor was it only on land that Spain had failed to maintain her position. A large squadron, posted in the Straits of Gibraltar to destroy the Dutch fleet as it issued from the Mediterranean, had been compelled to allow the enemy to sail out in safety. About the same time, another large fleet of twenty-two galleons suddenly appeared on the English coast, eager to make havoc amongst the Dutch trading vessels which thronged the channel. In the hope that a safe basis of operations might be gained, Coloma was instructed to demand shelter for his master's ships in the English ports. This time he asked in vain. In the excitement caused by the loss of Heidelberg, James forgot his old design upon

<small>Relief of Bergen-op-Zoom.</small>

<small>A Spanish fleet in the Channel.</small>

---

* Nethersole to Carleton, Oct. 18. *S. P. Germany.*
† Calvert to Carleton, Oct. 9. *S. P. Holland.* Calvert to Buckingham, Oct. 12. *Harl. MSS.* 1580, fol. 175.

Holland, and the demand was peremptorily refused. In a day or two, the mighty fleet which had terrified England with the prospect of a new armada, sailed back without doing damage to any one.* The misfortunes of Spain did not end here. The Mexico fleet was overtaken by a storm before it left the West Indies, and the damage suffered was so great, as to cause the postponement of the voyage till another season. This winter the Spanish Treasury would have to do as best it might, without the annual influx of silver.

Such a combination of disasters was not without its influence upon the Council of State at Madrid, and rendered them more than usually impatient of a policy which threatened to prolong the war in which the country was engaged. It was therefore with surprise not unmingled with indignation, that an accident revealed to them that Zuñiga had been playing them false, and had been encouraging the Emperor in his design of bestowing Frederick's Electorate upon Maximilian. Khevenhüller had recently received instructions to explain to Philip that the Emperor's resolution was unalterable, and Zuñiga had again replied that the course proposed would be most agreeable to the King of Spain, though he doubted its practicability in the face of the opposition which was certain to arise. If he would promise to keep the whole affair a profound secret, he would be allowed to state his wishes before the King.

Not long after this conversation, Zuñiga was seized with a fever, and as he lay tossing on his sick-bed, he pointed out to an attendant a bundle of papers which were to be laid before the Council, amongst which had been placed by mistake the memorial to the Imperial Ambassador. When the mystery was thus unexpectedly revealed, those members of the Council who were opposed to his policy, did not measure their words in reprobating the concealment which had been practised. It was thought that the harsh language then used had a serious effect upon his health. At all events from that moment

* The Dutch Commissioners to the States General, Oct. $\frac{4}{14}$. *Add. MSS.* 17,677 K, fol. 229. Salvetti's *News-Letter*, Oct. $\frac{18}{28}$.

he grew rapidly worse, and on the 27th of September, he died.*

By the death of his uncle Zuñiga, Olivares obtained the virtual control of the government of Spain. Hitherto he had been content to be what Buckingham was in England, the channel through which the favours of the Crown were distributed. He now became the medium for all political communications between the King and the various councils by which the affairs of the Spanish monarchy were conducted. From henceforth it was by Olivares that the opinions of these consultative bodies were laid before Philip, and it was through his hands that the orders passed by which such resolutions as proved acceptable were carried into execution. With a sovereign who, like Philip, hated the very name of business, such a position was equivalent to the possession of Royal power. From this moment Olivares was practically King of Spain, as Lerma had been king before him.

In many respects, the new minister was far superior to the avaricious favourite of Philip III. He had a ready tongue and a quick apprehension. Caring little for pleasure and amusement, he turned his back upon everything that might stand in the way of his devotion to state affairs, excepting so far as he was required to join in the diversions of the King.† To bribes he was entirely inaccessible, and, in the opinion of those who were best able to judge, he was honestly desirous of doing good service to his king and country.‡ If he was incapable of rising to those heights from which a genial statesman, raised like Bristol above the passions and prejudices of the world, looks serenely down upon the strife of men, he was, at least within the limitations of his age and country, an intelligent and resolute politician. If there were many things which he did not see at all, he was at least able to see clearly whatever came within the sphere of his vision;

Ch. X.
1622.
Sept. Olivares succeeds to his position.

His character.

---

* *Khevenhüller*, ix. 1780—1784.
† *Relazione Veneta Spagna*, i. 650.
‡ "Il fine delle sue intenzioni non credo che non sia il servizio del Rè."
"Il Conte Duca . . . non riceve doni, vuole il servizio del Rè. *Ib.* i. 653, 686.

Ch. X.
1622.
Sept.

and plans.

Bristol's
confidence.

and even if he had not been the favourite of his sovereign, he might have ruled the Spanish councils by virtue of that supremacy which is assigned by the ancient proverb to the one-eyed man in the kingdom of the blind. Suddenly raised in youth to the direction of affairs, he had never had an opportunity of learning to estimate the weight of opposition which would be brought against him by men of other races, and of other principles of action than his own. He was consequently, when by his uncle's death he was brought face to face with the problems of actual politics, in a position not unlike that of a theoretical mathematician of recognised ability, who might be called upon to conduct the siege operations of an army in real warfare. It has frequently been taken for granted by those who have judged only by the result, that the policy of Olivares was a warlike policy from the beginning. It was nothing of the sort. If there was any object for which he earnestly strove in order to heal the economical wounds of his country, it was peace, and especially peace with England. But he had clearly made up his mind that even war was to be preferred to national dishonour, whilst, on the other hand, he never arrived at anything like an accurate conception of the terms upon which peace was to be obtained. The limits of Protestantism, he imagined, could be driven back in Germany with the assent of the German Protestants; and the religion of England could be undermined and overthrown without wounding the susceptibilities of Englishmen. It was possible, he thought in his youthful ardour, to secure all the fruits of victory without the risks and anxieties of war.

The day before Zuñiga's death, the despatch which had been written in London on the 9th of September was placed in Bristol's hands.* He immediately demanded an audience, to lay his master's requirements before Philip. He wrote at once to Calvert that he would do everything in his power. For any want of fidelity in himself, he would "willingly undergo all blame and censure. But for the errors of other men, as the indirect course taken from Rome, or what was done in Germany," he could not

* P. 239.

be answerable. He understood that there were some in England, who held him responsible for the success of the business. "I know," he said, "I serve a wise and a just master, whom I have and ever will serve honestly and painfully. And I no way fear but to give him a good and an honest account both of myself and my proceedings. And, whereas it is objected that I have written over confidently of businesses, I write confidently of them still, if our own courses mar them not by taking alarms and altering our minds upon every accident." He concluded by saying that the two months within which he was ordered to expect the conclusion of the marriage treaty, would hardly be sufficient for the purpose. Letters to Rome must be written and answered, and he hoped to receive instructions not to break with Spain for a month more or less.*

On the 3rd of October, Bristol, accompanied by Aston, was received by Olivares at the Escurial, with the most profuse expressions of goodwill. As soon as he had explained his master's annoyance at the addition of new and unheard of demands to the original marriage articles, the Spanish minister assured him that the Pope should be brought to reason. Then passing to the larger question, he declared that the Emperor's proceedings were entirely disapproved of at Madrid, and that, if it were necessary, Philip would come to James's aid, and "would infallibly assist his Majesty with his forces." Being then introduced to the presence of the King, Bristol repeated his complaints. The same language was used by Philip which had previously been employed by his minister. According to Bristol's report of the interview, "he expressed an earnest desire that the match should be concluded, and that therein no time should be lost. He utterly disliked the Emperor's proceedings, and said he would procure his Majesty's satisfaction, and when he could not obtain it otherwise, he was resolved to procure it by his arms."

The very next day the ambassador was officially informed that the Pope's resolutions upon the marriage articles would at once be taken into consideration.

* Bristol to Calvert, Sept. 28, 29. *S. P. Spain.*

Ch. X.
1622.
October.

But before anything could be done, news of the fall of Heidelberg reached Madrid, and Bristol, who saw in the intelligence an excellent opportunity for putting the Spanish professions to the test, at once wrote to Olivares requesting that the King's garrisons in the Palatinate might be ordered to co-operate with Vere in maintaining Mannheim and Frankenthal against the Emperor.* To an assurance that a letter had been written to the Infanta, he replied that he had had enough of vague declarations of orders given, and that he should not be content unless the despatch were placed in his hands to be sent by a courier of his own. He must be allowed to read it, in order that he might see whether it really contained instructions to the Infanta to intervene by force if Tilly refused obedience. His resolute bearing was not without its effect. His demand was taken into consideration by the Council of State, and it was there unanimously resolved, "that, in case the Emperor should not condescend unto reason, this King should then assist his Majesty with his arms for the restitution of the Prince Palatine." Even this, however, was not sufficient for Bristol. He found that the Spaniards wished to interpret this resolution as referring to assistance to be given at some future time, and that they were proposing, so far as immediate action was concerned, to content themselves with what they called "earnest and pressing mediation." But he told them plainly that he would not accept an answer in such terms. His demand was at once acceded to.† Letters were despatched immediately to the Emperor and the Duke of Bavaria, urging them to the concessions required, whilst another letter, intended for the Infanta, was entrusted to Bristol's courier, so that he might be able to assure himself that she was really directed, in case of Tilly's refusal to raise the sieges of Mannheim and Frankenthal, to employ Spanish troops in support of the beleaguered garrisons.‡

* Bristol Memorial, Oct. 3. Bristol to Calvert, Oct. 8. *S. P. Spain.*
† Bristol to Calvert, Oct. 21. *S. P. Spain.*
‡ "Caso que los que governaren las dichas armas pongan alguna difficultad en el cumplimiento dello, V. A. les hará decir que, sino lo executaren, no permitirá otra cosa; y, si fuere necessario, mandará V. A. de la gente de guerra que por mi horden se entretiene en el Palatinado, que

Nor was it only in Bristol's presence that the Spanish Government drew back from the position which had been assumed by Zuñiga. Khevenhüller was distinctly told that whatever message might have been carried by the Friar Hyacintho, was to be understood at Vienna as it was interpreted by Oñate and the Infanta Isabella ; or, in other words, that the King of Spain would give no support, open or secret, to the transference of the Electorate. Philip, it was added, hoped that whatever was done, would be done in agreement with the Princes assembled at Ratisbon. If his advice were not followed, no further assistance was to be expected from Spain.*

<small>Ch. X.
1622.
October.
Language used to the Emperor.</small>

A year afterwards, the declaration made by Philip, that he would assist the King of England, if necessary even with his arms, was made the subject of grave complaint. The King of Spain, it was said, had engaged to compel the Emperor to restore the Palatinate to Frederick, and in refusing to fulfil his obligations, he had violated his most solemn promises. It is, indeed, impossible to acquit Philip and Olivares of concealing their wishes and intentions. But it cannot be said that in this matter, at least, they were guilty of wilfully deceiving James. It was not the question of the ultimate disposal of the Palatinate which was now before them. It was the question of enforcing a suspension of arms in order to make room for subsequent negotiation. And that, for the moment at least, they were ready to fulfil their promises is evident from the language which they used in their despatches.

Of many things the Spanish ministers were grossly ignorant ; but they saw clearly that the settlement of Germany was only possible if it proceeded from Germany itself. If James could have understood this, it

<small>Recall of Chichester.</small>

<small>no solo tenga muy buena correspondencia con la que alli ay del Rey de la Gran Bretaña, pero que si conveniere se entreponga y procure que no recivia daño de otro ; porque es justo se vea que de nuestra parte se hace esto, y todo lo que se puede." Philip IV. to the Infanta Isabella, Oct. $\frac{19}{29}$. S. P. Spain. The original is in the Archives at Brussels. It might be suspected that the instructions here given were countermanded by a secret despatch ; but this is put out of the question by the Infanta's reply of Nov. $\frac{6}{16}$. Brussels MSS.

* Khevenhüller, ix. 1784.</small>

Ch. X.
1622.
October.

would have mattered little that the concessions made to Bristol had been wrung from the fears of Olivares against his secret wishes. If he could have sent a minister to Ratisbon to proclaim loudly his son-in-law's resolution to abide by the terms to which he had set his hand in the preceding winter, he would undoubtedly have won over to the side of peace most of those who were present. Unless he could do that, if Frederick still cherished designs of continuing the war, or if he refused to make that submission which was considered by a great majority of the Princes of Germany to be nothing more than the Emperor's due, James had better have washed his hands of the whole affair. James, as usual preferred leaving the future to chance. On the first news of the fall of Heidelberg he had recalled Chichester to England. When the Assembly met, it would meet without the presence of a single representative either of Frederick or of James. If Oñate were there to counsel moderation on the part of Spain, it was not from him that a guarantee for the future good behaviour, or even for the present intentions of the exiled Elector, could proceed. It would be left to Frederick's enemies to proclaim his misdeeds, and judgment would go by default.

Discussion on the marriage articles.

In the meanwhile the Junta appointed to consider the marriage articles had been proceeding seriously with its work. Since Zuñiga's death, Gondomar was, without dispute, the ablest man amongst the Commissioners, and Gondomar had been of opinion from the beginning that, in order to effect the conversion of England, it was unnecessary to resort to those startling demands which were regarded at Rome as indispensable. Under his influence, therefore, the Junta lent itself without difficulty to Bristol's suggestions, and the ambassador, finding that his objections to the requirements of the Cardinals were regarded with a favourable ear, was enabled to augur well of the result of the negotiation.*

November.
Porter at Madrid.

Such was the position of affairs when, on the first day of November, Porter made his appearance at Madrid. The letter which he brought for Gondomar from Bucking-

* Bristol to Calvert, Oct. 21. *S. P. Spain.*

ham, was well received, and the bearer was assured that the Prince would be welcome in Spain. To the demand for instant action in the Palatinate, it was less easy to obtain an answer. The King was away, hunting in the mountains, and for some days nothing could be done. Forgetting that he was a messenger and not an ambassador, and fancying that Bristol was lukewarm in the business, Porter went straight to Olivares, and asked for an engagement that the Spanish forces in the Palatinate would give their support to Vere.

Such a demand, coming from such a man, roused all the indignation which, in his conversations with Bristol, Olivares had so carefully suppressed. It was preposterous, he said, to ask the King of Spain to take arms against his uncle,* the Catholic League, and the House of Austria. "As for the marriage," he ended by saying, "I know not what it means."†

It was not long before the Spaniard repented the passionate outburst in which his secret feelings had been so openly laid bare. To Bristol's inquiries, he answered coolly that Porter was not a public minister, and that it was unfit to entrust state secrets to such a man. A day or two afterwards, as if to repair his minister's error, the King expressly reiterated to Aston his assurance that, if necessary, the aid of his armies should not be wanting in the Palatinate.‡

It was now Bristol's turn to test the intentions of the Spanish Court. On the 18th of November, he presented a formal demand for the restitution of the towns in the Palatinate, within seventy days. The summons, he soon found, was received with an universal outcry of disapprobation. The King of Spain, he was told, was as firmly resolved as ever to abide by the resolutions which he had taken. But to ask him to engage that Heidelberg and Mannheim should be restored within seventy days, was a

---

* The Mother of Philip IV. was the Emperor's sister.
† Bristol afterwards asserted that the phrase about the match had not been reported to him, "as far as he remembereth" (*Hardwicke State Papers,* ii. 501); but it seems likely enough to have been said. Porter's own story (*S. P. Spain*) was transferred by Buckingham to his relation before the Parliament of 1624.
‡ *Hardwicke State Papers,* i. 504.

mere insult. "When these instructions were given you in England," said one of the Spanish ministers to Bristol, "they must have been very angry." In reporting what he heard to Calvert, the English Ambassador expressed his opinion that the Spaniards still wished to give satisfaction to his master, but that they were "in great confusion how to answer to the particulars."*

Bristol, in truth, was unwilling to acknowledge to himself how untenable his position was becoming. His original policy of an alliance between Spain and England, grounded upon mutual respect, and used for the benefit of European peace, had broken down completely when the Parliament of 1621 was dissolved. He had then warned James how thoroughly the conditions of his mediation had changed. England could no longer meet Spain upon equal terms. She must supplicate for peace now that she was no longer in a position to demand it. That in Spain there was a great dread of war, and above all, of war with England, he had every reason to know, and he believed that, partly by appealing to that feeling, partly by holding out hopes that the marriage treaty would be accompanied by benefits to the English Catholics, he could still induce Spain to throw its weight into the scale of peace.

That such a policy was a rational one under the circumstances few candid persons will deny. Its weak point was that it depended for success altogether upon the behaviour of Frederick and his allies. Unless James could so restrain the words and actions of his son-in-law, as to make it evident to the world that the restoration of the Palatinate would not be the signal for a fresh war, leaving the Imperial forces to do all their work over again, it was ridiculous to expect that either Spain or the Emperor would consent to the terms proposed. Above all, it was most absurd that James, who had shown himself utterly unable to control his son-in-law's proceedings, should now be urging the Spanish Government to sacrifice all its principles and interests, by taking up arms against its own allies in such a cause.

Between the hallucination of James, that the Spaniards

---

* Bristol to Calvert, Nov. 26. *S. P. Spain.*

would fight for the re-establishment of his son-in-law, and the hallucination of the Spaniards that the Protestants of Europe would look on unmoved whilst the heir of the Palatinate was being educated in the Roman Catholic faith, Bristol's negotiation was in evil plight. Yet the mere fact that the Spaniards had seriously promised to employ force for the preservation of the towns in Germany, is sufficient proof that if his master had been able to control events upon the Protestant side, it was not at Madrid that any serious opposition would be encountered.

_{Ch. X.
1622.}

A few days after Bristol's demands were presented, news arrived that Mannheim had fallen into the hands of Tilly.

With a garrison of fourteen hundred men, Vere had found it impossible to defend the extensive fortifications of the place; and, after setting fire to the town, had retired into the castle. But even there his troops were all too few for the work before them. Mansfeld had long before swept away the stores which had been laid up for the siege; and the blockade had been too strict to permit of the introduction of fresh supplies in sufficient quantity. Provisions and fuel were running short, and there was only powder enough to last for six or seven days. Hope of succour there was none, the German soldiers were beginning to talk of surrender, and Vere had every reason to suppose that they would refuse to stand to their guns. Under these circumstances, there was nothing to be done but to come to terms with the enemy, and a capitulation was accordingly signed which allowed the garrison to march out with the honours of war.*

_{Oct. 23.
Fall of Mannheim.}

Immediately after receiving the keys of the citadel, Tilly marched upon Frankenthal, the only place still occupied in Frederick's name. Advanced as the season was, he at once commenced the siege, in the hope of reducing the place before winter came. To a letter from Brussels, acquainting him that it was the King of Spain's wish that he should leave the place untouched, he had

_{Siege of Frankenthal.}

---

* Vere to Calvert, Oct. 30. *S. P. Germany.* Carleton to Calvert, Dec. 27. *S. P. Holland.*

replied with a blunt refusal to accept orders from any one but the Emperor.

If the Infanta had now been prepared to carry out the orders which she had received from Madrid, she would at once have given directions to the Spanish troops to break up the siege by force. But there were limits even to the power of a King of Spain. The Infanta informed her nephew that he had given orders which it was impossible to execute. The few Spanish troops left in the Palatinate were not sufficiently numerous to relieve the garrison of Frankenthal; and even if this had not been the case, it was preposterous to imagine that Spain could ever be found fighting against the Catholic League. She hoped that his Majesty would use all good offices in favour of peace; but assuredly he could do nothing more.*

In truth, no one but James could ever have dreamed of anything else. It was his business to make peace desirable. At the head of the neutral Protestants of Germany his word would have been worth listening to; but it was mere fatuity to expect the Spaniards to extricate him from the difficulty into which his own indolence had brought him.

The Infanta's letter, reaching Madrid at a time when Bristol was pressing for an answer to the demand which he had been instructed to make, was not calculated to diminish the hesitations of the Spanish ministers. Nor was their course rendered less difficult by the arrival of a despatch from Oñate, announcing that the Emperor was not to be moved from his design of conferring the Electorate upon Maximilian.† Evidently the problem of keeping on good terms with James and Ferdinand at the same time was becoming more insoluble every day.

It was not only from the side of foreign politics that danger was to be apprehended to the good understanding which Olivares wished to establish between the Courts of London and Madrid. The Infanta Maria, whose hand

---

* The Infanta Isabella to King Philip IV., Nov. $\frac{3}{13}$, $\frac{6}{16}$. Memoir for A. de Lossada. *Brussels MSS.*

† Ciriza to Philip IV., Nov $\frac{15}{25}$. *Simancas MSS.* Est. 2507.

was to be the pledge of its continuance, had now entered upon her seventeenth year. Her features were not beautiful, but the sweetness of her disposition found expression in her face, and her fair complexion and her delicate white hands drew forth rapturous admiration from the contrast which they presented to the olive tints of the ladies by whom she was surrounded.* The mingled dignity and gentleness of her bearing made her an especial favourite with her brother. Her life was moulded after the best type of the devotional piety of her Church. Two hours of every day she spent in prayer. Twice every week she confessed, and partook of the Holy Communion. Her chief delight was in meditating upon the Immaculate Conception of the Virgin, and preparing lint for the use of the hospitals. The money which her brother allowed her to be spent at play, she carefully set aside for the relief of the poor.

Her character was as remarkable for its self-possession as for its gentleness. Excepting when she was in private amongst her ladies, her words were few; and though those who knew her well were aware that she felt unkindness deeply, she never betrayed her emotions by speaking harshly of those by whom he had been wronged. Any one who hoped to afford her amusement by repeating the scandal and gossip of the Court, was soon taught, by visible tokens of her disapprobation, to avoid such subjects for the future. When she had once made up her mind where the path of duty lay, no temptation could induce her to swerve from it by a hair's breadth. Nor was her physical courage less conspicuous than her moral firmness. At a Court entertainment given at Aranjuez, a fire broke out amongst the scaffolding which supported the benches upon which the spectators were seated. In an instant the whole place was in confusion. Amongst the screaming throng the Infanta alone retained her presence of mind. Calling Olivares to her help, that he might keep off the pressure of the crowd, she made her escape without quickening her usual pace.†

* Bristol to the Prince of Wales, Dec. 25, 1622 ; Feb. 22, 1623. *S. P. Spain.*
† Description of the Infanta, by Toby Matthew, June 28, 1623. *S. P. Spain.*

There were many positions in which such a woman could hardly have failed to pass a happy and a useful life. But it is certain that no one could be less fitted to become the wife of a Protestant King, and the Queen of a Protestant nation. On the throne of England her life would be one continual martyrdom. Her own dislike of the marriage was undisguised, and her instinctive aversion was confirmed by the reiterated warnings of her confessor. A heretic, he told her, was worse than a devil. "What a comfortable bedfellow you will have," he said. "He who lies by your side, and who will be the father of your children is certain to go to hell."*

It was only lately, however, that she had taken any open step in the matter. Till recently, indeed, the marriage had hardly been regarded at Court in a serious light. But the case was now altered. A Junta had been appointed to settle the articles of marriage with the English Ambassador, and although the Pope's opinion had been given, it seemed likely that the Junta, under Gondomar's influence, would urge him to reconsider his determination. Under these circumstances the Infanta proceeded to plead her own cause with her brother. She found a powerful support in the Infanta† Margaret, the youngest daughter of the Emperor Maximilian II., who had retired from the world to a Carmelite nunnery at Madrid. This lady now put forth all her influence to induce the King to return to the scheme which had received his father's approval,‡ to marry his sister to the Emperor's son, the Archduke Ferdinand, and to satisfy the Prince of Wales with the hand of an archduchess.§

---

* Bristol to the King, Aug. 18, 1623. *S. P. Spain.*

† So termed at Madrid, though strictly speaking she should be called the Archduchess Margaret. Her mother was a Spanish Infanta.

‡ Vol. i. p. 351.

§ "Ho anco inteso per sicurissima via che scrive il Nontio di Spagna trattarsi in quella Corte nell apparenza molto alle secrette questo matrimonio con Inghilterra, et ch'era molto portato dal Conte di Codmar," *i.e.*, Gondomar, "dicendosi d'alcuni che seguira certo, et da altri che tutta era una fintione per addormentar Inghilterra, et che lui ne ha parlato secrettissimamente con detto Conte, et con li ministri, accio che non si faccia senza la saputa del Pontefice, et cosi ne havea riportata parola et promessa;—che questa voce era arrivata sino all' Infante, et che si dovesse presto preparar per quel Regno ; la qual ne mostrava dispiacere, ma che era stata consolata dalla Contessa di Lemos, et dal Infante Cardinale, et da tutte le dame del Palazzo, essortandola ad andar allegra-

The tears of the sister whom he was loath to sacrifice were of great weight with Philip; but she had powerful influences to contend with. Olivares, upon whose sanguine mind the hope of converting England was at this time exercising all its glamour, protested against the change; and Philip, under the eye of his favourite, made every effort to shake his sister's resolution. The confessor was threatened with removal from his post if he did not change his language; and divines of less unbending severity were summoned to reason with the Infanta, and were instigated to paint in glowing colours the glorious and holy work of bringing back an apostate nation to the faith.

For a moment the unhappy girl gave way before the array of counsellors, and she told her brother that, in order to serve God and obey the King, she was ready to submit to anything.*

In a few days, however, this momentary phase of feeling had passed away. Her woman's instinct told her that she had been in the right, and that, with all their learning, the statesmen and divines had been in the wrong. She sent to Olivares to tell him that if he did not find some way to save her from the bitterness before her, she would cut the knot herself by taking refuge in a nunnery;† and when Philip returned from his hunting in November, he found himself besieged by all the weapons of feminine despair.

Philip was not proof against his sister's misery. Upon

---

mente;—che all' Ambasciatore Inglese era stato promesso il vederla e visitarla, et che all' officio lei mai rispose, tenendo sempre gli occhi in terra;—che l'Infante Discalza," i.e., the Infanta Margaret, " insieme col Rè pur le hanno parlato di queste nozze, dicendole essa Discalza che le pensasse bene, poiche si trattava di lei sola ; et che lei habbi detto al Rè che in gratia non le lasciasse : onde persuadeva essa Discalza che gia che si vede non mostrar questa figliuola inclinatione a queste nozze, ben sarà maritarla in Germania, et dar la figliuola dell' Imperator ad Inghilterra, onde da questi concetti dubbiosi che si introducono si va argomentando che possino Spagnoli in fine, quando non possino far altro, et cavatone (?) il frutto che desideranno, liberarsi dalla promessa col dir che la figliuola non vuole maritarsi in Inghilterra, et addonar a lei tutto." Zen to the Doge, $\frac{\text{Oct. 29}}{\text{Nov. 8}}$. *Venice MSS.* Desp. Roma.

* Corner to the Doge, $\frac{\text{Oct. 29}}{\text{Nov. 8}}$. *Venice MSS.* Desp. Spagna. Bristol to the King, Aug. 18, 1623. *S. P. Spain.*

† Francisco de Jesus, 48.

> Ch. X.
> 1622.
> Nov. 25.
> Philip's letter to Olivares.

the political effect of the decision which he now took he scarcely bestowed a thought. It was his business to hunt boars or stags, or to display his ability in the tilt-yard; it was the business of Olivares and the Council of State to look after politics.

The letter in which he announced his intention to Olivares was very brief. "My father," he wrote, "declared his mind at his death-bed concerning the match with England, which was never to make it; and your uncle's intention, according to that, was ever to delay it; and you know likewise how averse my sister is to it. I think it now time that I should find a way out of it; wherefore I require you to find some other way to content the King of England, to whom I think myself much bound for his many expressions of friendship."*

> Nov. 28.
> Olivares' change of policy.

Such a letter as this would have been irresistible, even if the minister's own opinions had remained unchanged; but during the last fortnight much had occurred to shake his determination. On the one hand, Bristol's peremptory demand for immediate co-operation against the Emperor had been presented; on the other hand, it was now known at Madrid that Tilly had not paid the slightest attention to the Infanta's remonstrances, and that nothing would induce the Emperor to postpone any longer the transference of the Electorate. Under these circumstances, it was evident that it was necessary to reconsider those wide-reaching plans which had a few weeks before seemed so easy of accomplishment, and the result of a little thought was a memorial addressed by Olivares to the King, and laid before the Council of State for its approval.†

---

* This letter is only known from an English translation. It was afterwards shown to the Prince of Wales by Olivares; but he was not allowed to take a copy. The letter as printed here differs from that to be found in many collections. It is from a paper amongst the Spanish State Papers in the Prince's own handwriting with interlineations and corrections, which leave scarcely any doubt as to its being the original draft which Charles is said to have written down immediately after the interview. The letter as usually given (in Cabala for instance, p. 314,) is longer. The changes may have been added for the purpose of making it clearer to an English audience, as when "Your uncle" becomes "Your uncle Don Baltazar," or they may have been simply added on further consideration. It is perfectly immaterial which view is adopted, as in all essential points the two letters agree. The question of the date will be discussed in a note to p. 278.

† Bristol to the King, Aug. 18, 1623. *S. P. Spain.*

"Sir," he began, "considering the present state of the treaty of marriage between Spain and England, and knowing certainly, as I understand from the ministers who treated of the business in the time of our lord the King Philip III.,—may he now be in glory,—that his meaning was never to effect it, unless the Prince became a Catholic, but only with respect to the King of England to prolong the treaty, and the consideration of its articles, till he could obtain the conditions at which he aimed; and also to retain the amity of that king, which was desirable in every way, and especially on account of the affairs of Flanders and Germany and the obligation under which he has placed us as regards the latter; and suspecting likewise that your Majesty is of the same opinion, although you have made no demonstration of any such intention, yet founding my suspicions on the assurance which I have received that the Infanta Donna Maria has resolved to enter a nunnery the same day that your Majesty shall press her to make the marriage without the above-mentioned conditions, I have thought fit to present to your Majesty that which my zeal has suggested to me on this occasion, and which I consider will give great satisfaction to the King of Great Britain."

CH. X.
1622.
Nov. 23.
His memorial.

The minister then proceeded to show that James was involved in two difficulties, the one that of the marriage; the other, that of the Palatinate; and that it was not to be supposed that, even if the marriage were effected, he would cease to require the restitution of his grandchildren. If, therefore, the Infanta were married before the other question was settled, his Majesty would find himself in a dilemma; for, argued Olivares with every show of reason on his side, "it will be necessary for you to declare against the Emperor and the Catholic League, a thing which, even to hear as a mere possibility, will offend your Majesty's pious ears; or to declare yourself for the Emperor and the Catholic League, as certainly you will, and to find yourself engaged in a war against the King of England, and your sister married to his son." Any other supposition, he went on to say, was inadmissible. Neutrality would be out of the question. The King of England had made up his mind that he was to

Ch. X.
1622.
Nov. 28.

recover the Palatinate with the help of Spain; the Emperor, on the other hand, would not give way, at least as far as the Electorate was concerned. It was, therefore, by no means easy to escape from the situation in which they were placed ; and, if something were not done at once, it would be impossible to extricate themselves at all. He ended by proposing once more the old plan which had found favour with Philip III.—the marriage of Prince Charles with the Emperor's daughter, and a Catholic education for Frederick's eldest son at Vienna, with the prospect of the hand of an archduchess when he came of age. Thus everybody would be satisfied, and Europe would be at peace.*

Character of the scheme.

Never before, in all probability, had so visionary a scheme been found side by side with such sturdy common sense. Olivares at least saw plainly that the great difficulty of the day was the German war, and that all questions about family alliances and the amelioration of the condition of the English Catholics were insignificant in comparison ; yet, true Spaniard as he was, he could not rise, as Bristol had risen, to a position from which the two parties could be regarded with an equal eye. His own religion was to resume its true superiority almost without a struggle. Protestantism was not a religion at all ; certainly not one for which anyone was likely to fight, excepting upon selfish motives. All that was needed was to throw a little dust in the eyes of the princes. Let Frederick be persuaded that his son would regain the inheritance of his family, and he would not stop to haggle over such a trifle as his education at a Roman Catholic Court. Let James be persuaded that his dynastic interest would be secured, and he would surely not trouble himself about religious changes in the Palatinate.

Utterly absurd as was Olivares' estimate of the

* The date of this memorial is always given in the English translations as Nov. 8. But the original Spanish (*Francisco de Jesus*, 48) gives Dec. 8, that is to say, $\frac{\text{Nov. 28}}{\text{Dec. 8}}$, and this is confirmed by Bristol's letter of Aug. 18, 1623. Evidently the translator altered the month from the new to the old style, and forgot to change the day. The same will hold good of Philip's letter to which I have assigned the date of $\frac{\text{Nov. 25}}{\text{Dec. 5}}$, instead of Nov. $\frac{5}{15}$. In the English copies all references to the Prince's becoming a Catholic are omitted. Was this deliberate excision Charles's work ?

power of resistance which Protestantism still possessed, he was undoubtedly in the right in holding that, with all its antecedents, Spain could not separate itself from the Emperor. Yet, when his memorial was read in the Council of State, that body unanimously refused to endorse it.* Objecting to the path upon which Olivares was entering as ultimately leading to war with England, the Councillors were nevertheless incapable of striking out an antagonistic policy. With the instinct of weak men, they preferred blundering on in the old track, in the hope that some lucky accident would occur to set them free from the consequences of their long duplicity.

When Olivares met with opposition in the Council of State, he never allowed his displeasure to be seen. To all outward appearance he gave way to the decision. It was in this spirit that he now set to work. Every public act was to be in accordance with the supposition that the marriage treaty was not to be abandoned. In consequence of this resolution, the negotiations with Bristol went on as before. The Junta reported the result to the King, and the King formally expressed a satisfaction which he was far from feeling. Royal letters were written to the Spanish Ambassador at Rome, urging him to hasten the dispensation by every means in his power. These letters were allowed to fall into Bristol's hands, so as to remove all possible doubt of Philip's sincerity from his mind; but all this was only a solemn farce. On the day after his memorial was written, Olivares sent for Khevenhüller, and requested him to lay his plan before the Emperor.† Of that which to ordinary eyes constituted the main difficulty, Olivares had no fear at all; of the popular resistance which was certain to arise in England, he had simply no conception whatever; nor did he even fancy that there would be any difficulty about the marriage. The Pope had declared that without liberty of worship he would not grant the dispensation, and if there was any fear of his giving way, it would be easy to convey to him a private hint that the despatches from Madrid were not intended to be seriously regarded; and that if he wished

* Bristol to the King, Aug. 18, 1623. *S. P. Spain.*
† Khevenhüller, ix. 1789.

Intrigues of Olivares.

Ch. X.
1622.

December.
The marriage articles amended.

to please the King of Spain, he must refuse the petitions which were presented by his ambassador.* Such was the strange compound of audacity and cajolery with which the affairs of Spain were from henceforth to be conducted. In all seriousness, Gondomar went backwards and forwards between Bristol and the Junta. At last, on the 2nd of December, Bristol received what, as he supposed, was the final resolution of the Spanish Government. On the question of the church in London, he was informed that the King of Spain was ready to give way, and to restrict its publicity to the household of the Infanta. But he was told that it was impossible to allow the ecclesiastics who were to attend her to be subject to the laws of England. If James pleased, he might have the option of banishing any one of them who might offend against his laws, and a private assurance would be given that if, in any very foul case, he chose to proceed to actual punishment, the King of Spain would wink at the violation of the article. With

* " It is true that the Conde of Olivares, upon some scruple which the Infanta seemed to make to marry with a Prince of a different religion, but especially for that he feared that if the match with the Infanta should be made, and the business of the Palatinate not be compounded, they should hardly obtain their end of a peace which they chiefly aim at, projected and thereupon wrote a kind of discourse, how much fitter it would be for this King taking a daughter of the Emperor's to match her with the Prince, and thereby both to make an alliance, and to accommodate the troubles of Germany ; and he proceeded so far in this conceit that privately he procured a commission from the Emperor to treat and conclude that match with me if occasion were offered. But when this discourse of his came to be seen in the Council of State, it was utterly disliked by all, and resolved that it should in no ways interrupt the going forward to a present conclusion of the match for the Infanta with me . . . . And divers of the Council have told me that this discourse was upon a false ground, pre-supposing that neither the last king nor this intended to proceed in the match unless the Prince would turn Catholic, which point had long before been cleared, and the mistake merely grew out of this Conde of Olivares being absolutely new in the business." Bristol to the King, Aug. 18, 1623. S. P. Spain. Of course Bristol may have been misinformed, but I do not suppose he was. The difference of opinion between the Royal family and the ministers is corroborated by a despatch of the Venetian Ambassador at Rome, who says that he was informed by Cardinal Ludovisi that the marriage " sia molto consigliato dalli ministri, ma che pero gli parenti, et quelli del sangre, non lo consigliano, ma piutosto nel figliuolo dell Imperatore." Zen to the Doge, Jan. $\frac{11}{21}$, 1623. *Venice MSS.* Desp. Roma. Though Olivares is not directly mentioned, there can be no doubt that he took the part of the Infanta, and it will be seen that, some time after this, he continued to be a warm advocate of the German marriage.

respect to the education of the children, James's secret engagement to leave them in the hands of their mother till the age of nine would be accepted, though it was hoped that one more year would be added. The last point to be decided, was the difficult one of the protection to be afforded to the English Catholics. What James had offered was a general promise that the penal laws should be mercifully administered, and that no one should suffer death for his religion. The least that the Pope had asked was that liberty of worship should be granted, and liberty of worship was understood at Rome to mean the free use of a public church in every English town.* Gondomar now proposed a middle course. Let James, he said, promise in general terms to avoid all persecution of the Catholics as long as they gave no scandal, or in other words, let him consent to permit them the free exercise of their religion within the walls of their own houses. If he would do that, it would be unnecessary for the stipulation to be included in the marriage treaty. A letter containing the engagement, and signed by the King and the Prince of Wales, would be sufficient.

With this declaration Bristol professed himself so far satisfied, that he would gladly see the articles thus modified sent to Rome. Till he had received fresh instructions from home, it would be impossible for him to give a formal assent to the changes proposed; but he was unwilling to cause any further delay. Promises were accordingly given to him that pressure should be put upon the Pope to induce him to accept the treaty as it now stood, and to give a final answer before the end of March or April. In the mean time, the questions relating to the Infanta's portion and dowry might be discussed and settled, and the marriage might take place before the spring was at an end.†

With respect to the Palatinate, a less decisive answer was given. Everything, it was said, should be done to

* Zen to the Doge, $\frac{\text{Dec. 28}}{\text{Jan. 7}}$. *Venice MSS.* Desp. Roma.
† Bristol to Calvert, Nov. 26, Nov. 28, Dec. 4. Bristol to the King, Dec. 10. *S. P. Spain* The accommodation of the differences in religion.—Answer given to Bristol, Dec. $\frac{2}{12}$. Prynne's *Hidden Works of Darkness*, 22, 23.

CH. X.
1622.
December.

satisfy the King of England, but it would be unseemly to call upon the Emperor to surrender the towns in the Palatinate at seventy days' notice. Nor was it possible for the King to take any decided resolution till a reply had been received to his last despatch.*

Bristol recommends the adoption of the amended articles.

Of all this Bristol was inclined to take a favourable view. He could not see, he said, how the Palatinate could be recovered without the aid of Spain, and it was ridiculous to suppose that Philip would send his sister, and 500,000*l.* as well, to a country with which, if he did not mean honestly about the Palatinate, he would certainly be at war in a very short time. The only real question, therefore, was whether the marriage was intended or not.

In expressing his belief that the Spanish Council of State was in earnest about the marriage, Bristol did not form his conclusions rashly. He had received good information of the language used by the members of that body at their sittings. He had seen their reports presented to the King, and he had also seen the notes written by Philip's own hand, by which those proceedings were approved.† Was it possible to suppose, he might well argue, that a king would carry out a deception so systematically, not only with foreign ambassadors, but even with his own ministers? And even if he did, what use would it be to him to trick the whole world, when he was certain to be unmasked in a few months at the latest?

Such arguments would have been sound enough, if Spanish statesmen had been governed by the rules which ordinarily influence human conduct. What it was impossible for Bristol to conceive, was that Gondomar, who was openly and honestly advocating the marriage, was under the delusion that the promised visit of the Prince of Wales would end in his conversion to the Catholic creed, and that Olivares, who was secretly opposing the marriage, was fully convinced that it was possible to break it off, and to obtain the education of the young Prince Palatine as a Catholic, without giving the slightest offence to James.

* Verbal answer given to Bristol's Memorial. *S. P. Spain.*
† Bristol to the King, Aug. 18, 1623. *S. P. Spain.*

Accordingly, Gage who had been sent to Madrid to watch the progress of the negotiation, was ordered to start at once for Rome, and on the 13th of December, Porter at last set out for England, carrying with him the amended articles, and a secret message from Gondomar, joyfully accepting the offer of a visit from the Prince.

<small>Ch. X.
1622.
Porter's return.</small>

On the 2nd of January, Porter arrived in England. On two of the alterations, that relating to the additional year for the education of the children, and the more important one, which exempted the ecclesiastics of the Infanta's household from secular jurisdiction, James had already given way on the first intimation from Bristol that these changes were desired in Spain.* No further difficulty was therefore made. James and Charles at once signed the articles, as well as a letter in which they engaged that Roman Catholics should no longer suffer persecution for their religion, or for taking part in its sacraments, so long as they abstained from giving scandal, and restricted the celebration of their rites to their own houses, and that they should also be excused from taking those oaths which were considered to be in contradiction with their religious belief. This letter, however, was to be retained in Bristol's hands till the dispensation had actually arrived.†

<small>1623. January. The amendments accepted by the King.</small>

Whilst James and his son were thus signing away the independence of the English monarchy, his subjects were regarding the proceedings of their sovereign with scarcely concealed disgust. This time it was reserved for the young lawyers of the Middle Temple to give utterance to the feelings which the preachers now hardly dared to mutter. At their Christmas supper, one of them, we are told, "took a cup of wine in one hand, and held his sword drawn in the other, and so began a health to the distressed Lady Elizabeth; and, having drunk, kissed the sword, and laying his hand upon it, took an oath to live and die in her service; then delivered the cup and

<small>1622. Revels at the Temple.</small>

---

* The King to Bristol, Nov. 24, 1622. Prynne's *Hidden Works of Darkness*, 22.

† Calvert to Gage, Jan. 5. Prynne's *Hidden Works of Darkness*, 25.

sword to the next, and so the health and ceremony went round."*

Such opposition as this would have been harmless enough if James had had any real understanding of the political situation. But the news which Porter had brought lulled him once more to sleep, and he was now ready, not merely as Bristol advised him, to make use of the good offices of Spain for whatever they might be worth, but to give himself up blindly into the hands of the Spanish Government; for he had now taken up warmly the plan for the sequestration of Frankenthal which he had denounced, a few months before in no measured terms, and had been surprised to find that the Infanta was not quite so ready to accede to his wishes as she had been when the walls of Heidelberg and Mannheim were still guarded by his soldiers.† Accordingly he appealed directly to Philip. Tilly had broken up the siege on the 24th of November, but the town was still blocked up by the troops of his lieutenant Pappenheim, and even if it were not assaulted by force, it would be compelled to surrender from want of provisions before the end of March.‡

In this matter, at least, James had hardly any choice. With the best will in the world it would be impossible for him to send an English army into the Palatinate before the end of March. His fault was, not that he advocated the sequestration of Frankenthal, but that he had allowed affairs to fall into such a deplorable state, that nothing better could be done.

Yet even now news came from Germany which would have been grateful to any one with a clear perception of the position of affairs. For it was now known that the Elector of Saxony, who in July had been thrown into the arms of the Emperor by Frederick's ill-advised proceedings at Darmstadt, was beginning in October to

---

* Mead to Stuteville, Jan. 25. *Harl. MSS.* 389, fol. 274.

† Coloma to the King, $\frac{Oct. 29}{Nov.}$. *Harl. MSS.* 1583, fol. 305. De La Faille to Trumbull, Dec. $_{15}$. *S. P. Germany.*

‡ The King to Bristol, Jan. 7. Calvert to Bristol, Jan. 7. Prynne's *Hidden Works of Darkness*, 27, 28.

doubt the wisdom of the course which he had been pursuing.

Ch. X. 1622. October. Expulsion of the Lutheran clergy from Bohemia.

Ferdinand, elated with success, had thought that the time was come to take one more step in the reduction of Bohemia to his own religion. In the spring he had expelled the native Bohemian clergy from the country, and he now gave orders that the German Lutheran churches should be closed, and that the last of the Protestant clergy should be sent into exile. Against this the Elector of Saxony protested. Special promises, he said, had been made to him that Lutheranism should be left untouched in Bohemia. He was answered, that those promises had only been given on condition that the Bohemians made their submission peaceably. As, however, it was notorious that this had not been the case, Ferdinand had as much right as any other of the Princes of the Empire to provide as he pleased for the religious teaching of his subjects. The special arrangements made in Silesia by the Elector in the name of the Emperor would be respected, but no interference with the other States of the Austrian monarchy could be permitted.*

State of the Palatinate.

The theory which strained to the uttermost the rights of territorial sovereignty in matters of religion, had been too long the basis of the whole political system in Germany to make it probable that John George would do more than make empty remonstrances against the persecution which was setting in in Bohemia. But it was different with the Palatinate, which was not yet legally in the hands of a Catholic sovereign. Tilly's first act after the surrender of Heidelberg, had been to found a college for the Jesuits, and it was not long before the churches were filled with Catholic priests. Unless something were done shortly, the Palatinate would be lost to Protestantism for ever.

Difficult position of the neutral Protestants.

Unfortunately, John George was no more likely than James to strike out a new and vigorous policy in accordance with the altered circumstances of the time. But the difficulties which beset him in common with the other neutral Protestants, were not altogether of his own

---

* *Londorp,* ii. 630—653. Hurter. *Gesch. Ferdinands II.,* ix. 213. Pescheck *Gegenreformation in Böhmen,* ii. 36.

creation. In leaning to the side of Ferdinand, he had been defending the cause of order against anarchy. If he was to change his attitude and to defend the cause of the religious independence of the Protestant States against the Emperor, what assurance could he have that he was not bringing back the anarchy which he detested? Nor was this a mere theoretical question; for long before the end of the year, Mansfeld, at the head of his free companies, was once more at his work of plunder and destruction within the limits of the Empire.

With the relief of Bergen-op-Zoom the need for Mansfeld's services in the Netherlands had come to an end, and it was not likely that the States-General, in the midst of their own financial necessities, would keep in pay an army which they no longer wanted, merely to suit the convenience of James. He was accordingly discharged on the 27th of October, and sent over the frontier to find support as best he could. An attempt upon the Bishopric of Münster brought him face to face with the enemy in superior force,* and he turned his steps towards East Friesland. To him it was a matter of perfect indifference that he had no cause of quarrel whatever with the unlucky Count of East Friesland or his subjects. It was enough for him that the country was rich in meadows and in herds of cattle, and that, surrounded as it was by morasses, it would form a natural fortress from which he might issue to plunder the neighbouring territories at his pleasure. He at once sent to the Count to demand quarters for 15,000 men, a loan of 30,000 thalers, and the possession of Stickhausen, a strong fort on the Soest, which commanded the only road by which the country was accessible from the south.† Before an answer could arrive, Mansfeld made himself master of the place; and in a few days his troops had spread over the whole country. The aged Count himself was placed under arrest with his whole family, and his money was confiscated for the use of the army. Heavy contributions were laid upon

---

* Carleton to Calvert, Nov. 5. *S. P. Holland.*
† Carleton to Calvert, Nov. 18. *S. P. Holland.* Uetterodt's *Mansfeld,* 525.

the landowners and farmers, whilst the soldiery were suffered to deal at their pleasure with the miserable inhabitants.*

Such were the proceedings of the man who, if James had listened to the advice of the Prince of Orange, would have been furnished with English gold, and sent to reconquer the Palatinate.† He was now looking to France for aid; for Lewis had at last made peace with his Huguenot subjects, and it was understood that the French ministers were beginning to view with jealousy the increasing vigour of the House of Austria.

Meanwhile Frederick had once more returned to the Hague. Still floating aimlessly, like a cork on the tumbling waves, he was as irresolute and as impracticable as ever. His own wishes would have led him to give full support to Mansfeld, and to proclaim war to the knife against the Emperor and Spain; but he was absolutely penniless himself, and there were no signs that his father-in-law would support him in any such enterprise. In the midst of his sorrows, the news of the change in the Elector of Saxony's feelings came like a gleam of sunshine across the watery sky; but Frederick never knew how to profit by his advantages when they came. He could not see that he must choose once for all between anarchy and order, and that alliance with Mansfeld's brigands and the hordes with which Bethlen Gabor was again proposing to sweep over the empire,‡ was utterly incompatible with the friendship of John George, and of those unenthusiastic princes and populations who wished to see the Emperor powerful enough to put down with a strong hand such atrocities as those of which Mansfeld had recently been guilty in East Friesland.

Under these circumstances, the long letter which Frederick despatched to the Elector of Saxony was only calculated to produce an effect the very opposite to that which he desired. Scarcely touching upon the catas-

* Uetterodt's *Mansfeld*, 526.
† The Prince of Orange to the King, Nov. $\frac{2}{12}$. *S. P. Holland.*
‡ Chichester to Carleton, Nov. 25. *S. P. Holland.*

1623.
January.

trophe of Bohemia, he dwelt at length upon the wrongs which he had suffered at the hands of the Emperor. He had been unjustly put to the ban unheard and uncondemned. His towns had been seized and plundered; his subjects ruined, and debarred from the exercise of their religion. The Emperor and the League were not in earnest when they spoke of peace. Yet, much as he had been injured, he was ready at the request of his father-in-law to surrender his private pretensions. John George, he was certain, would acknowledge that the ban was utterly illegal, and would do his best to induce the Emperor to withdraw it and to issue a general amnesty. In that case, if not required to do anything contrary to his honour and his conscience, he would be prepared, as soon as he was perfectly restored to his lands and dignities, to acknowledge all due respect and obedience to the Emperor.*

Terms proposed by him unacceptable.

That Frederick should have entertained such views of his rights and duties is not to be wondered at. But it is strange that he did not see that John George's alliance was not to be won on such terms as these; for the question whether his submission was to be made before or after the grant of the amnesty, involved the whole matter at issue, not merely with Ferdinand, but also with the great majority of the Princes of the Empire. Before they could give any support to the injured Protestants of the Palatinate, the German neutrals wanted to know whether Frederick had renounced the right of making war upon any other prince who happened to displease him; and unless he was ready to do this, he had small chance of obtaining a hearing wherever the right of private war was regarded as an intolerable nuisance. Nor was it only by reference to the existing political necessities of Germany, that Frederick stands condemned; for he had distinctly promised his father-in-law to accept peace on the principles which he now repudiated, and he had never informed James that he had retracted his promise.

How fatal an enemy Frederick was to his own cause

* Frederick to the Elector of Saxony, Jan. $\frac{12}{22}$. *Londorp*, ii. 653.

was now, not for the first time, to be seen. On the 14th of November Ferdinand had reached Ratisbon, eager to force upon the assembly which he had summoned the acceptance of the act by which he had privately conferred the Electorate upon the Duke of Bavaria. But the ill treatment of the Bohemian Lutherans had robbed the gathering of its character as an impartial representative of the two religions. The Electors of Saxony and Brandenburg were present only by their ambassadors. The Dukes of Brunswick and Pomerania were not present at all. The only Protestant who appeared in person was the Landgrave of Hesse-Darmstadt.

From an assembly thus constituted Frederick could hope for little favour. Yet scarcely had the Emperor announced his intention than opposition arose on every side. It was not till the 20th of January that the answer of the assembly was delivered to him. Ferdinand's treatment of Frederick was approved of; but he was nevertheless recommended to lay the question of his deposition before the Electoral College; and a strong opinion was expressed as to the impolicy of passing over his immediate relations in favour of Maximilian.

Such an answer from such a body leaves no doubt that the peace of Germany was in Frederick's hands. If he had sent a representative to Ratisbon to offer any reasonable guarantees of his intention to keep the peace, he could by no possibility have failed in carrying the assembly with him. But Frederick made no sign, and James, who was accustomed to make such lavish promises on behalf of his son-in-law, had, on a foolish punctilio, refused to allow Chichester even to appear at the assembly. Amongst the foreign ambassadors, Oñate stood alone in protesting against the transference of the Electorate.

As it was, the conflict of opinion was embittered by the obstinate firmness of the Emperor. On the 13th of February Ferdinand pronounced his final decision. Whenever Frederick thought proper to seek for pardon, he would gladly give ear to his request for restoration to his lands and territories; but he would never tolerate him again in the Electoral College. He would, however, content himself with limiting the Electorate which he was about to confer to the lifetime of Maximilian. In the meanwhile, the rights of Frederick's children and relations should be subjected to judicial inquiry, in order that they might receive their due, after the death of the Duke of Bavaria.

Two days afterwards, the Electorate was solemnly conferred upon Maximilian, in spite of the protests of the ambassadors of Spain, of Saxony, and of Brandenburg.*

The significance of the act which had thus been accomplished in spite of all opposition, could hardly be fully appreciated at the time. To those who witnessed it, it seemed an act of triumph, proclaiming Ferdinand's ascendancy in the Empire. Of the six Electors who would now gather round his throne, two only would in future be Protestants. Yet, in reality, in the eyes of those who could penetrate beneath the surface, that day was of evil augury for the fortunes of the Empire. On it the seeds were sown which were to ripen to a bloody harvest at Leipzic and Lutzen. It was now that the first open blow was struck which was to dissipate the idea to which Ferdinand owed his strength,—the idea that his throne could ever become the fountain of justice and the centre of unity to a distracted nation. In his battle against turbulence and disorder, it was in the spirit of a partizan that he had conquered; it was in the spirit of a partizan that he would maintain the high place which he had gained. Therefore it was that the work which is now being accomplished by the Hohenzollerns fell to pieces in the hands of the descendants of Rudolph of Hapsburg.

Weakness of Saxony and Brandenburg.

If either of the two remaining Protestant Electors had been men of energy and decision, something might yet have been done to save the Empire from the obstinacy of Ferdinand and the pertinacity of Frederick. But both John George and George William were without earnestness of purpose or strength of will. They saw that they could not aid Ferdinand without countenancing the encroachments of the Catholic clergy. They saw that they could not aid Frederick without countenancing

---

* Hurter's *Geschichte Ferdinands II.*, ix. 152—180.

anarchy. After blustering for a few months they settled down lethargically into silence, well content if, as they fondly hoped, they could avert the ruin from their own dominions.

Utterly futile as was Frederick's notion of reconquering his position by Mansfeld's help, it was at least not so futile as James's notion of reconquering it by the help of Spain. Already Frederick had been begging his father-in-law for a large sum of money to enable him to take Mansfeld into his pay, and had been protesting vigorously against the plan for the sequestration of Frankenthal.* At last, on the 23rd of January, James vouchsafed him an answer. He had now, he said, received information from the Infanta, that she was ready to accept the sequestration on his own terms, and that she would engage to restore it if the negotiations for a general peace should come to nothing. It was impossible to preserve the town in any other way. As for Mansfeld, he wanted 500,000*l.* a year; and such a sum was not to be found in the exchequer. He was sorry to discover that he had been listening to bad advice, and was giving his ear to projects which were not likely to bring him any good.†

Frederick was deeply annoyed by this letter. In his reply, he recapitulated all the wrongs which he had suffered from the Emperor, and expressed an opinion that it was immaterial whether Frankenthal fell into the hands of Tilly or into those of the Infanta. He was quite ready to do anything that his father-in-law wished; but he must say that, in his opinion, a very small force would suffice for the relief of Frankenthal. No one could be more desirous of peace than himself; but peace was to be best won by arms. He certainly did not expect 500,000*l.* a-year, but he hoped to have some smaller sum allowed him.‡

From two such men what hope of success could possibly be entertained? Frederick's only notion of policy

Ch. X.
1623.

January.
James proposes to Frederick the sequestration of Frankenthal.

February.
Reply of Frederick.

---

* Calvert to Carleton, Dec. 16, 1622. *S. P. Holland.*
† The King to Frederick, Jan. 22. *S. P. Holland.*
‡ Frederick to the King, Feb. $\frac{4}{14}$. *S. P. Holland.*

Ch. X.
1623.
February.

was by a succession of petty acts of brigandage to force the Emperor to beg his pardon for proscribing him. James's only notion of policy was to sit still whilst Spain induced Ferdinand to readmit the unrepentant Frederick to the Electorate. He was quite right, no doubt, in judging that it was useless to suppose that England was strong enough to overcome the resistance of Germany; but in spite of his dissatisfaction with the incoherent schemes of his son-in-law, it never occurred to him to suggest that Frederick's abdication in his son's favour would be the shortest path to the pacification of Europe.

January. Settlement of the East India disputes.

The only spot in the political horizon upon which the English opponents of the Spanish alliance could look with pleasure was the close of the long dispute with the Dutch Commissioners upon the East India trade. On the 25th of January an accord was signed, by which an indemnity, far less than was claimed, was assigned to the English Company,* and it was further agreed that the island of Pularoon, which had been seized by the Dutch soon after Courthope's death, should be given back to its rightful possessors, and that the English should be allowed to erect a fort in the neighbourhood of the rising town of Batavia.† But such agreements, unhappily, were of little worth. It had taken many weary hours of hot debate to obtain the consent of a few cool and wary diplomatists to such concessions.‡ What chance was there that they would still the strife which was once more waxing loud amongst the rude mariners and the sturdy factors of the two great companies in the East? Proud of the vigour with which they had driven the Spaniards from those wealth-producing shores, of their own maritime superiority and commanding position, the servants of the Dutch company never ceased to look down upon the English as interlopers. A rooted feeling of hostility on the one side, and of distrust on the other, made all real confidence impossible. Under these circumstances, the treaty of 1619, and the accord of 1623, could only serve to aggravate the evil, by bringing into

---

* *Add. MSS.* 22,866, fol. 466 B.
† Bruce's *Annals of the East India Company*, i. 235.
‡ Aerssens' *Journal.* Aerssens' *Report. Add. MSS.* 22,864—65—66.

close commercial intercourse the rivals whom it would have been wise to keep at the greatest possible distance from one another.

<small>CH. X. 1623. January.</small>

James's mode of dealing with the mercantile antagonism of the Netherlands was, in truth, an exact counterpart of his mode of dealing with the religious antagonism of Spain. In both instances, in spite of occasional inconsistencies, he looked upon bloodshed and contention as a hateful and unnecessary concomitant of the prevailing differences. On both these points his views were rather in accordance with those which prevail in the nineteenth century, than with those which found credence in the seventeenth. But, with characteristic thoughtlessness, he leapt far too hastily at the conclusion at which he was anxious to arrive. To prepare the way for toleration, in order that toleration might in its turn give way to religious liberty, would have been a task which might well have taxed the energies of the wisest of statesmen. To lay down a territorial limitation for the possessions of England in the East, which might in time have led to the acquisition by England of a fair share in the trade of the Indian Archipelago, would have been an achievement which would have adorned the annals of the most illustrious reign. By grasping at too much, James ruined his own cause. He began at the end instead of at the beginning. He sought, not merely to put an end to the strife between the two religions, by a gradual relaxation of the penal laws, but to bring them face to face in the closest and most intimate alliance of which human nature is capable; and, in the same manner, instead of contenting himself with seeing that the English Company and the Dutch Company did not come to blows, he attempted to fuse them into one under the most unequal and irritating conditions. The foundations of this work were laid upon the shifting sands, and were ready to be swept away by the returning tide.

<small>Similarity of the religious and commercial policy of James.</small>

For the present, however, nothing could be further from James's thoughts than the evil which was already knocking at the doors. The negotiations for the sequestration of Frankenthal were going gaily on, and Boischot, one of the Infanta's commissioners at the conference at

<small>Vere's reception.</small>

Ch. X.
1623.
January.

Buckingham to fetch the Infanta.

Conway Secretary.

Brussels, was to come over to England to agree upon the terms of its surrender. As if all danger of war had been thereby averted, Vere was ordered to disband the soldiers of the late garrison of Mannheim, which he had brought with him as far as Holland,* and he was himself received in England with a full acknowledgment of his long and meritorious services.† At the same time, Chichester was honoured with a seat in the Privy Council.‡ But whilst those who were the warmest advocates of a war policy were treated with respect, it was taken for granted that warlike preparations were entirely unnecessary. Orders were given to get ready a fleet of ten ships to fetch the Infanta home, and it was publicly announced that Buckingham, as Lord High Admiral, was to command in person.§ But there can be no better evidence of the want of earnestness with which the dark and threatening future was regarded than is furnished by the choice of successor to Naunton, who had at last been allowed to retire from office upon the promise of a grant of land, which was afterwards commuted for a pension of 1000*l*. a year. The proposal had first been made to him at the time when Buckingham had turned away from Spain, and he had then entreated for a respite, on the ground that Lady Naunton was about to give birth to a child, and that she had in the preceding year been frightened into a miscarriage by a rumour that he was to lose his office. His prayer had been granted at the time; but the child was now born, and he was able to tender his resignation without further anxiety. The new Secretary of State was to be Sir Edward Conway, a man whose opinions, so far as he had any, had been usually supposed to be in favour of a close alliance with the Dutch. But it was soon understood at Court that he had in reality no opinions of his own. His thoughts as well as his words were at the bidding of the great favourite. In an age when complimentary expressions, which in our

---

* Calvert to Carleton, Dec. 28, 1622. Carleton to Calvert, Jan. 17, 20, 1623. *S. P. Holland.*
† —— to Mead, Jan. 31. *Harl. MSS.* 387, fol. 276. Chamberlain to Carleton, Feb. 10. *S. P. Dom.* cxxxviii. 23.
‡ Privy Council Register, Dec. 31, 1622.
§ Chamberlain to Carleton, Jan. 4. *S. P. Dom.* cxxxvii. 5.

time would justly be considered servile, were nothing more than the accustomed phrases of polite society, Conway's letters to Buckingham stood alone in the fulsome and cloying flattery with which they were imbued. He had attracted much attention and had caused some amusement by his efforts to fasten upon the favourite the title of "Your Excellency," which had hitherto been unknown in England, and he afterwards scandalised grave statesmen, who were accustomed to regard the Crown as the only fountain of official honour, by addressing Buckingham as "his most gracious patron." But it was less by such trifles as these, as by the agility with which his views changed with every shifting fancy of the great man to whom he owed his office, that his utter want of independence of character was shown. Not, indeed, that he was, in any sense of the word, a bad man. He was not one of those who acquire power by cringing to the great, in order that they may enjoy the satisfaction of trampling upon the small. He was neither extortionate nor harsh. All that was amiss with him was that he had no ideas of his own, and that he was impressed by nature with the profoundest admiration for any feather-brained courtier who happened to enjoy the favour of the King.

Such was the man who was at once admitted to the strictest intimacy by James and Buckingham. Calvert was to remain in London, to write despatches, to confer with foreign ambassadors, and to attend to the details of business. Conway was to be the private and confidential secretary, to move about with the Court, to convey the wishes of the King to his more experienced colleague, and to jot down, in his own abominable scrawl, whatever information it might please James to entrust to his keeping.

It is, indeed, intelligible enough that James should have been unwilling to admit any one of moral or intellectual superiority to his intimacy. Even Calvert, accustomed to obey orders as he was, could not avoid intimating that the time was come for a more decided policy in Germany,* and though the news from Madrid

* Expressions to this effect are constantly occurring in his correspondence with Carleton. *S. P. Holland.* I may take this opportunity of stating that

was decidedly favourable to the prospects of the marriage, it required all James's supereminent power of shutting his eyes to the facts of the world around him not to see that unless he could raise up a party in Germany for his son-in-law, all that Spain could do for him would be absolutely thrown away.

It was hardly possible that the day of disenchantment could be postponed much longer. If James succeeded in bringing the representatives of his son-in-law and of the Emperor to meet in a diplomatic encounter, even he might perhaps learn that diametrically opposite opinions are not to be reconciled by well-intended commonplaces, and then, if not before, he would discover how little good he was likely to derive from his connection with Spain. Yet foolish as James's policy was, there was a lower depth of folly to be disclosed. If the Spanish match and its accompanying advantages were a pure delusion, he had at least never projected anything so hopelessly insane as the scheme which had been gradually ripening in the mind of his favourite and his son.

it is quite a mistake to suppose that because Calvert afterwards became a Roman Catholic, he was ready to betray English interests into the hands of the Spaniards.

CHAPTER XI.

THE JOURNEY TO MADRID.

ALMOST a year had passed since Gondomar received from the lips of the Prince of Wales the assurance of his intention to visit Spain. To Baby Charles, as his father appropriately named him, the impolicy of the step which he was about to take appeared not to be worth a moment's consideration. Of the intrigues which would gather round him, of the strange expectations to which his mere presence at Madrid would give rise, he had simply no conception whatever. What he saw before him was a gay ride across a continent, a lovers' meeting, a brilliant adventure, with the spice of peril which made it all the more attractive to that irresolute mind, incapable, as it was, of weighing calmly the advantages and the dangers of the enterprise. And if he had not himself approved of the plan, doubt would have been impossible in the presence of that brilliant creature, so self-confident and so insinuating, to whom his father in his weakness had entrusted the companionship of his tender years. A worse guide for such a youth it was impossible to select. Charles, ready now, as in future life, to resent opposition which presented itself in the name of popular rights, or of a higher wisdom than his own, had no objection to raise against the boisterous familiarity of his friend. For Steenie, as he was called, from some real or imaginary resemblance to a picture of St. Stephen in the King's possession, never asked him to trouble himself with the painful operation of thinking, whilst he took care to represent his own forgone conclusions with all outward forms of respect. He had early discovered how easy it was to make a tool of Charles. The inertness of the father, which had so often refused to comply with his sudden freaks, had no place in the son.

<small>CH. XI.
1623.
January.
The projected journey.</small>

<small>Charles and Buckingham.</small>

Ch. XI.
1623.
January.

The journey proposed to James.

Had Charles been on the throne in James's place, there can be little doubt that England would have been engaged in a war with the Emperor in 1620, in a war with the Netherlands in 1621, and in a war with Spain in 1622.

At what time the King was first acquainted with the plan is uncertain; but, on the whole, it is most probable that before the end of the year his consent had been won to the project in a different shape from that which it afterwards assumed. If Buckingham was to go as Admiral of the Fleet to fetch the Infanta home in May, there would be comparatively few objections to his taking the Prince on shipboard with him. By that time the dispensation would have arrived, and the conditions of the marriage would be irrevocably settled. It could not, therefore, be said that there was any likelihood of Charles being treated as a hostage for the enforcement of new and exorbitant conditions.*

They ask leave to go at once.

This was not, however, what Charles and Buckingham wanted. To arrive after all difficulties were at an end was far too commonplace an arrangement to suit their fiery imaginations. One day in February, after binding the King to secresy, they told him that what they asked for was leave to go at once. It would be a long time before the fleet could be ready. A pass to travel through France would not be granted without delay. Why should they not travel incognito? It would surely not be difficult,

* "And I have it *de bonâ manu*, and under the rose, that the Prince himself goes in person." Chamberlain to Carleton, Jan. 4. *S. P. Dom.* cxxvii. 5. This puts out of the question Clarendon's story of the journey being suggested at once just before the Prince started. It must be remembered that our only knowledge of these scenes is derived from him. He undoubtedly obtained his information from Cottington, and that part of his narrative which relates to things which passed before Cottington's own eyes may be at once accepted. But the remainder of his story, though doubtless generally true, is liable to error whenever it touches upon those circumstances of general history with which Clarendon had not made himself familiar. Clarendon, for instance, incorrectly asserts that the Marquis and the Prince had been at variance up to this time, that the journey to Spain was the beginning of James's dissatisfaction with Buckingham, and that Frederick had already "incurred the ban of the Empire in an Imperial diet," all of which statements are manifestly incorrect. I suspect that the first conversation took place about New Year's Day, and related only to going with the fleet, and that there was an interval of some weeks before the question of the journey by land was mooted. Bristol was informed of Buckingham's intention to come to Spain to the Infanta's marriage.

by hard riding, to reach the Spanish frontier before they were missed at Whitehall.

CH. XI.
1623.
February.
James consents.

Never in the whole course of his life did James find it easy to say "No," to those with whom he was on terms of familiar intercourse. And of late years his fatal habit of irresolution had increased. His body was racked with terrible attacks of gout, and his mind was deadened by a sense of failure, which did not exercise the less influence upon his temper because he was unwilling to confess its existence. If he had been asked to do anything himself, he would undoubtedly have resisted any pressure that could be brought to bear upon him. As it was, he gave way without difficulty, and the fatal permission was accorded.

But before the morrow came, the mistake which he had committed rose before his mind. As soon as the spell of the young men's presence was removed, he was able to think of the dangers into which his beloved son was about to run, and of the extreme probability that the Spanish ministers would raise their demands, as soon as they had such a hostage in their hands.* Accordingly, when the Prince returned with the Marquis the next morning to make arrangements for the journey, James adjured him to think of the danger into which he was running. If any evil befel the Prince, he added, turning to Buckingham as he spoke, it was at his door that the blame would be laid, and his ruin would be unavoidable. Then, bursting into tears, he begged them not to press him to a thing so mischievous in every way, the execution of which was sure to break his heart.

Hesitation of the King.

Neither Charles nor Buckingham took the trouble to argue the question. With Buckingham, at least, it was a fundamental article of faith that opposition and difficulty must give way before him. The Prince contented himself with reminding his father of the promise which he had given the day before, and with assuring him that if he were forbidden to go to Spain, he would never marry

Language of Charles and Buckingham.

---

* I do not insert the whole of the arguments used by James as given by Clarendon, as I have a suspicion that they were embellished by knowledge acquired after the event. But so much as I have assigned to him may fairly be attributed to him as rising from the circumstances.

Ch. XI.
1623.
February.

Cottington's opinion.

James gives his final permission.

at all. The insolent favourite took higher ground. He told the King that if he broke his promises in this way, nobody would ever believe him again. He must have consulted some one in spite of his engagement to secresy. If he could find out who the rascal was who had suggested such pitiful reasons, he was sure the Prince would never forgive him.

The poor King was completely cowed. He swore that he had never communicated the secret to any one, and he allowed the young men to discuss the details of the journey, as if there had been no question of stopping it. Cottington and Porter were soon mentioned as proper persons to accompany the Prince. Once more the King caught at a straw, and sent for Cottington, in the hope that he would prove more successful than himself in combating the idea.

As Cottington entered the room, Buckingham turned to Charles. "This man," he whispered in his ear, "will be against the journey." "No," answered the Prince, "he dares not." "Cottington," said the King, after engaging him to silence, "here are Baby Charles and Steenie, who have a great mind to go by post into Spain, to fetch home the Infanta, and will have but two more in their company, and have chosen you for one. What think you of the journey?" In his amazement, Cottington, cool as he generally was, could scarcely speak. It was only upon the question being repeated that he answered, in a trembling voice, that he could not think well of it. In his opinion it would render everything that had been done fruitless. As soon as the Spaniards had the Prince in their hands, they were certain to propose new articles, especially with respect to religion. When he heard these words, the King threw himself upon his bed. "I told you this before," he shrieked out passionately. "I am undone. I shall lose Baby Charles."

Buckingham turned fiercely upon Cottington. It was his pride, he told him, which had led him to condemn the journey because he had not been sooner consulted. No one had asked for his opinion upon matters of state. The King only wanted to know which was the best road to Madrid. It was in vain for some time that James tried to take Cottington's part. In the end he was obliged to confess himself beaten and gave his final consent to the journey.*

Headlong as he was, there was one precaution which Buckingham did not omit to take before starting. For some days it had been observed that he seemed more than usually anxious to be reconciled with all to whom he had given any cause of offence. On the 28th of January, Mallory, one of the four members of the late House of Commons who were still restrained to their country houses, received permission to go where he would, though a similar relaxation was not accorded either to Coke, to Phelips, or to Pym. A few days afterwards, Lord Say, who was still in the Tower for his opposition to the Benevolence, was allowed to go down into the country to remain in confinement in his own house.† At last, too, Buckingham had begun to make preparations for repaying, or for giving security for the repayment of the purchase-money with which Mandeville had bought the temporary possession of the White Staff, upon the understanding that the late Lord Treasurer would consent to a marriage between his eldest son, the future general of the parliamentary armies, and Susan Hill, one of the many penniless kinswomen of the favourite.‡ At the same time, young Monson, who five years before had been selected by the Howards as a possible rival to Buckingham in the King's good graces, was knighted, and sent to travel on the Continent. A more formidable opponent was treated in the same way. For some time the discordance between the parsimony of Middlesex and the lavish ostentation of Buckingham had threatened to lead to an open rupture,

*Clarendon, i. 15. Cottington's objections are mentioned by Valaresso, Feb. 28 / March 10. *Venice MSS.*, Desp. Ingh. and in a letter of Dudley Carleton's, Feb. 27. *S. P. Dom.* cxxxviii. 99.

† Privy Council Register, Jan. 28, Feb. 4.

‡ Chamberlain to Carleton, Feb. 10. *S. P. Dom.* cxxxviii. 23. It appears from Buckingham's defence (*Rushworth*, i. 387), that the King promised to grant lands in fee farm of his own instead. It also appears from the Patent Rolls that a large grant was passed, under the Great Seal, to Mandeville by Charles almost immediately after his accession, and it was expressly stated that this was done in fulfilment of James's promises. It is true that money was paid for the land. But this may easily have been a mere blind, the land being undervalued. Pat. 1 *Charles I.*, Part 2.

Ch. XI. 1623.	and it was even supposed that the Lord Treasurer had fixed his eye upon his brother-in-law, Arthur Brett, a handsome gentleman of the bedchamber, as one who might possibly supplant the favourite. Of the particulars of the quarrel we have no information. Just as he was ready to start, Buckingham sought a reconciliation. Brett, like Monson, was knighted, and recommended to keep out of the way.
Feb. 17. The Prince sets out.	On the 16th, Cottington, who had by this time made his peace with Buckingham, was created a baronet, and was ordered to take Porter with him to Dover, and to hire a vessel for crossing the straits. The next day Charles took leave of his father at Theobalds, and rode off, accompanied by Buckingham, to the Marquis's house in Essex. On the morning of the 18th, the real difficulties of the adventure began. Disguised with false beards, the two young men started from Newhall, under the names of Tom and John Smith. They had no one with them but Sir Richard Graham, the Marquis's Master of the Horse and confidential attendant. At the ferry opposite Gravesend they surprised the boatman by ordering him to put them ashore on the outskirts of the town instead of at the usual place of landing. His astonishment was complete, when one of the party handed him a gold piece, and rode away without asking for change. Supposing that the two principal gentlemen were duellists, about to cross the sea for the purpose of settling their differences with the sword, he at once gave information to the magistrates, who sent off a postboy to Rochester, with orders to stop them. But the freshest horse in Gravesend was no match for the picked steeds from Buckingham's stable, and the party had left Rochester long before the arrival of their pursuer. A little later they were exposed to a more serious risk. Just as the three riders got out of the town, they saw advancing to meet them a train, in which they recognised the royal carriage, which was conveying the Infanta's ambassador, Boischot, under the escort of Sir Lewis Lewknor, the master of the ceremonies, and of Sir Henry Mainwaring, the Lieutenant of Dover Castle. To avoid detection, they spurred their horses over the hedge, and galloped across
Feb. 18. Adventures on the way.	

the fields. Mainwaring, who fancied that the party might contain two of Barneveldt's sons, who had been recently concerned in an attempt to assassinate the Prince of Orange, sent a messenger back to Canterbury with orders to detain them. It was only by pulling off his beard, and by assuring the mayor that he was the Lord Admiral going down to Dover to make a secret inspection of the fleet, that Buckingham obtained leave to continue his journey. At Dover, Cottington and Porter had a vessel in readiness, and early the next morning the whole party, five in number, put off without further hindrance for Boulogne, from whence they pushed on in the afternoon to Montreuil. Two days more riding brought them to Paris.*

The next day they spent in strolling about the French capital. They caught a sight of the King and of Mary de Medici; and in the evening, upon the plea that they were strangers in Paris, they contrived to obtain admission to the rehearsal of a masque, in which the Queen and the Princess Henrietta Maria were to take part. Of his future wife, Charles seems to have taken but little notice. "There danced," he wrote, as soon as he had left the scene of gaiety, "the queen and madame, with as many as made up nineteen fair dancing ladies; amongst which the queen is the handsomest, which hath wrought in me a greater desire to see her sister."† The next day they were up at three in the morning, riding hard for Bayonne.

Meanwhile James, who had gone down to Newmarket to be out of the way, put the best face possible upon the business. As soon as the news had spread, those of the Privy Councillors who were on the spot fell upon their knees, and implored him to inform them whether the Prince was really gone. He assured them that there was no doubt about the matter. His son was only imitating the example of his father, of his grandfather,

---

* *Reliquiæ Wottonianæ* (1672), i. 212. Mainwaring to Zouch, Feb. 22. Chamberlain to Carleton, Feb. 22. Dudley Carleton to Carleton, Feb. 27. *S. P. Dom.* cxxxviii. 58, 59, 99. Calvert to Carleton, Feb. 27. *S. P. Holland.*

† The Prince and Buckingham to the King, Feb. 22. Goodman's *Court of King James*, ii. 253. Ellis, series i. vol. iii. 121.

Ch. XI.
1623.

Darnley, and of his great-grandfather, James V., who had all gone into foreign countries to fetch home their wives. Beyond all doubt a general peace in Christendom would be the result. To prevent all danger, however, he would send Lord Carlisle to Paris to interpose his good offices on behalf of the Prince's journey.

Feeling in England.

With this answer the Council was forced to be content. But they did not conceal the apprehensions which they felt, and those apprehensions were shared by the whole country. Prayers were put up in all the churches for the Prince's preservation. If the marriage, it was said, were forward enough to justify the presence of the Prince at Madrid, why did he not go on board a fleet with an equipage suitable to his station? If everything was still uncertain, why should he risk his person, and give such an advantage to the King of Spain, by putting himself in his hands? It was generally felt that from this dilemma no escape was possible.*

Feb. 25. Letter of Williams to the Prince.

The popular dislike found a mouthpiece in the shrewd and cautious Williams. "Your journey," he wrote to the Prince, "is generally reputed the depth of your danger, which in my fears and representations your arrival should be. You are in a strange state—for aught we know uninvited, business being scarce prepared—subject to be stayed on many and contrary pretences; made a plot for all the wisdom of Spain and Rome, for all the contemplations of that state and that religion to work upon. And peradventure the detaining of your Highness's person may serve their turn as amply as their marriage, at leastwise for this time, and the exploits of the ensuing summer."†

Outcry against Buckingham.

Especially loud was the outcry against Buckingham. Great lords, who were not afraid to say what they meant, declared their opinion that he had been guilty of high treason in carrying the Prince out of the realm, and that he would one day have to answer in Parliament for what he had done. Even James began to hesitate, and seemed

* Calvert to Carleton, Feb. 27. *S. P. Holland.* D. Carleton to Carleton, Feb. 27. *S. P. Dom.* cxxxviii. 99. Salvetti's *News-Letter*, $\frac{\text{Feb. 28}}{\text{March 10}}$.

† Williams to the Prince, Feb. 25. *Hacket*, 116.

THE PRINCE'S ARRIVAL. 305

inclined to cast the blame from his own shoulders upon those of his favourite and his son.*

Ch. XI.
1623.

Whilst James was fretting at home, his "sweet boys, and dear venturous knights, worthy to be put in a new romanso,"† were speeding across France, leaving to Carlisle the empty task of demanding at Paris a safe conduct which was no longer necessary. A few miles beyond Bayonne they met Bristol's messenger, Gresley, carrying despatches to England. They opened his packet, but found that the greater part of the enclosed papers were in a cypher which they were unable to read. They then told Gresley that he must come back with them as far as Irun, as they wished him to be the bearer of a letter written to the King upon Spanish soil. The Marquis, Gresley afterwards reported in England, looked worn and weary with his long ride; but he had never seen the Prince so merry. As soon as he stepped on the southern bank of the Bidassoa, he danced about for joy.

March 2. The Prince arrives at Irun.

And yet even in that part of Bristol's letter which he was able to read, there was enough to have made Charles doubt the wisdom of his enterprise. "The temporal articles," he now told his father, "are not concluded, nor will not be till the dispensation comes, which may be God knows when; and when that time shall come, they beg twenty days to conceal it, upon pretext of making preparations." These difficulties, however, he was sanguine enough to imagine would vanish in a moment before the sunlight of his presence.‡

About eight o'clock in the evening of the 7th of March, the two young men, having outridden their companions, knocked for admittance at Bristol's door at Madrid. No one knew better than the ambassador what mischief was likely to result from the giddy exploit; but he had long learned to command his countenance, and he

March 7. And reaches Madrid.

---

* Williams to Buckingham, Feb. 25. *Hacket*, 116. Valaresso to the Doge, Feb. 28 / March 10. *Venice MSS.*

† The King to the Prince and Buckingham, Feb. 26. *Hardwicke S. P.* i. 399.

‡ The Prince and Buckingham to the King, March 2. *Hardwicke S. P.* i. 403. Salvetti's *News-Letter*, March 7/17.

VOL. II. X

took good care to receive his unexpected guests with all the deference due to their rank.*

For that night at least, as he fondly hoped, the secret would be kept; but Gondomar was not to be so deceived. In a few minutes he had learned that his long-cherished wishes had been gratified, and he at once proceeded to the Royal Palace, where he found Olivares at supper. "What brings you here so late?" said the favourite, astonished at his beaming face; "one would think that you had got the King of England in Madrid." "If I have not got the King," replied Gondomar, "at least I have got the Prince." Olivares, stupified with what he heard, remained silent for some time. At last he congratulated Gondomar on the news he brought. It could not be, he thought, but that the Prince's arrival would in some way redound to the advantage of the Catholic Church. Olivares then went to find the King, and the strange news was discussed between them in the royal bedchamber. On one point they were soon agreed. If Charles had not made up his mind to change his religion, he would not have come to Spain. Philip, turning to a crucifix which stood at the head of his bed, addressed Him whom the image represented. "Lord," he said, "I swear to Thee, by the crucified union of God and man, which I adore in Thee at whose feet I place my lips, that the coming of the Prince of Wales shall not prevail with me, in anything touching Thy Catholic religion, to go a step beyond that which Thy vicar the Roman Pontiff may resolve, even if it may involve the loss of all the kingdoms which, by Thy favour and mercy, I possess. As to what is temporal and is mine," he added, looking at Olivares, "see that all his wishes are gratified, in consideration of the obligation under which he has placed us by coming here."† With these words he dismissed Olivares for the night. During the first months of the year, the position of the Spanish minister had been one of extreme difficulty. If, indeed, a choice became inevitable, he would undoubtedly elect to stand by the side of the Emperor in war, rather than leave the

---

* A true relation, &c. Nichols' *Progresses*, iii. 818. This account was compiled by Bristol himself.
† Roja. *Add. MSS.* 25,689, fol. 65. Appendix to Francisco de Jesus.

cause of his Church without support. But the prospect was most unwelcome, and he had strained every nerve to bring Ferdinand and James to consent to terms, which, in his ignorance of the temper of Protestant nations, he fancied would prove acceptable to both parties. Already his dream had begun to melt away before the hard realities of life. It was known at Madrid that the Emperor was not to be bribed to relinquish his fixed intention by the promise of the Infanta's hand for his son. For some weeks Olivares had been tormented with renewed demands that the Spanish Government should take a side. Khevenhüller, the Imperial Ambassador, and De Massimi, the Papal Nuncio, had been urging him, in no measured terms, to secure his master's approbation for the transference of the Electorate, whilst Bristol had been no less persistent in pressing him to take active steps in thwarting a measure which he truly represented as ruinous to the prospects of peace. Under the circumstances, the perplexities of the Spanish Government had been overwhelming. If the Emperor would not yield, it might be possible, it was thought, to induce him to create an eighth Electorate, and this proposal had been allowed to reach Bristol's ears, coupled with the suggestion that Frederick's son should be educated at Vienna; but it is needless to say that no hint was given him of the scheme for bringing up the boy in the Roman Catholic religion.* Sanguine as his temperament was, Olivares can hardly have concealed from himself during these weeks that there was at least a possibility that his efforts to patch the rent might not be so successful as he had wished; nor were the prospects of the marriage more favourable than those of his German diplomacy. The Infanta, as he well knew, had set her face against it as sternly as ever; and yet he could not draw back from the treaty if he would. The penalty of his own dissimulation, and of the dissimulation of those who had gone before him, was being exacted to the uttermost. With a smiling face, he had to await the coming of the evil day which, unless the Pope chose to come to his help, would expose his falsehood to

Ch. XI.
1623.
March 7.
Difficult position of Olivares.

* Bristol to Calvert, Feb. 23. *S. P. Spain.* *Khevenhüller,* x. 71—79.

the world. At one time he had been obliged to make arrangements for the Infanta's voyage and for the selection of the noblemen who were to take charge of herself and her attendants; at another time he had been compelled to look on whilst the King wrote an autograph letter to the Pope pressing him to accord the dispensation, although the Pope must have been perfectly aware that the granting of the dispensation was the last thing that Philip really wished.*

From this horrible dilemma he was now, as he fancied, relieved for ever. The Prince, he supposed, was come with the intention of professing himself a convert to the Catholic Church. Every difficulty, therefore, was now at an end. The marriage would be concluded to the satisfaction of all parties; the Emperor would concede the point of the eighth Electorate, and the Prince of Wales would use all his influence in favour of the education of his nephew in the religion which would now be his own; the Palatinate and the British Isles would, within a few years, be added to the spiritual dominions of the Roman see; Spain, so long maligned as aspiring to universal monarchy, would not ask for a foot of territory which was not legitimately her own. If she was from henceforth to look down upon the other kingdoms of the world, it would be from the height of the moral supremacy which self-abnegation alone could give. Olivares would be the Philip II. of peace.†

Such was the last form of the long-enduring Spanish hallucination. The next morning Gondomar, summoned to Bristol's house, was, for the first time, as the English Ambassador imagined, entrusted with the great secret. He was to tell Olivares that Buckingham had arrived, but he was to say nothing about the Prince. Accordingly in the afternoon, the two favourites met in the palace gardens. Every form which the most precise rules of Spanish courtesy demanded was observed between them; and, as soon as it was dark, Buckingham was admitted

---

* Bristol to the King, Feb. 22. *S. P. Spain.*

† The scheme of Olivares may be not unaptly compared to the ideas which dictated the maps of Europe which have been published in Paris, during the second Empire. In them France always appears without additional territory though everything else is changed.

to the royal apartments to kiss his Majesty's hands. The next day, although the secret of the Prince's arrival had been communicated to Philip, a mysterious silence was ordered to be preserved upon the subject. Philip, accompanied by the Queen and the Infanta as well as by his two brothers, the Infants Charles and Ferdinand, drove backwards and forwards through the streets, whilst the Prince of Wales, whose arrival was supposed to be still unknown, was placed in another coach, from which he might catch a sight of the royal family as they passed. Once the King took off his hat to him, but there was no other sign of recognition. The streets were thronged, but no outward demonstrations were allowed, though everyone knew who the stranger in the coach was. Amongst that vast crowd there was not one whose heart did not swell with triumph at the thought that the Prince of heretic England had come to bow his knee at the altars of the national faith.

<small>Ch. XI. 1623. March 8. Buckingham presented to the King.</small>

When the procession was ended, Olivares joined the Prince, and assured him that his master was dying to speak to him, and intended to visit him in the evening. But Charles would not hear of this, and offered to pay his compliments to the King at once. The proposal was, however, declined on the ground that the Prince's retinue was not sufficiently numerous to enable him to appear with the dignity befitting his rank; and it was finally arranged that the meeting should take place in the open air.

As soon as they met, Philip invited Charles to come into his coach. Bristol was taken with them as an interpreter, and they remained together in friendly conversation for half an hour.*

<small>March 9. Meeting of Philip and Charles.</small>

In the midst of these ceremonies Olivares had an eye to business. "Let us despatch this matter out of hand," he said to Buckingham, "and strike it up without the Pope." "Very well," replied the Englishman; "but how is it to be done?" "The means," replied Olivares, "are very easy. It is but the conversion of the Prince, which we cannot conceive but his Highness intended upon his resolution for this journey." Against this idea, it would

<small>Olivares' conversation with Buckingham.</small>

---

* A true relation, &c. Nichols' *Progresses*, iii. 818. Spanish Account. Guizot. *Projet de Mariage Royal*, 107. Francisco de Jesus, 54.

seem, Buckingham protested, doubtless in less vehement language than he took credit to himself for after his return to England. "Then," said Olivares, "we must send to Rome."

The next morning Olivares appeared with a letter which he had written to the Pope's nephew, Cardinal Ludovisi. The King of England, he told him, had put such an obligation on his master by sending his son, that he trusted there would be no further delay in granting the dispensation, for there was nothing in his kingdom which he could now deny him. Some months afterwards, Buckingham asserted that he found the Spaniard's language "heavy and ineffectual," and that he had all but quarrelled with him about it. In a letter written to James that very day, by himself and the Prince, nothing of the kind is to be found. "We find," they say, "the Count Olivares so overvaluing our journey, that he is so full of real courtesy, that we can do no less than beseech your Majesty to write the kindest letter of thanks and acknowledgment you can unto him." That very morning, he had said, with truly Spanish exaggeration, that if the Prince could not have the Infanta as his wife, he should have her as his mistress. "We must hold you thus much longer to tell you," the writers went on to say, "the Pope's Nuncio works as maliciously and as actively as he can against us, but receives such rude answers, that we hope he will be soon weary on it. We make this collection of it, that the Pope will be very loath to grant a dispensation; which, if he will not do, then we would gladly have your directions how far we may engage you in the acknowledgment of the Pope's special power. For we almost find it, if you will be contented to acknowledge the Pope chief head under Christ, that the match will be made without him."*

The old King was sadly puzzled by this last paragraph when it arrived in England. "I have written," he replied, "a letter to Conde de Olivares, as both of you desired me, as full of thanks and kindness as can be devised, and indeed he well deserves. But in the end of

---

* Buckingham's relation. *Lords' Journals*, iii. 222. The Prince and Buckingham to the King, March 10. *Hardwicke S. P.* i. 401.

your letter, ye put in a cooling card, anent the Nuncio's averseness to this business, and that thereby ye collect that the Pope will likewise be averse; but first ye must remember that, in Spain they never put doubt of the granting of the dispensation; that themselves did set down the spiritual conditions, which I fully agreed unto, and by them were they sent to Rome, and the Consulta* there concluded that the Pope might, nay ought, for the weal of Christendom, to grant a dispensation upon these conditions. These things may justly be laid before them, but I know not what ye mean by my acknowledging the Pope's spiritual supremacy. I am sure ye would not have me renounce my religion for all the world, but all that I can guess at your meaning is that it may be ye have an allusion to a passage in my book against Bellarmin, where I offer, if the Pope would quit his godhead and usurping over kings, to acknowledge him for the Chief Bishop, to which all appeals of churchmen ought to lie *en dernier resort*, the very words I send you here enclosed, and that is the farthest that my conscience will permit me to go upon this point, for I am not a monsieur who can shift his religion as easily as he can shift his shirt, when he cometh from tennis." †

It is not probable that either Charles or Buckingham was seriously thinking of acknowledging the authority of the Pope. A game of duplicity was being carried on on both sides. By constantly referring to the reluctance of the Pope to grant the dispensation, Olivares, no doubt, hoped to terrify Charles into the hoped-for conversion, whilst, at the same time, if he found his religious convictions to be unassailable, he was preparing him for the announcement that the Pope had refused to grant the dispensation. Charles, on the other hand, instead of meeting the difficulty in the face, was inclined to temporise, thinking it

---

* *i.e.* The Junta at Madrid.

† "As for myself, if that were yet the question, I would with all my heart give my consent that the Bishop of Rome should have the first seat. I being a Western King, would go with the Patriarch of the West. And for his temporal principality over the Signores of Rome, I do not quarrel at either. Let him, in God's name, be *primus Episcopus inter omnes Episcopos, et princeps Episcoporum*, so it be no otherwise but as St. Peter was *princeps Apostolorum*." The King to the Prince and Buckingham, March 25. *Hardwicke S. P.* i. 411.

good policy to allow hopes to be entertained which he never intended to realise. Not long after his arrival, he threw away a splendid opportunity of clearing his position. Olivares was talking to him about his grandmother. The Queen of Scots, he said, had suffered for the true faith, and her blood which had been shed would not cease to cry to heaven, till her children who came after her were brought back to a knowledge of the faith. Instead of taking the chance thus thrown in his way, of stating plainly what his religious position was, Charles affected in his reply to treat the whole matter as a mere historical question, offered to show the Spaniard a portrait of his grandmother, and to enlighten him on some points relating to her execution.*

The Spanish ministers were much perplexed. At last they came to the conclusion that Charles was afraid of Bristol. Gondomar accordingly undertook to remove the obstacle, and going one morning to the ambassador's house, adjured him not to hinder the pious work of the Prince's conversion, to which, as he said, Buckingham was ready to give his aid. Bristol, knowing what the common rumour was, and having no doubt noticed the Prince's deportment, accepted Gondomar's account without difficulty, little dreaming that his mistake would one day be imputed to him as a crime. Going straight to the Prince, he asked him with what object he had come to Spain. "You know as well as I," answered Charles, briefly. "Sir," said Bristol, who was too much a man of the world to be surprised at anything, "servants can never serve their masters industriously, unless they know their meanings fully. Give me leave, therefore to tell you what they say in the town is the cause of your coming : 'That you mean to change your religion, and to declare it here.' I do not speak this that I will persuade you to do it, or that I will promise you to follow your example, though you will do it. But, as your faithful servant, if you will trust me with so great a secret, I will endeavour to carry it the discreetest way I can." By this time Charles began to show signs of vexation, hardly

---

* Francisco de Jesus, 57. Compare Roja's narrative in the Appendix.

knowing, perhaps, how much he was himself to blame for the suspicions to which he had given rise. " I wonder," he broke in, indignantly, " what you have ever found in me that you should conceive I would be so base and unworthy as for a wife to change my religion." Bristol replied that he hoped he would pardon what he had said, and then proceeded to give him some good advice. Unless he let it be known plainly that he had no intention of allowing himself to be converted, there would be no real effort made to obtain the dispensation. Nothing would be settled as long as that question remained open.*

It can hardly be doubted that both Gondomar and Olivares were well pleased when the day came on which the Prince was to be removed from Bristol's house. On the 16th of March he was conducted in state to the apartments prepared for him in the Royal Palace. The King himself came to accompany him, forcing him to take the right hand as they rode. A week before, Gondomar had been created a Councillor of State, and had been ordered to accept his dignity at the Prince's hands. All prisoners, who were not confined on account of the most heinous crimes, were now set at liberty. The English galley slaves, who had been captured when serving in pirate vessels, saw hope beam on them once more, and were freed for ever from their life of wretchedness. The sumptuary laws which had been recently imposed in the vain hope of restoring by such expedients the exhausted finances, were relaxed, and the Court was ordered to deck itself in all its ancient splendour.† As Charles passed through the streets, the populace applauded him to the echo, and the song of Lope de Vega, which told how Charles had come, under the guidance of Love, to the Spanish sky, to see his star Maria, was sung by high and low.‡

---

* Seventh Article against Bristol. Answer to the Seventh Article. Charles I. to Bristol, Jan. 20, 1626. *State Trials*, ii. 1285, 1406, 1277.

† A true relation, &c. Nichols' *Progresses*, iii. 818.

‡ " Carlos Estuardo soy
Que, siendo amor mi guia,
Al cielo d'España voy
Por ver mi estrella Maria."

Ch. XI.
1623.
March 17.
The conversion still looked for.

Yet even amidst the gorgeous festivities which followed, the old question was ever returning. "For our main and chief business," wrote the two young men to the King, "we find them, by outward shows, as desirous of it as ourselves, yet are they hankering upon a conversion; for they say that there can be no firm friendship without union in religion, but put no question in bestowing their sister, and we put the other quite out of question, because neither our conscience nor the time serves for it, and because we will not implicitly rely upon them." This was certainly but a faint resistance, and it is hardly to be wondered at that Charles added in his own hand, " I beseech your Majesty advise as little with your Council in these businesses as you can."*

Charles's opinion of the Infanta.

In truth, Charles was more than ever anxious to avoid giving offence to the Spaniards. He had found an opportunity of seeing the Infanta more closely than when she had passed him in her brother's coach. "Without flattery," wrote Buckingham, "I think there is not a sweeter creature in the world. Baby Charles himself is so touched at the heart, that he confesses all he ever yet saw is nothing to her, and swears that, if he want her, there shall be blows."† Of love, in the higher sense of the word, there can have been no question between two persons who had never exchanged a syllable with one another in their lives; but it is impossible to doubt that Charles's fancy and imagination were deeply impressed, even if something is to be set down to his reluctance to return to England baffled and alone.

Buckingham as a diplomatist.

At last, however, the time came when it was necessary to think of more serious business. Buckingham was now, for the first time in his life, to try his powers as a diplomatist. He began by requesting Olivares to join him in putting the marriage treaty into its final shape, the Prince having come to Spain upon the understanding that the King had already given his sincere assent to the match.‡

---

* The Prince and Buckingham to the King, March 17. *Hardwicke S. P.* i. 408.
† Buckingham to the King, March 17 (?). *Hardwicke S. P.* i. 410.
‡ Corner to the Doge, $\frac{\text{March 27}}{\text{April 6}}$. *Venice MSS.* Desp. Spagna.

It is not to be supposed that Olivares would leave anything unattempted to obtain better terms from Buckingham than those which he had wrung from Bristol. Before him rose the dreaded phantom of a war with England, a war which could hardly be averted if Charles were sent back with wounded feelings. And yet, in the Infanta's present temper, the marriage was impossible. One expedient only seems to have presented itself to his mind. It was almost certain that if the dispensation were granted at all it would be accompanied by a reiteration of the old demand for liberty of worship in England. If Charles could at least be persuaded to concede this, was it likely that the Infanta would persist in her opposition to terms which had received the hearty approbation of the Vatican?*

The Spaniard, accordingly, informed Buckingham that the King was most anxious for the conclusion of the marriage. It depended, however, entirely on the Prince whether it would take place or not. The King had done his best to obtain the dispensation from the Pope; but it was thought at Madrid that, if a favourable answer was to be obtained, it would be necessary for the King of England to grant liberty of worship according to the Pope's request. In this way all other difficulties would be easily surmounted.†

Buckingham was ignorant of much; but he at least knew England better than Olivares. It was impossible, he replied, for the King to admit such a proposition without danger of tumult, and even of rebellion, from which the Catholics would be the first to suffer. He

---

* In ascribing this reasoning to Olivares, I have not followed any authority. But it appears to be the only possible way of accounting for his actions, taking them into consideration as a whole.

† "Olivares rispose, che il Rè persisteva non solo nell' assento, et lo confermeva a pieno, ma che gradendo appunto la dimostratione del Prencipe di trasferirse qui, desiderava medesimamente che si concludesse et s'ultimasse: che tuttavia questi stava solo nella volontà del Prencipe; perchè si era sempre con tal conditione trattato per il che più volte havea S. Mtà. supplicato il Papa della gratia, et che rinoverebbe con efficace colore le supplicationi; ma acciò più facilmente fossero essaudite, si stimava necessario che il Rè d'Inghilterra si risolvesse permettere la libertà della conscienza nella maniera che insta il Pontifice, sperandosi che così tutte le altre difficoltà si superebbono." Corner to the Doge, March 27 / April 6. *Venice MSS.* Desp. Spagna.

had no power to promise anything beyond that which was contained in his master's letter. James was ready to promise that the Catholics should not be persecuted, and that they should not be meddled with as long as they confined their religious observances to their private houses. It was possible that time might bring them further advantages; but, for the present, nothing more could be done.

It is communicated to the Nuncio;

With this reply, Olivares betook himself to the Junta of the Council of State for English affairs, which had recently been formed by excluding the ecclesiastics who had taken part in the original Junta to which the marriage articles had been submitted, and received authority to consult the Nuncio on the subject.

It is better to see many things clearly than to be a man of one idea; but a clear-sighted ecclesiastic like De Massimi possesses an undeniable advantage over a shifty politician like Olivares. What Olivares wanted might vary at any moment, according as the danger of offending the Emperor, or the danger of offending the King of England, was uppermost in his mind. The Nuncio's object was ever the same. To the Infanta's feelings, and to the impending bankruptcy of the Spanish monarchy, he was entirely callous. All he wanted to know, as each proposition was brought before him, was, how far it would conduce to the extension of his Church. Under his scrutiny, therefore, it is not to be wondered at if Buckingham's proposal was weighed and found wanting. The Pope, he told Olivares, would do everything for the King of Spain that his honour and conscience would permit. But the decision had been entrusted to the Congregation of Cardinals, and it must be some very extraordinary cause which would move the Pope to set aside the resolution which they had taken. For his part, he thought that, unless liberty of worship were accorded, the dispensation would not be granted. If James did not choose to render real and effective service to the Catholics at a moment when he was so eager to gain the Pope's consent to the marriage, it was vain to expect his good will at a future time. Was it not ground for suspicion that he acknowledged that

who raises objections.

he was afraid of his own subjects, and that he was unable to induce them to consent to the very change which he professed himself to be most anxious to grant? If it were true that the King of England's power was limited by the will of his Parliament, was it likely that, when the Infanta was once in England, he would be able to keep any promises which he might now make.

Ch. XI.
1623.
March.

This was, indeed, going to the root of the matter. After all, the liberty accorded to the Catholics would depend upon the will of the English people. If Gondomar and Olivares had been able to understand this, they would have saved themselves much discredit.

Olivares, however, was not yet ready to acknowledge the weight of the Nuncio's objections. He tried to turn the subject, by alleging that he had not come to ask advice upon the general question. That had been carefully examined by the Council of State. All he wanted to know was, whether the Pope would assent to its decision.*

The Nuncio's reply showed that if he was more alive than Olivares to the general conditions of human action, his knowledge of special English feeling was limited in the extreme. Without some benefit to religion, he said, success was unattainable. If it were granted that, from fear of the Puritans and other heretics, the King of England was unable to permit the free exercise of the Catholic religion in his dominions, it was all the more necessary that he should give security that the concessions which he was willing to make would not be withdrawn. Let him, therefore, make over some fortified towns to the Catholics, to be held by them in the same way that Rochelle was held by the French Huguenots.†

Proposes the cession of a fortress to English Catholics.

---

* Corner to the Doge, March 27/April 6. *Venice MSS. Desp. Spagna.*

† "Monsignor Nuntio replicò che, senza beneficare la Religione et assicurarla, non sarebbono riusciboli i tentativi. Propose che, escusandosi il Rè di Inghilterra che in se non stava di ammettere publicamente l'essercitio Cattolico per non pericolarsi coi Puritani, et con gli altri Heretici; che, almeno, perchè vi fosse sicurtà che non venissero fra poco tempo di novo travagliati et molestati i Cattolici, et al exempio di Francia con gli Ugonotti, conseguesse alcuna fortezza o luogo da fortificarsi in mano di esse Cattolici per sicuro ricovero et difesa loro." *Ibid.*

CH. XI.
1623.
March.
Rejection of the proposal by Buckingham.

Charged with this monstrous proposition, the Spanish minister hurried back to Buckingham, who at once made short work of the proposal. The circumstances of the French Huguenots and of the English Catholics, he said, were not the same. When the strong places were granted to the Protestants in France, it was done as a means of obtaining peace from a powerful body, who not only had the fortresses already in their hands, but were well able to keep them. The English Catholics were in a very different case. Living a retired and timid life in private, they had no following in the kingdom. The King could find no pretext to submit the proposition just made to Parliament. If Olivares thought of bringing forward any such demands as these, it would save trouble if he understood at once that they would not even be taken into consideration.*

It is withdrawn by Olivares.

Olivares saw that he had made a mistake. He threw the blame of all that he had said upon the Nuncio, and assured Buckingham that he would write at once to the Pope to hasten the dispensation.†

March 25.
Satisfaction of Buckingham.

Everything now appeared to Buckingham's inexperienced eye to be going on smoothly. On the 25th, he received from Olivares an engagement that no time should be lost in making preparations for the Infanta's journey.‡

March 27. Two days afterwards, his Majesty's humble and obedient son and servant, Charles, and his humble slave and dog, Steenie, were able to send home still more favourable news. "We think it not amiss," they wrote, "to assure you that, neither in spiritual nor in temporal things there is anything pressed upon us more than is already

---

* "Il Conte di Olivares riportò il pensiero a Buckingham, qual maravigliendosene, esplicossi che non concorrea in parità di case lo succeduto nella Francia con quello che si ricercava deliberare il Rè suo Signore, perchè la consegnatione delle Piazze a quelli della Religione Reformata fu da stimolo et da desiderio di quiete del Regno, perchè si ritrovavano armati in furore, et con acquisti di Piazze ; cosa che non era de' Cattolici in Inghilterra, che nascosti, timidi, et senza alcuna existimatione viveano ; onde che il Rè, non havendo pretesto, non ardirebbe portar nel Parlamento simil propositione ; manifestando al Conde che, quando si pretendesse di novo queste dimande, si poteva riputar caduta e svanita qualunque trattica, ancorche avanti si trovasse." *Ibid.*

† *Ibid.*

‡ The Prince and Buckingham to the King, March 25. *Harl. MSS.* 6987, fol. 44.

agreed upon. Fain would they, in this time of expecting the dispensation, have treated upon the ends and effects of friendship; but we have avoided it with so many forcible arguments, that they now rest satisfied. They were likewise in hope of a conversion of us both, but now excuses are more studied than reasons for it, though they say their loves shall ever make them wish it. To conclude, we never saw the business in a better way than now it is; therefore, we humbly beseech you, lose no time in hasting the ships, that we may make the more haste to beg that personally which now we do by letter—your blessing." *

For some weeks the Duke of Pastrana, a Spanish grandee—the natural son, if rumour was to be trusted, of Philip II.—had been preparing to start on a mission to Rome. He was now ordered to leave Madrid at once, and it was given out that he was to use every means in his power to hasten the dispensation. Before he left Madrid, he came to kiss the Prince's hand, and assured him that "the chiefest errand of his employment was to do his Highness service." † No one would have been more startled than Charles, if he had known that Pastrana carried secret instructions from the King of Spain, requiring him to inform the Pope of the state of affairs at Madrid, and to urge him to refuse to grant the dispensation, which was no longer desired, now that all hope of the Prince's conversion was at an end.‡

* The Prince and Buckingham to the King, March 27. *Hardwicke S. P.* i. 413.
† Aston to Carleton, April 2. *S. P. Spain.*
‡ "Tardandosi tanto a sentire la nuova della conclusione del matrimonio del Principe d'Inghilterra, et sapendosi che la dispensa di quà fu inviata gran tempo fu, habbiamo procurato d'intendere con fondamento il vero stato di questo importante negotio, et da persona principalissima che ha havuto gran parte in questi maneggi habbiamo havuto la seguente relatione:—che la dispensa fu inviata in Spagna quasi contra la volontà de Spagnuoli, che per loro interessi tenevan volontieri questo negotio in piedi, ma anco per lor importanti rispetti non volevan per adesso venir a conclusione alcuna, et volevan servirse con Inghilterra per pretesti che non potevano cavar il consenso Pontificio nè la dispensa, et che questo era uno de' principali negotii che portasse il Duca di Pastrana." Soranzo and Zen to the Doge, July $\frac{5}{15}$. *Venice MSS.* Desp. Roma. Compare note to p. 326, and the extract from Zen's former despatch quoted at p. 274.

1623.
March.
Olivares' anxiety about the Palatinate.

That the secret was not communicated to the majority of the Spanish ministers there can be little doubt. It was a private arrangement between the favourite and the King. Knowing what was impending, Olivares, constant to his original policy, began to show renewed anxiety on the subject of the Palatinate. The war with England which, in any case, was probable enough, would be inevitable unless he could manage to smooth matters down in Germany. The news of the actual transference of the Electorate had by this time reached Madrid, and Buckingham had been speaking warmly about it. Olivares hurried to the Nuncio, and begged him to urge the Pope to put forward his influence in favour of peace, and to invent some scheme by which the Catholic religion could be promoted, and the promise given by the King of Spain to James in favour of his son-in-law might be at the same time fulfilled. The best thing, he said, would be that the Emperor should deposit the whole of the Lower Palatinate in the hands of the Infanta Isabella, with a view to its restitution either to Frederick or to his son. He hoped that the Emperor would give an express engagement that after Maximilian's death the Electorate should return either to the Count Palatine or to the young Prince, leaving, however, the selection between the two an open question, till it was known what were the final wishes of the King of England.

His conversation with the Nuncio.

Olivares was now to learn once more how little a Roman ecclesiastic cared for the interests of Spain apart from the interests of the Church. De Massimi answered coldly that the Pope would doubtless do everything in his power to keep up a good understanding between the Emperor and the King of Spain, but that it would never do to treat the new Elector of Bavaria with disrespect. It would be well if Oñate received instructions to congratulate him on his advancement.*

March 29.
Discussion in the Council of State.

Two or three days after this interview the subject came on for discussion in the Council of State. It would be in vain to look for an original or statesmanlike view of affairs from any one of the members of that body.

* Corner to the Doge, March 27 / April 6. *Venice MSS*. Desp. Sp.

There was a general feeling that a continuation of the war was almost unavoidable, and that the only chance of averting the calamity lay in getting as much of the Palatinate as possible into Spanish hands, in order that James might in due time be propitiated by its surrender. Olivares concurred in this advice, but he added an opinion that a great error had been made in form, if not in substance, by the irritating language which Oñate had used in dealing with the Emperor. It would have been far better to have acted in harmony with Ferdinand and Maximilian; and he would now recommend that whilst the fortresses in the Palatinate were brought as far as possible into Spanish hands, their surrender to the King of England should be made a matter of friendly negotiation with the Emperor.* Olivares' faith in the possibility of patching up the peace of Europe was not yet completely overthrown.

Scarcely had Pastrana left Madrid when news arrived from Rome that, though the dispensation was not yet drawn up, the Cardinals had made up their minds not to withhold it any longer.† It was a sad blow for Olivares, for he could not now hope, by throwing blame upon the Pope, to soften down in the Prince's eyes the asperity of the impending announcement that the marriage was impossible, excepting upon conditions to which even he could hardly expect a Protestant to consent; and the effect of the intelligence was easily to be perceived in the spasmodic efforts which he once more made to smooth away the almost insuperable obstacles by which the progress of the match was obstructed.

The Infanta, as was well known to the few who were allowed to penetrate the secrets of her domestic life, had fallen into a profound melancholy. She warmly protested that, unless the Prince became a Catholic, she would never consent to be his wife. To Olivares and Gondomar she spoke in terms of the strongest condemnation of the mischief they had done both to the King and to herself. Olivares, who seems merely to have wished to extricate himself from the entanglement in which he

* Consulta of the Council of State, March 29/April 8. *Simancas MSS.* Est. 2404.
† Aston to Carleton, April 2. *S. P. Spain.*

Ch. XI.
1623.
April.
Arguments of Olivares.

was involved, did his best to quiet her. He tried to impress upon her a sense of the merit which she would acquire, both in this world and in the next, by assisting in the spread of the faith. Nor was it impossible, he added, that the Prince might still become a Catholic, although he was too much in dread of his father to make a public acknowledgment of his conversion.* To the Infanta such arguments were addressed in vain. Strong in her own feelings of right, she was not left without warm sympathy from other members of the Royal family. The Queen, Elizabeth of France, took up her cause, and the King himself was disposed to share her ideas. But her stoutest champion was her second brother, Charles, who threw himself with all the ardour of his boyish nature into the struggle, and who saw clearly how little reality there was in the supposition that the Prince of Wales intended to become a Catholic. Already, when after his first interview with the Prince, Philip expressed his belief that his guest had come with the intention of acknowledging his conversion, the boy had muttered that it would be well for his Majesty to take care that his sister were not carried away into heresy; and he now lost all patience when he heard some one telling the Infanta that she was elected by God to be the means of redeeming England. "I hope," he said, "that the devil may not tempt us to send her there to her own destruction."†

Olivares hopes for a private conversion of the Prince.

In despair of prevailing with the Infanta, Olivares turned once more to the Prince, hoping that he might win from him at least a private acknowledgment of a change of religion. His first step was to appeal to the Nuncio. If the Prince, he said, would give the private assurance required of him, would it not be possible to proceed to the marriage at once without waiting for the dispensation.‡

* "Et segli da anco speranza, che il Prencipe possa anchè inclinar ad essere Cattolico ; ma che, per timor del Padre, non lo pubbliche.", Corner to the Doge, April 4. *Venice MSS.* Desp. Spagna.
† *Ibid.*
‡ "Il Conde de Olivares nondimeno ha ricercato Monsignor Nuntio, se il matrimonio si poteva effettuare senza permissione del Pontefice, mentre il Prencipe occultamente abjurasse o di segreto professasse la nostra religione, non comportando gli interessi suoi pubblica professione nè palese culto." *Ibid.*

The Nuncio replied in the negative; but Olivares was not discouraged. He determined to make his first attempt upon Buckingham, who had, whilst repelling the overtures of the Spaniards, been doing his best to simulate the appearance of one who was not unwilling to be converted, whenever the proper time should arrive. He had taken good care never to attend the Protestant service, which was regularly celebrated at the English Embassy by Bristol's chaplain. When he visited a church he did not omit to bow the knee reverently before the Sacrament on the altar.* So successful had he been in conveying the desired impression, that the Imperial Ambassador, writing to his master about this time, informed him that the English were assuming, as much as possible, the appearance of Catholics.†

Thus encouraged, Olivares lost no time in talking to Buckingham on the subject. What a pity it was, he said, that the Prince should not seize the opportunity of informing himself on the doctrines of the Catholic faith. No compulsion was intended; but it could not be taken otherwise than as an insult, if he refused even to listen to what was to be said in its favour. Buckingham was all politeness. Truly or falsely, he asserted that he had brought orders not to throw obstacles in the way of a discussion upon religious subjects. He should be glad, however, to try the effect of such a conversation upon himself before he recommended it to the Prince. It did not occur to Olivares that all that Buckingham wanted was to gain time. The offer was thought to be a serious one, and on the 4th of April the Marquis was carried in profound secresy to the monastery of San Geronimo, to engage in a theological disputation with Francisco de Jesus, a Carmelite friar, who had taken a principal part in the discussions upon the marriage treaty. For four hours the debate lasted. Buckingham listened patiently, said something whenever he could find anything to say in a paper which he had brought with him, and when he could not find an argument to the purpose, held his

---

* Articles against Buckingham. *State Trials*, ii. 1288.
† " Stellen sich sehr Catholisch." Khevenhüller to Ferdinand II., April 7/17. *Khevenhüller*, x. 79.

tongue. At last the friar began to suspect that he had taken all this trouble for nothing. Buckingham did not appear to understand that he had been well beaten according to all the rules of logic, and that it was his business to surrender at discretion.*

A few days before this curious scene was enacted, the Marquis of Inojosa, the Viceroy of Navarre, was ordered to prepare to go as Extraordinary Ambassador to England,† ostensibly to thank James for allowing his son to visit Madrid. He was, however, privately instructed to urge James to make yet further concessions to his Catholic subjects.‡

Nor was it possible any longer to avoid coming to a conclusion on a point still more delicate. As yet Charles had never been allowed to see the Infanta except in public, and had never had an opportunity of speaking to her at all. Every excuse which Spanish customs could suggest had been made without giving the slightest satisfaction. The knotty point was seriously debated in the Council of State, and it was at last decided that on Easter Day the long desired visit should take place. Accordingly the King, accompanied by a long train of grandees, came to fetch him, and led him to the Queen's apartment, where they found her Majesty seated with the Infanta by her side. After paying his respects to the Queen, Charles turned to address his mistress. It had been intended that he should confine himself to the few words of ceremony which had been set down beforehand, but in the presence in which he was, he forgot the rules of ceremony, and was beginning to declare his affection in words of his own choice. He had not got far before it was evident that there was something wrong. The bystanders began to whisper to one another. The Queen cast glances of displeasure at the daring youth. Charles hesitated and stopped short. The Infanta herself looked seriously annoyed; and when it came to her turn to reply, some of those who were watching her expected her

---

* Francisco de Jesus, 58.
† Aston to Carleton, April 2. *S. P. Spain.*
‡ Corner to the Doge, April $\frac{13}{23}$. *Venice MSS.* Desp. Sp.

to show some signs of displeasure. It was not so very long ago that she had been heard to declare that her only consolation was that she should die a martyr. But she had an unusual fund of self-control, and she disliked Charles too much to feel in the slightest degree excited by his speeches. She uttered the few common-place words which had been drawn up beforehand, and the interview was at an end.*

The unlucky termination of this visit did not hinder Olivares from making one more attempt upon Buckingham's religion. Before Easter week was over, he invited him to a second disputation. Seeing that the friar's eloquence produced but little effect, Olivares himself came to the rescue, and took part in the argument. Of course it was all in vain, and no further assault was made upon the conscience of the magnificent Englishman.†

Such were the expedients by which Buckingham hoped to occupy the attention of the Spanish ministers till the dispensation arrived. He could not now, he thought, have much longer to wait. On the 18th of April he wrote to England, to countermand the sending out of some horses for tilting, which had been ordered for Charles. Before they could possibly reach Spain the Prince would have left Madrid.‡ On the same day he wrote to Conway, informing him that he had been privately assured that the dispensation had been conceded at Rome.§

Margin: Ch. XI. 1623. April 7.

Margin: Fresh attempts to convert Buckingham.

Margin: He expects to return soon.

---

* Doppo molte consulte fu gratiato, il giorno dietro Pasqua di cumplire con essa per l'uso dell' annuntio delle SSme. Feste, accompagnandolo il Rè con seguito di tutti li Grandi et comitiva de' Cavalieri nell' appartamento della Regina, appresso la quale si pose a sedere il Prencipe, et il Rè a canto alla sorella. Annuntiato che hebbe felicità alla Regina si approssimò il Prencipe alla Infanta, et gli espose complimento assai lungo, et con maniera affettuosa, di che si susurrava nella stanza, et perciò finì prima dele suo gusto vedendo anco certi segni della Regina, et che si annoiava la Infanta : qual ispose compitamente et con la puntualità prescrittale di pochissime parole d'ufficio, et si notò per osservatione prencipale che ella si tenne tanto composta et senza minimo segno di mutatione, che tutte gli astanti rimasero stupidi, parlandosene con maraviglia universale, perchè è certissimo che ella ha una estrema antipathia et timore di queste nozze, non si consolando con altro se non col dire che morirà martire." Corner to the Doge, April $\frac{13}{23}$. *Venice MSS.* Desp. Spagna. As might be expected, Bristol passes over the Prince's repulse. Bristol to Calvert, April 8. *S. P. Spain.*

† Francisco de Jesus, 58.
‡ Buckingham to Graham, April 8. *S. P. Spain.*
§ Buckingham to Conway, April 8. *Harl. MSS.* 6987, fol. 65.

Ch. XI. 1623. March. The dispensation granted.	Buckingham's information was correct. The news of the Prince's arrival in Spain reached Rome on the 15th of March. There, too, as at Madrid, it was the universal opinion that he intended to become a Roman Catholic, or at least to grant extraordinary concessions to the professors of that religion. On the 19th,* the question was solemnly discussed by the Congregation of Cardinals. Under the impression caused by the Prince's journey, they resolved not to be content with the articles to which James had signified his assent in January, and though they no longer pressed their original demand for public liberty of worship, they put forward several by no means unimportant amendments of the treaty. Such questions as these, however, were very far from forming their chief difficulty. For though Pastrana had not yet arrived, care had been taken to let the cardinals know that Philip had no real wish to have the dispensation granted. Yet it was impossible for them to look upon the question with Philip's eyes. No one who was not a Spaniard could imagine that if Charles returned without his bride, he would return otherwise than filled with indignation against those by whom his disappointment had been caused. Nor, on the other hand, was the comfortable arrangement by which Olivares proposed to discharge that indignation upon the broad shoulders of the Pope likely to be received with much favour at the Vatican. If James were led to understand that his failure was owing to the obstinacy of the Pope, he would be sure to vent his displeasure upon his Catholic subjects. It would be better, therefore, so to arrange matters that his quarrel—if quarrel there was to be—should be a personal one with Philip.†
April. But the responsibility cast upon Philip.	

* Francisco de Jesus. *Add. MSS.* 60.
† The passage, part of which has been already quoted at p. 319, goes on as follows :—"Ma stimandosi qui pregiudicialissimo à Cattolici, che questa tardanza fusse tutta caricata al Pontifice, perchè ciò levarebbe dall' animo del Rè della Gran Bretagna qualche inclinatione ch' egli tiene alla sede Apostolica, et haverebbe potuto venir a qualche severa risolutione contra li Cattolici che si trovano sparsi per l'Inghilterra che sono infiniti ; per il che si risolvi sua Santità," etc. Soranzo and Zen to the Doge, July $\frac{5}{15}$.
Venice MSS. Desp. Roma. That the belief that Pastrana had a secret mission really prevailed at Rome is shown from a decypher of an extract from a letter of his which I found on a scrap of paper at Simancas (Est. 1869),

With amusing gravity, therefore, which recalls the well-known formula with which the clergy were wont to hand over offenders to the secular arm, the cardinals proceeded to wash their hands of the whole business. They were shrewd enough to suspect that as soon as he was safe in England with his bride, Charles would forget all the promises which he had made in Spain; and they entirely refused to be in any way responsible for the consequences. All they had to say about the matter was, that Charles must give some sort of security for his fidelity to his engagements. What that security ought to be it was not their business to judge. All such questions must be referred to the consideration of his Catholic Majesty. The dispensation would be placed in the hands of the Nuncio at Madrid, who was to have orders not to part with it till Philip had sworn, in his own name and in that of his successors, that the promises made in accordance with the treaty would be faithfully observed by both parties; and that neither his Catholic Majesty, nor the King of Great Britain, nor any of their successors, would "do or execute anything, nor consent that any should do or execute anything to the contrary; though it should concern the conservation of their kingdoms." Moreover, within one year, so concluded this strange proposal, the King of Spain "shall send unto his Holiness the said capitulations, approved, confirmed, and assured by the King of Great Britain, and also allowed and received by his Councils, and Parliament; and besides this, his said Catholic Majesty shall promise and swear that he and his successors in that Crown shall always be ready with their arms, army, and armadas, to the end that, so soon as any of the conditions shall be broken, without any delay he oppose himself with all his power and force against that Prince or King which shall break it, or not observe it."

Cardinal Ludovisi at once wrote to De Massimi announcing the decision.* The dispensation, he informed

Olivares tells the news to the Prince.

"Entráron en recato de que los queriamos por disculpa, y no para facilitar el negocio ; y este fué la razon de aprocurar la dispensacion pasada, sin aguardar á que yo llegase, porque dessean siempre quedar bien con Inglaterra."

* Cardinal Ludovisi to De Massimi. Translation in Cottington's hand. *Harl. MSS.* 1583, fol. 297.

him, would shortly be sent, though it would be accompanied by certain conditions, upon which he was at all hazards to insist. The letter, immediately upon its arrival, was imparted by the Nuncio to Olivares, with the strictest injunctions to secresy. But, much to De Massimi's disgust, the Spaniard could not resist the temptation of currying favour with Charles, by being the first to acquaint him with the news. The Prince was soon overwhelmed with congratulations on every side, as if all difficulties had been now surmounted.*

It is only by conjecture that we can penetrate the secret feelings of Philip when he learned that the long intrigue had finally broken down, and that the Pope had refused to stand between his sister and her unwelcome lover. The only symptom of his agitation which came to the surface, was one more desperate attempt to convert the Prince. A third theological discussion, in which Charles himself was to take part, was fixed for the evening of the 23rd of April.

That day, St. George's day, the Prince and Buckingham dined in state. Some weeks before, his father, in one of his garrulous letters, had encouraged them to keep the festival of the patron of England with unusual magnificence. "I sent you," he wrote, "your robes of the order, which ye must not forget to wear on St. George's day, and dine together in them, if they can come in time, which I pray God they may, for it will be a goodly sight for the Spaniards to see my two boys dine in them." The Spaniards, however, did not appear to appreciate the display.† They had been thoroughly digusted by Buckingham's proceedings with respect to the religious conferences, and they began now to take it for granted that it was by his arts that the Prince's conversion had been hindered. Before the day ended a violent quarrel had broken out between the English favourite and Don Fernando Giron, a member of the

---

* Corner to the Doge, May $\frac{10}{20}$. *Venice MSS.* Desp. Roma. De Massimi to Olivares, April $\frac{14}{24}$. *Bibl. Imp. MSS.* Harl. 228, 16. fol. 183. The King to the Prince and Buckingham, March 17. *Hardwicke S. P.* i. 408.

† Corner to the Doge, May $\frac{10}{20}$. *Venice MSS.* Desp. Spagna.

Council of State, and the angry disputants were only pacified by an assurance that the misunderstanding had been caused by the ignorance of an interpreter.

As soon as the evening came, Charles and Buckingham were carried off to the appointed conference. The King himself accompanied them to the place, though he withdrew immediately on the plea that it was unfit for a King of Spain to listen to a single word directed against his religion.

One friar had been thought sufficient to confront Buckingham. No less than four were summoned to convince the Prince. For some minutes after Charles had taken his seat, there was complete silence. At last one of the friars asked him if he had no matter to propose for their consideration. "Nothing at all," replied the Prince, "I have no doubts whatever." Olivares then suggested that an attempt should be made to enlighten him. Upon this Antonio de Sotomayor, the King's confessor, struck in, and argued at some length in behalf of the Pope's claim to be the Vicar of Christ. To clinch the argument, Father Zacharias chimed in with the passage in which the Saviour addressed the failing apostle, "And thou, when thou art converted, strengthen thy brethren." Charles at once replied that they were straining the text by forcing such an interpretation upon it, and requested that it might be read again in French. After it had been twice repeated, he said something to Buckingham in English. Regardless of those decencies of life, which were so dear to the Spanish heart, Buckingham leapt from his seat, and, after expressing his contempt for the friars by unseemly gesticulations, threw his hat upon the ground, and stamped upon it. After this the conference was of course brought to an end.*

That Charles gave any direct support to the prevailing opinion that he intended to change his religion, is contradicted by every scrap of evidence which exists. He was ready, he told one of the friars who had taken part in the discussion, to abjure his religion as soon as he was convinced of its falsehood. Under ordinary circumstances, such language is usually taken as a polite form of refusal. But,

* Francisco de Jesus, 58.

Ch. XI.
1623.
April.

Chaplains sent by James.

situated as he was, it would have saved much misapprehension, if he had absolutely declined to take part in religious conversations, lest they might give rise to those false hopes to which it was his duty to put an end.*

It was not with James's good will that the slightest ground was given to the Spaniards for supposing that they could effect a conversion of the Prince. A ship which sailed from England, crowded with attendants in order to enable Charles to keep his Court in state, carried also two of the Prince's chaplains, Mawe and Wren. From these men James had expected great things. When they arrived at Madrid they were to take care to have "a convenient room appointed for prayer," which was to "be decently adorned, chapel wise, with an altar, fonts, palls, linen coverings, demy carpet, four surplices, candlesticks, tapers, chalices, patens, a fine towel for the Prince, other towels for the household, a traverse, wafers for the Communion, a basin, flagons, and two copes." The chaplains were further directed to see that prayers "be duly kept twice a day, that all reverence be used by every one present being uncovered, kneeling at due times, standing up at the creeds and gospel, bowing at the name of Jesus." The Communion was to "be celebrated in due form, with an oblation of every communicant, and admixing water with the wine." In the sermons there were to be "no polemical preachings," but the doctrine of the Church of England was to be confirmed "by all positive arguments either in fundamental or moral points, and specially to apply ourselves to moral lessons to preach Christ Jesus crucified." The chaplains were not to engage in disputation, excepting at the request of Bristol or Cottington; and, lastly, they were to carry with them the articles of "religion in many copies, the book of Common Prayer in several languages, store of English service books," and "the King's own works in English and Latin."†

Exhorts his son not

"The Spanish Ambassador," wrote James a month

---

* "Le voci continuano che il Prencipe inclina assai all abjurare le heresie, quando ne sia illuminato, cosi si è espresso col Capucino." Corner to the Doge, May $\frac{10}{20}$. *Venice MSS. Desp. Spagna.*

† Directions to the Prince's chaplains, March 10. *S. P. Spain.*

later, "let fall a word to Gresley, as if there would be some question made that my baby's chaplains should not do their service in the King's palace there; but he concluded that that business would be soon accommodated. Always in case any such difficulty should be stuck at, ye may remember them, that it is an ill preparation for giving the Infanta free exercise of her religion here, to refuse it to my son there; since their religion is as odious to a number here as ours is there. And if they will not yield, then, my sweet baby, show yourself not to be ashamed of your profession; but go sometimes to my Ambassador's house and have your service there, that God and man may see ye are not ashamed of your religion. But I hope in God this shall not need."*

No doubt there was enough of folly in the idea that it was possible to make a Protestant service palatable to the Spaniards; but there are few persons of upright minds who will not prefer the folly of the father to the prudence of the son.

James's plan for exhibiting what he considered to be a service "decent and agreeable to the purity of the Prince's Church, and yet as near the Roman form as can lawfully be done,"† was never carried into execution. Olivares sent for Cottington, and told him plainly that any attempt of the chaplains to enter the Royal Palace would be resisted by force.‡ Against this intimation Charles was powerless. Once, indeed, it appears, in a moment of pique, Buckingham caused Charles to attend the ministrations of his religion in Bristol's house; but the practice was not continued, and a month later, in the instructions given to Cottington when he was about to return to England, the Prince charged him "to give his Majesty satisfaction in that his Highness hath not had the exercise of his religion in hearing sermons."§

On the 24th of April the dispensation was placed in the hands of the Nuncio at Madrid, accompanied by a

---

* The King to the Prince and Buckingham, April 7. *Goodman's Court of King James*, ii. 297.

† The King to the Prince and Buckingham, March 17. *Hardwicke S. P.* i. 406.

‡ Francisco de Jesus, 59.

§ Instructions to Cottington, May 21. *Clarendon S. P.* i. App. xviii.

Ch. XI.
1623.
April.
Oath required of Philip.

letter to Philip from the Pope, exhorting him to do everything in his power for the advantage of the Catholic religion in England, and by secret instructions in which the Nuncio was recommended to urge the concession of complete freedom of worship. He was also informed that the dispensation was absolutely null till the King of Spain had sworn that the King of England would perform his obligations, and would obtain the consent of the Privy Council and the Parliament to the articles, and had engaged that he would himself keep his fleets ready to enforce at any time the execution of the treaty.*

Quarrel between Buckingham and Olivares.

That Olivares should object strongly to such a startling demand as derogatory to the honour of his master was natural enough; but the Nuncio simply referred to his orders, and the Spanish minister was forced to inform the Prince of Wales how matters stood. The reception with which he met, as may well be supposed, was not a favourable one. The alterations made at Rome in the articles themselves were by no means unimportant. The age at which the education of the children by their mother was to cease was now fixed at twelve; whilst James had only expressed his willingness, as an extreme concession, to go as far as ten. The Infanta's church, it was again required, was to be open to all, and the oath drawn up by the Pope for the servants of the Infanta was to be substituted in the case of every English Catholic for that oath of allegiance which had been settled by act of Parliament. After such demands as these, the question of the King of Spain's oath, excepting so far as it led to fresh claims, was in reality unimportant. The articles themselves were utterly incompatible with James's notion that he was about to grant favours to his Catholic subjects of his own free grace. For a sovereign to agree with a foreign power to set aside the laws is to sign away the independence of his Crown, whatever may be the form in which the concession is couched; and the Pope's demand that Philip should become a guarantee for James's conduct, and should hold himself in readiness to enforce the execution of his engagements, merely ripped away the veil from the ill-concealed monstrosity behind.

* Francisco de Jesus, 64.

The meeting between Olivares and Buckingham was a stormy one, and for two days after it the favourites refused even to speak to one another. By the English it was alleged that when the Prince came to Madrid he did not expect to be asked to make fresh concessions. But they were told that the Prince had come of his own accord; that, if Gondomar had spoken to him on the subject, he had done so merely as a private individual, and that, as it had always been understood that the Pope was to be satisfied, nothing added at his request could be properly regarded as a new demand.*

<small>Ch. XI.
1623.
April.</small>

The quarrel thus begun was hushed up for the time, and on the 3rd of May the whole question was referred to the Marquis of Montesclaros, the Count of Gondomar, and the Secretary Ciriza, who were appointed to treat as Commissioners with Buckingham, Bristol, Aston, and Cottington on behalf of the Prince.

<small>May 3. The marriage referred to Commissioners.</small>

Before this body Charles appeared. He and his father, he said, were ready to swear that the penal laws should be suspended, and they would also do their best to obtain as soon as possible from Parliament a confirmation of the articles and of the suspension of the laws, if it were impossible to have them altogether repealed. To this offer the Spanish Commissioners replied by asking how soon all this was likely to happen, and Charles, who knew perfectly well that there was not the slightest chance that Parliament would do anything of the sort, answered boldly that it might possibly be in three months, or in six. It would probably be in a year; but it would certainly, and without fail, be done in three.

<small>Charles offers to try to induce Parliament to repeal the penal laws.</small>

The next day was taken up with hearing Charles's arguments against the additional articles. It was needless, he observed, to state that the nurses of the children must necessarily be Catholics, as they were in any case to be selected by the Infanta herself. To admit the Catholics generally to the Infanta's church was an uncalled for innovation, as they would have the benefit of their religion in their own houses. He would promise, however, to connive at their occasional presence. To do

<small>May 6. His offer refused by the Council of State.</small>

---

* Du Fargis to Puisieux, May $\frac{3}{13}$. *Bibl. Imp. MSS. Harl.* 228, 16, fol. 190.

Ch. XI.
1623.
May 6.

more would amount to a public toleration of the free exercise of the Roman Catholic religion, to which, as the King of Spain knew well, his father had always refused to accede. To the universal application of the new oath he also objected as unnecessary. Besides, he added, it was unfit that the Pope should dictate the form of oath due to the King of Great Britain by his subjects. With respect to the concession of two additional years of education he would intercede with his father, but he could not engage what the result would be.*

The declaration thus made was duly reported to the Council of State, where it was resolved that the articles must be accepted as they came from Rome, or not at all; and that the Prince's offer was altogether insufficient. The oath required from the King of Spain must be sworn if the marriage was to take place, and the question what the conditions were which would justify him in swearing should be referred at once to a Junta of forty theologians, to be summoned for the purpose.†

Olivares advises that the Infanta shall be retained.

Yet this decision, unacceptable as it was certain to be to Charles, did not go far enough for Olivares. It was impossible, he urged in a private paper addressed to the King, that James could be serious in the promises that he was willing to make, for it was altogether contrary to his interests to allow a religion differing from his own to grow up in his State. It would, therefore, be well to retain the Infanta in Spain till the engagements of the King of England had been actually put in execution.

May 7.
His speech in the Council of State.

It was, no doubt, under the impression caused by this opinion that the whole question was brought up again for discussion on the following day, when Olivares reproduced his ideas at greater length. "This marriage," he said, "has been treated of solely with a view to the good of the English Catholics. Yet, though the King of Great Britain desires its accomplishment with all the anxiety which he has already shown, and with such eagerness as may be understood from the pledges which he has given; he says that he is unable to do more for the Catholics in

---

* Account of the negotiation. Translated from the original at Simancas, by M. Guizot. *Un Projet de Mariage Royal*, 132.
† Francisco de Jesus. *Add.* 66.

his kingdom than to extend to them a mere connivance, and that without force of law, nor any confirmation greater than his own word, and that of the Prince, and although that is of great value, nevertheless, as it is in opposition to what they hold to be right, it is not obligatory on them in conscience, especially as oaths to the contrary have been made, and legally established, in so many Parliaments; it is, therefore, to be supposed that everything that is now offered is only done in order to obtain the marriage; for if, though the King desires it so much, he can do no more than this; and if we are told that the people may become so unruly at his mere condescension to a simple connivance that it may be impossible for him to do even this, how can it be argued that, after the marriage is over, either the King or the Prince will wish to preserve, or to favour, in their kingdoms a religion which they consider in their conscience to be contrary to their own? And so little power have they, according to their own public acknowledgment, that even with the best wishes of the King and the Prince, they cannot introduce the free exercise of religion now. How, then, is it to be supposed that they will do it after the marriage?"

If he could hear that either the King or Prince was likely to become Catholic, Olivares went on to say, it would be a different thing; as it was, it was impossible to trust their mere word. Let us propose to them to celebrate the marriage at once; but let us at the same time inform them that the Infanta must remain here till we see them act as well as talk. When the release of the Catholics from the penal laws is accepted by the Council, and confirmed by Parliament; when offices of trust are placed in the hands of declared Catholics, then, and not till then, it will be safe to allow the Infanta to go. For by this means the Catholics would increase in number and strength, so that it would no longer be in the King's power to depress them again. He would then be obliged to temporise, and perhaps even to adopt their religion for his own safety.*

In the Council of State Olivares found himself alone.

* Francisco de Jesus, 66—71.

CH. XI.
1623.
May 7.

It was not that the other ministers were less desirous to impose their own religion upon a foreign nation, but that they underrated the difficulties in their way. The idea of securing toleration for their co-religionists in England was utterly foreign to the Spanish mind. They wanted supremacy for their Church, and they were on the whole inclined to think with Gondomar, that a little more cajolery would be sufficient to obtain it.

The Prince makes fresh offers.

Olivares waited his time. Favourite as he was, it was not his habit to take violent measures with men who disagreed with him; and he was anxious to be regarded by the English as the firm friend of the match. He determined to apply once more to Charles, and asked him what in his opinion would be sufficient security to enable the King of Spain to take the oath? His father's oath and his own, he now said, should be confirmed by that of the Privy Council, and he would do his best that it should be confirmed by Parliament as well. Shortly afterward he declared himself ready to engage that he would never allow a word to be breathed in the Infanta's presence which was prejudicial to her faith; and that on the other hand he would be ready, whenever his wife requested him, to listen privately to the discourses of Catholic theologians.

The Nuncio refuses to dispense.

Upon this reply the Spanish Commissioners met once more, and laid the Prince's propositions before the Nuncio. De Massimi's answer was decisive. On these terms the dispensation could not be granted. The articles must be accepted precisely in the form in which they had been sent from Rome. Such a reply was peculiarly irritating to Buckingham. Confident, as usual, of the irresistible weight of his personal influence, he sought a secret interview with the Nuncio at the dead of night. For three hours he poured forth every form of argument and entreaty, descending even to threats. "There is no way," he said at last, "to treat for this marriage, but with the sword drawn over the Catholics."* Bristol was next sent to the Nuncio with no better success. Charles was plainly told that without the consent of the Pope the articles could not be restored to their original form. The

* Francisco de Jesus, 72.

King of Spain would indeed be ready to refer the matter again to Rome, and it would be well if Charles would send to England to obtain his father's consent to the concessions which were required. As for the King's oath, the question would be laid before the theologians.

It was not only by the slow progress of his wooing that Charles was made to feel how isolated he was at Madrid. Scarcely had he heard of the impending arrival of the retinue with which he had thought of keeping up his princely state, than he was given to understand that the presence of so many Englishmen would not be well taken by the Spanish Court. He accordingly despatched orders to meet them at Santander, commanding the greater part of them to return at once to England. Some few, including the two chaplains, got as far as Burgos, and made their homeward journey through France, carrying with them many strange stories of the rough fare with which they had met in Spain. A few, more lucky than the rest, were allowed to make their way to the capital. But they soon found that their services were not needed. The rooms assigned to the Prince in the royal palace were few and small, and it had been arranged that his attendants should sleep at the other end of the town, with the evident intention of making their stay as inconvenient as possible. For six or seven days they were to be seen strolling about Madrid. But the greater part of their time they passed in playing cards, and in grumbling at their enforced idleness. At last, Charles came to the conclusion that it was useless to detain them any longer, and ordered them, with one or two exceptions, to hasten home as soon as possible.

It was afterwards stated with great glee in England that one of these attendants, James Eliot by name, being admitted to take leave of the Prince, expressed a hope that his Highness would not remain much longer in Spain. "It is a dangerous place," he said, "to alter a man and turn him. I myself in a short time have perceived my own weakness, and am almost turned." To the Prince's demand, what he meant by being turned, he replied, that he was turned in his religion. "What motive," said Charles, "had you; or what hast thou seen

Ch. XI.
1623
May.

which should turn thee?" "Marry," replied Eliot, "when I was in England I turned the whole Bible over to find Purgatory, and because I could not find it there, I believed there was none. But now I have come to Spain, I have found it here, and that your Highness is in it; whence that you may be released, we, your Highness's servants, who are going to Paradise, will offer unto God our utmost devotions." So little, however, did Charles understand in what a net his feet were entangled, that he actually laid a wager with another of his followers that he would be in England before the 10th of July.*

Yet, to all who were not utterly blinded, the blunder which he had committed in coming to Spain at all was now plainly visible. If he had never left England, either the dispensation would have been refused, or the conditions with which it was accompanied would have been quietly referred by Bristol to his master, to be discussed in England upon their own merits. If it were not hazardous to affirm that James would have come to a settled resolution upon anything, there could be little doubt what the result of that discussion would have been. For weak as his conduct had been, he was not prepared for so barefaced an attempt to ride roughshod over the prerogatives of his Crown, as well as over the laws of his kingdom. The leading idea with which he had entered into the treaty had been a readiness to offer in return for political support, and for the large portion which was to be brought by the Infanta, a full guarantee for the free exercise of her own religion, and a considerable alleviation of the condition of the English Catholics. That he had been led step by step to offer more than this is certain; but it is no less certain that he had never intended to bargain for the opening of a public church, and still less to enter into any discussion about the abolition of the penal laws, a question which, as he well knew, it was useless to moot in the presence of the House of Commons, and which he would himself have been indisposed to consider, regarding, as he did, the

---

* Mead to Stuteville, June 21. Ellis's *Orig. Letters*, Ser. i., vol. iii. 152. Gwynne's Relation in the Appendix to Hearne's edition of *Vita Ricardi II.*, 299.

retention of the power of putting those laws in force as a safeguard against possible disloyalty.

"Do you think," said James to Williams, "that this knight-errant pilgrimage will be lucky to win the Spanish lady and to convey her shortly into England?" "Sir," replied the Lord Keeper, "if my Lord Marquis will give honour to the Count Duke Olivares; or if Olivares will show honourable civility to my Lord Marquis, remembering he is a favourite of England, the wooing may be prosperous. But if my Lord Marquis should forget where he is, and not stoop to Olivares; or if Olivares, forgetting what guest he hath received with the Prince, bear himself haughtily and like a Castilian grandee to my Lord Marquis, the provocation may be dangerous to cross your Majesty's good intentions."* The observation, shrewd as, like most of Williams' recorded sayings, it undoubtedly was, was only superficial. Buckingham's temper, exasperating as it was to those who had to deal with him, was very far from being the cause of the ultimate failure of the negotiation. What the Spaniards wanted was to accomplish by intrigue what Philip II. had failed to accomplish by force, namely, to make England once more a Roman Catholic country. Gondomar and Olivares might differ as to the means to be used, but there was no difference as to the end. And yet, with the evidence of this before his eyes, Charles could see nothing but the lovely vision of his hoped-for bride. For months he lingered at Madrid, sacrificing his country to his love—making promises, into the full meaning of which he did not care to inquire, and satisfying himself with the prospect of being able to explain them away, if at any time they should prove inconvenient; thus confirming the Spanish ministers in their belief that he was of so malleable a nature that, with careful manipulation, he might be led to promise anything, whilst at the same time he failed to impress them with the slightest confidence in the probability of his ever keeping his promises, excepting under compulsion.†

If it had been in his power, Buckingham would have

* Hacket, 115.
† Francisco de Jesus, 73.

broken off the treaty at once.* It was enough for him that the additional articles were a personal insult to himself, and to the Prince who had taken the trouble to come to Madrid on the understanding that the old ones were to form the basis of the treaty. But great as his influence was with Charles, it was not enough to tear him away so easily from the neighbourhood of the Infanta. The answer given by the Prince to the last resolution of the Spanish Government, was indeed sufficiently decisive in appearance. He was quite willing, he said, that a courier should be despatched to Rome, in order to induce the Pope to give way. He was also willing to communicate with his father, but he considered that he was himself the only fit person to carry the communication. He, therefore, requested permission to return at once to England.

The next day Buckingham sent a message to Olivares, informing him that the Prince intended to leave Madrid immediately. But it soon appeared that all this meant nothing. The messenger was delayed for some hours, and before he met with Olivares, Gondomar had made the discovery that Charles only needed a little pressure to induce him to remain.

The pressure which Charles required was extremely slight. A few friendly words from the King, begging him to stop at least till the Junta of Theologians had delivered its report, was sufficient to make him alter his determination. Nor was it only from the irresolution of the Prince that the Spaniards derived encouragement. Buckingham was the least reticent of men, and in the course of a conversation with Francisco de Jesus, the friar discovered two important facts, the one that he was chiefly moved by pique in his dislike of the additional articles; the second, that the Prince was not likely to make any difficulty in surrendering all other objections, if he could only escape from an obligation to procure the repeal of the penal laws.† Even on this last point the Spanish ministers had no reason to expect to find him obstinate. For within the last few days Buckingham had offered to engage that the King would see that the laws were

---

* Corner to the Doge, May $\frac{17}{27}$. *Venice MSS.* Desp. Spagna.
† Francisco de Jesus, 73.

repealed, though he added that it would require some time before he could obtain the assent of Parliament to the change. "Will he do it," said the Nuncio, "within a year?" Buckingham answered that it was impossible to fix a time, as the longer the appeal to Parliament was delayed, the more chance there would be of obtaining the consent of the Houses.*

Ch. XI. 1623. May. Question of the repeal of the penal laws,

The extreme readiness of Charles and Buckingham to make concessions, was probably caused by the care which Olivares had taken to allow the news of the proposed detention of the Infanta to reach their ears. He himself, he declared, was quite satisfied that the King of England's bare engagement was enough to enable his own sovereign to take the required oath. But the Nuncio was of a different opinion. It is probable that the course which had been adopted by Olivares in the Council, had been suggested by De Massimi. At all events, the Nuncio now came forward to defend it.† The marriage, he said, might take place, but it must be a mere ceremony. The Prince must go back at once to England, to obtain from his father the execution of the promises made. As might have been expected, both Charles and Buckingham were enraged at the very notion of delay, and the Nuncio, fearing that if he said anything more on the subject, the Prince would really return to England, consented, in appearance at least, to give way.

and of the Infanta remaining in Spain.

Yet the threat, though abandoned for the present, had done its work. Rather than go home without the Infanta, Charles was ready to agree to anything. His wife, he now said, might have the care of her children till they were twelve : the oath of allegiance should be altered so as to please the Pope. The Infanta's church should be open to the public. He and his father would bind themselves to the immediate suspension of the penal laws, and the King would engage to persuade Parliament to repeal them in three years.

Charles gives way on every point.

* Corner to the Doge, May $\frac{14}{24}$. *Venice MSS.* Desp. Spagna.

† In the letter just quoted, it is said impersonally " si respondi." But the despatch of May $\frac{17}{27}$ attributes the idea to De Massimi. " Perche la negativa di dar subito la Infanta al Principe era persuasa del Nuncio," etc. It had been suggested to the Nuncio by the Congregation of Cardinals. Francisco de Jesus, 60.

Ch. XI.
1623.
May.
Pedrosa's
sermon.

With such concessions as these Philip professed himself satisfied. If James confirmed his son's engagements, he would himself be ready to take the oath, and would allow his sister to accompany the Prince to England. But just as Cottington was about to start with the news, a fresh obstacle arose. A certain Father Pedrosa, a great opponent of the match, had been appointed to preach in the royal chapel. He did not throw away his opportunity. Turning to the King, he warned him not to decide from considerations of state policy, rather than from the interests of religion. Jehu, who had slaughtered Ahab and the priests of Baal, had met with disasters because, however good in itself the action was, he had not served God with his whole heart. In the present case, it could not even be said that the action was good. To marry the Infanta to a heretic was doubtful, and to take an oath that this heretic would keep his word, was more doubtful still. Philip, whose conscience was always sensitive to such considerations as these, was the more ready to take alarm, as he knew that the marriage was generally unpopular amongst his subjects, now that it was known that Charles had not come to be converted. People were every day talking about the prophecy of Daniel, who had predicted ruin to fall upon the King of the South, that is to say upon the King of Spain of the House of Austria — *Rex Austri*, as it stood in the Vulgate— for giving his daughter in marriage to the King of the North. Under these circumstances, Philip hesitated and drew back, waiting to see what relief the Junta of Theologians would bring.

Unpopularity of the marriage.

A letter from the Pope presented to Charles.

Even this rebuff could not cure Charles of his incorrigible habit of holding out hopes which he had no intention of gratifying. When the Nuncio presented him with a letter from the Pope, in which he was exhorted to return to the true Church, he not only spoke respectfully of the writer, but he added that, although he could not listen to any theological discussion now, he would be willing to hear anything as soon as the marriage was over.* In the written answer which he returned to the

* Corner to the Doge, May $\frac{14}{24}$, $\frac{17}{27}$, $\frac{May 24}{June 3}$. *Venice MSS. Desp. Spagna.*

Pope, he expressed himself in more guarded terms. Yet even then, his letter contrasts most unfavourably with that which had been written a few months previously by his father. James had urged the Pope not to allow difference of religion to stand in the way of a common understanding for the re-establishment of the peace of Christendom. Charles talked of those differences as the seed sown by the inveterate malice of Satan, and promised to employ all his energies in effecting a reconciliation in the Church. So far, he said, was he from feeling any abhorrence for the Roman Catholic religion, that he would take every opportunity, with the help of time, to remove all sinister suspicions, "so that as we all publicly confess one undivided Trinity, and one Christ crucified, we may unite with one mind in one only faith, and in one Church."† If Charles only meant that he looked forward to the establishment of a re-united Church, such as that which De Dominis had lately advocated to unwelcome ears, why did he not say so, except because though he objected to a downright falsehood, he had no objection to an equivocation? Of all men who have expressed an opinion on Charles's actions, surely no one was so likely to form a favourable judgment of them as Clarendon, and yet it was from that statesman, at a time when he was in exile for his devotion to his sovereign, that the bitterest condemnation of this letter proceeded. "The letter to the Pope," he wrote to Edward Nicholas, "is, by your favour, more than compliment, and may be a warning that nothing is to be done and said in that nice argument but what will bear the light."

At last, on the 23rd of May, the Junta of Theologians pronounced its sentence. They held that if Philip was to take the oath with a good conscience, the Infanta must remain in Spain for at least a year after the marriage

Ch. XI. 1623. May. The Prince's answer.

Decision of the Theologians to keep the Infanta for a year.

Corner's authority is quite good enough, and is not invalidated by the fact that there is no mention of the engagement to listen to discussion in the answer as given in *Goodman* ii. 260. Charles may have said it in conversation after the formal reply was given.

† The Prince to Gregory XV. *Hardwicke S. P.* i. 452. The letter, contrary to the general belief in England at the time, was written either by the Prince himself, or by his direction, without any reference to his father. See the letter of June 6. *Hardwicke S. P.* i. 419.

ceremony had been performed; within which time the suspension of the penal laws, and the concessions to the Catholics of the free exercise of their religion in private houses, must be publicly proclaimed in England. The King, the Prince, and the Privy Council, must swear that the favours thus accorded would never be withdrawn; and, finally, they must manage either to obtain the assent of Parliament to what they had done within the year, or at least they must have proceeded so far that there could no longer be any doubt that it would not be refused.

Olivares had his way, without violence or menace. In the face of the opposition of the Council he had summoned to his aid the Junta of Theologians.

In the hands of the Spanish minister, these learned canonists and divines now occupied the place which had been previously assigned to the Pope. From them could come the demands to which it might well be thought even Charles would find it impossible to agree. It would then be the turn of Olivares to express his regret for the decision taken, at the same time that he announced the necessity of conforming to whatever it might be. In the presence of such a bold and decided politician, with a definite scheme of action before him, and who shrank from no deception, however gross, in the attainment of the objects he had in view, a poor lovesick youth like Charles, with his petty reticences and dissimulations, had no chance whatever. Whether even he might not at last be roused to resistance, was a question which could not long be left undecided.

The very evening on which the Theologians had delivered their sentence, Olivares presented himself before the Prince with a smiling face, to inform him of their decision.* Furious at the news, Buckingham lost his temper, and poured forth a torrent of abuse. There was nothing but trickery and deceit, he said, in the whole business. "It would have been better," replied Olivares, coldly, "if you had never meddled with it, but had left it in Bristol's hands." The next day Cottington was sent once more to ask leave for the Prince to return to England. The request was politely received, but Charles

* Francisco de Jesus, 76.

was entreated not to forget his promise to remain at least till he had time to communicate with his father. As usual, Charles gave way, and Cottington was ordered to make every preparation to start for England as soon as the Spanish ministers could find time to furnish him with copies of the documents in which the late proceedings were recounted.

Ch. XI. 1623. May.

It was apparently about this time, that in defending the right of the King of Spain to make fresh demands, Olivares resorted to the perilous course of referring to the words which had been spoken by Philip III. upon his deathbed, and proceeded to argue that as the match was not really intended by the late King, his son was perfectly at liberty to propose new conditions.* As soon as this outrageous inference was reported to Bristol, he at once appealed to Sir Walter Aston, who repeated the strong language in which the present King had, within eight days after his father's death, declared his intention of going on seriously with the marriage treaty. Olivares then changed his tone, and began talking of the Infanta's aversion to marry any one who was not a Catholic. Upon this, Bristol produced the paper containing the opinion delivered by Olivares on the 28th of November, in which he had recommended that the Prince of Wales should be married to an Archduchess, and showed that the opinion thus given was rejected by the Council of State, and that the articles which Olivares now wished to set aside, had been officially agreed to four days afterwards. As to the Infanta's alleged dislike of the marriage, he attributed it entirely to the influence of her confessor, who was now dead.†

Olivares urges the Prince to concessions.

---

* The conversation is given by Hacket, 146, as taking place at a later date. But this writer is not to be trusted for details, and Valaresso writing on the $\frac{20\text{th}}{30\text{th}}$ of June, says that in a letter written to him by some one about the Prince on $\frac{\text{May 8}}{\text{June 7}}$, he was told "che Spagnoli portando l'affare come non più lor ma fatto del Pontefice, aggionti ai proprii moti anco gl' eccitamenti degli Inglesi Catolici, lasciassero il vecchio trattato con la stabilita convenenza, ed in suo luogo dimandassero aperta libertà de conscienza : che ad indolenza del Principe di questa innovatione fosse risposto che le trattationi prima della sa andata si tenevano di sola mostra, et esser falso opinione che nella sua ultima volontà il Rè ordinasse questo matrimonio : mentre anzi lasciò l'Infanta al figliuolo del Imperator." Valaresso to the Doge. *Venice MSS.* Desp. Ingh.

† Bristol to the King, Aug. 18. *S. P. Spain.*

Bristol's inference from all this was evidently that Charles should withstand the temptations of Olivares, and summon the Spanish ministry to abide by the articles as they originally stood. If indeed, he had been allowed to take the matter into his own hands, it is almost certain that nothing more would have been heard of the marriage treaty. But Charles was not so to be dealt with. Deaf to all questions of policy, he could neither think nor speak of anything but the Infanta. It was but a day or two since that he had startled the rigid propriety of the Spanish Court, by leaping into a garden in which the lady of his affections was walking. The poor girl shrieked and fled, and it was with some difficulty that the Prince was persuaded by the supplications of her guardian, to leave the place.*

Under these circumstances, Charles had recourse to Bristol, in the vain hope that he might be able to obtain what had been refused to Buckingham. The Ambassador, ever ready to carry out his orders, went to the Nuncio, and painted in glowing colours the great things that would be done for the Catholics as soon as the Infanta was safely in London. If they had any doubt, he said, on this point, they might at once send the Bishop who was to preside over the clergy of her household, whose admission to the country would be a sure proof of the King's sincerity. Finding no signs of yielding in De Massimi, Bristol next asked to plead his master's cause before the Junta of Theologians. It was all in vain. The Infanta, he was told, would certainly not be allowed to leave Spain for a year; though a hint was dropped that the Prince might be married at once, if he would be content to remain with his wife in Spain.† Finding that nothing was to be done, Charles desisted from his efforts for the time, and on the 31st of May, Cottington at last started for England. The Marquis of Inojosa left on his special mission a day or two later.

---

* The story is told by Howel in a letter said to have been written on the 10th of July. It is however referred to by Corner in his despatch of June $\frac{3}{13}$. *Venice MSS.* Desp. Spagna.

† *Ibid.* Aston to Calvert, June $\frac{10}{20}$.

Cottington had been hastened away before the Spaniards had furnished the promised documents. When they at last came they were forwarded by a special messenger, accompanied by a letter which bears in every line the impress alike of the vain hopes with which Charles was accustomed to solace himself, and of the petty trickery by which he fancied that he could deceive such a bold dissembler as Olivares. "We make no doubt," wrote the young man, "but to have the opinions of these busy divines reversed, so your Majesty will be pleased to begin to put in execution the favour towards your Roman Catholic subjects that ye will be bound to do by your oath, as soon as the Infanta comes over; which we hope you will do for the hastening of us home with this protestation, to reverse all, if there be any delay of the marriage. We send you here the articles as they are to go, the oaths private and public, that you and your Baby are to take, with the Council's, wherein, if you scare at the least clause of your private oath, where you promise that the Parliament shall revoke all the penal laws against the Papists within three years, we sought good to tell your Majesty our opinions, which is, that if you think you may do it in that time,—which we think you may,—if you do your best, although it take not effect, you have not broken your word, for this promise is only as a security that you will do your best."*

James was beginning at last to open his eyes to the difficulties with which his darling scheme was surrounded. When the news of his son's arrival at Madrid first reached him he ordered bells to be rung, and bonfires to be lighted. For some time, no one who wished to be in favour at Court, spoke otherwise than hopefully of the marriage. None but the envious, wrote Conway, or vile almanack-makers, who argue from the conjunction of the planets, talked of delay any longer.† James's chief occupation during the month of April, consisted in hastening on the equipment of the fleet which was to sail in May, under the command of the Earl of Rutland, who, as Bucking-

---

* The Prince and Buckingham to the King, June 6. *Hardwicke S. P.* i. 419.
† Conway to Wentworth, April 4. *S. P. Dom.* cxlii. 34.

ham's father-in-law, was preferred before all other competitors. To the complaints which were everywhere to be heard against his favourite, he resolutely turned a deaf ear. He amused himself with writing gossiping letters to Lady Buckingham, and in playing with her child.* He raised Christopher Villiers to the Earldom of Anglesea. To Buckingham himself he gave the proudest title which was in the gift of an English sovereign. Since Norfolk's execution, there had been no dukes in England. The high dignity was now revived in the person of the Duke of Buckingham. In order to save the feelings of Lennox, whose connection with the royal family made him unwilling to yield precedence to a subject, the Scotch nobleman was first created Duke of Richmond.

Preparations for the Infanta's reception were now hurried on with speed. Denmark House and Saint James' were ordered to be made ready for her reception by the skilful hand of Inigo Jones. The Prince's ship, men said, was as richly furnished as if it was intended to receive a goddess.†

In the midst of the bustle of preparation, James first heard of the conditions with which the dispensation was clogged; but his son had treated them lightly, and he was not inclined to attach much more importance to them himself.‡ The intimation had been followed in a few days by a strange letter from Charles. "Sir," he had written almost immediately after the terms of the dispensation were known to him, "I do find that if I have not somewhat under your Majesty's hand to show whereby that ye engage yourself to do whatsoever I shall promise in your name, that it will retard the business a great while; wherefore I humbly beseech your Majesty

---

* "This day . . . his Majesty came to Hyde Park, at the entry whereof he found a fair lady, indeed the fairest Lady Mary in England, and he made a great deal of love to her, and gave her his watch, and kept her as long pleased with him as he could, not without expression to all the company that it was a miracle that such an ugly, deformed father, should have so sweet a child." Conway to Buckingham, May 3. Goodman's *Court of King James*, ii. 290.

† Chamberlain to Carleton, May 3. *S. P. Dom.* cxliv. 11.

‡ The Prince and Buckingham to the King, April 22. *Hardwicke S. P.* ii. 414. The King to the Prince and Buckingham, May 9. Halliwell's *Letters of the Kings*, ii. 203.

to send me a warrant to this effect:—'We do hereby promise by the word of a King, that whatsoever you or son shall promise in our name, we shall punctually perform.' Sir, I confess this is an ample trust that I desire, and if it were not mere necessity I should not be so bold."* To this exorbitant request the fond father had at once acceded. "It were a strange trust," he answered, "that I would refuse to put upon my only son and upon my best servant. I know such two as ye are will never promise in my name but what may stand with my conscience, honour, and safety, and all these I do fully trust to any one of you two."†

On the 11th of May, the powers thus demanded were sent to Madrid. The secret was closely kept; but sharp-sighted observers detected that the King was growing anxious. He seemed like a man who was doing things against his will. He was continually showing signs of ill humour. In speaking of the chapel which he was to build for the Infanta, he could not avoid crying out,— "We are building a temple to the devil."‡

In spite, however, of the King's occasional despondency, the preparations went gaily on. He visited the building at St. James' of which he had spoken so harshly, and gave money to the workmen to encourage them to haste. Richmond, Middlesex, Pembroke, and Hamilton, were sent down to Southampton to see that everything was in readiness to greet the Infanta on her landing.§ On the 26th of May, instructions were issued to Rutland, ordering him to proceed at once to Corunna, and but for the contrary winds which detained him for a whole fortnight in the Downs, he would soon have dropped down the Channel on his way to the coast of Spain.§

All this time the King's anxiety must have been daily increasing. For four whole weeks not a single letter

Ch. XI.
1623.
May.

Preparations for the Infanta's arrival.

June 14. Arrival of Cottington.

---

* The Prince to the King, April 29. *Hardwicke S. P.* ii. 417.
† The King to the Prince and Buckingham, May 11. *Hardwicke S. P.* 46. The King to the Prince, May 11. Goodman's *Court of King James*, ii. 298.
‡ Valaresso to the Doge, May $\frac{16}{26}$. *Venice MSS.* Desp. Ingh.
§ Rutland's Instructions, May 26. Chamberlain to Carleton, May 28. D. Carleton to Carleton, June 3. *S. P. Dom.* cxlv. 33, 65; cxlvi. 6. Salvetti's *News-Letter*, June $\frac{13}{23}$.

Ch. XI.
1623.

June 14.
James begs his son to return.

reached him from Madrid. It was not till the evening of the 14th of June that Cottington appeared at Greenwich and told him the whole wretched story.*

James's worst fears were realised. The refusal to send the Infanta at once; and, above all, the suggestion that Charles might remain a year longer at Madrid, pierced him to the heart. That very night he poured out his grief. "My sweet boys," he wrote: "Your letter by Cottington hath strucken me dead. I fear it shall very much shorten my days; and I am the more perplexed, that I know not how to satisfy the people's expectation here; neither know I what to say to our Council for the fleet that stayed upon a wind this fortnight. Rutland, and all aboard, must now be stayed, and I know not what reason I shall pretend for the doing of it. But as for my advice and directions that ye crave, in case they will not alter their decree, it is, in a word, to come speedily away if ye can get leave, and give over all treaty. And this I speak without respect of any security they can offer you, except ye never look to see your old dad again, whom I fear ye shall never see, if you see him not before winter. Alas! I now repent me sore that ever I suffered you to go away. I care for match, nor nothing, so I may once have you in my arms again. God grant it: God grant it: God grant it: Amen, Amen, Amen. I protest ye shall be as heartily welcome as if ye had done all things ye went for, so that I may once have you in my arms again, and God bless you both, my only sweet son, and my only best sweet servant: and let me hear from you quickly with all speed, as ye love my life. And so God send you a happy and joyful meeting in the arms of your dear dad." †

But engages to confirm the articles.

The next day James had time to look into the affair with greater deliberation. For two hours he was closeted with Cottington and Conway. But it was the tenderness of a father, not the regret of a statesman, which was uppermost in his mind. Of the hard terms which the Spaniards were exacting, of the impolicy of the conces-

* Valaresso to the Doge, June $\frac{6}{10}$, June $\frac{20}{30}$. *Venice MSS.* Desp. Ingh.
† The King to the Prince and Buckingham, June 14. *Hardwicke S. P.* ii. 421.

sions which were wrung from him, he had not a word to say. If the Spanish ministers, he now wrote, could not "be moved to reverse the conclusion of their devils," he would confirm the articles as they came from them. Charles might then be married at once, and come away immediately upon receiving security that the Infanta would follow in due time with her portion. He need not be afraid to marry her, he went on to say, lest they should afterwards "free her by a dispensation from the Pope, for I will warrant you our Church shall free you better here; and I am resolved, if God shall spare me days, to become a Master Jack Cade myself, and the great governor of the mutineers in England. For, believe me, I can turn myself in any shape but that of a knave, in case of necessity." *

"His Majesty," wrote Conway at the same time to his patron, "desires your speedy return before all other respects, and your honour's counsel. He presseth you to admit of no delays. If his Majesty ratify the articles propounded, and the King and Council of Spain will not recede from the forced and devised delay of the Junta, you must apparel necessity like virtue, and make choice of continuing the treaty, by according to their time for the solemnising of the marriage in all the requisite parts by proxy, as is used in marriage of most kings and princes; or by his Highness espousing of her personally, and presently to come thence to give life and being to the performance and execution of the things contracted, which will not, cannot, in his Highness's absence be executed. There is nothing can be of so evil consequence as admittance of delay. I protest my heart can not think that the worst of men, or better sort of devils, could practise so base and monstrous falsehood and unthankfulness as to stop his Highness' return." †

Never were the evils of personal government presented in a clearer form. Neither James nor Conway appear to have bestowed one thought upon the English nation.

---

* The King to the Prince and Buckingham, June 15. *S. P. Spain.* Compare Instructions to Cottington, May 28. *Clarendon S. P.* App. xviii.
† Conway to Buckingham, June 15. Goodman's *Court of King James,* ii. 291.

Ch. XI.
1623.
June.

Never, since the days of Pandulph, had there been so gross a violation of its independence than these articles contained. The rights, and it might be the religion, of the country were to be sacrificed for the sake of securing the safe return of a headstrong young man who was really in no danger whatever. No wonder that James tried to wrap his proceedings in profound secresy, and that for some days even Calvert was kept in ignorance of what had taken place.* The fleet, indeed, which had just left the Downs, was intercepted and ordered to return. But it was merely announced that a temporary delay had occurred in the arrangements.† James went about with a smiling face, hunting as usual every day ; yet, when men's eyes were not upon him, the thought that he might never again see his beloved son seemed to break him down. "The King," said a keen-sighted observer, "is now grown quite stupid."‡ "Do you think," said James one day to a confidential attendant, bursting into tears as he spoke, "that I shall ever see the Prince again ?" At another time, Holderness, venturing upon his long familiar service, blamed the King to his face for his weakness in suffering himself to be tricked by the Spaniards. A month earlier, James would have rated him soundly for his insolence : now, he only turned away in disgust, and asked to be allowed to go to sleep in quiet.§

The Prince attempts to obtain better terms.

Whilst James was thus wasting his time in unprofitable regrets, his son was occupied, with Bristol's assistance, in unavailing efforts to induce the Spanish government to alter its decision. A long paper was drawn up under his directions, in which he proved to his own satisfaction that his word was the best possible guarantee for the fulfilment of any promises which he might think fit to make.|| But the Theologians could not be induced to

* Salvetti's *News-Letter*, Jan. $\frac{20}{30}$.
† Rutland to Conway. Conway to the Navy Commissioners, June 15. *S. P. Dom.* cxlvi. 93, 94.
‡ "Già fatto stupido." Valaresso to the Doge, June $\frac{20}{30}$. *Venice MSS.* Desp. Ingh.
§ Valaresso to the Doge, $\frac{\text{June } 27}{\text{July } 7}$. *Venice MSS.* Desp. Ingh.
|| The Prince's Reply, June. *Clarendon S. P.* i. App. xxiii.

agree with him; and the Prince was forced to wait in patience for his father's reply.

From all these efforts Buckingham stood aloof.* He had quarrelled with Olivares, and he had quarrelled with Bristol, whom he had accused of placing too great trust in Spanish promises. Like so many others, he was to find that, though there was no difficulty whatever in instilling the most pernicious advice into the mind of Charles, it was very difficult to lead him right. Charles would not hear of breaking off the treaty. His state of mind, indeed, was most miserable. He no longer took pleasure in amusements of any description; he spent his time, whenever he had a chance, in gazing upon the Infanta;—Olivares sarcastically said, as a cat watches a mouse;—he wrote verses in her praise, which, if she ever cared to read them, she would need an interpreter to understand; and was frequently seen stretching forward out of the window of his own apartment, in the hope of catching sight of her as she was sitting in her own room.

Ch. XI.
1623.
June.

Olivares was playing with Charles as a fisherman plays with a salmon. He had, indeed, a difficult part to act. Again and again voices were raised in the Council of State against the folly of exasperating the Prince in deference to a pack of theologians who knew nothing about State affairs. Gondomar declared himself on the side of a policy of confidence.‡ But Olivares knew his ground. Sure of the support of the King, he never ceased to screen himself behind the authority of the Junta. With a grave face, he informed Charles that he was doing his best to convert the Theologians. §

Intentions of Olivares.

There can be no doubt that if the general voice of the English Catholics had been listened to, Gondomar's opinion

* Corner to the Doge, $\frac{\text{June 21}}{\text{July 1}}$. *Venice MSS.* Desp. Spagna.

† "Non sta mirando se non la Infanta, et con ogni licentia nella conspicua piazza si facea fuori della sua finestra per colpire con l'occhio in quella dove ella sedea, sfogando poi anco al solito delle inamoratile fiamme in versi." *Ibid.*

‡ Consulta of the Council of State, $\frac{\text{June 25}}{\text{July 5}}$. *Simancas MSS.* Est. 2516. Corner to the Doge, July $\frac{5}{15}$. *Venice MSS.* Desp. Spagna.

§ The Prince and Buckingham to the King, June 26. *Hardwicke S. P.* i. 122.

would have prevailed. Sir Toby Matthew, the sharp-witted and intelligent son of the Archbishop of York, who had lost his father's favour by his desertion to the Church of Rome, was now in Madrid, having been despatched by Williams with the hope of inducing the Spanish ministers to listen to reason.* The advice which he gave was such as to deserve attention. If the match were broken off, he said, the King would be thrown into the hands of the Parliament, and from the Parliament what Catholic could expect anything but the extremity of rigour. If the Catholics suffered persecution, their blood would be required at the hands of those who advised the rejection of the reasonable terms to which the Prince was ready to consent.†

Such arguments fell flat upon Olivares. The two men were not aiming at the same object. Whilst Matthew was pleading for relief from persecution for the English Catholics, Olivares had his eye fixed upon the Palatinate, and as far as England was concerned, he would be content with nothing short of the absolute predominance of his Church.

It may be considered as certain that Olivares at this time did not expect that the marriage would ever take place. Four weeks before, he had requested Khevenhüller to renew the proposal for a marriage between the Prince of Wales and the Emperor's daughter.‡ Seeing that he was not likely to have his own in this way, he was probably now content with aiming at breaking off the marriage with as little offence as possible.

Charles was, however, too deeply in love to be easily shaken off. On the 26th of June, Sir William Croft arrived with James's promise to agree to the articles as they stood, and with directions for his son's immediate return. The next morning the Prince sent for Olivares, thinking, no doubt, that all resistance to the Infanta's journey would now be at an end. "This morning," wrote the Prince and his companion, "we sent for the Conde of Olivares, and, with a sad countenance, told

---

* Hacket, 135.
† Matthew to Philip IV. *Cabala*, 303.
‡ *Khevenhüller*, x. 255.

him of your peremptory command, entreating him in the kindest manner we could to give us his advice how we might comply with this and not destroy the business. His answer was, that there were two good ways to do the business, and one ill one; the two good ones were either your Baby's conversion, or to do it with trust, putting all things freely, with the Infanta, into our hands; the ill one was, to bargain and stick upon conditions as long as they could. As for the first, we absolutely rejected it, and for the second, he confessed if he were king, he would do it; and, as he is, it lay in his power to do it; but he cast many doubts lest he should hereafter suffer for it, if it should not succeed; the last he confessed impossible, since your command was so peremptory. To conclude, he left us with a promise to consider of it, and when I, your dog, conveyed him to the door, he bade me cheer up my heart, and your Baby's both. Our opinion is, that the longest time we can stay here will be a month, and not that neither without bringing the Infanta with us. If we find not ourselves assured of that, look for us sooner."*

After some further fencing,† Olivares returned on the 6th of July with the final resolution of the Theologians and the King. It was impossible, he told the Prince, that his wish could be gratified. The utmost that could be done would be to shorten the delay by four months. The marriage might take place in September, and the Infanta would then sail for England in March. His master could not act otherwise, as he was bound by the oath imposed upon him by the Pope. Charles received the message very quietly, and asked if this was a final determination. Being told that it was, he requested to have it in writing. He had, he said, received orders from his father not to consent to leave the Infanta behind him, and he must consider the treaty at an end. To Aston, who was sent to demand a reply, Olivares spoke in the most friendly manner. The King, he said, could never

Ch. XI.
1623.
June 27.

July 6. Charles informed of Philip's final determination.

Declares his intention of leaving.

---

* The Prince and Buckingham to the King, June 27. *Hardwicke S. P.* i. 423.

† The Prince and Buckingham to the King, June 29. *Hardwicke S. P.* i. 425.

1623.
July 6.

abate anything of his demands; but if the Prince liked to leave, no obstacle whatever would be thrown in his way. His Majesty would accompany him many days' journey in order to show the respect in which he held him. Still he would be much grieved if he refused to consent to so brief a delay, as it would seem to the world as if he had no real intention of carrying out his engagements.*

July 7.
Changes his mind;

and accepts the terms offered.

The next morning Charles sent to demand audience of the King, in order that he might take leave. He was accordingly admitted the same evening to the Royal presence, where he found Philip fully prepared to bid him adieu; but, to the King's inconceivable astonishment, it soon appeared that the Prince had come on a very different errand. "I have resolved," said Charles, "to accept with my whole heart what has been proposed to me, both as to the articles touching religion, and as to the security required." He had found great difficulties, he proceeded to say, and he had done his best to lessen them; but it was better to consent to all that was required, rather than to abandon the hope of so close an alliance with the Spanish Crown. Some of the bystanders who had heard him speak so differently a few days before, naturally asked one another how they were to know what they were really to believe.† The truth was that Charles had been merely haggling over the bargain, and he fancied that, by yielding now, he might perhaps win back some of the price hereafter.‡

The marriage agreed upon.

For the time, Charles was allowed to dream that the prize, for which he had sacrificed so much, was all his own. Philip embraced him as a brother. For four successive nights the streets of Madrid were ablaze with illuminations. The President of the Treasury, venturing to speak against the match, was summarily dismissed

---

* Corner to the Doge, July $\frac{9}{19}$. *Venice MSS.* Desp. Spagna.

† Francisco de Jesus, 81.

‡ Writing two days earlier, the Venetian Ambassador shows that there was a general impression amongst those best able to judge, that the Prince would give way. "Quei di più fondato discorso," he says, "stimano impossibilità che una delle parti non declini dal presuposto, ma dal Principe si pensa sarà la declinatione, et che si accomoderà al volere di quà." Corner to the Doge, July $\frac{5}{15}$. *Venice MSS.* Desp. Spagna.

from his post. The Infanta was openly spoken of as the Princess of England, and was allowed to appear in public at the Court Theatre.* Lord Andover was at once despatched to bear the happy news to England.† So decided were the advances made to him that Charles imagined he would have little difficulty in obtaining the removal of the bar placed upon the Infanta's journey. He fancied that if only his father performed his part of the stipulations punctually, there would be little more heard of the demand for a Parliamentary confirmation, and that he would be permitted to take his bride home with him at Michaelmas.‡ He did not know that Olivares, Spaniard though he was, had a clearer idea than himself of the place and functions of Parliament in the English Constitution.

<small>CH. XI.
1623.
July.</small>

Whilst Andover was on his way to England with the news, James was still hesitating before he could make up his mind to take the required oath to those articles to which he had already given his consent. To many of them, against which objections might reasonably be raised, he seems to have felt no repugnance; but he considered it an insult to himself that he should be bound to obtain an oath from the Privy Council in confirmation of his own, and, what was of far greater importance, he objected strongly to the engagement that the penal laws should never be reimposed under any circumstances, and to the promise to do his best to obtain from Parliament a confirmation of the articles.

<small>Discussion at Wanstead on the articles.</small>

<small>James's hesitation.</small>

"In the first," wrote Conway, "his Majesty foresaw an infinite liberty and a perpetual immunity granted to the Roman Catholics; which if it should bring them to a dangerous increase, or encourage them to the acting of insolencies, his conscience opposeth his wisdom of government, and his sovereignty runs a danger."

"Touching the Parliament, his Majesty saw it impossible for him to effect, neither did his affection and

---

* Aston to Conway, July 8. Bristol to Carleton, July 9. *S. P. Spain.* Bristol to Cottington, July 15. Prynne's *Hidden Works of Darkness,* 49.

† Williams to Buckingham, July 21. Hacket, 145.

‡ The Prince and Buckingham to the King, July 15. *Hardwicke S. P.* i. 426.

Сн. XI.
1623.
July.

July 13.
The principal councillors consulted.

Advice of Williams.

reason incline to exercise his power that way if it were in his hand."*

It was to this he had come at last. Nine months before he had soothed himself with the dream that the Infanta and her ducats were to be had for a mere connivance at the breach of the penal laws, which he would be at liberty to withdraw if matters took a serious turn. Yet how could he now go back? In an evil moment he had pledged his honour that he would confirm whatever promises his son might make; and even if he could be brought to understand that it was better that he should break his word than that he should inflict so serious a wound upon the nation entrusted to his care, he could not forget that his son's liberty might depend upon his decision. For, in common with almost everyone with whom he conversed on the subject, he fully believed that if the articles were now rejected the Prince would never be allowed to leave Madrid.

It was, therefore, with a heavy heart that he summoned his principal councillors to meet him at Wanstead on the 13th of July, and after laying his perplexities before them, left them to consider the advice which they might decide upon giving him. He had no sooner quitted the room, than it became evident that they, too, shared in his perplexity. But it had been long since the Councillors had been asked by their hitherto self-sufficient monarch to take a decisive step in a matter of such importance, and scarcely one of them could think of anything better than to suggest some scheme or other for getting the Prince out of Spain before the oath was taken.

Never was the extraordinary ability with which Williams managed to smooth away a difficulty which he did not attempt to overcome more conspicuously exhibited than on this occasion. It can hardly be doubted that he saw that James was only looking out for an excuse to yield, and that, in the opinion which he delivered, he was influenced by this supposition. After what they had heard from the King, he said, he did not see how they could give any advice at all; for they must

* Conway to Buckingham, July 17. *Ellis*, Series 1, vol. iii. 154.

first know whether his Majesty had any conscientious scruple against the oath. Until they had received information on that point, they could not tell what to recommend. The councillors, glad to relieve themselves from the responsibility of advising the King either to act against his conscience or to leave his son a prisoner for life, leapt at Williams's suggestion, and replied, as soon as James returned, by asking whether he felt any conscientious scruples. "My conscience," said the King, turning to the Lord Keeper as he spoke, "stands as I said before; but I am willing to hear anything that may move me to alter the same." Upon this hint Williams spoke. He was aware, he said, how little it became him, whose studies had been so frequently interrupted, to discuss a point of divinity with one of his Majesty's deep learning. Yet he could not but remember that the Prince had already acceded to the articles, and he was sure that the Prince was as good a Protestant as any one in the world; and he must say that he thought he was in the right; for he had not been asked to be slack in the advancing of the true religion, or even to give his consent to the predominance of Popery. All that was demanded was that he would withdraw from any attempt to suppress or to extirpate the Roman Catholic faith. No one thought of accusing the King of France of sinning against his conscience because he did not suppress the Protestants in his dominions; nor were the States General thought to be false Protestants because they did not suppress the Roman Catholics. Even his Majesty himself had often relaxed the penal laws, and it was inconceivable that in so doing he had offended against his conscience. "I conclude, therefore," he ended by saying, "that his Highness having admitted nothing in these oaths or articles, either to the prejudice of the true, or the equalising or authorising of the other religion; but contained himself wholly within the limits of penal statutes and connivances, wherein the State hath ever challenged and usurped a directing power, hath subscribed no one paper of all these against his own; nor—I profess it openly—against the dictamen of my conscience."

Ch. XI.
1623.
July 13.
The King satisfied.

As a speech in favour of the principles of toleration the Lord Keeper's argument was an admirable one; but anything more utterly alien to the point at issue it is impossible to conceive. For, as Williams must have known perfectly well, the question was not whether it was wise to relax or repeal the penal laws, but whether it was wise to enter into an engagement with a foreign power that they should never again, under any circumstances, be put in force.

Yet, beside the mark as Williams's reasoning was, it was enough for James. It gave him what he wanted—an excuse for a questionable act, which he regarded as the insuperable condition of his son's return. With a cheerful countenance he declared himself fully satisfied, and the councillors present, as in duty bound, coincided with the opinions of their master.*

July 16.
Assent of the Council.

Three days later the whole Council were summoned to Wanstead. Almost with tears in his eyes, James told them that he knew he had been hardly dealt with by Spain; but what could he do, if he did not mean to desert the Prince? He wished now to have their opinion whether they thought good to take the oath which would be required of them. He would tell them, however, that he meant to give explanations to the Spanish Ambassadors to the effect that he could not bind himself to obtain the consent of Parliament, and that the safety of the realm must always be paramount to any obligation entered into by treaty in favour of the Catholics.† As soon as he had finished, Abbot, who, for obvious reasons,

---

* Williams to the Prince, July (?). Hacket, 141. Conway to Buckingham, July 17. *Ellis*, Series 1, vol. iii. 154.

† "Invitò bene ogn'uno a consigliarlo liberamente in si importante occasione; ma artificiosamente li constrinse, per non mostrarsi poco desiderosi del ritorno d'esso Principe et male amatori del loro futuro Rè, di approbar propositione et di essibirse pronti a suoi comandi in ogni punto. Disse delli due articoli più importanti, cioè di convocare il Parlamento, et del non offender Cattolici, che li ammetterebbe con le restrittioni; a quello di procurarlo a suo potere, et a questo di farlo salva la salute del Regno. I Consiglieri eccettuatine due che fecero in contrario alcune poche considerationi prometterono cieca ubbidienza ad ogni volere di Sua Maestà. Certo del Rè si può ben dire che ne' proprii danni tenghi un eccelente artificio, et de' Consiglieri ch' habbino dato l'ultimo saggio della loro debolezza, havendo perduto quest' opportunità di parlar liberamente a servicio del Regno et di far conoscer al Rè che il vero mezzo, non di ricuperar il Principe, ma di far crescer le dimande a Spagnuoli, sia questa facilità alle

had not been asked to attend the former deliberation, led
the way by asking inconvenient questions. He was at
once interrupted by the King, who told him that the
matter was already settled, and that all that was wanted
was to know if he was willing to join in taking the oath.
No further opposition was offered, and the whole Council
agreed to swear to the articles on condition of receiving
orders to do so under the great seal.

CH. XI.
1623.
July 16.

The King's authority, and the fear of leaving the Prince
a hostage in Philip's hands, had prevailed over every other
consideration. Yet it was with no good will that the
great majority of the Privy Councillors had given their
consent. Questions were asked in a whisper amongst
them which showed that they were ill at ease. What,
it was said, had become of the temporal articles in which
the amount of the dowry was to be settled? What obligation
had the King of Spain entered into? When was
the marriage to be performed? "All which," adds the
reporter, "ended with wishes that the Prince were well
returned, with much doubt what use will be made of his
being there."*

Dissatisfaction of the Councillors.

Sunday, the 20th of July, was fixed for the important
ceremony. In the Royal Chapel at Whitehall, after
the morning sermon was ended, the public articles of the
treaty were read by Calvert in the presence of the Spanish
Ambassadors, Inojosa and Coloma, and of the great majority
of the Privy Council. When Calvert had finished,
James swore to observe them, thereby engaging that,
not only should his son's wife be surrounded by a
household nominated by her father, the King of Spain,
but that for the spiritual guidance of this little knot of
foreigners there should be kept up the exorbitant number
of twenty-four priests and a bishop, not one of whom
were to be amenable to the laws of England, or to any
jurisdiction excepting that of their ecclesiastical superiors;
and that wherever the Infanta might fix her
dwelling, there should be erected a public church to

July 20.
The articles sworn to.

oro sodisfattioni." Valaresso to the Doge, July $\frac{18}{28}$. *Venice MSS.* Desp. Ingh.

* Conway to Buckingham, July 17 (a different letter from the one quoted in the last note). *Harl. MSS.* 1580, fol. 309.

CH. XI.
1623.
July 20.

The banquet.

The oath of the Council.

The King's oath to the private articles.

which all Englishmen who pleased might have access. To these and to other relatively unimportant engagements, James added a promise that he would do everything in his power to obtain the confirmation of these stipulations by Parliament.*

The solemnity was followed by a banquet, given by the King to the ambassadors; but it was observed that of the English who were present, only two appeared in that gay attire which was usually worn on occasions of rejoicing, and that those two were the Roman Catholic Gage, who had lately returned from Rome, and Carlisle, who would probably have decked himself with gold and jewels if he had been invited to a funeral.†

As soon as the banquet was at an end, the Privy Councillors went into their usual place of meeting, where they one after another took the required oath not only to observe the public articles, but also to abstain, either personally or by their officers, from exacting any penalty imposed upon the Catholics by the penal laws.

Of the whole number, six were absent. Naunton was now only nominally a member of the Council, and had not been asked to attend. Arundel was at Ghent, hanging over the deathbed of his eldest son; Pembroke and Brooke were detained by serious illness, whilst the absence of Southampton and Zouch can hardly be explained on any other ground than that of disinclination to take the oath.‡

James kept the ambassadors with him till the evening, when he informed them that he was now ready to proceed to swear to the private articles. They were four in number. He was to promise that no law which pressed upon the Catholics, without affecting their fellow-subjects, should ever be put in force against them; that whilst no fresh laws should be passed against them in future, a perpetual toleration to extend to Scotland and Ireland as

---

* "Insuper verbo regio fidem daturi sumus, nos omnem operam navaturos ut omnia suprà capitulata per Parlamentum stabiliantur." *Clarendon State Papers,* i. App. 25.
† Chamberlain to Carleton, July 26. *S. P. Dom.* cxlix. 48.
‡ The oath seems finally to have been taken by all except perhaps Zouch, who was about to take it when the breach with Spain took place. Whether he did it or not does not appear.

well as to England should leave them free to exercise
their religion in private houses; that neither he nor the
Prince would ever allow the Infanta to witness anything
repugnant to her faith, or attempt to induce her to
renounce it; and, finally, that they would interpose their
authority, and do their utmost, to obtain a parliamentary
confirmation of these private articles; that they would
ask Parliament to repeal the penal laws, and that, at
all events, they would never give the royal assent to
any fresh ones directed against the Catholics.*

Ch. XI. 1623. July 20.

James's word was not always to be trusted; for it was
but seldom that, when the time came for the performance
of his promises, some new gust of feeling had not swept
over his mind; but to deliberate hypocrisy, such as that
which seemed to be the natural element of his son's life,
he never stooped. It was abhorrent to his nature to
enter into an engagement which he had no intention of
performing. He, therefore, took good care to explain to
the Spanish Ambassadors, in the hearing of Cottington
and the two secretaries, in what sense he understood the
oath which he was about to take. When he promised to
obtain the consent of Parliament, he said he merely meant
that he would do his best. As to the relaxation of the
penalties imposed on the Catholics, he did not mean to
bind himself never, in any case, to reimpose them. If a
great state necessity occurred, he should hold himself free
from any engagement now made. With this explanation
he took the oath, and with this the ambassadors were
forced to be content.†

Explanation given by the King.

James had, indeed, paid a heavy price for his son's
freedom. Since the days of King John, no act so
imprudent had been committed by any English sovereign.
He had taught his Catholic subjects that it was better
for them to depend upon the favour of a foreign state
than upon their own King. He had made it a matter
of bargain with a foreign Government that he would
rule at variance with the wishes of his people lawfully
expressed in Parliament. He had expressly stipulated
that he would never put in force the existing laws,

Consequences of the treaty.

* *Clarendon State Papers*, i. App. 25.
† Conway to Buckingham, July 23. *Hardwicke S. P.* i. 429.

although in the eyes of his subjects it was most important for the safety of the nation that they should be executed with rigour. If he had of his own motion adopted the policy which was shadowed out in the private articles, he might have had a hard struggle before he could carry it into execution; but he would probably at least have gained the respect of his contemporaries, and he would certainly have earned the admiration of posterity. But by making the progress of religious liberty dependent upon a treaty with Spain, he struck a deadlier blow against the rising spirit of tolerance than if he had been in league with all the fanatics in the world. From henceforth the religious Protestant, and the patriotic statesman, would be banded together in a common determination that a Church which sought to win its way by foreign aid, and which publicly professed its contempt for the laws of England and for the independent action of Parliament, should not be allowed to enjoy even that ordinary fair play for which, under other circumstances, it might have asked. The Spanish marriage treaty was the signal that the milder spirit of the new age had received a check, and that all hope of smoothing down religious differences, and of quenching the fires of religious bigotry, must be indefinitely postponed.

Popular excitement.

All through the past week the popular mind had been more than usually excited. The acts, the words, the very countenances of the members of the Privy Council, had been eagerly scanned by multitudes who were anxious to draw from them an augury of the fate of the country. Never were the newsmongers more busy. Strange tales of what had happened in the Council and at Court passed from mouth to mouth, some of them perhaps true, but the greater part of them evidently invented for the occasion. It was thus that James was said to have exclaimed triumphantly, after signing the articles, that all the devils in hell could not now prevent the marriage; and that one of the courtiers, who heard what he said, whispered to another that there were none left there, for they had all gone to Spain to assist in making the match.

At last some one, bolder than the rest, forged a letter to the King, in the name of the Archbishop of Canterbury.

"Your Majesty," Abbot was supposed to say, "hath propounded a toleration of religion. I beseech you to take into your consideration what your act is, and what the consequence may be. By your act you labour to set up that most damnable and heretical doctrine of the Church of Rome, the whore of Babylon. How hateful will it be to God, and grievous to your subjects, the true professors of the gospel, that your Majesty who hath often defended and learnedly written against those wicked heresies, should now show yourself a patron of those doctrines which your pen hath told the world, and your conscience tells yourself, are superstitious, idolatrous, and detestable. Also what you have done in sending the Prince, without consent of your council, and the privity and approbation of your people. For although, sir, you have a large interest in the Prince, as the son of your flesh, yet have your people a greater, as a son of the kingdom, upon whom, next after your Majesty, are their eyes fixed, and their welfare depends. And so slenderly is his going apprehended, that, believe it, sir, however his return may be safe, yet the drawers of him into that action so dangerous to himself, so desperate to the kingdom, will not pass away unquestioned and unpunished.

"Besides, this toleration you endeavour to set up by your proclamation, it cannot be done without a Parliament, unless your Majesty will let your subjects see that you now take unto yourself a liberty to throw down the laws of the land at your pleasure. What dreadful consequences these things may draw after, I beseech your Majesty to consider, and above all, lest by this, the toleration and discountenance of the true profession of the gospel, wherewith God hath blessed us, and under which the kingdom hath flourished these many years, your Majesty doth draw upon the kingdom in general, and yourself in particular, God's heavy wrath and indignation.

"Thus, in discharge of my duty to your Majesty, and the place of my calling, I have taken the humble boldness to deliver my conscience. And now, sir, do with me what you please."*

* Printed with the name of the Archbishop of York. *Cabala*, 108.

CH. XI.
1623.
July.
Disavowed
by Abbot.

The letter was at once disavowed by Abbot to the King,* and attempts were made to discover the author. When these were found to be unavailing, some dissatisfaction was expressed at Court with the Archbishop, who appears to have been backward in making a public declaration that he had no hand in the authorship of the letter. It is possible, indeed, that he was unwilling to make a statement which could hardly fail to be accompanied with something like a disavowal of the opinions contained in it; and there can be little doubt that however much he had lately withdrawn himself from opposition to James, he continued to nourish those sentiments which had been put forward in his name. But, however this may have been, it is certain that whether the forger had accurately adopted the ideas of the Archbishop or no, he had felicitously expressed the thoughts of the great majority of the people of England.

James complains of the expense to which he will be put.

Meanwhile James was doing his best to make light of what he had done. In the letter which he wrote to his son and his favourite, the day after he had taken the oaths, he had a word to say in praise of the unexpected compliance of Pembroke and Abbot, but he had nothing to say about that of which every one else was talking. In truth his thoughts were running upon the expense to which he was likely to be put by the delay in the Infanta's voyage. "Since it can be no better," he wrote, "I must be contented; but this course is both a dishonour to me, and double charges if I must send two fleets. But if they will not send her till March, let them, in God's name, send her by their own fleet; and forget not to make them keep their former conditions anent the portion, otherwise both my Baby and I are bankrupts for ever." Other matters of infinitely greater importance were passed over in far fewer words. "This bearer," he informed his son, "will bring you power to treat for the Palatinate, and the matter of Holland."†

---

* Valaresso to the Doge, Aug. $\frac{1}{11}$. *Venice MSS.* Desp. Ingh. This shows that the letter must have been written in July. Mrs. Green places it conjecturally under the date of Aug. 8.

† The King to the Prince and Buckingham, July 21. *Hardwicke S. P.* i. 428.

The wretched affair of the Palatinate was at this moment more hopelessly entangled than ever. Almost the first thing which James had been called upon to do, after his son had left him, was to open negotiations with Coloma and Boischot, for the sequestration of Frankenthal, and these were to be followed by an agreement for a suspension of arms, to make room for a congress to discuss the final terms of peace in the Empire. Commissioners were appointed to treat and the first conference was held on the 3rd of March.* But the discussions had not proceeded far when the news of the transference of the Electorate reached England, and the Commissioners at once wrote to the King. "We cannot," they said, "with our duties, but humbly deliver our opinions unto your Majesty, that as things now stand, we hold it most dishonourable for you, and unworthy your greatness to hearken to any further treaty of the suspension of arms."† Being asked to reconsider their advice, they repeated it more emphatically than before. Frankenthal, they said, had better be delivered to the Infanta on any terms that could be had, in order to keep it out of the hands of the Duke of Bavaria. But a suspension of arms would only serve to ruin the Protestants of Germany. Nor were the men who unanimously tendered this advice, by any means partizans of either side. Together with the names of Pembroke and Hamilton, of Chichester, and of Viscount Grandison, who as Sir Oliver St. John, had succeeded Chichester in Ireland, appeared those of Arundel, of Middlesex, of Calvert, and of Weston.‡

As might be expected, however, the protest of the Commissioners went for nothing. The treaty of sequestration was signed on the 19th of March. Frankenthal was to be placed in the hands of the Infanta Isabella for eighteen months. If at the end of that time no reconciliation had been effected between Frederick and the Emperor, an English garrison was to be re-admitted. In the meanwhile the religious worship of the inhabitants

---

* The Commissioners for the treaty to the King, March 3. *S. P. Germany.*
† The Commissioners to the King, March 6. *S. P. Germany.*
‡ The Commissioners to the King, March 9. *S. P. Germany.*

was to be secured from attack.* The treaty was carried into immediate execution. On the 14th of April, the Spanish commander, Verdugo, entered the town, and Sir John Buroughs, with his garrison, prepared to march out with the honours of war.

The treaty for a suspension of arms was the next to follow. On the 21st of April it was agreed to by the Commissioners.† It bound James and his son-in-law to enter into no leagues or confederacies by which the peace of the Empire might be disturbed, and to abstain from actual hostilities for fifteen months, during which time negotiations were to be opened at Cologne for a definite peace. The article relating to the associates of Frederick, that is to say to Christian and Mansfeld, was purposely left in obscurity. If they continued to carry on war, they were to be considered as enemies of the Empire, and to be disavowed by James and his son-in-law. Three months were to be allowed for completing the arrangements for the conferences at Cologne.

Saving so far as it might pave the way to a general treaty, this agreement was evidently of no importance whatever. James had no intention of sending an army into the Empire if he could by any possibility avoid it, and Frederick, who would have been delighted to send as many armies as he could, was unable to dispose of a single man.

Scarcely, however, had the treaty been ratified by the Infanta, when it appeared that the prospect of a general peace was as distant as ever. Without Frederick's signature the treaty was worth no more than the paper on which it was written, and that signature Frederick resolutely refused to give. Then ensued a long and bitter controversy between James and his son-in-law, James imperiously insisting upon negotiation as the only way in which past losses could be made good, and Frederick no less obstinately refusing to believe that anything could be regained excepting by force of arms.

In truth the controversy was one of those the details of which are worthy only of oblivion. Both parties were

---

* Treaty of Sequestration, March 19. *S. P. Germany.*
† Treaty of Suspension, April 21. *S. P. Germany.*

thoroughly in the wrong. There was doubtless large scope in Germany for diplomacy. There was doubtless large scope for military resistance. But nothing but ruin could come either from an attempt to make peace under the guidance of James, or from an attempt to carry on war under the guidance of Frederick.

For what James proposed was, not to strike out an arrangement which would suit the altered circumstances of the case, and which would have been acceptable in the existing state of opinion to the German princes and the German people, but simply to blot out the history of the last four years as though they had never been. He fancied with the help of Spain he could wring from the Emperor a complete restitution of all of which his son-in-law had been in possession before his acceptance of the Bohemian crown. Against this, as the Commissioners for the treaty wisely asserted, the transference of the Electorate effected at Ratisbon was a complete bar. It was certain that Ferdinand would never be induced solely by diplomatic pressure to undo that day's work; and when James, in his folly, continued to speculate on the possibility of such a concession, he was plainly talking in ignorance both of the special facts of the case, and of the general laws by which human nature is guided.

Frederick was therefore undoubtedly in the right in pronouncing against his father-in-law's proposal. He saw clearly that the complete restitution which he sought was only to be obtained by victory. How victory was to be obtained he was the last man in Europe to know. In fact, there were two courses before him, neither of which was likely to yield the results at which he was aiming. He might hound on Mansfeld and Christian to their bloody work, and might once more summon Bethlen Gabor with his hated allies, the Turks, to pour ruin and desolation over Ferdinand's hereditary dominions. Or, on the other hand, by an almost superhuman effort of self-sacrifice, he might have declared that his own personal claims should not be an obstacle to a general pacification, and might thus have paved the way by his own abdication for that reconciliation with the Lutheran states of Northern Germany which would have given the surest guarantee for the future stability of Protestantism in the Empire.

Such was the choice which lay before Frederick; but the unfortunate man did not even comprehend that there could be any choice at all. What he pictured to himself was a general league in which the Electors of Saxony and Brandenburg, the Kings of England and Denmark, and the States General of the Netherlands, should agree, in loving union with Christian and Mansfeld, to fight out the quarrel which he had done more than any living man to embitter. Of course all this was but a dream. The Lutheran Princes may have been sluggish and unwarlike. They may have cared quite as much about the security of their domains as they cared about their religion. But if one thing was clearer than another, it was that they detested the freebooters which Frederick was ready, without the slightest compunction, to pour over Germany, far more than they detested the Emperor's treatment of their fellow-Protestants in Bohemia and the Palatinate. A meeting of the two Protestant Electors ended in nothing more than a resolution to levy troops enough to protect their own territories from invasion. A meeting of the States of Lower Saxony ended in an almost similar manner. From all this, however, Frederick learned nothing. He had not indeed much to expect from Mansfeld, who was not likely to quit his comfortable quarters in East Friesland as long as anything remained to plunder. But from Christian he hoped great things. That headlong warrior had been taken into pay by his brother the Duke of Brunswick, and efforts had been made, not without success, to obtain his pardon from the Emperor. But all the while his head had been teeming with vaster projects. Covering himself with the negotiations for a pardon, he intended to wait till Bethlen Gabor was ready to move. He would then throw himself suddenly upon Silesia, and before their joint efforts Bohemia and Moravia would once more be snatched from the House of Austria.

These wild plans received a sudden check. The Elector of Saxony prudently refused to Christian and his men permission to pass through his territories.* Yet something must be done. Tilly was approaching, and Christian was ordered to leave the circle of Lower Saxony, and not to presume to make those countries the seat of war. His first thought was to throw himself upon Tilly's army, and he succeeded in obtaining an advantage over a detachment of the enemy. But the old general knew his man. Placing his troops in an unassailable position, he waited till Christian was compelled to retreat for want of supplies. He had not long to remain in inaction. As usual, Christian had no money to pay his men or provisions with which to feed them. In the face of such an enemy it was impossible to scatter them in search of spoil.† An immediate retreat was necessary, and Christian had nothing before him but to hurry on for the Dutch frontier, with Tilly following hard upon his heels. Before he reached the boundary, Tilly had been joined by reinforcements which gave him a decided superiority. At Stadtloo, with the Dutch territory almost in sight, Christian reached a heath to which the only entrance was a narrow road amongst the marshes. There, on the 27th of July, he took up a position which he fondly imagined to be unassailable, but the troops which he had placed to guard the entrance, whilst the rest of the army continued its march, gave way almost at the first shock, and the whole of the cavalry, seized with sudden panic, fled at the sight. Christian, seeing that the day was lost, followed their example. A terrible butchery ensued amongst the infantry, which was only stopped by the personal interference of Tilly. Of the whole army which had marched against the enemy little less than twenty thousand strong, five thousand five hundred men alone sought refuge under the flag of the Republic.‡

Ch. XI.
1623.
July.

As in 1622, so in 1623, Frederick's thought of reconquering his position by the help of adventurers without money or means had ended in disaster. As in 1622, so in 1623, a defeat wrung from him a grudging

Aug. 16.
Frederick signs the treaty of suspension of arms.

---

* Frederick to Bethlen Gabor, June 17, July 3. Nethersole to Calvert, July 1. *S. P. Germany.*
† Nethersole to Calvert, July 25. *S. P. Germany.*
‡ Carleton to Calvert, July 30, Aug. 1, Aug. 16. *S. P. Holland.*

compliance with his father-in-law's wishes. The battle of Stadtloo was fought on the 27th of July. On the 16th of August Frederick signed the treaty for the suspension of arms.* It was too late. The three months prefixed for making the arrangements for the conference at Cologne had already expired, and all that the Infanta could say when the treaty was presented to her at Brussels was that she wished well to the success of the negotiations, but that it would now be necessary to consult the Emperor afresh.†

CH. XI. 1623. August.

Such were the results of the divergent efforts of James and Frederick during the summer of 1623. It would be strange, indeed, if his son at Madrid were able to reduce the chaos into order.

The proposed attack upon the Dutch.

It might be thought that in his treatment of the affairs of Germany James had done his worst, but in dealing with the other difficulty to which he had referred in his letter of the 21st of July‡ he had strayed even farther from the paths of common sense. For it might well have been supposed that after the final settlement of the long disputes between the two East Indian Companies, nothing more would have been heard of that senseless project for a joint invasion of the free Netherlands by Spain and England. Yet it was this very project which James chose to revive at the critical moment when he was talking of engaging in a Continental war, unless the Emperor gave his consent to abandon all the advantages which he had gained during so many weary years.

The Flemish privateers.

The renewal of the war between Spain and Holland had been accompanied by the imposition of a strict blockade upon the Flemish ports. Deprived of all share in the commercial enterprise upon which their Northern kinsmen were thriving, the sea-faring populations of Dunkirk and Ostend gave themselves up to privateering. The swift-sailing vessels which from time to time contrived to slip through the blockading squadron were the terror of the smaller Dutch trading vessels and especially of the fleet of herring boats, which, as James had bitterly

* Carleton to Conway, Aug. 16. *S. P. Holland.*
† Trumbull to Calvert, Sept. 5. *S. P. Flanders.*
‡ P. 366.

complained, were engaged in reaping the harvest of the sea along the whole line of the east coast of England. It happened that in the summer of 1622, two of these privateers chased by Dutch men-of-war took refuge, the one in Aberdeen and the other in Leith, and that in the ardour of the chase, the Dutch captain, who was in pursuit of one of them, had continued to fire his guns after entering Leith harbour, and had even struck with his balls some of the houses in the town. Against this outrage James had remonstrated with the Dutch Commissioners, who were at that time in England, and had demanded that their countrymen should remain in port two tides after the Dunkirk vessels had sailed.* The demand was however rejected, and during the winter months the Dunkirk vessels at Leith and Aberdeen were closely watched by Dutch men-of-war lying in the harbour.†

At last, after some months' delay, James sent orders to Carleton to repeat his demand in the presence of the States General, and Carleton in addition to his public declaration spoke in private to the Prince of Orange. Maurice, he found, was not inclined to yield. He reasonably enough declared that what was now asked would be the ruin of the Dutch commerce. If every Flemish privateer could be certain of a refuge in an English harbour, from which it might issue forth unmolested by the enemy till two tides were past, there would no longer be a chance left to the honest trader.‡

Thus pressed, James withdrew his most arrogant pretentions. He laid down the rule which even now prevails in maritime warfare. He had never meant, he said, to deny the Dutch their right of blockade. As long as they remained outside a harbour, they were at liberty to pursue their enemies wherever they could find them. It was only when they entered his ports that they were bound to wait two tides after the enemy's vessel had

---

* *Aitzema*, i. 200. The vessel is called in the correspondence sometimes a Dunkirker, and sometimes an Ostender.
† The Council of Scotland to the King, Feb. 15. *Melros Papers. Abbotsford Club*, ii. 497. Best to Conway, July 23. *S. P. Dom.* cxlix. 28.
‡ Carleton's Proposition, March 5. Carleton to Calvert, March 6. *S. P. Holland.*

<small>CH. XI.
1623.
March.</small>

sailed. The present case, however, was not a mere case of blockade. The Dutch captain had fired guns in his harbour and had knocked down some chimneys in the town. It was in reparation for this wrong that he expected that the blockaded vessels at both ports should be allowed to escape.*

To this declaration the States General returned answer, accepting at once the King's exposition of maritime law, and apologizing for the error of their sailors. On the mode of reparation suggested by James they were altogether silent, hesitating naturally enough to let the caged privateers loose upon their fishermen who were toiling on the billows of the North sea.†

<small>Two ships ordered to Scotland.</small>

To such considerations as these James refused to listen. Both at Leith and at Aberdeen the Dutch vessels had actually entered his harbours, and they must be prepared to take the consequences of relinquishing the blockade. He ordered two ships of the Royal Navy to be got ready for service in Scotland. He would set his ports free, he said, one way or other.‡

<small>April.
Seizure of a ship at Cowes by the Dutch.</small>

As ill luck would have it, just at the moment when James's displeasure was at its height, news arrived of a fresh violation of an English harbour. A few days before two Dutch captains, one of whom was the noted Moy Lambert, came to an anchor in Cowes roads. Their sight was at once arrested by a vessel manned by countrymen of their own which they knew to have been engaged in piracy. As soon as they notified the fact, the pirate officers were arrested by the Commander of the Castle, and information was sent to London. The question whether the ship and its crew should be delivered up to the Dutch was being examined by the Privy Council, when Lambert, acting on his own authority, took possession of the vessel and sailed away with it to Holland.§

Worse than this was to come. On the night of the

<small>* Conway to Carleton, March 19. *S. P. Holland.*
† Carleton to Calvert, April 7. Answer to the States General, April 16. *S. P. Holland.*
‡ Conway to Carleton, May 6. *S. P. Holland.* Calvert to Buckingham, April 24. Conway to Buckingham, May (?). *Harl. MSS.* 1580, fol. 158, 287.
§ Conway to Carleton, May 15, with enclosed statement of the proceedings of the Dutch. *S. P. Holland.* Caron to the States General, April 17. *Add. MSS.* 17,677 K, fol. 278.</small>

3rd of May the captain of the Dunkirk ship at Leith, weary of his long detention, made an effort to escape, and ran his vessel aground upon a sandbank. Just as it had passed the pier-head, when the morning dawned, the crews of the Dutch men-of-war caught sight of their enemy in this disabled position. Ranging up alongside, they poured broadside after broadside into the stranded vessel, till the falling tide compelled them to sheer off. So close were they to the shore that a man standing on the pier-head had been killed by the shot. In vain the Lord Chancellor, Sir George Hay, with other members of the Privy Council, had hurried down from Edinburgh to stop the slaughter. Before noon the Dunkirker was lying a hopeless wreck, abandoned by her crew.

Ch. XI.
1623.
May 4.
Attempt of the Dunkirker at Leith to escape.
Attacked by the Dutch.

The fugitive sailors had no sooner reached the shore than a new danger awaited them. Nowhere was the Spanish flag more thoroughly detested than in Scotland. By the ties of religious and of commercial sympathy the inhabitants of Leith and Edinburgh were brought into close communication with the Dutch. The moment, therefore, that the unfortunate sailors set foot on shore they were set upon by an angry mob, and were robbed and illtreated in every possible manner. The Councillors were powerless. No one would assist them in maintaining order or would give information where the stolen property had been concealed.

The sailors robbed on shore.

The next day, in spite of repeated orders, it was found that no aid was to be got in Leith, for the preservation of the abandoned ship. Equally in vain was an attempt to obtain assistance from Edinburgh. The Provost came, but scarcely a man accompanied him. Guns were at last brought down from the castle, and on the following day, after the King's flag had been hoisted on the wreck, an attempt, which proved fruitless, was made to get the vessel into the harbour. The Lord Chancellor himself lent a hand to the work, only to find on his return to land that the Edinburgh men, who had been induced with much difficulty to guard the cannon, had gone off leaving the guns to their fate. His labours were at last drawing to a close. That night the Dutchmen set fire to the wreck, and spared him any further trouble.

May 5.

May 6.
The ship burnt.

CH. XI.
1623.
May.
Melrose suggests the levy of a standing force.

The Council contented themselves with reporting to the King the misconduct of the Dutch. The Secretary, Melrose, could not help following the dictates of his harsh and despotic nature. His bitterest indignation was reserved for his unruly countrymen. The only remedy for the evil, he said, lay in the possession of sufficient treasure to enable the King to keep on foot a standing force, which could be trusted to obey orders, whether they were pleasing to the populace or not. Utterly impracticable as the suggestion was for the moment, it was one which, without fail, would be heard of again, if the antagonism between the Stuart Kings and their subjects proved to be of long continuance.*

Carleton's remonstrances.

The infraction of English neutrality by the Dutch had now reached such a pitch as to be intolerable to any Government which retained the slightest feeling of self-respect. Carleton was directed to remonstrate seriously at the Hague, and to demand the arrest of the captains in command of the ships at Leith, and the withdrawal of the Dutch men-of-war from Aberdeen.† About the same time Conway wrote a private letter to the Prince of Orange, adjuring him to avert so great a disaster as a war between England and the Netherlands.‡

June 10.
The Prince of Orange's letter.

It was not long before an answer came from Maurice. The seizure of the ship at Cowes he declared to have been the result of a pure mistake. With respect to the affair at Leith, he did his best to explain it away. The captains, he said, had been unable to restrain their too fervent zeal when they saw themselves in the presence of men who had exercised such cruelties upon the poor fishermen. About a fortnight later, a formal letter from the States General, acknowledging the fault which had been committed, and expressing a hope that the King would pass it over, was placed in Carleton's hands.§

This letter the ambassador refused to accept. There

* The Council of Scotland to the King, May 7. *S. P. Dom.* cxliv. 20. Melrose to the King, May 7. *Melros Papers*, ii. 512. Statement of Juan de Sagasticaval, May 7. *S. P. Flanders.*
† Carleton's Proposition, May 23. *S. P. Holland.*
‡ Conway to the Prince of Orange, May 22. *S. P. Holland.*
§ The Prince of Orange to Conway, June $\frac{10}{20}$. The States General to the King, $\frac{\text{June } 27}{\text{July } 7}$. *S. P. Holland.*

was nothing in it, he said, about allowing the ship at Aberdeen to proceed to sea.* Great was the perplexity of the Dutch. They were evidently prepared to offer any reasonable reparation; but they could not forget that to allow the privateer to set sail unpursued from Aberdeen, would subject hundreds of poor fishermen to utter ruin, if not to a cruel death.

{Ch. XI. 1623. July. Hesitation of the Dutch.}

For all this, in his present state of exasperation, James was without the slightest consideration. His two ships were already on the way to Scotland, under the command of Captain Best. Scarcely had they started, when news arrived that four more Dutch men-of-war had cast anchor in Aberdeen roads. Immediate orders were despatched to send four more ships from the Royal Navy to join Best in the North.†

{Best sails for Aberdeen.}

{July 17.}

The King's wrath was not appeased by the active measures which he had taken. Scarcely had the order been given, when he wrote to his son to look after the matter of Holland; and by looking after the matter of Holland, he meant nothing short of putting into execution the old scheme for the partition of the Netherlands.‡

{July 21. Renewal of the scheme for an attack upon the Netherlands.}

Two days later, formal powers were despatched to Buckingham and Bristol, directing them to enter upon negotiations with the Spanish ministers for the attainment of this object.

{July 23. Formal powers sent to Spain.}

"Having now brought," he wrote, "the main and principal business, which is the match of our son, to a happy conclusion, as we have lately understood both from himself and by your despatches; there riseth two other particulars of great importance, as you know: the one whereof is public, namely, the restitution of our son-in-law and his posterity to the Palatinates and dignity electoral; the other private, concerning the transposing of some part of the Netherland Provinces, and annexing them to our Crown, both which will now fall fitly to be treated on. And, because this letter is a matter of supreme secresy, and not communicable to many, we

---

* Carleton to Calvert, July 5. *S. P. Holland.*
† Conway to Calvert, July 17. *S. P. Holland.*
‡ The King to the Prince and Buckingham, July 21. *Hardwicke State Papers,* i. 428.

Ch. XI.
1623.
July 23.

have thought fit only at this time to give you authority by this letter, under our hand and signet, as hereby we do give you full authority and commission jointly and severally, to proceed to the treaty of both those particulars aforementioned with the commissioners to be appointed on that side by our good brother the King of Spain, according to such instructions or directions as you have heretofore had from us. And whatsoever further powers shall be necessary to be given you in this behalf, you may cause it to be drawn up there formally and legally, transmitting the same hither unto us, whereupon we shall pass the same under our signature and great seal of England, and so return it back unto you. In the meantime, you may proceed to the treaty according to the authority here given you, and whatsoever you shall thereupon conclude in our name, we shall ratify and confirm; not doubting but that you will acquaint our dear son, the Prince, with all your proceedings, from time to time, whilst he remains in that Court, and assist yourselves also continually with his advice and directions, for so is our pleasure."*

They are never acted on.

Never probably in the history of the civilised world was a war of conquest against a neighbouring nation projected so lightly, and on so utterly inadequate grounds. That the consequence of this wild and iniquitous proceeding, if by any strange chance it happened to be successful, would have been the ruin of both England and Holland, and the unchecked supremacy of the Pope and the Catholic monarchies in Europe, James never paused to consider for an instant. Fortunately, he had at least one amongst his servants who was able to think for him. The letter bears on the back the brief indorsement, in Bristol's handwriting, "The King's letter touching Holland, 23rd of July, 1623. His Majesty's pleasure to be first known."

Compromise with the Dutch.

Long before an answer could be received from England, James's anger had cooled down. Upon Caron's assurance that the Dutch captains would refrain from further aggression, the preparation of the four additional ships was countermanded. In point of fact, in the very midst of the quarrel, a compromise had been struck out which, if

* The King to Buckingham and Bristol, July 23. *Sherborne MSS.*

James had not been too angry to understand what was passing before him, would have saved him from disgracing himself by his ignoble despatch to his ambassadors in Spain. For Best had carried with him orders not, as had been James's original intention, to let loose the privateer upon the fishing-boats of his neighbours, but to convoy her safely to Dunkirk or Ostend, without suffering her to do any damage by the way. In a Flemish port she would be watched closely by the blockading squadron, and the Dutch would be in no worse position than they had been before.* Nor was there any fear that the States General would be dissatisfied with this solution. As early as the 7th of June they had issued directions to their captains to accompany the privateer to the Flemish coast, without firing a shot, unless she attempted to leave the convoy.† Fearing lest this should not be enough, they placed in Carleton's hands on the 9th of August a passport, by which their commanders on the Flemish coast were directed to allow the vessel from Aberdeen to pass unharmed through the blockading squadron.‡

But for the folly of the Dunkirk captain, this affair, which had at one time threatened to embroil two nations in war, would have given no further trouble to anyone. Best and the Dutch captains came to a mutual understanding before they left Aberdeen, and the convoy sailed away, steering south, accompanied by four out of the six vessels which were watching over the interests of the Republic. Unluckily, the privateer captain was not content with the humble position assigned to him, and, wishing to show that he could go faster through the water than any of the others, crowded all sail, and speedily outstripped both friends and enemies. The Dutch captains, either fearing for the fishing-boats, or, simply from the pleasure of catching their enemy unprotected, started in pursuit, and came up with the privateer after he had shortened sail, and was waiting for the English convoy, which was already nearly two miles astern. Before Best's

marginalia: Ch. XI. 1622. Best's orders. August. July. The voyage from Aberdeen. Fight between the Dunkirker and the Dutch.

---

* Conway to the Prince of Orange, July 26. *S. P. Holland.*
† Best to Conway, July 23. *S. P. Dom.* cxlix. 28.
‡ Carleton to Calvert, Aug. 9. Carleton to Conway, Aug. 16. *S. P. Holland.*

slow-sailing vessels had come up, the Dutch ships opened fire, shot away the main yard of the Dunkirker, and killed the captain and five men. The English vessels now appeared upon the scene, and poured in their fire in return; but they soon found that they were no match for their adversary in speed. The Dutchmen sheered off, and keeping well out of gunshot, amused themselves by sailing round his Majesty's ships at a respectful distance, till Best anchored in the Downs, when they took up a position of observation near the South Foreland.*

Best could not be ignorant that the Dunkirk captain had no one but himself to blame; yet the old sailor was filled with indignation at the attack which had been made upon a vessel under his charge. By daylight, as he was aware, it was impossible to bring the Dutch captains to task, unless they chose to await the coming of the sluggish vessel with which the Navy Commissioners had provided him. He, therefore, waited for a dark night, and dropping down unperceived amongst the Dutch squadron, fired a broadside into their hulls, and drove them triumphantly out of the roads.†

A fortnight earlier this thoughtless act of violence upon the crews of a friendly nation who had been doing no more than their duty, would probably have met with the warmest approbation at Court. But it was not in James's nature to retain his indignation long. Already he had forgotten all about his instructions to his ambassadors in Spain. Orders were sent down to Best to bring his own ship and the Dunkirker up the Thames, where they would be in safety from the vengeance of the Dutch, and to present himself before the Council in order to give an account of his proceedings.‡

Two or three days later, Carleton's messenger arrived with the fresh passport from the States. With this, and with the accompanying acknowledgment of the justice of his demands, James was highly delighted. He now began to speak of the Republic in the most friendly terms, and

---

* Best to Conway, Aug. 4, 11. *S. P. Dom.* cl. 18, 83.
† Best to Conway, Aug. 6. Best to the Council, Aug. 11. *S. P. Dom* cl. 33, 84.
‡ Calvert to Conway, Aug. 12. *S. P. Dom.* cl. 86.

even went so far as to declare openly, that as soon as his son came home, he was "firmly minded to do something" for the States.* Best was, therefore, superseded in his command by Sir Richard Bingley, who carried the vessel which had been the cause of so much contention into the Flemish harbour of Mardike, without any further interruption from the Dutch.†

So ended James's scheme for subduing the Netherlands with Spanish aid. It could hardly be long before his other scheme for regaining the Palatinate with the same assistance, would break down still more ignominiously.

* Dudley Carleton to Carleton, Aug. 21. *S. P. Holland.*
† Locke to Carleton, Sept. 14. *S. P. Dom.* clii. 40. The Infanta Isabella to the King, $\frac{\text{Sept. 20}}{\text{Oct. 10}}$. *S. P. Flanders.*

CHAPTER XII.

THE BREACH WITH SPAIN.

<small>Ch. XII.
1623.
July.
Position of Olivares.</small>

Seldom has there been a stranger position than that occupied by Olivares in the July of this extraordinary year. Like a dishonest jockey, he had ridden the race with the settled purpose of losing it; but, do what he would, he had won every heat, in spite of all his efforts. It was in vain that he had trusted to the obduracy of the Pope. It was equally in vain that he had strained his demands upon Charles to the uttermost. There had been hesitation and distrust; but in the end neither the Pope nor Charles had ventured to deny him anything.

<small>Fresh secret articles presented to Charles.</small>

Even the secret articles sworn to in England had not contained the whole of the demands of the Spanish minister. As the treaty was now drawn up at Madrid it included four additional engagements, which Olivares declared it to be necessary for Charles to take.

"Moreover," he was required to declare, "I Charles, Prince of Wales, engage myself, and promise that the most illustrious King of Great Britain, my most honoured lord and father, shall do the same both by word and writing, that all those things which are contained in the foregoing articles, and concern as well the suspension as the abrogation of all laws made against the Roman Catholics, shall within three years infallibly take effect, and sooner, if it be possible, which we will have to lie upon our conscience and Royal honour.

"That I will intercede with the most illustrious King of Great Britain, my father, that the ten years of the education of the children which shall be born of this marriage with the most illustrious Lady Infanta, their mother, accorded in the twenty-second article, which term the Roman Pontiff desires to have prorogued to twelve years, may be lengthened to the said term; and

I promise freely and of my own accord to swear that, if it so happen that the entire power of disposing of the matter be devolved to me, I will also grant and approve the said term.

"Furthermore I, Prince of Wales, oblige myself upon my faith to the Catholic King that, as often as the most illustrious Lady Infanta shall require that I should give ear to divines or other whom her Highness shall be pleased to employ in matters of the Roman Catholic religion, I will hearken to them willingly without all difficulty, and laying aside all excuse.

"And for further caution in point of the free exercise of the Catholic religion and the suspension of the laws above named, I Charles, Prince of Wales, promise and take upon me in the word of a king, that the things above promised and treated concerning those matters shall take effect and be put in execution as well in the Kingdoms of Scotland and Ireland as of England." *

Of the articles thus offered to Charles, the first three were such as no man of honour could accept. In the first he promised that which, as he well knew, he would never be able to perform. In the second he gave a secret engagement which converted the public one into a mere deception. In the third he not only sacrificed his own self-respect in his domestic relations, but he held out hopes of future conversion which he had no intention of justifying. But Charles was deeply in love, and unhappily he was not a man of honour. At first, indeed, if it is to the formal presentation of these articles that we must refer a rather vague account which has reached us, he shuffled, and asked leave to refer the question to his father. When this was refused, he said that he would return an answer in a few hours. Before the day was over he sent Gondomar to Olivares to tell him that he would give way once more. So astonished was Olivares when he heard it, that it was some time before he could speak. "Is it possible?" he cried out at last; "I should as soon have expected my death." †

* *Rushworth*, i. 89. The original marriage contract is in Latin. *Add. MSS.* 19,271.

† *Khevenhüller*, x. 271. The additional demands are not specified, and are said to have been made after Cottington's return. But I can find no

Ch. XII.
1623.
July.
Olivares changes his plans.

From that moment Olivares changed his tactics. He had at last discovered, what he ought to have known long ago, that a man who could bear such treatment as this was not to be easily shaken off. The idea of marrying the Infanta to the son of the Emperor must be definitively abandoned. The marriage must in some way or other be made palatable to the Infanta, and the six months which had been gained by the refusal of the Theologians to allow her to leave Spain at once, must be made use of to come to a definite understanding upon the terms which the King of England was willing to impose upon his German son-in-law.

Persuades the Infanta to accept the marriage.

His first difficulty was with the Infanta herself. Fortunately for his object, he would now have a warm ally in his own wife, who was constantly in attendance on the Princess, and who had always wished well to the match as a means of the conversion of the Prince. Whatever opposition there was, he took immediate steps to quell. Sending for one of the Infanta's ladies who had encouraged her in resistance, he charged her in the King's name to be more discreet for the future. One morning, as the Infanta was preparing for confession, the Countess of Olivares had a long interview with her, and it was observed that she left her in tears. At the same time her confessor* was closeted with Olivares himself. As far as it is possible to judge, all this was not without effect. She may have been in some degree impressed by the assiduous attention shown to her, and though the marriage was still personally distasteful to her, it was easy to pass to the conclusion that she would find in the handsome youth who loved her so well, a fit instrument for bringing back the whole of England to the bosom of the Church.†

trace of any such demands after Cottington came back, on the 5th of August, and those above given were undoubtedly accepted before the 25th of July. Whatever date may be given to the story, the facts of Charles' acceptance of the articles, and of Olivares' change of policy about this time, are beyond a doubt.

* He was a different man from the one who had warned her against the marriage so strongly, and who had lately died.

† "A che," i.e. to assent to the marriage, "sebene gia stava lontanissima, essendo stata tuttavia impressa che grandissimo merito acquisterebbe appresso il Signor Dio col maritarsi con questo Principe, perche beneficava tanto la Religione, si havea ella accommodato l'animo, confidando che ritrovan-

On the 25th of July the marriage contract with its additional clauses was duly signed by Charles and Philip. It now included a special acknowledgment by the Prince that he was willing that the Infanta should not commence her journey till the following spring, though the marriage was to take place as soon as news arrived that James had sworn to the articles, and that the Pope had given his consent to the celebration of the rite. With regard to the last condition some slight delay was expected, as the death of Gregory XV. had been known at Madrid for some days; but it was considered probable that the Dean of the College of Cardinals would think himself justified in giving his approbation, and that, even if it were necessary to wait for the approbation of the new Pope, no serious delay was to be apprehended.*

Once again Charles was to show how little he understood the binding nature of an engagement. If anything was to be considered as settled it was that the Infanta's journey must be delayed till the spring. Again and again he had given his word that he would accept this condition. Yet, at the very time that he was affixing his signature to the marriage contract, in which his acquiescence was most solemnly reaffirmed, he was wearying Olivares with renewed supplications, whilst the Spaniard, true to his old policy of deceit, professed his readiness to oblige him—a profession which he was enabled to make without fear of consequences, from his knowledge that the Theologians were always at his back as a last resort.

On the 28th a messenger arrived with the intelligence that the English Council had consented to take the required oath. The next day Charles and Buckingham returned answer to the King's letter. That James should have entertained any conscientious objections to his oath was perfectly unintelligible to his favourite and his son. "We are sorry," they wrote, "that there arose in your conscience any scruples; but we are confident, when we

Ch. XII.
1623.
July 25. Signature of the marriage contract.

Death of Gregory XV.

Charles again urges immediate delivery of the Infanta.

July 28. He is astonished at his father's scruples.

July 29. Hopes to bring the Infanta with him.

---

dosi da dovero esso Principe inamorato di lei, con progresso di tempo gli sia per esser facile anco il ridurlo con tutto il Regno alla chiesa." Corner to the Doge, Aug. $\frac{8}{18}$. *Venice MSS.* Desp. Spagna.

* Bristol to Cottington, July 15. Prynne's *Hidden Works of Darkness*, 49.

Ch. XII.
1623.
July 29.

see your Majesty, to give you very good satisfaction for all we have done." They then proceeded to speak of their hopes and designs. "Sir," they wrote, "we have not been idle in this interim, for we can now tell you certainly that, by the 29th of your August, we shall begin our journey, and hope to bring her with us .... Marriage there shall be none without her coming with us; and, in the meantime, comfort yourself with this, that we have already convinced the Conde of Olivares in this point, that it is fit the Infanta come with us before winter. He is working underhand with the divines, and, under colour of the King's and Prince's journey, makes preparation for hers also. Her household is a-settling, and all other things for her journey; and the Conde's own words are, he will throw us all out of Spain as soon as he can. There remains no more for you to do, but to send us peremptory commands to come away, and with all possible speed. We desire this, not that we fear that we shall have need of it, but in case we have, that your son, who hath expressed much affection to the person of the Infanta, may press his coming away, under colour of your command, without appearing an ill lover." *

Charles and Buckingham

The letter, indeed, was in Buckingham's handwriting; but the thoughts which it contained, the little contrivances and the empty hopes with which it is full, came straight from the brain of Charles. After his return to England, it suited the favourite to declare that both he and the Prince had stood together in manful resistance to the trickery of Olivares; and, as a natural result, those who have been unable to reconcile his narrative with admitted facts, have thrown the whole blame of the breach upon Buckingham's insolence. "If the Prince," said the Spaniards, when all was over, "had come alone, he would not have returned alone." Yet, natural as the explanation was, it was not in accordance with the truth. The real cause of Charles's failure lay partly in the exorbitant pretensions of the Spaniards to religious supremacy in England, but still more in the belief which Olivares

* The Prince and Buckingham to the King, July 29. *Hardwicke S. P.* i. 432.

had always consistently held, that the terms which he himself regarded as indispensable would not prove acceptable in England. Annoyed as he was at being unable to relinquish a negotiation which he disliked, the Spanish minister was likely to look with especial disfavour upon Buckingham's insolence. Different as they were in every other respect, Bristol and Buckingham had been of one mind in objecting to the fresh terms imposed upon the Prince in consequence of his presence at Madrid; but what Bristol had said gravely and respectfully, Buckingham had said petulantly and rudely. Ill at ease in the part which he was playing, he had vented his displeasure upon all towards whom he dared to show his real feelings. He had quarrelled with Bristol, and he had quarrelled with Olivares; but even he, utterly void of self-restraint as he was, dared not quarrel with Charles. In all ordinary matters he could impose his will upon him by sheer force of audacity. The rude familiarity with which he treated the Prince caused the greatest astonishment to the Spaniards. Accustomed as they were to the most rigid etiquette, it was with the deepest disgust that they saw a subject sitting without breeches in his dressing-gown at the Prince's table, or standing in public with his back towards him, or rudely leaning forward to stare at the Infanta.* All this he allowed himself to do. But he knew that he could not thwart Charles in the one object upon which he had set his heart; that he must carry his messages, and make himself the instrument of all those petty compliances which were so dear to the heart of the youth whom he served, knowing all the while that he was regarded at home as the author of those concessions which, in reality, he detested.

Sometimes, indeed, his feelings were too strong for him. Once, on receiving a visit from Khevenhüller, he showed his consciousness of being duped. "The affairs of our masters," he said, "appear to clash at present. I hope that this marriage will accommodate them. If not, before a year is over, an army will be sent into Germany strong enough to set everything right by force." The

Who caused the failure of the match?

Buckingham and Khevenhüller.

---

* Wadsworth to Buckingham, Nov. 11. Goodman's *Court of King James*, ii. 314.

Ch. XII.
1623.
July.

Imperial Ambassador replied, that the door of grace had been opened to Frederick, but that he had refused to walk in ; and Buckingham, who probably could not trust himself to pursue the conversation further, changed the subject to an inquiry about Khevenhüller's horses.*

July 30. His account of the state of the negotiation.

Even in writing to James this feeling of doubt as to the ultimate issue of the business pierces through the surface. It was thus that, on the 30th of July, he allowed adverse details which had been absolutely banished from the joint composition of the day before, to find a place in his private letter to the King. "In the mean time, sir," he wrote, "know that, upon the King's Council's and Court's expression of joy that the Prince had come into and accepted of their own offers here to be contracted and stay for the Infanta's following him at the beginning of the spring, we thought it a fit time, in the heat of their expressions, to try their good natures,

He is sent to urge Olivares to give way.

and press the Infanta's present going. Whereupon the Prince sent me to the Conde of Olivares with these reasons for it: that, first, it would lengthen much your days, who best deserved of them in this and many other businesses ; it would add much to the honour of the Prince, which otherwise must needs suffer ; the Infanta would thereby gain the sooner the hearts of the people, and so consequently make her desires and their ends sooner and easier to be effected in favour of the Catholics ; that otherwise we should compass but one of those ends for which we came, for marriage, and not friendship, and so it would prove but like the French alliance;† that the affairs of Christendom would easilier and sooner be compounded ; that if he had any reason of state in it which he hoped to gain at the spring, I would show him how he would better compass it now than when distrust would beget the same in us ; how your Majesty had been this year at a great charge already, and how this delay would but be of more to both kingdoms. With this I entreated him to think of my poor particular, who had waited upon the Prince hither, and in that distasted

---

* Khevenhüller to Ferdinand II. *Ann. Ferd.* x. 271.
† That is to say the alliance between France and Spain by the double marriages of Lewis XIII. and Philip IV. with each other's sisters.

all the people in general; how he laid me open to their malice and revenge, when I had brought from them their Prince a free man, and should return him bound by a contract, and so locked from all posterity till they pleased here; how that I could not think of this obligation, if he would not* relieve me in it, without horror or fear, if I were not his faithful friend and servant, and intended thankfulness. He interrupted this with many grumblings, but at last said I had bewitched him; but if there was a witch in the company, I am sure there was a devil too.

"From him I repaired to his lady, who, I must tell you by the way, is as good a woman as lives, which makes me think all favourites must have good wives; whom I told what I had done. She liked of it very well, and promised her best assistance. Some three or four days after, the Prince sent to intreat him to settle her house, and to give order in other things for their journey. He asked what day he should go away: but himself named the 29th of your August, which the Prince accepted of.

"Some two days after, the Countess sent for me, the most afflicted woman in the world, and told me the Infanta had told her the Prince meant to go away without her; and, for her part, she took it so ill, to see him so careless of her, that she would not be contracted till the day he was to take his leave. The Countess told me, the way to mend this was to go to the Conde, and put the whole business in the King's hands, with this protestation, that he would rather stay seven years than go without his mistress, he so much esteemed her; and if I saw after that this did not work good effects, that the Prince might come off upon your Majesty's command at pleasure.

"With this offer I went to the Conde. He received it but doggedly. The next day I desired audience of the Infanta. To taste her, I framed this errand from your Majesty, that you had commanded me to give her a particular account of what you had done, and that you

---

* "If he would releeve me," in Buckingham's hand. *Harl. MSS.* 6987, fol. 129 b.

Ch. XII.
1623.
July.

had overcome many difficulties to persuade the Council to come into these articles, and that you yourself was come into them merely in contemplation of her; and that you had given order for present execution, and since you had done thus much to get her, you made no question but her virtues would persuade you to do much more for her sake. When I had done this, I told her of the Prince's resolution, and assured her that he never spake of going but with this end, to get her the sooner away; but that hereafter he durst use no diligences for her and himself, since he was subject to so ill offices; except she would take this for granted, that he would never go without her, which she liked very well of. When I had done this, I told her, since she was the Prince's wife, all my thoughts were bent to gain her the love of that people whither she was to go; and I showed her how the articles contained no more than for the time to come, but there were many Catholics who at this day were fined in the Exchequer, and though it would be some loss to your Majesty,—though I think it would be none,—yet, if she would make a request to the Prince for them, your Majesty would quit it.

Assurance from the Countess that the Infanta will be allowed to go.

"I hope I have not done ill in this: but sure I am it hath not done ill to our business; for what with this, and that news of the sending the four ships to Leith, this morning the Countess hath sent the Prince this message, that the King, the Infanta, and the Conde, are the best contented that can be; and that he should not now doubt his soon going away, and to carry the Infanta with him." *

July 24. The fleet ordered to sail.

Already, some days before this letter reached England, the suggestion thus thrown out by Buckingham about the Recusancy fines, had been carried out by the King. Almost immediately after the solemnity at Whitehall, James had set out on his progress towards Salisbury, where the Spanish Ambassadors were invited to join him on the 4th of August. Orders were at once sent off to Rutland to set sail for Santander as soon as possible, and Conway, in his usual hyperbolical language, had wished him for his return " a wind like lovers' embrace-

* Buckingham to the King, July 30. *Hardwicke S. P.* i. 433.

ments, neither too strong nor too slack, and a sea as smooth as a lady's face so embraced."

In the meanwhile,* Calvert, who had remained in London, was busily engaged in consulting with other members of the Council in what mode the favours recently promised to the Recusants should be granted;† and their deliberations had ended in an appeal to the King for further instructions. If James fancied it was still possible to win the consent of the Spanish Government to the immediate delivery of the Infanta, his reply was singularly unfortunate. Disgusted with the necessity of bargaining at all over his dealings with his own subjects, he determined to reserve at least some show of independent authority, by adding to his order to Calvert to draw warrants releasing the Catholics from future penalties, a statement that, though he had resolved to give up the fines of such Recusants as had been already convicted, he meant to reserve this act of grace for some future occasion of public rejoicing. This subtle distinction between convicted and unconvicted Recusants was of course lost upon the ambassadors, and James soon found that in his attempt to maintain his dignity he had laid himself open to the charge of having refused to fulfil his obligations. Inojosa at once wrote to Calvert to complain of a decision which he was able to represent as a breach of promise. If it were not remedied, he proceeded to hint, it would be impossible for him to make a satisfactory report to his master.‡ Thus pressed, James gave way at once, and Calvert was ordered to include in the warrants offences committed in times past, as well as those which might be committed in time to come.§

Yet even with this the ambassadors were not contented. They demurred to the proposal that the pardon should be issued under the Great Seal, accompanied by a dispensation for the future from all penalties which might be incurred. What they wished was a public proclamation

* Conway to Rutland, July 24. *S. P. Dom.* cxlix. 36, 37.
† Calvert to Conway, July 24. *S. P. Dom.* cxlix. 38.
‡ Inojosa to Calvert, July 27, 28. *S. P. Spain.* Calvert to Conway, July 28. *S. P. Dom.* cxlix. 79.
§ Conway to Buckingham, Aug. 1. *S. P. Spain.*

Ch. XII.
1623.
August.

declaring his Majesty's purpose to grant relief from the penal laws. It was not till some time had been spent in explaining to them that a proclamation, according to English law, had no binding effect whatever, whereas a pardon under the Great Seal might safely be pleaded in court, that they consented to give way.* Yet it is impossible to resist the conviction that more was meant by the ambassadors than they chose to avow. What they wanted was a public and notorious act, which would ring in the ears of all men, and which would test the readiness of the English people to submit to the repeal of the obnoxious laws by Parliament. For such a purpose a proclamation would undoubtedly have served far better than hundreds of pardons quietly granted to individuals.

Aug. 8.
Agreement made at Salisbury.

As soon as the ambassadors reached Salisbury, Conway and Carlisle were appointed to treat with them on this important matter. At last, after some discussion, an agreement was come to, and was signed by both parties. A pardon was to be passed under the Great Seal of which all Roman Catholics who had been convicted or had been liable to be convicted in past times, would be allowed to take the benefit at any time during the next five years. A declaration should be issued, under his Majesty's seal, suspending for the future all the penal laws by which the Roman Catholics were affected, and at the same time they should be released from all penalties to which they might be subject " by reason of any statute or law whatsoever for their consciences, or exercise of their Roman Catholic religion in their private houses without noise and public scandal, or for any other matter or cause whatsoever for their consciences, by what law or ordinances soever to the observation whereof the rest of his Majesty's subjects are not bound." The King would, after conference with the Bishops, contrive a way for relieving the Catholics from the penalties consequent upon excommunication. Orders should be sent to Ireland to grant similar concessions there. As for Scotland, his Majesty would "according to the con-

* Conway to Calvert, Aug. 5. *S. P. Spain.* Conway to Buckingham, Aug. 5. *Hardwicke S. P.* i. 436.

stitution of affairs there, and in regard to the public good and peace of that kingdom, and as soon as possible, do all that shall be convenient for the accomplishment of his promise."*

Two points only amongst the ambassadors' demands† had been passed over. To a request that the forfeited rents and fines which had been given away by patent should be restored, James could only reply by giving permission to the aggrieved persons to try the question at law. The other claim was of a more serious nature. Not content with the immunity which they had secured for those who refused to take the oath of allegiance, the ambassadors pressed hard that schools and colleges might be rendered accessible to the Roman Catholics. On this point James stood firm. It would not look well, he held, "that he should not only at one instant give unexpected grace and immunity to his subjects the Roman Catholics, but seem to endeavour to plant a seminary of other religion than he made profession of."

To this answer Coloma raised no objection; but Inojosa, who no doubt had been to some extent initiated into the plans of Olivares, was evidently dissatisfied. Yet, at last, he promised to write to Madrid that James had done all that was to be expected, and, on leaving Salisbury, both the ambassadors joined in expressions of hope that the immediate marriage and departure of the Princess would be the result of these negotiations.‡

On the 10th of August, two days after the signature of the agreement, Buckingham's letter arrived with renewed hopes of the immediate delivery of the Infanta. James was of course delighted with the news.§ In return, he sent the order to leave Spain immediately, which Charles had asked for in order to excuse his rudeness to the Infanta. "My dearest son," he wrote, "I sent you a commandment long ago, not to lose time where ye are, but either to bring quickly home your mistress, which is my earnest desire; but if no better may be, rather than

---

* Agreement made at Salisbury, Aug. 8. *Harl. MSS.* 1583, fol. 287.
† Demands of the ambassadors, Aug. *Harl. MSS.* 1583, fol. 285.
‡ Conway to Buckingham, Aug. 5, Aug. 10. *Hardwicke S. P.* i. 436. *Harl. MSS.* 1580, fol. 326.
§ The King to Buckingham. Aug. 10. *Ellis's Ser.* i., iii. 158.

_{Ch. XII.}
_{1623.}
_{August.}

to linger any longer there, to come without her, which, for many important reasons, I am now forced to renew; and therefore I charge you, on my blessing, to come quickly either with her or without her. I know your love to her person hath enforced you to delay the putting in execution of my former commandments. I confess it is my chiefest worldly joy that ye love her; but the necessity of my affairs enforceth me to tell you that you must prefer the obedience to a father to the love ye carry to a mistress." *

_{Spanish proposal that Charles shall be married in Spain.}

Before this letter reached Madrid, there had been a fresh struggle between Charles and the Spanish Court. The conferences with Olivares and the messages to the Infanta had failed in producing the expected result. Philip utterly refused to give up his sister a day sooner than he had promised; but in one respect he now changed his tactics. If Charles would consent to remain in Spain till Christmas, he might then be married in person, and would be allowed to live with the Infanta as his wife, though she would not be permitted to leave Madrid till the appointed time in the spring.

_{Accepted by Charles.}

That there were the gravest objections to such a plan as this was evident to anyone who was less deeply in love than Charles; and no doubt there were not a few around him who reminded him that, if he accepted the offer, he would not only be placing himself in Philip's hands as a hostage for another half year, but that if, before the spring came, there were a prospect of the Infanta becoming a mother, fresh excuses for delay would arise, which would, in all probability, end in placing in Spanish hands another heir to the English throne — another hostage for James's subserviency to Spain in the affair of the Palatinate. Yet to all this Charles was blind. He told Philip that he was ready to accept the conditions, and he even sought an audience of the Queen in order to assure her, in the Infanta's presence, that he had made up his mind to remain.†

_{He changes his mind.}

Scarcely was this resolution taken when Cottington arrived, bringing with him the signatures of the King

---

* The King to the Prince, Aug. 10. *Hardwicke S. P.* i. 447.
† Francisco de Jesus, 32.

and Council to the marriage articles. Once more Charles tried, by a renewed threat of immediate departure, to induce the Spaniards to give way, and to allow him to carry home his bride at once. The request was referred to the Theologians, and the Theologians, as usual, proved obdurate, and refused their consent.*

Ch. XII. 1623. August.

But cannot prevail upon himself to go.

Charles could not make up his mind what to do. If he was unable to resist the impression that he was being made a tool of by Olivares, neither could he resolve to tear himself away from the Infanta. It was observed that when the refusal of the Theologians was brought to him, he did not repeat his threat of leaving Madrid; yet he had hard work to hold his own. Buckingham had again lost his temper, and had for some days been talking of setting out alone to meet Rutland's fleet at Santander.† All the Prince's little Court were of one mind in denouncing the hypocrisy of the Spaniards, and the hard words which were freely used were returned with interest by those who were assailed. One day a Spanish gentleman going into the Prince's room found on the table a richly-bound copy of a translation of the English Catechism into his own language, and carried it off in triumph to Philip; whilst at the same time charges, true or false, of an attempt to make proselytes to their faith were brought against Charles's attendants. The accusation might certainly have been retorted upon the Spaniards. One day Cottington was suddenly taken ill, and believing himself to be dying, sent for Lafuente, and was by him reconciled to the Church of Rome. A few days afterwards, as soon as he began to get better, he declared himself a Protestant again. The next case was that of Henry Washington, a dying youth, who summoned an English Jesuit, named Ballard, to his bedside. The little company of English were terribly excited. Gathering in a knot about the door, they barred the entrance, as they said, by the Prince's orders; and one of them, Sir Edmund Verney, struck the priest on the face with his fist. The people without, seeing what had happened, naturally took the

Behaviour of the Prince's attendants.

Temporary conversion of Cottington.

A priest struck by Sir E. Verney.

---

* Corner to the Doge, Sept. $\frac{10}{20}$. *Venice MSS. Desp. Spagna.*
† Aston (?) to Trumbull, Aug. 13. *S. P. Spain.*

part of the priest, and, but for the timely arrival of the alcalde, backed by the interposition of Gondomar, the tumult which ensued would hardly have been quieted without bloodshed.

Dissatisfaction at Court.

It was no doubt with a feeling of triumph, mingled with sorrow, that Verney and his friends attended the funeral of Washington in the burial-ground in the garden behind Bristol's house, which was the only resting-place allowed to him whom they had snatched from the jaws of the Papacy. At Philip's Court the tidings were received with indignation. How can it be expected, it was asked, that these men should behave better to the Catholics in England than they do in Spain? To meet the opposition which had been raised, Charles ordered Verney to leave Madrid; but this was not enough to satisfy the Nuncio; and, at his complaint, the King sent Gondomar to demand that the offender should be rigorously punished. The Prince was deeply annoyed, and demanded in return that the alcalde should be punished for laying hands upon his servant. At last Philip cut the matter short by sending a message to Charles, to tell him that if he wished to spend the winter at Madrid he must dismiss all his Protestant attendants.*

Dispute about punishing Verney.

Aug. 20. Charles writes that he will leave Madrid.

Such a collision between the two Courts made Charles's stay at Madrid more difficult than ever. At last, therefore, he gave way to the solicitations of those around him, and announced to his father his resolution to leave Spain. "The cause," he explained, "why we have been so long in writing to you since Cottington's coming, is that we would try all means possible, before we would send you word, to see if we could move them to send the Infanta before winter. They, for form's sake, called the divines, and they stick to their old resolution; but we find, by circumstances, that conscience is not the true but seeming cause of the Infanta's stay. To conclude, we have wrought what we can, but since we cannot have her with us that we desired, our next comfort is that we hope shortly to kiss your Majesty's hands." †

---

* Francisco de Jesus, 83. Corner to the Doge, Sept. $\frac{10}{20}$. *Venice MSS. Spagna.* Howell's *Letters.* Book i., Ser. 3, Letter 20.

† The Prince and Buckingham to the King, Aug. 20. *Hardwicke S. P.* i. 448.

Such was the meagre account which Charles thought fit to give to his father of that fortnight of weakness and vacillation, of promises unfulfilled, and of words only uttered to be recalled. What he meant by the circumstances which, in his opinion, were the cause of the Infanta's stay, it is impossible to tell; but those who have attentively perused the true narrative of his proceedings will hardly join in the cry, which has been repeated from century to century, that the Spaniards were deeply to blame in refusing to send the Infanta at once to England, excepting so far as they deserve blame for not taking a wider and more generous view than they did of the crisis through which the world was in that day passing. For there can be little doubt that they would have preferred not to send the Infanta at all, if it could have been done without exasperating Charles and his father into war, and that they looked upon her detention, not merely as affording them time to ascertain how James would treat his Catholic subjects, but as enabling them to come to some definite understanding as to the resistance which he was likely to offer to their scheme for the forced conversion of the Palatinate to their creed. Viewed from the higher standing-ground at which we have arrived, the whole policy of Olivares was altogether indefensible; looked at from the point of view of a Spaniard of the seventeenth century, he omitted nothing which could be done in order to attain an object which would be most beneficial to the world. If, however, we look merely at the consequences which the refusal to deliver the Infanta at once produced in Charles's mind, it is impossible to say that Olivares was wrong; for he had learned by a strange experience to know Charles as his countrymen were, to their sorrow, to know him in coming years. He had learned that he was at the same time weak as water and obstinate as a mule. How was Philip to entrust his sister to such a man? Who was to guarantee that the moment the wedded pair landed in England the whole of the edifice of religious liberty, which was one day to become the edifice of religious supremacy for the Catholics, would not be overthrown with a shout of triumph?

Ch. XII.
1623.
August.
Olivares brings on the subject of the Palatinate.

Olivares was a liar of a very different stamp from Charles. He, at least, was perfectly aware whether his words were intended to be true or not, whilst Charles was, probably, perfectly unconscious of his prevarications. As far as the marriage went, the course was now straight before him. He had only to keep the English to the very hard bargain which he had driven, and to make use of the winter to drive an equally hard bargain for the Palatinate. Strange to say, however, the irresolution of Charles had at last beguiled him into the idea that the task of gaining his consent to his scheme for the pacification of Germany was a mere trifle in comparison. On the 12th of August, in the midst of all his difficulties with Charles, he calmly gave it as his opinion that it would be well to interest the Prince of Wales in the marriage of Frederick's son with the Emperor's daughter. As for James, he added, he would accept the scheme with gladness. It would relieve him from all further annoyance, and, after all, it was certain that he would rather see his grandchildren Catholic than Puritan. To Gondomar the future did not present itself in quite so rosy a light. The chief thing, he observed, was to contrive that the boy should be brought up as a Catholic. It would, therefore, be well to have him sent to Vienna before the Prince left the country; for, if Charles were once gone, it was probable that he would take arms against the Emperor and the King of Spain.*

Olivares proposes the marriage of Prince Frederick Henry with the Emperor's daughter.

Olivares did not know how completely Charles had set his heart upon his sister's restoration, and that since his arrival in Spain he had twice despatched a special messenger to assure her that she should not be forgotten.† Not long ago he had told the Prince, in his grand Spanish way, that his master was ready to place a blank sheet of paper in his hands, which he would be at liberty to fill up with what conditions he pleased about the Palatinate. He now recited the old scheme which had been originally sketched out by his uncle, of course taking care to say nothing about the boy's conversion. The Electoral

* Consulta of the Council of State, Aug. $\frac{12}{22}$. *Simancas MSS.* Est. 2404.
† Sir W. Croft and Sir George Goring.

Prince, he said, was to be educated at Vienna, and married to the Emperor's daughter. "But," replied Charles, "if the Emperor proves refractory, will the King your master assist us with arms to reduce him to reasonable terms?" "No," replied Olivares, in a moment of frankness, "we have a maxim of state, that the King of Spain must never fight against the Emperor. We cannot employ our forces against the House of Austria." "Look to it, sir," said the Prince, "for if you hold yourself to that, there is an end of all; for without this, you may not rely upon either marriage or friendship."* It was probably after this conversation had taken place, that the question was once more brought before the Council of State. By this time Olivares' faith in his powers of cajolery had been somewhat shaken, and he had fallen back upon his old position. "Even if the Emperor," he said, "were to give the King a blow in the face, and to call him a knave, it would be impossible for his Majesty to abandon him or to become his enemy. If he can preserve the friendship of the King of England as well as that of the Emperor, well and good. But if not, we ought to break with England, even if we had a hundred Infantas married there. Such conduct is necessary for the preservation of Christendom and the Catholic religion, and of the glorious House of Austria." The King, he went on to say, was much indebted to the Elector of Bavaria, and he must not take part against him. The proposed marriage between the Emperor's daughter and the Palatine's son, should not be left out of consideration. But it must be brought about by his Majesty's intercession. The boy must be educated as a Catholic, and either the Emperor or the Elector of Bavaria must have the administration of the Palatinate during his minority. It was impossible that the father should be restored. But he might have a certain portion of territory assigned to him. The number of Electors might be raised to nine, the Landgrave of Hesse Darmstadt being rewarded by this honour for his fidelity.

The question was then put to the vote, and the proposition of Olivares, counting his own voice, was

Ch. XII.
1623.
August.

* Buckingham's Relation. *Lords' Journals*, iii. 226.

approved by a majority of one, Gondomar voting in the minority.*

Nine months before, the Council of State had declared in opposition to Olivares in favour of a temporising policy, and had driven him to take refuge in a series of intrigues by which he had hoped first to get rid of the marriage altogether by the intervention of the Pope, and then to make the acceptance of his terms by Charles as difficult as possible. But in these intrigues he had been signally foiled. The Pope had refused to take upon himself the burden of withholding the dispensation, and Charles had been ready to promise anything that was asked of him. Very few months now remained before the time would come for the Infanta's marriage, and before that time came the affairs of the Palatinate must be arranged one way or the other. It is easy to say that the decision adopted by the Council of State produced the exhaustion and ultimate ruin of the Spanish monarchy. But this is only to say, in other words, that the Spanish ministers ought to have risen above the traditions of their creed and country. Frederick had for months refused to set his hand even to the preliminary suspension of arms, and he had only been induced to sign the treaty at last by the terrors of Tilly's victory at Stadtloo. It was therefore more than ever evident that no real peace was to be purchased in Germany on any reasonable terms, and the Spanish ministers, being what they were, naturally preferred oppressing Protestants in the name of their own creed, to standing by whilst Protestants were plundering Catholic lands, and annexing Catholic dioceses by force of arms.

It was by these considerations, no doubt, that in opposition to Gondomar's plea for further procrastination, the Spanish Council of State adopted the more decisive policy of Olivares. The question to which they now required an answer, was whether James and his son would consent to such a settlement as would please the Emperor; and, excepting upon grounds far higher than any of which a

---

* *Kherenhüller*, x. 95. There is some confusion about the dates; but I think that I am following the probabilities of the case in placing Olivares' declaration here.

Spaniard was likely to take cognizance, there can be little doubt that they were in the right.

The Prince was accordingly given to understand that he must not expect to have everything his own way in Germany. The King of Spain, he was told, would not engage to obtain for Frederick himself a restitution of the Electorate. But he might have the territory, and after Maximilian's death his son should have the title.

Charles was very sore. He had come to Spain with the idea that he would find the whole world at his feet. He had assured his sister that he would take care of her interests as his own, and now he was told that the decision rested in the hands of the Emperor, and that the Emperor would not admit his brother-in-law into the Electoral College. It was therefore not without the gravest dissatisfaction that, when talking over the proposal with Bristol, he found that, after making some reservations, the ambassador had much to say in its favour. He thought, he said, that his Majesty would not be averse to the boy's education at Vienna, if only the dignity as well as the land were at once restored, and if the young Prince "might be brought up in his own religion, and have such preceptors and such a family as his Majesty and his father should appoint, and they to have free exercise of their religion."* At this unexpected declaration, Aston, who happened to be present, was startled. "I dare not," he said, "give my consent, for fear of my head." "Without some such great action," answered Bristol, "the peace of Christendom will never be had."†

As is well known, these words were long afterwards raked up by Charles and Buckingham, and were made by them the subject of a grave charge against the ambassador. It is indeed impossible to acquit him entirely at least of an error in judgment. It was true, no doubt, as he afterwards explained, that the sons of Protestant princes‡ were at that very time being brought up at Vienna,

---

* Bristol's Answer to his Impeachment. *State Trials*, ii. 1411.
† Charles I. to Bristol, Jan. 20, 1626. Ninth Article of Bristol's Impeachment. *State Trials*, ii. 1278, 1286.
‡ The son of Christian of Anhalt, for instance.

Ch. XII.
1623.
August.

His policy with respect to the marriage.

without danger to their religion. But the stake to be played for in the present case was a far higher one, and with the religion of the whole of the two Palatinates depending on the issue, a skilful Jesuit, supported as he would be by the bright eyes of the young archduchess, would probably find little difficulty in eluding the vigilance of the prince's Protestant tutors. But, in spite of this, the spirit of Bristol's advice was undoubtedly right. No man who knew what human nature was, could fancy that without some serious guarantee for the future, the Emperor would ever again place power in the hands of the ally of Mansfeld and of Bethlen Gabor; and, however lightly Charles and Buckingham might talk about using compulsion, Bristol was justified in shrinking from a renewal of the conflict in which the great cause of Protestantism had been stained with greed and cruelty and with every anarchical passion.

In truth, it is impossible to do justice to this great statesman without recollecting that at every step he was liable to be controlled by others, who had not a tithe of his sagacity. It was against his recommendation that the Spanish match had originally been accepted by the King; but when once it had been accepted, he proceeded to carry out his instructions, and to manage the negotiations so that the greatest possible good might accrue to his country. Resisting any direct interference of Spain with the internal affairs of England, he was in favour of any alleviation of the bitter lot of the English Catholics, which might proceed from the spontaneous act of his own sovereign. It was in this spirit that, when he returned to Spain in 1622, he had attempted to carry on the negotiations entrusted to him. When, after the unexpected demands by the Pope, alterations were made in the treaty by which the King was bound to a special mode of dealing with his Catholic subjects, it was only upon Gondomar's assurance that he had often heard James express his willingness to consent to these conditions that the changes were even acknowledged by Bristol, as fit to send home for his master's approval. And after that approval was given, he then believed, and it is certain that he was right in so believing, that but for the

unlucky arrival of the Prince at Madrid, the affair would Ch. XII.
have been settled one way or another in the spring of 1623.
1623. Either the Pope and the King of Spain would August.
assent to the marriage on the conditions agreed to in the
preceding winter, or they would not. If they did, the
whole question was settled. If they did not, it would
have to be considered afresh with reference to any new
conditions that might be laid down. But his expectations had been baffled by the sudden arrival of the Prince.
New demands were made, which he evidently considered
to be exorbitant, but which he was powerless to resist.
Questions which would affect deeply the future welfare of
the English nation, were taken out of the hands of grave
diplomatists and statesmen to be settled in accordance
with the fleeting desires of a love-sick youth, and of an
ignorant, headstrong courtier. Charles himself behaved in
such a manner as to tempt the Spanish ministers to put
forward the most indefensible propositions. With the
acceptance of these propositions, Bristol had nothing whatever to do. Treated with studied rudeness by the insolent
Buckingham, he was shut out from any serious part in
the negotiations which ensued. But, like a man of honour
as he was, he held that a marriage treaty which had been
sworn to in the most solemn manner, was intended to
be kept. In his eyes, it was now too late for the Prince
to break off the marriage without the deepest discredit
to himself. That it might be for the interest of the
English people that its future sovereign should cover
himself with disgrace, was an idea which was hardly
likely to commend itself to his mind.

Straightforward as Bristol's conduct had been in rela- And with
tion to the marriage, it was equally straightforward in respect
relation to the Palatinate. Ever since the failure, through latinate.
James's fault, of his plan for imposing by the sword a
compromise upon the contending parties in Germany, he
had advocated a close understanding with the Spanish
Government, and had hoped that if his master at home
could succeed in bringing his son-in-law to reasonable
terms, it might be possible, partly by the fear of a ruinous
contest with England, partly by the wish to retain the
advantages which were offered by the proposed marriage,

D D 2

1623.
August.

to induce Philip to lend his assistance to the attempt to bring about a pacification in Germany upon some rational basis. Unhappily, such a policy had one irreparable fault. It was too much in advance of the times to meet with acceptance on either side. In spite of all that Bristol could say, in spite of the conviction of the advantages, and even of the necessity of peace, which was cherished by Philip's ministers, they would not cease to believe that it was possible by some petty diplomatic contrivance, to snatch a glorious victory for their Church; and, equally, in spite of all that might be urged in favour of concession, Frederick and his confederates would never cease to sow discord in the Empire and to forward that reign of plunderers and bandits, which some of them at least imagined in all sincerity to be the highest achievement of patriotism.

His policy compared with that of Charles and Buckingham.

But however impractical Bristol's ideas had by this time become, they were the highest wisdom when contrasted with those passing fancies which floated in the brains of Charles and Buckingham. To Bristol the question of the restitution of the Palatinate was one to be entertained on its own merits. It depended partly on the nature of the concessions which Frederick was willing to make, partly on the state of public feeling in Germany, and it was therefore impossible to make the settlement of an intricate European problem a condition of the marriage treaty. And yet this was precisely what Charles, if his words meant anything, was prepared to do. What he expected was that Frederick should be replaced in his old position, without the slightest reference to the interests of the Empire, on the mere ground of his happening to be the brother-in-law of the Prince of Wales. It was with this expectation that he had come to Madrid, and he felt that it would be an insult to himself if, when the time came for his departure, the question were still unsettled.

Olivares produces the King's letter.

Carried about by every breath of feeling as Charles was, and unable, like a true son of his father, to grasp anything beyond the purely personal side of a policy, he was at least in the right in thoroughly distrusting Olivares. The Spaniard, adept at falsehood as he was, had been too early in life a favourite of fortune to make a good hypocrite. After weeks of flattery and dissimulation, he would overthrow, in some moment of confidence or of passion, the edifice of deceit which he had raised so painfully. At an interview with the Prince and Buckingham, he cried out that it must certainly be a match now, for the devil himself could not break it. "I think so too," said Buckingham, ironically. "It had need to be firm and strong, for it has been seven years in soldering." "Nay," replied Olivares, forgetting all that was implied by his words, "it has not really been intended these seven months." To this Buckingham answered, that in that case the settlement was plainly the result of his negotiations, and he must therefore have the credit of it. Stung by the tone in which the words were uttered, Olivares walked to his desk and produced not only his own written opinion against the marriage which had been placed by Bristol in Charles's hands some months before, but even the short letter in which Philip himself had ordered him to break off the match; and that neither the late King nor Zuñiga had ever really intended to allow the marriage to take place.

Well may Aston, when he heard of this letter, have held up his hands in astonishment, remembering as he did the assurances which he had so often received from Philip's own lips. The importance of the revelation it is impossible to estimate too highly. It could no longer be held, as Bristol had supposed, that the plan for throwing off the Prince of Wales had originated either in Olivares' newness to business or in a passing fancy of the Infanta's. Philip himself stood convicted as having taken part in the long deceit.

Of this letter Charles was not allowed to take away a copy. But, with Aston's assistance, he carried with him the meaning of the words in English, and wrote them down as soon as he had left the room.*

---

* Buckingham's Relation. *Lords' Journals*, iii. 226. A difficulty arises as to the date of this extraordinary revelation. Hacket apparently places it in July (p. 146). But he is no authority whatever in details. A more serious question arises as to the probability of its having been made during the conversations in May which have been narrated at p. 345. But if so, it would surely have been mentioned in Bristol's letter of Aug. 18, which is there quoted, unless Charles concealed it from him. This, however, is very unlikely, as he seems at that time to have spoken freely with him.

Yet, in spite of all that had now occurred, Charles could scarcely make up his mind. Almost at the last moment, Bristol wagered with him a ring worth 1,000*l*., that he would spend his Christmas at Madrid.* It is possible, that, but for one circumstance, he might still have resolved to disregard his father's commands. But the new Pope, Urban VIII., had fallen ill almost immediately after his election, and till he was able to send the necessary powers by which the Nuncio would be authorised to hand over the dispensation to Philip, the marriage could not take place. Whilst Charles was thus kept in inaction, he asked leave of Philip to present to his future bride a magnificent chain of pearls, a pair of diamond earrings, and another single diamond of priceless value. The King took them from him, showed them to his sister, and returned him word that he would keep them safely for her till after the marriage. Annoyed at the fresh rebuff, he once more announced his positive intention of returning; yet those who watched him closely doubted whether he would not have lingered on, if Philip, who was by this time thoroughly tired of his guest, had not taken him at his word, and assured him that his presence with his father would be the best means of facilitating those arrangements which were the necessary conditions of the Infanta's journey in the spring.†

It was now therefore arranged that the Prince, being unable to wait any longer for tidings from Rome, should make out a proxy in the names of the King of Spain and his brother the Infant Charles, and that this proxy should be lodged in Bristol's hands. Before he went, he was himself to swear solemnly to the marriage contract which he had signed on the 4th of August.

If Charles had possessed one spark of that heroical

Again, there is this to be said in favour of placing it, as I have done, where it is placed by Buckingham, that if it came just before the Prince's departure, it supplies an explanation for the sudden question raised about the Infanta going into a nunnery, of which nothing had been heard for months, but which would have been brought freshly before his mind by the reading of these papers.

* Buckingham's Relation. *Lords' Journals*, iii.

† Corner to the Doge, Sept. $\frac{10}{20}$. *Venice MSS.* Desp. Spagna.

virtue for which he allowed himself to take credit a few months later, he would surely have paused here. For many months he had known that the Spaniards were not dealing fairly by him. He had now learned that whatever might have been said when they were hard pressed, they had not the slightest intention of assisting his brother-in-law to recover the Palatinate by force of arms. That he was thoroughly dissatisfied with the discovery, there can be no doubt whatever.* Still less can there be any doubt that it was his plain duty to make up his mind before he took the oath, whether or no he meant to demand a promise of armed assistance as a condition of his marriage. But in Charles's mind such considerations found no place. On the 28th he took the solemn oath binding himself to the marriage, and engaged to leave his proxy behind to be used within ten days after the arrival from Rome of the Pope's consent.†

margin: Ch. XII. 1623. Aug. 28. Charles takes the oath to the marriage contract.

The next day Charles went to take his leave of the Queen, in whose presence he saw the Infanta for the last time. With his parting words he assured her that he had taken the Catholics of England under his protection, and that they should never again suffer persecution. The rest of the day was spent in giving and receiving presents, and on the following morning he started for the Escurial, accompanied by Philip and his brothers.

margin: Aug. 29. Takes leave of the Infanta. Aug. 30. And leaves Madrid.

It is probable that in expressing his wish that Charles should go home to see the marriage treaty carried out, Philip was giving vent to his real wishes: but whatever may have been his exact feelings about Charles, there can be no doubt whatever as to the disgust with which he regarded Buckingham. His insolence was every day becoming more and more unbearable. Strange words were now heard from the lips of the polite and courteous Spaniards. "We would rather," said one of them, speaking of Buckingham to Bristol, "put the Infanta headlong into a well, than into his hands." Bristol was in great distress. Ever since he had had the misfortune

margin: Arrogance of Buckingham.

---

* In a letter written about the end of September to Aston (S. P. Spain), Buckingham reminded Aston that the Prince had expressed himself to this effect before leaving Madrid.
† Francisco de Jesus, 54. Spanish Narrative in Nichols' Progresses, iii. 907.

CH. XII.
1623.

Aug. 29.
Bristol
informs
the King
of it.

to differ from the favourite he had, as he said, been treated worse than a dog; but he had never allowed his resentment to get the better of him, and had, if possible, been more respectful than before.* But he now saw that it was time to speak out. "I must here," he wrote to his master, "like a faithful and much obliged servant unto your Majesty, presume to deal freely and clearly with you, that if your Majesty's great and high wisdom find not means to compound and accommodate what is now out of order,—although I conceive it not to be doubted that the match will, in the end, proceed,—yet your Majesty will find yourself frustrated of those effects of amity and friendship which by this alliance you expected. For the truth is, that this King and his ministers are grown to have so high a dislike against my lord Duke of Buckingham, and, on the one side to judge him to have so much power with your Majesty and the Prince, and, on the other side, to be so ill affected to them and their affairs, that if your Majesty shall not be pleased in your wisdom either to find some means of reconciliation, or else to let them see and be assured that it shall no way be in my lord Duke of Buckingham's power to make the Infanta's life less happy unto her, or any way to cross and embroil the affairs betwixt your Majesties and your kingdoms, I am afraid your Majesty will see the effects which you have just cause to expect from this alliance to follow but slowly, and all the great businesses now in treaty prosper but ill. For I must, for the discharge of my conscience and duty, without descending to particulars, let your Majesty truly know that suspicions and distastes betwixt them all here and my Lord of Buckingham cannot be at a greater height."†

It is certain that no other man amongst the ministers of the Crown would have been bold enough to write such a letter.

Two whole days were spent by Charles at the Escurial, and, according to one account, he did not omit to plead once more for the Palatinate, and received in return

* Bristol to the King, Aug. 20. *Cabala*, 95.
† Bristol to the King, Aug. 29. *Hardwicke S. P.* i. 476.

an assurance from Philip that he would leave no means untried to obtain its cession from the Emperor in order that he might bestow it upon the Prince as a marriage gift.* When, on the 2nd of September, the moment of parting came, nothing could exceed the effusion of cordiality between the two young men. Philip pressed Charles to allow him to attend him to the coast, and Charles in refusing the offer pointed to the effect which the journey might have upon the Queen, who was daily expecting her delivery. At last the moment for separation came. The King and the Prince enjoyed one last hunt together, and after a repast which had been prepared for them under the shadow of a wood, they took an apparently affectionate farewell of one another, by the side of a pillar which had been raised to commemorate the event.†

Ch. XII. 1623. Sept. 2. Charles leaves the Escurial.

Buckingham had not been present at this last interview. Fierce words had passed that morning between him and Olivares. He was going away, he said, under the greatest obligations to his Majesty. As to himself, he had come with the hope of making him a friend; but he had found it impossible to carry out his intention, as he had discovered the bad offices he had done him both with the King of Spain and with his own master. He hoped however, that in spite of this he would hasten on the conclusion of the marriage with all his power. To this petulant outbreak Olivares replied with offended dignity. The marriage, he said, was for the good of the Catholic religion. As for the friendship which he had lost, he looked upon it as of no importance. It was enough for him that he had always acted as a gentleman, and as a man of honour.

Buckingham insults Olivares.

The loud tone in which these words were spoken attracted the attention of the bystanders, and the King called Olivares away to put an end to this unseemly altercation.‡ Soon afterwards Buckingham rode away on horseback, in spite of all remonstrances against the imprudence of exposing himself to the heat, leaving the

* Hacket, 163.
† Narrative in Nichols' *Progresses*, iii. 907.
‡ Corner to the Doge, Sept. $\frac{10}{20}$. *Venice MSS.* Desp. Spagna.

Prince to follow in the coach which had been provided for him.*

The Prince's journey. The Prince's journey resembled a Royal progress. The President of the Council of the Indies, with three members of the Council of State, accompanied him to do him honour, and a large retinue of officials had been sent to make the way easy for him and to see that he wanted nothing. After their return they were loud in praise of his courtesy and liberality.† Only once did he betray the sentiments which were lurking beneath the smooth surface of his speech. Cardinal Zapata had asked him whether he wished the carriage to be open, "I should not dare," he replied, "to give my assent without sending first to Madrid to consult the Junta of Theologians."‡

In truth Charles's feelings towards the Infanta were rapidly undergoing a change. At the best, his love for her had been largely compounded of vanity, and it was a sore blow to him after giving way to every exorbitant demand till he had all but crawled in the dust at Philip's feet, to be sent back to England without the bride whom he had sacrificed every honourable consideration to win. If he had expressed himself openly in indignant remonstrance, no one would have thought the worse of him. Even if he had simply restrained his impatience, and had confined himself to unmeaning compliments till he was safely out of Spain, wise men might have shaken their hands at a prudence which did not promise well for the future of so young a man; but nothing more would have been said. As it was, he did that which forces us to regard Buckingham, petulant and arrogant as he was, as a model of virtue by his side.

His doubt about the Infanta. It seems that the reference to the possibility of the Infanta's taking refuge in a nunnery from dislike of the marriage, which was contained in the papers produced by Olivares a few days before, had sunk deeply into his mind, and that he now fancied it possible that she would be allowed thus to dispose of herself even after the marriage.

* Francisco de Jesus. *Add. MSS.* 14,043, fol. 238.
† Bristol to Calvert, Oct. 24. *Hardwicke State Papers,* i. 473.
‡ Corner to the Doge, Oct. $\frac{6}{16}$. *Venice MSS.* Desp. Spagna.

With this thought he was undoubtedly justified in asking for an explanation; but to speak out where he felt doubts was not in his nature. It is true that he said something on the subject to Bristol before he left the Escurial, but he took no further action in the matter at the time. On the 3rd, the day after he had parted from Philip, he reached Segovia, where he found a friendly letter from the King. He at once sat down to answer it. "I have," he wrote, after expressing his regret for the necessity which compelled him to leave Spain, "a firm and constant resolution to accomplish all that my father and I have treated of and agreed with your Majesty; and, moreover, to do everything else that may be necessary as far as possible to draw tightly the bonds of brotherhood and sincere amity with your Majesty. Even if all the world conjoined were to oppose itself, and seek to trouble our friendship, it would have no effect upon my father or myself; but we would rather declare those who attempted it to be our enemies."*

Ch. XII. 1623.

Sept. 3. His letters to Philip from Segovia.

Within a few hours† after this letter was written, Edward Clarke, a confidential servant of Buckingham's, started for Madrid with another of widely different import. "Bristol," wrote Charles, "you may remember that a little before I came from St. Lorenzo,‡ I spake to you concerning a fear I had that the Infanta might be forced to go into a monastery after she is betrothed; which you know she may do with a dispensation. Though at that time I was loath to press it, because I thought it fit, at the time of my parting, to eschew distastes or disputes as much as I could; yet, since, considering that, if I should be betrothed before that doubt be removed, and that upon illgrounded suspicions, or any other cause whatsoever, they should take this way to break the marriage, the King my father, and all the world might justly condemn me for a rash-headed fool, not to foresee and prevent this in time; wherefore I thought it necessary by this letter to command you not to deliver my proxy to the King of

His letter to Bristol asking whether the Infanta will go into a nunnery.

---

* The Prince to Philip IV., Sept. 3. *S. P. Spain.*
† It was written from Segovia. Francisco de Jesus, 87.
‡ The Escurial.

Ch. XII.
1623.
Sept. 3.

Spain, until I may have sufficient security, both from him and the Infanta, that, after I am betrothed, a monastery may not rob me of my wife; and after ye have gotten this security send with all possible speed to me, that, if I find it sufficient, as I hope I shall, I may send you order, by the delivery of my proxy, to despatch the marriage."*

Clarke ordered not to deliver it at once.

The worst is yet to come. Clarke was ordered to inform the ambassador that he had been sent back to Madrid on Buckingham's private business, whilst he kept the precious document in his pocket till the arrival of the Pope's approbation. He was then to hand it to Bristol, when, as the date had been intentionally omitted, he would be able to represent it as having only just come to hand. The meaning of this manœuvre is unfortunately but too easy to understand. Bristol would be compelled to postpone the betrothal for more than three weeks, whilst he was communicating with Charles in England, although the Prince had solemnly consented to the arrangement by which the ceremony was to be performed ten days after the arrival of the news from Rome. It would seem, therefore, that the scheme was one carefully prepared by Charles in order to take revenge for the slights which he had received, by the outrageous device of rendering the redemption of his own promise impossible; if, indeed, the explanation is not rather to be sought in his burning desire to throw off his engagements, without the slightest consideration for the nature of the method by which he proposed to gain his object.†

The Prince continues his journey.

Unconscious of the disgrace which he was bringing upon himself in the eyes of all honourable men, Charles pursued his way to Santander, taking care every day to indite a few words of greeting to the Sovereign who little dreamed of the insult which had been so elaborately prepared for him. As he drew near the coast his anxiety increased to know whether the fleet, which had been long detained by contrary winds in the English channel,

* The Prince to Bristol, Sept. 3 (?). *S. P. Spain*. The original is amongst the *Sherborne MSS*.
† Francisco de Jesus says that the letter was to be kept back till one or two days before the marriage; but from Clarke's own letter to Buckingham (*Cabala*, 199), there can be little doubt that his orders were as I have given them.

had yet arrived to bear him away from the now detested soil of Spain. Early in the morning of the 12th, when he was about six leagues from Santander, he was met by Sir John Finett, and Sir Thomas Somerset, who had been riding all night to greet him with the welcome tidings. The news, he afterwards assured Finett, made him look upon him "as one that had the face of an angel."* As the train entered Santander, the bells were rung, and the cannon of the fort were fired, in honour of the Prince's coming; but his heart was in the fleet which bore the English flag. Late as it was in the afternoon, he put off to Rutland's ship, the Prince, which was appointed to have carried him home, and which had been fitted up with a gorgeously decorated cabin for the Infanta. As he was returning in his barge, after nightfall, the wind rose, and the rowers found it impossible to make head against the tide, which was sweeping them out to sea. Fortunately, Sir Sackville Trevor, in the Defiance, was aware of the danger, and threw out ropes attached to buoys with lanterns, which might attract the notice of the Prince amidst the increasing gloom. One of these ropes was seized by the crew, and Charles, saved from imminent danger, passed the night on board the Defiance.

For some days the fleet remained wind-bound at Santander. Between Charles and his Spanish train, the utmost cordiality appeared to prevail. There were festivities in the town, and festivities on board. At last, on the 18th, the wind changed. Orders were given to weigh anchor, and this strange episode of the Spanish journey was at an end.†

No doubt, as he was tossing upon the waves of the Bay of Biscay, Charles did not cease to brood over the prospects of his scheme for springing a mine under Philip's feet. Happily, however, for his own reputation, his deep-laid plot had already been disconcerted by a lucky accident. Almost immediately after he reached Madrid, Clarke was taken ill, and was thus unable to

Ch. XII. *1623.* *Sep. 12.* His embarkation.

Sept. 18. He sails for England.

Sept. 11. Clarke gives Bristol the Prince's letter.

* Finetti *Philoxenis*, 120.
† Pett's Autobiography. *Harl. MSS.* 6279, fol. 86. Compare Nichols' *Progresses*, iii. 920.

glean the news of the day by his own personal observation. About a week after he appeared at the Embassy, Bristol, either suspecting that he had been entrusted with a secret mission, or being himself under some misapprehension, told him that the Pope's approbation had arrived. Clarke, supposing that the time indicated had now come, produced the letter as one which he had just received. Bristol looked very grave when he had read it, and charged him not to breathe a word about it to any one. " If the Spaniards," he said, " should come to the knowledge of it, they might give orders to stay the Prince."*

He promises to make inquiries.

Bristol at once despatched a courier to England, acknowledging the receipt of the letter, and assuring Charles that as soon as he heard that he was out of Spain, he would make every inquiry on the subject which he had named.†

Sept. 21. The result communicated to Charles.

Ten days afterwards he communicated to Charles the result of his investigations. "Since your Highness's departure," he wrote, "there have been divers suspicions raised, which chiefly have grown from letters of some that accompanied your Highness to Santander, as though there might a doubt be made of your Highness's affection to the Infanta, and of the real performance on your Highness's part of what had been capitulated; which some of your Highness's old friends about the Infanta have taken several occasions to intimate unto her; but, I dare assure your Highness, it hath not been possible for any to raise in her the least shadow of mistrust or doubt of want of your Highness's affection, but she hath with show of dis-

---

* Clarke to Buckingham. Oct. 1. *Cabala*, 199. Clarke says this took place on the day that the Prince arrived at Santander, *i.e.* the 12th. But Bristol's letter shows that it must have been on the 11th.

† " This day Mr. Clarke, that lyeth sick in my house, delivered me a letter from you; but without date either of time or place. The contents of it your Highness will remember, and I will see as faithfully performed as God willing all your commandments to me shall be; though, for just respects, I shall forbear the clearing of that doubt your Highness maketh for some few days, until I heare of Lewis Dyve." Bristol to the Prince, Sept. 11. *S. P. Spain*. The allusion is obscure, but it is explained by a passage in the letter of the 21st, which is quoted in the text further on. Lewis Dyve was no doubt attached to the embassy, and may very well have been sent to accompany the Prince to Santander. Bristol may well have shrunk from saying plainly that he could not do anything till Charles had left Spain, as it would convey an indirect censure on the letter which he had received.

pleasure reproved those that have presumed to speak that kind of language; and herself never speaketh of your Highness but with that respect and show of affection that all about her tell me of it with a little wonder.

"There was of late in some a desire here that, before your Highness's embarking, the Princess might have sent unto your Highness some token; whereunto I assure your Highness that the Countess of Olivares was not backward; nor, as I am assured, the Princess herself; but this was not to be done without the allowance of the Junta;* and they, for a main reason, alleged that, in case your Highness should fail in what had been agreed, she would by these further engagements be made unfit for any other match; which coming to her knowledge, I hear she was infinitely much offended, and said that those of the Junta were blockheads.† to think her a woman for a second wooing, or to receive a congratulation twice for several husbands. The truth is that, now in your Highness's absence, she much more avowedly declareth her affection to your Highness than ever she did at your being here; and your Highness can not believe how much the King and she and all the Court are taken with your Highness's daily letters to the King and her.

"Since I understood of your Highness's embarking, I have begun to speak of the doubt which your Highness seemeth to make, that the Infanta might enter into religion after the marriage. The Countess of Olivares broke it unto the Infanta, who seemed to make herself very merry that any such doubt should be made, and said that she must confess that she never in all her life had any mind to be a nun, and thought she should hardly be one now only to avoid the Prince of Wales, to whom she had such infinite obligation. After this, I replied that your Highness no way doubted of the favour that the Infanta did you; but she might be forced to that which others would have her; for that you said there was

---

* Not the Junta of Theologians, which was now dissolved, but the Junta of Councillors of State and others, who were appointed to treat on all things connected with the marriage.

† "Maxaderos" in the original.

nothing done but either what the Theologians or the Junta ordained. Hereupon it was answered me, after conference with the Princess, that, after the marriage the Princess would be her own woman, and that the King neither would, nor the Junta should, have to do with her in things of that nature; but that she doubted not but, when it were fitting for her to write unto the Prince herself, she would both quickly clear that doubt, and any other that should be made, of her affection to the Prince of Wales. And the truth is that I never speak of this marriage but the Countess of Olivares falleth a laughing extremely, and telleth me that the Princess doth so too. And, to tell your Highness my opinion, like an honest servant, if this doubt should be insisted upon, I conceive there will at the instant be such satisfaction given, as to stand upon it would rather seem a colour or pretext sought than otherwise; and therefore, once again, I humbly crave your Highness's speedy direction herein.

"I shall conclude this letter by telling your Highness that commonly once a day I wait upon the Princess on the Queen's side.* I receive from her most gracious usage, and ever affectionate and sometimes long messages.† I pray God send your Highness as happy in everything else as you are like to be in a wife; for certainly a worthier or more virtuous Princess liveth not."‡

It is true that for his knowledge of the Infanta's secret feelings, the ambassador was altogether dependent upon the reports which it pleased the Countess of Olivares to put in circulation. But there is no reason to doubt that the statements in his letter were at least in the main correct. Whether any trace of her original repugnance to Charles still lurked in her mind it is impossible to say; but it is certain that she now regarded the marriage as a settled thing, and it is by no means impossible that, as Bristol suggested, Charles's absence may have fanned into life the sparks of affection which the daily sight of her hoped-for convert had kindled into a flame within her bosom. She was now officially styled Princess of England, and she was

---

* The Queen's side of the palace.
† "Recandos" in the original.
‡ Bristol to the Prince, Sept. 21. *Clarendon State Papers,* i. App. 19.

diligently occupied in studying the language of her future country. Nor was it merely by the help of dictionaries and grammars that she was preparing herself for her new position. For she was now, by her brother's command, receiving instructions from the Bishop of Segovia, and from two of the royal preachers, by which, as it was hoped, she would be prepared to fulfil those duties of her married life, of which such great expectations had been formed.*

<small>CH. XII.
1623.
Sept.</small>

Yet already doubts were beginning to be entertained at Madrid whether, after all, those expectations would be realised. Led on step by step by Charles's supine indifference to dishonour, Olivares had committed the blunder of forgetting the large part which vanity had in his professions of love for the Infanta. He had calculated that because Charles was ready to do anything, and to swear to anything, in order to carry with him his promised bride, he would therefore be equally ready to redeem his engagements in the hope of obtaining her in the spring. Having omitted in his calculations the consequences of offended pride, he was now to learn that Charles, who would have accepted all his terms in order to obtain the credit of success, would be equally ready to shake off the most binding engagements in the vain hope of wiping away the disgrace of failure.

<small>Doubts of the Spanish Ministers.</small>

In one respect, at least, the Spanish minister appears to have resolved to bend before the coming storm. From the moment that Charles began to show any spirit of independence, nothing more was heard about the Parliamentary repeal of the penal laws, which had been so marked a feature in the previous discussions. It almost seems as if Olivares would have been content to allow that point to drop out of sight, in spite of the long and arduous struggle which it had cost him.

<small>Intentions of Olivares.</small>

For even before Charles arrived in England, the news forwarded by the Spanish Ambassadors must have created some doubt in the mind of Olivares whether even the ground which had been gained by the agreement of Salisbury was not slipping from under his feet. For three weeks after the signature of that agreement the form in which the promises then made were to be clothed

<small>August. The pardon and dispensation.</small>

---

* Francisco de Jesus, 88.

VOL. II. E E

in legal phraseology had been the subject of warm discussion; and, though there does not appear to have been any intention to raise delays, the length of time thus occupied brought forth grievous complaints from the Spanish ambassadors, and especially from the hot-tempered Inojosa.* At last, on the 28th of August, Conway was able to inform the Lord Keeper that the pardon and dispensation had been signed by the King, and at the same time he directed him to prepare a warrant for the liberation of the imprisoned priests, and to write a letter to the Judges and magistrates, desiring them to take note of the pardon which had been granted, and to allow it to be pleaded in court.†

The instructions thus conveyed by Conway were themselves a concession to Williams. The ambassadors had been asking for something very different—for a direct command restraining the Judges from allowing the institution of proceedings against the Catholics. To this the Lord Keeper, not without reason, objected. It was customary, he urged, to grant dispensations from penalties incurred by the breach of the laws, and such dispensations would render any judicial sentence inoperative. He was, therefore, willing to write to the Judges, informing them that the dispensation had been granted, and directing them to take note of the fact whenever it was pleaded in arrest of judgment. But it was utterly contrary to reason and precedent to forbid the Judges and the Justices of the Peace to execute that law which they were sworn to administer. Such a proceeding, he justly declared, would provoke a storm of reprobation from one end of England to the other.

Through the efforts of Williams, the ambassadors were induced to postpone their demands. It was agreed that the question should not be mooted again till the Infanta had been six months in England.‡

---

* The correspondence on both sides is amongst the State Papers, but has unfortunately been divided without any sufficient motive. Some of the letters will be found in the Domestic Series, others in the Spanish.
† Conway to Williams, Calvert and Weston, Aug. 28. *S. P. Dom.* cli. 77. Conway to Gage, Aug. 29. *S. P. Spain.*
‡ Williams to Buckingham, Aug. 30. Printed with a wrong date in *Cabala*, 272.

If Williams had stopped here he would have done nothing more than his duty as a guardian of constitutional right. But it soon became evident that he had something more than the mere exercise of his duty in his mind. Knowing, as he did, that the Prince would in all probability soon be home from Spain, he turned all the resources of his brain to the one object of postponing the settlement of any single question by which the Recusants were affected till Charles was once again in England. Shrewd enough to foresee that the Prince would probably come back in a high state of discontent, the Lord Keeper was already trimming his sails to suit the changing breeze; but in this, as in most other human actions, there was, no doubt, a mixture of motives at work. The last concessions to the Catholics had been wrung out of the King by the fear that a refusal would be visited upon his son. Would James not therefore, Williams may have thought, be justified in replacing himself in the position which he would have occupied if the Prince had remained quietly in England? To do this, indeed, would cost some amount of manœuvring, from which an honourable man would have shrunk. But the Episcopal Lord Keeper was ready to take all this upon his own shoulders, and it is probable that the game which he proposed to play was all the more enjoyable to him because it involved a trial of skill which was not restrained within the limits of truthfulness and honesty.

Thus far, at least, Williams had the clear support of the King. James was really desirous of fulfilling his promises, but he wished first to make sure that the King of Spain was in earnest too. The instrument containing the pardon and dispensation was therefore ordered to be got ready on the distinct understanding that it was not to be published or in any way made use of until the return of the Prince, or the arrival of satisfactory tidings from Spain. An exemplification of it was, however, to be made under the great seal for the purpose of being placed in Inojosa's hands, though he was strictly charged to keep his possession of it a profound secret.* A day

Ch. XII.
1623.
Aug.
Manœuvres of Williams.

The publication of the pardon delayed.

* Conway to Williams, Calvert, and Weston, Sept. 1. Conway to Gage, Sept. 1. Conway to Calvert, Sept. 4. *S. P. Dom.* Conway's Letter Book,

CH. XII.
1623.
August.

Preston's pardon.

Delays of Williams.

or two afterwards he was told that this restriction would be taken off, and the Catholics would be allowed to benefit by the pardon as soon as it was known that the marriage ceremony had taken place at Madrid.*

Great as must have been the annoyance felt by Inojosa at the delay, it was as nothing to his disgust at what followed. It happened that a certain Preston was one of the very few Roman Catholic priests who had taken the King's side in the controversy on the oath of allegiance. He was in consequence excessively unpopular amongst the members of his own Church, and was living under the constant fear of punishment by his ecclesiastical superiors for the courageous firmness with which he had maintained his opinions in the face of the worst of oppositions, the opposition of those who had once been his intimate friends. He had now for some time been imprisoned in the Marshalsea with his own consent, in order that if he were summoned to Rome to give an account of his actions, he might be able to plead the bar of physical impossibility.

This was the man, of all others, who was selected by James and Williams to be named in the first pardon, a copy of which was to be placed in Inojosa's hands. Care was taken at the same time that he should not be sent away from England without the King's permission.†

A day or two after Williams received orders to get this pardon ready, news arrived that the Prince had left Madrid. From that moment the Lord Keeper set himself resolutely to evade, and even to disobey, the orders which he received from his Sovereign. Again and again Inojosa complained that no copy of the pardon had been given to him, and that the promises which he had received in the King's name had not been fulfilled. Again and again James sent messages to assure him that he had given distinct orders, and that it was not his fault if they had not been carried out.‡ Williams, when-

---

81, 82. Calvert to Conway, Sept. 2. *S. P. Dom.* clii. 4. Conway to Calvert, Aug. 31. Conway to Inojosa, Sept. 4. *S. P. Spain.*
* Conway to Inojosa, Sept. 6. *S. P. Spain.*
† Conway to Williams, Sept. 6. Warrant, Sept. 8. *Hacket*, 158.
‡ Calvert to Conway, Sept. 12. *S. P. Dom.* clii. 36. Conway to Calvert.

ever he was applied to, answered unblushingly that it was impossible to get ready such a multitude of instruments in so short a time. At last, however, James, who did not like to see his orders disobeyed, sent peremptory commands to the Lord Keeper to do as he had been told. Williams, thus thrown back upon himself, acknowledged that there had not been a word of truth in the excuses which he had made, and pleaded the danger of incurring opposition in a future Parliament by too great readiness to give way in matters of religion. Such underhand proceedings were not to the taste of James. All this, he said, would have been good counsel if no promises had been passed. As it was, "the truth of a King must be preferred before all other circumstances," and within three days the ambassadors must be satisfied.* Thus pressed, Williams replied that he was ready to obey orders. The copy of the pardon was given to Inojosa, and the letter directing the Judges to admit its validity was to follow as soon as possible.†

<small>Ch. XII.
1623.
Sept.</small>

At last, on the 5th of October, the Prince landed at Portsmouth. Hurrying up to London, he reached York House a little after daybreak on the following morning. Already the news of his arrival had spread like wildfire. That he had come without the dreaded Infanta by his side was sufficient to awaken the long-suppressed loyalty of the English people. They saw in it a pledge that the prolonged rule of Spanish ministers and of Spanish counsels was coming to an end. At last, they believed, the Prince had burst the bonds which had been woven around him by designing men, and had come back free to withstand the insidious aggressions of Popery. When Charles landed from the barge in which he crossed the Thames, he found that the news of his coming had preceded him. The bells rang out their merriest peals on

<small>Oct. 5.
Arrival of the Prince.</small>

<small>Rejoicings in London.</small>

<small>Sept. 12. Inojosa to Conway, Sept. 15. Conway to Inojosa, Sept. 16. S. P. Spain. Conway to Williams, Sept. 17. Hacket, 158.
* Conway to Williams, Oct. 18, Oct. 19. Hacket, 159. Williams to Conway, Oct. 18. S. P. Dom. clii. 46.
† Hacket (i. 159), states that everything was put off till the return of the Prince; but he himself admits that the order for the letter had been given; and Salvetti, in his News-Letter of the 24th of October, distinctly states that the pardon was in the ambassador's hands.</small>

every side. The streets were thronged with happy faces. But he did not care to linger in London. After receiving complimentary visits from the Privy Councillors, he rejected an ill-timed demand that he would give audience to the Spanish Ambassadors, and ordered a coach to be got ready that he might join his father at Royston with all possible speed. As he drove out into the Strand, it was with the utmost difficulty that he could make his way through the enthusiastic crowd. "Long live the Prince of Wales," was heard on every side, from voices whose notes were mingled in one universal roar of gladness. When he was gone, men felt that it was impossible to settle down to their usual avocations. Wealthy citizens brought out tables laden with food and wine, and placed them in the streets. Prisoners confined for debt were set at liberty by the contributions of persons whose names were utterly unknown to them. A cartload of felons wending its melancholy way to Tyburn, and happening to cross the Prince's path, was turned back, and the condemned men were astonished by an unexpected release from death. When the evening closed in, lighted candles were placed in every window, and the sky was reddened with bonfires. One hundred and eight blazing piles were counted in the short distance between St. Paul's and London Bridge. Carts laden with wood were stopped by the populace, and as soon as the horse had been taken out, a light was applied to the load as it stood. Never before, according to the general testimony of all who have left a narrative of the scenes which passed before their eyes, had rejoicing so universal and so spontaneous been known in England.*

Charles at Royston. With the shouts of welcome, which had been so ill-deserved, still ringing in his ears, Charles hastened to meet his father. After the first warm greetings were over, the King took his son and his favourite with him, and closed the doors of the room. The courtiers without listened long to the outbursts of merriment or of indignation which expressed the varying feelings of the

---

* Nichols, iii. 935. Valaresso to the Doge, Oct $\frac{10}{20}$. *Venice MSS.* Desp. Ingh. Salvetti's *News-Letter*, Oct. $\frac{10}{20}$.

speakers, in the vain hope of catching some indication of the turn which the conversation was taking. At last the doors were thrown open, and the King came forth to supper. Once more all ears were on the alert, and it was not long before the listeners were rejoiced by the sound of words to which they had been long unused from Royal lips. James, it seemed, after all, was not displeased at the delay of the marriage, as long as he had no better satisfaction about the Palatinate. "I like not," he said, "to marry my son with a portion of my daughter's tears."*

Yet, if Buckingham's vehement denunciations of Spanish perfidy had shaken James from the calm and self-satisfied repose in which he had long been slumbering, they were not of a nature to open his eyes to the true position of affairs. Still, as before, the restitution of the Palatinate was a mere trifle, which the King of Spain could not courteously refuse to a friendly sovereign. For James, all the physical and moral difficulties which stood in the way had no existence whatever. If Philip did not comply with his wishes at once, it was simply because he had made up his mind to insult him.

Out of this miserable blindness nothing which he now heard was likely to deliver him; for both Charles and Buckingham believed, as firmly as he did, that Philip could do anything he would in Germany. The only point on which they differed was, whether he was willing to do it or not.

The doubts of Spanish sincerity, to which James was now compelled to listen, must have been the more distressing to him, as he had just given his sanction to a plan for the settlement of Germany, which was, as he fondly hoped, to free Europe from war, and himself from all further trouble. On the 2nd of October, three days before the Prince's return to England, the Spanish Ambassadors had a long interview with Calvert in London. The scheme which they proposed was couched in the very form which had been suggested by Bristol in Spain. It would be well, they said, if the King would write to his son-in-law to recommend the marriage of the young

---

* *Hacket*, 165.

Prince with the Emperor's daughter. If, as was probable, the Emperor wished to have the education of the boy, he might be gratified on condition that his governor was appointed by his father, and that neither he nor any of his household were to be "forced in point of their conscience." To an inquiry from Calvert whether the King of Spain would, under these circumstances, give assurance of the "full restitution of the inheritances and dignities," the Ambassadors replied evasively that "it was a needless thing to take it into thought." If the marriage took place, there could be no doubt that the Emperor "would restore all."*

It is difficult to regard this concession of a guarantee for the religion of the Prince as seriously made. It is just possible that Olivares may have been frightened by the feelings which the Prince had manifested at his departure from Madrid; but it is more likely that he calculated upon Frederick's resistance, and that he hoped by moderating his own terms, once more to draw James over to his side.

The next day Conway replied, in his master's name, to Calvert's report of the conversation. "His Majesty's judgment," he wrote, "is that it is an honourable and fair way to the ends of restoration; and that his Majesty will have clear and full assurance of an honourable, total, and punctual restitution in all points before he deliver his grandchild into their hands; and also take as punctual provision for the demands and limitations in point of freedom of conscience which shall be agreed on for his grandchild, as is here done for those that are accorded for the Infanta." †

Thus it was that when Buckingham returned he found his master still busy, as of old, in the vain attempt to strike out a middle path between irreconcilably opposite pretensions. The day after his return was spent in anxious deliberation. If Buckingham had had his way, no doubt all further negotiation would have been broken off at once; but James's mind was not yet ripe for this, and he was obliged to wait a little longer till

---

* Calvert to the King, Oct. 2. *S. P. Spain.*
† Conway to Calvert, Oct. 3. *S. P. Spain.*

events forced on the inevitable decision. On one point at least there was no hesitation. Williams was ordered to open the prison doors, and to set the priests at liberty that they might join in the general rejoicing.*

CH. XII.
1623.

On the following day couriers were despatched in every direction. A letter to Frederick, laying before him plainly and distinctly the Spanish proposal for his son's marriage, was easy enough to write.† It was far more difficult to know in what terms the Court of Spain was to be approached.

Oct. 9. Proposal made by James to Frederick.

In considering this all-important question, James had before him a bundle of despatches which had recently arrived from Bristol, written on the 24th of September. A difference had arisen about the Infanta's portion, which Bristol had proposed to receive, at stated terms, in ready money, whilst Olivares, who knew well how empty his master's treasury was, would only agree to pay a small part of the sum in money, whilst the rest was to be commuted partly for its worth in jewels, partly for a yearly rent, calculated at five per cent. upon the capital, and secured upon landed property in Spain.‡ In writing both to the King and to the Prince, Bristol reverted to the question which had been raised about the possibility of the Infanta's betaking herself to a nunnery. On this point, he said, the King would give any security that might be desired. "I must now crave leave," he continued in his letter to the Prince, "to speak unto your Highness like a faithful, plain servant, which is, if your Highness's pleasure be to have use made of the powers you have left in my hands, I no way doubt but, in this particular, such satisfaction will be given as will appear reasonable to all the world. But, if your Highness desire that these powers should not be used, they may be detained upon other just reasons which will arise in the treaty of the temporal articles; and I doubt not but the marriage may be deferred for some few days upon other fair pretexts. But these inconveniences I conceive will follow :— First, it

Sept. 24. The Infanta's portion.

Question of the Infanta going into a nunnery.

---

* Conway to Coloma, Oct. 7. *S. P. Germany.*
† The King to Frederick, Oct. *S. P. Germany.*
‡ Bristol to the Prince, Sept. 24. *Cabala, 94.* Bristol to Calvert, Sept. 24. *S. P. Spain.*

Ch. XII.
1623.
Sept. 24.

will be of great discomfort to the Infanta, who, until the marriage is past, is not her own woman, but must be governed by the pleasure of the Junta, which, I think, she is very weary of; neither till then may she declare herself to be yours, nor comply with your Highness in answering of your letters and messages, and giving you those respects and comforts which I know she would be glad to do; but if she would any way judge that the delay of the marriage should arise from your Highness's part, I conceive she would take it most heavily. Secondly, it will certainly raise great jealousies in this King and his ministers, and retard the resolutions that are fit to be taken with speed, for the putting in execution that which is capitulated. I therefore offer it unto your Highness's wisdom whether, upon the satisfaction which they will give in this particular, which will be whatsoever you can desire, and upon the agreement of the temporal articles your Highness would, upon the coming of the Pope's approbation, make any further scruple in the delivering of your Highness's powers."*

To the King, Bristol spoke of his own difficult position even more explicitly. "I must further," he wrote, "let your Majesty understand that the first of the temporal articles is that the marriage shall be within ten days after the arrival of the Pope's approbation, which is hourly expected; so that I must deal like a faithful servant with your Majesty. If, upon the coming of the Pope's approbation, I should withhold the powers, and they understand that it is by a secret order of the Prince's, there being a clause in the said powers that the Prince shall no ways, either in part or whole, revoke the said powers, or detract from them, but that they shall be in force till Christmas, I fear your Majesty will find your business much disturbed and retarded by it." †

Oct. 8.
The marriage to be postponed till assurance

To Bristol's assurances about the Infanta there was nothing more to be said. "We have resolved," wrote James, "with the great liking of our son, to rest upon that security in point of doubt of the Infanta's taking a

* Bristol to the Prince, Sept. 24. *Clarendon State Papers*, i. App. xx.
† Bristol to the King, Sept. 24. *Hardwicke State Papers*, i. 481.

religious house, which you, in your judgment, shall think meet." The ambassador's statement that any postponement of the marriage would be attended with grave difficulties was utterly thrown away upon James. He went on to say that it was his special pleasure that it should take place shortly after Christmas, "that holy and joyful time best fitting so notable and blessed an action."

"But first," he continued, "we will that you repair presently to that King and give him knowledge of the safe arrival of our dear son to our Court, so satisfied and taken with the great entertainments, personal kindness, favour, and respect he hath received from that King and Court, as he seems not able to magnify it sufficiently, which makes us not know how sufficiently to give thanks; but we will that by all means you endeavour to express our thankfulness to that King, and the rest to whom it belongs, in the most ample manner you can. And hereupon you may take occasion to let that King know that, according to our constant affection, to make a firm and indissoluble amity between our families, nations, and crowns, and not seem to abandon our honour, nor, at the same time we give joy to our only son, to give our only daughter a portion in tears, by the advice of that King's ambassadors, we have entered a treaty concerning the restitution of the Palatinate and Electoral dignity to our son-in-law to be really procured by that King, according to the obligation of our honour, as you have well expressed in your reasons why the person of our son-in-law should not be left out of the treaty; but that the Emperor should find out a great title, or by increasing the number of Electoral States wherewith to satisfy the Duke of Bavaria. We now, therefore, require you that presently on your first audience you procure from that King a punctual answer what course that King will take for the restitution of the Palatinate and Electorate to our son-in-law; and in case that either the Emperor or the Duke of Bavaria oppose any part of the expected restitution, what course that King will take to give us assurance for our content on that point, whereof we require your present answer; and that you so press expedition herein that we may all together receive the full joy of both in

Ch. XII.
1623.
Oct. 8.

Christmas, resting ourself upon that faithful diligence of yours we have approved in all your service; though almost with the latest we must remember to you as a good ground for you to work on, that our son did write us out of Spain that that King would give us a blank, in which we might form our own conditions concerning the Palatinate, and the same our son confirms to us now. What observation and performance that King will make we require you to express, and give us a speedy account." *

Intentions of James.

It is seldom that a letter testifies so completely as this to the utter bewilderment of the writer. Practically, James meant to make the marriage dependent upon a fresh and more binding engagement for the restitution of his son-in-law; but he did not say anything of the kind. Passing by, as entirely unworthy of notice, Bristol's statement that a postponement of the marriage would be regarded in Spain as a personal insult, he quietly fixed, as if it were a mere matter of course, upon a day subsequent to the date at which, as he must have known if he had read his ambassador's despatch with the slightest attention, his son's proxy would expire. The remainder of the letter was no less characteristic of the man. Still, as ever, credulous of words, and closing his eyes to facts, he actually believed that the King of Spain would be able and willing to effect what was now equivalent to a revolution in Germany as a personal favour to himself. For him to take part in the German war on behalf of his kindred and religion was a task which was, in his eyes, surrounded by ever increasing difficulties; for the King of Spain to throw himself into the strife on the side opposite to his own family interests and his own warmest convictions, was a mere trifle, from which it would be ridiculous to expect him to shrink.

Charles writes to Bristol.

James's letter was accompanied by one from the Prince. "The King," wrote Charles, "has thought good in this interim of expectation for my mistress, to give you a command to try what the King of Spain will do concerning the business of the Palatinate before I be contracted, and his reason is—which I could not reply to—

* The King to Bristol, Oct. 8. *Cabala*, 241.

that, having but two children, he would be loath that one of them should have cause to weep when the other has reason to laugh; and I was the rather induced to yield unto it, because the King may very well have a positive answer of this before Christmas, so that it will lose no time in that business I desire so much. Although this be a needless office, because I am sure you will understand this more amply by the King's own letters, yet I have written this that ye may know from me as well as from the King my father, the intent of this direction, which I assure you is in no way to break the marriage, but, in this dull interim of looking for my mistress, to put an end to the miseries of my sister and her children, which I should have done if I had stayed this winter."*

Another letter, written to Aston on the same day, is far more indicative of Charles's real feelings. "Honest Watt," he wrote, "the King, my father, has sent a command to Bristol not to deliver my proxy until we may know certainly what the King of Spain will do concerning the Palatinate. If you find that this do make them startle, give them all the assurance that you can think of, that I do really intend to desire this match; and the chief end of this is that we may be as well hearty friends as near allies; and, to deal freely with you, so that we may have satisfaction concerning the Palatinate, I will be content to forget all ill-usage and be hearty friends; but, if not, I can never match where I have had so dry entertainment, although I shall be infinitely sorry for the loss of the Infanta."†

It is not probable, that if Charles had been allowed to bring the Infanta with him in September, he would have expressed himself so strongly about the Palatinate. But all his self-love was in arms to avenge the slight which had been put upon him. Now that the remembrance of the wounds which had been inflicted upon his vanity in Spain was rankling in his breast, his sense of his sister's wrongs became more vivid than before.

To the summons thus peremptorily addressed to

---

* The Prince to Bristol, Oct. 8. *Sherborne MSS.*
The Prince to Aston, Oct. 8. *S. P. Spain.*

Ch. XII.
1623.
Oct. 20.
Frederick's reply.

Madrid and to the Hague, Frederick was the first to reply. After thanking his father-in-law profusely for his good-will, and especially for his declaration that he would obtain for him an entire restitution, he touched upon the important demand which had now been made. "As to the overture," he wrote, "of a marriage between my eldest son and the Emperor's daughter, when I have obtained that full and entire restitution of which I have spoken, if your Majesty judges it expedient to insist upon the point, I shall always be very willing, through my duty and filial respect, to yield to whatever may tend to the advancement of the glory of God, and which is in conformity with your Majesty's good advice, and is necessary for the public good, and the particular interests of my House." *

His impracticable demands.

However courteous may have been the forms in which it was expressed, the letter contained what was virtually a decided refusal to listen to James's proposal. No candid person, indeed, would think of blaming Frederick for his objection to marry his son to a Roman Catholic wife. Every day it was becoming more plain that the Protestant religion was in real danger in Germany. But what the fugitive Prince could not see was, that he was himself in a great measure to blame for the change which had come over his country. As long as he persisted in claiming total restitution as a right, so long would those moderate men who looked upon the Imperial institutions as the only bulwark against anarchy, be lukewarm in his cause, if they were not absolutely hostile. What was needed now was, that he should himself retire altogether from the scene, and leave the championship of his religion to men whose names would not sound in the ears of their countrymen as a challenge to sedition. Unhappily such patriotism as this is hardly to be expected from the majority of men, and least of all from such as Frederick.

Mediation now impossible.

But however much opinions may differ as to Frederick's duty, there can be no doubt whatever that this letter was a deathblow to any vitality which may have been left in James's mediation. Further negotiation was

* Frederick to the King, Oct. $\frac{20}{30}$. *S. P. Germany.*

now rendered altogether hopeless. If Philip had been Ch. XII.
the most conscientious man in Europe, he would not 1623.
have considered himself bound by promises made under Oct. 20.
other circumstances, either to persuade or to compel the
Emperor to replace Frederick in his old authority, on
the mere chance that, having given no guarantees for his
future conduct, he would not think it right to send out
fresh hordes of plunderers to devastate the territories of
his neighbours. If Frederick was to some extent in the
right, so far as the quarrel concerned religion, Ferdinand
and Philip were altogether in the right so far as it concerned the political security of Germany.

On the 21st, the day after Frederick's letter was Oct. 21.
written, the King of Spain's intentions with respect to the Philip's
Palatinate were made known to Bristol. With respect to tion about
the proposed marriage, he declared himself ready to do the Pala-
all good offices with the Emperor, if it were understood
that the young Prince was to be educated at Vienna. It
would then be for his father to make due submission, and
to give guarantees that he would from that time become
the firm ally of the House of Austria. Then everything
possible would be done to meet James's wishes, and in
proportion as the Palatine gave satisfaction, his States
would be restored either to himself or to his children. After
the death of the Duke of Bavaria, the Electorate would
revert to Frederick's eldest son. But, to quote the words
of the document itself, "as the aforesaid Count Palatine
has up to this time shown so little sign of submission or
repentance, and as he has made such notorious attempts
upon his lord the Emperor, it seems that it would be of
very ill example that he should not retain in his individual person some mark of punishment." *

As far as Frederick's own position was concerned,
nothing more could fairly be expected. Ignorant as the
Spanish ministers necessarily were of the letter which
had been written the day before at the Hague, they
were not ignorant that it was not till after Christian's
defeat at Stadtloo that Frederick had been brought to

* Ciriza to Bristol, Oct. $\frac{21}{31}$. *S. P. Spain.* Olivares to Cottington, *Ib.*.
Oct. $\frac{21}{31}$. *Hacket*, 483.

Ch. XII.
1623.
Oct. 21.

consent to any negotiation at all. The really serious point in the King of Spain's declaration was the total omission of any reference to the Protestant governor who was to have superintended young Frederick-Henry's education at Vienna. The omission was evidently intentional; and, in fact, Olivares, sanguine as usual, was already communicating to Khevenhüller a plan by which Frederick might be induced to travel to Vienna in order to throw himself at the Emperor's feet, and to leave, not only his eldest, but also his second son, to be educated in the Catholic religion.*

Such were the secret plans of Olivares and his master, when, on the 21st of October, the despatches written in England on the 8th were placed in Bristol's hands. Ignorant as he was, alike of Frederick's last impracticable demands, and of the no less impracticable designs of the Spanish Government, he still cherished the belief that, when once the Prince of Wales was married, Philip could not fail to exert himself on behalf of the interests of his brother-in-law on the Continent. Himself without any religious enthusiasm whatever, and being accustomed to regard passing events from the point of view of a secular politician, he was always too apt to leave out of consideration the action either of genuine religious feeling, or of that theological partizanship which follows like a ground-swell the storm which has been already hushed. But mistaken as he was in his interpretation of the purposes of the Spanish Court, he knew far better than to imagine that the war which had now been raging for five disastrous years could be allayed in a few weeks by Philip's mere word.

Oct. 24.
Bristol complains of the postponement of the marriage.

He was under these impressions when he received directions to put off the marriage till after Christmas. Such a step, he told his master plainly, would throw back into uncertainty all that had been covenanted in prospect of the marriage. The proxy with which he was entrusted would then have expired. Nor was this the worst. This question of the Palatinate had often been under debate, but it had never been insisted upon as a ground for postponing the marriage. If it were now

* *Khevenhüller*, x. 99.

brought forward, it could not be but that the Spaniards would suspect that it was a mere pretext, and nothing more; for there could be no doubt that to make the match conditional upon the restoration of the Palatinate was a totally new demand. His own instructions had been "to insist upon the restoring of the Prince Palatine, but not so as to annex it to the treaty of the match, as that thereby the match should be hazarded;" his Majesty having "seemed confident they here would never grow to a perfect conclusion of the match, without a settled resolution" to give him "satisfaction in the business of the Palatinate." Both the Prince and Buckingham had treated the business in a similar spirit, and they might remember that "Olivares often protested the necessity of having this business compounded and settled before the marriage, saying, otherwise they might give a daughter and have a war within three months after, if this ground and subject of quarrel should be still left on foot."

Bristol then proceeded to point out in the most guarded terms the absurdity of the course which he was asked to take. The restoration of the Palatinate, he showed, was not an affair to be hustled over in a day; it was a question in which many great Princes were interested, and it certainly could not be obtained excepting after long and formal negotiations. If the Prince were to wait for his wife till these were brought to an end, he might wait long. He had no doubt that the King of Spain would really assist in obtaining that which had been asked; but to demand a peremptory answer, under the penalty of retaining the proxy, was to fling an insult in his face and in the face of his sister, an insult which was certain to be bitterly resented. He therefore hoped that orders would at once be sent him to make use of the proxy when called for, and in the same time to use every means in his power to obtain a better answer about the Palatinate.*

However respectfully Bristol's letter had been worded, it evidently bore but one interpretation. The ambassador had contrived to tell his sovereign that he had done a

* Bristol to the King, Oct. 24. *Hardwicke State Papers,* i. 483.

very foolish thing, and that he had better undo it as soon as possible.

It is not necessary to share Bristol's confidence in the reality of Spanish promises—to agree with him in his estimate of James's letter. It might be wise to break off his son's marriage at any cost. It might be wise to obtain a distinct engagement from Philip about the Palatinate. But to expect to wring such an engagement from Philip by the studied insult of postponing the betrothal, and at the same time to talk about the most perfect amity and friendship, was mere infatuation.

Yet, infatuation as it was, it was a dream to which James clung with his usual tenacity. Every day, indeed, Buckingham, and the Prince under Buckingham's guidance, were urging him to make the restitution of the Palatinate the indispensable condition of the marriage. But neither Buckingham nor Charles cared for anything larger than the immediate interests of the hour; whereas James, in his uncertain and helpless way, had been labouring for years to promote the peace and well-being of Europe. Whilst he was waiting for the replies from the Hague and from Madrid to the despatches which he had sent forth as the messengers of peace, his anxiety brought on a fit of the gout, which rendered him more than ever incapable of coming to a decision.

In the meanwhile, the Spanish Ambassadors were treated with all outward show of respect. But, beyond the liberation of the priests, nothing was done to satisfy their demands. The pardon and dispensation remained unused in the Lord Keeper's hands.* The promised letters to the judges were not written.† Encouraged by the support of Buckingham, men now allowed themselves to talk more freely than they had dared before. Strange tales were told by those who had returned with the Prince of the ignorance and superstition of the Spanish people, and of the beggarly fare and discourteous treatment to which they had been exposed in Spain.‡ The

---

* Salvetti's *News-Letter*, $\frac{Oct\ 24}{Nov.\ 3}$.

† Williams to Conway, Oct. 10. Conway to Williams, Oct. 11. *S. P. Dom.* cliii. 38, 39.

‡ Chamberlain to Carleton, Oct. 25. *S. P. Dom.* cliv. 98.

air was thick with rumours. The words and actions of the men who seemed to have the destiny of England in their hands were noted as if they had been the oracles of fate. Charles, reserved and silent as usual, gave few tokens of his real feelings. Yet even Charles was unable altogether to conceal the change which had come over him. "It is certain," said a keen observer, "that he does not love the Spaniards; and if he loves the Infanta, his affection is very moderate.*

In the midst of these uncertainties, an accident occurred, which, if it threw no new light upon the intentions of the Court, might at least have served to open the eyes of the Spanish Ambassadors to the opposition which their scheme for securing a Catholic domination would be certain to meet with in England. It happened that a large number of persons were assembled one Sunday afternoon, to hear a Jesuit preach in a large garret attached to the French Embassy at Blackfriars. In the midst of the sermon the beam on which the flooring rested gave way, and about a hundred and fifty persons were hurled in a confused, shrieking mass below. The next story, too, was carried away by the falling ruin, and when the living had been separated from the dead, ninety-one crushed and blood-stained corpses were drawn out from amongst the mass.

In the presence of such a scene of misery, even religious bigotry might well have been silent for a time: but the age was not one in which there was much charity to spare for Jesuits, and the dread of Papal encroachment was, thanks to James, rooting itself more firmly than ever in the English mind. As soon as the news was known, a howling mob gathered round the doors, and threatened to break into the ambassador's house. The Bishop of London refused to allow the dead to be buried in the churchyards. In order to escape insult and ill-usage, it was found necessary to dispose of the greater number of the bodies in pits dug in the court-yard of the French Embassy. Men who should have known better pointed out

---

* "Il Principe è al solito cupo et usa gran silentio. Certo non ama Spagnuoli; et se ama l'Infanta, l'amor è temperato." Valaresso to the Doge, Oct. 24 / Nov. 3. *Venice MSS.* Desp. Ingh.

with triumph that the 26th of October, the day on which the accident happened, was the 5th of November in the Roman calendar, and stated, in utter disregard of the fact, that the broken beam was a perfectly sound one. The inference from these two propositions was, of course, that the occurrence was a direct judgment of God.*

The time was rapidly approaching when it was to be decided whether the privilege of openly receiving Catholic preachers, which had been grudgingly connived at in the case of foreign ambassadors, was to be extended to every Catholic gentleman in England. On the 31st of October the Prince suddenly arrived in London, and the next day twelve members of the Privy Council, who were specially entrusted with Spanish business, were summoned to meet him. After swearing, by the special command of the Prince, not to repeat a word of anything that they might hear, they were called upon to listen to a long narrative from Buckingham about his proceedings in Spain, which was no doubt as highly coloured by his personal resentment as his subsequent report to the Houses of Parliament. As soon as the statement had been made, he returned to Newmarket to visit the King, by whom he was probably taken to task for his want of courtesy in refusing to receive a visit from the Spanish Ambassadors. At all events, he suddenly reappeared in London on the 9th, and lost no time in paying a formal visit to the Spaniards.†

The King's gout had passed away for the time, and he was able to come up to London. He had by this time received the replies of Bristol and Frederick to his letters, and even if it could be supposed that neither party in the dispute would ever put forward further claims than they now asserted, the discrepancy between the views of Philip and of Frederick was sufficiently wide to startle the most lethargic politician. What Philip asked was that Frederick and his children should be put upon their

---

* A relation of the fall of the room at Blackfriars. *Court and Times of James I.*, ii. 428. Salvetti's *News-Letter*, $\frac{Oct. 31}{Nov. 10}$. ——— to Mead, Oct. 29. *Harl. MSS.* 389, fol. 374. D. Carleton to Carleton, Nov. 1. *S. P. Dom.* cliv. 2.

† Salvetti's *News-Letters*, $\frac{Oct. 31}{Nov. 10}$, Nov. $\frac{7}{17}$, $\frac{14}{24}$.

good behaviour, and readmitted to their former possessions as a matter of grace, in proportion as they appeared to deserve it. What Frederick asked was, that he should be at once reinstated as a matter of right, and that he should then be allowed to consider what was the nature of that ill-defined submission which he owed to the Emperor. It is evident that, even leaving the religious question out of sight for the moment, the two views of the respective rights of the head and of the members of the Empire were wide asunder as the poles.

To a man with any capabilities for thought, it would have been of infinite service to have had these two ideas of the constitution of the Empire thus boldly presented before him. He would have seen that he must make up his mind either to adopt one of the two views, or to strike out some new theory for himself. In coming to his decision, he would not forget to investigate the consequences of the victory of one side or the other, and, above all, he would ask himself whether he was prepared to take any part at all in the conflict. But for such considerations there was no room in the mind of James. He had always insisted that his son-in-law must make submission to the Emperor. He had always insisted that, in some way or another, his son-in-law's restitution was to be the consequence of the Prince's marriage. The only result, therefore, of his present cogitations, was another long rambling letter to Bristol, in which he once more called upon the King of Spain to get him out of his difficulties.

He would never have written to defer the marriage till after Christmas, he said, if he had known that the proxy would have expired. He now sent a fresh proxy, which would continue in force till March. There would, therefore, be plenty of time to obtain entire satisfaction. Yet he could not but have doubts as to the intentions of the King of Spain. News had just arrived that the rich lands about the Bergstrasse, which had been given up by the Elector of Mentz more than a century and a half before, had now been reclaimed from the Palatinate, and had been surrendered into the Elector's hands with the connivance of the Spanish garrisons. Bristol was, there-

Ch. XII.
1623.
Nov. 13.

fore, before he delivered the proxy, to procure a written declaration from Philip of his determination to obtain a complete restitution of the Palatinate and the Electorate by mediation, and to give assistance to obtain that object by other means, if mediation failed. He was also to be required to state "within what time the mediation shall determine, and the assistance of arms begin."

In order, however, to show that he was not exorbitant in his demands, James expressed his readiness to propound a plan for satisfying the Duke of Bavaria, and to go on with the negotiation for his grandson's marriage. In deference, however, to his son-in-law's objections, the offer of sending the boy to Vienna must be withdrawn. He now proposed that he should be educated in England, under the eye of the Prince of Wales and the Infanta.

Having thus disposed of the interests of Europe, James returned with unusual vigour to his own. He would have nothing to do, he said, with the proposal for sending any part of the Infanta's portion in jewels, or with the substitution of a yearly rent for the payment of the capital. He must have the whole sum in ready money.*

This letter was accompanied by another from Conway, ordering Bristol to come away from Spain, if he did not receive a satisfactory answer within twenty days.†

Character of the letter.

Such was the despatch which, no doubt, much to James's astonishment, proved to be an ultimatum, the rejection of which broke up the whole edifice of the Spanish alliance. It has, perhaps, been usual to lay too great stress upon the influence of Charles and Buckingham in bringing about the change in his method of proceeding. For in point of fact there was very little change at all, and what there was, was the result far more of circumstances than of any alteration in James's opinions. Always inclined to look upon the great religious and political questions of the age very much as a lawyer looks upon an action for the possession of an acre of ground, and leaving out of consideration the interests, the feelings, and the passions of nations and of men, he had for years been under the impression that if only a

* The King to Bristol, Nov. 13. *Clarendon State Papers,* i. 13.
† Conway to Bristol, Nov. 13. *Sherborne MSS.*

suspension of arms could be effected, everything else would be easy. At last he had got his wish. There was to be a great diplomatic meeting at Cologne, where all difficulties were to be surmounted. Unhappily for James, he had now to find some middle term which would satisfy the disputants, and a very few weeks were sufficient to show that he could do nothing of the kind. All that was left, therefore, was to call upon the King of Spain to come to his help, or to forfeit his friendship for ever.

<small>Ch. XII.
1632.
Nov. 13.</small>

The King's despatch was followed by one much shorter and sharper from his son. "Bristol," wrote Charles, "the false interpretation of the King's and my directions concerning the not delivering of my proxy, has made me in such haste to send away this bearer, that by this I can only give you a command, without giving any reasons at this time, which is not to deliver my proxy until you hear further from the King and myself. Make what shifts or fair excuses you will, but I command you, as you answer it upon your peril, not to deliver my proxy till you hear further from hence. So, hoping you will obey this command punctually, I rest your friend, CHARLES, P."*

<small>Nov. 14.
Letter from Charles.</small>

The next day another letter from the Prince followed in the same tone. "Whatsoever answer ye get," he wrote, "ye must not deliver the proxy till ye make my father and me judge of it. As for the whole business, ye must deal freely with them in as civil terms as ye will, that except that King will promise under his † hand to help my father with his arms, in case mediation fail, to restore my brother-in-law to his honours and inheritances, there can be neither marriage nor friendship ; and, as to ‡ the breeding up of my nephew in the Emperor's Court, avoid it handsomely as ye can, but I assure you it shall never be. And if they will do all that my father desires, they may not only be sure of an alliance, but of a hearty sincere friendship. Make no replies. Suffer no delays."§

<small>Nov. 15
A second letter.</small>

The day on which this letter was written, Inojosa and

---

* The Prince to Bristol, Nov. 14. *Sherborne MSS.*
† The word "his" is not in the original.
‡ The word "to" is also omitted.
§ The Prince to Bristol, Nov. 15. *Sherborne MSS.*

Ch. XII.
1623.
Nov. 15.
Audience of the Spanish Ambassadors.

Coloma were received by the King in the presence of the Prince and Buckingham. For four long hours the discussion lasted. James was forced to admit that he had never asked that the restitution of the Palatinate should be made a condition of the marriage, and even that it was unreasonable to expect the King of Spain to take up arms against the Emperor;[*] but, he added, in his usual inconsecutive way, that his daughter and his grandchildren were dear to him,—he could not bear to abandon them,—he had promised that by fair means or by foul he would recover all that they had lost,—his reputation was engaged, and he could not break his word.

Oct. 30.
Fresh answer about the Palatinate.

Whilst James was making these ineffectual representations in London, the question of the marriage was being decided at Madrid. On the 30th of October, Bristol received a fresh reply on the subject of the Palatinate: Philip now affirmed that he would try to get the Electorate restored after the death of Maximilian to Frederick himself instead of to his son, but he gave no hope of taking arms against the Emperor. He would continue, he said, to interpose his good offices. To ask him for more, was to ask for impossibilities.[†]

Nov. 1.
The dispensation approved at Rome.

Whilst Bristol was waiting for a reply to a fresh application for a better answer,[‡] tidings reached Madrid that the new Pope had given his approval to the dispensation granted by his predecessor, and that the documents necessary for the accomplishment of the marriage ceremony would soon be on their way from Rome. The Ambassador who had at this time only received the despatch of the 8th of October, in which he was commanded to postpone the marriage till after Christmas, at once communicated his difficulties to James. "There is an intention," he wrote, "to call presently upon me for the Prince's powers for the marriage left in my hands, the which I know not upon what ground or reason to detain, the Prince having engaged in the said powers the faith

---

[*] This particular admission is referred to in the King of Spain's reply to the ambassadors on the 9th of December. For the rest of the conversation see Salvetti's *News-Letter*, $\frac{\text{Nov. 21}}{\text{Dec. 1}}$.

[†] Ciriza to Bristol, $\frac{\text{Oct. 30}}{\text{Nov. 9}}$. *S. P. Spain.*

[‡] Bristol to Calvert, Oct. 31. *S. P. Spain.*

and word of a prince no way to revoke and retract from them, but that they should remain in full force till Christmas; and delivered unto me a politic declaration of his pleasure, that, upon the coming of the dispensation, I should deliver them unto this King that they might be put in execution, and hereof, likewise was there, by Secretary Ciriza, as a public notary, an instrument drawn and attested by all the witnesses present. If I shall allege your Majesty's pleasure of having the marriage deferred till one of the holidays, although they should condescend thereunto, that is impossible, for the powers will be then expired. If I shall insist upon the restitution of the Palatinate, this King hath therein declared his answer; and it would be much wondered why that should be now added for a condition of the marriage, having hitherto been treated of as a business apart, and was in being at the granting of the said powers, and hath been often under debate, but never specified, nor the powers delivered upon any condition of having any such point first cleared; and I must confess unto your Majesty I understand not how with honour, and that exact dealing which hath ever been observed in all your Majesty's actions, the powers can be detained, unless there should appear some new and emergent cause since the granting of them, whereof as yet I hear none specified. Therefore, being loath to be the instrument by whose hands anything should pass that might have the least reflection upon your Majesty's or the Prince's honour, which I shall ever value more than my life or safety, and judging it likewise to conduce more to your service, and assuring myself that your Majesty's late direction to have the marriage upon one of the holidays in Christmas, was for want of due information that the powers will be then expired, I have thought it fit, with the advice of Sir Walter Aston, to raise no scruple in the delivery of the said powers; but do intend, when they shall be required, to pass on to the nominating of a prefixed day for the marriage, but I shall endeavour to defer the time until I may be advertised of your Majesty's pleasure, if it may be within the space of twenty-four days, and will labour to find some handsome and fair occasion for the deferring of them, without alleging

Ch. XII.
1623.
Nov. 1.
Was Charles dishonoured?

any directions in that kind from your Majesty or the Prince."*

This was plain speaking. The King, and the Prince through him, were told that the course which they had adopted was utterly dishonourable. With full knowledge that Spain would not give armed assistance for the recovery of the Palatinate, Charles had chosen to swear that he would fulfil the marriage contract in every particular, and it was monstrous that he should now repudiate his obligations on account of an obstacle which he had foreseen when he undertook them. If indeed he had chosen to plead that he had subsequently been enlightened, and that since his return to England he had learned that the engagements which he had formed were ruinous to his country, he might fairly have asked to be relieved from a promise which he had given through ignorance or inadvertence. But nothing of the kind was the case. With him there was no admission of error, no confession of heedlessness. He was in the right when he had sworn, he was equally in the right when, without a word of explanation, he broke his oath.

Bristol's policy right in the main.

On the question of personal honour, few will probably be found to hesitate in deciding between Charles and Bristol. Opinions are likely to be more divided on the larger question of the general policy of the ambassador; for it is plain that Bristol considered the offers of the Spanish Court on the whole satisfactory, and that he was prepared to enter upon the negotiations in Germany, with confidence in the diplomatic support of Spain. That he was wrong in supposing that Spain had renounced all exorbitant pretensions is, to us at least, undeniable; for we know that it would have been difficult to content either Spain or the Emperor without imposing a Catholic Prince upon the Palatinate. But in the main point, Bristol was undoubtedly in the right. Standing almost alone amongst his countrymen, he never ceased to maintain that there were faults on both sides, and he saw in the promised negotiations at Cologne a golden opportunity for putting his master's son-in-law in the right.

* Bristol to the King, Nov. 1. *Cabala,* 95. Compare Aston to Buckingham, Nov. 1 (?). *Cabala,* 11.

If Frederick had been other than himself,—that is to say, if he could have understood the times in which he lived; if he could have cast away those pretensions to independence which had been so ruinous to himself and to his country; if, in short, he could have separated the cause of his religion from the cause of anarchy, he would either have forced both Spain and Austria to relinquish their schemes of armed proselytism, or would have united all Protestant States in a resistance to which his enemies would be compelled to bow. If, therefore, Bristol failed signally, it was because he was so entirely unsupported. The part which Frederick was called upon to play, was one which he regarded with the utmost loathing, and signs were not wanting that it would not be long before James, long suffering as he had been, would throw up the game in despair.

At last, on the 12th of November, the Pope's approbation arrived at Madrid,* and the 19th, the Prince's birthday, was talked of as the day for the ceremony of the marriage; but Bristol discovered means to delay it a little longer. Fresh conditions had been sent, together with the approbation, and till it was ascertained whether they would be accepted, the Nuncio refrained from placing the papal brief in the King's hands. His orders were, however, not to insist upon them if he found that they were likely to be refused, and after a week had passed away, he retired from the contest.† On the 19th he surrendered the document to Philip, who at once took the required oath to the observance of the articles by the King of England.

Bristol did his best to put off the ceremony as long as possible. It would be well, he said, to give time for the news to reach England, before the day appointed, in order that it might be celebrated there as a day of triumph and festivity; but to all such suggestions, the Spaniards turned a deaf ear. The King, he was told, intended punctually to perform his own engagements, and he expected the same accuracy on the other side. It had been expressly agreed that the marriage should take

---

* Bristol to Calvert, Nov. 13. *S. P. Spain.*
† Bristol's Answers to the Interrogatories. *Hardwicke State Papers,* i. 520.

place within ten days after the arrival of the dispensation, and though he had consented to reckon the time from the day on which it was given into his hands, no further concession would be made. He would not force his sister upon the Prince, but if the marriage had not taken place on the 29th it must be understood that the promises made were no longer binding. Thus pressed, Bristol consented to fix the ceremony for the 29th, and waited anxiously for the courier, which, unless some unusual accident occurred, would be certain before that day to bring him more precise orders than had yet been sent.*

Answer promised about the Palatinate. That those orders would be otherwise than favourable to the marriage, he could not bring himself to believe. The Council of State, he was informed, had lately taken into consideration his renewed application about the Palatinate, and the King's answer would be in his hands before the day appointed for the ceremony. That answer he was solemnly assured should be everything that he could desire.† It was indeed not likely that Philip would again engage to take up arms against the Emperor, but it is not improbable that an effort would have been made to obtain some further concessions to Frederick.

Whether, under existing circumstances the attempt to obtain the conversion of the young Prince would have been abandoned, it is impossible to say; but it is certain that Olivares was beginning to open his eyes to much to which, six months before, he had been wilfully blind. In the summer he had imagined that the conversion of England and the Palatinate were such mere trifles as to be hardly worth any extraordinary effort. Since the Prince had left Madrid he had begun to suspect that the prize might even now elude his grasp. He had begun to conceive the possibility that Charles might have ceased to set his heart upon the Infanta, and not a word was now uttered of those Parliamentary guarantees for religious liberty, for the sake of which he had done so much to alienate the Prince. Upon the failure of the marriage, indeed, both he and Philip would probably have looked

---

* Bristol to the King, Nov. 23. *S. P. Spain.* Aston to Buckingham, Nov. 23. *Harl. MSS.* 1580, fol. 10.
† Bristol to Conway, Jan. 23, 1624. *S. P. Spain.*

with considerable equanimity. What they really dreaded was a war with England, and as the tales reached them of Buckingham's frenzied denunciations, and of Charles's moody silence, they could not but regard such a war as likely to break out at no distant time. To avert such a catastrophe, then, it may safely be concluded, they were ready to make any reasonable concession. There were some things, indeed, that they could not do. They could not re-admit Mansfeld into the heart of Germany; they could not, whatever they might have said in a moment of heedlessness, take arms against the Emperor. But whatever gave promise of a firm and stable peace, they were prepared to advocate. Let Frederick show that he could again be trusted in the Palatinate, and the Court of Madrid would not have been the last to relinquish those airy dreams of ecclesiastical supremacy which had seemed so lifelike a few short months before.

Ch. XII. 1623.

But it is seldom possible for one who has woven such a web of falsehood as Olivares had been labouring at ever since his uncle's death to regain the solid ground of truth. Even now, when Bristol was nodding approbation at his golden promises, the blow reached him which levelled his toilfully constructed edifice to the dust. His empty professions, which had been intended to serve the purpose of the moment, had been taken as equivalent to the most solemn covenant. On the 26th of November, three days before the ceremony of the marriage was to have taken place, the despatches containing peremptory commands for its postponement were placed in Bristol's hands.

Nov. 26. The order for the postponement of the marriage reaches Madrid.

The ambassador was deeply chagrined at an order which was so fatal to his policy and his hopes. He at least did not, like his master or Olivares, flatter himself with the idea that it was possible to insult a friendly sovereign, and at the same time to retain his friendship. Never doubting for an instant that the letter which he held in his hands was ominous of evil for his own country and for the whole of Europe, his first act was to write back to James an announcement that his directions would be punctually carried into effect. His next act was to

Postponement of the marriage.

Ch. XII.
1623.
Nov. 26.

inform Olivares that the marriage must be postponed, on the ground that his master wished the ceremony not to be separated from the foundation of a thorough amity between the Crowns.

Such an insult, thus publicly administered in the sight of the world, was not likely to lay the foundation of a thorough amity. The temporary gallery, along which the Infanta was to have walked to the church in which the ceremony was to be performed, was dismantled and removed. She herself ceased to be addressed by the style of Princess of England. The Prince's letters were no longer allowed to reach her. Her English grammars and dictionaries were restored to the shelf. The marriage was considered as indefinitely postponed, if not as broken off altogether.*

Nov. 29.
The summons to restore the Palatinate.

It was with little hope, therefore, that Bristol and Aston delivered the summons for the restitution of the Palatinate, which they had been instructed to present. They first asked for an explicit answer to their last request, in which they had begged for information as to what the King would do if the Emperor refused to grant entire restitution to Frederick upon due submission?† They then proceeded to complain generally of Philip's conduct, of his allowing the reduction of Heidelberg and Mannheim, of his permitting the surrender of the Bergstrasse, and of his recognising the Electoral title of the Duke of Bavaria. They now wished to ask for his Majesty's good offices and mediation, and begged him to fix a time, after which, if no satisfactory result followed, he would assist the King of Great Britain with his arms.‡

Dec. 2.
Philip's first answer.

Three days after this decisive summons was delivered, the ambassadors received an evasive answer to their former proposition, stating that it was unbefitting for a mediator to take part in a quarrel. Bristol was plainly told that this was not the reply which had been prepared for him a week before: and that, even as it was, it had been antedated, so as to appear to have been written

---

* Bristol to James, Nov. 26. *Hardwicke State Papers*, i. 488. Bristol and Aston to Calvert, Nov. 30. *S. P. Spain.*
† Proposition of the Ambassadors, Nov. 13. *S. P. Spain.*
‡ Proposition of the Ambassadors, Nov. 29. *S. P. Spain.*

before he had given information of his last orders from England. How was it possible, it was added, for the King to give a more pleasing answer, when he was summoned to do so on pain of his sister's rejection?*

The tone of the reply to the last memorial was far more defiant. If Heidelberg and Mannheim had been taken, said Philip, it was the fault of the Count Palatine himself, who had continued to call himself King of Bohemia, had had two armies fighting on his side, and had tried to rouse the Princes of Germany, with Bethlen Gabor and the Turks, against the Emperor. As to his recognition of the Elector of Bavaria, it was a courtesy due to him on account of the many services done by him to the House of Austria, though it could never be said that his private interests had ever been considered at Madrid to the injury of the public good and the peace of Germany.

"As to the proposition of giving armed assistance against the Emperor," the King proceeded to say, "it is an unnecessary demand, and one which is impracticable on account of the great obligations under which his Catholic Majesty lies towards him. This was said to the Prince of Wales when the matter was discussed here; and lately the same declaration was repeated by the Marquis of Inojosa to the King of Great Britain, when, at his last audience, they were conversing on the subject, and his Majesty declared himself satisfied.

"As to the alliance and amity required, and the novelty of introducing the settlement of this question as a condition of the marriage, it is answered that this business of the settlement of the Palatine's affairs has altogether changed both in form and substance by this new and unexpected course which the ambassadors have attempted to introduce, it being now asked as a condition of the marriage. On this point, therefore, his Majesty has nothing more to say than that he will on all occasions wish well to the prosperity of the King of Great Britain; and that that which would be most conducive to his

---

* Reply to the Ambassadors' Proposition, Dec. 2. Dated $\frac{\text{Nov. 26}}{\text{Dec. 6}}$. Bristol to the King, Dec. 6. *S. P. Spain.*

security, and to the better success of this business, might easily be done. His Majesty, therefore, replies forthwith formally to the proposition made to him, that there is need of forethought; and his Majesty is still considering of giving a good direction, not only to this business of the Palatine, but to all those matters from which any inconvenience may spring to the perpetuity of this friendship and alliance. As his Majesty looks upon this amity with so great affection and desire for its perfect attainment, it would be an error not to forestall, and to arrange everything that was conducive to this end, as his Majesty the King of Great Britain, and the Prince his son did in the present business; a resolution which his Catholic Majesty approves and praises much."*

Such was the answer by which James's hopes were finally extinguished on the side of Spain. That the insult which he received had sunk deeply into Philip's mind is most certain. But, though the form of his reply would undoubtedly have been more courteous if the marriage had taken place, there is no reason to suppose that the substance would have been very different. To ask the King of Spain to take arms against the Emperor was to ask a moral impossibility.

Nor was this the only rebuff to which James exposed himself by his inconsiderate persistence in a policy which was, in reality, no policy at all. On the 20th of November, he wrote once more to his son-in-law, laying before him in greater detail than in his former letter the terms which the Court of Madrid had at that time agreed to support. "We present to you," he wrote, "these propositions—to wit, in the first place, a due submission to the Emperor, under convenient limitations, which first shall be granted and agreed in conformity to that which is noble, with a safe conduct and assurance requisite and sufficient for the free and safe going and return of your person and train. This being done, we make you offer of a present and full restitution of all the Palatinate unto the person of your son, and that you shall be his administrator during your life: and that, after the death of

* Reply of the King of Spain, Dec. $\frac{9}{19}$. *S. P. Spain.*

the Duke of Bavaria, your son be re-established in the Electoral dignity, and for the better confirming the sound amity and assuring your possession, and enjoying of all according to the contract which is presently to be made; and also to serve for a preparation for the bettering of the said conditions to your person, which will be in all likelihood when the marriage will be resolved and concluded to be made betwixt your eldest son, our grandchild, and one of the Emperor's daughters. In contemplation whereof, they have approached a degree nearer, to wit, that the Electoral dignity shall come again to your person after the Duke of Bavaria's death. In which treaty of marriage, to clear the principal difficulty, which consisted in the education of your son with the Emperor, we have taken from them all hope herein, wherein we assure ourselves you will be content, and are purposed that he shall have his education with our son, and with and in the presence of the Infanta, when she shall be at our Court."*

It is evident from these last words that James had no clear idea before his mind of the state of feeling at Madrid. The marriage, he seems to have fancied, could be indefinitely deferred, with the sole result of bringing Philip down upon his knees. Yet in one respect the uncertainty of his position was beginning to tell upon him. Six months before, he would have accompanied such a scheme as that which his letter contained, with a threat of withdrawing his support if it were not accepted at once. Now everything was changed. His old self-confidence was gone. His favourite and his son had taken part against him, and the King of Spain, in whom he had trusted, had turned his back upon him. He, therefore, contented himself with recommending his son-in-law to weigh the arguments on both sides thoroughly, and to let him know the result.

Whilst he was waiting for the answer, James underwent all the daily torments of uncertainty. At one time he talked of lighting up the flames of war, and of calling Bethlen Gabor and the Turks to his aid. But it was

* The King to Frederick, Nov. 20. *Cabala*, 245.

Ch. XII.
1623.
November.

December.
Talk about summoning Parliament.

seldom that he used such language as this. One day his son adjured him to open his eyes to the trickery of the Spaniards. "What," replied James, reproachfully, with tears in his eyes, "would you engage me in a war in my old days, and make me quarrel with Spain?"* To the urgent entreaties of Buckingham and Charles that he should summon a Parliament, he turned a deaf ear as long as he could. At last he consented to name a day on which the question might be debated in the Council; but when the day arrived, it only brought a message from James, declaring that nothing could be done till an answer to his last propositions had been returned from Spain.†

Dec. 20.
Frederick's reply to his father-in-law.

It was not long before James heard that his demand for an armed intervention had been utterly rejected by Philip, and the news was soon followed by a letter from Frederick. That letter contained, as might have been expected, a complete refusal of the terms proposed. Nor did the exiled Prince content himself, as he might well have done, with raising objections to the marriage of his son with a Roman Catholic Princess. He took higher ground than this. His own restitution, he said, was a reality; the submission to the Emperor was but a ceremony. The restitution must, therefore, precede the submission, and might well enough be performed by deputy, as he dared not trust the Emperor by placing his own person in his power. But he soon showed that what he wanted was war. Now, as ever, his easily excited imagination was filled with the wildest hopes. It was nothing to him that Christian had been driven headlong out of Germany in the autumn, and that Mansfeld, after committing unheard-of cruelties, was preparing to abandon the devastated meadows of East Friesland. It was not, according to Frederick, his alliance with these marauders that had left him without a friend in the Empire. It was by his too great readiness to seek for peace that his natural allies had been alienated. If James would but declare in his favour, the Electors of Saxony and Branden-

---

* Rusdorf to Frederick, Nov. 26. *Rusdorf. Memoires*, i. 145.
† Rusdorf to Frederick, Dec. 16. *Ibid.* i. 156. Conway to Buckingham, Dec. 20. *S. P. Dom.* clv. 65.

burg would come to his aid. The King of Denmark would be certain not to hang back. And if this were not enough, it was notorious to all the world, that the majority of the troops which marched under the banners of the Catholic League, were Protestants, and were more inclined to its ruin than to its preservation.*

If James had merely been called upon to answer his son-in-law's arguments, he would have made short work with such absurdities as these; but, unhappily for him, he had to deal with them not in the region of logic, but in the region of facts. It was a fact that neither Ferdinand nor Philip would agree to any peace which did not give sufficient guarantees for the predominance of the Imperial authority and the supremacy of law in the Empire. It was a fact, that Frederick would not agree to any peace which did not place himself and the other Princes of the Empire in a position of virtual independence, which would enable them to retain in their hands the right of peace and war. The radical difference which had long ago existed had now come to an open and avowed expression. There was a great gulf between the two, which no diplomatic arts, no well intended commonplaces, could ever even hope to fill up.

What Bristol would have said, if he had been consulted at this crisis, can hardly be doubted. He would have told James that it was no fit part for England to take to become the champion either of the religious encroachment of the Emperor, or of the political anarchy of Frederick, and that it was his duty as a statesman and as an honest man to remain neutral, at least for the present, in the coming strife; but James was not the man to say anything of the kind. Never having taken the trouble to master the simplest elements of the political question, he had boasted again and again, with his accustomed garrulity, that he would accomplish everything upon which he had set his heart. Frederick and Ferdinand should be once more fast friends; his son-in-law, without any effort of his own, should again enjoy his lands and his honours; the marriage tie, which bound the Prince of Wales to the

---

* Frederick to the King, Dec. $\frac{20}{30}$. *Cabala*, 246.

Infanta, was to be the bond of amity within which pacified Europe would be encircled: and now all this bright vision had faded away, and in its stead there stood the furies of war and faction hounding on the suffering millions to their ruin. How could he, being what he was, stand forth and acknowledge his blindness? How could he even comprehend, with his poor confused brain, in what his blindness really consisted? There was nothing for it left but to give way at once, to allow his son and his favourite, with the nation at their backs, to work their will, whatever it might be.

On the 28th of December, James signed the warrant commanding the Lord Keeper to issue writs for a new Parliament.* On the 30th, he despatched a courier to Bristol reproving him for his conduct in agreeing to the betrothal, and ordering him to return immediately to England to give an account of his behaviour.†

The same courier conveyed a long letter to Aston, written in a greater state of bewilderment than usual. James was, beyond all measure, astonished at the interpretation put by the Spaniards on his order for postponing the betrothal. Both he and his son were more than ever anxious for the marriage. He had never meant to make the assurance for which he asked a condition of the marriage with the Infanta. He only intended it to be "as a fruit and blessing of the alliance with her, and an eternal pawn to this people of the constancy and faithful execution of that King's promises, and our expectation grounded upon those promises."

James might write in this style as much as he pleased; but it was none the less certain that the Spanish match was at an end. Nor was that the only thing which had passed away from the world of reality in those last days of December. For fifteen months more James was to sit upon the throne, and men would continue to style him King of England; but in the eyes of those who think more of the actual possession of power than of its semblance, he ceased to rule when he issued orders for the

---

* The King to Williams, Dec. 28. *Hacket*, 173.
† The King to Bristol, Dec. 30. *S. P. Spain.*

convocation of a Parliament. On that day the reign of Buckingham began.

So miserable had been the failure, so rapid the downfall of that self-sufficient monarch, that it is difficult to give him credit for those good intentions which were marred by the cloudiness of his intellect and the infirmity of his will. Yet even to him belongs a place amongst those who heralded the dawn of the new era, when difference of religion should no longer be regarded as a motive for war. Intolerant of opposition to his personal claims, he had now and again appeared on the stage as a persecutor. He had struck at Puritans on the one hand, and at Roman Catholics on the other; but his tendency was towards peace and quiet, and not towards violence; and stained as his foreign policy was throughout with selfish aims, no candid mind will fail to recognise in it an effort, ignorant and ineffectual it may be, but still an effort, towards that better day when the spiritual and eternal hopes and consolations of mankind would cease to form a rallying cry for blood-stained armies. It was by the consciousness that in this at least they stood upon a common ground, and not by any mere cringing adulation of the crowned monarch, that he succeeded in attaching to his throne the two most prescient statesmen of the age; and that he counted Bacon and Bristol amongst his ministers.

Of the two men, it is to Bristol rather than to Bacon that we must turn as the representative of the higher tendencies of his age. The sweep of Bacon's thoughts was too wide, whilst he was too often oblivious to that which was actually passing before his eyes not to render him a figure apart, whose position must be laid down in the chart of time on the scale of centuries and not of years. The mind of Bristol, on the other hand, was intensely practical: no visions of future glory thronged before his eyes; no general conceptions of law or policy ever exercised his intellect. From the hundreds of his letters which have been preserved, it would be difficult to reconstruct the theory upon which he acted; but he had that strong power of intuition which is accorded to some men, by which they are enabled to single out from all others the one predominant evil which is weighing down upon their time, and to discern instinctively the remedies which alone are applicable. Gradually as we read the long series of his despatches, the grand form of the noble-hearted man stands revealed before us, and we see him ever varying his means, as the events drifted before him with their changing forms, but never losing sight of the object at which he aimed.

If his own unalloyed wishes had been carried into execution, he would have gladly seen a gradual modification of the harsh treatment to which the English Catholics were exposed; and he would have based his foreign policy upon a friendly understanding with Spain, which would have made a continental war impossible. It was not his fault that this friendly understanding was exchanged for a marriage treaty, and for some time he seems to have exercised whatever influence he might possess in restricting within the narrowest limits the concessions which it would be requisite to make. For many years both he and his master concurred in refusing to make any express stipulation for those who were beyond the pale of the Infanta's household, though they were willing to promise that, as a matter of favour, the lot of the English Catholics should be alleviated. It was on this rock that the negotiations had almost split when the war in Germany broke out. A Protestant Prince, in the hope of protecting the followers of his own creed, engaged in a rash attempt to overturn the whole political fabric of the Empire, without even proposing to substitute anything better in its room. Borne back by the almost universal indignation which his rashness had excited, he was wandering about a fugitive, whilst the victorious Emperor was converting his recovered power into an engine of religious persecution. It was at this moment that the English statesman stepped upon the scene. Seizing at a glance the difficulties of the work of pacification, he proposed a compromise, which, whether it were logically defensible or not, would have been in the highest degree satisfactory to the vast majority of the German nation. Let the Emperor, he said in effect, blot the past out of his memory, and replace his rival in the position which he occupied before the war; let Frederick not only renounce the title of King of Bohemia which he had assumed, but let him, by making due submission to the Emperor, abandon the right of private war within the limits of the Empire.

Ch. XII.
1623.
December.

That such a compromise would have conduced alike to the peace of Europe and the independence of Protestantism it is impossible to doubt. Relieved from the dread of anarchy, Lutherans and Calvinists would have presented an united front to Catholic aggression, and the provocation which roused the final opposition by which the Imperial power was crushed, would never have been given. Unhappily the English Ambassador stood alone. His master had sent him to speak words of wisdom, but he had taken no care to support his representations by the argument of the sword; and he therefore hastened back to England to hurry on those preparations which had been too long delayed. The flames of war were already blazing behind him. Ferdinand could see no law but the written one, and no basis of authority excepting in the Church of Rome. Frederick had thrown himself into the arms of a needy adventurer, who was prepared, in order to advance his own ends, to spread fire and slaughter over the fair fields of his native land.

The day when the great advocate of peace learned that Parliament had been dissolved without granting a penny to the public service, must have been the saddest in the life of the patient, much-enduring man. Every difficulty had been surmounted; all opposition had been silenced, when he saw his dearest hopes wrecked on his sovereign's infirmity of temper.

It would have been well for him if his public career had ended there. After his return to Spain he was rather hoping against hope than pursuing any rational scheme. He learned to look with trust upon Spanish promises, though he had no longer the hope which he had once cherished, that his master would stand forward to enforce their performance. Yet, after all, his error was the error of a noble mind. He could not bear to think that others were less honest or less clear-sighted than himself. Against Frederick he maintained that no

His return to Spain.

peace was to be had unless he would restore the reign of order in the Empire. Against Ferdinand and Philip he maintained that no peace was to be had without guarantees for religious independence. For the sake of the benefits which would be accorded to the English Catholics, Spain would, he trusted, support him in imposing his compromise upon Germany, and it was only too late that he learned how unconquerable was the perversity of Frederick's nature, whilst he never learned at all that the Spanish ministers had been aiming, not merely at the alleviation of the sufferings of the few Catholics who were left in England, but at the reduction, by fraud or by force, of England itself to the creed of the Roman Catholic Church.

Failure of his hopes.

And so it came to pass that Bristol saw the bark which bore his political fortunes go down before his eyes; wrecked, not as he himself imagined, upon the petulance of Buckingham and the imbecility of Charles, but upon the inherent difficulties of the task which he had undertaken. The terms which he proposed may easily be criticised, and might probably have been amended with advantage. But his chief fault was that he attempted to impose terms at all upon those who were unwilling to assent to any reasonable compromise whatever.

1624. Jan. 14. Bristol's letter to Buckingham.

He was now to take leave of the scene in which he had played so distinguished and so honourable a part. To the last he preserved the full dignity of his character. Buckingham he had never flattered; but he had never ceased to treat him with respect. The letter which he wrote to him soon after the postponement of the marriage would surely have touched the heart of any man who was not lost to all sense of public duty. "The present estate of the King's affairs," he said, "requireth the concurrency of all his servants, and the co-operation of all his ministers, which maketh me desirous to make your Grace this tender of my service; that if there have happened any errors or misunderstandings, your Grace would for that regard pass them over; and for anything that may personally concern my particular, I shall labour to give you that satisfaction as may deserve your friendship. And if that shall not serve the turn, I shall not be found unarmed with patience against anything that can happen unto me."*

Language such as this was absolutely thrown away upon Buckingham. The favourite was not to be propitiated by anything short of the most cringing subservience, and it was not long before it was known all over Europe that when Bristol returned to London it would be, if Buckingham could have his way, to find ruin and disgrace before him. With the best intentions, but with very questionable taste, Olivares stepped forward to save him. In the presence of Gondomar and Aston he assured him that he was ordered to express his master's gratitude for the services which had been rendered to both Crowns, and that he was directed to place in his hands a sheet of white paper, which he was at liberty to fill up as he pleased in his own favour. He might ask either for lands or for honours, with the full assurance that nothing would be denied him. If he could further suggest any means by which he might be defended against his enemies at home, it should be put into execution at once.

To this strange proposal Bristol replied with dignity. The offer, he said, he could not but esteem as it deserved, but it troubled him more than the malice of his enemies had ever done; for against that he could appeal to the security of a good conscience and of his sovereign's justice; whereas what had now been said to him forced him to consider whether he had not been serving Spain rather than his own country. Spain, he proceeded to say, was not indebted to him the value of a leaf of paper. Whatever he had done, he had done because he thought it to be the best for England. He went home perfectly contented, and fully satisfied that he would meet with justice and protection from his sovereign. He was not, therefore, under the necessity of seeking the favour of another Prince. To speak plainly, he ended by saying, he would rather offer himself to the slaughter in England than be Duke of Infantado in Spain.†

* Bristol to Buckingham, Dec. 6. *Cabala*, 96.
† Account of the offers made by Olivares, Jan. $\frac{14}{24}$, 1624. *Sherborne MSS.*

CH. XII.
1624.
Jan. 28.
He takes leave of Philip.

A few days later, on the 28th of January, Bristol took his formal leave of Philip. As he went the King drew off from his own finger a valuable ring to present to the ambassador, an honour before unheard of at the Court of Spain. The next day Philip left Madrid for Seville on a journey of inspection into the state of the navy. It was the public signal that, though no formal notice had been given, the marriage treaty was practically at an end.

1623.
December.
His presentiment of coming evil.

Whatever Bristol may have thought of the causes of his failure, he had at least a clear presentiment of its results. "I will heartily pray to God," he wrote, in one of his last letters from Madrid, "to prevent that miserable storm, which is like suddenly to be raised in Christendom, if it be not speedily prevented by his especial goodness."* The war which was now about to blaze up once more from its smouldering ashes was indeed one which no one, who was acquainted with the real merits of the parties, could look upon without horror. On one side the cause of German nationality and of legal order was bound in an inextricable bond with an ecclesiastical despotism which was sapping the root of all moral and intellectual vigour. On the other side was a Protestantism which had lost all respect for law, and which had allied itself with the selfish greed of princes, and with the marauding instincts of the plunderers by whom the honourable name of soldiers was disgraced. The coming miseries of

The future of the Thirty years' War.

that war were beyond even Bristol's vision. The help, indeed, which Charles was eager to render to his brother-in-law proved to be in vain. No cause could support the accumulated burden of Frederick's incapacity, of Charles's weakness, and of the selfishness of Mansfeld and Christian. But when the victory had been won by the sword of Tilly, and the whole of Northern Germany lay at the Emperor's feet, then was revealed in turn the incapacity of Ferdinand to become the second founder of the Empire. He might have been the head of an united Germany; he might have given renewed life to the old national institutions, and have made the cold and calculating aggressions of Richelieu and of Lewis XIV. impossible. Lorraine and Alsace would still have remained

* Bristol to Calvert, Jan. 22, 1624. *S. P. Spain.*

German soil, and, what was of far greater consequence, two centuries of moral and political anarchy would have been spared to the noble German nation. But Ferdinand was still the Ferdinand of old. The Edict of Restitution replaced the two religions upon that legal basis which, in his eyes, was all in all. In the composition of his mind there was no room for the political element which weighs the feelings, the hopes, the passions of men before proceeding to action. He cared little that his extremity of law was held by half the nation to be the extremity of injustice. And thus it was that instead of standing, as he might have stood, at the head of an united people, he found himself coercing a divided nation, by the sword of an army which represented nothing but a faction. And what an army it was! Mansfeld and Christian were no longer alive, and their misdeeds had ceased to be a terror to German citizens and peasants. Frederick was living in hopeless exile unregretted and forgotten. It was round Wallenstein, the general, who represented the majesty of the Imperial name, and the cause of order against anarchy, that every element of anarchy and villany was gathered. During years of strife, men of every creed had cast yearning eyes towards him who wore the crown of the Othos and the Fredericks, to seek for that help which might reduce the chaos into order. They would never look with hope to Vienna again. The Empire had survived external contempt and internal dissolution; but the iniquities of Wallenstein laid it in the dust.

For a moment, the avenging arm of the great Swede was raised to redress the balance of the war, and to re-establish the Empire upon a Protestant basis. With the genius to construct as well as to destroy, it is probable that if he had been born a German prince, he might have stood at the head of a new and happier era. As it was, his career, even if his days had been prolonged, was predestined to failure. It was the last effort, almost till our own day, to establish any national order in Germany. After him came that waste and howling wilderness, resounding with shrieks and bitter cries, and filled with the struggles of brutal and degraded beings, who seemed

Ch. XII.
1623.
December.

Feeling in England.

Change in the condition of progress.

in form alone to resemble human kind. The hideous misery of that war, if war it can be called, no writer would willingly descend to recount; no reader would care to hear recited.

Yet, if Bristol was in the right in holding that the sword of England could not be drawn in such a war to the advantage of herself or of the Continent, he was scarcely conscious of the wide basis upon which rested that uneasy dissatisfaction with the existing state of things which had spread amongst all classes of the population at home; for he was hardly aware how completely the conditions of European politics had changed since he first arrived at Madrid in 1611. Then the evil, before which the rising intellect of the time shrunk with horror, was the prolongation of the religious strife. Everywhere the tendency of the age was towards an obliteration of the line drawn with such marked distinctness between the two creeds. In the field of speculation, the historian of the progress of tolerance can point to the spread of the Arminian theory. In the field of practical politics, he can trace the growing preponderance of political over theological arguments for persecution. Differing in everything else, Pym and Ferdinand II. would have repudiated with horror the notion that a heretic ought to be imprisoned or put to death simply because he was a heretic.

Before 1623 a great change had passed over the scene. Divide the blame as we may, the fact was undoubted that the old religion was encroaching upon Protestant soil. The evil most to be dreaded was no longer the continuance of war, but the imminence of defeat. In Germany the rashness of Frederick had betrayed the key of the Protestant position into Catholic hands. In England the weakness of James had granted to Spain a basis of operations against his own faith. For the interests of the human race, a barrier must be raised against the great enemy of its progress.

It was this alteration of circumstances, far more than his personal quarrel with Buckingham, which threw Bristol into discordance with the spirit of the age. Partly from the habitual deference to the home government which is the inevitable law of an ambassador's life, partly from his own mental constitution, his eyes were fixed too exclusively upon the horrors of a religious war. He saw all that was evil in those who had aroused it. He did not see that resistance to Catholic supremacy was rapidly becoming a necessity. He adopted, without a thorough examination of their ultimate tendencies, schemes for pacification which had not originated with himself, but which, faulty as they were, might perhaps lead to the consummation which he so ardently desired.

In truth, the balance of the two religions was only to be redressed by means which did not lie within the sphere of Bristol's intellect. No candid person can survey the world at the beginning of the seventeenth century without acknowledging that as far as the leaders were concerned, moral superiority was not on the Protestant side. It would be an insult to Ferdinand, to Maximilian, and to Tilly, to compare them for an instant with Frederick, with James, or with Mansfeld. Even Philip IV. and Olivares were vastly superior to their English visitors. Liars as they were, they hoped to achieve by their falsehoods something more than the gratification of their own immediate interests, or of their personal vanity. The great question which the Protestants of that age were called upon to solve was the eternal question which presents itself to all who have embraced freedom in any form. Would they regard their liberty as a means by which to grasp the conception of a higher order than they had known before? Would they learn discipline and obedience? Would they reverence law, and count truth as a most precious jewel? If they could do this, then the victories of Wimpfen and Höchst, of Stadtloo and Lutter, would have been won in vain. If not, the world would turn in disgust to the deathlike stillness of Papal absolutism, that it might escape from the miseries which the abuse of liberty had set before it.

Such was the question which Germany had failed to comprehend, but to which England was ready to respond. The men of that generation were prepared to build upon the foundations of that reverence at once for justice and for freedom which the events of centuries had laid deep

Ch. XII.
1623.
December.

Position of Charles.

Character of the past history,

in the English character. The world was to learn that there were men who were ready to suffer and to die, if need be, on behalf of principles more true, and of an order more fruitful of good and noble life than anything which Ferdinand and Maximilian had found it possible to conceive. From the study of Bacon, from the parsonage of George Herbert, from the pulpit of Baxter, from the prison of Eliot, a light was to break forth upon the world splendid in its multiplicity of colour and of brilliancy. It was to teach that world to shrink from anarchy and despotism alike, and to entrust the treasure of its moral and intellectual progress to ordered liberty.

How long the conflict thus entered upon would last, and to what issues it might finally be conducted, it was impossible to foretell. But to any one who had watched the events which had recently been passing in Spain, it must have been evident that the league which appeared to be springing up between Charles and the English nation could not by any possibility be long-lived. It was to no purpose that he had listened to the explosion of loyalty which had greeted his return; it was to no purpose that he found himself accidentally thrown into a fortuitous accordance with the deeper feelings of the nation. In all this there was no abiding security. Once before in English history had a giddy youth won a fleeting popularity by stepping forward to declare himself the leader of the multitudes whose sufferings had never touched his heart; and those who could look most deeply into the character of Charles might well dread lest the tragical story of the second Richard would be repeated in the face of an earnest and long-suffering nation.

If for a moment we turn back to look upon the years that had passed by as Charles was growing up to manhood, it is impossible to resist the feeling of discouragement. Not a hope had been formed which had not been baffled; not a man had stepped forward to guide the English nation who had not been thrown back into obscurity. Bacon was banished for ever from public life; Bristol's career had been cut short, and he was looking forward to the future with more anxiety than he was willing to express; Pym was solacing himself in the seclusion of a country life, and was waiting for better times. The wish to send forth an English army to the help of the Continental Protestants, and the wish to put an end by mediation to the miserable war by which Germany was devastated, had alike been uttered in vain. Seven years had gone by since the negotiation for the Spanish match had been formally opened, and it seemed as if, since that day, nothing had been done.

Yet it was not really so. The worth of an individual or of a nation lies not so much in what they achieve, as in what they are. Ignorance enough there had been, and sloth; but the will to do right was there. Bacon and Bristol, Pym and Phelips, and even (whenever his better nature was in the ascendant) James himself, were filled with a desire that their country, and the world, might be better and happier than it was. There was no petty desire of national aggrandizement in the English demand for war; there was no mere shrinking from laborious toil in the English demand for peace. And so it was that the seeds sown in these wintry days would bear precious fruit; that the silenced speakers of the Parliament which had been dissolved by the irritable King would gather to their side comrades as noble as themselves to bear in common the burden of the new struggle, into which they were to enter with clearer perceptions and with higher aims; and that the frustrated advocates of peace, when they had passed away from earth, would leave behind them men who would take up their work when the time came for it to be accomplished.

INDEX.

ABB

ABBOT, George, Archbishop of Canterbury, his dislike of Spain, i. 8. Obtains an order for the imprisonment of Luisa de Carvajal, i. 11. Refuses to read the Declaration of Sports, i. 203. His letter to Naunton on the war in Bohemia, i. 293. Accidental homicide by, ii. 31. Hospitable reception of De Dominis by, ii. 172. Issues the directions to preachers, ii. 233. Asks questions about the marriage treaty, ii. 360. Forged letter attributed to him, ii. 365

Aberdeen, Dunkirk ship at, ii. 373

Ainsworth, Henry, minister of a Separatist congregation at Amsterdam, ii. 36

Albert, the Archduke, receives Doncaster at Brussels, i. 281. Advocates the invasion of the Palatinate, i. 305. Answers Trumbull's inquiries about the invasion, i. 326. Rejects James's plan for a partition of the Netherlands, i. 335. Supports the suspension of arms in the Palatinate, ii. 80. Orders Spinola to aid the Duke of Bavaria, ii. 97. His death, ii. 98

Alehouses, patent for, i. 358. Inquiry into by the House of Commons, i. 412. Condemned by the Commons, ii. 3

Alford, Edward, congratulates Coke, i. 410. Defends liberty of speech, ii. 121

Algiers, becomes a nest of piracy, i. 70. Proposed expedition against, i. 76. Conferences between Digby and the Spanish ministers, i. 112. The fleet got ready against, i. 276. Cessation of preparations against, i. 281. Fresh preparations against, i. 348. Mansell's operations before, ii. 113

Aliaga, Luis de, appointed to negotiate with Digby, i. 109. Joins Uzeda in supplanting Lerma, i. 267. Opposes the invasion of the Palatinate, i. 306

VOL. II.

AST

Amsterdam, Separatist congregation at, ii. 36, 43

Ancre, Marquis of, his murder, i. 114

Andrewes, Lancelot, Bishop of Winchester, contrasted with Laud, i. 195. Preaches at the opening of Parliament, i. 394. His opinion of De Dominis, ii. 176

Anne, Queen (wife of James I.), her secret profession of the Roman Catholic religion, i. 14. Interferes in Raleigh's favour, i. 145. Her last illness, i. 238; and death, i. 239. Verses on her by her husband, i. 240

Anne, the Infanta, offered in marriage to Prince Henry, i. 6. Engaged to Lewis XIII. i. 7

Anstruther, Sir Robert, mission to Copenhagen, i. 310. Sent back to borrow money from the King of Denmark, i. 388. His interview with Christian IV. ii. 71

Antwerp, the Truce of, expiration of, ii. 77

Aremberg, Count of, extracts from his despatches, i. 46, note

Argall, Samuel, his abduction of Pocahontas, i. 212. His administration in Virginia, i. 214

Argyll, Earl of (Archibald Campbell), levies Scottish troops for the Spanish service, ii. 192

Arminianism, spread of, in the Netherlands, i. 209. Its acceptance in England, ii. 233

Arundel, Earl of (Thomas Howard), visits Raleigh, i. 65. Presides over a committee for taking evidence against Bacon, i. 458. Takes part in the discussion on Bacon's case, i. 462, 471. His quarrel with Spencer, ii. 7. Is sent to the Tower, ii. 8. Made Earl Marshal, ii. 30

Asti, Treaty of, i. 57

Aston, Sir Walter, sent ambassador to Madrid, i. 303. Receives assurances

B II

ATT

of goodwill from Philip IV., ii. 81. Objects to the education of the Electoral Prince at Vienna, ii. 401. His astonishment at Olivares' revelations, ii. 405
Attorney-General. See Bacon, Yelverton, Coventry
Aubrey's case against Bacon, i. 426
Augsburg, Peace of, i. 245. Its revision demanded, i. 247
Austria, the House of, causes of its growth, i. 251. Condition of Protestantism in its dominions, i. 252

BABWORTH, Clifton's preaching at, ii. 39
Bacon, Sir Francis, Attorney-General, recommends an active policy, i. 16. His position as an adviser of the Crown, i. 33. His argument about the position of Raleigh's mine, i. 54, note. His alleged conversation with Raleigh, i. 55, note. Talks with Raleigh about the Mexico fleet, i. 56. His views on the Spanish alliance, i. 68, 69. Proposes additional instructions to Digby, i. 70. Becomes Lord-Keeper, i. 86. Takes his seat in Chancery, i. 89. His hopefulness, i. 90. His objections to Sir J. Villiers' marriage, i. 95. His quarrel with Winwood, i. 96. Remonstrates with Buckingham on his brother's marriage, i. 97. Irritates the King, i. 100. Withdraws his opposition, i. 101. Regains the King's favour, i. 102. Becomes Chancellor, and created Lord Verulam, i. 106. Supposed misrepresentation of an incident in Raleigh's life examined, i. 138, note. Appointed a commissioner to take evidence against Raleigh, i. 141. Draws up the report, i. 145. Prepares the King's declaration, i. 152. Recommends economy, i. 167. His conduct at Suffolk's trial, i. 178, 179. Supports Shute's candidature for the Recordership, i. 186. Draws up a draft proclamation for summoning Parliament, i. 352. His statement about the prerogative, i. 353. His connection with the monopolies, i. 355, 357, 363, 366. Advises the withdrawal of the patents, i. 372. His remark on Montague's promotion, i. 376. Created Viscount St. Alban, i. 377. Publishes the "Novum Organum," i. 378. Harmony between his philosophy and his politics, i. 379. His views on parliamentary government, i. 381; and on foreign policy, i. 382. His opinion of Cadenet, i. 391. His conduct as a referee of the patents questioned, i.

BES

415. Called to order in the House of Lords, i. 420. Charged with bribery, i. 426. Examination of Aubrey's case, i. 426—428; of Egerton's case, i. 428—432. His appeal to Buckingham, i. 434. His illness, i. 435. His case carried to the Lords, i. 439. Lady Wharton's case examined by the Commons, i. 440. He protests his innocence, i. 450. Makes notes in his case, i. 456. His interview with the King, i. 457. Hears of the evidence against him, i. 459. Abandons his defence, i. 460. Is required to answer the charges particularly, i. 463. His full confession, i. 468. The Great Seal taken from him, i. 469. His sentence, i. 471. Imprisoned and released, ii. 24. His "History of Henry VII.," ii. 25. Jests at Mandeville's resignation, ii. 116. Objects to giving up York House, ii. 164. Surrenders York House, ii. 166
Baden-Durlach, Margrave of. See George Frederick
Bailey, Captain, deserts Raleigh, i. 118
Ballard, an English Jesuit, assaulted by Sir E. Verney at Madrid, ii. 395
Banda Isles, the, produce nutmegs, i. 218. Partial conquest of by the Dutch, i. 219. See Puloway and Pularoon
Bandino, Cardinal, his instructions to Gage, ii. 237
Bantam, proceedings of the Dutch at, i. 225
Barbary pirates. See Algiers
Barneveldt, John van Olden, supports the Arminians, i. 209. Is deprived of power, i. 250. Execution of, i. 211
Bedford, Earl of (Edward Russell), ii. 119.
Bedford, Lady, takes part in the patent for gold and silver thread, i. 362
Belle, Captain, reveals Raleigh's plans to the Spaniards, i. 116
Ben, Sir Anthony, death of, i. 186
Benevolence, for the Palatinate, the first, i. 347, 354. The second, ii. 182
Bennett, Sir John, offers to purchase the Chancellorship, i. 86. Charge of corruption against him, ii. 1, 18. Sentenced in the Star-Chamber, ii. 236
Bergen-op-Zoom, siege of, ii. 227. Relief of, ii. 261
Berkshire, Earl of (Francis Norris), his quarrel with Scrope, i. 408. Commits suicide, ii. 164
Berreo, Spanish governor of Trinidad, gives information to Raleigh, i. 40
Berry, Captain, sent by Raleigh to Guiana, i. 45
Best, Captain, sent to Aberdeen, ii. 377. Convoys a Dunkirk vessel, ii. 379.

BET

Attacks the Dutch ships in the Downs, ii. 380. Is superseded by Bingley, ii. 381

Bethlen Gabor, Prince of Transylvania, his attack upon Vienna, i. 299. Elected king of Hungary, i. 384

Bills of Conformity, i. 425

Bingley, Sir John, accused of malpractices, i. 158. Proceedings against in the Star-Chamber, i. 178

Bingley, Sir Richard, convoys a Dunkirk vessel to Mardike, ii. 381

Blackfriars, accident at, ii. 435

Bohemia, Protestantism in, i. 252. Aristocracy of, i. 253. The Royal Charter of, 254. Question of the right of church-building in, i. 255. Ferdinand accepted as King of, i. 256. Revolution in, i. 259. Commencement of hostilities in, i. 260. Proposed mediation, i. 264, 266. Successes of the revolutionists, i. 267. Defeat of their army, i. 284. Election of Frederick, i. 288. Disorganization of the state and army, i. 289. Conquest of, by the Imperialists, i. 383. Expulsion of the Lutheran clergy from, ii. 285

Bowes, Sir Jerome, his patent for the manufacture of glass, i. 362

Brackley, Viscount (see Ellesmere, Lord), his death, i. 85

Bradford, William, attends Clifton's preaching, ii. 39. Chosen Governor of the New England colony, ii. 60

Brett, Anne, her marriage to Cranfield, i. 182

Brett, Arthur, suspected of a design to rival Buckingham, ii. 302

Brewster, Captain, condemned to death by Argall, i. 215

Brewster, William, postmaster at Scrooby, ii. 39. Opens his house to the Separatists, ii. 41. His position in New England, ii. 60

Bridgewater, Earl of (John Egerton), reported payment by, i. 85

Bristol, Earl of (see Digby, Lord), ordered to lay a summons before Philip, ii. 256, 259. His confidence in ultimate success, ii. 264. Receives fresh assurances from Philip, ii. 265. Obtains orders to the Infanta Isabella to intervene in James's behalf, ii. 266. Formally demands the restitution of the Palatinate, ii. 269. Receives an answer, ii. 281. Informed of the scheme for educating the Electoral Prince at Vienna, ii. 307. His conversation with Charles about his conversion, ii. 312. Repels Olivares' argument that he is at liberty to make fresh demands, ii. 315. Advocates the

BUC

education of the Electoral Prince at Vienna, ii. 401. Review of his policy, ii. 402. Acquaints the King with Buckingham's insolence, ii. 405. Inquires into the design of going into a nunnery attributed to the Infanta, ii. 414. Writes about delaying the marriage, ii. 425. Receives Philip's declaration about the Palatinate, ii. 431. He complains of the postponement of the marriage, ii. 432. Announces that he shall go on with it unless he hears further, ii. 440. Fixes the day, ii. 444. Receives orders to postpone it, 445. Summons Philip to restore the Palatinate, ii. 446. Is recalled, ii. 452. Pleads with Buckingham, ii. 456. Rejects the offers of Olivares, ii. 457. His presentiment of coming evil, ii. 458

Brooke, Lord (Fulke Greville), i. 377

Brown, Rawdon, his discovery of the evidence of a proposed attack upon Genoa, i. 59

Brussels, movement of troops at, i. 302

Buckingham, Countess of (see Lady Compton), requested to leave the Court, i. 177. Interferes with her son's patronage, i. 182. Tries to find a wife for her son Christopher, i. 241. Interferes in Buckingham's courtship, i. 328, 331. Her conversion by the Jesuit Fisher, ii. 167. Listens to the conference between Fisher and Laud, ii. 168

Buckingham, Duke of (see Buckingham, Marquis of), fails in inducing Charles to break off the marriage, ii. 353. His arrogant conduct, ii. 386. Threatens Khevenhüller, ii. 387. Is sent to Olivares to persuade him to allow the Infanta to come, ii. 388. His interview with the Infanta, ii. 389. His ironical compliment to Olivares, ii. 405. His continued arrogance, ii. 407. Information of his conduct given by Bristol to the King, ii. 408. Insults Olivares on taking leave, ii. 409. His arrival in England, ii. 421. Takes part against Spain, ii. 434. Makes a report to the committee of the council, ii. 436. Urges James to summon Parliament, ii. 450

Buckingham, Earl of (see Villiers, Viscount), opposes Yelverton's promotion, i. 86. Receives Bacon's remonstrances against his brother's marriage, i. 97, 100. His anger with Bacon, i. 101. Is reconciled to him, i. 102. Created Marquis of Buckingham, i. 106. See Buckingham, Marquis of

Buckingham, Marquis of (see Bucking-

H H 2

468   INDEX.

BUC

ham, Earl of), his jealousy of the Howards, i. 155. His quarrel with the Prince, i. 157. His lease of the Irish customs, i. 157, note. Quarrels with Lake, i. 158. Appointed Lord High Admiral, i. 175. Asks for leniency to Suffolk, i. 179. Supports Shute's candidature for the Recordership of the City, i. 186. Puts forward Heath, i. 187. Takes part with the popular party, i. 303. Deserts the war-party, i. 328. His courtship, i. 329. Quarrels with Rutland, i. 331. His marriage, i. 332. Supports Cecil for the command of the volunteers, i. 332. Complains of the Dutch to Gondomar, i. 333. His language about the invasion of the Palatinate, i. 340. His conversation with Cadenet, i. 391. His alarm at the proceedings against Mompesson, i. 414. His attack upon the referees, i. 415. His alarm, i. 421. Declares against the monopolies, i. 422. His quarrel with Southampton, i. 423. His conversation with Bacon, i. 434. Advocates a dissolution, i. 453. Blames Bacon, i. 455. Defends him in the House of Lords, i. 462, 471, 472. Listens to Yelverton's attack, ii. 5. Sets the political prisoners at liberty, ii. 29. His language about the Palatinate, ii. 76. His hostility to the Dutch, ii. 115. Rides in a litter with Gondomar, ii. 116. Urges the dissolution of Parliament, ii. 153. Bargains with Bacon for York House, ii. 164. Buys Wallingford House, ii. 167. Is confirmed by the Bishop of London, ii. 167. Is present at Laud's conference with Fisher, ii. 168. Writes to Gondomar on the marriage, ii. 240. His eagerness for war, ii. 250. Selected to command the fleet in which the Infanta is to come, ii. 256. Wants to ask for another benevolence, ii. 260. His appointment to command the fleet announced, ii. 294. Joins in asking leave for Charles to go through France, ii. 298. Adventures on the way, ii. 302. Arrives at Madrid, ii. 305. Is presented to the King, ii. 309. His conversation with Olivares on the Prince's conversion, ii. 309. His negotiation with Olivares, ii. 315. His satisfaction with his position, ii. 318. Engages in a religious discussion with a friar, ii. 323. Discusses theology with Olivares, ii. 325. Quarrels with Don Francisco Giron, ii. 328. His insolent conduct at a religious conference, ii. 329. His quarrel with Olivares, ii. 332. His anxiety to break

CAR

off the treaty, ii. 339. Offers that the present laws shall be repealed, ii. 340. Created a Duke, ii. 348. See Buckingham, Duke of
Bucquoi, Count, commands the Imperialists in Bohemia, i. 260. Defeats Mansfeld, i. 284. Defeated and slain, ii. 94
Burroughs, Sir John, commander of Frankenthal, ii. 111. Prevented from taking his troops to Mannheim, ii. 248
Bushel, his story about Bacon examined, i. 458
Buwinckhausen de Walmerode, Benjamin, his mission to Holland and England, i. 307

CADENET, Marquis of, his embassy to England, i. 390
Calvert, Sir George, appointed Secretary of State, i. 164. Asks the House of Commons for supply, i. 397. Brings a message on liberty of speech, i. 399. Asks for supply, i. 400. Explains Sandys' imprisonment, ii. 121. Begs the Commons to grant a supply, ii. 125. Accepts Coke's explanation of the King's attack upon the privileges of the House, ii. 145. Advises a more active policy in Germany, ii. 295. Takes part in preparing the pardon and dispensation for the Recusants, ii. 391. Listens to a proposal from the Spanish ambassadors for the pacification of Germany, ii. 423
Canaries, Raleigh's visit to, i. 118
Carapana's village on the Orinoco, i. 40
Carey, Sir Henry, created Viscount Falkland, i. 408
Carleton, Sir Dudley (Ambassador at the Hague), a candidate for the secretaryship, i. 105. Complains of Frederick, ii. 101. Remonstrates about the Dutch attack upon the Dunkirk ship at Leith, ii. 373
Carlisle, Earl of (James Hay), sent to Paris to ask for a safe conduct for the Prince, ii. 303. Takes part in the negotiation with the Spanish ambassadors, ii. 392
Caron, Noel de, Dutch ambassador in England, proposes a negotiation on the East India quarrel, i. 226. Complains of the ill-feeling caused by the delays of the Dutch, ii. 115
Carvajal, Luisa de, imprisonment of, i. 11
Carver, John, first Governor of the New England colony; ii. 54. His death, ii. 60

CAS

Castleton, Samuel, his proceedings at Puloway, i. 222
Catholics, the English, their condition, i. 18. Prospects of the conversion of England to their religion, i. 24, 189. Their ill treatment by the pursuivants, i. 319. Petition of the Houses against, i. 398. Reply of the King to the petition, i. 402. Their position in the country, ii. 177. Favours accorded to, ii. 391
Cavendish, Lord (William Cavendish), purchases the earldom of Devonshire, i. 184
Cayenne, the, Raleigh's visit to, i. 120
Cecil, Sir Edward, aspires to the command of the troops in the Palatinate, i. 332. Quarrels with Dohna, i. 333. Member of the Council of War, i. 389. Speech in Parliament falsely attributed to him, i. 397. Approves Perrot's motion for a declaration, ii. 22
Cham, surrender of, to the Bavarians, ii. 108
Chancellor, Lord High. See Ellesmere; Bacon
Chancery Reform, Bill for, ii. 2
Charles, Emmanuel I., Duke of Savoy, his war with Spain, i. 57. Sends Scarnafissi to England, i. 58. Makes peace with Spain, i. 61. Offers to make over Mansfeld's regiment to the Elector Palatine, i. 265. Refuses to take part in the war in Bohemia, i. 279
Charles, the Infant, his hostility to the English marriage, ii. 322
Charles, Prince of Wales (see marriage treaty with France, Savoy, and Spain). Early quarrel and reconciliation with Buckingham, i. 157. Is present at his mother's death, i. 238. Takes his sister's part, i. 303. Hears the scheme for the partition of the Netherlands, i. 334. Subscribes to the benevolence, i. 347. His distress on hearing of the battle of Prague, i. 387. Carries Bacon's letter to the Lords, i. 462. His feelings about his marriage, ii. 253. His character, ii. 251. He promises Gondomar that he will visit Madrid, ii. 254. Sees the Princess Henrietta Maria at Paris, ii. 303. Reaches Madrid, ii. 305. Expectations of his conversion, ii. 308. His con-

CHI

versation with Bristol on the subject, ii. 312. He is lodged at the Palace, ii. 313. Pays a formal visit to the Infanta, ii. 324. Congratulated on the grant of the dispensation, ii. 325. Dines in state on St. George's day, ii. 328. Enters upon a religious discussion, ii. 329. Is not allowed to admit his chaplains to the Palace, ii. 331. Offers made by him to justify the King of Spain's oath, ii. 333. Makes further concessions, ii. 336. Dismissal of his retinue, ii. 337. Declares his intention of leaving, which he afterwards retracts, ii. 340. Agrees to all demands, ii. 341. His letter to the Pope, ii. 342. Asks to return to England on hearing that the Infanta is to be detained, ii. 344. Promises to remain, ii. 345. Leaps over the wall of the Infanta's garden, ii. 346. Asks his father for full powers, ii. 348. Tries to induce the Spaniards to reconsider their decision, ii. 352. Declares the treaty at an end, ii. 355. Accepts the terms proposed, ii. 366. Accepts additional articles, ii. 383. Signs the marriage contract, ii. 385. Hopes to take the Infanta with him after all, ii. 386. Agrees to be married and to remain till the spring, ii. 394. Changes his mind again, ii. 394. Finally determines to go, ii. 396. His conversation with Olivares about the Palatinate, ii. 399. Is shown Philip's letter by Olivares ii. 405. Sends a present to the Infanta, ii. 406. Swears to the marriage contract, and leaves Madrid, ii. 407. Spends two days at the Escurial, ii. 408. Takes leave of Philip, ii. 409. Fears that the Infanta will go into a nunnery, ii. 410. His letter to Bristol by Clarke, ii. 411. Sails for England, ii. 413. Arrives in London, ii. 421. Meets his father, ii. 422. Writes to Bristol to postpone the marriage, ii. 428. Shows signs of coolness towards Spain, ii. 435. Repeats his orders to Bristol to postpone the marriage, ii. 439. Urges his father to summon Parliament, ii. 450. His future prospects, ii. 462
Chichester, of Belfast, Lord (Arthur Chichester), his mission to the Palatinate, ii. 191. He arrives at Mannheim, ii. 202. Fails in negotiating an armistice, ii. 203. His opinion of Mansfeld's army, ii. 204. His position at Frankfort, ii. 248. Sends Nethersole to England, ii. 249. Is recalled, ii. 268. Appointed a Privy Councillor, ii. 294

CHR

Christian IV., King of Denmark, lends money to James, i. 388. Reproves Frederick, ii. 70. Lends more money to James, ii. 71. Complains of the inertness of James, ii. 85. Offers mediation, ii. 203

Christian of Anhalt, his intrigues, i. 250. His mission to Turin, i. 279

Christian of Brunswick, Administrator of Halberstadt, his ravages in Germany, ii. 181, 189. Marches towards the Main, ii. 203. Is defeated at Höchst, ii. 205. Takes no part in the Conference at Brussels, ii. 209. Shares in the Battle of Fleurus, ii. 227. His campaign in North-west Germany, ii. 370. His defeat at Stadtloo, ii. 371

Christina, the Princess, her proposed marriage with Prince Henry, i. 7; and afterwards with Prince Charles, i. 7

Churchill, John, Registrar in Chancery, malversation of, i. 424. His connection with Lady Wharton's case, i. 442, 443, 444. Presents a list of charges against Bacon, i. 430

Clarke, Edward, conveys the Princess's letter to Bristol, ii. 411. Is taken ill, ii. 413. Gives the letter to Bristol, ii. 414

Clayton, Mr., imprisoned for attacking Spain in a Sermon, ii. 232

Clifton, Richard, his preaching at Babworth, ii. 38. Ejected from his rectory, ii. 39. Becomes minister of the Separatists at Scrooby, ii. 41. Settles at Amsterdam, ii. 43

Cobham, Lord (Henry Brooke), Death of, i. 153

Coke, Clement, joins in carrying off his sister from Oatlands, i. 98

Coke, Frances, asked in marriage by Sir John Villiers, i. 93. Signs a contract of marriage with the Earl of Oxford, i. 97. Is carried to Oatlands, i. 97. Seized by her father, i. 98. Her marriage, i. 103

Coke, Sir Edward, his treatment after his disgrace, i. 91. Quarrels with his wife about the Hatton estate, i. 92. Haggles with Lady Compton over his daughter's marriage, i. 95. Carries off his daughter from Oatlands, i. 98. Appears before the Council, i. 99. Is favourably received by the King, i. 102. Restored to the Council Table, i. 103. Votes for a harsh sentence upon Suffolk, i. 179. His opinion on the patent for mines, i. 351. His position in the House of Commons, i. 409. Moves that Michell be sent to the Tower, i. 412. Reports the opinion of the Committee against Mompesson, i. 413.

COM

His argument upon the jurisdiction of the Commons, i. 414. Brings in a bill against Monopolies, i. 423. Objects to the King's plan for a new tribunal, i. 437. His opinion on the jurisdiction of the Commons, ii. 15. Repeats the prayer for the Royal Family, ii. 23. Attacked by Lepton and Goldsmith, ii. 128. His speech against Spain, ii. 129. Excuses James's attack on the privileges of the House, ii. 145. Moves for a Protestation, ii. 147. Is committed to the Tower, ii. 154. Set at liberty, ii. 236

Coloma, Carlos, Spanish ambassador in England, ii. 221. Asks for the opening of the ports to a Spanish fleet, ii. 261. Negotiates the pardon and dispensation for the Recusants, ii. 391. Presents a plan for pacifying Germany, ii. 423

Commons, House of, its quarrel with the King in 1614, i. 17. Its first debate in 1621, i. 397. Petitions against the Recusants, i. 398. Grants a supply, i. 400. Debate on Gondomar's licence to support ordnance, i. 401. Expulsion of Shepherd, i. 402. Its foreign policy, i. 403. Debates on Monopolies, i. 409—424. Proceedings against Michell and Mompesson, i. 412—413. Its jurisdiction questioned, i. 413. Demands inquiry into the conduct of the referees, i. 418. Sends up the charges against Mompesson to the Lords, i. 423. Examines the charges against Bacon, i. 426. Sends them up to the Lords, i. 433. Debate on the King's scheme for a new tribunal, i. 437. Refuses fresh supplies, ii. 2. Condemns the patent for alehouses, ii. 3. Is exasperated with Floyd, ii. 13. Its jurisdiction questioned, ii. 14. Patents condemned by, ii. 18. Declaration of, ii. 22. Adjourned, ii. 33. Called by the Lords to hear a statement on the King's behalf, ii. 120. Discussion on Sandys' imprisonment, ii. 121. Takes into consideration the King's demand for a supply, ii. 122. Resolves to grant a supply, ii. 129. Goes into Committee on religion, ii. 130. Debate on the clause relating to the Prince's marriage, ii. 135. Reception of the King's letter, refusing to receive the petition, ii. 138. Draws up an explanatory petition, ii. 139. Sends a deputation to the King, ii. 140. Debate upon the King's answer, ii. 142. Claims the right of petition and freedom of speech, ii. 143. Unanimity of, ii. 145. Resolves to consider its privileges in Committee, ii.

145. Receives a fresh communication from the King, ii. 146. Resolves upon a protestation, ii. 149. Necessity of guarding its privileges, ii. 150. The last sitting, ii. 152

Compton, Bacon's interference in his favour, i. 466

Compton, Lord (William Compton), created Earl of Northampton, i. 184

Compton, Lady, supports Sir J. Villiers's offer of marriage with Frances Coke, i. 94. Strikes a bargain with Coke, i. 95. Appeals to Bacon and Winwood against Lady Hatton, i. 98. Created Countess of Buckingham, i. 177. See Buckingham, Countess of

Compton, Sir Thomas, i. 95.

Conway, Sir Edward, ambassador to Germany, with Sir R. Weston, i. 336. Visits Brussels, i. 337. Gives advice to the Union at Oppenheim, i. 342. Arrives at Prague, i. 385. Is recalled, i. 338. Appointed Secretary of State, ii. 294. Assures Buckingham of the King's anxiety for his return, ii. 351. Takes part in the negotiation with the Spanish ambassadors, ii. 392

Cooke, his treatment by the Commissioners of the patent for inns, i. 411

Cordova, Gonzalo Fernandez de, Spanish commander in the Lower Palatinate, ii. 98. Seizes Stein, ii. 104. Ravages the Palatinate, ii. 202. Commands at the Battle of Fleurus, ii 227

Cottington, Francis, urges Sarmiento to propose a Spanish marriage, i. 15. Agent at Madrid, i. 268. Brings despatches from Spain, ii. 258. Is consulted by James about the Prince's journey, ii. 300. Is created a Baronet, and accompanies the Prince, ii. 302. Returns with the Spanish terms, ii. 346. Arrives in England, ii. 350

Cotton, Sir Robert, his secret negotiation with Sarmiento, i. 29. Assures Sarmiento that he is a Roman Catholic, i. 32. Sent to search Coke's papers, ii. 154

Council of War, formed, i. 389. Its report considered in the House of Commons, i. 399

Courthope, Nathaniel, his defence of Pularoon, i. 223, 229. His death, i. 236

Coventry, Sir Thomas, becomes Solicitor-General, i. 88. Takes part in the proceedings against Raleigh, i. 142. Becomes Attorney-General, i. 376. Sent with a message from the King to the Commons, i. 420

Cowes, ship seized by the Dutch at, ii. 374.

Cranfield, Lord (Lionel Cranfield), made Lord Treasurer, ii. 117. Asks the Commons for a supply, ii. 121. Created Earl of Middlesex, ii. 256. See Middlesex, Earl of

Cranfield, Sir Lionel, his rise, i. 168. Takes the lead in administrative reform, i. 170. Appointed Master of the Wardrobe, i. 172. Becomes Master of the Wards, i. 182. Attacks Bacon as a referee of the patents, i. 415. His jealousy of Bacon's interference with the Courts of Wards, i. 416. Complains of Bacon's procedure with respect to Bills of Conformity, i. 435. Attempt to hinder an adjournment, ii. 20. Speaks on the state of trade, ii. 21. Named for the Lord Keeper's place, ii. 27. Created a Peer, ii. 33. See Cranfield, Lord

Cranmer, Archbishop, his opinion on the introduction of innovations, i. 197, note

Crew, Thomas, carrying to the Lords charges against the referees, i. 415, 420. Asks who is the enemy against whom the Commons are to prepare, ii. 125

DALE, Sir Thomas, his administration in Virginia, i. 211. His expedition to the East Indies, i. 225. His Victory over the Dutch, i. 234. His Death, i. 235

Dansker, a Dutch pirate, i. 72

Declaration of Sports, the, issue of, i. 202.

De Dominis, Marco Antonio, his early life, ii. 170. Takes refuge in England, ii. 170. Returns to Rome, ii. 175

De La Warr, Lord (Thomas West), his death, i. 215

Delft Haven, sailing of the emigrants from, ii. 49

De Massimi, Papal Nuncio in Spain, urges Olivares to approve of the transference of the Electorate, ii. 307. Refuses to make concessions about the marriage treaty, ii. 316. Demands the cession of fortified towns to the English Catholics, ii. 317. Converses with Olivares about the Electorate, ii. 320. Displeased with Olivares for announcing the dispensation, 328. Insulted by Buckingham, ii. 336

Denham, Sir John, i. 88

Desmarets, his interview with Raleigh, i. 62

Deux Ponts, Duke of, Administrator of the Palatinate, i. 344. Urges Vere to occupy the lands of the Bishop of Spires, ii. 103

Devonshire, Earl of (Charles Blount), receives a Spanish pension, i. 14, note

Digby, Lord (John Digby), his policy,

INDEX.

DIG

i. 310, 311, note. His conversation with Gondomar, i. 313. Is present when Gondomar proposes a War with the Dutch, i. 334. His views on the Spanish Alliance, i. 337. Repels Gondomar's objections to the expedition against Algiers, i. 349. His mission to Brussels, ii. 79. Receives instructions for his embassy to Vienna, ii. 89. His negotiations at Vienna, ii. 93. Complains of his difficulties, ii. 104. His interview with Mansfeld, ii. 107. Visits Heidelberg and Brussels, ii. 112. His return to England, ii. 118. His speech on Foreign Affairs, ii. 120. His vexation at the dissolution of Parliament, ii. 156. His policy compared with that of Gondomar, ii. 157. His return to Madrid, ii. 216. Obtains fresh assurances about the marriage, ii. 219. Urges that the King of Spain shall enforce a cessation of arms, ii. 221. Created Earl of Bristol, ii. 250. See Bristol, Earl of

Digby, Sir John, sent Ambassador to Spain to open the marriage treaty, i. 7. His return to England in 1614, i. 21. His views on the marriage, i. 27. He resumes his negotiation at Madrid, i. 29. Returns to England in 1615, and discovers Somerset's intrigues with Sarmiento, i. 33. Sent to Madrid to open formal negotiations for the marriage, i. 68. Sails for Spain, i. 107. His negotiation with Aliaga, i. 110. Returns to England, i. 111. Created Lord Digby, i. 112. See Digby, Lord

Digges, Sir Dudley, complains of Bacon's procedure with respect to Bills of Conformity, i. 425. Calls the attention of the Commons to the imprisonment of Sandys, ii. 121. Supports the King's demand for Supply, ii. 122. Supports the petition on Religion, ii. 136. Seconds Philip's motion for adjournment, ii. 139. Expresses satisfaction with the King, ii. 142. Sent to Ireland, ii. 154

Dixon, W. Hepworth, examination of statements by, i. 425, 442, 455

Dohna, Baron Achatius of, his mission to England, i. 308. Attempts to raise a loan in the City, i. 316. Receives permission to ask for a contribution and to levy volunteers, i. 326. Selects Vere for the command in the Palatinate, i. 332. Insulted by Sir E. Cecil, i. 333. Gives offence and is obliged to leave England, i. 393

Dohna, Baron Christopher of, his first mission to England, i. 273. His second mission, i. 291

Doncaster, Viscount (Sir Hay, Lord), his

ELE

mission to Germany, i. 277. Receives his instructions, i. 280. Visits Brussels, i. 281. Supports Frederick's demand for English aid, i. 282. His meeting with Ferdinand and Oñate, i. 285. Rejection of his overtures to the Bohemians, i. 287. Retires to Spa, i. 287. Ordered to congratulate Ferdinand, i. 302. Returns to England, i. 308. His mission to France, ii. 178. Created Earl of Carlisle, ii. 250. See Carlisle, Earl of

Dorset, first Earl of (Thomas Sackville), receives a Spanish pension, i. 14, note

Dorset, third Earl of (Richard Sackville), his contribution for the Palatinate, i. 322

Dort, Synod of, i. 210

Drummond, Mrs. receives a Spanish pension, i. 14

Du Buisson, his mission to England, i. 390

Dunkirk vessels in Scotland, i. 373

Dutch. See Netherlands, States General of the

EAST INDIA COMPANY. See East Indies

East Indies, disputes between the English and Dutch in the, i. 217. Protection of the East India Company, i. 223. Proposed Negotiation, i. 226. Reprisals on the Dutch, i. 227. Negotiations opened, i. 229. Continued discussions, i. 230. The King's arbitration, i. 233. Signature of a treaty, i. 234. Fresh quarrels, i. 235. The treaty known in the East, i. 236. Fresh dispatches, ii. 161. Settlement of the disputes, ii. 292

Ecclesiastical preservation, the, i. 246

Edmondes, Sir Thomas (Treasurer of the Household), his interview with Scarnassi, i. 60

Edwards, E., his argument on the date of one of Raleigh's letters, i. 47, note. Date assigned by him to Raleigh's release, i. 48, note. His statement about the geographical position of San Thomé, i. 55, note. Date assigned by him to a conversation between Raleigh and Bacon, i. 56, note. His remarks on Raleigh's Genoa scheme, i. 60, note. Examination of a charge brought by him against Bacon, i. 138, note

Egerton, Edward, his gratuity to Bacon, i. 428

Egerton, Sir Roland, his gratuity to Bacon, i. 464

El Dorado, i. 39

Elector Palatine. See Frederick V.

ELE

Electress Palatine. See Elizabeth
Eliot, James, story of his discovery of Purgatory, ii. 337
Eliot, Sir John, mistake in his account of Parliamentary proceedings in 1614, i. 17, note
Elizabeth, Electress Palatine, her marriage, i. 7. Advises her husband to accept the Crown of Bohemia, i. 259. Her language after the Battle of Prague, ii. 66. Is forbidden to visit England, ii. 73. Protests against her husband's visit to the Dutch camp, ii. 100. Her health drunk at the Middle Temple, ii. 283
Elizabeth, Queen, her reception of Raleigh, after his return from Guiana, i. 42. Her treatment of the claim of the House of Commons to liberty of speech, ii. 144
Ellesmere, Lord (Thomas Egerton), his opposition to the Spanish party, i. 8. Created Viscount Brackley, i. 84. See Brackley, Viscount
Essex, Earl of (Robert Devereux), serves in the Palatinate, i. 339. Returns to England, i. 389
Everard, Dr., imprisoned, ii. 11, 232
Exeter, Countess of, charges brought against her by Lady Roos, i. 161
Exeter, Earl of (Thomas Cecil), interferes in his grandson's dealings with the Lakes, i. 160
Exportation of gold, i. 237

FAIGE, Captain, sent by Raleigh to France, i. 63, 113. Entrusted with bringing reinforcements, i. 115, 117, note
Ferdinand II., Emperor, his visit to Munich, i. 297. His secret compact with Maximilian, i. 298. Defends Vienna, i. 299. Advocates the invasion of the Palatinate, i. 305. His position after the Battle of Prague, ii. 63. Proposes to transfer Frederick's Electorate to Maximilian, ii. 83. Authorises Maximilian to attack Mansfeld, ii. 93. Inclines to an accommodation, ii. 95. Secretly transfers the Electorate upon Maximilian, ii. 109. Gives instructions to the Infanta Isabella, ii. 192. His indignation against Mansfeld, ii. 225. Confers Frederick's Electorate upon Maximilian, ii. 289
Ferdinand, the Archduke, (afterwards King of Hungary and Bohemia), acknowledged King of Bohemia, i. 256. His character, i. 257. His pilgrimage to Loretto, i. 258. Expels the Protestants from his Duchies, i. 259. His reception of Doncaster, i. 285. He is

FRA

elected Emperor, and deposed from the throne of Bohemia, i. 255. See Ferdinand II., Emperor
Ferdinand, the Archduke (son of Ferdinand II.), proposed marriage between him and the Infanta Maria, i. 351
Ferrett, his behaviour as an agent of the Commissioners of the patent for inns, i. 411
Field, Theophilas, Bishop of Llandaff, his connection with the Egerton case, i. 432; ii. 18
Fielding, Lord (William Fielding), becomes Master of the Wardrobe, and is created Viscount Fielding, ii. 164. See Fielding, Viscount
Fielding, Sir William, created Lord Fielding, ii. 164. See Fielding, Lord
Fielding, Viscount (William Fielding), created Earl of Denbigh, ii. 250
Finances, state of the, i. 165. Improvement in the, i. 176
Finch, John, speaks in Bacon's favour, i. 432
Finch, Sir Heneage, Recorder of the City of London, i. 376. Carries up to the Lords the charges against the referees, i. 418, 420
Finch, Sir Henry, a referee for the patent for inns, i. 356
Fisher, the Jesuit, his conference with Laud, ii. 168
Fishery, the herring, Dutch claims to, i. 227
Fishery, the Spitzbergen, i. 227, 234
Fleetwood, Sir Miles, speech of, in the debate in supply, ii. 123
Flemish ports, blockade of the, ii. 115, 160, 372
Fleurus, battle of, ii. 227
Floyd, Edward, insults Frederick and Elizabeth, ii. 12. Sentenced by the Commons, ii. 14. Sentenced by the Lords, ii. 16. Set at liberty, ii. 20
Forster, J., quotation by him from a speech of Eliot's, i. 17. His view of the circumstances of the grant of supply in 1621, i. 100. His statement respecting the date of a letter, ii. 146
France (see Marriage Treaty with). Civil war in, ii. 177
Francisco de Jesus, holds a theological discussion with Buckingham, ii. 323
Frankenthal besieged by Cordova, ii. 111. Siege of, raised by Mansfeld, ii. 113. Sequestration of, proposed, ii. 222. The citizens prevent Burroughs from leaving, ii. 218. Siege of, ii. 271, 284. Its sequestration objected to by Frederick, ii. 291. Treaty for its sequestration signed, ii. 367. Surrendered to Verdugo, ii. 368

474   INDEX.

FRE

Frederick IV., Elector Palatine, i. 249
Frederick V., Elector Palatine. His marriage, i. 7. His character, i. 263. His intrigues with the Duke of Savoy, i. 265. Sends Christopher Dohna to England, i. 273. Sends Mansfeld to Turin, i. 279. His reception of Doncaster, i. 283. His election to the Bohemian crown, i. 288. Accepts it, i. 289. Sends Dohna back to England, i. 291. His journey to Prague, i. 294. Goes to the assembly at Nuremberg, i. 295. His defeat at Prague, i. 384. His plans after the battle of Prague, ii. 63. Takes refuge at Breslau, ii. 66. Ban pronounced upon him, ii. 67. Goes to Lower Saxony, ii. 68. Receives Sir E. Villiers, ii. 69. Appears at Segeberg, ii. 70. Refuses to go to the Palatinate, ii. 72. Arrives at the Hague, ii. 74. Issues a warlike manifesto, ii. 84. Supports Mansfeld and Jägerndorf, ii. 99. Joins the Dutch camp at Emmerich, ii. 100. Returns to the Hague, ii. 110. His unpopularity in Germany, ii. 111. Accepts his father-in-law's terms, ii. 187. Goes to the Palatinate, ii. 195. Takes the field, ii. 196. Retreats to Alsace, ii. 198. Declares against a truce, ii. 199. Joins Mansfeld in his attack upon Darmstadt, ii. 200. Retires to Mannheim, ii. 201. Refuses to remain in the Palatinate, ii. 205. Dismisses the army, and retires to Sedan, ii. 210. Returns to the Hague, ii. 247. Is deprived of his Electorate, ii. 289. Objects to the sequestration of Frankenthal, ii. 291. Refuses to sign the treaty for a suspension of arms, ii. 368. Signs the treaty, ii. 372. Returns an evasive answer to James's proposal of a marriage between his son and an archduchess, ii. 430. Refuses to accede to the plan, ii. 450.
Frederick Henry, Prince, eldest son of the Elector Palatine, proposal for his education at Vienna, ii. 109, 214, 278, 307.
French merchants, company of, the dispute with the Vintners referred to Bacon's arbitration, i. 467
Furatta, Madame, see Turatta

G AGE, George, sent by James to watch the negotiations at Rome, ii. 119. Sent back to England by the Cardinals, ii. 236. Returns to Rome, ii. 283
Gainsborough, congregation of Separatists at, ii. 37, 41
Genoa, proposed attack upon, by Ra-

GON

leigh, i. 59. Designs of the Duke of Savoy on, i. 279
George Frederick, Margrave of Baden-Durlach, joins Mansfeld, ii. 196. Is defeated at Wimpfen, ii. 197.
Giron, Don Fernando, quarrels with Buckingham, ii. 328
Glass, patents for the manufacture of, i. 362.
Gloucester, the Cathedral of, removal of the communion table in, i. 196.
Gold and silver thread, patent for, i. 363. Debate upon, in the House of Commons, i. 417
Gold mine. See Mine
Gondomar, Count of (see Sarmiento,) objects to the proposed expedition against Algiers, i. 76. Urges James to repeal the penal laws against the Catholics, i. 111. Demands justice upon Raleigh, i. 133. Leaves England, i. 135. His report on English affairs, i. 270. Comments on James's mediation in Bohemia, i. 272. His conversation with Sir H. Mainwaring, i. 275. Sets out to return to England, i. 301. Arrives in London, i. 312. His conversation with Digby, i. 313. His interview with the King, i. 314. Intercedes for Lady Lake, i. 320. Listens to Buckingham's complaints, i. 333. Recommends an attack upon the Dutch, i. 334. His language on the invasion of the Palatinate, i. 338, 340. Repels James's complaints, i. 345. Attempts to stop the expedition against Algiers, i. 348. Complains of Naunton, i. 349. Makes James contradict himself, i. 351. Carries on further negotiations on the marriage treaty, i. 351. Fears assassination upon the news of the battle of Prague, i. 38 . Obtains a licence to export ordnance, i. 401. His conversation with James on the Papal claims, i. 405. Is insulted by the apprentices, ii. 11. His credit with Buckingham, ii. 115. Protests against the proceedings of the Commons, ii. 136. Rejoices at the dissolution of Parliament, ii. 153. Urges James to punish the leading members, ii. 154. His policy compared with that of Digby, ii. 157. His plan for breaking the blockade of the Flemish ports, ii. 160. Is recalled from England, ii. 220. Obtains from Charles a promise to visit Madrid, ii. 254. Assures James that he hopes to bring the Infanta in the spring, ii. 259. His views on the marriage treaty, ii. 268. Carries the news of the Prince's arrival to Olivares, ii. 306. Visits the Prince, ii. 308. Declares in favour of

GRA

showing confidence in Charles, ii. 353.
Is in a minority against Olivares in the Council of State, ii. 400.
Gray, Sir Andrew, asks leave to levy troops for Bohemia, i. 309
Green, Mrs., date assigned by her to a forged speech of Sir E. Cecil, i. 397. Date given by her to an assignment of fines to Cranfield, i. 425.
Gregory XV., Pope, appoints a Congregation to consider the marriage treaty, ii. 119. Writes to Charles, ii. 342. Dies, ii. 385.
Gresley, Walsingham, meets the Prince at Irun, ii. 309
Greville, Sir Fulk, Chancellor of the Exchequer, created Lord Brooke, i. 377.
Grotius, Hugh, his "Mare Liberum," i. 219
Guiana, the seat of the fabled El Dorado, i. 39. Raleigh's first voyage to, i. 40. Keymis's voyage, i. 44. Berry's voyage, i. 45. Explorations of Leigh and Harcourt, i. 45. A fresh voyage planned by Raleigh, i. 47. Theories on the ownership of the territory, i. 50. Ascent of the Orinoco by Raleigh's expedition, i. 125
Gwilliams committed to prison by Sir T. Lake, i. 162

HADDINGTON, Viscount (John Ramsay), appealed to by Raleigh, i. 47. Created Earl of Holderness, i. 377. See Holderness, Earl of
Hallam, H., his statement relating to the supply granted by the Commons, ii. 129.
Hansby, Ralph, said to have bribed Bacon, i. 465
Harcourt, his voyage to Guiana, i. 45
Harvey, Sir Sebastian, proposed marriage between his daughter and Christopher Villiers, i. 241
Hatton, Elizabeth, Lady, her marriage and quarrel with Coke, i. 91. Supports her daughter's refusal to marry Sir J. Villiers, i. 96. Draws up a contract of marriage for her daughter, i. 97. Appeals to the Council against her husband, i. 99. Her temporary favour at Court, i. 104. Refuses to make over estates to her son-in-law, i. 242
Hatton, Luke, supports Lepton and Goldsmith, ii. 128; his connection with the quarrel between the Lakes and Lady Exeter, i. 160
Hay, Lord (James Hay), his mission to Paris, i. 35. His courtship and marriage, i. 170. Resigns the Mastership of the Wardrobe, i. 172. Is created

IMP

Viscount Doncaster, i. 173. See Doncaster, Viscount
Heath, Robert, elected Recorder of the city, i. 187. Solicitor-General, i. 376. Urges an immediate supply, ii. 128. Moves an explanatory clause in the petition on religion, ii. 136. Supports the Commons' claim to liberty of speech, ii. 145.
Heidelberg, departure of Frederick from, i. 295. Visit of Digby to, ii. 112. Siege of, begun and interrupted, ii. 207. Siege and surrender of, ii. 247.
Heilbronn, assembly of the Union at, i. 281, ii. 75
Henrietta Maria, the Princess (see Marriage treaty with France), her opinion on the marriage, i. 390. She is seen by Charles at Paris, ii. 303
Henry VIII., his treatment of the claim of the House of Commons to freedom of speech, ii. 143
Henry, Prince of Wales, proposed marriage with the Infanta Anne, i. 6, and with the Princess Christina, i. 7. His death, i. 7
Herbert, George, his lines on the observance of Sunday, i. 201
Herbert, Sir Gerard, killed at Heidelberg, ii. 247
Herbert, Sir Edward (ambassador in France), supports the French marriage, i. 390. His quarrel with Luyne, ii. 178
Hesse-Cassel, Landgrave of. See Maurice.
Hesse-Darmstadt, Landgrave of. See Lewis
Hobart, Sir Henry, Chief Justice of Common Pleas, spoken of as Ellesmere's successor, i. 86. His vote on Suffolk's trial, i. 179
Höchst, battle of, ii. 205
Holderness, Earl of (John Ramsay), blames James's weakness, ii. 302
Holland. See Netherlands.
Holman's case against Raven, i. 143
Houghton, Lord (John Holles), offers a bribe for the Secretaryship, i. 106
Hunt, Robert, factor at Puloway, i. 222
Hutton, Serjeant, made a judge, i. 89
Hyacintho, the Friar, urges Ferdinand not to treat, ii. 95. Seizure of his despatches by Mansfield, ii. 188. His negotiations at Madrid, ii. 215. Explanation given to the message sent by him, ii. 262

IMPOSITIONS, right of levying, discussed in the Parliament of 1614, i. 17

Infanta. See Anne, Maria, Isabella, Margaret

Inns, patent for, delayed by Ellesmere, i. 85, note. Brought forward by Mompesson, i. 356. Condemned by the Commons, i. 416

Inojosa, Marquis of, recalled from the Governorship of Milan, i. 57. Sent on a special mission to England, ii. 324. Takes part in the negotiation for a pardon and dispensation for the recusants, ii. 391. His displeasure at the delays in his way, ii. 418, 420. Presents a plan for pacifying Germany, ii. 423

Irun, the Prince's arrival at, ii. 305

Isabella, the Infanta, Governor of the Netherlands after her husband's death, ii. 98. Empowers Chichester to negotiate an armistice, ii. 203. Despairs of peace, ii. 209. Urges a suspension of arms, ii. 214. Rejects Weston's terms, ii. 229. Refuses to intervene in the Palatinate, ii. 272. Raises difficulties to the sequestration of Frankenthal, ii. 284

JACATRA, victory of Dale at, i. 234

Jägerndorf, the Margrave of, his proceedings in Silesia, ii. 92, 105

James I. of England, and VI. of Scotland, result of the first fourteen years of his reign, i. 1. His schemes for Prince Henry's marriage, i. 6. His alliance with the German Protestants, i. 7. His love of peace, i. 8. Liberates Luisa de Carvajal, i. 12. Summons Parliament in 1614, i. 16. Resents the conduct of the Commons, i. 17. Looks to the Catholics and to Spain for support, i. 18. Makes overtures to Sarmiento, i. 21. Opens a secret negotiation through Cotton, i. 29. His hesitation on reading the proposed marriage articles, i. 30. He finally accepts them with modifications, i. 32. Fresh hesitations, i. 36. He liberates Raleigh, i. 48. His theory on the tenure of colonies in America, i. 50. Issues a commission to Raleigh, i. 51. Assures Sarmiento of his intention to give satisfaction to Spain, i. 57. His offers to Scarnafissi, i. 58. Rejects Raleigh's plan for an attack upon Genoa, i. 60. Takes up the marriage treaty again, i. 61. Rejects Sarmiento's last protest against Raleigh's voyage, i. 63. Lays the marriage treaty before a Commission, i. 66. Instructs Digby to open the negotiation formally at Madrid, i. 68, and to propose an attack upon Algiers, i. 78. His supineness in the face of official corruption, i. 81. His irritation at Bacon's resistance to Sir J. Villiers' marriage, i. 100. Receives Coke with favour, i. 102. Admits Bacon's excuses, i. 102. Restores Coke to the Council-Table, i. 103. Promises justice upon Raleigh, i. 134. Liberates the priests, i. 135. Punishes the rioters at the Spanish Embassy, i. 136. Appoints a Commission to examine Raleigh, i. 141. Offers to deliver him to the King of Spain, i. 145. Resolves to send him to the scaffold, i. 146. Reconciles the Prince with Buckingham, i. 157. Sends for Lord Roos, i. 162. Pronounces sentence on the Lakes, i. 163. Proposes to economise, i. 167. Interferes in the election to the Recordership of the City, i. 186. Considers the question of the observance of the Sabbath in Lancashire, i. 200. Enjoins the reading of the Declaration of Sports, i. 202. His treatment of Selden, i. 206. Sends deputies to Dort, i. 210. His dispute with the Dutch on the herring-fishery, i. 228. Appealed to on the East India negotiation, i. 233. His illness, i. 239. Thanksgiving for his recovery, i. 240. Interferes in favour of the marriage of Christopher Villiers, i. 241. Receives overtures from Spain to mediate in Bohemia, i. 268. Accepts the mediation, i. 271. Receives Christopher Dohna, i. 273. His naval preparations, i. 275. Gives Doncaster his instructions, i. 280. Receives Dohna, i. 291. Declares his intentions to the Council, i. 292. His anxiety to convince the world that he is not in collusion with his son-in-law, i. 307. His continued irresolution, i. 303. Refuses to Frederick the title of King of Bohemia, i. 304. His "Meditations," i. 304. Hears of the projected invasion of the Palatinate, i. 307. Investigates Frederick's title, i. 308. Orders Trumbull to protest against the invasion of the Palatinate, i. 310. Receives Buwinckhausen, i. 310. His undignified reception of Gondomar, i. 314. His treatment of Buwinckhausen, i. 315. Takes up the marriage treaty again, i. 318. Rejects Gondomar's intercession for Lady Lake, i. 320. Visits St. Paul's, i. 321. Converses with Gondomar about the Palatinate, i. 325. Refuses to take part in the war, i. 326. Rejects the offers of the Dutch, i. 327. Assents to Gondomar's proposal for a partition of the Netherlands, i. 334. Sends embassies to Germany, i. 336. His language about the invasion of the Palatinate, i. 338, 340. Complains to Gondomar of Spinola's attack, i. 344. Makes promises to Dohna and Caron, i. 345. His declaration before the Council, i. 346. Retracts his assertions to Gondomar, i. 350. Rejects Bacon's draft proclamation summoning Parliament, i. 353. Talks of demanding Spinola's head, i. 354. Summons Parliament, i. 354. Complains of the alehouses, i. 358. Hears the news of the Battle of Prague, i. 387. Sends out fresh embassies, i. 388. His reception of Cadenet, i. 392. Opens Parliament, i. 394. His conversation with Usher, i. 398. Replies to the petition against the Recusants, i. 402. His conversation with Gondomar on the Papal claims, i. 405. Resists inquiry into the conduct of the referees, i. 418. Promises to redress grievances, i. 422. Proposes a new tribunal to enquire into Bacon's case, i. 436. His speech to the Houses, i. 451. Cancels the three obnoxious patents, i. 453. His interview with Bacon, i. 457. Addresses the Houses on their grievances, ii. 2. Issues a proclamation against speaking on State affairs, ii. 10. Questions the jurisdiction of the Commons over Floyd, ii. 14. Directs an adjournment of the Houses, ii. 19. Is satisfied with the Declaration of the Commons, ii. 24. His remark on the accident at Bramshill, ii. 32. His conversation with a deputation from the Separatists at Leyden, ii. 47. Advises Frederick to go to the Palatinate, ii. 70. Forbids Elizabeth to visit England, ii. 73. His language to the Dutch Commissioners, ii. 76. Obtains a prolongation of the truce in the Palatinate, ii. 84. Expostulates with Frederick, ii. 104. Gives money for the defence of the Palatinate, ii. 117. Sends a categorical demand to the Emperor, ii. 118. Assures Gondomar that nothing shall be done against Spain in Parliament, ii. 119. Writes to the Speaker refusing to receive the petition on religion, ii. 137. His answer to their explanatory petition, ii. 140. His letter to Calvert explaining his views of the privileges of the House, ii. 146. Offers to relinquish the subsidy, ii. 148. Destroys the protestation of the Commons, ii. 152. Dissolves Parliament, ii. 153, 155. Falls into the New River, ii. 155. Revives the scheme for the invasion of the Netherlands, ii. 161. Recalls Oxford from the command in the Narrow Seas, ii. 162. His treatment of De Dominis, ii. 172, 174. Proposes to send an English force to the Palatinate, ii. 182. Increasing unpopularity of, ii. 183. Regulates the studies of the University of Oxford, ii. 186. Requires Frederick to assent to his terms, ii. 187. Receives the Emperor's ambassador, ii. 191. Objects to the assembly at Ratisbon, ii. 212. Refuses to listen to the proposal for the sequestration of the towns in the Palatinate, ii. 223. Orders the issue of directions to preachers, ii. 233. Receives Gage, ii. 236. Sends an answer to the amendments in the marriage treaty, ii. 239. His visit to New Hall, ii. 256. Writes to the Pope, ii. 257. Asks the Dutch to keep Mansfeld in their pay, ii. 261. Refuses to allow a Spanish fleet to enter his ports, ii. 261. Recalls Chichester, ii. 268. Accepts the marriage treaty as revised at Madrid, ii. 283. Proposes to Frederick the sequestration of Frankenthal, ii. 291. Hears of his son's proposed journey, ii. 248. Gives his permission to it, ii. 300. Announces it to the Council, ii. 303. Replies to his son's letter about the claims of the Pope, ii. 311. Sends out chaplains to his son, ii. 330. Exhorts the Prince not to be ashamed of his religion, ii. 331. Converses with Williams about the two favourites, ii. 339. Prepares for the Infanta's reception, ii. 348. Grants full powers to Charles, ii. 349. Entreats his son to return, ii. 350. Promises to confirm the articles, ii. 351. Fancies that he shall never see his son again, ii. 352. Hesitates to take the oath to the treaty, ii. 357. Determines to swear, ii. 360. Takes the oath, ii. 361. Explains his meaning, ii. 363. Complains of the expense to which he has been put, ii. 366. Signs a treaty for the sequestration of Frankenthal, ii. 367. And another for a suspension of arms, ii. 368. Remonstrates against the Dutch blockade of the Scottish ports, ii. 373. Grants favours to the Catholics, ii. 391. Orders his son to return, ii. 393. Signs the pardon and dispensation for the Recusants, ii. 418. Receives the Prince at Royston, ii. 423. Accepts a Spanish plan for pacifying Germany, ii. 424. Liberates the priests in prison, ii. 425. Asks Frederick to accept the Spanish

JOH

plan, ii. 425. Orders the postponement of the marriage, ii. 426. Waits anxiously for replies to his proposals, ii. 434. Comes up to London, ii. 436. Orders the marriage to be postponed till after Christmas, ii. 437. Lays once more the Spanish terms before Frederick, ii. 448. Summons Parliament, ii. 452

John, The Archduke, his proposed marriage with the Infanta Maria, i. 108

John George, Elector of Saxony, his political position, i. 261. His advice on hearing of the Bohemian revolution, i. 264. His conduct before Ferdinand's election, i. 288. Agrees to attack Lusatia, i. 342. His position after the Battle of Prague, ii. 65. His disgust on hearing of the seizure of Darmstadt, ii. 202. His anger at the expulsion of the Lutheran clergy from Bohemia, ii. 285. His reception of the transference of the Electorate, ii. 290

Johnson, Francis, minister of a Separatist congregation at Amsterdam, ii. 37

Jourdain, voyage of, to the Spice Islands, i. 221

Junta of theologians. See marriage treaty with Spain

KEEPER, Lord High. See Bacon; Williams

Kennedy, Sir John, his gift to Bacon, i. 464

Keymis, Lawrence, shown the site of the gold mine on the Orinoco, i. 42. Returns to Guiana, i. 44. Has the gold mine again pointed out to him, i. 45. Raleigh proposes to send him back, i. 47. Entrusted with the supervision of Raleigh's force on the Orinoco, i. 123. Attacks San Thomé, i. 125. Retreats, i. 128. Commits suicide, i. 129

Khevenhüller, Count of, urges the Spanish Government to invade the Palatinate, i. 306. Proposes a marriage between the Infanta and the Archduke Ferdinand, i. 351. Urges Olivares to obtain the assent of Spain to the transference of the Electorate, ii. 307. Is requested by Olivares to support a marriage between Charles and the Emperor's daughter, ii. 355. Converses with Buckingham, ii. 387

King, Captain, makes arrangements for Raleigh's escape, i. 137

Kinloss, Lord Bruce of, his name suggested for a Spanish pension, i. 14, note

Knight, his sermon at Oxford, ii. 184

LEY

LA CHESNÉE, his dealings with Raleigh, i. 139. Summoned before the Council, i. 143

Lafuente, Diego de, Gondomar's confessor, i. 271. His mission to Rome, i. 351. Arrives at Rome, ii. 119

Lake, Arthur, interferes in his sister's quarrel with her husband, i. 160. His sentence in the Star-Chamber, i. 163, 320

Lake, Sir Thomas, Secretary of State, accepts a Spanish pension, i. 34. Loses Buckingham's favour, i. 158. His explanations listened to, i. 159. Takes part in the quarrel between his daughter and Lord Roos, i. 158. Commits Hatton and Gwilliams, i. 162. His sentence in the Star-Chamber, i. 163. Deprived of the Secretaryship, i. 164

Lancashire, the observance of the Sabbath in, i. 199

Laud, William, his views, i. 193. Appointed dean of Gloucester, i. 196. Removes the Communion table, i. 197. Made Bishop of St. David's, ii. 30. His conference with Fisher, ii. 168. His views on intellectual liberty, ii. 169. The two sides of his character, ii. 235

Le Clerc, his interview with Raleigh, i. 139. Examined by the Council, and obliged to leave England, i. 144

Leicester, Earl of (Robert Sidney), member of the Council of War, i. 389

Leigh, Captain, his voyage to Guiana, i. 45

Leith, Dunkirk vessel at, ii. 373

Lennox, Duke of (Lewis Stuart), supports Yelverton's appointment, i. 87. Makes an offer to Bacon for York House, ii. 166. Created Duke of Richmond, ii. 348

Leonard, the Indian, i. 46

Leopold, the Archduke, put to flight by Mansfeld, ii. 198

Lepton and Goldsmith, case of, ii. 128

Lerma, Duke of, his foreign policy, i. 4. Encourages James to reopen the marriage treaty, i. 21. Disgrace of, i. 267

Lewis, Landgrave of Hesse Darmstadt, captured by Frederick, ii. 200

Lewis XIII., King of France, takes part in the murder of Ancre, i. 114

Ley, Sir James, offers a bribe for the Attorney-Generalship, i. 87. Becomes Chief Justice, i. 377. Appointed Speaker of the House of Lords during Bacon's illness, i. 435. Continued in the place after Bacon's disgrace, i. 470

Leyden, Separatist congregation at, ii. 43. Emigration of part of, to America, ii. 45. See New England, the founders of.

LIN

Lindsay, Sir James, his name suggested for a Spanish pension, i. 14, note
Lisle, Lord (Robert Sydney), created Earl of Leicester, i. 184. See Leicester, Earl of
Lope de Vega, his verses on the Prince's visit, ii. 314
Lords, House of, rise of opposition in, i. 407. Question of the precedency of Scotch Peers, i. 408. Receives the complaints of the Commons against Michell and Mompesson, i. 418. Examines the charges against Bacon, i. 440. Delivers sentence upon him, i. 472. Sentences Mitchell, ii. 1. Examines Yelverton, ii. 4. Debate on his attack upon the King, ii. 6. Takes Floyd's case into its hands, ii. 15. Considers the question of adjournment. ii. 19. Meeting of, after the adjournment, ii. 120
Luynes, Duke of, rise of, at the French Court, i. 114. His quarrel with Herbert, ii. 178. Death of, ii. 179

MAINWARING, Sir Henry, i. 278
Mallory, William, sent to the Tower, ii. 154. Set at liberty, ii. 236. Released from his restraint, ii. 301
Mandeville, Viscount (Henry Montague), called to order in the House of Lords, i. 420. Enforced resignation of, ii. 116.
Money to be repaid to him, ii. 201
Manners, Lady Catherine, her marriage with Buckingham, i. 329
Mannheim, besieged by Tilly, ii. 247. Capitulation of, ii. 271
Mannouric, his intrigue with Raleigh, i. 138
Mansell, Sir Robert, his share in the glass patent, i. 363. His operations against Algiers, ii. 113
Mansfeld, Count Ernest of, taken into the service of the Union, i. 266. Sent on a mission to Turin, i. 279. Employed against Bucquoi, i. 282. Is defeated, i. 284. Posted at Pilsen, i. 384, 385. Character of, ii. 85. His conduct in Bohemia, ii. 87. Retreats to the Upper Palatinate, ii. 88. His violence to the neighbouring Catholics, ii. 93. His position in the Upper Palatinate, ii. 102. Is attacked, ii. 107. Engages to disband his troops, ii. 108. Marches into the Lower Palatinate, ii. 112. Quarters his troops in Alsace, ii. 181. Plans the plunder of the Bishoprics, ii. 190. Demands the cession of Haguenau to himself, ii. 191. His intrigue with Raville, ii. 193. Takes the field, ii. 196. Retreats to Alsace, ii. 197. Seizes Darmstadt,

MAR

ii. 200. Retreats to Mannheim, ii. 201. Invades Lorraine, ii. 224. Fights his way through the Spanish Netherlands, ii. 226. Assures Weston that his negotiations are useless, ii. 230. Transfers his army to East Friesland, ii. 286
Margaret, the Infanta, death of, i. 108
Margaret, the Infanta (daughter of Maximilian II.), supports the Infanta Maria in her resistance to the marriage, ii. 274
Maria, the Infanta. See Marriage Treaty with Spain. Khevenhüller proposes that she shall marry the Archduke Ferdinand, i. 351. Her interview with Digby, ii. 219. Her dislike of the marriage, ii. 272. Her character, ii. 273. Remonstrates with her brother, ii. 274. Talks of going into a nunnery, ii. 275. Accompanies her brother in a coach to meet the Prince, ii. 309. Her continued abhorrence of the marriage, ii. 321. Receives a visit from Charles, ii. 324. Question of her detention after the marriage, ii. 334, 341. Attempt of the Prince to speak to her, ii. 346. Styled Princess of England, ii. 357. Grows more satisfied with the marriage, ii. 384. Her interview with Buckingham, ii. 389. Idea of going into a nunnery attributed to, ii. 410, 414. Her feelings towards Charles, ii. 416. Day fixed for her marriage, ii. 443. The marriage postponed, ii. 445
Marriage treaty with France proposed for Prince Henry, and transferred to Prince Charles, i. 7. Breach of the negotiations, i. 35, 37. Attempts to re-open them, i. 272, 390
Marriage treaty with Savoy, i. 15
Marriage treaty with Spain, proposed by Villa Medina, i. 6. Negotiations for it formally opened by Digby, and broken off, i. 6, 7. Fresh overtures from Lerma listened to by James, i. 21. Recommendations of Sarmiento, i. 23. The Pope's opposition, i. 26. Approbation of the junta of the theologians, i. 26. Preparation of the articles, i. 27. Secret negotiation of Cotton, i. 29. The articles sent to England, i. 29. Remarks of James, i. 30. He accepts them with modifications, i. 32. Fresh hesitations of James, i. 35. Assurances given by him to Sarmiento, i. 57. New difficulties, i. 58. Final determination of James to open negotiations, i. 61. Commissioners appointed to consider the question, i. 66. The

MAT

question again referred to the Pope, i. 107. Extreme expectations of the Spanish Theologians, i. 107. Discussions between Digby and Aliaga, i. 110. Suspension of the negotiations, i. 111. Hopes held out to James that they will be re-opened, i. 272. Resumption of the negotiations, i. 317. Lafuente sent to Rome, i. 351. The treaty taken up by Philip IV., ii. 81. Referred to a congregation of Cardinals at Rome, ii. 119. Its effect in stopping the progress of toleration, ii. 133. Digby obtains fresh assurances of Philip's intention to go on with it, ii. 219. Discussed at Rome, ii. 237. The articles altered, ii. 238. Revised at Madrid, ii. 280. Sent back to Rome, ii. 281. Agreed to by James and Charles, ii. 283. Discussed between Buckingham and Olivares, ii. 314. Probability of the dispensation being granted, ii. 321. Grant of the dispensation, ii. 326. Oath required from Philip, ii. 327, 332. The terms referred to commissioners, ii. 333. The detention of the Infanta advocated by Olivares, ii. 334. The Theologians resolve upon detaining her, ii. 343. Acceptance of their terms by Charles, ii. 356. Oath taken to the treaty by James and the Privy Council, ii. 361. It is signed by Charles, ii. 385. Sworn to by him, ii. 407

Matthew, Toby (Archbishop of York), announces his own death, ii. 172

Matthew, Sir Toby, his mission to Madrid, ii. 354

Matthias, King of Hungary and Bohemia (afterwards Emperor), confirms the Royal Charter, i. 254.—(Emperor). Opposes the Protestant view of the right of church building, i. 255. Appeals for help against the revolutionists, i. 261. His death, i. 278

Maurice, Landgrave of Hesse-Cassel, his advice to the Elector Palatine, i. 282. Dissuades him from accepting the Crown of Bohemia, i. 289. Is compelled to abandon the Union, ii. 81

Maurice of Nassau. See Orange, Prince of

Maximilian, Duke of Bavaria, his reception of Doncaster, i. 285. His character, i. 296. His secret compact with Ferdinand, i. 297. Prepares for war, i. 300. His designs on the Palatinate, i. 305. Invades Upper Austria, i. 342. Attacks Bohemia, i. 383. Proposed transference of Frederick's Electorate to, ii. 82. His suspicions of Mansfeld, ii. 92. Begins hostilities

MOR

in the Upper Palatinate, ii. 94. Protests against Digby's mediation, ii. 95. Prepares to attack Mansfeld, ii. 97. Receives the Electorate in secresy, ii. 109. Has it publicly conferred on him at Ratisbon, ii. 287

Mayflower, the. See New England, founders of

Mentz, treaty of, ii. 81

Michell, Sir Francis, a Commissioner for gold and silver thread, i. 369, 417. Sent to the Tower, i. 412. Sentence pronounced on, ii. 6. His degradation, ii. 25

Middlesex, Earl of (Lionel Cranfield), suspected of a design to overthrow Buckingham, ii. 31

Middleton, David, his voyage to the Banda Isles, i. 219

Mine in Guiana, pointed out to Keymis, i. 42. Again shown to him, i. 45. Its geographical position discussed, i. 53, note

Mohaes, battle of, i. 251

Moluccas, the, i. 218

Mompesson, Sir Giles, his connection with the patent for inns, i. 356 ; with his patent for gold and silver thread, i. 369, 417. Examined by the House of Commons, i. 411, 413. Escapes to the Continent, i. 414. His case carried before the Lords, i. 423. His sentence, i. 452. His fine granted to trustees, ii. 25

Monopolies, (see Patents). Bill against, i. 423. Proclamation against, ii. 33.

Monson, Sir William, receives a Spanish pension, i. 14. His advice on marriage to his son, i. 98, note

Monson put forward in rivalry to Buckingham, i. 156. Knighted and sent abroad, ii. 301

Montague, Sir Henry (Chief Justice of the King's Bench), asks Coke for his official collar, i. 91. Awards judgment against Raleigh, i. 148. A referee for the patent for inns, i. 356. Supports the patent for gold and silver thread, i. 364. Lord Treasurer and Viscount Mandeville, i. 376. See Mandeville, Viscount

Montague, Viscount (Anthony Brown), his gratuity to Bacon, i. 464

Montgomery, Earl of (Philip Herbert), his quarrel with Southampton, i. 76. His share in the glass patent, i. 363.

Montmorency, Duke of, Admiral of France, promises Raleigh a commission, i. 113, 131, note

More, Sir George, his language in the debate upon the charges against Bacon, i. 433

MOR

Morton, Sir Albertus, his mission to the Palatinate, i. 388, ii. 75
Morton, Thomas, Bishop of Lichfield and Coventry; his advice on the observance of the Sabbath, i. 200. Remonstrates with De Dominis, ii. 174
Müller, Professor Max, quotation from, i. 191

NAUNTON, Sir Robert, appointed Secretary of State, i. 106. Lays an account of the negotiations in Germany before the Council, i. 292. Is complained of by Gondomar, i. 349. Suspended from office and confined to his own house, i. 393
Navy, investigation into the state of, i. 172. Proposed reforms in, i. 175
Neile, Richard, Bishop of Lincoln, afterwards of Durham, insults the House of Commons, i. 17
Netherlands, States General of the, suggested co-operation of, in the expedition against Algiers, i. 76. Their refusal, i. 112. Religious commotions in, i. 208. Disputes with, on the East India trade, i. 217. Negotiations opened with, i. 227. Signature of a treaty with, i. 234. Alarm of, at the movement of Spanish troops, i. 302. Propose to James joint action in Germany, i. 327. Proposed attack upon, by England and Spain, i. 334. Make a fresh effort to engage James in the war, i. 341. Send Commissioners to England to treat on East India affairs, ii. 76. Refuse to renew the truce of Antwerp, ii. 79. Claim a right of blockading the Flemish ports, ii. 115. Revival of the scheme for an attack upon, ii. 161. Negotiate about the Dunkirk vessels blockaded in Scotland, ii. 374. Instructions sent by James to revive the negotiation for the attack upon, ii. 377
Nethersole, Sir Francis, his gloomy despatches from Bohemia, i. 383. Is sent to England, ii. 84. Sent by Chichester to explain the state of the Palatinate, ii. 249. His interview with Buckingham, ii. 250
Nevers, the Duke of, defends France against Mansfeld, ii. 227
New England, the founders of, their early history, ii. 34—45. Determine to emigrate to America, ii. 46. Obtain a patent from the Virginia Company, ii. 47. Leave Leyden, ii. 48. Sail from Delfthaven, ii. 49. Sail from Southampton in the Mayflower, ii. 51. Arrive at Cape Cod, ii. 52. Draw up an instrument of government, ii. 53. Explore the country,

OLI

ii. 54. Land at Plymouth, ii. 56. Sickness during the winter, ii. 55. The return of the Mayflower, ii. 59
Norris, Elizabeth, her proposed marriage with Edward Wray, i. 408. Her marriage, ii. 163
Norris, Lord (Francis Norris), created Earl of Berkshire, i. 408. See Berkshire, Earl of
North, Captain Roger, announces Raleigh's failure, 134. His expedition to the Amazon, i. 320. Imprisoned, i. 393. Set at liberty, ii. 30
Northampton, Earl of (Henry Howard), accepts of a Spanish pension, i. 14
Northampton, Earl of (William Compton), bribe paid at his creation, i. 184
Northumberland, Earl of (Henry Percy), objects to his daughter's marriage with Hay, i. 171. Is set at liberty, ii. 30
Nottingham, Earl of, Lord High Admiral, his name mentioned for a Spanish pension, i. 14, note. His objection to the appointment of a commission on the Navy, i. 173. His resignation, i. 175
Noy, William, moves for an inquiry into the monopolies, i. 409
Nuncio at Madrid, the. See De Massimi.
Nuremberg, assembly of Protestants at, i. 293

OLIVARES, Count of, Duke of San Lucar (Gaspar de Guzman), the favourite of Philip IV., ii. 80. Succeeds to Zuñiga's influence, ii. 263. Assures Bristol of his master's sincerity, ii. 265. Urges Philip to go on with the marriage, ii. 279. Changes his policy, ii. 276. His memorial to the King, ii. 277. Intrigues against the Council of State, ii. 279. Carries the news of the Prince's arrival to Philip, ii. 306. Expects the Prince to change his religion, ii. 308. His conversation with Buckingham on the Prince's conversion, ii. 309. His letter to Cardinal Ludovisi, ii. 310. His negotiation with Buckingham, ii. 315. Proposes the cession of fortified towns to the English Catholics, ii. 318. Converses with De Massimi about the Palatinate, ii. 320. Gives his opinion in the Council of State, ii. 321. Argues with the Infanta in favour of the marriage, ii. 322. Attempts to convert Buckingham, ii. 323, 325. His quarrel with Buckingham, ii. 332. Advises the detention of the Infanta, ii. 334. Informs Charles of the decision of the Theologians, ii. 344. Urges further concessions, ii. 345. Asks Khevenhüller to support a marriage

OLI

between the Prince of Wales and the Emperor's daughter, ii. 354. Changes his policy and supports the Intanta's marriage, ii. 384. His interview with Buckingham, ii. 388. Brings forward the subject of the Palatinate, ii. 398. Obtains a majority in the Council of State, ii. 399. Effect of his policy, ii. 400. Shows Philip's letter to Charles, ii. 404. Doubts whether Charles will fulfil his engagement, ii. 417

Olivares, Countess of, carries a message from the Infanta, ii. 389

Oñate, Count of, his conversation with Doncaster, i. 285. Opposes the transference of the Electorate, ii. 83. Ordered to refuse all extension of Spanish territory, ii. 214

Orange, Prince of (Maurice of Nassau), overthrows the Arminian party, i. 210. His conversation with Dohna, i. 291. Recommends James to attack Flanders, ii. 77. His reception of overtures from Brussels, ii. 77. His camp at Emmerich, ii. 100. Insists upon the right of blockade, ii. 115, 373. Excuses the attack upon the Dunkirk ships at Leith, ii. 376

Ordnance, licence for the exportation of, granted to Gondomar, i. 401

Orinoco. See Raleigh; and Guiana.

Oxford, Earl of (Henry Vere), serves in the Palatinate, i. 339. Returns to England, i. 389. Imprisoned in the Tower, ii. 26. Set at liberty, ii. 29. Commands the fleet in the Narrow Seas, ii. 102. His second imprisonment, ll. 103

Oxford, University of, regulation of the studies of the, ii. 186

Oyapok, the, Raleigh's visit to, i. 120

PADRE MASTRO, the. See Lafuente, Diego de

Palatinate, the Lower, projected invasion of, i. 305, 307. Proposed loan for the defence of, i. 316. Contribution for the defence of, i. 322. Departure of the volunteers for, i. 339. Invasion of, i. 344. Defence of, discussed in the House of Commons, i. 399. Declaration of the Commons in favour of, ii. 22. Suspension of hostilities in, ii. 82. Prolongation of the armistice, ii. 84, 181. Recommencement of hostilities in, ii. 103. Tilly's campaign in, ii. 181, 193, 199, 246, 271. Condition of, ii. 289

Palatinate, the Upper, occupied by Mansfeld, ii. 88. Invaded by Maximilian, ii. 106. Subdued, ii. 108

Pareus, his commentaries burnt, ii. 185

PHE

Parima, fabulous lake of, i. 39

Parliament of 1614, meeting of, i. 16. Dissolution of, i. 22

Parliament of 1621. Summoned by proclamation, i. 354. Meeting of, i. 394. Adjournment of, ii. 23. Dissolution of, ii. 155. See Commons, House of; and Lords, House of

Pastrana, Duke of, his mission to Rome, ii. 319, 326

Patents, complained of, i. 353. The patent for inns, i. 356; for alehouses, i. 358; for the importation of salmon and lobsters, i. 361; for the manufacture of glass, i. 362; for the manufacture of gold and silver thread, i. 363. Debates on, in the House of Commons, i. 409, 424. The patents for inns, alehouses, and gold and silver thread, cancelled, i. 453. Other patents condemned by the Commons, ii. 18. Proclamation against, ii. 33

Paul V., Pope, his objections to the marriage of the Infanta Maria with a Protestant, i. 26. Renews his opposition, i. 107. His remarks on Frederick's acceptance of the crown of Bohemia, i. 296. His death, ii. 119

Pawel, Andrew, his mission to Vienna, ii. 101

Peacock, Reginald, money lent by him to Bacon, i. 466

Pecquius, his mission to the Hague, ii. 78. Takes part in the conference at Brussels, ii. 209, 223

Pedrosa, Father, his sermon, ii. 342

Pembroke, Earl of (William Herbert), carries a message to young Monson, i. 156. Urges on the benevolence, i. 354. Calls Bacon and Mandeville to order, i. 420. Demands further inquiry into Bacon's case, i. 462. Objects to calling him to the bar of the House, i. 462. Regrets the dissolution of Parliament, ii. 153

Pennington, Captain John, in want of money for his ship, i. 113. His evidence against Raleigh, i. 142

Pensioners of Spain in England, i. 13, 34

Percy, Lady Lucy, her marriage, i. 170

Perrot, Sir James, moves that the Commons receive the communion together, i. 397. Accepts the King's plan for a new tribunal, i. 437. Proposes a declaration on the war in the Palatinate, ii. 21. Supports a war with Spain, ii. 123. Asks for guarantees against Popery, ii. 142

Phelips, Sir Robert, speaks against the Catholics, ii. 297. Moves inquiry into the gold and silver thread patent, i. 417. Brings in the report on the cases

PHI

of Aubrey and Egerton, i. 433. Carries the charges against Bacon to the Lords, i. 439. Attack upon Floyd, ii. 13. Objects to the adjournment of the Houses, ii. 20. Argues against the grant of a supply, ii. 124. Reiterates his arguments, ii. 129. Supports the petition on religion, ii. 136. Moves the adjournment of the House, ii. 138. Loyal expressions of, ii. 142. Sent to the Tower, ii. 154. Set at liberty, ii. 236

Philip II., King of Spain, abandonment of his policy, i. 3

Philip III., King of Spain, attitude of his government towards foreign nations, i. 4. Demands the conversion of Prince Henry as a condition of his marriage with an Infanta, i. 7. Consults the Pope, i. 26. Refers the question of the marriage to a junta of theologians, i. 26. Sends again to the Pope, i. 107. Raises his demands, i. 108. Consents to the invasion of the Palatinate, i. 306. His apprehension of English interference. Assents to a plan for his daughter's marriage with the Archduke Ferdinand, i. 351. Expresses a desire for peace, ii. 74. His death, ii. 86

Philip IV., his accession, ii. 80. Declares his readiness to go on with the marriage treaty, ii. 81. Objects to the transference of the Electorate, ii. 97, 109. His character, ii. 218. Gives fresh assurances about the marriage, ii. 219, 265. Writes to the Infanta Isabella to intervene in James's behalf, ii. 266. Declares against the transference of the Electorate, ii. 267. His letter to Olivares, ordering him to break off the marriage, ii. 276. Hears of the Prince's arrival, ii. 306. His meeting with Charles, ii. 309. Oath required from him by the Pope, ii. 327, 332. Hesitates to allow the Infanta to go immediately on her marriage, ii. 342. Signs the marriage contract, ii. 385. Requests Charles to send away his Protestant attendants, ii. 396. Takes leave of Charles, ii. 409. His declaration about the Palatinate, ii. 431. His second declaration, ii. 440. Receives the dispensation from the Nuncio, and fixes the day for the marriage, ii. 443. Answers the summons to restore the Palatinate, ii. 446. Refuses to arm against the Emperor, ii. 447

Pirates. See Algiers

Plessen, Volrad von, his mission to England, i. 280

RAL

Pocahontas, her visit to England, i. 212. Her death, i. 213

Pope, The, see Paul V., Gregory XV., Urban VIII.

Porter, Endymion, Buckingham's follower, i. 187. Selected for a mission to Madrid, ii. 255. Writes to Gondomar, ii. 256. Sets out for Spain, ii. 260. Arrives at Madrid, ii. 263. His conversation with Olivares, ii. 269. Returns to England, ii. 283

Prague, Battle of, i. 384. Agitation in London at the news, i. 386

Preston, Thomas, liberation of, ii. 420.

Privy Council, its want of influence, i. 79

Pularoon, surrendered by the natives to the English, i. 222. Defence of, by Courthope, i. 223, 229

Puloway, opening of trade with, by the English, i. 222. Conquered by the Dutch, i. 223

Purbeck, Viscount (John Villiers), i. 242

Puritan Conformists, i. 191

Pursuivants, their treatment of the Catholics, i. 318

Pym, John, his speech in the Committee on religion, ii. 130. His political position, ii. 131. Confined to his house, ii. 154

RALEIGH, Elizabeth Lady, advances money for her husband's voyage, i. 55. Helps Pennington to borrow money, i. 113. Visits her husband in the Gatehouse, i. 148.

Raleigh, George, commands the land forces on the expedition up the Orinoco, i. 123

Raleigh, Walter, accompanies the expedition to San Thomé, i. 123. His death, i. 127

Raleigh, Sir Walter, a fit representative of the Elizabethan age, i. 37. His projects of conquest in the Indies, i. 38. His first voyage to Guiana, i. 40. Ascends the Orinoco, i. 41. Publishes his discovery of Guiana, i. 42. Sends Keymis to Guiana, i. 44. Sends Berry, i. 45. His imprisonment, i. 46. Offers to send Keymis again to Guiana, i. 47. Appeals for liberty to Winwood and Villiers, i. 47. Allowed to leave the Tower to prepare for his voyage, i. 48. Protests that the mine of which he is in search is not on Spanish territory, i. 49. Receives a commission for his voyage, i. 51. Makes his preparations, i. 54. Thinks of seizing the Mexico fleet, i. 56. Proposes an attack upon Genoa, i. 59. Released from the charge of a keeper,

RAM

i. 60. His communications with the French Protestants, i. 61. His interview with Desmarets, i. 62. Sends Faige to Montmorency, i. 63, 113, 131, note. Allowed to sail in spite of Sarmiento's renewed protests, i. 64. Leaves London, i. 65. His difficulties at Plymouth, i. 113. His satisfaction at Ancre's murder, i. 114. His arrangements with Faige and Belle, i. 115. He sails from Plymouth, i. 117. His voyage across the Atlantic, i. 118. Arrives at the Oyapok, i. 120. Makes preparations for ascending the Orinoco, i. 121. Talks of an attack upon the Mexico fleet, i. 122. Is left at the mouth of the river, i. 123. Hears the news of the disaster at San Thome, i. 128. His harsh language to Keymis, i. 129. His desperation, i. 130. His return to England, i. 132. Seizure of his ship, i. 136. His attempt to escape from Plymouth, i. 137. Feigns illness, i. 138. Attempts to escape from London, i. 139. Is lodged in the Tower, i. 140. Writes the Apology, i. 140. Examined by a Commission, i. 141. Acknowledges his dealings with the French, i. 144. Charges Winwood with complicity, i. 145. Brought before the King's Bench, i. 147. Prepares for death, i. 148. His execution, i. 150

Ramsay, Sir John, his name suggested for a Spanish pension, i. 14, note. See Haddington, Earl of

Ratisbon, Assembly at, projected by the Emperor, ii. 94, 211. Its meeting, ii. 289

Raville, Sieur de, his negotiation with Mansfeld, ii. 193

Recordership of the City, election of, i. 185

Recusants. See Catholics

Referees of the patents, their conduct questioned by the Commons, i. 409, 415, 418

Reynell, Sir George, said to have bribed Bacon, i. 466

Rich, Lord (Robert Rich), buys the Earldom of Warwick, i. 184. See Warwick, first Earl of

Rich, Lord (Robert Rich), his piratical speculations, i. 185. Succeeds his father in the earldom, i. 216. See Warwick, second Earl of

Ridgway, Lord, his evidence against Suffolk, i. 179

Robinson, a London citizen, refuses to pay his share of the City Loan, i. 167

Robinson, John, ejected at Norwich, i. 40. Assistant minister of the Separatists at Scrooby, ii. 41. Succeeds Clifton as their minister, ii. 43. His influence at Leyden, ii. 44. Preaches to the emigrants, ii. 49. His views compared with those of Selden, ii. 61

Rolfe, Thomas, his marriage to Pocahontas, i. 212

Rome, opening of negotiations for the dispensation at, ii. 119. Progress of the negotiations, ii. 237. Grant of the dispensation, ii. 326. Dispensation approved at, ii. 440

Roos, Lady, her quarrel with her husband, i. 159. Brings calumnious charges against Lady Exeter, i. 161. Her sentence in the Star Chamber, i. 162

Roos, Lord (William Cecil), his mission to Spain, i. 58. His quarrel with his wife, i. 159. Flies to Rome, i. 161. His death, i. 163

Rudyard, Sir Benjamin, expresses his joy at the King's declaration in favour of the Palatinate, i. 346. Urges the Commons to grant a supply, ii. 123

Rusdorf, John Joachim, his advice to Frederick, ii. 68

Rutland, Earl of (Francis Manners), his quarrel with Buckingham, i. 331. Commands the fleet which is to fetch the Prince, ii. 347. Sets sail for Spain, ii. 390

SAI

SABBATH the, observance of, in Lancashire, i. 198. Publication of the Declaration of Sports on, i. 202. Debate upon, in the House of Commons, i. 401

Sackville, Sir Edward, incorrectly said to have accompanied Vere to the Palatinate, i. 340. His duel with Lord Bruce, i. 438. Objects to the King's plan for a new tribunal, i. 439. Advises an immediate grant, ii. 123. Reiterates his arguments, ii. 127. Objects to the clause in the petition on religion relating to the Prince's marriage, ii. 135. Supports the claim of the House to freedom of speech, ii. 145. Takes Bacon's part with Buckingham, ii. 166. Visits De Dominis at Rome, ii. 175

St. Alban, Viscount. See Bacon, Sir Francis

St. John, J. A. His argument on a supposed early voyage of Raleigh, i. 40, note. His assertion about Raleigh's letters to Montmorency, i. 116, note

St. John, Sir William, story of his interference with Raleigh's release examined, i. 47, note. Gives information of Raleigh's plans, i. 139.

SAI

St. Leger, Sir Warham, detained in the Downs, i. 113. Left at the mouth of the Orinoco, i. 123. His evidence against Raleigh, i. 142
St. Paul's Cathedral, ruinous state of, i. 321
St. Valery, proposed attack on, i. 61
Salisbury, agreement made at, ii. 392
Salisbury, Earl of (Robert Cecil), his acceptance of a Spanish pension, i. 7, note. Asks for a declaration of war against Spain, i. 8, note. Appealed to by Raleigh, i. 47
Salmon and lobsters, patent for the importation of, i. 361
Sandys, Sir Edwin, elected Treasurer of the Virginia Company, i. 217. His observations on Floyd's case, ii. 14. Laments the state of the country, ii. 20. Imprisoned in the Tower, ii. 26. Set at liberty, ii. 29. His imprisonment discussed by the Commons, ii. 121
San Thome, deserted by Berreo, i. 40. Visited by Raleigh, i. 41. Its geographical position discussed, i. 53, note. Attacked and burnt by Keymis, i. 125
Sarmiento de Acuña, Diego, ambassador in England, i. 9. Protects Luisa de Carvajal, i. 11. Watches an opportunity for proposing the resumption of the marriage treaty, i. 13. His reluctance to increase the pension list, i. 14. Receives a visit from Cottington, i. 15. His intercourse with Somerset, i. 16. Receives an overture from the King, i. 21. His views of the future of England and Europe, i. 23. Expects to accomplish the conversion of England, i. 24. Urges Philip to forward the marriage, i. 25. Receives a visit from Cotton, i. 29. Welcomes Cotton's announcement that the King will pursue the marriage treaty, i. 32. Protests against Raleigh's voyage, i. 49, 53. Created Count of Gondomar, i. 69. See Gondomar, Count of
Savage, Sir Thomas, appointed a commissioner of the Prince's revenue, ii. 254
Saville, Sir Henry, predicts evil times, ii. 160.
Savoy, marriage treaty with, i. 15. War with Spain, i. 57. Peace concluded, i. 61. See Charles Emmanuel
Saxony, Elector of. See John George
Say and Sele, Lord (William Fiennes), urges that Bacon shall be summoned to the bar, i. 462. Imprisoned for attacking the Benevolence, ii. 182. Al-

SOU

lowed to go to his country house, ii. 301
Scarnafissi, Count of, his embassy in England, i. 58. Joins Raleigh in a scheme for attacking Genoa, i. 59
Schwarzenberg, Count of, his mission to England, ii. 191
Scot, Thomas, author of the "Vox Populi," i. 394, ii. 10
Scrooby, Brewster's house at, ii. 39. Separatist congregation at, ii. 41. Emigration from, ii. 42
Scrope, Lord (Emanuel Scrope), his quarrel with Berkshire, i. 408
Secretary of State. See Winwood; Lake; Naunton; Calvert; Conway
Selden, John, his "History of Tithes," i. 204. Is forced to make submission, i. 206. Sent to the Tower, ii. 26. Set at liberty, ii. 29. Comparison between his views and those of Robinson. ii. 61.
Separatists, their doctrines, ii. 34. Their persecutions, ii. 36. Emigrations of, ii. 37, 60
Sheldon, Dr., reprimanded for a sermon, ii. 233
Shepherd, member of the House of Commons, expulsion of, i. 402
Ship money, levy of, i. 276
Shute, Robert, candidate for the Recordership of the City, i. 186. Becomes Recorder, i. 376. His connection with Lady Wharton's case, i. 445
Sitva Torok, Peace of, i. 251
Skinner, voyage of, to the Spice Islands, i. 221
Smith, Captain John, receives Pocahontas in England, i. 213. Explores New England, ii. 46
Smith, John, minister of a Separatist congregation at Gainsborough, ii. 37, 41
Smith, Miles, Bishop of Gloucester, his opposition to Laud, i. 196
Smith, Sir Thomas, treasurer of the Virginia Company, i. 216
Smithwick, his charge against Bacon, i. 449
Solicitor-General. See Coventry; Heath
Somerset, Earl of (Robert Carr), advocates the Spanish alliance, and the Savoy marriage, i. 15. Urges Sarmiento to beg James to break with France, i. 16. Authorised to treat secretly with Sarmiento, i. 29. His fall and imprisonment, i. 32. Is released from the Tower, ii. 167
Southampton, Earl of (Henry Wriothesly), his character, i. 75. Supports a proposal for an expedition against Algiers, i. 76. Becomes a Privy Councillor, i. 281. His name put forward for the

SPA

command of troops in the Palatinate, i. 326. Urges on the Benevolence, i. 354. His quarrel with Buckingham, i. 423. Is sent to the Tower, ii. 26. Set at liberty, ii. 29

Spain, its foreign policy after the death of Philip II., i. 4. Proposed alliance with, i. 6. Possibility of war with, i. 7. Poverty of, i. 9. Sends money to the Emperor, i. 261. Miserable condition of, i. 267. Further aid sent to the Emperor, i. 272. Naval armaments of, i. 274. Hesitation of the government to attack the Palatinate, i. 305, 311. Pacific tendencies of, ii. 74, 97. See Zuñiga, Bathazar de; and Olivares, Count of

Spanish Embassy, riot at the, i. 135

Spedding, J. His argument on Bacon's conduct in 1613, i. 17, note. Quotation from his preface to the New Atlantis, i. 43. His remarks on a conversation between Raleigh and Bacon, i. 56, note

Spencer, Lord (Robert Spencer), calls Pembroke to order, i. 420. Asks whether Bacon shall be summoned to the Bar, i. 462. His quarrel with Arundel, ii. 7

Spinola, Ambrosio, his march to Mentz, i. 342. Invades the Palatinate, i. 344, 389. Receives orders to support the Duke of Bavaria, ii. 97. His excitement at Mansfeld's proceedings, ii. 98. Doubts the reality of Mansfeld's dismissal, ii. 211. Besieges Bergen-op-Zoom, ii. 227

Spires, the Bishop of, his lands occupied by Vere, ii. 103

Stadtloo, Battle of, ii. 371

Standish, Miles, joins the emigrants to New England, ii. 51. Appointed military commander, ii. 60

Star Chamber, proceedings threatened against Coke, i. 99. Against the Lakes, i. 161. Against Suffolk, i. 177. Against the exporters of gold, i. 237. Against Yelverton, i. 375

States General. See Netherlands, States General of the

Stukely, Sir Lewis, ordered to bring Raleigh to London, i. 137. Gives information of Raleigh's plans, i. 139. His downfall and death, i. 152. His guardianship of the child of Pocahontas, i. 213

Suffolk, Countess of (Katherine Howard), receives a Spanish pension, i. 14. Account of malpractices, i. 158. Proceedings against, in the Star Chamber, i. 178

Suffolk, Earl of (Thomas Howard), dis-

USH

missed from the Treasurership, i. 158. Sentence in the Star Chamber, i. 178. Obtains a mitigation of his fine, i. 179. Urges that Bacon shall be sent for to the bar, i. 462

Swarton, Sarah, bears false witness against Lady Exeter, i. 162. Her sentence, i. 163

THEOLOGIANS, Junta of. See Marriage Treaty with Spain

Thurn, Count, heads the Bohemian revolutionists, i. 260. Attacks Vienna, i. 282

Tilly commands the forces of the Duke of Bavaria, i. 297. His army in the Lower Palatinate, ii. 181, 193. Defeats the Margrave of Baden at Wimpfen, ii. 197. Overthrows Mansfeld's rearguard at Lorsch, ii. 201. Refuses to grant an armistice, ii. 203. Gains a victory over Christian of Brunswick at Höchst, ii. 205. Besieges Heidelberg, ii. 207, 246. Takes Heidelberg, ii. 247. Takes Mannheim, ii. 271. Defeats Christian at Stadtloo, ii. 371

Toledo, Pedro de, appointed Governor of Milan, i. 57

Toleration, difficulties of, i. 19

Tom Tell-Truth, ii. 183

Topiawari, an Indian chief visited by Raleigh, i. 41

Treasurer, Lord High. See Suffolk, Mandeville, Cranfield, Middlesex

Trevor, Sir John, his gratuity to Bacon, i. 464

Trinidad, Raleigh's visit to, i. 40

Trumbull, William, agent at Brussels, ordered to protest against the invasion of the Palatinate, i. 325. Converses with Spinola about the truce, ii. 98

Tserclaes, Madame, carries messages from Brussels to the Hague, ii. 77

Turata, Madame (see Errata), teaches the art of making silver and gold thread, i. 364

ULM, the treaty of, i. 338

Union, the Protestant, its origin, i. 249. Assembly of, at Heilbronn, i. 281. Sends Buwinckhausen to England, i. 307. Makes a fresh application to James, i. 324. Concludes a treaty with the League at Ulm, i. 338. Its army retires before Spinola, i. 344. Assembly of, at Heilbronn, ii. 75. Dissolution of, ii. 81

Urban VIII., Pope, his illness, ii. 406. Approves his predecessor's grant of a dispensation for the marriage, ii. 440

Usher, James, Bishop of Meath, his sermon to the House of Commons, i. 398

VAL

VALTELLINE, the, occupied by the Spaniards, i. 289
Van der Merven, (Governor of Heidelberg, ii. 240
Vane, Sir Henry, declares the liberties of the Commons to be their inheritance, ii. 145
Vanlore, Peter, lends money to Bacon, i. 466
Vaux, Lord (Edward Vaux), levies English troops for the Spanish service, ii. 192
Venice, the Bedmar conspiracy at, i. 275
Vere, Sir Horace, appointed to command the volunteers for the Palatinate, i. 332. Leaves England, i. 339. Arrives in the Palatinate, i. 389. Breaks the truce, ii. 103. Despairs of Mansfeld's mode of fighting, ii. 193. Hopelessness of his position, ii. 206. Besieged at Mannheim, ii. 247. Despairs of his prospects, ii. 248. Surrenders Mannheim, ii. 271. Returns to England, ii. 294
Verney, Sir Edmund, assaults a priest at Madrid, ii. 395
Verney, Sir Francis, joins the pirates of Algiers, i. 172
Versillini introduces improvements in the manufacture of glass, i. 362
Verulam, Lord. See Bacon
Villa Mediana, Count of, proposes a marriage, i. 6
Villiers, Christopher, marriages proposed for, i. 241. His share in the patent for alehouses, i. 359. His pension from the gold and silver thread, i. 366. Marriage with Elizabeth Norris proposed for, ii. 164. Created Earl of Anglesea, ii. 348
Villiers, Sir Edward, story of his interference with Raleigh's release examined, i. 47, note. His part in the gold and silver thread patent, i. 365. His embassy to Frederick, i. 388. Takes his seat in the House of Commons, ii. 9. His mission to the Hague, ii. 116
Villiers, Sir George, his name placed by Sarmiento on the pension list, i. 34. Supports Raleigh's petition for release, i. 48. Declares for the Spanish marriage, i. 57. See Villiers, Viscount
Villiers, Sir John, offers marriage to Frances Coke, i. 93. His marriage, i. 103. Created a viscount, i. 242. See Purbeck, Viscount
Villiers, Viscount. (See Villiers Sir George.) Patronage in his hands, i. 83. Created Earl of Buckingham, i. 84. See Buckingham, Earl of
Vintners, their dispute with the French merchants referred to Bacon's arbitration, i. 467

WIL

Virginia, colony of, i. 211. First colonial Parliament of, i. 216
Virginia Company, election of treasurer of, i. 216
Vox Populi, the, i. 394

WAKE, Sir Isaac, ordered to return to Turin, i. 280
Wallingford, Viscount (William Knollys), forced to surrender the Mastership of the Wards, i. 165. Objects to summoning Bacon to the bar, i. 462
Walter, Sir John, his hopes of the Solicitor-Generalship, i. 88. Put forward as candidate for the Recordership of the City, i. 188
Ward, Dr. Samuel, imprisonment of, ii. 11
Ward, Thomas, the pirate, i. 72
Warwick, first earl of (Robert Rich), his speculations in piracy, i. 185. His death, i. 216
Warwick, second earl of (Robert Rich), takes part in the disputes of the Virginia Company, i. 216
Washington, Henry, asks to see a priest on his deathbed, ii. 391
Weiss, Captain, sent by Mansfeld to Brussels, ii. 260
Wentworth, Sir Thomas, his character, ii. 125. Proposes to the Commons to adjourn, ii. 127. Recommends an immediate grant, ii. 128. His opinion on the best way of dealing with the Church of Rome, ii. 133. Supports the claim to freedom of speech, ii. 145. Suggests a protestation, ii. 145
Weston, Sir Richard, his embassy to Germany with Conway, i. 336. (See Conway, Sir E.) Made Chancellor of the Exchequer, ii. 117. Urges an immediate supply, ii. 128. His negotiations at Brussels, ii. 198, 208, 211, 222, 226, 228. Reports his proceedings to the Council, ii. 256
Wharton, Lady, her case, i. 440
White, Dr. Francis, his Conference with Fisher, ii. 168
Whitehall, the banqueting-house at, i. 242
Whitelocke, James, candidate for the Recordership of the City, i. 186
Wiesloch, combat of, ii. 197
Williams, John, part taken by him in Buckingham's marriage, i. 329. Made Dean of Westminster, i. 332. Objects to Usher's preaching, i. 398. His advice to Buckingham, i. 121. Becomes Lord Keeper and Bishop of Lincoln, ii. 27, 28. His remark on the accident at Bramshill, ii. 32. His speech to the Commons, ii. 120. Attempts to

mediate between James and the Commons, ii. 145. Warns the Prince of his dangers in Spain, ii. 304. Talks about the two favourites, ii. 339. Recommends James to swear to the treaty, ii. 358. Opposes the demands of the Spanish Ambassadors, ii. 418

Wilson, Sir Thomas, set as a spy over Raleigh, i. 143

Wimpfen, battle of, ii. 197

Winniffe, Dr. Thomas, preaches against Spinola, ii. 192

Winslow, Edward, joins the emigrants to New England, ii. 51, 60

Winwood, Sir Ralph, Secretary of State, proposes a vote of supply, i. 17. Supports Raleigh's petition, i. 47. Favours the plan for an attack upon Genoa, i. 60. Supports Raleigh against Spain, i. 61. His interview with Sarmiento, i. 64. Quarrels with Bacon, i. 96. Supports Coke in the affair of his daughter's marriage, i. 97. His death, i. 105

Withipole, Sir Edmund, takes charge of Frances Coke, i. 97

Wotton, Sir Henry, proposed for the embassy to Germany, i. 277. His visit to Heilbronn, i. 281. His embassy to Vienna, i. 336, 337. Sent on to Venice, i. 388

Wray, Edward, proposed marriage between him and Elizabeth Norris, i. 408. His marriage, ii. 163.

YEARDLEY, his first administration in Virginia, i. 213. His second administration, i. 214

Yelverton, Sir Henry, appointed attorney-general, i. 86. Makes a present to the King, i. 88. Appears against Coke before the Council, i. 99. Defends Bacon's conduct, i. 102. Brings charges against Raleigh, i. 142. His behaviour in the affair of the gold and silver thread, i. 365, 369, 376. Sentenced in the Star-Chamber, and deprived of his office, i. 375. His attack upon the King and Buckingham, ii. 4. His sentence, ii. 9. Set at liberty, ii. 29

ZOUCH, Sir Edward, his patent for the manufacture of glass, i. 362

Zuñiga, Balthazar de, minister of Philip IV., ii. 80. Puts forward a plan for Frederick's abdication, ii. 109. His plan adopted by the Council of State, ii. 214. Carries on a secret negotiation with the Emperor, ii. 216, 218. Discovery of his intrigues by the Council of State, ii. 262. His death, ii. 263

THE END.

www.ingramcontent.com/pod-product-compliance
Lightning Source LLC
Chambersburg PA
CBHW021419300426
44114CB00010B/555